Benchmark Papers in Animal Behavior

Series Editor: Martin W. Schein
West Virginia University

Volume

1 HORMONES AND SEXUAL BEHAVIOR / *Carol Sue Carter*
2 TERRITORY / *Allen W. Stokes*
3 SOCIAL HIERARCHY AND DOMINANCE / *Martin W. Schein*
4 EXTERNAL CONSTRUCTION BY ANIMALS / *Nicholas E. Collias and Elsie C. Collias*
5 IMPRINTING / *Eckhard H. Hess and Slobodan B. Petrovich*
6 PSYCHOPHYSIOLOGY / *Stephen W. Porges and Michael G. H. Coles*
7 SOUND RECEPTION IN FISHES / *William N. Tavolga*
8 VERTEBRATE SOCIAL ORGANIZATION / *Edwin M. Banks*
9 SOUND PRODUCTION IN FISHES / *William N. Tavolga*
10 EVOLUTION OF PLAY BEHAVIOR / *Dietland Müller-Schwarze*
11 PARENTAL BEHAVIOR IN BIRDS / *Rae Silver*
12 CRITICAL PERIODS / *John Paul Scott*

RELATED TITLES IN BENCHMARK PAPERS IN ECOLOGY

Volume

1 CYCLES OF ESSENTIAL ELEMENTS / *Lawrence R. Pomeroy*
2 BEHAVIOR AS AN ECOLOGICAL FACTOR / *David E. Davis*
3 NICHE: Theory and Application / *Robert H. Whittaker and Simon A. Levin*
4 ECOLOGICAL ENERGETICS / *Richard G. Wiegert*
5 ECOLOGICAL SUCCESSION / *Frank B. Golley*
6 PHYTOSOCIOLOGY / *Robert P. McIntosh*
7 POPULATION REGULATION / *Robert H. Tamarin*
8 PATTERNS OF PRIMARY PRODUCTION IN THE BIOSPHERE / *Helmut H. Lieth*

Benchmark Papers in Animal Behavior / 12

A BENCHMARK® Books Series

CRITICAL PERIODS

Edited by
JOHN PAUL SCOTT
Bowling Green State University

Dowden, Hutchinson & Ross, Inc.
STROUDSBURG, PENNSYLVANIA

Benchmark Papers in Animal Behavior, Volume 12
Library of Congress Catalog Card Number: 78-632
ISBN: 0-87933-119-4

80 79 78 1 2 3 4 5
Manufactured in the United States of America.

LIBRARY OF CONGRESS CATALOGING IN PUBLICATION DATA
Main entry under title:
Critical periods.
(Benchmark papers in animal behavior ; 12)
Includes index.
1. Critical periods (Biology)—Addresses, essays, lectures. I. Scott, John Paul, 1909-
QL962.C74 591.3'3 78-632
ISBN 0-87933-119-4

Distributed world wide by Academic Press,
a subsidiary of Harcourt Brace Jovanovich,
Publishers.

SERIES EDITOR'S FOREWORD

It was not too many years ago that virtually all research publications dealing with animal behavior could be housed within the covers of a very few hard-bound volumes which were easily accessible to the few workers in the field. Times have changed! The present day students of animal behavior have all they can do to keep abreast of developments within their own area of special interest, let alone in the field as a whole; and of course we have have long since given up attempts to maintain more than a superficial awareness of what is happening "in biology," "in psychology," "in sociology," or in any of the broad fields touching upon or encompassing the behavioral sciences.

It was even fewer years ago that those who taught animal behavior courses could easily choose a suitable textbook from among the very few that were available; all "covered" the field, according to the bias of the author. Students working on a special project used *the* text and *the* journal as reference sources, and for the most part successfully covered their assigned topics. Times have changed! The present day teacher of animal behavior is confronted with a bewildering array of books to choose among, some purported to be all encompassing, others confessing to strictly delimited coverage, and still others being simply collections of recent and profound writings.

In response to the problem of the steadily increasing and overwhelming volume of information in the area, the Benchmark Papers in Animal Behavior was launched as a series of single-topic volumes designed to be some things to some people. Each volume contains a collection of what an expert considers to be *the* significant research papers in a given topic area. Each volume, then, serves several purposes. To teachers, a Benchmark volume serves as a supplement to other written materials assigned to students; it permits in-depth consideration of a particular topic while at the same time confronting students (often for the first time) with original research papers of outstanding quality. To researchers, a Benchmark volume serves to save countless hours digging through the various journals to find *the* basic articles in their area of interest; often the journals are not easily available. To students, a Benchmark volume provides a readily accessible set of original papers on the topic, a set that forms the core of the more extensive bibliography that they are likely to compile; it also permits them to see at first hand what an "expert" thinks is important in the area, and to react accordingly. Finally, to librarians, a Benchmark volume represents a collection of important papers from many diverse sources, thus making readily available materials that might otherwise not be economically possible to obtain or physically possible to keep in stock.

The choice of topics to be covered in this series is no small matter. Each of us could come up with a long list of possible topics and then search for potential volume editors. Alternatively, we could draw up long lists of recognized and prominent scholars and try to persuade them to do a volume on a topic of their choice. For the most part, I have followed a mix of both approaches: match a distinguished researcher with a desired topic, and the results should be outstanding. So it is with the present volume.

Dr. John Paul Scott has been deeply involved for many years in critical period research in conjunction with his interest in the effects of early experience on subsequent social behavior. One of the early leaders in the field of animal behavior and sociobiology, Dr. Scott was a student of the late W. C. Allee at the University of Chicago. Following a long and productive tenure at the R. B. Jackson Memorial Laboratory at Bar Harbor, Maine, he moved to Bowling Green State University in Ohio and continued his active program in research on social behavior and social interactions of dogs. Because of his widespread interest in animal behavior and his great familiarity with the literature, Dr. Scott was a natural choice for the task of selecting appropriate articles for this Benchmark volume on critical periods.

MARTIN W. SCHEIN

PREFACE

When Martin Schein asked me to edit a volume containing significant papers on critical periods arranged according to historical principles, I thought that this would be relatively easy to do, as critical periods had been the central theme of one of my major fields of research. Actually, the limitations of space and finances have made the task of choosing appropriate papers a very difficult one. I have had to omit or abridge many important and significant papers, and to their authors I tender my regrets and apologies. Wherever possible, I have retained the complete bibliographies of reprinted papers. This will at least serve as reference resources for other significant papers.

As the book has turned out, I have tried to give an overall historical picture of the concept of critical periods as it has been discovered, has matured, and has been elaborated on in embryology and developmental psychobiology. With respect to special fields, I have had to be content in some cases with the inclusion of one or two papers, and in others with brief descriptions.

Papers on imprinting in birds, which are highly relevant to the concept of critical periods, may be found in Hess' companion volume in this series. Similarly, papers on the prenatal critical period for the determination of secondary sex organs and associated behavior are included in Carter's *Hormones and Sexual Behavior.* I have also omitted any papers on the behavioral development of nonhuman primates, including the major studies of Mason, Harlow, Hinde, and others, because research that precisely defines critical periods is still to be done in these species, if indeed such periods exist.

Although research on critical periods is a mature field, it is by no means exhausted. Practical applications are numerous and, from a theoretical standpoint, critical periods should be found in any newly studied organizational process on any level, from genetic systems up through social and ecological ones. These studies in turn lead to research on the nature of organizational processes, and this is the trend of the future.

J. P. SCOTT

CONTENTS

PART III: CRITICAL PERIODS IN THE DEVELOPMENT OF SOCIAL ATTACHMENT

PART IV: CRITICAL PERIODS FOR LEARNING

PART V: CRITICAL PERIODS IN PHYSIOLOGICAL ORGANIZATION

CONTENTS BY AUTHOR

INTRODUCTION*

Of all the known phenomena of development, that of critical periods lends itself most readily to practical applications, both for preventive mental hygiene and for positive control of behavioral development. Once a critical period has been identified, there is little difficulty in putting the information to use. Until recently, however, our understanding of this phenomenon has progressed very little further than its description and the recognition of its generality. It is the principal purpose of this Introduction to develop and illustrate its underlying theoretical principles.

PHYSICAL GROWTH AND BEHAVIORAL DEVELOPMENT—A COMPARISON

The Concept of Systems

A system may be defined as a group of interacting entities. As such, it is one of our most general scientific concepts, applying to both living and nonliving phenomena and ranging in size from an atom to the solar system and perhaps to the universe beyond. I shall limit my discussion to living systems and point out only their most basic characteristics: reciprocal stimulation between the units of the system; a tendency for organization to change toward increasing complexity, and, concurrently, toward stability; the differentiation of function between units; and finally, a tendency for the interactions between the units to favor the survival of the system, or in biological terms, to be adaptive.

There are various dimensions along which the organization of a system can be measured, but two of the most important are the predictability of the interactions and the differentiation of function between the individuals. Another basic characteristic of

*This is an abridged version of the introductory material in "Critical Periods in Organizational Processes" that will appear in *Human Growth: A Comprehensive Treatise*, Vol. III, F. Falkner and J. M. Tanner, eds., Plenum Press, in press.

systems which is implicit in the concept of interaction is communication, which can be measured in various ways, the simplest of which is mere quantity. Without some form of mutual stimulation, there can be no system.

The Concept of Development

Within the framework of the systems concept, development can be defined as change in the organization of systems that persists for only one generation. The qualification differentiates development from evolutionary change and ecological change, both of which persist over more than the lifetime of an individual. Generally, the organizational changes that we call development are in the direction of increasing complexity of organization and, as such, involve greater adaptivity and more efficient functioning. They are wholly or partially irreversible, which is related to the general systems characteristic of stability. One cannot take an adult human and reprocess him back to an embryo, attractive as this idea might be to a student of science fiction.

Growth and Behavioral Development

Both of these are organizational processes, but they take place on different levels of systems organization. Growth is largely a process of organization taking place within subsystems of an organism, whereas behavioral development, although it involves internal physiological processes and systems, is primarily a process of organizing the organismic system as a whole with respect to the external world and, in particular, to other living systems. Both of these organizational processes are still incompletely known except on a descriptive basis. Growth involves changes in an enormously complex set of physiological systems and subsystems. We have determined some of the methods through which units of these systems interact, but we are still very far from being able to understand the process as a whole. From a descriptive viewpoint we can say that physical growth is a cumulative process, is an integrative process in that the units become increasingly related to each other and react in a more and more predictable fashion, and finally, that it is a process of specialization of function. We also know in general that the last process—specialization or differentiation—is opposed to the cumulative part of the process, or growth in size.

Actually, behavioral development could be described in much

the same terms. It is cumulative in that more and more behaviors are added, and as these are added, they are integrated into systems and subsystems of behavior. Finally, the development of specialized sorts of behavior may interfere with the acquisitions of new behaviors.

Besides the differences with respect to levels of organization, behavioral development and physical development are different with respect to time relationships, since behavior is defined as the activity of an organism as a whole which can only be expressed when the organismic system is sufficiently well organized to be capable of activity, whereas growth takes place from the very outset of development. Although there is a considerable period during which these two processes overlap, the processes of physical growth must be initiated earlier and generally achieve complete stability and so cease development before the process of behavioral development reaches a similar stability.

Seen within the concept of developmental change in systems, an infant is born with its internal physiological organization already far advanced, although not complete, but with no organization with respect to the social systems of which it will become a part. This suggests that the important problems are the time relationships between behavioral and physiological organizational processes and their effects on each other, for it is not only the entities within a system that interact with each other but also systems at higher and lower levels.

These considerations place the old "innate-acquired" problem in a modern focus. The central problem now becomes one of empirically determining the time relationships between the organizing processes of growth and behavioral development, and the nature of the interactions between the systems produced by each. This replaces the older dichotomy, which was at best merely descriptive.

Theory of Organizational Change

Since organizational processes on different levels have similar general characteristics, it should be possible to formulate general theories of organization as well as descriptive laws.

The Concept of Processes

In its most general definition, a process is something that

proceeds or goes forward. In a system the thing that proceeds is organizational change. Therefore, to call something a process is simply to give it a name; we must discover the nature of the change or changes. An initial step in this direction is to divide processes into classes. A mature system must process outside materials and alter their organization in order to maintain the system. We can, therefore, make a distinction between *maintenance processes* that do not alter the organization of the system, and *developmental processes* that result in the organization of the system itself.

We know that maintenance processes are not unitary but consist of many different ongoing processes. Likewise, it is highly unlikely that developmental processes are simple and unitary even within a relatively simple system. Developmental change results in a single overall system, the organism, but we know that this consists of many subsystems. Therefore, any theory of organizational change must include the possibility of multiple processes.

The Concept of Time

A fundamental dimension of organizational change is time, and no study of development can omit it. It is important both in a relative and an absolute sense. However, anyone who studies the development of more than one organism is immediately confronted with the problem of variation.

The Concept of Variation

Differences in the state of development of individuals can result from a variety of causes, the most obvious of which are differences in starting points. In addition, various environmental accidents can speed up or slow down developmental rates. Similarly, genetic variation can effect developmental change. Variation in organizational change is, therefore, inevitable; and this brings up the question of the role of genetics relative to such changes.

The Role of Genetics

The genes are the fundamental units of organizational change. Without going into the details of gene structure and gene action, concerning which so many fundamental discoveries have been made in recent years, we can say that genes are large organic molecules. The genes not only reproduce themselves but produce enzymes, substances that alter the speed of chemical reactions. Each gene produces one primary enzyme (Beadle and Tatum, 1941). Therefore, each gene represents not only a structure but a different organizing process. This confirms the conclusion that multiple organizing processes must be involved in development. To some extent genetic processes go forward independently, resulting in variation in degrees of organization in different parts of an organism. Since each gene is subject to mutational change, variation in rates of development are inevitable, not only within an individual but between individuals.

In a higher organism there may be 100,000 or more genes, each controlling a different organizational process but interacting with others to produce an integrated whole. How integration is accomplished is still much of a mystery. We are only beginning to make progress in understanding gene action in bacteria, which are little more than collections of a few genes with very little higher organization. Thus, while the genes are the fundamental units of organizational change, progress in understanding developmental change must involve the study of organizing processes at higher levels, both in order to achieve more rapid progress and in order to understand the activities of the genes themselves. Furthermore, genes can affect both developmental processes and maintenance processes, and these two functions must be considered separately.

GENERAL THEORY OF CRITICAL PERIODS

The Nature of Critical Periods

The term "critical" is derived from the Greek word *krisis,* and its basic meaning is that it involves a decision. A critical period is therefore one in which a decision is made, but in its more restricted meaning it involves a decision that cannot be repeated or reversed at a later time. For example, contact with a newly hatched turkey may produce an adult bird that will be attached to humans and will even attempt to mate with them (Schein, 1963). Similar contact with an adult bird will not produce such an effect. The irreversibility of decisions is even more strikingly illustrated by embryological examples. There is only a brief period in embryological development when an individual can be influenced to develop more than the normal number of digits. No interference in later periods can modify the number so produced except by amputation. Waddington (1962) has used the metaphor of canalization to describe such effects. Early in development organizational changes may proceed in many directions, but as they proceed it is as if the process is following a deeper and deeper canal whose boundaries limit further choices.

From an analytical viewpoint, developmental organizational processes tend to be irreversible simply because such processes produce more and more stable systems; thus, the phenomenon of critical periods is inherent in the concept of systems. It therefore becomes important to determine the stability of any system that is analyzed.

It is obvious that species may vary with respect to stability of organization. For example, a *Planaria* worm can be cut into small pieces, each of which will regenerate into an entire worm. In the higher vertebrates, regeneration is largely limited to healing of minor wounds. Any drastic disorganization such as produced by a major wound usually results in the destruction of some vital organ and death. This is one of the penalties of complex organization. It produces greater stability and greater efficiency of function but inhibits the power of regeneration, i.e., reorganization. Similar species differences can be seen in behavior. Most birds, which have evolved a relatively rapid course of development in connection with acquiring the ability for flight, show much more stability of behavioral organization than do mammals, whose behavior can be extensively modified even as adults. We must conclude that the stability of a system can be modified by genetics, at least between species and, by implication, with species.

The Theory of Critical Periods

This theory, which has been developed in detail elsewhere (Scott et al., Paper 38), is largely based on the empirical finding that organizational processes are modified most easily at the time that they are proceeding most rapidly.

The Nature of Organizational Processes Involved in the Development of Behavior

Behavior is defined as the activity of the entire organism and, therefore, is dependent on all those organizing processes that have produced a functioning organism. Of particular relevance to behavior is the development of the capacity for movement which is, of course, dependent upon the organization of the muscular and skeletal systems. These systems are particularly responsive to functional differentiation. Muscles not only increase in size but also develop additional circulation in response to exercise, and there is an increasing body of evidence that indicates a critical period for this effect in young rats (Rakusan and Poupa, Paper 27). Another system that is concerned with behavior is the endocrine system. This system also can be organized in response to function. The critical period for the effects of handling in young rats appears to involve this phenomenon (Denenberg and Zarrow, Paper 35). The most essential physiological system involved in behavior integration is, of course, the nervous system. As with other systems, it becomes more and more stable in its organization with maturity and has quite limited powers of regeneration or reorganization in the adult mammal.

In addition to the above, the process of learning has major relevance for behavorial organization. In spite of its importance, we still do not know its precise physiological basis. We know that it must be biochemical in nature and we know that it is related to the organization of nerve tracts produced by other organizing processes, but its mode of function is still known largely through description.

The major characteristics of the learning process are, first, that it may occur very rapidly, in fact, within a fraction of a second in one trial learning. It can be organized in a more stable fashion, however, by repetition.

Second, the evidence from higher organisms indicates that learning is permanent and that forgetting is not a matter of erasure but of inability to retrieve information. This implies that learning is a cumulative process.

Considered in more detail, the process consists of: (1) attempts at adaptation, (2) varying these attempts, (3) the choice of one of these attempts as a solution, and (4) the fixing of this solution by habit formation. This implies that there is a critical period involving the choice or decision between adaptive behaviors.

Still another characteristic of learning is that it tends to be self-limiting. That is, the formation of certain habits inhibits the formation of conflicting new ones. In this way, the learning process shares the general characteristic of systems organization of producing stability. Finally, in contrast to most growth processes, considerable but not complete reorganization may be possible, even in adulthood.

Learning is, therefore, an example of an organizational process that involves repeated or intermittent critical periods. Each new problem that is solved involves a new critical period for that particular organization of behavior. On a higher level, the early period of mutual adjustment seen in the formation of a social relationship is a critical period for determining the nature of that relationship.

From the nature of the process in higher vertebrates, decisions made in the learning process are not as critical as those that are involved in growth. Nevertheless, the same general principle applies; there can be *no reorganization without disorganization.*

The flexibility of behavior organized by the process of learning is dependent upon the fact that each system tends to be organized around a particular environmental situation. Thus, new behavioral organization is created in each new situation. Behavioral organization becomes less flexible when many subsystems of behavior are organized around a particular event. Human language lends itself to generalization based on verbally stated principles around which very extensive organization of behavior can occur. If such a principle is found to be false or ineffective, the resulting organization is faulty and presents great difficulty if it is to be modified. One suspects that there may be a critical period shortly after verbal capacities are fully developd that may be critical for the establishment of such generalizations.

Part I

CRITICAL PERIODS IN EMBRYONIC DEVELOPMENT: DISCOVERY OF THE PHENOMENON AND EARLY STATEMENTS OF THE CONCEPT

Editor's Comments on Papers 1 Through 4

1 **STOCKARD**
Developmental Rate and Structural Expression: An Experimental Study of Twins, 'Double Monsters' and Single Deformities, and The Interaction Among Embryonic Organs During Their Origin and Development

2 **LANDAUER**
Studies on the Creeper Fowl. III. The Early Development and Lethal Expression of Homozygous Creeper Embryos

3 **SCOTT**
The Embryology of the Guinea Pig. III. The Development of the Polydactylous Monster. A Case of Growth Accelerated at a Particular Period by a Semi-Dominant Lethal Gene

4 **MOORE**
Malformations Caused by Environmental Factors

The *concept* of critical periods relates time to organizational change. The *phenomenon* of critical periods was first discovered through the study of experimental embryology. Like so many exciting discoveries in the early part of the twentieth century, this one was made at the Marine Biological Laboratory at Woods Hole, Massachusetts. C. R. Stockard had become interested in the production of monsters and used the eggs of a minnow, *Fundulus heteroclitus,* as a convenient model.

As his early papers showed, he first believed that specific kinds of abnormalities such as cyclopea could be produced by specific chemicals dissolved in sea water, and he originally referred to one of these as the "magnesium embryo." Further experiments, however, convinced him that similar monsters could be produced by a large number of injurious chemical and physical agents, provided they were applied at the same time in development. Reprinted here (Paper 1) are extracts from Stockard's classic monograph that summarize his research and the theories that grew out of it.

All of the general concepts concerning critical periods are found in this monograph: the term "critical period" (for which he also used the synonym "sensitive period"), the idea that critical stages occur at times when rapid cell proliferation and rapid developmental changes are occurring, and the finding that more general and serious results occur early in development.

In his later work, Stockard became convinced that the basic phenomenon was one of developmental arrest. He therefore used two general techniques of inducing the stoppage of development: the lowering of the temperature of the water in which the eggs were developing, and the reduction of the oxygen supply rather than the use of chemical substances. This foreshadowed the later discovery that even a relatively short stoppage of oxygen may be a cause of serious or fatal brain injuries to human fetuses and infants.

As Stockard pointed out, he was not the first to think of developmental arrest as a cause of abnormal development. In a still earlier work on experimental embryology, Dareste (1891) recounted the results of a lifetime of research on the production of monstrosities, mostly in chick embryos. His book gives an excellent summary of the history of embryology up to that date. Dareste not only pointed out that most single monsters can be classified as cases of arrested development but also that some abnormalities, such as hermaphroditism, can be explained as cases of excessive development.

In his experimental work, Dareste principally used changes in incubation temperature and interference with respiration to modify development. The idea of critical periods had occurred to him in connection with the development of the allantois, the respiratory organ of the chick embryo, without which development cannot proceed further. However, he was unable to demonstrate such a critical period, probably because he was unable to induce rapid and precise temperature changes at particular times with the crude equipment available to him. The principal credit therefore goes to Stockard, who was the first to delineate this idea clearly and to substantiate it with numerous experiments that are presented with detailed protocols in the original monograph.

A few years later, Landauer analyzed the development of an inherited anomaly in the domestic fowl, a short-legged variety of chickens known as "Creepers" (Paper 2). Landauer showed that the condition was produced by a dominant gene that was lethal in the homozygous condition. Most of these abnormal embryos died after about four days of incubation, but a few survived to hatch as phocomelic monsters, having very short legs close to the body with the feet attached by a single bone. Consistent with genetic theory, when two creepers were mated together, about 25 percent of the eggs failed to hatch in addition to the normal mortality of 6 to 7 percent. These homozygous embryos could be easily recognized at three days of incubation. When Landauer studied them in detail, he found evidence of a general retardation in growth, but much more pronounced retardation in those organs, such as the limb buds, that were rapidly developing at that time. Thus, he showed that developmental arrest in a critical period could be produced by genetic factors as well as by environmental ones. The reprinted material includes part of the discussion and summary sections of one of Landauer's papers which is most relevant to the theory of critical periods.

One limitation of Stockard's theories was that he did not consider the possibility that developmental acceleration as well as developmental arrest could produce defective development. This discovery came about through a study of the development of the polydactylous monster of the guinea pig, which I made under the direction of Sewall Wright. Part of this study is reprinted here (Paper 3). The monster was produced by the homozygous condition of a dominant gene which, in the heterozygous condition, causes one or two extra toes on each foot. Since guinea pigs normally have four toes in front and three behind, the result often looked like a more or less normal five-toed foot as seen in other rodents. The monsters, however, had enormous paddle-shaped feet bearing fifteen to twenty toes on each.

Detailed studies of normal and abnormal embryos revealed the fact that the monsters were larger than normal littermate controls, indicating that the cause of the condition was acceleration of growth at a time when the limb buds were first developing. Thus, abnormal development of an organ can be produced by stimulation as well as by inhibition of growth, although the latter is more common.

The final portion of this section is a summary of the practical knowledge concerning critical periods in human embryonic development (Paper 4). As the years have gone by, more and more cases of abnormalities produced by toxic environmental substances have accumulated, of which the thalidomide disaster was an example. Infants affected by this drug showed phocomelia similar to that produced by a genetic factor in the creeper fowl.

At the present time, physicians advise that pregnant mothers avoid the use of any drugs, except in cases of real emergencies concerning the mother's life and health. Mothers are also advised not to go to high altitudes or to go on high altitude airplane flights during the later stages of pregnancy because restriction of oxygen supply may be harmful to the baby. The phenomenon of critical periods thus involves more than an interesting theoretical concept, as it has highly important medical applications. Its chief use is to avoid conditions that may be harmful but, in the future, it may be possible to produce desirable developmental change, as is suggested in studies of the later physiological development of the nervous system.

1

Reprinted from *Am. J. of Anat.* **28**:115, 116–126, 138–139, 152–153, 263–267 (1921)

DEVELOPMENTAL RATE AND STRUCTURAL EXPRESSION: AN EXPERIMENTAL STUDY OF TWINS, 'DOUBLE MONSTERS' AND SINGLE DEFORMITIES, AND THE INTERACTION AMONG EMBRYONIC ORGANS DURING THEIR ORIGIN AND DEVELOPMENT[1]

CHARLES R. STOCKARD

Cornell University Medical College, New York City

1. INTRODUCTION

In the present contribution an endeavor will be made to analyze the causes and conditions which determine the usual type of structural expression or form. The ordinary progress of embryonic development gives rise to individuals of rather uniform structure, yet there may be numerous slight variations and defects in the structural composition of various organs and parts. Minor defects in structure are found in almost every individual of a group, but rarely do two individuals present exactly the same kind or degree of defects. These facts are readily recognized in a group of human beings where small differences are easily appreciated,

[1] This investigation has been aided by the Memorial Foundation of St. Bartholomew's Hospital for Diseases of the Alimentary Canal, of New York City. The author expresses his appreciation for this valuable support.

but no doubt the same conditions obtain among vertebrate animals in general, although in lower forms such differences in developmental results are more difficult to detect.

The end products of development differ from one another to varying degrees, slight differences are of little concern and are classed as ordinary variations, but when the same deviations become exaggerated they may be ranked as serious deformities or anomalies. This fact renders the analysis of normal developmental processes and the experimental study of monstrous development one and the same problem. It should be understood that the present study is not intended solely as a contribution to so-called 'teratology,' but is an experimental analysis and consideration of the processes involved in all normal embryonic development and growth. The experimental treatments have in many of the cases caused the formation of well-known monstrous structures, but the point of importance is not the production of the monster, but the simple alterations in the usual course of events which have induced the modified structural expression.

For the past ten years I have claimed that all types of monsters not of hereditary origin are to be interpreted simply as developmental arrests. Such a position has been taken by others (Dareste, '91). However, I propose at this time to present evidence which clearly demonstrates the truth of the claim. By arresting development in very simple ways all types of monsters may be obtained. The experiments have now reached such a degree of exactness that the following propositions may be stated as true, the evidence for which is recorded in the body of this paper.

First, all types of monster, double as well as single, may be caused by one and the same experimental treatment; second, any one type of monster, such as cyclopia, may be produced by a great number of different experimental treatments; third, all effective treatments tend primarily to lower the rate of development, and, fourth, the type of monster induced depends upon the particular developmental moment or moments during which the developmental rate was reduced. Slowing the rate at one moment will produce a double monster or identical twins and at another moment slowing by the same method will give rise to the cyclopean defect. In fact, the same thing which causes the double monster may later in development induce one of its heads to be cyclopean.

Thus there is no longer any ground for considering certain defects as specific responses to particular treatments. And there is as little reason for further descriptions of individual monsters, since all belong to the same class and the individual differences simply result from the different moments during which the developmental interruptions have acted.

The important consideration then arises as to what internal and external factors may tend to introduce the developmental arrests. Does one growing part in any way inhibit the activity of other developing organs? We shall devote a section to a consideration of the interaction among the developing and growing organs within the embryo. The study of the growth influences of one embryonic organ on another is one of the most important problems in the analysis of structure.

Finally, the interaction among growing parts and the inhibiting effects of one rapidly proliferating region over other regions will be very briefly considered in connection with abnormal and malignant growths.

2. THE SPECIFIC RATE OF DEVELOPMENT IN A GIVEN SPECIES

It is a generally known fact that the eggs of different species do not progress at the same rate of development even during comparable stages. The lengths of time between fertilization and the first cleavage and the rates at which the early cleavages follow one another may differ decidedly among the eggs of even closely related forms. These differences in developmental rate are probably fundamentally connected with differences in chemical structure of the egg substances, and in particular with the different rates of oxidation of certain stuffs. It is a well-known chemical fact that very slight differences in composition between substances may cause very great differences in their oxidation capacities.

The efforts on the part of numerous embryologists to associate the differences in rate of cleavage and time required to attain certain stages of development with the size of the egg, the amount and position of the yolk substances, or even the types of cleavage have not been satisfactory. Certain meroblastic eggs develop much faster than certain holoblastic ones, while other holoblastic eggs have a rate of cleavage far more rapid than the meroblastic types. All of the so-called laws of cleavage rates based on morphological differences among egg types have been found to fail so decidedly when applied in general that one is forced to seek more deep-seated causes for the differences in developmental rate.

At the present time we can only state that such causes probably reside in the differences in chemical make-up of the several species of eggs. The rate of development certainly depends, particularly during later stages, on the amount of food available, but the supply of oxygen and the degree of temperature at which development is taking place have a far more striking influence on the rate. Cessation of development also occurs much more promptly from absence of oxygen or sudden changes in temperature than from any other natural modifications which happen in the environment. These facts point decidedly to the rate of development as being dependent upon kind and rate of chemical change, most particularly upon rate of oxidation. The egg probably has a definite coefficient of metabolism dependent upon the interaction of its specific chemical structure and the given environment in which it normally develops. The rate of development results from both the internal qualities of the egg and the nature of the surrounding environment.

The present extremely crude state of our knowledge of the chemistry of development will permit of no more satisfactory statements of the principles underlying differences in developmental rate than those which have been attempted above. The inadequacy of such statements is as keenly appreciated by the writer as by the critical reader, but this inadequacy concerns chiefly the absence of the details involved, while the statements in general I believe are correct.

Although there is a definitely normal rate of development for a given egg, this rate is frequently subject to wide variations, usually as a result of variations in the surrounding conditions. The two chief, or most frequent, modifying causes are a change in oxygen supply or a change in temperature. An acceleration of the usual rate only takes place to a limited degree under natural conditions and but slight increases in developmental rate have been experimentally obtained. On the other hand, a very wide range of decrease in developmental rate is readily brought about. Slight changes in the surrounding temperature or reduction in the oxygen supply will readily tend to slow the rate of development to a marked degree. Finally, the entire progress of development is frequently stopped in nature by removing the supply of oxygen or by sufficiently lowering the surrounding temperature, as will be discussed in subsequent sections.

3. CONTINUOUS AND DISCONTINUOUS MODES OF DEVELOPMENT

Although, as stated in the foregoing section, each egg has a more or less characteristic rate of development, this rate is not uniform throughout the different developmental stages. All eggs develop with rythmical changes in rate, going alternately faster and slower from stage to stage. Certain stages are passed very rapidly, almost suddenly, while others are slowly attained in a tedious manner, yet the process of development is as a whole continuous. That is, development begins with fertilization which is soon followed by cleavage, and then continues without interruption until a free living larva or young embryo is formed. This then proceeds to grow and change until the adult structure is attained. Such a continuous mode of development is most common, indeed so common, that it is often carelessly considered to be universal, while a discontinuous mode is looked upon as something very strange or unusual and not as a phenomenon extremely important in an understanding of the more common continuous type of development.

The continuous mode is found among the great majority of those animals in which the eggs develop in a uniform or homogeneous environment, such as the sea-water. The general conditions of moisture, oxygen supply, and temperature are comparatively uniform, and although the eggs may develop faster or slower under slightly different conditions of temperature, etc., yet the variations in the medium are rarely sufficient to inhibit or stop development entirely, and when they are the eggs usually die.

On leaving the sea the fresh-water and land-living invertebrates and vertebrates show most varied and complex methods and arrangements for insuring an environment of sufficient uniformity to permit an uninterrupted development. Many forms, as is also the case in certain sea-living animals, have evolved a method for the development of the embryo within the body of the mother. Such an internal environment tends to control very effectively the conditions of moisture and in mammals also the temperature, but at times, as we shall see beyond, the oxygen supply is not properly adjusted and the continuity of development may be interrupted or interfered with on this account.

The land-living animals have not always succeeded in obtaining an ideal developmental environment, and there are many examples of a discontinuous mode of development as a result of environmental breaks in the strictest sense. That is, the egg begins to develop and attains a certain stage, when a more or less sudden change or break in the environment occurs and development stops completely and may remain at a standstill for various lengths of time—days or possibly weeks. Another alteration in the environment then occurs which again permits development to start and continue until the fully formed animal is obtained. Such a discontinuous mode of development is universal among one great class of vertebrates, the birds. Among the birds development, as far as studied, is invariably interrupted when about the stage of gastrulation, at which time the egg is laid or passed out of the warm body of the mother. The fall in temperature causes development to stop and the egg remains in the gastrular stage until incubated by the heat of the parent's body or until artificially incubated at a similar temperature.

The means of interrupting development seem to reside entirely outside the egg itself, they are properties of the environment. As far as is known, all eggs having once begun to develop will proceed in a continuous manner from stage to stage until the larva or free living embryo is formed, the environment permitting. Stops in development take place through lack of oxygen, unfavorable temperature, insufficient moisture, or shortage of available nutriment, but the egg itself is wound or set for development so as to continue through if possible. Thus experiments on discontinuous development must apply as methods various means for modifying the environment, and the results will depend upon the power of the egg to adjust itself to or withstand these changes. Being unable to meet the situation, abnormal or unusual developmental productions may arise.

The question then presents itself as to whether the development of any egg may be interrupted for definite lengths of time and later be allowed to finish or proceed. What would be the consequences of such interruption in the case of a normally continuous mode of development? Would the effects of the manner of development be the same following interruptions at different stages, or would the effects vary depending upon the stage of development at which the interruption occurred? In other words, are there indifferent and critical moments of developmental interruption? Would a complete stop in development have an effect similar to a decided slowing of the rate, or would the one be more effective than the other? The experiments recorded in the following sections were devised in order to answer these and other queries.

4. EXPERIMENTALLY CHANGING A CONTINUOUS INTO A DISCONTINUOUS MODE OF DEVELOPMENT

a. The method of experiment

The continuous mode of embryonic development is the more common type in nature. We are, therefore, warranted to some extent in assuming that the discontinuous mode is nature's experimental modification of the continuous. What methods of modification has nature employed that may be artificially imitated? The simplest, commonest, and most evident natural method is change in temperature which causes the interruption of development in the eggs of all birds.

Changing the temperature of the environment and, therefore, of the egg, is the method employed in most of the present experiments in order to interrupt or make discontinuous a normally continuous development.

There are several definite natural cases of discontinuous development among mammals, the significance of which will be considered in another section of this paper. But in the present connection we may be certain that nature has here employed another method than temperature change in causing the interruption. The temperature of the maternal body in which the mammalian embryo is developing is sufficiently uniform never to interrupt the progress of the egg. For reasons to be more fully cited beyond, changes in the supply of oxygen would seem to be the most probable cause of interrupted development in the rare cases of this phenomenon among mammals. Lack of oxygen or excess of CO_2 has also been resorted to in the present experiments as a means of interrupting or retarding the rate of a normally continuous development.

Neither of the two methods is new. A number of experimenters have studied the influence of temperature changes on the manner of development of different eggs. The effects of abnormally high and low incubator temperature on the development of the hen's egg have been recorded by Dareste and many others, most recently by Miss Alsop ('19). The development of amphibian eggs under unusual temperature conditions has been considered by O. Hertwig ('96), King ('04), and others. The influences of low temperatures on the development of the fish's egg have been investigated by Loeb ('16) and Kellicott ('16).

These studies on temperature, however, are of interest in the present connection only in so far as they almost all show how readily abnormal development of the embryo may be induced by unfavorable temperature conditions. The attempted explanations of the deformities which were given in only a few cases, as by Kellicott, entirely disregard or dismiss the real point of fundamental importance; that is, the induced change in the rate of development resulting from the modified temperature. Kellicott attempted to refute the slow rate as a cause of structural modification in discussing my assumption of arrested development. The present experiments differ from the previous temperature experiments in that they were undertaken with an almost completely different problem in view. The former experiments will be considered only as they bear on the specific questions in the discussion to follow.

Numerous studies on the behavior of eggs deprived of oxygen as well as in the presence of various reducing and anaesthetic substances have been conducted. All of these oxygen studies have little or no bearing on the immediate problems and are not treated in this connection.

The material used in the present experiments were the eggs of the common minnow Fundulus heteroclitus. I have studied and experimented with these eggs for a number of years and am familiar with a great many common deformities which they may be induced to present. The exact method of experimentation with temperature change was as follows: the eggs were taken from the female and fertilized in a 'dry bowl.' About fifteen minutes later they were rinsed free of foreign material with sea-water and left standing under water. The first cleavage takes place after about two hours, varying a little with the season and the temperature. The next cleavage follows after another hour, and development proceeds in a continuous fashion from then on until the fully formed fish hatches from the egg membrane and swims freely about within from eleven to eighteen or twenty days, depending again upon the season and temperature. There is a wide variation in the rate of development of these eggs, yet under all usual conditions after development once starts it is continuous.

The eggs were placed during different stages of development in compartments of a refrigerator at temperatures of 5°, 7° and 9°C. and left for varying lengths of time, from one to five days. At the lowest temperature development was almost if not completely stopped, while in the other two compartments it was slowed down to from one-twentieth to one-fiftieth of the normal rate. The responses shown in the manner of development are so different in eggs stopped or slowed at different stages that the exact time of treatment will be considered in connection with the different effects obtained. The difference in effects between slowing and actually stopping development will also be considered.

Other eggs were crowded close together in bunches and developed in bowls at room temperature. The eggs near the center of the masses or bunches obtained much less oxygen and were in a higher concentration of CO_2 than the more superficial ones. These were slowed in their rate of development. Sea-water was boiled so as to drive out most of the air and afterward kept stagnant. Egg masses were developed in this water and the inner eggs of the mass were almost completely stopped in many cases. In all such arrangements the rate of development was so retarded that many abnormal and deformed embryos resulted.

These in general are the methods employed; the different times of application and the results will be discussed in the particular cases below.

b. Stopping or retarding the progress of development at stages of apparent indifference to such interruption

In order to successfully change a continuous into a discontinuous mode of development, without producing ill effects on the resulting embryos, it becomes necessary to locate certain indifferent periods during embryonic development at which the interruption may be induced. Certain of these indifferent periods are those moments at which the interruptions of development occur in nature. Should the stoppage naturally take place during a sensitive period, the species would readily be eliminated on account of the high proportion of abnormal embryos which would result.

When the eggs of Fundulus are placed in low temperatures after having passed through the earliest active stages of development, cleavage, gastrulation, the formation of the germring and early appearance of the embryonic shield, they may be stopped for several days, or caused to develop at an extremely slow rate, without marked injury to the resulting embryos. In fact, when such eggs are returned to room temperature after being in the refrigerator for three or four days, they may often resume development at such a fast rate, probably as a result of the stimulation of raising the temperature, that they may hatch only a day or so later than control embryos. The percentage of such eggs that do hatch may also be equally as high as that from the control.

[*Editor's Note:* Material has been omitted at this point.]

c. Stopping or retarding the progress of development at stages of critical susceptibility to developmental interruption

From facts we know of development in nature, as well as, from the experiments discussed in the preceding section, it becomes evident that the course of embryonic development need not necessarily progress in a continuous manner, but may be stopped entirely for a considerable length of time or may be decidedly reduced in rate without necessarily injuring the end result. On the other hand, it is equally well known in a general way, and even more widely believed, that when a developing egg is injured in such a manner as to cause its development to stop, it is usually incapable of resuming development at all, or if it does start again to develop it will only continue for a short time and often in a very abnormal fashion.

These two apparently contradictory statements are equally true. This is due to the fact that the way in which a developing egg responds after having had the progress of its development stopped or arrested by any unfavorable condition depends entirely upon the stage in development at which the interruption occurred. In the first case stated above, the interruption is introduced at a stage in development when no unusually rapid changes are taking place, a comparatively quiescent moment during which all parts are developing, but during which no particular or important part is going at an excessively high rate. Such a time we may term a 'moment of indifference.'

In the second case, the interruption occurs at a time when certain important developmental steps are in rapid progress or are just ready to enter upon rapid changes, a moment when a particular part is developing at a rate much in excess of the rate of the other parts in general. Gastrulation is an important developmental step which apparently cannot be readily interrupted without serious effects on subsequent development. Many of the chief embryonic organs seem also to arise with initial moments of extremely high activity, processes of budding or rapid proliferation and growing out. During these moments a given organ may be thought of as developing at a rate entirely in excess of the general developmental rate of the embryo. Such moments of supremacy for the various organs occur at different times during development. As is well known, a certain organ arises much earlier or later in the embryo than certain others. When these primary developmental changes are on the verge of taking place or when an important organ is entering its initial stage of rapid proliferation or budding, a serious interruption of the developmental progress often causes decided injuries to this particular organ, while only slight or no ill effects may be suffered by the embryo in general. Such particularly sensitive periods during development I have termed the 'critical moments.'

[*Editor's Note:* Material has been omitted at this point.]

This series of experiments further shows the possibility of almost stopping, or reducing to an extreme degree, the rate of development during the earliest cleavage stages and again resuming a more or less normal rate on the part of a few individuals. An almost complete stoppage at an early cleavage stage results in a very high mortality ranging from as great as 78 per cent and 54 per cent, down to 34 per cent. However, the reduction in rate brought about by a less severe temperature of 9°C. does not cause so great a mortality and does not prevent the resumption of development of almost normal rapidity.

It is clearly shown, however, that although certain specimens may resume a fairly normal developmental rate after such treatments, the early arrests have had injurious effects upon the quality of the resulting embryos. A considerable percentage of gross abnormalities occurs in all of the groups, and even those embryos which appear on close examination to be normal in structure are extremely slow in hatching and are not in all cases capable of typical swimming reactions and perfect behavior as young fish.

A point of particular importance is that in such a series as this which had been arrested during an early cleavage stage, the monsters resulting are not limited to any particular type, but exhibit, in a series of sufficient extent, almost all known types. There may occur double monsters of varying degrees, from separate twins, fused but with complete bodies and tails, to double bodies and single tails, and finally different degrees of double-headedness on single bodies. There are specimens exhibiting anophthalmia, monophthalmia, microphthalmia, cyclopia, and all types of malformed eyes. The brains may be slightly asymmetrical, irregular, tubular with no primary ventricles, or deformed in various ways. The mouth and branchial region may exhibit almost any known defect. The fins may be poorly developed and the bodies ill-shaped and twisted. The tails may be short, bifed, and undeveloped due to a slow or arrested descent of the germ-ring. And finally there may be such minor defects as would escape observation until the hatched embryos were found to be unable to right themselves and swim. These are the defects to be seen on simple external examination, the internal structures are as frequently abnormal. The latter fact is borne out by numerous examinations of these monsters in sections. I have studied a great many of the sectioned specimens during the past number of years.

The reason for this great variety of monsters following arrests during cleavage stages is that the development of all organs or parts must subsequently take place and all may thus become arrested and deformed. When eggs are treated at later stages, as at the beginning of gastrulation, no double monsters will occur, their moment has passed, though the various brain, branchial, and other defects mentioned may exist. When treated after the embryonic axis is visible, it is most difficult to get any gross eye defects and so on.

Thus it may be said that the earlier the arrest the more numerous will be the type of defects found and the later the arrest the more limited the variety of deformities, since there are fewer organs to be affected during their rapidly proliferating primary stages.

The same treatment that causes a gross deformity when applied during an early stage, will during a later embryonic stage often give only a minor effect.

[*Editor's Note:* In the original, material follows this excerpt.]

LITERATURE CITED

ALSOP, F. M. 1919 Abnormal temperatures on chick embryos. Anat. Rec., vol. 15, no. 6, p. 307.

ARNOLD, L. 1912 Adult human ovaries with follicles containing several oöcytes. Anat. Rec., vol. 6, p. 413.

ASSHETON, R. 1908 A blastodermic vesicle of the sheep of the seventh day, with twin germinal areas. Jour. Anat., 32.

BISCHOFF, T. L. W. 1854 Entwicklungsgeschichte des Rehes. Giessen.

CHILD, C. M. 1915 Individuality in organisms. Univ. of Chicago Press.

1916 Experimental control and modification of larval development in the sea-urchin in relation to the axial gradients. Jour. Morph., vol. 28, no. 1.

CONKLIN, E. G. 1905 Mosaic development in ascidian eggs. Jour. Exp. Zool., vol. 2.

1906 Does half an ascidian egg give rise to a whole larva? Roux's Arch., vol. 21, p. 725.

1912 Experimental studies on nuclear and cell division in the eggs of Crepidula. Jour. Acad. Nat. Sci., Philadelphia, ser. 2, vol. 15.

DARESTE, C. 1891 Mode de formation de la Cyclopie. Annales d'Oculist, vol. 106.

1891 Recherches sur la production artificielle des monstruosités. 2d edition, Paris.

DAVENPORT, C. B. 1920 Heredity of twin births. Proc. Soc. Exp. Biol. and Med., vol. 17.

DRIESCH, H. 1892 Entwicklungsmechanische Studien: I, II. Zeit. wiss. Zool., Bd. 53, S. 160.

1895 Von der Entwickelung einzelner Ascidienblastomeren. Arch. Entw.-Mech., vol. 1.

DONALDSON, H. H. 1915 The rat. Memoir, Wistar Institute.

FERRET, P., ET WEBER 1904 Malformations du système nerveux central de l'embryon de poulet obtenues expérimentalement. C. R. Soc. de Biol., vol. 56.

GEMMILL, J. F. 1901 The anatomy of symmetrical double monstrosities in the trout. Proc. Roy. Soc. London, vol. 68, no. 444.

1912 The teratology of fishes. Glasgow (James Maclehose & Sons).

HARPER, E. H. 1904 The fertilization and early development of the pigeon's egg. Am. Jour. Anat., vol. 3, p. 349.

HERLITZKA, A. 1897 Sullo sviluppo di embrioni completi da blastomeri isolati di uova de tritone. Arch. Entw.-mech., Bd. 4, S. 624.

HERTWIG, O. 1892 Urmund und Spina Bifida. Arch. f. mikrosk. Anat., vol. 39.

1895 Beiträge zur experimentellen morphologie und entwicklungsgeschichte. Arch. f. mikrosk. Anat., Bd. 44.

1898 Ueber den Einfluss der Temperatur auf die Entwicklung von Rana fusca and Rana esculenta. Arch. f. mikrosk. Anat., vol. 51.

1911 Die Radiumkrankheit tierischer Keimzellen. Ein Beitrag zur experimentellen Zeugungs- und Vererbungslehre. Arch. f. mikr. Anat., vol. 77.

KAESTNER, S. 1898 Doppelbildungen dei Wirbelthieren. Ein Beitrag zur Casuistik. Arch. f. Anat. u. Physiol., S. 81.
1899 Neuer Beitrag zur Casuistik der Doppelbildungen bei Hühnerembryonen. Arch. f. Anat. u. Physiol., S. 28.
1907 Doppelbildungen an Vogelkeimscheiben. Fünfte Mitteilung. Arch. f. Anat. u. Phys.

KELLICOTT, WM. E. 1916 The effects of low temperature upon the development of Fundulus. Am. Jour. Anat., vol. 20, p. 449.

KING, H. D. 1903 The influence of temperature on the development of the toad's egg. Biol. Bull., vol. 5.

KOPSCH, FR. 1895 Ueber eine Doppel-Gastrula bei Lacerta agilis. Kgl. preuss. Akad. Wissensch.
1899 Die Organisation der Hemididymi und Anadidymi der Knochenfische und ihre Bedeutung für die Theorien über Bildung und Wachstum des Knochenfischembryos. Internat. Monatsschr. f. Anat. u. Phys., Bd. 16.

LEPLAT, G. 1914 Localisation des premières Ébauches oculaires. Pathogénie de la Cyclopie. Anat. Anz., Bd. 46.
1919 Action du milieu sur le développement des larves d'amphibiens. Localisation et différenciation des premiéres ébauches oculaires chez les vertébrés. Cyclopie et Anophtalmie. Arch. de Biol., T. 30, p. 231.

LEUCKART AND SCHROHE 1891 Die Organisation der Hemididymi und Anadidymi der Knochenfische. Internat. Monatsch. f. Anat. u. Physiol., Bd. 16.

LEWIS, W. H. 1904 Experimental studies on the development of the eye in Amphibia. Am. Jour. Anat., vol. 3.
1909 The experimental production of cyclopia in the fish embryo (Fundulus heteroclitus). Anat. Rec., vol. 3, p. 175.

LILLIE, RALPH S. 1917 The formation of structures resembling organic growths by means of electrolytic local action in metals, and the general physiological significance and control of this type of action. Biol. Bull., vol. 33, p. 135.

LOEB, J. 1895 Beiträge zur Entwickelungsmechanik der aus einem Ei entstehenden Doppelbildungen. Arch. Entw.-Mech., Bd. 1.
1915 The blindness of the cave fauna and the artificial production of blind fish embryos by heterogeneous hybridization and by low temperatures. Biol. Bull., vol. 29.
1916 Further experiments on correlation of growth in Bryophyllum calycinum. Botanical Gaz., vol. 62, p. 293.
1918 Chemical basis of correlation. I. Production of equal masses of sister leaves in Bryophyllum calycinum. Botanical Gaz., vol. 65, p. 150.
1918 The law controlling the quantity and the rate of regeneration. Proc. Nat. Acad. Sci., vol. 4, p. 117.
1919 The physiological basis of morphological polarity in regenerations. II. Jour. of Gen. Phys., vol. 1, p. 687.

MALL, F. P. 1908 A study of the causes underlying the origin of human monsters. Jour. Morph., vol. 19.
1917 Cyclopia in the human embryo. Publication 226 of Carnegie Institution of Washington, p. 5.
1917 On the frequency of localized anomalies in human embryos and infants at birth. Am. Jour. Anat., vol. 22, p. 49.

MITROPHANOW, P. 1895 Teratogenetische Studien. Arch. Entw.-Mech., vol. 1.

MORGAN, T. H. 1893 Experimental studies on teleost eggs. Anat. Anz., Bd. 8, S. 803.
1895 Half-embryos and whole-embryos from one of the first two blastomeres of the frog's eggs. Anat. Anz., Bd. 10, S. 623.

MORRILL, C. V. 1919 Symmetry reversal and mirror imaging in monstrous trout and a comparison with similar conditions in human double monsters. Anat. Rec., vol. 16, no. 4, p. 265.

NEWMAN, H. H. 1917 The biology of twins. Univ. of Chicago Press.
1917 On the production of monsters by hybridization. Biol. Bull., vol. 32, p. 306.

NEWMAN, H. H., AND PATTERSON, J. T. 1910 Development of the nine-banded armadillo from the primitive-streak stage to birth; with special reference to the question of specific polyembryony. Jour. Morph., vol. 21, p. 359.

OPPERMANN, K. 1913 Die Entwicklung von Forelleneiern nach Befruchtung mit radiumbestrahlten Samenfäden. Arch. f. mikr. Anat., Bd. 83.

PATTERSON, J. T. 1907 On gastrulation and the origin of the primitive streak in the pigeon's egg. Preliminary notice. Biol. Bull., vol. 13, p. 251.
1909 Gastrulation in the pigeon's egg—a morphological and experimental study. Jour. Morph., vol. 20, p. 65.
1913 Polyembryonic development in Tatusia novemcincta. Jour. Morph., vol. 24, p. 559.

SCHULTZE, O. 1895 Die künstliche Erzeugung von Doppelbildungen bei Froschlarven mit Halfe abnormer Gravitationswirkung. Arch. Entw.-mech., Bd. 1.

SPEMANN, H. 1901–1903 Entwicklungsphysiologische Studien am Triton-Ei. I, Arch. Entw.-mech., Bd. 12; II, Arch. Entw.-mech., Bd. 15, 1903; III, Arch. Entw.-mech., Bd. 16, 1903.

STOCKARD, C. R. 1907 The artificial production of a single median cyclopean eye in the fish embryo by means of sea-water solutions of magnesium chloride. Arch. f. Entw.-mech., Bd. 23.
1909 a The origin of certain types of monsters. Amer. Jour. Obs., vol. 59.
1909 b The development of artificially produced cyclopean fish, 'The magnesium embryo.' Jour. Exp. Zoöl., vol. 6, p. 285.
1910 a The influence of alcohol and other anaesthetics on embryonic development. Am. Jour. Anat., vol. 10, p. 369.
1910 b The independent origin and development of the crystalline lens. Am. Jour. Anat., vol. 10, p. 393.
1913 a The artificial production of structural arrests and racial degeneration. Proc. N. Y. Path. Soc., vol. 13, N. S.

STOCKARD, C. R. 1913 b An experimental study of the position of the optic anlage in Amblystoma punctatum, with a discussion of certain eye defects. Am. Jour. Anat., vol. 15, p. 253.

1914 A study of further generations of mammals from ancestors treated with alcohol. Proc. Soc. Exp. Biol. and Med., vol. 11, p. 136.

1919 Developmental rate and the formation of embryonic structures. Proc. Soc. Exp. Biol. and Med., vol. 16, p. 93.

STOCKARD, C. R., AND PAPANICILAOU, G. N. 1918 Further studies on the modification of the germ-cells in mammals: the effect of alcohol on treated guinea-pigs and their descendants. Jour. Exp. Zoöl., vol. 26, p. 119.

TANNREUTHER, G. W. 1919 Partial and complete duplicity in chick embryos. Anat. Rec., vol. 16, no. 6.

THORNDIKE, E. L. 1905 Measurements of twins. Arch. Phil., Psych. and Sci. Methods, vol. 13, no. 3.

VEJDOVSKÝ, FR. 1888–1892 Entwicklungsgeschichtliche Untersuchungen. 2 vols. text and atlas, Prag.

VON JHERING, H. 1885 Ueber die Fortpflanzung der Gürteltiere. Sitzungsb. d. konigl. Akad. d. Wiss., Bd. 47, S. 105.

WILDER, H. H. 1904 Duplicate twins and double monsters. Am. Jour. Anat., vol. 3.

1908 The morphology of cosmobia; speculations concerning the significance of certain types of monsters. Ibid., vol. 8.

WILSON, E. B. 1893 Amphioxus and the mosaic theory of development. Jour. Morph., vol. 8, p. 604.

1904 Experimental studies in germinal localization. I. The germ-regions in the egg of Dentalium. Jour. Exp. Zoöl., vol. 1, p. 1.

WINDLE, B. C. A. 1895 On double malformations amongst fishes. Proc. Zool. Soc. London, pt. 3.

ZOJA, R. 1895–1896 Sullo sviluppo dei blastomeri isolati delle uova di alcune Meduse. Arch. Entw.-mech., Bd. 1, u. 2.

2

Reprinted from *J. Genetics* **25**:367, 388–394 (1932)

STUDIES ON THE CREEPER FOWL.

III. THE EARLY DEVELOPMENT AND LETHAL EXPRESSION OF HOMOZYGOUS CREEPER EMBRYOS.

By WALTER LANDAUER.

(*Storrs Agricultural Experiment Station, Storrs, Conn.*)

In an earlier report we have offered genetic proof that the gene determining the typical features of the Creeper variety of fowls is lethal when present in homozygous condition (Landauer and Dunn, 1930). We have stated already in that report that the typical lethal period of homozygous Creeper embryos is to be found at the beginning of the fourth day of incubation, and that at this stage the homozygous embryos appear to be considerably smaller and less well differentiated than normal ones. We have also stated that under favourable conditions some of the homozygous Creeper embryos survive the critical period at the beginning of the fourth day, and that such embryos later exhibit morphological features resembling phokomelia.

Our present report is concerned with a more detailed description of those homozygous Creeper embryos which die at the beginning of the fourth day of incubation. The phokomelia-like homozygous Creeper embryos will be discussed in a future report.

[*Editor's Note:* Material has been omitted at this point.]

It appears from our discussion that the lethal action of the homozygous Creeper condition does not consist in the production of specific abnormalities, but that it must be brought about by fundamental factors affecting embryonic growth. The nature of these factors remains unknown[1]. It seems probable that what is true for the homozygous Creeper condition holds true also for the heterozygous state. We are thus led to believe that the skeletal peculiarities of the Creeper fowl (and probably of chondrodystrophy in general) are not brought about by specific factors acting upon the growth of certain parts of the skeleton, but by agencies which influence body growth in general. These agencies must realise their influence *at a time when the growth rate of the extremities is at a maximum*, thereby exerting a specific inhibitory action upon the formation of these parts of the body.

There are further facts pointing to the conclusion that neither the homozygous nor the heterozygous Creeper condition *directly* cause specific malformations, but that both exert a general growth-inhibiting action. The fact that the *lethal* effect is not a *direct* consequence of

[1] An attempt is being made in our laboratory to analyse experimentally (tissue culture, chorio-allantoic grafting) the nature of these growth-inhibiting factors.

cumulative inhibitory action of two Creeper genes is demonstrated by the observation that this lethal effect may be considerably postponed by the presence of many genes (other than the two Creeper genes) in a heterozygous condition. The progressive retardation of growth, of which death is a consequence, may thus be influenced by other genes.

A duplication of many features of the histological skeletal abnormalities brought about by one Creeper gene may be found in cases of chrondrodystrophy occurring in chicken embryos (Landauer, 1927) which Dunn has shown to be non-genetic. This similarity may be taken as evidence for the non-specific, growth-inhibiting nature of the effect of one Creeper gene and of the agencies which cause the appearance of sporadic, non-hereditary chondrodystrophy. In human chondrodystrophy there are obviously also hereditary and non-genetic cases, and it is suggested that, as in our material, the etiological factors in both instances are of a non-specific, growth-inhibiting type.

Jansen and others have proposed to explain the origin of chondrodystrophy through the effect of pressure exerted by a too narrow amnion. Dietrich believes that Jansen's hypothesis, improbable enough for various other reasons, became definitely impossible after chondrodystrophy had been found in chicken embryos (Landauer, 1927). We are not convinced that the occurrence of chondrodystrophy in chicken embryos as such constitutes critical evidence against Jansen's explanation. In fact, it seems that Jansen received the suggestion for his hypothesis from publications by Blanc and Dareste in which these authors proposed to explain certain monstrosities of chicken embryos as a consequence of the mechanical forces which a too small amnion had brought to bear upon these embryos. Rabaud, later on, presented critical evidence against this explanation.

On the other hand, we think that the observations reported here provide evidence against Jansen's hypothesis for the explanation of the origin of chondrodystrophy. A comparison of the findings in homozygous Creeper embryos and in heterozygous Creepers leads to the conclusion that these two groups are differentiated by the presence of two Creeper genes in the former and of one in the latter; both the chondrodystrophy which we have shown to exist in the heterozygous Creepers (Landauer, 1931) and the phokomelia-like condition of homozygous Creepers appear to have their origin in non-specific factors inhibiting growth of the embryos at a certain period. The abnormalities of the homozygous Creeper embryos appear during the second and third day of incubation, that is at a time when the head and tail-folds of the amnion are still separate and do not cover the places of origin of the wing and tail-buds. Our evidence thus excludes peculiarities of the amnion as a possible cause for the origin of the phokomelia-like condition of homozygous Creeper embryos, and, for genetic reasons, this conclusion may be applied also to chondrodystrophy as represented by the heterozygous Creeper fowl.

Our observations concerning the effects of two Creeper genes throw some light upon the intricate relations which exist between growth and organ formation. *In vitro* growth of tissue cells may take place for long periods without leading to morphogenetic differentiation. On the other hand, the formation of organs and tissues of developing organisms, obviously depends to a certain extent upon previous growth which furnishes the substratum for the processes of morphogenesis. Our material demonstrates, however, that there is a certain degree of independence between the events of growth and organ formation which, in the case of inhibited growth, makes it possible that the processes of morphogenesis proceed at a relatively normal rate, thus leading to the appearance of organs and parts of the body which are more abnormal in size than in structure.

Summary.

It has been shown in an earlier contribution that the dominant factor responsible for the traits of the Creeper fowl has recessive lethal action. Homozygous Creeper embryos usually die at the beginning of the fourth day of incubation, but in rare instances such embryos may live until shortly before hatching time. These latter embryos exhibit a phokomelia-like condition of the extremities and malformations of the head.

A study of the early development of homozygous Creeper embryos (between 36 and 72 hours' incubation) led to the following conclusions:

1. At the age of 36 hours homozygous Creeper embryos are slightly smaller than normal ones from the same mating. Their average total body length amounts to about 86 per cent. of normal embryos. The anterior and posterior part of the body show the normal size relations with regard to total body size. The size differences between homozygous Creeper and normal embryos probably begin to appear at least as early as the formation of the primitive streak.

2. This early general retardation in growth is followed by unequal retardation in different parts of the body of homozygous Creeper embryos. Thus, we find that at the age of 48 hours the anterior part of the body (anterior end of head to first somite) is more retarded than the posterior

one (first somite to posterior end of body). The length of the anterior part at this time averages about 68 per cent. of normals, that of the posterior part is about 78 per cent. of normals.

3. This unequal retardation is still much more pronounced at the age of 72 hours. The posterior part of the body now averages 74 per cent. of normals, while the average head length amounts to only 59 per cent. of the normal one. The head length usually resembles that of normal embryos between 48 and 60 hours' incubation, but is nearer to 48 hours. The cranial and cervical flexures are about as in 60-hour normal embryos. In some homozygous Creeper embryos of 72 hours a head length is found which is smaller than the smallest head length observed in normal embryos at the time when head length first becomes measurable by the establishment of the cranial flexure (43 hours). Obviously, there is a certain degree of independence of growth of the head region and of the formation of the cranial flexure.

4. A comparison of the number of somites shows the following average differences between homozygous Creeper and normal embryos from the same matings: at 36 hours homozygous Creepers 7·3, normal 10·5; at 48 hours homozygous Creepers 13·9, normal 21·4; at 72 hours homozygous Creepers 29·5, normal 34·4. These differences correspond to approximately 8, 10–12 and 12–14 hours' normal development respectively. At the age of 72 hours homozygous Creeper embryos have 89 per cent. of the somites of normal embryos. With regard to the number of somites the homozygous Creeper embryos lag most conspicuously behind the normal ones during the period when in normal development a rapid multiplication in somite number takes place (close of the second day). The fact that in spite of their smallness the homozygous Creeper embryos become nearly normal again in somite number demonstrates that the processes of morphogenesis are but little affected by the homozygous Creeper condition.

5. The conclusion that organ formation is more nearly normal in the homozygous Creeper embryos than is growth, is attested by other observations: the primordia of the eyes are more retarded in growth than in morphogenetic differentiation. The same, although to a much lesser degree, is true for the otocyst. The distance from the last somite to the posterior end of the body is smaller in 72-hour homozygous Creeper than in normal embryos of 48 or even 60 hours, although the latter are much larger in total body size.

6. Homozygous Creeper embryos of 72 hours' incubation usually have wing-buds about equal in size, and in differentiation of the mesen-

chyme cells, to those of 48-hour normal embryos. The leg-buds are extremely small or absent.

7. The heart of 72-hour homozygous Creeper embryos shows much variation. Most frequently the cardiac tube still has the U-shape of a normal earlier period, but exceeds the size of the cardiac tube in normal embryos of structurally comparable stages. This is probably to be explained by a more extreme growth retardation of the normally faster growing atrial over the ventricular region, thereby preventing the loop formation of the cardiac tube.

8. The vitelline blood vessels of 72-hour homozygous Creeper embryos usually show about the developmental stage of 60-hour normal embryos but in some instances they resemble those of 48-hour normal embryos.

9. The allantois usually is not yet present in 72-hour homozygous Creeper embryos. The amnion folds are still separate.

10. Hybrid vigour appears to have a favourable influence on body growth but not on morphogenetic differentiation (*e.g.* somite number).

11. No gross malformations have been found in those homozygous Creeper embryos which die during the typical lethal period at the beginning of the fourth day of incubation. The lethal action appears to be brought about by cessation of growth.

12. The peculiarities of homozygous Creeper embryos may be understood on the basis of Stockard's hypothesis that during embryogeny the faster growing regions are more inhibited by adverse conditions than the slower growing ones. Our observations, especially the fact that homozygous Creeper embryos, which under favourable conditions survive the early lethal period, later show a phokomelia-like malformation, militate against Stockard's assumption that a complete stop of development is necessary to produce malformations. It is probable, therefore, that no sharp line can be drawn between the effects of an extreme retardation and a complete stop upon later development.

13. Since the homozygous Creeper condition appears to be expressed chiefly by a retardation of growth in general (but at a time when the extremities and the head are most susceptible to such influences), it seems also probable that the characters of the heterozygous Creeper fowl and of chondrodystrophy in general are brought about by general growth-inhibiting factors rather than by specific ones.

14. The places of origin of the wing and leg-buds in 72-hour homozygous Creeper embryos are not yet covered by the amnion. Amnion pressure, therefore, cannot be responsible for the smallness of the wing-

buds and the frequent complete lack of the leg-buds of these embryos, nor for the phokomelia-like condition of older embryos of this type. On the basis of the assumption that the homozygous and heterozygous Creeper conditions are only quantitatively different expressions of the same factor, it seems impossible to explain the origin of the heterozygous Creeper traits with the amnion hypothesis of Jansen and others. Further, since the heterozygous Creeper condition and human chondrodystrophy are very similar in expression, Jansen's hypothesis becomes also improbable as an explanation of the etiology of human chondrodystrophy.

15. While it is known that growth *in vitro* may take place without leading to morphogenetic differentiation, the present study demonstrates that morphogenesis of organs and parts of developing embryos may to a certain extent be independent of growth.

REFERENCES.

BLANC, L. (1892). "Transformation cutanée de l'amnios chez un monstre célosomien chilonisome." *Ann. de la Soc. linnéenne de Lyon.*

CHILD, C. M. (1929). "Physiological dominance and physiological isolation in development and reconstitution." *Archiv für Entwick.* CXVII.

DARESTE, C. (1891). *Recherches sur la production artificielle des monstruosités ou essais de tératogénie expérimentale.* Deuxième édition. Paris.

DIETRICH, A. (1929). "Die Entwicklungsstörungen der Knochen." *Handbuch der speziellen und pathologischen Anatomie und Histologie,* IX, 1 Teil, Berlin.

DUNN, L. C. (1927). "The occurrence of chondrodystrophy in chick embryos. II." *Archiv für Entwick.* CX.

FISCHEL, A. (1896). "Ueber Variabilität und Wachstum des embryonalen Körpers." *Morphol. Jahrb.* XXIV.

JANSEN, M. (1913). *Das Wesen und Werden der Achondroplasie.* Stuttgart.

KEIBEL, F. und ABRAHAM, K. "Normentafel zur Entwicklungsgeschichte des Huhnes (Gallus domesticus)." Jena, 1900.

LANDAUER, W. (1927). "Untersuchungen über Chondrodystrophie. I." *Archiv für Entwick.* CX.

—— (1931). "Untersuchungen über das Krüperhuhn. II." *Zeit. für mikr.-anat. Forschung,* XXV.

LANDAUER, W. and DUNN, L. C. (1930). "Studies on the Creeper fowl. I." *Journ. Gen.* XXIII.

LEVI, G. (1922). "Per la migliore conoscenza del fondamento anatomico e dei fattori morfogenetici della grandezza del corpo. L'accrescimento dei somiti mesodermici e di altre individualità morfologiche." *Archiv. Ital. di Anat. e di Embriol.* XVIII, Supplemento.

—— (1925). "Wachstum und Körpergrösse." *Ergebnisse der Anat. und Entwick.* XXVI.

LILLIE, F. R. (1919). *The Development of the Chick.* New York.

Mehnert, E. (1897). *Kainogenesis als Ausdruck differenter phylogenetischer Energie.* Jena.

Patten, B. M. (1915). *The Early Embryology of the Chick.* Philadelphia.

Rabaud, E. (1902–3). "Essai sur la symélie. Son évolution embryonnaire et ses affinités naturelles." *Bull. de la Soc. Philomath. de Paris,* 9e série, v.

Scammon, R. E. and Calkins, L. A. (1929). *The Development and Growth of the External Dimensions of the Human Body in the Fetal Period.* Minneapolis.

Schmalhausen, J. und Stepanowa, J. (1926). "Das embryonale Wachstum des Extremitätenskeletts des Hühnchens." *Archiv für Entwick.* cviii.

Sieglbauer, F. (1911). "Zur Entwicklung der Vogelextremität." *Zeit. für wissenschaftl. Zool.* xcvii.

Stockard, C. R. (1921). "Developmental rate and structural expression: An experimental study of twins, 'double monsters' and single deformities, and the interaction among embryonic organs during their origin and development." *Amer. Journ. Anat.* xxviii.

3

Reprinted from *J. Exp. Zool.* 77:123, 126, 147–157 (1937)

THE EMBRYOLOGY OF THE GUINEA PIG

III. THE DEVELOPMENT OF THE POLYDACTYLOUS MONSTER. A CASE OF GROWTH ACCELERATED AT A PARTICULAR PERIOD BY A SEMI-DOMINANT LETHAL GENE [1]

J. P. SCOTT

Whitman Laboratory, The University of Chicago

THIRTY-THREE FIGURES

INTRODUCTION

It has long been realized that the limitations of both physiological genetics and experimental embryology can be defined by the gap in knowledge between the evidence for the existence of hereditary factors and the observation of their final visible effects. That is, the chief concern of these two sciences is the problem of how hereditary factors act, singly in genetics and collectively in embryology. One science attempts to vary the causal agents by selection, the other to modify their effects by environmental interference. An anomaly produced by a single gene provides a controlled variation of heredity comparable to the controlled variations of environment used in experimental embryology and has been so employed in many recent studies.

Such an anomaly was discovered and described by Wright ('34, '34 a, '35), who reported that in the guinea pig the semi-dominant lethal factor *Px* produced extra toes in the heterozygous condition and a polydactylous monster in the homozygous condition. The anatomy of those monsters which lived up to the time of birth has since been described in detail (Scott, '37 a). All organ systems except the circulatory, reproductive and endocrine (the last not studied) showed serious

[1] This paper comprises the third part of a doctoral thesis in zoölogy submitted to the faculty of The University of Chicago. The author is indebted to Dr. Sewall Wright for suggesting the problem and for advice and criticism.

abnormalities. These were attributed to an arrest of morphogenesis plus an alteration of relative growth rates.

Wright ('35) has suggested that the primary effect of the *PxPx* genes is a general inhibition of development at a particular moment, following Stockard's theory. Such a general inhibition could be produced by interference with general processes going on in all cells (metabolism), or with specific processes going on in certain cells having control over general processes.

However, unlike most monsters produced by inhibitory influences, this type exhibits excessive growth as well as suppression of certain organs.

MATERIALS AND METHODS

Monstrous embryos were obtained by mating heterozygote with heterozygote within the I and ID stocks of Wright's Chicago guinea pig colony. The ID stock (Wright, '35) was produced by a cross between the D and I stocks—showing respectively multiple factor and single factor (*Pxpx*) polydactyly—and exhibits additive effects of both sets of factors. The I stock probably carries a considerable number of unfavorable hereditary qualities (table 1) and possibly other lethal factors, but there is no evidence of interference with the expression of the *PxPx* genes.

Most of the embryos were prepared by the method previously described (Scott, '37)—removal by caesarian section, fixation in Bouin's fluid, and staining in Mallory's phospho-tungstic haematoxylin. The exact copulation age was obtained for all litters and the position in the uterus of each embryo noted.

Thirty-three litters were so obtained, ranging from 11½ to 43 days copulation age. The first recognizable monster (fig. 4) was obtained at 18 days, 12 hours and 15 minutes (18–12–15). The neural folds in the region of the cervical flexure were thrown into irregular wavy lines (fig. 2). Older monsters also show microphthalmia and paddle-shaped limbs. Table 1 gives a classification of all embryos of 18½ days and over, including cross-bred non-polydactylous material. Twenty-three monsters were obtained, confirming Wright's theory of a lethal gene (expectation $= 16.5 \pm 3.5$). Ten litters contained living monsters, and a study of nine of these provided the basis for the present paper. The most advanced normal embryo in each of six of the nine has been described in the author's table of normal development (Scott, '37).

TABLE 1

Classification of embryos of 18½ days and over

TYPE	STOCK I	STOCK ID	STOCK Random cross-bred
PxPx			
Dead *PxPx* monsters	6	3	0
Living *PxPx* monsters	3	9	0
Allantois a solid bud	0	1	0
Retarded 2 days	1	0	0
Total *PxPx*	10	13	0
Pxpx* or *pxpx			
Pxpx polydactyls	4	6	0
Retarded 2 days	1	0	0
—*px*, no toes developed	6	18	24
In double decidua	1	1	0
Allantois a solid bud	0	1	0
Retarded 2 days	2	0	0
pxpx non-polydactyls	2	1	17
Total not *PxPx*	16	27	41
Unclassified as to *Px*			
Possible *PxPx*	0	1	1
Retarded 2 days (doubtful)	2	0	0
Grossly abnormal, allantois not attached to placenta	2	0	0
Undifferentiated cell mass	1	0	0
Empty decidua	2	2	2
Unclassified dead	1	0	2
Total not classified	8	3	5
Total	34	43	46

The most advanced monster of each litter was compared externally and in section with its most advanced normal litter mate. The method would be unfair, there being an expectation of three times as many normal animals as monsters, were it not that litters containing no monsters were omitted, and the numbers were nearly equal (fourteen and twelve).

This method of paired comparisons controls variable intra-uterine environmental factors by selection of the most advanced embryos and inter-uterine factors by avoidance of comparisons between members of different litters. Extraneous hereditary factors were slightly controlled by inbreeding. An ideal experiment of this type should use: 1) inbred stocks, 2) exact timing, 3) identical treatment of embryos, and 4) comparison of the most advanced representative of each type within a litter. Other controls, such as age of mother and type of food, are probably not so important.

No correlation between uterine position and size or abnormality was discovered.

[*Editor's Note:* Material has been omitted at this point.]

SIZE AND GROWTH RATE

The above data indicate decided differences in the growth pattern of monsters, as well as interference with the type of morphogenesis dependent upon differential growth. Wright ('35) found the newborn heterozygous animals to be heavier than the normals, and one would expect the *PxPx* embryos to be heavier than either of the other types. But the embryos were not weighed, for fear of injury, and other measurements of size must be used.

It can be seen by a glance at table 3 that there is no significant difference in crown-rump length between monsters and their

TABLE 3

Average crown-rump lengths for normal and monstrous litter mates

AGE	C.R. LENGTH IN CENTIMETERS		DIFFERENCE
	Monster	Normal	
18–12–15	0.51	0.47	0.04
19– 2–45	0.71	0.64	0.07
19–16–55	0.70	0.764	— 0.064
21–15–15	0.95	1.13	— 0.18
22–17–35	1.12	1.00	0.12
23–16– 5	1.53	1.51	0.02
24–13– 1	1.31	1.412	— 0.102
26– 3–45	1.892	1.814	0.078
		Total	— 0.018
		Mean	— 0.002

litter mates. This result is misleading in that crown-rump length is dependent upon the flexure of the body, and the monsters are flexed for a longer period than the normal embryos. Table 4 shows that there is a considerable average difference in area as obtained from scale drawings, but this is still not significant with the numbers available. The monsters average 10% larger in area, which would probably mean about 15% by volume. Finally, in only three comparisons out of sixteen was a normal embryo found to be larger in area than a monstrous litter mate. Assuming that there is an equal chance of its being smaller or larger, the probability of obtaining this result is 0.025.

It is thus reasonable to conclude that there is some stimulation of growth in the monsters. The size of newborn monsters is not noticeably increased, but this may be attributed to injury at the time when the majority of monsters die.

There is no indication that the relative size of the monsters increases greatly during the period studied. Rather, the fact that morphogenetic processes which are going on most rapidly when the abnormalities first appear are most seriously affected indicates that the increase in growth *rate* is temporary and gradually disappears.

TABLE 4

Average area of sagittal sections of normal and monstrous litter mates

AGE	AREA IN SQUARE CENTIMETERS		DIFFERENCE
	Monster	Normal	
18–12–15	0.1477	0.1370	0.0107
19– 2–45	0.3300	0.2607	0.0693
19–16–55	0.2831	0.3402	— 0.0571
21–15–15	0.4970	0.5581	— 0.0611
22–17–35	0.6824	0.4791	0.2033
23–16– 5	0.9696	0.8148	0.1548
24–13– 1	0.7659	0.6518	0.1141
26– 3–45	1.4829	1.2874	0.1955
		Total	0.6295
		Mean	0.0787

The fact that monsters in retarded litters (such as 24–13–1) are of the usual type indicates that the time of increased growth is correlated with embryonic developmental processes, and tends to eliminate the possibility of an extra-embryonic cause.

CRITICAL PERIODS

There are always two important times in the development of an animal carrying a lethal factor: the time of first action of the factor and the time of death. In the *PxPx* monster there are three such periods. The onset of abnormality is first apparent at 18½ days copulation age; the lethal period for about 92% of the monsters occurs at approximately 26 days; the lethal period for the remaining 8% is the time of birth. This last 'critical period' has been described elsewhere (Scott, '37 a).

When first detectable the monsters show a state of development comparable to that of 17½-day normal embryos, and it is probable that the *PxPx* genes first act at this stage. Their primary effect appears to be stimulation of growth. Growth-promoting substances may either be admitted from the outside or manufactured in the embryo.

Outside substances must come through the allantoic placenta or the yolk sac. The former is ruled out because of two embryos in which the allantois had not become attached to the placenta, one being a monster and one normal. The latter, however, is functional at the critical period, and in the later stages the placental edge of the yolk sac of monsters is less constricted than the normal. No histological defects of the yolk sac were discovered. The possibility of the admission of a maternal hormone must be dismissed because of the irregularity of cyclical humeral function.

The hypothesis of embryonic endocrine activity is untenable. At 17½ days both the thyroid and pituitary bodies are still open diverticulae, and when the aortic bodies appear at 18½ days they are if anything less well developed than in normal embryos. None of these show any indication of function. If a growth-promoting substance is formed within the embryo it is probably produced throughout the body, perhaps entirely intra-cellularly.

The only plausible theories are: 1) admission of a maternal growth-promoting substance through the yolk sac, and 2) production of a growth-promoting substance throughout the body or in the yolk sac, probably intra-cellularly since there is no evidence of unusual secretory activity. The latter is to be preferred, since the former offers no explanation for a particular time of action.

The immediate cause of death of the monstrous embryos appears to be the bursting of small blood vessels in the region of the shoulder hump, a mass of loose connective tissue back of the brain which is the site of a large fat body in the newborn animal. The hemorrhage spreads to other parts of the body, death resulting within a few hours. Monsters recently dead appear pale and oedematous, with patches of clotted blood beneath the skin.

Two normal events are associated with death: the appearance of large amounts of loose dermal connective tissue all over the body, and the straightening of the cervical flexure. In normal development the latter precedes the former. In addition, the dying monsters show a reduction of the post cava and of the sinuses of the liver, and the loss of a direct route through the liver by the allantoic veins. This might be caused by inadequate growth of the ventral side of the body or by retention of flexure, both of which would tend to put mechanical pressure upon the liver; or the escape of blood may lower blood pressure, resulting in small size of certain channels.

The straightening of the cervical flexure plus excessive size of the nerve cord in this region (there being no corresponding growth of surrounding mesodermal tissue) should produce considerable mechanical stress in the dorsal neck region, which may be sufficient to produce lesions, perhaps assisted by raised blood pressure. The chance of recovery would be small because the continued straightening of the flexure would increase stress.

This mechanical theory of death is supported by the fact that normal embryos are very easily bruised by handling at this period, especially around the head. A small outside pressure might be necessary to start off bleeding, the lack of which would account for those monsters which survive to birth.

DISCUSSION

The essential parts of the theory developed above to explain the action of the gene *Px* are the differential stimulation of growth at a particular time in development, and that increased growth rate inhibits the type of morphogenesis which is produced by differential growth. The facts are that the organs growing most rapidly at a particular period begin to show excessive growth, and that these organs are subsequently delayed in morphogenesis roughly proportionally to the amount of increased growth.

Polydactylous monsters are very rare (Scott, '37 a), but most of the abnormalities are found, differently combined, in other genetically produced monsters.

The irregular polydactylous feet of Bagg's mouse strain are produced by bleb formation according to Bonnevie ('31, '34), but Plagens ('33) attributes them to clots. One or the other probably produces either mechanical isolation or physiological inhibition of the controlling center.

Landauer's ('31, '33) descriptions of the homozygous monsters produced by the Creeper fowl are at first glance strikingly similar to those of the polydactylous monster. The Creeper monsters show a dome-shaped forehead, microphthalmia, and clubbed feet. But the initial effect is a stoppage of growth at about the time of first appearance of the limb buds (Landauer, '32) followed by a later failure of histogenesis in the long bones, resulting in a chondrodystrophic condition. The Creeper monster is thus essentially unlike the polydactylous monster, and the similarities between the two can be attributed to agents acting at corresponding periods in development. It is here suggested that some of the characteristics of homozygous Creepers may be caused by retention of embryonic form.

Chesley ('35) described the development of a tailless monster in the mouse which is characterized by lateral folding of the nerve cord and failure of the underlying notochord. This folding is similar to that found in the cervical region of *PxPx* monsters, where there is no failure of the notochord. Chesley probably correctly considered the failure of the notochord to be primary, but he apparently thought of the result as an induction phenomenon. It is suggested that the similarity between the two cases is produced by opposite causes giving the same mechanical result: disproportionate growth between the nerve cord and the notochord. In the guinea pig the nerve cord is hypertrophic; in the mouse the notochord and surrounding tissues are hypotrophic.

Snell et al. ('34) have figured a type of monster occasionally obtained from the descendants of x-rayed mice which shows folding of the entire nervous system and an extreme type of flexure. No details are given, but it appears to be inhibited rather than stimulated.

Reed ('33) has described development in a race of mice producing individuals with harelip and cleft palate. He regards it as a case of local retardation of growth and morphogenesis. There is no accompanying defect of the eye, nor any indication of accelerated growth.

All of the above cases are essentially different from the polydactylous monster in that abnormality is produced by inhibition rather than stimulation. Child ('24) has stated that when development is environmentally modified differential acceleration produces a change in form opposite to that produced by differential inhibition, active regions being enlarged in one case and reduced in the other. Inactive regions develop more or less normally in both cases. This statement is correct when applied to a simple unchanging growth pattern, but where there is morphogenesis produced by a change in growth patterns it must be modified. Acceleration should preserve the original growth pattern by causing the rapidly growing portions to escape control, while inhibition prevents a change in growth pattern by stopping growth. Thus both acceleration and inhibition of growth can arrest morphogenesis in active regions.

Because the eye, digestive and respiratory tracts are reduced in size in the polydactylous monster it might be assumed that these organs were originally inhibited and that other parts of the body afterward escaped from their control and became enlarged. However, the reduced parts are not growing rapidly just before the abnormality appears, and unlike typical cases of inhibition there is no reduction in total size of the embryo. Taken together these facts rule out the application of any theory involving inhibition of growth or metabolism to the *PxPx* monster. There is, of course, an inhibition of morphogenesis.

The theory accounting for the polydactylous foot—a lateral dominant growing center which loses its control over the median side of the foot because of separation by distance—can also be reconciled with environmental experiments. The reduplicated limbs so often resulting from grafting amphibian limb buds may in some cases be caused by mechanical division of the controlling center. The fact that grafting one limb bud upon another produces a larger normal limb at first seems puzzling, but here there is no modification of the shape of the bud previous to digit formation.

Ruud ('29) was able to restore the thumb of the axolotl by grafting a fore limb bud in place of a hind one. She attributed her results to the tendency of the sciatic nerve to divide into five parts, but local conditions may have simply produced a wider bud. The latter theory seems preferable, since limbs differentiate normally in the absence of nerves. In the polydactylous monster the first effects on the limb buds are visible before nervous connections are established, and there is no apparent hypertrophy of the peripheral nerves.

The above theory is consistent with Wright's ('35) idea that multiple factor polydactyly is produced by the suppression of a digit suppressor, as the latter could be a local inhibitor of growth. But in *Pxpx* and *PxPx* animals there is almost undoubtedly a general stimulation of growth at a time when the limb buds are susceptible. The fact that heterozygous show less than half the variation from the normal found in the monsters indicates the existence of a threshold phenomenon.

Of the three unique features of the polydactylous monster—extreme polydactyly, telescoped sternum, and missing tibia—two have been explained. The condition of the tibia remains mysterious.

CONCLUSION

The physical and chemical nature of a gene cannot be established until it or its immediate products can be physically isolated. The futility of attempting to physically identify things by comparing their biological functions was originally pointed out by Owen, and the non-specific biological results obtained by Child with known physical and chemical agents has extended the basic principle, that biological processes may be produced by a variety of agents, to include similar modification by a variety of others. The gene *Px* can be defined only biologically, but such a definition throws some light on the possible nature of primary life processes.

It is concluded that the polydactylous monster of the guinea pig is probably produced by a growth stimulating substance manufactured throughout the embryo by the *PxPx* genes for a short time after approximately 17½ days copulation age; that the effect of this substance is greatest upon those organs growing most rapidly at the time—the limb buds, nerve cord in the cervical region, roof of the diencephalon, and visceral arches—with the result that morphogenesis is retarded in these organs proportionately to the rate of growth (the general effect being to maintain the relative growth pattern of the original period); that this results in uncoordinated development of certain related parts, eventually ending in disrupted function and death for most of the monsters between 26 and 27 days of age; that the size of certain embryonic organs thus becomes unusually large and that of others remains relatively small; and because histogenesis is uniformly and relatively little delayed complete recovery is impossible and the monster retains certain characteristics of embryonic form even if it survives till birth.

The case demonstrates that genes can accelerate as well as inhibit embryonic growth and supports the theory that an extensive modification of development is injurious, no matter what the nature of the effect. The polydactylous monster probably represents an instance of direct interference with a general process going on in all cells.

SUMMARY

1. The paper attempts an analysis of the embryonic action of the semi-dominant lethal gene *Px* in producing the polydactylous monster of the guinea pig.

2. The essential methods employed were exact timing and identical treatment of embryos, and the comparison of the most advanced normal and abnormal embryos within a litter.

3. The number of monsters obtained was consistent with genetic theory.

4. A table of differences between monsters and normals at specific ages is presented.

5. The monsters are first recognizable at 18½ days copulation age and usually die shortly after 26 days.

6. The first visible effects are excessive growth and halted morphogenesis of those parts normally growing fastest at about 17½ days.

7. In subsequent development morphogenesis is delayed approximately as follows: general body form, 2 days; limb buds, 2½; sense organs and visceral arches, 1; coelom, 1; diencephalon 4; telencephalon, 2; ear, 3; gut, 1; all organs, except those of the circulatory system, to some extent.

8. The most rapidly growing organs are in general the most delayed and become most abnormal; those organs normally developing later than the critical period show delayed morphogenesis without increased growth or extreme malformation.

9. The abnormalities of newborn monsters (except for the missing tibia) are accounted for on the bases of disproportionate growth and adjustments to it, and the relatively early onset of histogenesis which 'freezes' embryonic form.

10. It is concluded that there is a controlling center of morphogenesis on the lateral side of the guinea pig foot and that polydactyly results from the excessive length of the marginal thickening which permits medial points of growth to escape from control.

11. Reduced points of growth representing the missing digits are found on the feet of non-polydactylous embryos.

12. It is concluded that delayed straightening of the cervical flexure produces an unusual strain on the loose connective tissue of that region, resulting in hemorrhage and death for most embryos.

13. It is concluded that total size of the monsters is increased over that of normal litter mates.

14. The primary visible effect of the gene *Px* is the differential stimulation of growth, inhibiting morphogenesis only where the process is one of differential growth.

15. Consequently, the polydactylous monster shows increased relative size of the most abnormal parts, whereas monsters produced by differential inhibition of growth usually show reduction of the most abnormal parts. Applied at the same time acceleration and inhibition should produce the same abnormalities but opposite proportions.

LITERATURE CITED

BONNEVIE, K. 1931 Vererbarer Cerebrospinaldefekt (?) bei Mäusen mit sekundären Augen- und Fuszanomalien, nebst Turmschädelanlage. Abh. N. Vidsk. Akad. Oslo. Kl. J., no. 13, 26 pp.

——— 1934 Embryological analysis of gene manifestation in Little and Bagg's abnormal mouse tribe. J. Exp. Zoöl., vol. 67, pp. 443–520.

CHESLEY, P. 1935 Development of the short-tailed mutant in the house mouse. J. Exp. Zool., vol. 70, pp. 429–459.

CHILD, C. M. 1924 Physiological foundations of behaviour. Henry Holt, New York.

LANDAUER, W. 1931 Untersuchungen über das Krüperhuhn. II. Morphologie und Histologie des Skelets, insbesondere des Skelets der Langen extremitätenknochen. Zeitsch. f. mikr.-anatom. Forschung., Bd. 25, S. 115–180.

——— 1932 III. The early development and lethal expression of homozygous creeper embryos. J. Genetics, vol. 25, pp. 367–394.

——— 1933 IV. Die Missbildungen homozygoter Krüperembryonen auf späteren Entwicklungsstadien. Zeitsch. f. mikr.-anatom. Forschung., Bd. 32, S. 359–412.

PLAGENS, G. M. 1933 An embryological study of a special strain of deformed x-rayed mice, with special reference to the etiology and morphogenesis of the abnormalities. J. Morph., vol. 55, pp. 151–183.

REED, S. C. 1933 An embryological study of harelip in mice. Anat. Rec., vol. 56, pp. 101–110.

RUUD, G. 1929 Heteronom-orthotopische Transplantation von Extremitätenanlagen bei Axolotlembryonen. Arch. f. Entwick., Bd. 118, S. 308–351.

SCOTT, J. P. 1937 The embryology of the guinea pig. I. A table of normal development. Am. J. Anat., vol. 60, pp. 397–432.

——— 1937 a II. The polydactylous monster: a new teras produced by the genes *PxPx*. (In press.)

SNELL, G. D., E. BODEMANN AND W. HOLLANDER 1934 A translocation in the house mouse and its effect on development. J. Exp. Zoöl., vol. 67, pp. 93–104.

STOCKARD, C. R. 1930 The presence of a factorial basis for characters lost in evolution: the atavistic reappearance of digits in mammals. Am. J. Anat., vol. 45, pp. 345–377.

WRIGHT, S. 1934 Polydactylous guinea pigs. J. Hered., vol. 25, pp. 359–362.
———— 1934 a Genetics of abnormal growth in the guinea pig. Cold Spring Harbor Symposia on Quantitative Biology, vol. 2, pp. 137–147.
———— 1935 A mutation of the guinea pig, tending to restore the pentadactyl foot when heterozygous, producing a monster when homozygous. Genetics, vol. 20, pp. 84–107.
YOUNG, W. C., E. W. DEMPSEY AND H. I. MYERS 1933 Some data from a correlated anatomical, physiological and behaviouristic study of the reproductive cycle in the female guinea pig. Am. J. Physiol., vol. 105, pp. 393–398.

4

Reprinted from pp. 133–144 of *The Developing Human: Clinically Oriented Embryology*, 2nd ed., K. L. Moore, W. B. Saunders Company, 1977, 411 pps.

MALFORMATIONS CAUSED BY ENVIRONMENTAL FACTORS

Keith L. Moore

SENSITIVE OR CRITICAL PERIODS

Environmental disturbances during the first two weeks after fertilization may interfere with implantation of the blastocyst or cause early death or abortion of the embryo or both, but they rarely cause congenital malformations in human embryos. Teratogens may, however, cause mitotic nondisjunction during cleavage, resulting in chromosomal abnormalities that then cause congenital malformations.

Development of the embryo is most easily disturbed during the *organogenetic period*, particularly from day 15 to day 60. During this period teratogenic agents may be lethal, but they are more likely to produce major morphological abnormalities. Physiological defects, minor morphological abnormalities, and functional disturbances are likely to result from disturbances during the fetal period. However, certain microorganisms are known to cause serious congenital malformations, particularly of the brain and eyes, when they infect the fetus (see Table 8–3).

Each organ has a critical period during which its development may be deranged (Fig. 8–14). The following examples illustrate the ways in which different teratogens may affect different organ systems that are developing at the same time. (1) Radiation tends to produce abnormalities of the central nervous system and eye as well as mental retardation; (2) the rubella virus mainly causes cataracts, deafness and cardiac malformations; and (3) thalidomide induces skeletal and many other malformations.

Warkany (1971) believes that embryological timetables (such as Figure 8–14) are helpful in studying the etiology of human abnormalities, but he stresses that it is wrong to assume that malformations are always due to a single event occurring during the sensitive period or that one can determine from these tables the exact day at which the malformation was produced. All that one can reliably say is that the teratogen probably had its effect before the end of the organogenetic period of the structure or organ concerned.

TERATOGENS AND HUMAN MALFORMATIONS

A teratogenic agent (teratogen) is any agent that can induce or increase the incidence of congenital malformations. The general objective of teratogenicity testing of chemicals as drugs, food additives, or pesticides is to attempt to identify agents that may be teratogenic during human development.

To prove that a given agent is teratogenic, one must show either that the frequency of malformations is increased above the "spontaneous" rate in pregnancies in which the mother is exposed to the agent (the prospective approach), or that malformed children have a history of maternal exposure to the agent more often than normal children (the retrospective approach). Both types of data are hard to get in an unbiased form. Individual case reports are not convincing unless both the agent and type of malformation are so rare that their association in several cases can be judged not coincidental.

—*Fraser*, 1967

Drug Testing in Animals. Although the testing of drugs in pregnant animals is important, it should be emphasized that the results are of limited value for predicting drug effects on human embryos. Animal experiments can only suggest similar effects in man. However, if a variety of species respond to a specific compound, then, even if the malformations differ between species, the probability of potential human hazard must be considered to be high.

DRUGS AS TERATOGENS

Relatively few drugs have been positively implicated as teratogenic agents during human development (Table 8–3). Discussions of these teratogenic drugs appear in large print.

Several drugs are suspected of having teratogenic potential, because of a few well-documented case reports (Wilson, 1973a). Still others must be regarded as possibly teratogenic on the basis of scattered evidence. Discussions of these drugs appear in small print.

Although much has been written about drugs as teratogens in man, it must be admitted that were it possible to withdraw all these drugs, "the effect on the frequency of malformations would be small" (McKeown, 1976).

Alkaloids. Caffeine and nicotine do not produce congenital malformations in human embryos, but nicotine has an effect on fetal growth. In heavy cigarette smokers (20+ per day), premature delivery is twice as frequent as in mothers who do not smoke, and their infants weigh less than normal (see Figure 6–12). Nicotine causes a decrease in uterine blood flow, thereby lowering the supply of oxygen in the intervillous space that is available to the fetus. The resulting oxygen deficiency in the fetus impairs cell growth and may have an adverse effect on the mental development of the fetus.

Alcohol. Infants born to chronic alcoholic mothers exhibit prenatal and postnatal growth deficiency and mental retardation (usually associated with microcephaly, as illustrated in Figure 18–31). Short palpebral fissures, maxillary hypoplasia, abnormal palmar creases, joint anomalies, and congenital heart disease were present in most infants (Jones et al., 1973).

Androgenic Agents. Administration of progestogens in an attempt to prevent abortion has produced masculinization of female fetuses (Fig. 8–15). The preparations most

TABLE 8-3 TERATOGENS KNOWN TO CAUSE HUMAN MALFORMATIONS

Teratogens	***Malformations***	***References***
Androgenic Agents		
Ethisterone Norethisterone	Varying degrees of masculinization of female fetuses: most have labial fusion and clitoral hypertrophy.	Federman (1967); Jones and Scott (1958); Stempfel (1975); Vaughan and McKay (1975); Venning (1965); Warkany (1971); Wilson (1973b)
Antitumor Agents		
Aminopterin	Wide range of skeletal defects and malformations of the central nervous system, notably anencephaly.	Shaw and Steinback (1968); Sokal and Lessmann (1960); Thiersch (1952); Warkany et al. (1960); Wilson (1973a)
Busulfan (Myleran) alternating with 6-mercaptopurine	Stunted growth, skeletal abnormalities, corneal opacities, cleft palate and hypoplasia of various organs.	Fraser (1967); Karnofsy (1965); Sokal and Lessmann (1960); Vaughan and McKay (1975)
Methotrexate	Multiple malformations, especially skeletal.	Milunsky et al. (1968); Vaughan and McKay (1975)
Thalidomide	Meromelia and other limb malformations, external ear, cardiac and gastrointestinal malformations.	Lenz (1966); Lenz and Knapp (1962); Moore (1963); Warkany (1971)
Infectious Agents		
Cytomegalovirus	Microcephaly, hydrocephaly, microphthalmia, microgyria and mental retardation.	Sever (1970); White and Sever (1967); Dudgeon (1976)
Rubella virus	Cataract, chorioretinitis, deafness, microphthalmia and congenital heart defects.	Gregg (1941); Sever et al. (1964); Cooper (1975); Dudgeon (1976)
Toxoplasma gondii	Microcephaly, microphthalmia, hydrocephaly and chorioretinitis.	Dudgeon (1976); Vaughan and McKay (1975); White and Sever (1967)
Herpes simplex virus	Microcephaly, microphthalmia, and retinal dysplasia.	South et al. (1969); Nahmias et al. (1975); Dudgeon (1976)
Therapeutic Radiation	Microcephaly and skeletal malformations.	Hicks and D'Amato (1966); Tuchmann-Duplessis (1970)

frequently involved were *ethisterone* and *norethisterone* (Venning, 1965).

Oral contraceptives, containing progestogen with estrogen, taken during the early stages of an unrecognized pregnancy, or started after conception has occurred, are strongly suspected of being teratogenic agents (Nora and Nora, 1975). The infants of 13 of 19 mothers who had taken progestogen-estrogen pills during the critical period of development exhibited the VACTERAL syndrome (in the term vacteral, the letters stand for *v*ertebral, *a*nal, *c*ardiac, *t*racheo*e*sophageal, *r*enal, and *l*imb malformations).

There is not sufficient evidence to indicate that diethylstilbestrol (DES) taken during pregnancy is teratogenic, but it is apparently carcinogenic. A number of young women aged 16 to 22 years have developed adenocarcinoma of the vagina after a common history of having been exposed to the synthetic estogen in utero (Herbst et al., 1973, and Hart et al., 1976).

Antibiotics. *Tetracycline* therapy during the second and third trimesters of pregnancy may cause minor tooth defects (e.g., hypoplasia of

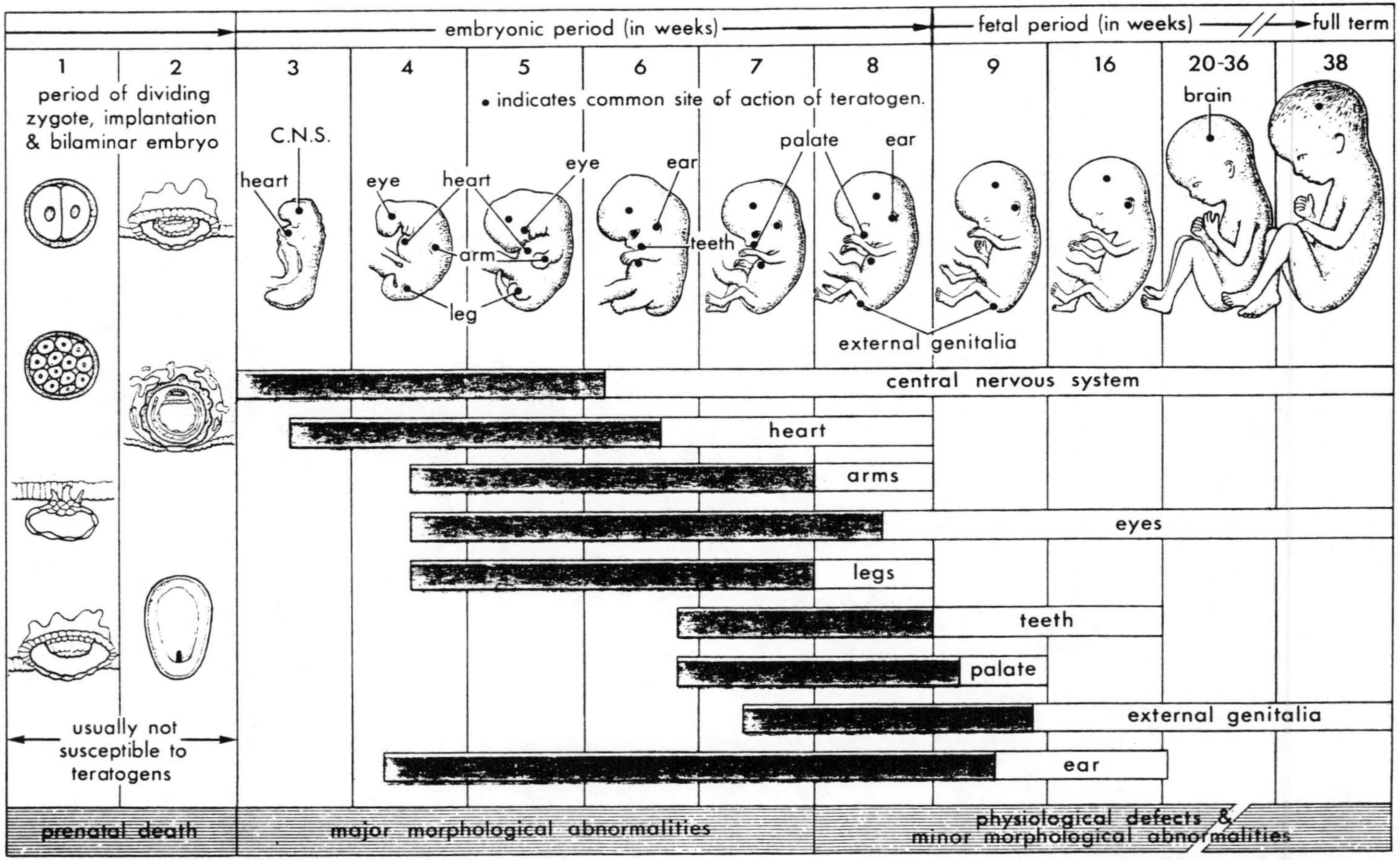

Figure 8–14 Schematic illustration of the sensitive or critical periods in human development. During the first two weeks of development, the embryo is usually not susceptible to teratogens. During these predifferentiation stages, a substance either damages all or most of the cells of the embryo, resulting in its death, or it damages only a few cells, allowing the embryo to recover without developing defects. Red denotes highly sensitive periods; yellow indicates stages that are less sensitive to teratogens.

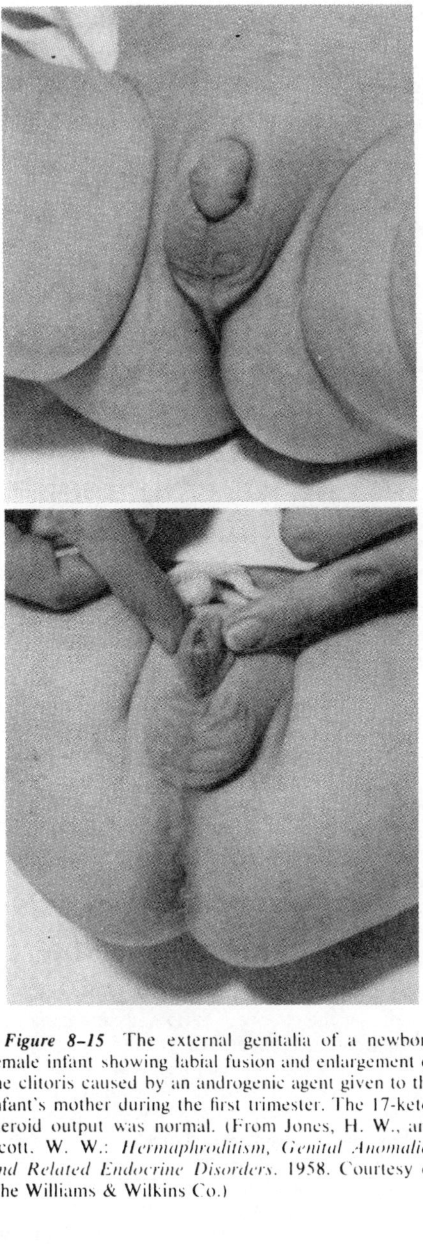

Figure 8–15 The external genitalia of a newborn female infant showing labial fusion and enlargement of the clitoris caused by an androgenic agent given to the infant's mother during the first trimester. The 17-ketosteroid output was normal. (From Jones, H. W., and Scott, W. W.: *Hermaphroditism, Genital Anomalies and Related Endocrine Disorders.* 1958. Courtesy of The Williams & Wilkins Co.)

enamel), yellow to brown discoloration of the deciduous teeth, and distortion of bone growth (Witkop et al., 1965). An association between administration of tetracycline and congenital cataracts has been reported (Harley et al., 1964) but not proved (Fraser, 1967). A few cases of deafness have been reported in infants of mothers who have been treated with high doses of streptomycin for tuberculosis, but the evidence is inconclusive. Penicillin has been used extensively during pregnancy and appears to be harmless to the human embryo (Tuchmann-Duplessis, 1970).

Anticoagulants. Most anticoagulants except heparin cross the placental membrane (barrier) and may cause hemorrhage in the fetus. *Warfarin* is strongly suspected of having teratogenic potential (Warkany, 1976, and Smithels, 1976). There are several reports of infants born with hypoplasia of the nasal bones whose mothers took this anticoagulant during the critical period of their embryo's development.

Anticonvulsants. There is strong suggestive evidence that *trimethadione* (Tridione) and *paramethadione* (Paradione) may cause fetal facial dysmorphia, cardiac defects, cleft palate, and intrauterine growth retardation when given to pregnant women (German et al., 1970). Other drugs (Dilantin, phenytoin) have produced cleft palate in certain strains of mice. Loughnan et al. (1973) reported seven cases of hypoplasia of the terminal phalanges in infants of epileptics. All mothers had taken phenytoin and a barbiturate.

In summary, it appears that cleft lip and palate, congenital heart disease, and digital hypoplasia are common malformations in infants of mothers who take anticonvulsants during pregnancy.

Antitumor Agents. Tumor inhibiting chemicals are highly teratogenic (Fraser, 1967). Although treatment with *folic acid antagonists* during the embryonic period usually results in intrauterine death of the embryos, 20 to 30 per cent of those that survive until term are malformed (Wilson, 1973b). *Busulfan* and *6-mercaptopurine* administered in alternating courses throughout pregnancy have produced multiple severe abnormalities, but neither drug alone appears to cause major malformations (Sokal and Lessman, 1960). *Aminopterin is a potent teratogen,* which can induce major congenital malformations (Fig. 8–16), especially of the central nervous system (Thiersch, 1952, and Warkany et al., 1960). *Methotrexate,* a derivative of aminopterin, is also teratogenic. Milunsky et al. (1968) described multiple skeletal and other congenital malformations in an infant born to a mother who attempted to terminate her pregnancy by taking this drug.

Corticosteroids. Cortisone causes cleft palate and cardiac defects in susceptible strains of mice and rabbits (Fraser, 1967). The scanty data concerning humans suggest that cortisone may be a weak teratogen (Karnofsky, 1965, and Fraser, 1967). There is little evidence to indicate that

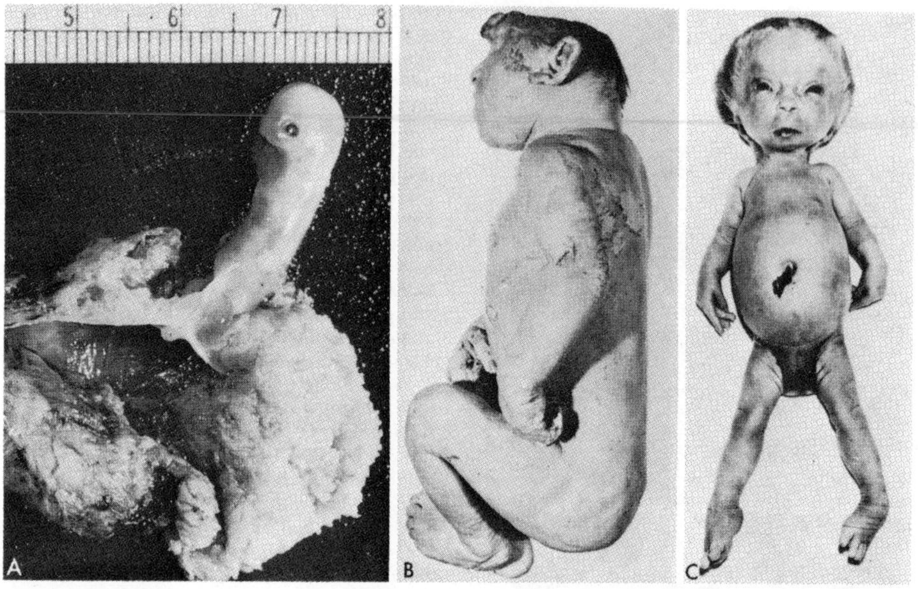

Figure 8–16 Aminopterin-induced congenital malformations. *A*, grossly malformed embryo and its membranes. (Courtesy of Dr. J. B. Thiersch, Seattle, Washington.) *B*, newborn infant with anencephaly or partial absence of the brain (From Thiersch, J. B., *in* Wolstenholme, G. E. W., and O'Connor, C. M. (Eds.): *Ciba Foundation Symposium on Congenital Malformations*. London, J. & A. Churchill, Ltd., 1960, pp. 152–154.) *C*, newborn infant showing marked intrauterine growth retardation (2380 gm), a large head, a small mandible, deformed ears, club-hands, and clubfeet. (From Warkany, J., Beaudry, P. H. and Hornstein, S.: *Am. J. Dis. Child.* 97:274, 1960.)

cortisone induces cleft palate or any other malformation in human embryos. It has been widely used during human pregnancy and has rarely been shown to have been associated with the birth of defective children (Wilson, 1973b).

Insulin and Hypoglycemic Drugs. Insulin is not teratogenic in human embryos, except possibly in maternal insulin coma therapy (Wickes, 1954). Hypoglycemic drugs (e.g., tolbutamide) have been implicated, but evidence for their teratogenicity is very weak.

Thyroid Drugs. *Potassium iodide* in cough mixtures and *radioactive iodine* (^{131}I) may cause congenital goiter (Fraser, 1967). *Propylthiouracil* interferes with thyroxin formation in the fetus and may cause goiter. Warkany (1954) reported that maternal iodine deficiency goiter may cause congenital *cretinism* (arrested physical and mental development).

Thalidomide. A mass of evidence has shown that this drug is a potent teratogen. Lenz (1966) estimated that 7000 infants were malformed by thalidomide. A characteristic feature of the *thalidomide syndrome* is meromelia (phocomelia or seal-like limbs, Fig. 8–17), but malformations range from amelia (absence of limbs) through intermediate stages of development (rudimentary limbs) to meromelia (short limbs). (See Chapter 17 for further discussion). Thalidomide also causes many other malformations (Lenz and Knapp, 1962).

LSD and Marijuana. There are still conflicting views about the effects of LSD and marijuana on embryonic development. An extensive literature has developed over the past few years suggesting that LSD may be teratogenic when taken during early human pregnancy. There have been reports of limb malformations (Zellweger et al., 1967) and severe abnormalities of the central nervous system (Berlin and Jacobson, 1970). From their own research and a review of the literature, Dishotsky et al. (1971) concluded that "pure LSD ingested in moderate doses does not cause detectable genetic damage, and is not a teratogen or carcinogen in man." Limb malformations have also been reported following the use of LSD and marijuana (Hecht et al., 1968, and Carakushansky et al., 1969). In summary, there is not enough evidence to indicate that LSD and marijuana are teratogenic, but there are grounds for caution.

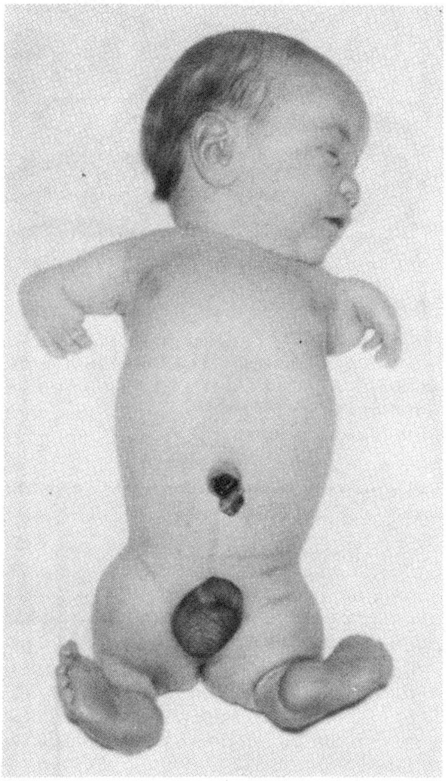

Figure 8–17 Newborn male infant showing typically malformed limbs (meromelia) caused by thalidomide. (From Moore, K. L.: *Manit. Med. Rev. 43*:306, 1963.)

ENVIRONMENTAL CHEMICALS AS TERATOGENS

In recent years there has been increasing concern over the possible teratogenicity of environmental chemicals, including industrial pollutants and food additives. At present, none of these chemicals has been positively implicated as teratogenic in man. However, infants of mothers whose diets during pregnancy consist mainly of fish containing abnormally high levels of organic mercury acquire fetal Minamata disease and exhibit neurological and behavioral disturbances resembling cerebral palsy (Matsumoto et al., 1965, Bakir et al., 1973). In some cases severe brain damage, mental retardation, and blindness are present (Amin-Zaki et al., 1974). Similar observations have been made in infants of mothers who ate pork that became contaminated when the pigs ate corn grown from seeds that had been sprayed with a mercury-containing fungicide (Snyder, 1971).

INFECTIOUS AGENTS AS TERATOGENS

Throughout prenatal life the embryo and fetus are assaulted by a variety of microorganisms. In most cases the assault is resisted; in some cases an abortion or stillbirth occurs; and in others, the infants are born with congenital malformations or disease.

The microorganisms cross the placental membrane (barrier) and enter the fetal blood stream. The fetal blood-brain barrier appears to pose little resistance to microorganisms since there is a propensity for the central nervous system to be affected.

Rubella (German Measles). Rubella virus is the outstanding example of an infective teratogen. About 15 to 20 per cent of infants born to women who have had German measles during the first trimester of pregnancy are congenitally malformed (Sever, 1970). The usual triad of malformations is *cataract* (Fig. 8–18*A*), *cardiac malformation*, and *deafness* (Dudgeon, 1976), but the following abnormalities are occasionally observed: chorioretinitis, glaucoma (Fig. 8–18*B*), microcephaly, microphthalmia, and tooth defects (Cooper, 1975).

The earlier in pregnancy the maternal rubella infection occurs, the greater is the danger of the embryo being malformed. Most infants have congenital malformations if the disease occurs during the first four to five weeks after fertilization; this is understandable, because this includes the most susceptible organogenetic periods of the eye, ear, heart, and brain (Fig. 8–14). The risk of malformations due to infections during the second and third trimesters is low, but functional defects of the central nervous system and ear may result if infection occurs as late as the twenty-fifth week (Sever, 1970).

Although there is no conclusive information about the teratogenic potential of *live attenuated rubella virus*, Larson et al. (1971) state that vaccination with live attenuated virus during early pregnancy is contraindicated. They further believe that women and adolescent girls should be immunized with live attenuated virus only when pregnancy is not planned during the following two months.

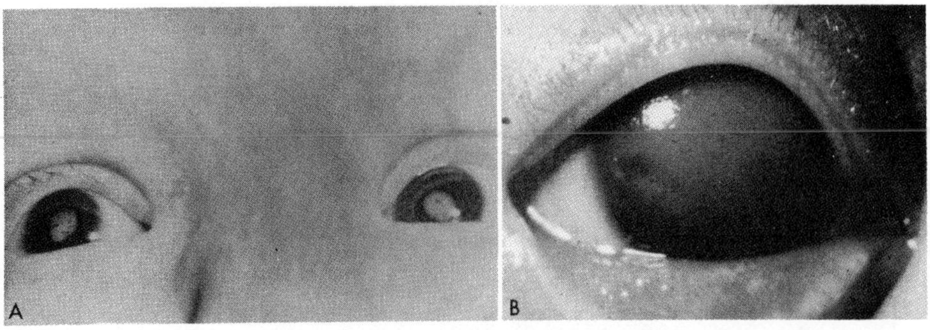

Figure 8–18 Congenital malformations of the eye caused by the rubella virus. *A*, Cataracts. (From Cooper, L. Z., *et al.*: *Am. J. Dis. Child. 110*:416, 1965. Courtesy of Dr. Richard Baragry, Department of Ophthalmology, Cornell–New York Hospital.) *B*, Glaucoma. (From Cooper, L. Z., *et al.*: *Am. J. Dis. Child. 110*:416, 1965. Courtesy of Dr. Daniel I. Weiss, Department of Ophthalmology, New York University School of Medicine.)

Cytomegalovirus. Infections during the embryonic period are not known to produce congenital malformations. It seems that infections occurring during the first trimester cause such severe damage to the embryo that abortion occurs. Most infections probably occur during the late fetal period. The principal abnormalities attributed to this virus involve the brain (microcephaly and hydrocephaly) and the eyes (microphthalmia). Microcephaly may be obvious at birth or may become apparent during infancy (Dudgeon, 1976).

Herpes Simplex Virus. Infection of the fetus with this virus usually occurs late in pregnancy, probably most often during delivery. The congenital abnormalities that have been observed in fetuses infected several weeks before birth are: microcephaly, microphthalmia, retinal dysplasia, and mental retardation (South et al., 1969, and Dudgeon, 1976). If the fetus acquires the infection from its mother's genital tract at birth, the abnormalities (e.g., chorioretinitis) result from inflammatory reactions.

Toxoplasma Gondii. This protozoan is an intracellular parasite. It can be contracted from eating raw or poorly cooked meat, by contact with infected animals (usually cats), or from the soil. It is thought that the soil becomes contaminated with infected cat feces carrying the oocyst (Dudgeon, 1976). This organism may cross the placental membrane and infect the fetus, causing destructive changes in the brain and eye resulting in microcephaly, microphthalmia and hydrocephaly (White and Sever, 1967). There is no proof that this parasite produces malformations during organogenesis in the embryonic period (Warkany, 1971).

Other Microorganisms. There is some evidence that other microorganisms may cause abnormalities. Recent reports suggest that varicella-zoster virus infection can cause congenital malformations similar to those produced by other viruses (Dudgeon, 1976). The syphilis microorganism may produce wasting of fetal tissues, malformed teeth, fetal meningitis, mental retardation, hydrocephalus, and deafness (White and Sever, 1967, and Vaughan and McKay, 1975).

RADIATION AS A TERATOGEN

Ionizing radiations are potent teratogens (Bartalos and Baramki, 1967, and Saxén and Rapola, 1969). Treatment of pregnant mothers during the embryo's susceptible period of development with large doses of roentgen rays and radium may cause microcephaly, mental retardation, and skeletal malformations (Hicks and D'Amato, 1966). An increase in these malformations was also reported following maternal exposure to atomic radiation in Japan (Fraser, 1967, and Makino, 1975).

There is no proof that congenital malformations have been caused by diagnostic levels of radiation (x-rays), but there are grounds for caution (Warkany, 1971), because actively proliferating cells of the central nervous system seem to be particularly susceptible to injury by x-rays. Interference with differentiation of these cells might lead to mental retardation.

In addition to the teratogenic effects on the embryo and fetus, radiation could cause mutations (heritable changes in genetic material) in the germ cells of the fetus. These chemical or structural transformations of genes or chromosomes could lead to the occurrence of congenital malformations in succeeding generations (Epstein, 1972).

MECHANICAL FACTORS AS TERATOGENS

The significance of mechanical influences in the uterus on congenital postural deformities is still an open question (McKeown, 1976). The amniotic fluid absorbs mechanical pressures, thereby protecting the embryo from most external trauma. Consequently, it is generally accepted that congenital abnormalities caused by external injury to the mother are extremely rare but possible (Hinden, 1965, and Warkany, 1971). Dislocation of the hip and clubfoot may rarely be caused by mechanical forces, particularly in a malformed uterus (Browne, 1960), but genetic factors appear to cause most of these abnormalities.

A reduced quantity of amniotic fluid *(oligohydramnios)* may result in mechanically induced abnormalities of the fetal limbs (Dunn, 1976) e.g., congenital genu recurvatum or hyperextension of the knee. Intrauterine amputations or other malformations caused by local constriction during fetal growth may result from amniotic bands or fibrous rings, presumably formed as a result of rupture of the fetal membranes (amnion and smooth chorion) during early pregnancy (Vaughan and McKay, 1975).

SUMMARY

Much progress has been made in recent years in the search for causes of congenital malformations, but satisfactory explanations are still lacking for most of them. Developmental abnormalities may be macroscopic or microscopic, on the surface or within the body. Some congenital malformations are caused by *genetic factors* (chromosomal abnormalities and mutant genes), and a few are caused by *environmental factors* (infectious agents and teratogenic drugs), but most common malformations probably result from a complex *interaction of genetic and environmental factors.*

During the first two weeks of development, teratogenic agents may kill the embryo or cause chromosomal abnormalities that give rise to congenital malformations. During the *organogenetic period,* particularly from day 15 to day 60, teratogenic agents may cause *major congenital malformations.* During the fetal period, teratogens may produce minor morphological and functional abnormalities, particularly of the brain and the eyes. However, it must be stressed that some teratogenic agents (e.g., drugs and infections) may adversely affect the fetus without causing congenital malformations.

SUGGESTIONS FOR ADDITIONAL READING

Berry, C. L.: Human malformations. *Br. Med. J. 3*:1–94, 1976. A special issue of the *British Medical Bulletin* devoted exclusively to problems of congenital malformations in man. Of special interest are the three papers concerned with etiological factors that may lead to birth defects. For the first time, the legal rights of the malformed infant are discussed in a most authoritative manner.

Langman, J.: *Medical Embryology, Human Development—Normal and Abnormal.* 3rd ed. Baltimore, The Williams & Wilkins Co., 1975. Read, in particular, Chapter 8, "Congenital Malformations and Their Causes," which is an excellent review by an eminent embryologist and teratologist of the causes of congenital malformations and the actions of teratogens. Especially recommended for the beginning medical student.

Persaud, T. V. N. (Ed.): Selected Readings in Teratology. New York, Simon and Shuster Inc., 1975. A compilation of articles covering the major aspects of teratology and providing the essential information on epidemiology, causes, mechanisms, and prenatal detection of birth defects.

Warkany, J.: *Congenital Malformations: Notes and Comments.* Chicago, Year Book Medical Publishers, Inc., 1971. An excellent reference text on human malformations. Contains data on congenital malformations gathered over a 35-year period by an outstanding professor of research pediatrics. It would be very difficult to find a congenital malformation that is not well covered in this book consisting of 1309 pages.

REFERENCES

Allderdice, P. W., Browne, N., and Murphy, D. P.: Chromosome 3 duplication q21-qter deletion p25-pter syndrome in children of carriers of a pericentric inversion inv (3) (p25 q21). *Am. J. Hum. Genet. 27*:699, 1975.

Amin-Zaki, L., Elhassani, S., Majeed, M. A., Clarkson, T. W., Doherty, R. A., and Greenwood, M.: Intrauterine methylmercury poisoning in Iraq. *Pediatr. 54*:587, 1974.

Bakir, F., Damluji, S. F., Amin-Zaki, L., Murtadha, M., Khalidi, A., Al-Rawi, N. Y., Tikriti, S., Dhahir, H. I., Clarkson, T. W., Smith, J. C., and Doherty, R. A.: Methylmercury poisoning in Iraq. *Science 181*:320, 1973.

Barr, M. L.: The sex chromosomes in evolution and medicine. *Can. Med. Assoc. J. 95*:1137, 1966.

Bartalos, M., and Baramki, T. A.: *Medical Cytogenetics*. Baltimore, The Williams & Wilkins Co., 1967.

Benirschke, K.: Teratology; *in* Reid, D. E., Ryan, K. J., and Benirschke, K.: *Principles and Management of Human Reproduction*. Philadelphia, W. B. Saunders Co., 1972, pp. 392–402.

Bennett, R., Persaud, T. V. N., and Moore, K. L.: Experimental studies on the effects of aluminum on pregnancy and fetal development. *Anat. Anz. 138*: 365, 1975.

Bergsma, D. (Ed.): The First Conference on the Clinical Delineation of Birth Defects. Part V: Phenotypic Aspects of Chromosomal Aberrations. The National Foundation–March of Dimes. Birth Defects: Original Article Series, Vol. V, No. 5, 1969.

Bergsma, D. (Ed.): *Birth Defects Atlas and Compendium*. The National Foundation–March of Dimes. Birth Defects: Original Article Series. Baltimore, The Williams & Wilkins Co., 1973.

Bergsma, D. (Ed.): *New Chromosomal and Malformation Syndromes*. The National Foundation–March of Dimes. Birth Defects: Original Article Series, Vol. XI, No. 5, 1975.

Berlin, C. M., and Jacobson, C. B.: Congenital anomalies associated with parental LSD ingestion. *Society for Pediatric Research Abstracts, Second Plenary Session*, 1970.

Breg, W. R.: Autosomal abnormalities; *in* L. I. Gardner (Ed.): *Endocrine and Genetic Diseases of Childhood and Adolescence*. 2nd ed., Philadelphia, W. B. Saunders Co., 1975, pp. 730–762.

Browne, D.: Congenital deformity. *Br. Med. J. 2*:1450, 1960.

Carakushansky, G., Neu, R. L., and Gardner, L. I.: Lysergide and cannabis as possible teratogens in man. *Lancet 1*:150, 1969.

Carr, D. H.: Heredity and the embryo. *Science J.* (London) 6:75, 1970.

Carr, D. H.: Chromosome studies in selected spontaneous abortions: Polyploidy in man. *J. Med. Genet. 8*:164, 1971.

Carr, D. H., Law, E. M., and Ekins, J. G.: Chromosome studies in selected spontaneous abortions. IV. Unusual cytogenetic disorders. *Teratology 5*:49–56, 1972.

Carter, C. O.: The genetics of congenital malformations; *in* E. E. Philipp, J. Barnes, and M. Newton (Eds.): *Scientific Foundations of Obstetrics and Gynecology*. London, William Heinemann, Ltd., 1970, pp. 665–670.

Challacombe, D. N., and Taylor, A.: Monosomy for a G autosome. *Arch. Dis. Child. 44*:113, 1969.

Cooper, L. Z., Green, F. H., Krugman, S., Giles, J. P., and Mirick, G. S.: Neonatal thrombocytopenic purpura and other manifestations of rubella contracted in utero. *Am. J. Dis. Child. 110*:416, 1965.

Cooper, L. Z.: Congenital rubella in the United States; *in* S. Krugman and A. A. Gershon (Eds.): *Progress in Clinical and Biological Research, Infections of the Fetus and Newborn Infant*. New York, Alan R. Liss Inc., 1975, Vol. 3, p. 1.

Dishotsky, N. I., Loughman, W. D., Mogar, R. E., and Lipscomb, W. R.: LSD and genetic damage. *Science 172*:431–440, 1971.

Dudgeon, J. A.: Infective causes of human malformations. *Br. Med. J. 32*:77, 1976.

Dunn, P. M.: Congenital malformations and maternal diabetes. *Lancet 2*:644, 1964.

Dunn, P. M.: Congenital postural deformities. *Br. Med. J. 32*:71, 1976.

Epstein, S. S.: Environmental pathology. *Am. J. Pathol. 66*:352, 1972.

Federman, D. D.: *Abnormal Sexual Development: A Genetic and Endocrine Approach to Differential Diagnosis*. Philadelphia, W. B. Saunders Co., 1967, pp. 121–133.

Ferguson-Smith, M. A.: Sex chromatin, Klinefelter's syndrome and mental deficiency; *in* K. L. Moore (Ed.): *The Sex Chromatin*. Philadelphia, W. B. Saunders Co., 1966, pp. 277–315.

Fraser, F. C.: Some genetic aspects of teratology; *in* J. G. Wilson, and J. Warkany (Eds.): *Teratology: Principles and Techniques*. Chicago, University of Chicago Press, 1965, pp. 21–37.

Fraser, F. C.: Etiologic agents. II. Physical and chemical agents; *in* A. Rubin (Ed.): *Handbook of Congenital Malformations*. Philadelphia, W. B. Saunders Co., 1967, pp. 365–371.

Fraser, F. C., and Nora, J. J.: *Genetics of Man*. Philadelphia, Lea and Febiger, 1975.

Gardner, E. J.: *Principles of Genetics*. 5th ed. New York, John Wiley & Sons, Inc., 1975.

Gardner, L. I.: *Endocrine and Genetic Diseases of Childhood and Adolescence*. 2nd ed. Philadelphia, W. B. Saunders Co., 1975.

German, J., Kowal, A., and Ehlers, K. H.: Trimethadione and human teratogenesis. *Teratology 3*:349, 1970.

Gray, J. E., Mutton, D. E., and Ashby, D. W.: Pericentric inversion of chromosome 21. A possible further cytogenetic mechanism in mongolism. *Lancet 1*:21, 1962.

Gray, S. W., and Skandalakis, J. E.: *Embryology for Surgeons. The Embryological Basis for the Treatment of Congenital Defects*. Philadelphia, W. B. Saunders Co., 1972.

Gregg, N. M.: Congenital cataract following German measles in the mother. *Trans. Ophthalmol. Soc. Aust. 3*:35, 1941.

Hamerton, J.: *Human Cytogenetics. Clinical Cytogenetics*. Vol. II. New York, Academic Press, Inc., 1971, pp. 169–195.

Harley, J. D., Farrar, J. F., Gray, J. B., and Dunlop, I. C.: Aromatic drugs and congenital cataracts. *Lancet 1*:472, 1964.

Harris, L. E., Stayura, L. A., Ramirez-Talavera, P. F., and Annegers, J. F.: Congenital and acquired abnormalities observed in live-born and stillborn neonates. *Mayo Clin. Proc. 50*:85, 1975.

Hart, W. R., Zaharrow, I., Kaplan, B. J., Townsend, D. E., Aldrich, J. O., Henderson, B. E., Roy, M., and Benton, B.: Cytologic findings in stilbestrol-exposed females with emphasis on detection of vaginal adenosis. *Acta Cytol. (Baltimore) 20*:7, 1976.

Hecht, F., Beals, R. K., Lees, M. H., Jolly, H., and Roberts, P.: Lysergic-acid-diethylamide and cannabis as possible teratogens in man. *Lancet 2*:1087, 1968.

Herbst, A. L. H., Ulfelder, H., and Poskanzer, D. C.: Adenocarcinoma of the vagina. *N. Engl. J. Med. 284*:878, 1971.

Hicks, S. P., and D'Amato, C. J.: Effects of ionizing radiations on mammalian development. *Adv. Teratol. 1*:195, 1966.

Hinden, E.: External injury causing foetal deformity. *Arch. Dis. Child. 40*:80, 1965.

Jones, H. W., Jr., and Scott, W. W.: *Hermaphroditism, Genital Anomalies and Related Endocrine Disorders.* Baltimore, The Williams & Wilkins Co., 1958.

Jones, K. L., Smith, D. W., Streissguth, A. P., and Myrianthopoulos, N. C.: Outcome in offspring of chronic alcoholic women. *Lancet 1*:1076, 1974.

Karnofsky, D. A.: Drugs as teratogens in animals and man. *Ann. Rev. Pharmacol. 5*:447, 1965.

Kucera, J., Lenz, W., and Maier, W.: Malformations of the lower limbs and the caudal part of the spinal column in children of diabetic mothers. *Ger. Med. Mon. 10*:393, 1965.

Larson, H. E., Parkman, P. D., Davis, W. J., Hopps, H. E., and Meyer, H. M., Jr.: Inadvertent rubella virus vaccination during pregnancy. *N. Engl. J. Med. 284*:870, 1971.

Laurence, K. M., and Gregory, P.: Prenatal diagnosis of chromosome disorders. *Br. Med. J. 32*:9, 1976.

Lenz, W.: Malformations caused by drugs in pregnancy. *Am. J. Dis. Child. 112*:99, 1966.

Lenz, W., and Knapp, K.: Foetal malformations due to thalidomide. *Ger. Med. Mon. 7*:253, 1962.

MacVicar, J.: Antenatal detection of fetal abnormality; physical methods. *Br. Med. J. 32*:4, 1976.

Makino, S.: *Human Chromosomes.* Tokyo, Igaku Shoin Ltd., 1975.

Matsumoto, H. G., Goyo, L., and Takevchi, T.: Fetal minamata disease. A neuropathological study of two cases of intrauterine intoxication by a methyl mercury compound. *J. Neuropathol. Exp. Neurol. 24*:563, 1965.

McKeown, T.: Human malformations: Introduction. *Br. Med. J. 32*:1, 1976.

McKusick, V. A.: *Mendelian Inheritance in Man. Catalogs of Autosomal Dominant, Autosomal Recessive, and X-linked Phenotypes.* Baltimore, The Johns Hopkins University Press, 1975.

Miller, O. J.: The sex chromosome anomalies. *Am. J. Obstet. Gynecol. 90*:1078, 1964.

Milunsky, A., Graef, J. W., and Gaynor, M. F., Jr.: Methotrexate-induced congenital malformations. *J. Pediatr. 72*:790, 1968.

Mims, C.: Comparative aspects of infective malformations. *Br. Med. J. 32*:84, 1976.

Mittwoch, U.: *Sex Chromosomes.* New York, Academic Press, Inc., 1967.

Moore, K. L.: The vulnerable embryo: Causes of malformation in man. *Manitoba Med. Rev. 43*:306, 1963.

Moore, K. L.: *The Sex Chromatin.* Philadelphia, W. B. Saunders Co., 1966.

Moore, K. L., and Barr, M. L.: Smears from the oral mucosa in the detection of chromosomal sex. *Lancet 2*:57, 1955.

Nahmias, A. J., Visintine, A. M., Reimer, C. B., Del Buono, I., Shore, S. L. and Starr, S. E.: Herpes simplex virus infection of the fetus and newborn; *in* S. Krugman and A. A. Gershon (Eds.): *Progress in Clinical and Biological Research, Infections of the Fetus and Newborn.* New York, Alan R. Liss Inc., 1975, Vol. 3, p. 63.

Neu, R. L., and Gardner, L. I.: Abnormalities of the sex chromosomes; *in* L. I. Gardner (Ed.): *Endocrine and Genetic Diseases of Childhood and Adolescence.* Philadelphia, W. B. Saunders Co., pp. 793–814.

Nishimura, H., and Tanimura, T.: *Clinical Aspects of the Teratogenicity of Drugs.* Amsterdam, Excerpta Medica, 1975.

Nora, J. J., and Fraser, F. C.: *Medical Genetics: Principles and Practice.* Philadelphia, Lea and Febiger, 1974.

Page, E. W., Villee, C. A., and Villee, D. B.: *Human Reproduction: The Core Content of Obstetrics, Gynecology and Perinatal Medicine.* Philadelphia, W. B. Saunders Co., 1976, pp. 201–222.

Patten, B. M.: Varying developing mechanisms in teratology. *Pediatrics 19*:734, 1957.

Persaud, T. V. N., and Ellington, A. C : Teratogenic activity of cannabis resin. *Lancet 2*:406, 1968.

Persaud, T. V. N., and Moore, K. L.: Causes and prenatal diagnosis of congenital abnormalities. *J. Obstet. Gynecol. Nursing 3*:40, 1974.

Poswillo, S.: Mechanisms and pathogenesis of malformation. *Br. Med. J. 32*:59, 1976.

Punnett, H. H., Kistenmacher, M. L., Toro-Sola, M. A., and Kohn, G.: Quinacrine fluorescence and giemsa banding in trisomy 22. *Theoret. Appl. Genet. 43*:134, 1973.

Ray, M.: Autosomal deficiencies in humans. *The Nucleus (Suppl.)*:275, 1968.

Rubin, A.: *Handbook of Congenital Malformations.* Philadelphia, W. B. Saunders Co., 1967.

Saxén, L., and Rapola, J.: *Congenital Defects.* New York, Holt, Rinehart and Winston, Inc., 1969, pp. 35–75.

Sever, J. L.: Rubella and cytomegalovirus; *in* F. C. Fraser, V. A. McKusick, and R. Robinson (Eds.): *Congenital Malformations.* Proc. Third. Internat. Conf. New York, Excerpta Medica Foundation, 1970, p. 377.

Sever, J. L., Nelson, K. B., and Gilkeson, M. R.: Rubella epidemic 1964: Effect on 6000 pregnancies. *Am. J. Dis. Child. 110*:395, 1964.

Shaw, E. B., and Steinbach, H. L.: Aminopterin-induced fetal malformation: Survival of infant after attempted abortion. *Am. J. Dis. Child. 115*:477, 1968.

Smith, D. W.: Autosomal abnormalities. *Am. J. Obstet. Gynecol. 90*:1055, 1964.

Smith, D. W.: The 18 trisomy and D_1 trisomy syndromes; *in* L. I. Gardner (Ed.): *Endocrine and Genetic Diseases of Childhood.* 2nd ed., Philadelphia, W. B. Saunders Co., 1975, pp. 715–729.

Smith, D. W.: *Recognizable Patterns of Human Malformation: Genetic, Embryologic, and Clinical Aspects.* 2nd ed. Philadelphia, W. B. Saunders Co., 1976.

Smithels, R. W.: Drugs and human malformations. *Adv. Teratol. 1*:251, 1966.

Smithels, R. W.: Environmental teratogens of man. *Br. Med. J. 32*:27, 1976.

Snyder, R. D.: Congenital mercury poisoning. *N. Engl. J. Med. 284*:1014, 1971.

Sokal, J. E., and Lessmann, E. M.: Effects of cancer chemotherapeutic agents on the human fetus. *J.A.M.A. 172*:1765, 1960.

South, M. A., Tompkins, W. A. F., Morris, C. R., and Rawls, W. E.: Congenital malformations of the central nervous system associated with genital type (type 2) herpesvirus. *J. Pediatr. 75*:13, 1969.

Speidel, B. D., and Meadow, S. R.: Maternal epilepsy and abnormalities of the fetus and newborn. *Lancet 2*:839, 1972.

Stempfel, R. S., Jr.: Disorders of sexual development; *in* L. I. Gardner (Ed.): *Endocrine and Genetic Diseases of Childhood*. 2nd ed., Philadelphia, W. B. Saunders Co., 1975, pp. 551–570.

Sutherland, J. S., and Light, I. J.: The effects of drugs upon the developing fetus. *Pediatr. Clin. North Am. 12*:781, 1965.

Thiersch, J. B.: Therapeutic abortions with a folic acid antagonist, 4-aminopteroylglutamic acid (4-Amino-PGA), administered by the oral route. *Am. J. Obstet. Gynecol. 63*:1298, 1952.

Thompson, J. S., and Thompson, M. W.: *Genetics in Medicine*. 2nd ed. Philadelphia, W. B. Saunders Co., 1973.

Thorburn, M. J., and Johnson, B. E.: Apparent monosomy of a G autosome in a Jamaican infant. *J. Med. Genet. 3*:290, 1966.

Tuchmann-Duplessis, H.: The effects of teratogenic drugs; *in* E. E. Philipp, J. Barnes, and M. Newton (Eds.): *Scientific Foundations of Obstetrics and Gynecology*. London, William Heinemann, Ltd., 1970, pp. 636–648.

Uchida, I. A., Ray, M., McRae, K. N., and Besant, D. F.: Familial occurrence of trisomy 22. *Am. J. Hum. Genet. 20*:107, 1968.

Vaughan, V. C., and McKay, R. J.: *Nelson Textbook of Pediatrics*. 10th ed., Philadelphia, W. B. Saunders Co., 1975.

Venning, G. R.: The problem of human foetal abnormalities with special reference to sex hormones; *in* J. M. Robson, F. M. Sullivan, and R. L. Smith (Eds.): *Embryopathic Activity of Drugs*. London, J. & A. Churchill, Ltd., 1965, pp. 94–104.

Warkany, J.: Congenital malformations induced by maternal dietary deficiency; Experiments and their interpretations. *Harvey Lect. 48*:383, 1954.

Warkany, J.: *Congenital Malformations: Notes and Comments*. Chicago, Year Book Medical Publishers, Inc., 1971.

Warkany, J.: Warfarin embryopathy. *Teratology 14*: 205, 1976.

Warkany, J., Beaudry, P. H., and Hornstein, S.: Attempted abortion with 4-aminopteroylglutamic acid (Aminopterin): Malformations of the child. *Am. J. Dis. Child. 97*:274, 1960.

Weiss, B., and Doherty, R. A.: Methylmercury poisoning. *Teratol. 12*:311, 1975.

White, L. R., and Sever, J. L.: Etiologic agents. I. Infectious agents; *in* A. Rubin (Ed.): *Handbook of Congenital Malformations*. Philadelphia, W. B. Saunders Co., 1967, pp. 353–364.

Wickes, I. G.: Foetal defects following insulin coma therapy in early pregnancy. *Br. Med. J. 2*:1029, 1954.

Wilkins, L., Jones, H. W., Jr., Holman, G. H., and Stempfel, R. S., Jr.: Masculinization of the female fetus in association with administration of oral and intramuscular progestins during gestation; non-adrenal female pseudohermaphroditism. *J. Clin. Endocrinol. Metab. 18*:559, 1958.

Wilson, J. G.: *Environment and Birth Defects*. New York, Academic Press, Inc., 1973a.

Wilson, J. G.: Present status of drugs as teratogens in man. *Teratol. 7*:3, 1973b.

Wilson, J. G.: Mechanisms of teratogenesis. *Am. J. Anat. 136*:129, 1973c.

Witkop, C. J., Jr., Wolf, R. O., and Mehaffey, M. H.: The frequency of discolored teeth showing yellow fluorescence under ultraviolet light. *J. Oral Therap. Pharmacol. 2*:81, 1965.

Zellweger, H., McDonald, J. S., and Abbo, G.: Is lysergic acid diethylamide a teratogen? *Lancet 2*:1066, 1967.

Part II

CRITICAL PERIODS IN BEHAVIORAL DEVELOPMENT

Editor's Comments on Paper 5

5 **SCOTT**
Critical Periods in Behavioral Development

The concept of development is most usefully defined in terms of the concept of systems. Seen as an attribute of living systems, development is defined as organizational change within an individual, in contrast to evolutionary change which is defined as organizational change in a species as a whole.

Organizational processes continue throughout the lifetime of an individual at greater or lesser speeds. The distinction between organizational change that takes place prior to birth or hatching and that which takes place later is largely an artificial one. While the event of birth or hatching produces great changes in possibilities for the expression of behavior and in the nature of the effects of the organizational process of learning, much behavior appears prior to birth or hatching. Conversely, many developmental processes based on physiological organization continue for weeks, months, or years thereafter, depending on the life span of the organism and the nature of the organizational processes concerned. The concept of "the innate" is therefore relatively superficial and can be discarded. What *is* important is the nature of the organizational processes that go on in development and their relationships to each other.

It has sometimes been alleged that the concept of critical periods is a crude analogy carried over from early embryology to behavioral phenomena. This is not the case. In every instance, the phenomenon of critical periods in behavioral development has been first recognized independently, and only thereafter has the resemblance to embryological phenomena been pointed out. On the basis of new knowledge concerning organizational processes, it is now possible to establish a theoretical framework embracing all such processes. As will be seen in the theoretical section of this book, there is an essential unity of organizational processes in living systems.

There is such a variety of behavioral and behavior-related processes that exhibit the critical period phenomenon that it would be impossible, in the space of this book, to present a detailed historical introduction to each. I have, therefore, selected papers of special interest to illustrate the most important cases of critical periods in behavioral development. As a general introduction, I can add little to my 1962 paper (Paper 5), which surveyed the literature available at that time.

5

Reprinted from *Science* **138**:949–958 (1962)

Critical Periods in Behavioral Development

Critical periods determine the direction of social, intellectual, and emotional development.

J. P. Scott

A number of years ago I was given a female lamb taken from its mother at birth. My wife and I raised it on the bottle for the first 10 days of life and then placed it out in the pasture with a small flock of domestic sheep. As might have been expected from folklore, the lamb became attached to people and followed the persons who fed it. More surprisingly, the lamb remained independent of the rest of the flock when we restored it to the pasture. Three years later it was still following an independent grazing pattern. In addition, when it was mated and had lambs of its own it became a very indifferent mother, allowing its offspring to nurse but showing no concern when the lamb moved away with the other members of the flock (*1*).

Since following the flock is such a universal characteristic of normal sheep, I was impressed by the extensive and permanent modification of this behavior that resulted from a brief early experience. The results suggested that Freud was right concerning the importance of early experience, and pointed toward the existence of critical periods in behavioral development. As I soon discovered, there is considerable evidence that a critical period for determining early social relationships is a widespread phenomenon in vertebrates; such a critical period had long been known in ants (*2*).

The theory of critical periods is not a new one in either biology or psychology. It was strongly stated by Stockard in 1921, in connection with his experiments on the induction of monstrosities in fish embryos, although he gave credit to Dareste for originating the basic idea 30 years earlier (*3*). In experimenting with the effects of various inorganic chemicals upon the development of *Fundulus* eggs, Stockard at first thought one-eyed monsters were specifically caused by the magnesium ion. Further experiments showed him that almost any chemical would produce the same effect, provided it was applied at the proper time during development. These experiments and those of Child (*4*) and his students established the fact that the most rapidly growing tissues in an embryo are the most sensitive to any change in conditions, thus accounting for the specificity of effects at particular times.

Meanwhile Freud had attempted to explain the origin of neuroses in human patients as the result of early experience and had implied that certain periods in the life of an infant are times of particular sensitivity. In 1935, Lorenz (*5*) emphasized the importance of critical periods for the formation of primary social bonds (imprinting) in birds, remarking on their similarity to critical periods in the development of the embryo, and McGraw soon afterward (*6*) pointed out the existence of critical periods for optimal learning of motor skills in the human infant.

Since then, the phenomenon of critical periods has excited the imagination of a large group of experimenters interested in human and animal development. In describing this fast-moving scientific field, I shall point out some of the most significant current developments. More detailed information is available in some excellent recent reviews (*7, 8*).

To begin with, three major kinds of critical-period phenomena have been discovered. These involve optimal periods for learning, for infantile stimulation, and for the formation of basic social relationships. The last of these has been established as a widespread phenomenon in the animal kingdom and consequently receives major attention in this article.

The author is senior staff scientist at the Roscoe B. Jackson Memorial Laboratory, Bar Harbor, Maine.

Periods Are Based on Processes

In the dog, the development of behavior may be divided into several natural periods marked off by important changes in social relationships (Table 1). Only a few other species have been studied in sufficient detail for making adequate comparisons, but enough data have been accumulated to show that similar periods can be identified in other mammals and in birds (*9, 10*). I originally expected to find that the course of postnatal development, like that of embryonic development, would be essentially similar in all vertebrates, and that while the periods might be extended or shortened, the same pattern of development would be evident in all (*11*). However, comparison of only two species, man and the dog, shows that the periods can actually occur in reverse order, and that there is an astonishing degree of flexibility in behavioral development (*12*).

This leads to the conclusion that the important aspect of each developmental period is not time sequence but the fact that each represents a major developmental process. Thus, the neonatal period is chiefly characterized by the process of neonatal nutrition—nursing in mammals and parental feeding in many birds. The transition period is characterized by the process of transition to adult methods of nutrition and locomotion and the appearance of adult patterns of social behavior, at least in immature form. The period of socialization is the period in which primary social bonds are formed. If we consider processes alone, it is apparent that they are not completely dependent on each other and that they can therefore be arranged in different orders. It is also apparent that certain of these processes persist beyond the periods characterized by them. For example, a mammal usually retains throughout life the ability to suck which characterizes the neonatal period, although in most cases this ability is little used.

Process of Primary Socialization

Since one of the first acts of a young mammal is to nurse, and since food rewards are known to modify the behavior of adult animals, it once seemed logical to suppose that the process of forming a social attachment begins with food rewards and develops as an acquired drive. However, the experimental evidence does not support this extreme viewpoint. Brodbeck reared a group of puppies during the critical period of socialization, feeding half of them by hand and the other half by machine, but giving all of them the same degree of human contact (*13*). He found that the two sets of puppies became equally attached to people. This result was later confirmed by Stanley and his co-workers (*14*), who found that the only difference in response between the machine-fed and the hand-fed puppies was that the latter yelped more when they saw the experimenter. Elliot and King (*15*) fed all their puppies by hand but overfed one group and underfed another. The hungry puppies became more rapidly attached to the handlers. We can conclude that, in the dog, food rewards per se are not necessary for the process of socialization, but that hunger will speed it up.

Fisher (*16*) reared fox terrier puppies in isolation boxes through the entire socialization period. The puppies were fed mechanically (thus, food was entirely eliminated as a factor in the experiment), but they were removed from the boxes for regular contacts with the experimenter. One group of puppies was always rewarded by kind social treatment. A second group was sometimes rewarded and sometimes punished, but in a purely random way. Still a third group was always punished for any positive approach to the experimenter. The puppies that were both rewarded and punished showed most attraction and dependency behavior with respect to the experimenter, and the puppies that were always punished showed the least. After the treatment was discontinued, all the puppies began coming toward the experimenter, and the differences rapidly disappeared. This leads to the surprising conclusion that the process of socialization is not inhibited by punishment and may even be speeded up by it.

At approximately 3 weeks of age—that is, at the beginning of the period of socialization—young puppies begin to bark or whine when isolated or placed in strange places. Elliot and Scott (*17*) showed that the reaction to isolation in a strange place reaches a peak at 6 to 7 weeks of age, approximately the midpoint of the critical period, and begins to decline thereafter. Scott, Deshaies, and Morris (*18*) found that separating young puppies overnight from their mother and litter mates in a strange pen for 20 hours per day produced a strong emotional reaction and speeded up the process of socialization to human handlers. All this evidence indicates that any sort of strong emotion, whether hunger, fear, pain, or loneliness, will speed up the process of socialization. No experiments have been carried out to determine the effects of pleasant types of emotion, such as might be aroused by play and handling, but these were probably a factor in Brodbeck's experiment with machine-fed puppies.

The results of these experiments on dogs agree with evidence from other species. While they were going on, Harlow (*19*) was performing his famous experiments with rhesus monkeys isolated at birth and supplied with dummy "mothers." When given the choice between a comfortable cloth-covered mother without a nipple and an uncomfortable mother made of wire screening but equipped with a functional nursing bottle, the young rhesus monkeys definitely preferred the cloth-covered models from which they had received no food rewards. Harlow concluded that the acquired-drive theory of the origin of social attachment could be discarded.

Later, Igel and Calvin (*20*) performed a similar but more elaborate experiment with puppies. These animals had more opportunity to choose, being provided with four kinds of mother models: comfortable and uncomfortable, each type with and without nipples. Like rhesus monkeys, the puppies preferred the comfortable "mother" but usually chose one with a nipple. Thus, it appears that food rewards do contribute something to the social relationship, although they do not form its prime basis.

Since then Harlow (*21*) has raised to maturity the monkeys raised on dummy mothers, has mated them, and has observed their behavior toward their own young. They become uniformly poor mothers, neglecting their offspring and often punishing them when they cry. In spite of such rejection, the young rhesus infants desperately crawl toward their mothers and give every evidence of becoming attached to them, although perhaps not as strongly as in the normal relationship. Here again punishment does not inhibit the formation of a social bond.

The hypothesis that the primary social bond originates through food rewards had already been shown to be invalid in the precocial birds, many of which form attachments prior to the time when they begin to feed. Lorenz (*5*) was the first to point out the significance of this phenomenon, which he called "imprinting." He also stated that it differed from conditioning, primarily in that it was very rapid and apparently irreversible. However, rapid formation and great persistence are also characteristic of many conditioned responses and other learned behavior. Fabricius (*22*) pointed out that no sharp line can be drawn between imprinting and conditioning, and Collias (*23*) concluded that imprinting is a form of learned behavior that is self-reinforcing.

The process of imprinting in young ducklings and chicks has since been experimentally analyzed in much detail, with results that invariably confirm the conclusion that it takes place without any obvious external rewards or reinforcement. Hess (*24*) found that if he caused young ducklings to follow a model over varying distances or over

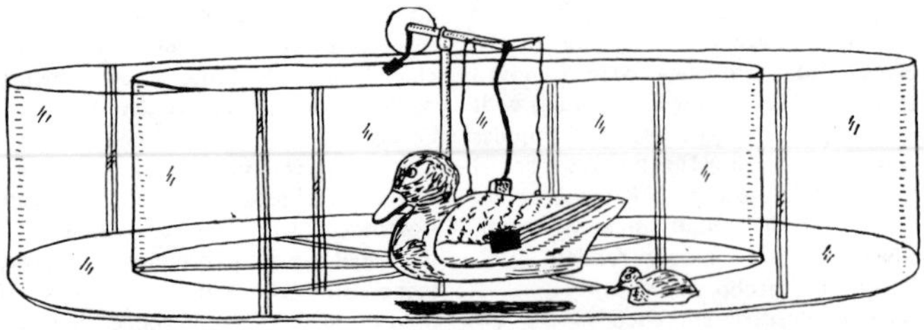

Fig. 1. Hess's apparatus for measuring the following response in ducklings and chicks. A decoy revolves on a circular path, the young duckling staying nearby. Other revolving objects may be substituted for the decoy, which is wired for sound. The following response is a major positive timing mechanism that initiates the critical period for imprinting; it is also an indicator that an attachment has been formed. [From a photo by E. H. Hess]

hurdles, the ducklings which had to make the greater effort became more strongly imprinted. He also found that the drug meprobamate and its congener carisoprodol, which are muscle relaxants as well as tranquilizers, greatly reduce imprinting if given during the critical period. James (*25*) found that chicks would become attached to an object illuminated by a flickering light, even though they were not allowed to follow, and Gray (*26*) later showed that they will become attached to a motionless object illuminated by a steady light and viewed from an isolation box. It is therefore apparent that chicks can become imprinted without following, although muscular tension may still be important.

Guiton (*27*) found that chicks allowed to follow a model in a group become less strongly imprinted than chicks exposed singly, and he attributed the results to the greater fear shown by the isolated chicks. Recently, Pitz and Ross (*28*) subjected young chicks following a model to a loud sound and found that this increased the speed with which they formed a social bond. Hess (*29*) (with the apparatus shown in Fig. 1) has given a mild electric shock to chicks following a model and finds that this also increases the strength of imprinting. Instead of avoiding the model, the distressed chick runs after it more closely.

We may conclude that these young birds become attached to any object to which they are long exposed during the critical period, even when their contact is only visual. We may also conclude that the speed of formation of a social bond is dependent upon the degree of emotional arousal, irrespective of the nature of that arousal. Whether attachment is the result of the emotion itself or of the reduction of emotion as the chick or duckling approaches the model is still a matter of conjecture (*30*).

Table 1. Periods of development in the puppy and song sparrow. The six periods of development described by Nice (*10*) for the song sparrow correspond to the first four periods in the puppy, as indicated in the table. The young of the two species are born or hatched in an immature state, require intensive parental care and feeding, and go through much the same stages before becoming independent. Development is much more rapid in the bird than in the puppy, although small mammals such as mice mature at about the same rate as birds.

Puppy			Song sparrow		
Name of period	Length of period (weeks)	Initial event	Name of period	Length of period (days)	Initial event
I. Neonatal	0–2	Birth, nursing	Stage 1 (nestling)	0–4	Hatching, gaping
II. Transition	2–3	Eyes open	Stage 2	5–6	Eyes open
III. Socialization	3–10	Startle to sound	Stage 3	7–9	Cowering—first fear reactions
			Stage 4 (fledgling)	10–16	Leaving nest—first flight
			Stage 5	17–28	Full flight
IV. Juvenile	10–	Final weaning	Stage 6 (juvenile)	29–	Independent feeding

Timing Mechanisms

The basic timing mechanisms for developmental periods are obviously the biological processes of growth and differentiation, usually called maturation. For various reasons, these are not precisely correlated with age from birth or hatching. For example, birds often retain newly formed eggs in their bodies overnight, thus incubating them for several hours before laying. By chilling duck eggs just before placing them in an incubator (thus killing all embryos except those in the earliest stages of development) Gottlieb (*31*) was able to time the age of ducklings from the onset of incubation rather than from hatching and found that variation in the timing for the critical period was much reduced. No such exact timing studies have been made in mammals, but I have estimated that there is at least a week's variation in development among puppies at 3 weeks of age, and the variation among human infants must be considerably greater (*32*).

Another approach to the problem is to try to identify the actual mechanisms which open and close a period. Since an important part of forming a primary social relationship appears to be emotional arousal while the young animal is in contact with another, it is obvious that the critical period for socialization could be timed by the appearance of behavioral mechanisms which maintain or prevent contact, and this indeed is the case. There are demonstrable positive mechanisms, varying from species to species, which bring young animals close to other members of their kind: the clinging response of young rhesus monkeys; the following response of chicks, ducklings, and lambs and other herd animals; the social investigation, tail wagging, and playful fighting of puppies; and the visual investigation and smiling of the human infant (*33*). These are, of course, accompanied by interacting responses from adult and immature members of the species: holding and clasping by primate mothers, brooding of mother hens and other birds, calling by mother sheep, investigation and play on the part of other young puppies, and the various supporting and nurturing activities of human mothers.

If contact and emotional arousal result in social attachment, there must be negative mechanisms which prevent such attachment once the critical period is past. Perhaps the most widespread of these is the development of a fear response which causes the young animal to immediately leave the vicinity of a stranger and hence avoid contact. This developing fear response is found in young chicks (*7*), ducklings (*22, 34*), dogs (*35*; Fig. 2), rhesus monkeys (*36*), and in many other birds and mammals. Even in children there is a period between the ages of 5 and 12 months in which there is a mounting fear of strangers (*37*), sometimes called "8-months anxiety" (*38*). As already pointed out, there is a time in development when certain fear responses actually facilitate imprinting, but, as they grow stronger, the escape reaction follows so quickly that it prevents contact altogether.

Another sort of negative mechanism is the rejection of strange young by adult sheep, goats, and many other herd animals (*39*). In these species the mothers become strongly attached to the young within a few hours after birth and refuse to accept strangers thereafter (Fig. 3). This indicates that the rapid formation of emotional bonds is not limited to young animals.

These timing mechanisms all depend primarily on the development of social behavior patterns, but both sensory and motor development can also influence timing. For example, a very immature animal cannot maintain contact by following, and in slowly developing altricial birds such as jackdaws and doves (*5, 40*), the period of imprinting comes much later than it does in the precocial species. In the human infant the process of socialization begins before the adult motor patterns develop, but contact is maintained by visual exploration and by the smiling response to human faces (*33*). Thus, understanding the process of socialization and its timing mechanisms in any particular species requires a systematic study of the development of the various capacities which affect the time of onset and the duration of the critical period. These include sensory, motor, and learning capacities as well as the ability to perform essential patterns of social behavior.

The fact that emotional arousal is so strongly connected with the process of primary socialization suggests that the capacity to produce emotional reactions may also govern the time of onset of a critical period. Figure 4 summarizes the results of a study of emotional development in the dog during the critical period. If puppies are kept in large fields, totally isolated from people, fear and escape responses toward human beings very nearly reach a maximum by the time the puppies are 14 weeks old—a finding that fixes the upper limit of the period of socialization (*35*). On the other hand, the peak of the emotional response to isolation in a strange place occurs when puppies are approximately 6 to 7 weeks old, as does the peak of the heart-rate response to handling. At this age, such emotional arousal actually contributes to the strength of the social bond. Fuller (*41*) was unable to condition the heart-rate response consistently until puppies were 5 weeks old. This indicates that one of the factors that brings the critical period to a close may be the developing ability of the young puppy to associate fear responses with particular stimuli.

All this suggests that if the development of the escape response to strangers could be held in check, the critical period might be extended indefinitely. Raising puppies in small isolation boxes during the critical period inhibits the development of the escape response, but they still show obvious signs of fear when they are first removed from their cages. Fuller (*42*) reports some success in socializing these older pups by

Fig. 2. Puppies reacting to leash training, according to their experience during the critical period (see *35*). (Top) Reaction of a puppy that had had contact with people for 1 week during the peak of the critical period. (Bottom) Reaction of a puppy that had had contact only with other dogs prior to the end of the critical period. This puppy shows an extreme fear reaction and refuses to follow.

overcoming their fear responses, either by careful handling or through the use of tranquilizing drugs.

Fear responses thus have the dual effect of facilitating the formation of the social bond during the critical period (along with other emotions) and of bringing the period to a close. This is understandable because the type of fear which terminates the critical period is a developing fear of strange animals. In the early part of the critical period the escape reaction is either lacking or is momentary and weak. At the close of the period it is strong enough to prevent contact altogether.

Formation of Affectional Bonds in Adult Life

Until recently, most investigators have concentrated their attention on the critical period for primary socialization or imprinting and few have gone on to study similar phenomena in later development. This field of investigation is just beginning to open up, though many related facts have long been known. For example, many birds form strong pair bonds which are maintained as long as both members survive. In studying the development of various types of social bonds in different species of ducks, Schutz (*43*) finds that, while attachments to particular individuals may be formed in the early critical period from 12 to 17 hours after hatching, the critical period for the attachment to the species may not come until sometime later, in some cases as late as 30 days after hatching, and the attachment to a particular member of the opposite sex, or the pair bond, does not come until the age of 5 months or so. Schutz also finds that female mallards cannot be sexually imprinted with respect to other species but always mate with other mallards no matter what their earliest experience has been. A similar phenomenon is reported by Warriner (*44*), who finds that male pigeons prefer to mate with birds whose color is similar to that of the parents who reared them, whether of the same or another color from themselves, but females show no preference.

Fig. 3. Rejection by a mother goat of a kid not her own. The behavior of adults terminates the critical period for primary socialization in sheep and goats. Immediately after giving birth the mother will accept any young kid, but within a few hours she will reject any strange kid that approaches. [From a photo by A. U. Moore]

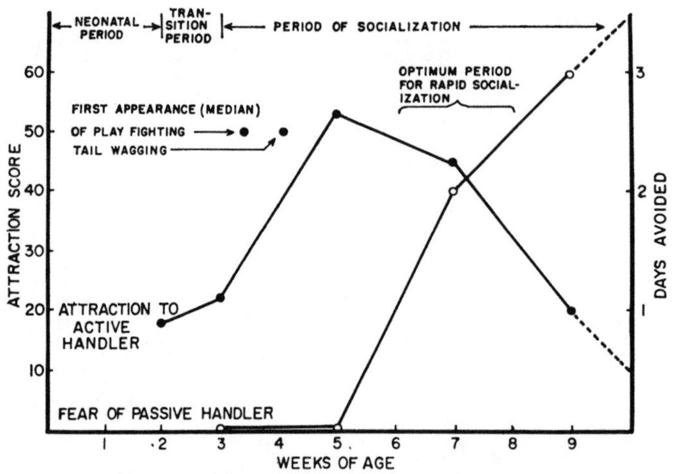

Fig. 4. Timing mechanisms for the critical period in puppies (see *35*). The period is initiated by positive behavior mechanisms, such as playful fighting, which result in attraction to a strange individual, and it is brought to a close by the development of a fear response which causes the attraction to decline. The optimum period for rapid and permanent socialization comes shortly after the appearance of prolonged avoidance reactions.

Certain species of mammals, such as foxes (*45*), form long-lasting mating bonds. It is possible that the violence of the sexual emotions contributes to the formation of the adult bond, just as other sorts of emotional arousal are important to the primary socialization of the infant. Klopfer (*46*) has suggested that the rapid formation of the social bond in a mother goat toward her kid is the result of the high degree of emotional arousal which accompanies the birth of the offspring.

In short, it seems likely that the formation of a social attachment through contact and emotional arousal is a process that may take place throughout life, and that although it may take place more slowly outside of certain critical periods, the capacity for such an attachment is never completely lost.

At this point it may be remarked that, in attempting to analyze the development of affection and social bonds objectively, scientists have often tried to simplify the problem by postulating various unitary, unromantic, and sometimes unesthetic explanations. One of these was the "acquired drive" hypothesis—that children love you because you feed them. Taking a more moderate view Harlow (*19*) has emphasized "contact comfort" as a major variable —that the young monkey begins to love its mother because she feels warm and comfortable—but that a number of other factors are involved. As this article indicates, evidence is accumulating that there is a much less specific, although equally unromantic, general mechanism involved—that given any kind of emotional arousal a young animal will become attached to any individual or object with which it is in contact for a sufficiently long time. The necessary arousal would, of course, include various specific kinds of emotions associated with food rewards and contact comfort.

It should not be surprising that many kinds of emotional reactions contribute to a social relationship. The surprising thing is that emotions which we normally consider aversive should produce the same effect as those which appear to be rewarding. This apparent paradox is partially resolved by evidence that the positive effect of unpleasant emotions is normally limited to early infancy by the development of escape reactions.

Nevertheless, this concept leads to the somewhat alarming conclusion that an animal (and perhaps a person) of any age, exposed to certain individuals or physical surroundings for any length of time, will inevitably become attached to them, the rapidity of the process being governed by the degree of emotional arousal associated with them. I need not dwell on the consequences for human behavior, if this conclusion should apply to our species as well as to other animals, except to point out that it provides an explanation of certain well-known clinical observations such as the development by neglected children of strong affection for cruel and abusive parents, and the various peculiar affectional relationships that develop between prisoners and jailors, slaves and masters, and so on. Perhaps the general adaptive nature of this mechanism is that since the survival of any member of a highly social species depends upon the rapid development of social relationships, a mechanism has evolved which makes it almost impossible to inhibit the formation of social bonds.

Critical Periods of Learning

Unlike the process of socialization, the phenomenon of critical periods of learning was first noticed in children rather than in lower animals. McGraw's *(47)* famous experiment with the twins Johnny and Jimmy was a deliberate attempt to modify behavioral development by giving one of a pair of identical twins special early training. The result varied according to the activity involved. The onset of walking, for example, was not affected by previous practice or help. Other activities, however, could be greatly speeded up—notably roller skating, in which the favored twin became adept almost as soon as he could walk. In other activities performance was actually made worse by early practice, simply because of the formation of unskillful habits. McGraw *(6)* concluded that there are critical periods for learning which vary from activity to activity; for each kind of coordinated muscular activity there is an optimum period for rapid and skillful learning.

In an experiment with rats, Hebb *(48)* used the technique of providing young animals with many opportunities for spontaneous learning rather than formal training. Pet rats raised in the rich environment of a home performed much better on learning tasks than rats reared in barren laboratory cages. Since then, other experimenters *(49)* have standardized the "rich" environment as a large cage including many objects and playthings and have gotten similar effects.

Forgays (see *50*) finds that the age at which the maximum effect is produced is limited to the period from approximately 20 to 30 days of age, immediately after weaning. A similar experience in adult life produces no effect. In rats, at any rate, the critical period of learning seems to coincide with the critical period of primary socialization, and it may be that the two are in some way related. Candland and Campbell *(51)* find that fearful behavior in response to a strange situation begins to increase in rats between 20 and 30 days after birth, and Bernstein *(52)* showed earlier that discrimination learning could be improved by gentle handling beginning at 20 days. It may well be that the development of fear limits the capacity for future learning as well as the formation of social relationships.

In addition to these studies on motor learning and problem solving, there are many experiments demonstrating the existence of critical periods for the learning of social behavior patterns. It has long been known that many kinds of birds do not develop the characteristic songs of their species if they are reared apart from their own kind *(53)*. More recently, Thorpe *(54)* discovered a critical period for this effect in the chaffinch. If isolated at 3 or 4 days of age, a young male chaffinch produces an incomplete song, but if he hears adults singing, as a fledgling 2 or 3 weeks old or in early juvenile life before he sings himself, he will the next year produce the song characteristic of the species, even if he has been kept in isolation. In nature, the fine details of the song are added at the time of competition over territory, within a period of 2 or 3 weeks, when the bird is about a year old. At this time it learns the songs of two or three of its neighbors, and never learns any others in subsequent years. The critical period for song learning is thus a relatively long one, but it is definitely over by the time the bird is a year old. There is no obvious explanation for its ending at this particular time, but it is possible that learning a complete song pattern in some way interferes with further learning.

King and Gurney *(55)* found that adult mice reared in groups during youth fought more readily than animals isolated at 20 days of age. Later experiments showed that most of the effect was produced in a 10-day period just after weaning, and that similar experience as adults produced little or no effect *(56)*. Thus, there appears to be a critical period for learning to fight through social experience, and this experience need be no more than contact through a wire. In this case the effect is probably produced by association with other mice before the fear response has been completely developed. Similarly, Fisher *(16)* and Fuller *(57)* inhibited the development of attacking behavior in fox terriers by raising them in isolation through the critical period for socialization. The animals would fight back somewhat ineffectually if attacked, but did not initiate conflicts. Tinbergen *(58)* found a critical period in dogs for learning territorial boundaries, coinciding with sexual maturity.

The results of corresponding experiments on sexual behavior vary from species to species. In mice, rearing in isolation produced no effects *(59)*. Beach *(60)* found that male rats reared with either females or males were actually slower to respond to sexual behavior than isolated males, and he suggested that habits of playful fighting established by the group-reared animals interfered with sexual behavior later on. In guinea pigs, contact with other young animals improves sexual performance *(61)*.

On the other hand, young chimpanzees *(62)* reared apart from their kind can only be mated with experienced animals. Harlow *(21)* discovered that his rhesus infants reared on dummy mothers did not develop normal patterns of sexual behavior, and he was able to obtain matings only by exposing females to experienced males (Fig. 5). Normal behavior can be developed by allowing 20-minute daily play periods with other young monkeys, but if rhesus infants are reared apart from all other monkeys beyond the period when they spontaneously play with their fellows, patterns of both sexual and maternal behavior fail to develop normally. These results suggest that play has an important role in developing adult patterns of social behavior in these primates, and that the decline of play behavior sets the upper limit of the critical period during which normal adult behavior may be developed.

Such great changes in the social environment rarely occur in humans even by accident, but Money, Hampson, and Hampson (*63*) have studied the development of hermaphroditic children who have been reared as one sex and then changed to the other. They find that if this occurs before 2½ years of age, very little emotional disturbance results. Thus, there is a critical period for learning the sex role, this capacity persisting unchanged up to a point in development which roughly corresponds to the age when children begin to use and understand language. Perhaps more important, this is the age when children first begin to take an interest in, and play with, members of their own age group.

It is difficult to find a common factor in these critical periods for learning. In some species, such as rats, mice, dogs, and sheep, certain critical periods for learning coincide with the period for primary socialization and seem to be similarly brought to a close by the development of fear reactions. Other critical periods, in chaffinches and dogs, coincide with the formation of adult mating bonds. However, the critical period for sexual learning in the rhesus monkey comes later than that for primary socialization (*64*), as do critical periods for various kinds of learning in human beings.

Part of this apparent inconsistency arises from our ignorance regarding timing mechanisms. One such mechanism must be the development of learning capacities, and we have evidence in dogs (*65*), rhesus monkeys (*66*), and human infants (*12*) that learning capacities change during development, sometimes in a stepwise fashion. One element in these capacities is the ability to learn things which facilitate subsequent learning.

It is equally possible, however, to "learn not to learn," and such a negative learning set may act to bring the critical period to a close. At this point, we can only state a provisional general hypothesis: that the critical period for any specific sort of learning is that time when maximum capacities—sensory, motor, and motivational, as well as psychological ones—are first present.

Critical Periods for Early Stimulation

Experiments to determine the effects of early stimulation have been mainly performed on infant mice and rats, which are usually weaned at about 21 days at the earliest, and have been concerned with the effect of stimulation during this pre-weaning period. All investigators beginning with Levine (*67*) and Schaefer (*68*), agree that rats handled during the first week or 10 days of life have a lessened tendency to urinate and defecate in a strange "open field" situation, learn avoidance behavior more readily, and survive longer when deprived of food and water. In short, early stimulation produces an animal that is less timorous, learns more quickly, and is more vigorous. Levine found that the effect could be obtained by a variety of stimuli, including electric shock and mechanical shaking as well as handling. This ruled out learned behavior as an explanation of the effect, and Levine, Alpert, and Lewis (*69*) discovered that animals handled in the early period showed a much earlier maturation of the adrenocortical response to stress. Levine interpreted these results as indicating that the laboratory environment did not provide sufficient stimulation for the proper development of the hormonal systems of the animals. This interpretation is in agreement with Richter's finding (*70*) that laboratory rats are quite deficient in adrenocortical response as compared with the wild variety.

Fig. 5. Through play behavior during a critical period young rhesus monkeys develop the capacity for adult sexual behavior. The two at right exhibit an approximation of the adult posture. It is almost impossible to mate monkeys raised with cloth "mothers" without an opportunity for play with other infants. [H. F. Harlow]

Schaefer, Weingarten, and Towne (*71*) have duplicated Levine's results by the use of cold alone, and have suggested temperature as a possible unitary mechanism. However, their findings are not necessarily in disagreement with those of Levine, as the hormonal stress response can be elicited by a variety of stimuli, and temperature may simply be another of the many kinds of stimuli which produce the effect.

According to Thompson and Schaefer (*72*) the earlier the stimulation the greater the effect. If the hormonal mechanism is the chief phenomenon involved, we can say that there is a critical period during the first week or 10 days of life, since the adrenal response in any case matures and becomes fixed by 16 days of age.

Denenberg (*73*) takes a somewhat different approach, pointing out that there should be optimal levels of stimulation, so that either very weak or very strong stimulation would produce poor results. He suggests that there are different critical periods for the effect of early stimulation, depending on the intensity of stimulation and the kind of later behavior measured. Working within the critical first 10 days, Denenberg found that the best avoidance learning was produced by stimulation in the second half of the period, whereas the best survival rates were produced by stimulation in the first half. Weight was approximately equally affected, except that there was little effect in the first 3 days (*74*).

Analyzing the effect on avoidance learning, Denenberg (*75*) and his associates found that both unhandled controls and rats handled for the first 20 days performed poorly, the former because they were too emotional and the latter because they were too calm to react quickly. An intermediate amount of emotional response produces the best learning, and this can be produced by handling only in the first 10 days of life; handling during the second 10 days has a lesser effect. No handling produces too much emotionality, and handling for 20 days results in too little. Irrespective of the effect on learning, the data lead to the important conclusion that emotional stimulation during a critical period early in life can lead to the reduction of emotional responses in later life.

More precisely, there appear to be two critical periods revealed by research on early stimulation of rats, one based on a physiological process (the development of the adrenal cortical stress mechanism) and extending to 16 days of age at the latest, the other based on a psychological process (the reduction of fear through familiarity) (*51*), beginning about 17 days when the eyes first open and extending to 30 days. The effects of handling during these two periods are additive, and many experiments based on arbitrary time rather than developmental periods undoubtedly include both.

The deleterious effects of excessive stimulation in the life of the infant may also be interpreted as a traumatic emotional experience. Bowlby (*76*), in studying a group of juvenile thieves, found that a large proportion of them had been separated from their mothers in early infancy, and he postulated that this traumatic emotional experience had affected their later behavior. Since this conclusion was based on retrospective information, he and his coworkers have since studied the primary symptoms of separation and have described in detail the emotional reactions of infants sent to hospitals, and thus separated from their mothers (*77*). Schaffer (*78*) found a difference in reaction to separation before 7 months and separation afterward. Both sets of infants were disturbed, but they were disturbed in different ways. Infants show increasingly severe emotional reactions to adoption from 3 through 12 months of age (*33*). It seems logical to place the beginning of the critical period for maximum emotional disturbance at approximately 7 months—at the end of the critical period for primary socialization, which Gray (*79*) places at approximately 6 weeks to 6 months. Infants whose social relationships have been thoroughly established and whose fear responses toward strangers have been fully developed are much more likely to be upset by changes than infants in which these relationships and responses have not yet been developed.

However, not all apparently "traumatic" early experiences have such a lasting effect. Experimental work shows that young animals have a considerable capacity to recover from unpleasant emotions experienced in a limited period in early life (*80*), and that what is traumatic in one species may not be in another. While young rats become calmer after infantile stimulation, young mice subjected to excessive auditory stimulation later become more emotional (*81*). At this point it is appropriate to point out that critical periods are not necessarily involved in every kind of early experience. Raising young chimpanzees in the dark produces degeneration of the retina, but this is a long and gradual process (*82*).

Another approach to the problem is to stimulate emotional responses in mothers and observe the effect on the offspring. Thompson (*83*) and other authors (*84*) have shown that the offspring of rats made fearful while pregnant are more likely to be overemotional in the open-field situation than the offspring of animals not so stimulated. Since any direct influence of maternal behavior was ruled out by cross-fostering experiments, it seems likely that the result is produced by modification of the adrenocortical stress mechanism—in this case, by secretion of maternal hormones acting on the embryo rather than by stimulation after birth of the young animal itself. No precise critical period for the effect has been established, but it is probably confined to the latter part of pregnancy. Similar effects have been obtained in mice (*85*), and if such effects can be demonstrated in other mammals, the implications for prenatal care in human beings are obvious.

It is interesting to note that, whereas shocking the mother both before and after parturition has the effect of increasing emotional responses in the young, the emotional responses of young rats are *decreased* when the treatment is applied directly to them. The explanation of this contradiction must await direct experiments on the endocrine system.

General Theory of Critical Periods

There are at least two ways in which experience during critical periods may act on behavioral development. The critical period for primary socialization constitutes a turning point. Experience during a short period early in life determines which shall be the close relatives of the young animal, and this, in turn, leads the animal to develop in one of two directions—the normal one, in which it becomes attached to and mates with a member of its own species, or an abnormal one, in which it becomes attached to a different species, with consequent disrupting effects upon sexual and other social relationships with members of its own kind.

The concept of a turning point applies equally well to most examples of critical periods for learning. Up to a certain point in development a chaffinch can learn several varieties of song, but once it has learned one of them it no longer has a choice. Similarly, the human infant can learn either sex role up to a certain age, but once it has learned one or the other, changing over becomes increasingly difficult. What is learned at particular points limits and interferes with subsequent learning, and Schneirla and Rosenblatt (*86*) have suggested that there are critical stages of learning—that what has been learned at a particular time in development may be critical for whatever follows.

A second sort of action during a critical period consists of a nonspecific stimulus producing an irrevocable result, not modifiable in subsequent development. Thus, almost any sort of stimulus has the effect of modifying the development of the endocrine stress mechanism of young rats in early infancy.

Is there any underlying common principle? Each of these effects has its counterpart in embryonic development. Up to a certain point a cell taken from an amphibian embryo and transplanted to a new location will develop in accordance with its new environment. Beyond this turning point it develops in accordance with its previous location. Some cells retain a degree of lability, but none retain the breadth of choice they had before. Similarly, specific injuries produced by nonspecific causes are also found in embryonic development: damage to an embryonic optic vesicle results in a defective eye, no matter what sort of chemical produces the injury. It is obvious that the similarity between this case and the critical period for early stimulation can be accounted for by the single common process of growth, occurring relatively late in development in the case of the endocrine stress mechanism and much earlier in the development of the eye. The effects are nonspecific because of the fact that growth can be modified in only very limited ways, by being either slowed down or speeded up.

Both growth and behavioral differentiation are based on organizing processes. This suggests a general principle of organization: that once a system becomes organized, whether it is the cells of the embryo that are multiplying and differentiating or the behavior patterns of a young animal that are becoming organized through learning, it becomes progressively more difficult to reorganize the system. That is, organization inhibits reorganization. Further, organization can be strongly modified only when active processes of organization are going on, and this accounts for critical periods of development.

Conclusion

The concept of critical periods is a highly important one for human and animal welfare. Once the dangers and potential benefits for each period of life are known, it should be possible to avoid the former and take advantage of the latter.

The discovery of critical periods immediately focuses attention on the developmental processes which cause them. As these processes become understood, it is increasingly possible to deliberately modify critical periods and their results. For example, since the development of fear responses limits the period of primary socialization, we can deliberately extend the period by reducing fear reactions, either by psychological methods or by the use of tranquilizing drugs. Or, if it seems desirable, we can increase the degree of dependency of a child or pet animal by purposely increasing his emotional reactions during the critical period. Again, if infantile stimulation is desirable, parents can be taught to provide it in appropriate amounts at the proper time.

Some data suggest that for each behavioral and physiological phenomenon there is a different critical period in development. If this were literally true, the process of development, complicated by individual variability, would be so complex that the concept of critical periods would serve little useful purpose. Some sort of order can be obtained by dealing with different classes of behavioral phenomena. For example, it can be stated that the period in life in which each new social relationship is initiated is a critical one for the determination of that relationship. Furthermore, there is evidence that critical-period effects are more common early in life than they are later on, and that the critical period for primary socialization is also critical for other effects, such as the attachment to particular places (*87*), and may overlap with a critical period for the formation of basic food habits (*88*).

We may expect to find that the periods in which actual physiological damage through environmental stimulation is possible will turn out to be similarly specific and concentrated in early life.

A great deal of needed information regarding the optimum periods for acquiring motor and intellectual skills is still lacking. These skills are based not merely on age but on the relative rate of maturation of various organs. Any attempt to teach a child or animal at too early a period of development may result in his learning bad habits, or simply in his learning "not to learn," either of which results may greatly handicap him in later life. In the long run, this line of experimental work should lead to greater realization of the capacities possessed by human beings, both through avoidance of damaging experiences and through correction of damage from unavoidable accidents (*89*).

References and Notes

1. J. P. Scott, *Comp. Psychol. Monogr.* **18**, 1 (1945).
2. A. M. Fielde, *Biol. Bull.* **7**, 227 (1904).
3. C. R Stockard, *Am. J. Anat.* **28**, 115 (1921).
4. C. M. Child, *Patterns and Problems of Development* (Univ. of Chicago Press, Chicago, 1941).
5. K. Lorenz, *J. Ornithol.* **83**, 137, 289 (1935).
6. M. B. McGraw, in *Manual of Child Psychology*, L. C. Carmichael, Ed. (Wiley, New York, 1946), pp. 332–369.
7. E. H. Hess, in *Nebraska Symposium on Motivation* (Univ. of Nebraska Press, Lincoln, 1959), pp. 44–77.
8. H. Moltz, *Psychol. Bull.* **57**, 291 (1960); J. L. Gewirtz, in *Determinants of Infant Behaviour*, B. M. Foss, Ed. (Methuen, London, 1961), pp. 213–299.
9. J. P. Scott, in *Social Behavior and Organization in Vertebrates*, W. Etkin, Ed. (Univ. of Chicago Press, Chicago, in press).
10. M. M. Nice, *Trans. Linnaean Soc. N.Y.* **6**, 1 (1943).
11. J. P. Scott and M. V. Marston, *J. Genet. Psychol.* **77**, 25 (1950).
12. J. P. Scott, *Child Develop. Monogr.*, in press.
13. A. J. Brodbeck, *Bull. Ecol. Soc. Am.* **35**, 73 (1954).
14. W. C. Stanley, private communication (1962).
15. O. Elliot and J. A. King, *Psychol. Repts.* **6**, 391 (1960).
16. A. E. Fisher, thesis, Pennsylvania State Univ. (1955).
17. O. Elliot and J. P. Scott, *J. Genet. Psychol.* **99**, 3 (1961).
18. J. P. Scott, D. Deshaies, D. D. Morris, "Effect of emotional arousal on primary socialization in the dog," address to the New York State Branch of the American Psychiatric Association, 11 Nov. 1961.
19. H. Harlow, *Am. Psychologist* **13**, 673 (1958).
20. G. J. Igel and A. D. Calvin, *J. Comp. Physiol. Psychol.* **53**, 302 (1960).
21. H. F. Harlow and M. K. Harlow, personal communication (1962).
22. E. Fabricius, *Acta Zool. Fennica* **68**, 1 (1951).
23. N. Collias, in *Roots of Behavior*, E. L. Bliss, Ed. (Harper, New York, 1962), pp. 264–273.
24. E. H. Hess, *Ann. N.Y. Acad. Sci.* **67**, 724 (1957); in *Drugs and Behavior*, L. Uhr and J. G. Miller, Eds. (Wiley, New York, 1960), pp. 268–271.
25. H. James, *Can. J. Psychol.* **13**, 59 (1959).
26. P. H. Gray, *Science* **132**, 1834 (1960).
27. P. Guiton, *Animal Behavior* **9**, 167 (1961).
28. G. F. Pitz and R. B. Ross, *J. Comp. Physiol. Psychol.* **54**, 602 (1961).
29. E. H. Hess, "Influence of early experience

on behavior," paper presented before the American Psychiatric Association, New York State Divisional Meeting, 1961.
30. H. Moltz, L. Rosenblum, N. Halikas, *J. Comp. Physiol. Psychol.* **52**, 240 (1959).
31. G. Gottlieb, *ibid.* **54**, 422 (1961).
32. J. P. Scott, *Psychosomat. Med.* **20**, 42 (1958).
33. B. M. Caldwell, *Am. Psychol.* **16**, 377 (1961).
34. R. A. Hinde, W. H. Thorpe, M. A. Vince, *Behaviour* **9**, 214 (1956).
35. D. G. Freedman, J. A. King, O. Elliot, *Science* **133**, 1016 (1961).
36. H. F. Harlow and R. R. Zimmermann, *ibid.* **130**, 421 (1959).
37. D. G. Freedman, *J. Child Psychol. Psychiat.* **1961**, 242 (1961).
38. R. A. Spitz, *Intern. J. Psychoanalysis* **31**, 138 (1950).
39. N. E. Collias, *Ecology* **37**, 228 (1956).
40. W. Craig, *J. Animal Behavior* **4**, 121 (1914).
41. J. L. Fuller and A. Christake, *Federation Proc.* **18**, 49 (1959).
42. J. L. Fuller, private communication.
43. F. Schutz, private communication.
44. C. C. Warriner, thesis, Univ. of Oklahoma (1960).
45. R. K. Enders, *Sociometry* **8**, 53–55 (1945).
46. P. H. Klopfer, *Behavioral Aspects of Ecology* (Prentice-Hall, New York, in press).
47. M. B. McGraw, *Growth: a Study of Johnny and Jimmy* (Appleton-Century, New York, 1935).
48. D. O. Hebb, *Am. Psychologist* **2**, 306 (1947).
49. D. G. Forgays and J. W. Forgays, *J. Comp. Physiol. Psychol.* **45**, 322 (1952).
50. D. G. Forgays, "The importance of experience at specific times in the development of an organism," address before the Eastern Psychological Association (1962).
51. D. K. Candland and B. A. Campbell, private communication (1962).
52. L. Bernstein, *J. Comp. Physiol. Psychol.* **50**, 162 (1957).
53. W. E. D. Scott, *Science* **14**, 522 (1901).
54. W. H. Thorpe, in *Current Problems in Animal Behaviour*, W. H. Thorpe and O. L. Zangwill, Eds. (Cambridge Univ. Press, Cambridge, 1961).
55. J. A. King and N. L. Gurney, *J. Comp. Physiol. Psychol.* **47**, 326 (1954).
56. J. A. King, *J. Genet. Psychol.* **90**, 151 (1957).
57. J. L. Fuller, "Proceedings, International Psychiatric Congress, Montreal," in press.
58. N. Tinbergen, *The Study of Instinct* (Oxford Univ. Press, Oxford, 1951).
59. J. A. King, *J. Genet. Psychol.* **88**, 223 (1956).
60. F. A. Beach, *ibid.* **60**, 121 (1942).
61. E. S. Valenstein, W. Riss, W. C. Young, *J. Comp. Physiol. Psychol.* **47**, 162 (1954).
62. H. Nissen, *Symposium on Sexual Behavior in Mammals, Amherst, Mass.* (1954), pp. 204–227.
63. J. Money, J. G. Hampson, J. L. Hampson, *Arch. Neurol. Psychiat.* **77**, 333 (1957).
64. H. Harlow, in *Determinants of Infant Behaviour*, B. M. Foss, Ed. (Wiley, New York, 1961), pp. 75–97.
65. J. L. Fuller, C. A. Easler, E. M. Banks, *Am. J. Physiol.* **160**, 462 (1950); A. C. Cornwell and J. L. Fuller, *J. Comp. Physiol. Psychol.* **54**, 13 (1961).
66. H. F. Harlow, M. K. Harlow, R. R. Rueping, W. A. Mason, *J. Comp. Physiol. Psychol.* **53**, 113 (1960).
67. S. Levine, J. A. Chevalier, S. J. Korchin, *J. Personality* **24**, 475 (1956).
68. T. Schaefer, thesis, Univ. of Chicago (1957).
69. S. Levine, M. Alpert, G. W. Lewis, *Science* **126**, 1347 (1957).
70. C. P. Richter, *Am. J. Human Genet.* **4**, 273. (1952).
71. T. Schaefer, Jr., F. S. Weingarten, J. C. Towne, *Science* **135**, 41 (1962).
72. W. R. Thompson and T. Schaefer, in *Functions of Varied Experience*, D. W. Fiske and S. R. Maddi, Eds. (Dorsey, Homewood, Ill., 1961), pp. 81–105.
73. V. H. Denenberg, in *The Behaviour of Domestic Animals*, E. S. E. Hafez, Ed. (Bailliere, Tindall and Cox, London), 109–138.
74. ——, *J. Comp. Physiol. Psychol.*, in press.
75. ——— and G. G. Karas, *Psychol. Repts.* **7**, 313 (1960).
76. J. Bowlby, *Intern. J. Psychoanalysis* **25**, 19, 107 (1944).
77. C. M. Heinicke, *Human Relations* **9**, 105 (1956).
78. H. R. Schaffer, *Brit. J. Med. Psychol.* **31**, 174 (1950).
79. P. H. Gray, *J. Psychol.* **46**, 155 (1958).
80. M. W. Kahn, *J. Genet. Psychol.* **79**, 117 (1951). A. Baron, K. H. Brookshire, R. A. Littman, *J. Comp. Physiol. Psychol.* **50**, 530 (1957).
81. G. Lindzey, D. T. Lykken, H. D. Winston, *J. Abnormal Soc. Psychol.* **61**, 7 (1960).
82. A. H. Riesen, in *Functions of Varied Experience*, D. W. Fiske and S. R. Maddi, Eds. (Dorsey, Homewood, Ill., 1961), pp. 57–80.
83. W. R. Thompson, *Science* **125**, 698 (1957).
84. C. H. Hockman, *J. Comp. Physiol. Psychol.* **54**, 679 (1961); R. Ader and M. L. Belfer, *Psychol. Repts.* **10**, 711 (1962).
85. K. Keeley, *Science* **135**, 44 (1962).
86. T. C. Schneirla and J. S. Rosenblatt, *Am. J. Orthopsychiat.* **31**, 223 (1960).
87. W. H. Thorpe, *Learning and Instinct in Animals* (Methuen, London, 1956).
88. E. H. Hess, in *Roots of Behavior*, E. L. Bliss, Ed. (Harper, New York, 1962), pp. 254–263.
89. Part of the research described in this article was supported by a Public Health Service research grant (No. M-4481) from the National Institute of Mental Health.

Part III

CRITICAL PERIODS IN THE DEVELOPMENT OF SOCIAL ATTACHMENT

Editor's Comments on Papers 6 Through 9

HISTORICAL AND GENERAL

Imprinting is the subject of another book in this series but is historically so important that it cannot be omitted here. Imprinting in domestic chicks was described by the British naturalist Spalding in 1873 and was repeatedly observed by Heinroth, as a result of handrearing, in the early years of the twentieth century (Gray, 1963; Hess, 1973). It was Konrad Lorenz, however, who first recognized its importance and gave it the name that it now bears.

Lorenz came from Vienna and received his primary scientific training in medicine. In the late 1920s, he was a medical student in New York City, where he acquired an excellent command of English. The real love of his life was ornithology and in 1935 he published his first major work, a monograph entitled *Der Kumpan in der Umwelt des Vogels.* Other ornithologists and research workers in the field of animal behavior almost immediately recognized its importance, and the editor of *The Auk* invited him to write an English summary of his paper for the benefit of American readers. This paper states his general theories concerning releasers and includes a relatively short section on imprinting, which is reprinted here. At that time, Lorenz considered imprinting to be a rather minor part of a general theory.

The fact that some of Lorenz's original concepts have not held up under detailed experimental analysis should not detract from the importance of the phenomenon and his recognition of it. In particular, imprinting in most cases does not appear to be completely irreversible. Organizational processes in living systems do tend to become stable, and the resulting organization is more and more difficult to modify as time goes on. Such processes as they affect behavior are seldom completely irreversible. The general importance of the phenomenon of imprinting is that it determines which shall be the close social relatives of the individual concerned.

Parallel to the research on imprinting in birds, and to some extent inspired by it, various workers began to investigate early attachment in human infants. As the paper by Gray (Paper 7) indicates, there are good reasons for postulating the existence of a critical period for social attachment and for primary socialization in human infants. Separation, institutionalization, and adoption interfere with normal human social development in ways that are the equivalent of results from experimental separation and deprivation in nonhuman animals. Spitz and Wolf (Paper 8) did one of the earliest descriptive studies of the normal process of human socialization, using the smiling response as an indicator. Children begin to smile at anything resembling a human face at approximately two months of age, and this response can be readily obtained up until approximately six months of age, when it begins to die away. This work was followed by numerous confirmatory studies on the smiling response.

Research in this area also received strong impetus from the work by Bowlby (Paper 9), who studied the effects of separation in human infants hospitalized for various reasons and reviewed this material in his book *Maternal Care and Mental Health.* Working with the effects of separation, Schaffer (1958) found that infants who had been separated from their mothers in hospitals showed strong emotional reactions upon their return to their parents. Under seven months of age, the infants became extremely preoccupied with environmental stimuli, constantly scanning it, sometimes with some indications of alarm. After seven months, the returning infants generally showed overdependence, as evidenced by excessive crying when left alone and by a fear of strangers.

This and other evidence suggests that the critical period for primary socialization in human infants extends from approximately six or seven weeks to approximately seven months (Scott, 1963). Schaffer and Emerson (1964) subsequently reported that children prior to seven months showed general attachments, in the sense that they would show distress whenever they were left alone. Schaffer and Emerson also found evidence of specific attachment to the mother after seven months. Fleener (1967) found that children 10–14 months would cry following separation from a stranger after 7½ hours of contact, indicating that attachments could still be readily formed. Subsequent work in this area, as reviewed by Bowlby (1969) and Ainsworth (1973), is in agreement with these conclusions. While many children show fear reactions to strangers in the third quarter of their first year, this is not universal and children generally become more tolerant of strangers as they become more mobile. Ainsworth suggests that babies find it progressively more difficult to form first attachments after seven months but that this difficulty does not become acute until approximately 3½ years in the case of institutionalized children who are placed in foster homes.

This evidence suggests that the critical period for social attachment in human infants may extend over a considerable time period, although the optimum period for initiating such an attachment is obviously between five or six weeks and seven months. I have also suggested (Scott, 1963) that humans undergo a special critical period of verbal socialization beginning at the time when the child first begins to communicate effectively with words around twenty-seven months of age.

6

Reprinted from *Auk* **54**:245, 262–271 (1937)

THE COMPANION IN THE BIRD'S WORLD

BY KONRAD Z. LORENZ

Introductory Note

WHEN Dr. Lorenz's paper on the 'Kumpan'[1] was published in 1935, it seemed to be such an original and important contribution to our knowledge of the instincts and behavior of birds, that I was anxious to have a summary of its theses and conclusions appear in the pages of 'The Auk'. Knowing that Dr. Lorenz was conversant with English, I wrote to him, asking if he would consent to prepare such an account of his own work, and he replied that he would be pleased to do so if given sufficient time.

Dr. Lorenz's paper was delayed in reaching me from various causes. He found difficulty in summarizing a work which consisted in so large a measure of observational detail, and accordingly has stressed those subjects of the most theoretical importance; and he added: "I shall not refrain from using some new observations, and the results of experiments which have come to my knowledge since the publication of my paper." My function has been mainly editorial; and although it has seemed best to condense some parts of the author's manuscript, I trust that its value has not been impaired.

The doctrine of 'releasers,' herein set forth,—or devices for the production of stimuli, which serve as the 'keys' to 'unlock' or release those 'innate perceptory patterns,' characteristic of the species and the individual, and which result in instinctive reactions,—seems at last to offer a sound and satisfying explanation of that riddle so long embodied in 'the secondary sexual characters of birds,' and one which I believe that Darwin, when struggling with his 'Theory of Sexual Selection,' would have welcomed with open arms.—FRANCIS H. HERRICK.

[*Editor's Note:* Material has been omitted at this point.]

IMPRINTING

It is a fact most surprising to the layman as well as to the zoologist that most birds do not recognize their own species 'instinctively', but that by far the greater part of their reactions, whose normal object is represented by a fellow-member of the species, must be conditioned to this object during the individual life of every bird. If we raise a young bird in strict isolation

[1] 'Der Kumpan in der Umwelt des Vogels (Der Artgenosse als auslösendes Moment sozialer Verhaltungsweisen)' [The Companion in the Bird's World; the fellow-member of the species as a releasing factor of social behavior.] Journ. f. Ornith., vol. 83, pt. 2–3, 1935.

from its kind, we find very often that some or all of its social reactions can be released by other than their normal object. Young birds of most species, when reared in isolation, react to their human keeper in exactly the same way, in which under natural conditions they would respond to fellow-members of their species. In itself this phenomenon is in no way surprising. We know of a great many reflex actions that can be conditioned to very different releasing factors without being changed as to their coordination of movement. Also we know that a great many animals, when deprived of the normal object of some instinctive reaction, will respond to a substitute object, or, to be more precise, will react to other than the usual set of stimuli. In all these cases the animal will prefer the normal object as soon as it is proffered, but the bird raised in isolation refuses to react to its kind. In most cases experimentally investigated, the biologically right object, that is, the fellow-member of the species, was not even accepted as a substitute for the abnormal object, acquired under the conditions of experiment, when the latter was withdrawn and the bird left severely alone with other individuals of its species. Heinroth failed to breed hand-reared Great Horned Owls, Ravens and other birds, for no other reason than that these tame individuals responded sexually to their keepers instead of to each other. In a very few cases known, the bird whose sexual reactions were thus directed toward man, finally accepted a fellow-member of the species which, however, was always regarded as a rather poor substitute for the beloved human and was instantly abandoned whenever the latter appeared. Portielje, of the Amsterdam Zoological Gardens, raised a male of the South American Bittern (*Tigrisoma*) who, when mature, courted human beings. When a female was procured, he first refused to have anything to do with her but accepted her later when left alone with her for a considerable time. The birds then successfully reared a number of broods, but even then Portielje had to refrain from visiting the birds too often, because the male would, on the appearance of the former foster-father, instantly rush at the female, drive her roughly away from the nest and, turning to his keeper, perform the ceremony of nest-relief, inviting Portielje to step into the nest and incubate! What is very remarkable in all this is that while all the bird's instinctive reactions pertaining to reproduction had been repeatedly and successfully performed with the female and not once had been consummated with a human being for their object, they yet stayed irreversibly conditioned to the latter in preference to the biologically proper object. The performance or better the successful consummation of an instinctive reaction is evidently quite irrelevant for this peculiar way of acquiring its object. The object-acquiring process can be completed months before the action is executed for the first time. I once had a pair of Greylag Geese hatch a Muscovy Duck's eggs. The parent-child relations in this artificial family dissolved sooner than is normal for any of the two species, owing to some hitches in mutual understanding which occurred because the key and lock of the releasers and innate perceptory patterns of both species did not fit. From the seventh week of their life, however, the young Muscovies had nothing more to do with their former foster-parents nor with any other Greylag Geese, but behaved socially toward one another, as well as toward other members of their species as a perfectly normal Muscovy Duck should do. Ten months later the one male bird among these young Muscovies began to display sexual reactions and, to our surprise, pursued Greylag Geese instead of Muscovy Ducks, striving to copulate with them, but he made no distinction between male and female geese.

These few observational examples are sufficient to illustrate in a general way the peculiarities of the acquiring process in question, but I wish to call the reader's attention more especially to the points in which this process differs from what we call associative learning. (1) The process is confined to a very definite period of individual life, a period which in many cases is of extremely short duration; the period during which the young partridge gets its reactions of following the parent birds conditioned to their object, lasts literally but a few hours, beginning when the chick is drying off and ending before it is able to stand. (2) The process, once accomplished, is totally irreversible, so that from then on, the reaction behaves exactly like an 'unconditioned' or purely instinctive response. This absolute rigidity is something we never find in behavior acquired by associative learning, which can be unlearned or changed, at least to a certain extent. In 1936, I kept a young Greylag isolated from its kind for over a week, so that I could be sure that its following-reaction was securely attached to human beings. I then transferred this young goose to the care of a Turkey hen, whom it soon learned to use as a brooding-Kumpan for warmth instead of the electric apparatus it had hitherto favored. The gosling then followed the Turkey hen, provided that I was not in sight, and kept this up for a fortnight; but even during that time I had only to walk near the two birds, to cause the gosling to abandon the hen and follow me. I did this but three times, to avoid conditioning the gosling to my person as a leader. When, after two weeks, the gosling began to become more independent of the warming function provided by the Turkey hen, it left her and hung around our front door, waiting for a human being to emerge and trying to follow it when it did so. Now this gosling, excepting the few necessary trial runs, each of which did not last more than about a minute, had never actually consummated its following-reaction with a human for its object. On the other hand, for more than two weeks, it had been in constant contact with the Turkey hen; yet its following-reaction did not become conditioned to the Turkey in preference to the human. I would even suspect that its instinctive following-reaction was never really released by the Turkey at all, and that its following the hen was predominantly a purposive act, directed to the necessity of getting a warm-up from time to time. It never ran directly after the Turkey hen in the intensive way in which it would follow me and in which Greylag goslings follow their normal parents, but just kept near her in a most casual and deliberate sort of way, quite different from the normal reaction. Most impressive is the fact of the irreversibility of imprinting in such cases, in which birds become conditioned to an inaccessible object or to one with which it is physically impossible to perform the reaction. (3) The process of acquiring the object of a reaction is in very many cases completed long before the reaction itself has become established, as seen in the observations on the Muscovy drake cited above. This offers some difficulties to the assumption that the acquiring process in imprinting is essentially the same as in other cases of 'conditioning', especially in associative learning. To explain the process in question as one of associative learning, one would have to assume that the reaction is, in some rudimentary stage, already present at the time when its object is irreversibly determined, an assumption which psychoanalysts would doubtless welcome, but about which I have doubts. (4) In the process of imprinting, the individual from whom the stimuli which influence the conditioning of the reaction are issuing, does not necessarily function as an object of this reaction. In many cases it is the object of the young bird's begging-reactions, or the following-reactions, in short the object of the reactions directed to the parent-companion, that irreversibly determines the conditions which, more than a year later, will release the copulating reactions in the mature bird. This is what we might call a super-individual conditioning to the species and certainly it is the chief biological task of imprinting to establish a sort of consciousness of species in the young bird, if we may use the term 'consciousness' in so broad a sense.

I would not leave the subject of imprinting without drawing the reader's attention to some very striking parallels existing between imprinting and a certain important process in the individual development of organs known in developmental mechanics (Entwicklungsmechanik) as indicative determination. If, at a certain stage of development, cellular material of a frog embryo be transplanted from one part of its body to another, the transplanted cells owing to influences emanating from their new environment, are induced to develop in a way fitting to it, and not in the way they would have developed in their original position. This process of being influenced by environment, termed 'induction' by Spemann and his school, is confined to very limited periods in the ontogenetic development of the embryo. After the lapse of this period, transplantation of tissue results in the development of abnormal monsters, because any transplanted material will develop in a way exactly fitting the place of its provenience. Also, cells transplanted before the critical time and afterward replaced in their original situation, will develop in harmony with the part of the embryo in which they are implanted during the critical period of inductive determination. It is certainly a very suggestive fact that the two chief characteristics of imprinting, in which it differs from associative learning, namely, in being irreversible and in being strictly confined to definite phases of ontogenesis, coincide with those which imprinting has in common with inductive determination in Spemann's sense of the word.

Of course, it is a matter of personal opinion how much or how little importance one should attribute to these differences from associative learning, and to analogies to inductive determination. My object in drawing the parallels to the latter, is to show that not only the phylogeny of instinctive reaction, but also its ontogeny more closely resemble those of an organ than those of any of the higher psychological processes. Also, it is a purely conceptional dispute whether imprinting is to be regarded as a special sort of learning, or as something different. The decision of this question depends entirely upon the content we see fit to assign to the conception of 'learning.' Imprinting is a process with a very limited scope, representing an acquiring process occurring only in birds and determining but one object of certain social reactions. Yet rarity does not preclude systematic importance, but I should think it rather unwise to widen the conception of learning by making it include imprinting. Such an increase of its content would bring the conception of associative learning dangerously near to including inductive determination as well, and experience has shown that this kind of stretching the boundaries of a conception is apt to destroy its value. This is exactly what has already happened to the conception of the reflex and to that of instinctive action. Since it determines the conditions for the releasing of a certain reaction, imprinting certainly must be regarded as 'conditioning' in a very broad sense of the word, but I think that English-speaking scientists should be glad to possess this term because it describes a conception less specific than that of learning.

Interaction between Innate Perceptory Patterns and Imprinting

There is a dual connection between innate perceptory patterns and the process of imprinting. On one side it is the normal function of innate perceptory patterns to guide a reaction to their biologically proper object, and we have already mentioned that sets of stimuli releasing one reaction are, strange as it may seem, factors inducing the choice-of-object of an entirely different action. For instance the sets of stimuli which, through innate perceptory patterns, release the following-mother reaction in many species of precocial birds, in doing so determine the object of sexual reactions not displayed until a year later. On the other hand, such characters of the object which are not present in the innate perceptory patterns, but to which the reactions must become conditioned in individual life, serve as a uniting factor to the different reactions once their acquisition is accomplished. This uniting of hitherto independent functions has already been illustrated by the example of the mother Mallard learning to know her ducklings individually. A very similar uniting function must be attributed to the process of imprinting as well, though it never concentrates reactions on one individual object, but only in the species as such. If normal imprinting is prevented experimentally, the social functions of a bird may be distributed between a considerable number of species. Thus, I had a tame Jackdaw, all of whose social reactions were, once for all, directed toward Hooded Crows as a species, while it would court human beings and respond with all its caring-for-progeny reactions to a young Jackdaw. One might say metaphorically, that imprinting fills out the spaces left vacant in the picture of the proper species, outlined in the bird's perceptory world by the data given by innate receptory patterns, very much as medieval artists in drawing astronomic maps, accommodated the pictures of the heraldic creatures of the zodiac between the predetermined points given by the position of the stars. Just as the imagination of such an artist is given the more freedom the smaller the number of stars which must be accommodated in the picture, so also is the scope of imprinting the greater, the fewer and the less specific are the characters of the species represented in innate perceptory patterns. With very many species it is practically impossible to direct experimentally the social reactions of the young to any but the normal object, because their innate perceptory patterns are so highly differentiated as to prevent the successful 'faking' of the corresponding sets of stimuli. This is the case with most birds of the Limicolae. Especially Curlews (*Numenius arcuatus*), even when hatched artificially and never having seen any living creature but their keeper, cannot be brought to respond to him with any reactions but those of escape. Most instructive are those cases where it is just possible to imitate releasing stimuli normally emanating from the parent bird, and thus to direct the imprinting of some reaction to a substitute object. This is the case with the following-mother reaction of young Mallards. It was long regarded by me as an established fact that Mallard ducklings would not accept their human keeper as a foster-parent, as would young Greylags, cranes and a number of other birds. I began experimenting by having Mallards hatched by a Muscovy Duck, with the result that they ran away from her as soon as they could, while she continued incubating on the empty shells. Foster-mother and young failed completely to respond to each other. Heinroth had exactly the same experience when he tried to let young Wood Ducks hatch under a Mallard. On the other hand I knew, from former experience, that young Mallards without any difficulty accept a spotted or even a white domestic duck as a foster-mother. The optical stimulation emanating from such a domestic duck was indeed more different from that provided by the small, brown mother Mallard, than was that of the small and rather shabby Muscovy with whom I had been experimenting. The characters relevant for the responding of innate perceptory patterns of the young must then, I concluded, be those common to the Mallard and the domestic ducks. These characters evidently were represented chiefly by the call note and by the general demeanor, both of which have not been changed much in the process of domesticating the Mallard. I decided to try experimenting on the call note which it is happily well within the powers of the human voice to imitate. I took seven young Mallards and while they were drying under the electric heater I quacked to them my imitation of the mother Mallard's call. As soon as they were able to walk, the ducklings followed me quite as closely and with quite the same reactional intensity that they would have displayed toward their real mother. I regard it as a confirmation of my preconceived opinion about the relevance of the call note, that I could not cease from quacking for any considerable period without promptly eliciting the 'lost peeping' note in the ducklings, the response given by all young anatides on having lost their mother. It was only very much later, probably after much conditioning to other characters inherent to my person, that they regarded me as their mother-companion even when I was silent.

The distribution of function between the innate perceptory patterns and the acquisition by imprinting is very different in different species. We find all possible gradations between birds like the Curlew whose innate perceptory patterns, corresponding to stimuli emanating from their own species, are so specialized as to leave hardly any room for the acquiring of characters by imprinting, up to birds like the Mallard, in which just one character, but a very 'characteristic' one, represents the evolutionally predetermined condition which must be fulfilled to make the object 'fit' into the general pattern of the companion. Finally we know of species whose innate perceptory patterns are so reduced as to form but a very rough and sketchy outline of the companion which, under the conditions of an experiment, may become filled out by a very different object. A good example of this is represented by the reactions of the newly hatched Greylag Goose who, on coming to the light of day for the first time, looks upward in a marked manner and will respond to actually any sound or movement by giving its specific greeting reaction. If the moving and sound-emitting object begins to move away from it, the gosling will instantly start in pursuit and will most stubbornly try to follow. It has been credibly reported that boats were followed by Greylag goslings when the parent birds had been driven away, very probably at exactly the right moment to elicit the looking-up reaction above described. I intend to experiment on the general form and on the limits of size which the object, thus releasing the young gosling's following-reaction, must possess. The lack of specificity which is so remarkable in the gosling's first responses to form and sound is, to an extent, compensated by its specificity in time. The looking-up reaction once performed, it is extremely difficult and possible only by very forceful means to induce the gosling to follow any other object than the one releasing its very first greeting reaction. In a natural environment it is extremely unlikely that a moving and sound-emitting object other than the parent bird ever encounters the gosling just at the critical moment and, even if some enemy of the species should do so, it does not matter whether the still very helpless gosling runs away from it or toward it.

Another example of a species with wide and little specific innate perceptory patterns is the Shell Parakeet (*Melopsittacus undulatus*). I raised in isolation a young bird of this species, which was taken out of the nest of its parents at the age of about one week. It was reared in such a way as to expose it to as little stimulation from the keeper's side as possible. When fledged it was confined to a cage in which a celluloid ball was so attached that it would swing to and fro for a considerable time if accidently touched by the bird. My intention to transfer the sexual and general social reactions of this bird to the very simple contrivance mentioned, succeeded beyond all expectations. Very soon the bird kept continuously near the celluloid ball, edged close up to it before settling down to rest and began performing the actions of social preening with the ball for an object. Notwithstanding the fact that the celluloid ball had no feathers, the bird minutely went through all the movements of preening the short plumage of another bird's head. One most interesting item in the behavior of this bird was that evidently he was treating the celluloid ball as the head of a fellow-member of the species. All actions which he performed in connection with it were such as are normally directed toward the head of another parakeet. If the ball was attached to the bars of the cage in such a manner that the bird was at liberty to take any position relative to it by holding on to the bars, he would always do so at such a level that his own head would be at exactly the same height as the celluloid ball. When I attached it closely to a horizontal perch, so that it was much lower than the head of the sitting bird, he would be at a loss what to do with his companion and looked 'embarrassed.' Throwing the ball loosely on the floor of the cage elicited the same response as the death of the only cage-mate does in Shell Parakeets, namely, the bird fell absolutely silent and sat still in the 'fright-attitude' with feathers depressed close to the elongated body. The only instinctive reaction not normally addressed to the head of a fellow-member of the species that I could observe in this isolated bird, was the following: males in courting a female excitedly run up and down a perch in a quick sidewise movement and finally sidling up to her, they grip in a playful way at her lower back or at the base of her tail, using one foot and standing on the other. When my parakeet grew to mature age and began more seriously to court the celluloid ball, he would execute exactly the same movements, but, as he was aiming them in such a way that the ball represented the female's head, his thrust-out claw would grip only vacancy below the celluloid sphere dangling from the ceiling of his cage. All this seems to indicate that some of the innate perceptory patterns of the Shell Parakeet must, in some way, be adapted to the *receiving of formed stimuli* representing, at least in rough outline, the head and body of a companion. Portielje got analogous results in his most interesting investigation of the European Bittern (*Botaurus stellaris*). This bird possesses an innate perceptory pattern corresponding to formed stimuli emanating from the enemy who releases its defence-reaction. This pattern also represents the head and body and also consists of a very rough outline only. The Bittern in defending itself, strikes at the head of the enemy, not at its eyes as was formerly believed. Portielje could show that the bird in this reaction was guided by the fact that a smaller shape representing the head of the enemy, was situated just above a larger one, representing the body. Two disks of cardboard were sufficient to meet the requirements of this simple innate perceptory pattern.

The observations of the Budgerigar[1] may serve us as an example, of how, under the abnormal conditions of captivity, the rough sketch representing the companion, outlined in the bird's perceptory world by innate patterns, may be 'filled out' in an incomplete way by accepting an object only partially corresponding to the innate sketch, so that some parts of the latter are left vacant, as the space reserved for the companion's body was left vacant by the celluloid ball. Instinctive reactions directed to such vacant spaces, as the one of gripping the female's tail in the Shell Parakeet, very often prove their fundamental independence by attaching themselves to an independent object, to a separate 'Kumpan.' The Jackdaw mentioned above supplies a good example of this. More transparent perhaps and susceptible of a simpler explanation is the behavior of man-reared young Greylag Geese. This species, as mentioned before, has particularly wide and sketchy innate perceptory inlets which, by reason of their very wideness enable the experimenting human to step in and supply all the needs a Greylag has for companionship, much more completely than is possible

[1] The Shell Parakeet, a corruption of Betcherrygah, native Australian for 'good parrot,' probably introduced into Great Britain at the time of the Crystal Palace Exhibition in Hyde Park, London, in 1851, when it soon became a favorite cage bird.

with any other species of bird hitherto investigated. There is, however, one reaction of the Greylag which constitutes an interesting exception to this rule by having a very definite and highly differentiated 'lock,' an innate perceptory pattern corresponding to the one and only structural releaser ever evolved by the species. I am referring to the reaction of flying after another member of the flock which is dependent upon a striking and beautiful grey-and-black color pattern on the wings of the preceding bird. This color pattern which represents one of the prettiest examples of an 'automatic releaser', is quite invisible in the sitting bird, as all the parts of the wings then open to view are colored in the same 'protective' gray-brown as the rest of the bird. It is only the plumage of the propatagial membrane, which disappears beneath the shoulder plumage when the wing is folded, and furthermore the base of the remiges of the hand and their primary coverts, then covered by the dull plumage of the arm, which display a light silvery gray appearing almost white when seen at a distance. The sudden transformation of a grayish-brown bird into one predominantly black and white at the moment of taking to wing, is very impressive, even for the human observer, and most probably is essential for the following-or flocking-together reaction of the fellow-member of the species. This highly differentiated way of releasing the reaction makes it impossible for the human companion to elicit it in the isolated goose, which results in an apparently inconsistent behavior on the part of such a bird. The young goose seems to undergo a complete mental transformation at the moment of taking to wing. While being completely indifferent to any fellow-member of the species and most intensely and affectionately attached to its keeper as long as it stays on the ground or on the water, it will suddenly and surprisingly cease to respond to the human in any way whatever at the moment it takes to wing in pursuit of another Greylag. My Greylags used to follow me on my swimming tours in the Danube as a dog would, and in walking and swimming, the leader-companion of a Greylag Goose releases its following-reaction without the use of specially differentiated bodily characters; therefore, when walking or swimming in front of the bird, it is able to supply the necessary stimulation, but leaves unfulfilled the conditions releasing the following-reaction of the bird on the wing, and leaves vacant a place which may be taken by any object which supplies specific stimulation.

The releasing of one separate social reaction independently of all others which normally cooperate with it in the social life of the species, as exemplified in these observations, is indeed a very common occurrence in birds reared by man. Abnormal though these phenomena undoubtedly are, they yet tend to throw some light on the normal processes upon which social life is built up in birds. As in the case of the reflex processes, our knowledge of what is the normal sequence of reactions is almost entirely founded on a careful analysis of abnormal reactions produced experimentally.

[*Editor's Note:* In the original, material follows this excerpt.]

7

Reprinted from *J. Psychol.* **46**:155–166 (1958)

THEORY AND EVIDENCE OF IMPRINTING IN HUMAN INFANTS*

Institute of Child Development, University of Washington

PHILIP H. GRAY[1]

A. INTRODUCTION

The concept of socialization attempts to account for events which are common and fundamental as well as events which are variable to the extreme. If one gathers under the rubric of acculturization those events which differ from culture to culture and from group to group, then the former term may be reserved for the primary attachment of the young to its kind.

Socialization is the result of an invariable sequence of events; without proper social contacts at biologically determined periods later social interaction is impaired and abnormal when it does occur. Although one expects this to be true for animals and humans alike, past efforts to isolate the mechanisms of socialization in human infants have not had phylogenetic significance. A theory of socialization applicable to humans alone is scornful of the continuity of species.

B. THEORY AND DEFINITION OF IMPRINTING

I wish to submit that socialization, whereby an immutable bond is fastened between the young and its kind, is essentially the same in most or all species where a social complex is an attribute of survival. In infancy there are specific and distinct periods for social development, and the relevant environmental occurrences in these periods are critical for the individual's welfare.

In species not born at an advanced stage of neural and motor maturation there is a pre-learning period; the higher parts of the brain are immature, conditioning is not possible, and events that might otherwise be stressful have no demonstrable effect.

The present evidence is explicit that the infant's first social response is directed toward learning its parent. This process, as it has been described in lower animals, is called imprinting.

*Received in the Editorial Office on May 7, 1958, and published immediately at Provincetown, Massachusetts. Copyright by The Journal Press.

[1]In the writing of this paper I have become indebted to a number of persons for their encouragement and critical appraisals: William C. Carson, Meyer Braiterman, Iris McKinney Gray, Stanley Matz, Roger Kelley, Jere Wilson, and Donald M. Baer. The first and last named I owe in a coin unrequitable.

Following this period is another, the period of infantile fear. The conditions of the fear period are little understood, but there is indication that some events during the fearfulness can become traumatic and remain so.

The fourth identifiable period is an in-group learning, when the infant learns the non-parental individuals around it.

The pre-learning period is of interest here to the extent that it sets a lower boundary for the imprinting period. In-group learning is undoubtedly important for the individual's social maturity, but it is manifestly of lesser importance than the imprinting period, when the parent is learned, or the period of infantile fear, when there is unusual susceptibility to stressful circumstances.

Imprinting[2] involves an innate disposition to learn the parent, or parent-surrogate, at a certain early period in life. The learning has a permanency of effect even if the imprinted individual does not remain materclinous. The critical period seems to have a gradient of effectiveness, only in the last part of the period does it appear that adequate learning is possible.

It appears, also, that imprinting need not be directed to one object but can encompass other individuals in the environment. Contrary to prevalent opinion, I must conclude that siblings can, and sometimes do, imprint on each other. The joining response of infant siblings is undoubtedly prompted by releasing stimuli similar to that which the normal parent possesses, but in reduced form so the young imprint mainly on the parent. If siblings are fostered on a parent-surrogate the siblings may themselves constitute more natural imprinting objects, so that attachment to the surrogate is minor.

Accidental imprinting to a false object is not likely to happen except by man's deliberate tampering. One of the paramount reasons why imprinting seldom goes wrong is the existence of what Lorenz has called releasers (25). These are particular aspects of an animal's morphology or behavior which have signal value: the young are born with the instinct to react to these signals. If releasing stimuli for imprinting are displayed by a mock parent the infantile responses will be directed to that mock parent. It is an error to suppose that a false parent-object will determine the kind of releasers to be efficacious; the young animal will react to the degree with which the false parent-object can supply the proper releasers, and will continue to so react when it is grown.

[2]For more than twenty years the theory of imprinting set forth by Lorenz has continued without major revision. The definition I give here departs from the ethological definition in several respects.

C. Imprinting in Birds

Imprinting has been discovered in birds on at least four separate and independent occasions (8, 17, 25, 33). Until recent years it attracted no attention from psychologists, with the exception of William James who was the first to attempt a formulation (18). But for the writings of Lorenz, a zoölogist, it is probable we today would know nothing of the matter (25).

1. *Critical Period for Imprinting*

When the study of imprinting was taken into the laboratory a minimum of criteria for testing was retained from the informal studies. The criteria involve little more than a presentation of the parent-object after some hours or days to see if the imprinted young will still follow. Logically one may consider following in most but certainly not in all circumstances as indicating imprinting; but duration, permanent effects, and magnitude of attachment remain unreported. The laboratory studies do show that in precocial birds the critical period is short, several days at the most (10, 16, 19, 20, 28). Good results of at least short term duration can be obtained by brief imprinting sessions, but I doubt that the effects are anywhere near as strong as those from natural imprinting.

Evidence on the development of the period falls short of desirability. Jaynes found the readiness of chicks to follow a model to be at a maximum after hatching but to decline steadily thereafter (20), as Fabricius had likewise found for ducklings (10). Jaynes hypothesized two simultaneous periods, an increment for effectiveness similar to that found in other studies, and a decrement for readiness to follow. If a decrement for response readiness does indeed exist (and it may for objects of slight releasing value) it cannot be verified when the subjects are kept in collective groups, as the animals used by Jaynes and Fabricius were. These animals would be less inclined to follow a model as they imprinted on each other. Had Jaynes isolated his chicks it is possible the peak of his critical period would have shifted toward the third day, and the readiness to follow would have increased.

2. *Releasers and Responses*

No study of the releasers necessary for the following response has been made. Jaynes did find that chicks imprinted to a model of a hollow cylinder will follow a cube-shaped model better than a chick imprinted to the cube will follow a cylinder. He thought this to mean that a cube is more like a hollow cylinder than a cylinder is like a cube (19). I suspect a different explanation: if the chick has differential responses to releasing stimuli it should respond better to a solid model; there are no hollow parents among the higher animals.

Both Spalding and Hudson were certain that even before a bird learns its parent it reacts innately to the parental calls (17, 33). When Ramsay and Hess imprinted chicks to a model emitting artificial calls, the chicks preferred in the test an incorrect model emitting authentic calls. In a preference test on naïve chicks 11 of 13 animals went to the model with authentic calls (28).

3. *Critical Period of Fear*

Spalding was the first to notice a specific time of fearfulness. He incubated chicks by a crude but effective method and hooded them as they hatched. Chicks unhooded before they were fully three days old would go to Spalding without fear and imprint to him, but if the hoods were removed a day later the animals tried to escape (33). William James, aware that animals are not afraid during their early infancy, stated that if an infant animal formed a habit to an object during this period the learning would limit the effects of the wildness to develop later. "In the chicks and calves above mentioned, it is obvious that the instinct to follow and become attached fades out after a few days, and that the instinct of flight then takes its place, the conduct of the creature toward man being decided by the formation or nonformation of a certain habit during those days" (18).

It has been assumed that the fear response remains at the same level throughout life. But Howard and I found a previously unnoticed event: that while the chick's fearfulness mounts to a peak sometime about the fourth day of life it then abruptly declines so that by about the fifth day the chick, in non-threatening situations, displays scarcely more than a mild caution. We suggested if an animal were exposed to particular situations in this period of extreme fear the situations might later be avoided (15). Recent evidence corroborates this. In a preliminary study, isolated chicks exposed to solid black circles or triangles during the fear period later spent significantly more time near a strange form than near the familiar form, but chicks exposed after the period had no preference for either the strange or the familiar form.

D. Imprinting in Mammals

Lorenz has been emphatic in his belief that imprinting is confined to birds. Certainly it is true that among the many developmental studies on mammals one must seek diligently to find mention of some event which bears on the problem of imprinting. Except for a few minor studies on "irrational fears" the period of fearfulness in infrahuman mammals has escaped notice altogether.

1. *Critical Period for Imprinting*

Allen could not force newborn guinea pigs to go to their mothers until the early part of the third day (1), while Seward was impressed that after several days of age guinea pigs had a strong drive toward their mothers which was independent of food-drive (31). Several years ago I successfully undertook to imprint hand-reared guinea pigs; strength of imprinting varied from a mere gentling to a readiness to follow me in field and building. From work with five litters it was possible to set a critical period for imprinting at the latter part of the second day. The imprinted animals never mixed well with their own kind and lived to old age without losing their unusual attachment to me.

Scott reared two lambs by hand, one from the fourth day and one from birth. They were returned to the flock on the twelfth and ninth day respectively. The male animal taken at the fourth day was usually to be found with the flock but grazing apart from it; in adulthood it did not fight nor evince other appropriate male actions. The female taken at birth "showed no tendency whatsoever to approach the flock until her first heat period and immediately thereafter left it" (30).

Kuo tried to prove that rat-killing in cats has a learned rather than an instinctive foundation, but he produced instead evidence of imprinting of kittens on rats. In one experiment, kittens when several days old were kept most of the time with rats, one kitten with one rat. As soon as the kittens could eat by themselves they were completely separated from the mother. The subsequent behavior of a kitten to a rat-companion was judged to be no different from the normal behavior of kitten to kitten. In rat-killing tests extending to the age of six months, 5 of 18 kittens finally killed wild rats, but they were kittens raised with albino rats. No kitten could be tempted to attack the kind of animal it had grown up with, while control kittens were predominantly rat-killers (22). Later Kuo modified his design by keeping several kittens at a time with several rats. No social bond was formed and these kittens could be induced to attack or kill rats of the kind they had lived with (23). The results of the second experiment bear out the contention made earlier: if the parent-object is so false it fits the young's innate schema less than a sibling the young will imprint on each other.

2. *Releasers and Responses*

Some filial behavior patterns demonstrated by mammals can be understood as imprinting behavior. One of the more notable occurs in herd animals. Beach and Jaynes have mentioned that females of two species leave the herd shortly before parturition and do not return until several days after the young are born; this could serve to let the critical events pass with only the mother in the vicinity of the young (4). The phenomenon is not restricted but may happen widely since Murie describes it in other species (27), and I have noticed similar behavior in farm mammals.

Innate reaction to calls in filial behavior seems to hold for mammals also. The shrill distress cry of the infant guinea pig brings its mother immediately, but when imprinting has run its course the mother merely replies to the pup's call and forces it to come to her.

E. Imprinting in Humans

One regrets that Chapin's demand for adequate statistics on infants in institutions, made over four decades ago, was not fulfilled (7). Were these data readily available it would be far easier to elucidate the socializing process of humans, for it is the incarceration of infants in institutions that provides us with the best evidence we have of imprinting in the human.

1. *Releasers and Responses*

Man is one of the few animals unable to walk immediately after the neonatal stage. In a manner of speaking, this uniqueness has forced the evolution of a different system of releasers and responses for imprinting. I propose that the smiling response in human infants is the motor equivalent of the following response in animals below the higher primates. In a general way in has been known for years that the true or social smile does not appear much before six weeks of age. Darwin reported the smile for two infants as first emerging at 45 and 46 days (9), and this is the typical age in most studies. One finds expressed opinions that the true smile is present even during the first month but the opinions do not seem to be based on careful observation.

The problem received little attention until Spitz and Wolf published their continuation of Kaila's work. Kaila had discovered that between the third and fifth months the smile is to a stimulus configuration of two eyes, nose and forehead, with motion of the face itself necessary to hold the infant's attention (21). Spitz wished to test if it is the human quality of the face or a configuration within the face which releases smiling. To accomplish this he used three stimulus situations: a rictus expression of the face, a human head covered with a grotesque mask, and a life-size dummy with the mask. As long as motion was present in the form of a nodding movement, the smile was rendered without discrimination until the fifth month when models would no longer elicit the response, although the human face continued effective as a releasing stimulus for another month (35). Banham noted that smiling is accompanied by the expenditure of energy in other overt acts (3). Spitz used the term "striving toward" and was aware that vocalization is a part of the total response (35). Wilson, using two dimensional models of the human face, found the incidence of vocalization to be highly correlated with smiling (37).

2. *Critical Period for Imprinting*

It is reasonable to place the critical period for imprinting in humans from about six weeks to about six months. It begins with the onset of learning ability (14), continues with the smiling response (35, 37), and ends with the fear of strangers (35). Were it not for a peculiar feature of western culture, which came about through a sense of charity, we might have no evidence of critical periods in humans. The feature is the various institutions where large numbers of children are cared for and reared by small staffs. One says "reared" with reluctance because until quite recent years, according to Bakwin, the death rate of infants under one year of age in most of these institutions approached 100 per cent. Application of modern knowledge of health and nutrition has been beneficial, at least for mere survival. But a substantial reduction of the mortality rate has come about only because "foundling homes have been in large part replaced by the much more suitable and less lethal foster homes" (2).

The syndrome remarked by Chapin and others is probably a variety of syndromes caused by several different conditions of social isolation or deprivation. First to be considered is the behavior during the critical period itself when infants are deprived of adequate social stimulation. The first three months are probably not critical; Bakwin is of opinion that infants under this age smile readily in institutions and are otherwise responsive to attention, but after a short time they undergo a process of withdrawal that becomes progressively worse (2). Levy tested children at six months of age who had been institutionalized since the second month; they showed a small but significant decline in developmental quotients when compared with infants of similar age in foster homes (24). Brodbeck and Irwin compared the speech sounds of family-reared infants with infants institutionalized from birth to six months; the latter were deficient in both frequency of sounds and types of sounds (6). Spitz and Wolf studied infants in a foundling home from the first through to the 12th month; the drop in development quotient from the third to the sixth month was precipitous, and gradual beyond the sixth month (34).

The second condition of deprivation is merely the first seen in retrospect: that of children deprived during the critical period and tested later. Durfee and Wolf found that infants kept in an institution not beyond three months of age showed no impairment, commensurate with Bakwin, but children institutionalized for more than eight months of the first year had such personality disturbances they could not later be tested (cited in 34). Of eight case histories presented by Lowery of problem children referred to him from an orphanage, six had been committed to the institution under the age of four months and one under the age of five and one-half months. The maladaptive behavior of these children, tested at about three and one-half years of age, is recounted in unhappy detail (26). In a final study of adolescents who had been removed from institutions to foster homes at ages under six months, the subjects were reported as having no great emotional disturbances. The writers perhaps did not realize the irony of their explanation that the children were adopted at unusually early ages due to the lack of standardization of adoption procedure at that time (32).

The most careful work on the effects of institutionalization is that of Goldfarb. An early study showed that children admitted to institutions at the age range of one to nine months compare unfavorably when tested at adolescence with other children who entered foster homes directly at one to 21 months of age. The institutional children were victims of apathy and lacked ability to feel guilt or shame or to compete (11). Goldfarb then bracketed a critical period. He compared two groups of adolescents who had been adopted at about three years of age. One group of 15 had been admitted to the institution at less than six months of age, the other group of 15 at six months or older. Eleven of the adolescents admitted at less than six months had severe behavior troubles and were considered to be poorly adjusted, while only four of the other group were maladjusted. Goldfarb could find no reason to believe that damage to the infant, once done, can ever be undone (13). One might be naïve to believe Ribble's anxious advice for proper "mothering" but one might not be wrong to follow it (29).

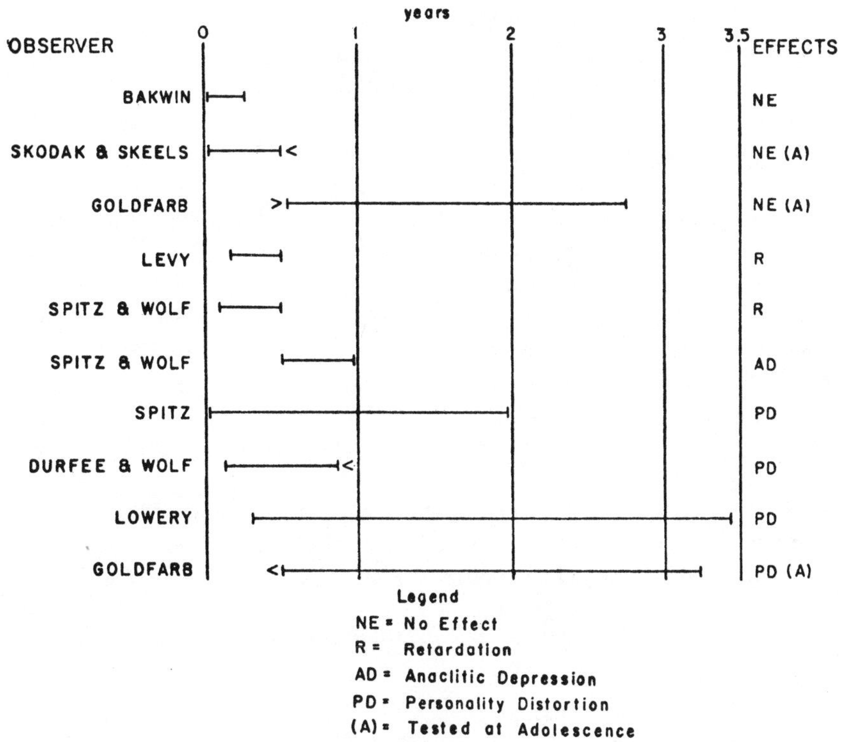

FIGURE 1
THE EFFECTS OF INSTITUTIONALIZATION OF HUMAN INFANTS AT DIFFERENT AGE PERIODS

3. *Critical Period of Fear*

Infants become shy, even fearful, of strangers soon after the sixth month (35). The latter are regarded with intense stares and actual unease if they come too close or if the parent moves from sight. Beyond six months the smile is seldom given to other than familiar persons. At this same time, the infant evinces the "irrational fears" to strange objects and animals. I expect the fears are all of one parcel and simply reflect the onset of the extreme fearfulness such as Howard and I saw in our chicks (15). Like the chick, the infant must soon pass the period of fear, but what occurs in the period is of the first importance.

The third condition of deprivation to be considered is that of infants who are not separated from their parent-objects until soon after the critical period for imprinting. Spitz and Wolf have spoken of the immediate symptoms of separation during the second half of the first year. These are depression, continual weeping, withdrawal, weight loss, and lack of health in general (36). In a word, the symptoms one could expect from an unprotected infant in a stage of innate fearfulness. And the suggested consequences have a dread undertone. Bowlby, on the basis of his own research, has hypothesized that it is these children deprived of parents and parental love at about this age who are most likely to become incorrigible delinquents (5). There are some indications from animal work, although minor at the moment, that tend to corroborate Bowlby's data.[3] Chicks which were kept in visual contact with (but bodily isolated from) guinea pig parent-surrogates through both periods of imprinting and fear were ambivalent in behavior when given free access to the guinea pigs. While the week-old chicks displayed the filial attention expected from imprinting they were also aggressive, so aggressive that they soon put the full-grown guinea pigs to rout. When removed from the situation the guinea pigs were in abject demoralization.[4]

Despite a lack of satisfactory proof, I should like to insist that certain experiences, we do not quite know what, in the period of infantile fearfulness will provoke a personality distortion of a psychopathological nature.

4. *Compound Effects of Deprivation*

Even in the most aseptic of social conditions, it is doubtful that a human infant would be totally unimprinted. The briefest contacts with caretakers should give some affiliation. The syndrome of deficit imprinting alone is probably social apathy and emotional withdrawal; while the syndrome of fear trauma is probably aggressiveness, an excessive demanding of attention, and moral delinquency. If harmful effects in the fear period are in any way due to a lack of parental protection then I do not suppose that an infant without full parental attachment can escape adverse consequences of the fear period. The obverse need not be true: a fully imprinted infant could still be victim to the latter period.

From the human deprivation studies I have selected what seems best to indicate compound effects. Goldfarb reported on 40 children who were returned to the institution from their adoptive homes because of an inability to adjust. These children had spent the first two or three years of their lives at the institution. Their behavior was aggressive, hyperactive, emo-

[3]But not his theory. Like other writers on this subject with the exception of Goldfarb, Bowlby concluded that the socializing events occur in the second half of the first year, but of course this was a confounding of two distinct periods at a time when only one period was assumed to exist.

[4]Baer, D. M., & Gray, P. H. Unpublished data.

tionally unresponsive, and characterized by a so-called peculiar or bizarre syndrome (12). Lowery spoke of some "extremely wild children" who were so beyond hope of redemption that they were taken from the institution to Bellevue Hospital, and thence to state incarceration. The causes of the wildness were unknown to Lowery but the antecedents were almost surely deprivational (26).

There is little more to say except this: it would be well for us to understand if and to what extent the criminal mind is a resultant of formative and stressful experiences during a few weeks of infantile fearfulness, and it would be well also if we knew to what extent we are making wild beings of children under the name of charity.

References

1. ALLEN, J. The associative processes of the guinea pig. *J. Comp. Neurol. & Psychol.*, 1904, **14**, 293-359.
2. BAKWIN, H. Loneliness in infants. *Amer. J. Dis. Child.*, 1942, **63**, 30-40.
3. BANHAM, K. M. The development of affectionate behavior in infancy. *J. Genet. Psychol.*, 1950, **76**, 283-289.
4. BEACH, F. A., & JAYNES, J. Effects of early experience upon the behavior of animals. *Psychol. Bull.*, 1954, **51**, 239-326.
5. BOWLBY, J. Maternal Care and Mental Health. Geneva: World Health Organization, 1951.
6. BRODBECK, A. J., & IRWIN, O. C. The speech behavior of infants without families. *Child Devel.*, 1946, **17**, 145-156.
7. CHAPIN, H. D. A plea for accurate statistics in infants' institutions. *Arch. Pediat.*, 1915, **32**, 724-726.
8. CRAIG, W. Male doves reared in isolation. *J. Anim. Behav.*, 1914, **4**, 121-133.
9. DARWIN, C. A biographical sketch of an infant. *Mind*, 1877, **2**, 285-294.
10. FABRICIUS, E. Zur Ethologie junger Anatiden. *Acta Zoöl. Fenn.*, 1951, **68**, 1-178.
11. GOLDFARB, W. The effects of early institutional care on adolescent personality. *J. Exp. Educ.*, 1943, **12**, 106-129.
12. ———. Infant rearing as a factor in foster home replacement. *Amer. J. Orthopsychiat.*, 1944, **14**, 162-167.
13. ———. Variations in adolescent adjustment of institutionally-reared children. *Amer. J. Orthopsychiat.*, 1947, **17**, 449-457.
14. GRAY, P. H. Experimental studies of learning in the neonate. (Unpublished manuscript.)
15. GRAY, P. H., & HOWARD, K. I. Specific recognition of humans in imprinted chicks. *Percept. & Mot. Skills*, 1957, **7**, 301-304.
16. HESS, E. H. Effects of meprobamate on imprinting in waterfowl. *Ann. N. Y. Acad. Sci.*, 1957, **67**, 724-733.
17. HUDSON, W. H. The Naturalist in La Plata. (3rd Ed.) New York: Appleton, 1895.
18. JAMES, W. Principles of Psychology. (Authorized reprint.) New York: Dover, 1950.

19. JAYNES, J. Imprinting: the interaction of learned and innate behavior: I. Development and generalization. *J. Comp. & Physiol. Psychol.*, 1956, **49**, 201-206.

20. JAYNES, J. II. The critical period. *J. Comp. & Physiol. Psychol.*, 1957, **50**, 6-10.

21. KAILA, E. Die reaktionen des Säuglings auf das menschlichs Gesicht. *Ann. Univ. Aboensis*, 1932, **17**, 1-114. (Cited in 35.)

22. KUO, Z. Y. The genesis of the cat's responses to the rat. *J. Comp. Psychol.*, 1930, **11**, 1-35.

23. ———. Further study on the behavior of the cat toward the rat. *J. Comp. Psychol.*, 1938, **25**, 1-8.

24. LEVY, R. J. Effects of institutional vs. boarding home care on a group of infants. *J. Pers.*, 1947, **15**, 233-241.

25. LORENZ, K. Z. The companion in the bird's world. *Auk*, 1937, **54**, 245-273.

26. LOWERY, L. G. Personality distortion and early institutional care. *Amer. J. Orthopsychiat.*, 1940, **10**, 576-585.

27. MURIE, A. The Wolves of Mount McKinley. U. S. Dept. Interior, Fauna Series No. 5, 1944.

28. RAMSAY, A. O., & HESS, E. H. A laboratory approach to the study of imprinting. *Wilson Bull.*, 1954, **66**, 196-206.

29. RIBBLE, M. A. The Rights of Infants. New York: Columbia Univ. Press, 1943.

30. SCOTT, J. P. Social behavior, organization, and leadership in a small flock of domestic sheep. *Comp. Psychol. Monog.*, 1945, **18**, No. 4.

31. SEWARD, G. H. Studies on the reproductive activities of the guinea pig: II. The role of hunger in filial behavior. *J. Comp. Psychol.*, 1940, **29**, 25-41.

32. SKODAK, M., & SKEELS, H. M. A final follow-up study of one hundred adopted children. *J. Genet. Psychol.*, 1949, **75**, 85-125.

33. SPALDING, D. A. Instinct, with original observations on young animals. *Macmillan's Mag.*, 1873, **27**, 282-293. Reprinted in *Brit. J. Anim. Behav.*, 1954, **2**, 1-11.

34. SPITZ, R. A. Hospitalism, an inquiry into the genesis of psychiatric conditions in early childhood. *Psychoanal. Stud. Child*, 1945, **1**, 53-74.

35. SPITZ, R. A., with WOLF, K. M. The smiling response: a contribution to the ontogenesis of social relations. *Genet. Psychol. Monog.*, 1946, **34**, 57-125.

36. SPITZ, R. A., & WOLF, K. M. Anaclitic depression. *Psychoanal. Stud. Child*, 1946, **2**, 313-342.

37. WILSON, J. Some conditions determining infant smiling. Unpublished master's dissertation, Univ. Chicago, 1957.

Department of Psychology
University of Washington
Seattle 5, Washington

8

Reprinted from *Genet. Psychol. Monogr.* **34**:71–75, 123–125 (1946)

IS THE SMILING RESPONSE UNIVERSAL?

Rene A. Spitz, M. D., and K. M. Wolf

With these points in mind, I devised a new series of experiments with the aim of clarifying the issue and following it up to its logical conclusion. We shall now describe our experimental sample and methods.

A. The Sample

A total of 251 children, 139 males and 112 females, was investigated. In any such experiment the problem of nature versus nurture arises, i.e., the question of congenital and that of environmental influences on individual response. With the intention of throwing some light on this question in regard to our problem we diversified our material according to two leading principles. (*a*) *According to heredity.* For this purpose we investigated children belonging to three races, distributed as follows: 105 white, 39 colored, 107 Indian. (*b*) *According to environment.* For the purpose of elucidating the possible effectiveness of environmental influence we investigated five different environments: private homes (upper class professionals), a baby nursery, a foundlings' home, a delivery clinic, and an Indian village.

Table 1 shows the total distribution of the children according to environment and race.

TABLE 1
Environment

Race	Nursery	Private home	Foundlings home	Delivery clinic	Village	Total
White	57	15	21	12	—	105
Colored	39	—	—	—	—	39
Indian	—	—	48	33	26	107
Total	96	15	69	45	26	251

Other than diversification as to race and environment no further selection was attempted. In each environment the *unselected total* of the available infants was examined. Within this unselected total four age groups were distinguished as the result of the average appearance and disappearance of the smiling reaction. They are:

1. A group of 54 children observed from birth to their 20th day.
2. One hundred and forty-four children observed from the age of 20 days to 60 days.
3. A group of 132 children (this group covers the previously mentioned 144, less 12 who for varying reasons could not be followed) tested during their third, fourth, fifth, and sixth month. To this has to be added a group of 13

[*Editor's Note:* In the original, material follows this excerpt.]

children who came under observation only after their third month, bringing the total of this group to 145.

4. A total of 147 children were followed from their sixth month to the completion of their first year. Of these 108 had already been followed from their third to their sixth month.

An additional group of 39 children came under observation for the first time only after their sixth month.

In all our experiments (both those mentioned up to now and those to be discussed subsequently) we introduced certain basic safeguards. As far as possible each experiment was performed on each child by a male experimenter and by a female experimenter separately, at different times to determine whether there were differences in reaction to one or the other sex. Talking to the child (or in its presence) or touching it either before or during the experiment was avoided. Where it was necessary to move the arm of the child for photographic purposes we were careful to take hold of the clothing only. Thus the exclusively visual quality of the stimulus offered to the children was preserved.

Finally we narrowed down the visual stimulus to that offered by the experimenter's face. To avoid falling into the error committed by Washburn (64) we were careful to perform our experiments in the absence of the mother or at least to exclude her from the visual field of the child during the experiment. We were investigating the nature of the stimulus of the child's smiling response and the presence of the mother would have introduced an unpredictable variable into the test situation, because the emotional relations of infants with their mothers vary from one emotional extreme to the other. Furthermore, a smile of the child in the presence of the mother would have to be interpreted in the light of the fact that a pre-existing emotional relation was coloring the child's attitude, whereas a smiling response to the experimenter is a response to a stimulus seen for the first time. Finally the difference between the mother as instigator (26) and the experimenter as stimulus of the baby's response varies greatly at different developmental levels of the infant, as we hope to show in subsequent publications.

With the exception of the 26 children in the Indian village, each child was submitted to the smiling stimulus from 5 to 30 times during the critical period of the third, fourth, fifth, and sixth months. Since each experiment was performed both by the male and the female experimenter, whenever both were available, the number of reactions is nearly double the above figures. Furthermore, as will be explained in the experiments described below, the smiling reaction of the babies was provoked 8 to 10 times in each experiment, as a consequence of the modifications which were added to the experiment. The very large number of experiments thus performed on each child excludes the possibility of accidental results. These repetitions bore valuable fruit in other directions too. They provided us, for example, with data which contribute to an understanding of the deviations in the usual pattern. Of these deviations, more later.

B. Method

In our first set of experiments we presented a smiling or nodding face as a stimulus fully "en face" so that the children could see both eyes simultaneously. When the child responded with a smile we slowly turned our face into profile, continuing either to smile or to nod. If the child now stopped smiling, we turned the face back "en face" and tried to provoke the smile again.

C. Results and Discussion

The first important result to emerge from our investigation is the age distribution of the smiling response, the rise and fall of which is vividly illustrated in Table 2.[4]

TABLE 2

Response	Age			
	Birth to 0;0+20	0;0+21 to 0;2+0	0;2+1 to 0;6+0	0;6+1 to 1;0+0
Smile	—	3	142	5
No smile	54	141	3	142
Total	54	144	145	147

The age limits indicated in this table should be considered as zones merging imperceptibly into each other. For instance, the smiling response does not disappear suddenly after the sixth month. This disappearance is a gradual one and becomes complete by the end of the 8th month. It should also be stressed that the significant contrast between the first and the second half year of life lies in the fact that in the first six months the infant smiles *indiscriminately* at *every* adult offering the appropriate stimulation, whereas in the second half it *may* smile at one person or another, if so inclined, but will not smile indiscriminately at everybody.

Perhaps it should also be mentioned that even during the peak of the

[4]Age is designated in years, months and days. Thus 1;3+16 means one year, three months and sixteen days.

smiling response infants will only respond if the experimenter has the ability to focus their attention, and if there are no gross interfering circumstances such as sickness, sleepiness, disturbances with screaming and crying, to inhibit the reaction of the child.

As expected, children of less than 20 days do not respond to the smiling stimulation. After all, it is generally conceded that during the first few weeks the infant's reactions are diffuse and uncoördinated, their perception inadequate, their attention unfocussed. The minimal necessary conditions for a stimulus to evoke a reaction are: (*a*) that the stimulus be perceived; (*b*) that the attention be focussed on it sufficiently to permit a reaction to take place; (*c*) that the neuromuscular reaction patterns be sufficiently coördinated to make reaction possible.

None of these conditions is fulfilled at this age and accordingly none of the infants examined by us showed any of these reactions. Of course, smiling as a spontaneous movement could sometimes be observed just as any other facial contortion.

We also expected to find the largest number of reactions in the group covered by the 3rd, 4th, 5th, and 6th months. All previous investigators spoke of these age levels as being the ones characterized by smiling; smiling has, therefore, been incorporated as a test for infant development in the testing procedures of Hetzer & Wolf (42), Gesell (35), and others. Again our expectation was fulfilled, though in a measure far surpassing anything we had imagined. The unfailing presence of the smiling reaction at these age levels makes the few exceptions, which comprise only 2.07 per cent, all the more significant and worthy of investigation.

The concentration of the smiling response on the age group between the third and sixth month induced us to limit the main body of our investigation to this period. The distribution of this age group according to environment, race, and presence of smiling response is shown in Table 3.

Table 3 shows that neither in regard to race nor in regard to the sociological structure of the environment was any gross difference in the reaction to the smiling stimulus discernible. We can, therefore, conclude that the smiling response is a universal human pattern, which is not influenced either by race or by environment.

As we shall see, there is good reason to believe that certain environmental factors can have a very marked effect indeed on the development of the smiling response. These particular environmental factors, however, were not operative in the environments which we studied, for age groups up to the point where the smiling response is at its peak.

TABLE 3
ENVIRONMENT AND RACE

Response	Institution White	Institution Colored	Institution Indian	Private home White	Private home Indian	Total
Smile	53	26	23	14	26	142
No smile	1	1	—	1	—	3
Total	54	27	23	15	26	145

These uniform results over a widely diversified range of subjects are strikingly consistent and contribute to our conviction of the universality of the smiling pattern; we are also impressed by the hardiness of this pattern, a finding which makes deviations all the more interesting for us.

As we have stressed above, these results were more or less to be expected, except for the extraordinary reliability of the presence of the smiling response during the second trimester of life.

We have, on the other hand, found some rather unexpected phenomena. One is the appearance of the smiling response in a few rare cases as early as the twenty-fifth day of life. In our material the cases in which the smiling response occurs before the end of the second month total 2 per cent. (The rarity of the phenomenon no doubt explains why it was not noticed by previous observers.) The scattered nature of its inception during this period places it into marked contrast with the uniformity of the reaction in the second trimester of life. We shall attempt to find an explanation for these exceptions later on.

Another unexpected result is the extinction of the smiling pattern after the sixth month. The proportion of children in the last third of the first year who smile indiscriminately at the approach of a smiling stranger is less than 5 per cent. In our later discussion we shall analyze these exceptions and try to find out whether factors within the individual history of these children offer any explanation of their divergent behavior.

All in all, we can say that this part of our investigation has shown us a phenomenon in infant behavior which is narrowly circumscribed as to the age levels at which it appears, but which within these age levels seems to be as unshakeably consistent as the patellar reflex. For this reason we shall be able to make use of it in the same manner as we make use of a tendon reflex: its absence, or its atypical manifestation, will call our attention to a dysfunction within a certain area of the personality.

[*Editor's Note:* In the original, material precedes this excerpt.]

REFERENCES

1. ALLPORT, G. W. The psychology of participation. *Psychol. Rev.*, 1945, **53**, 117-132.

2. AMENT, W. Die Entwicklung des Sprechens und Denkens beim Kinde. Leipzig: Wunderlich, 1899.

3. ———. Die Seele des Kindes. Stuttgart: Franckh, 1906.

4. BAKWIN, H. Loneliness in infants. *Amer. J. Dis. Child.*, 1942, **63**, 30-40.

5. BELL, SIR CH. The Anatomy and Philosophy of Expression as Connected with the Fine Arts. London: Murray, 1847.

6. ———. The Hand; Its Mechanism and Vital Endowments as Evincing Design: The Bridgewater Treatises on the Power, Wisdom and Goodness of God as Manifested in the Creation. Philadelphia: Carey, Lea & Blanchard, 1833.

7. BERNFELD, S. Psychologie des Säuglings. Wien: Springer, 1925.

8. BLANTON, M. G. The behavior of the human infant during the first thirty days of life. *Psychol. Rev.*, 1917, **24**, 456-483.

9. BRAINERD, P. P. Some observations of infant learning and instincts. *Ped. Sem.*, 1927, **34**, 231-254.

10. BROAD, C. D. The Mind and Its Place in Nature. London: Kegan Paul, 1925.

11. BÜHLER, CH. The social behavior of children. In *A Handbook of Child Psychology*. Worcester, Mass.: Clark Univ. Press, 1933. (Pp. 374-417.)

12. ———. From Birth to Maturity. London: Kegan Paul, 1937.

13. ———. The First Year of Life. London: Kegan Paul, 1937.

14. ———. Die ersten sozialen Verhaltungsweisen des Kindes. *Quellen und Studien zur Jugendkunde*, Jena, Heft 5, 1927.

15. BÜHLER, CH., HETZER, H., & MABEL, F. Die Affektwirksamkeit von Fremdheitseindrücken im ersten Lebensjahr. *Zeit. f. Psychol.*, 1928, **107**, 21-38.

16. CANESTRINI, S. Ueber das Sinnesleben des Neugeborenen. *Monog. a.d. Geb. d. Neur. und Psychiat.*, 1913, No. 5.

17. CANNON, W. B. Organization for physiological homeostasis. *Physiol. Rev.*, 1929, **9**, 399-431.

18. ———. The Wisdom of the Body. New York: Norton, 1932.

19. DARWIN, CH. Der Ausdruck der Gemüthsbewegungen bei dem Menschen und den Thieren. Stuttgart: Schweizerbart'sche Verlagshandlung, 1872.

20. DEARBORN, G. V. N. The emotion of joy. *Psychol. Rev. Monog.*, 1897, No. 2.

21. ———. Moto-Sensory Development: Observations on the First Three Years of Childhood. Baltimore, Md., Warwick & York, 1910.

22. ———. The nature of the smile and laugh. *Science*, 1900, **11**, 851-855.

23. DENNIS, W. The effect of restricted practice upon the reaching, sitting, and standing of two infants. *J. of Psychol.*, 1935, **47**, 17-32.

24. ———. An experimental test of two theories of social smiling in infants. *J. Soc. Psychol.*, 1935, **6**, 214-223.

25. ———. Infant development under conditions of restricted practice and of minimum social stimulation. *J. Genet. Psychol.*, 1938, **53**, 149-159.

26. DOLLARD, J. Frustration and Aggression. New Haven: Yale Univ. Press, 1939.

27. FECHNER, G. TH. Einige Ideen zur Schöpfung und Entwicklungsgeschichte der Organismen. Leipzig, 1873.

28. FRANKL, L., & RUBINOW, O. Die erste Dingauffassung beim Säugling. *Zschr. f. Psychol.*, 1934, **133**, 1-71.

29. FREUD, S. Civilization and Its Discontents. London: Hogarth, 1939.

30. ———. Jenseits des Lustprinzips. *Ges. Schriften* VI, 1925, 191-193.
31. ———. Zum ökonomischen Problem des Masochismus. *Ges. Schriften* V, 1924, 374-376.
32. ———. Wit and Its Relation to the Unconscious. In *The Writings of Sigmund Freud.* New York: Modern Library, 1938.
33. GESELL, A. The Mental Growth of the Preschool Child. New York: Macmillan, 1925.
34. ———. Wolf Child and Hùman Child. New York: Harper, 1941.
35. GESELL, A., & AMATRUDA, C. S. Developmental Diagnosis. New York and London: Harper, 1941.
36. GESELL, A., & ILG, F. Feeding Behavior of Infants. Philadelphia: Lippincott, 1937.
37. GESELL, A., & THOMPSON, H. Infant Behavior, Its Genesis and Growth. New York and London: McGraw-Hill, 1934.
38. GOODENOUGH, F. Anger in Young Children. Minneapolis: Univ. Minnesota Press, 1931.
39. ———. The expression of the emotions in infancy. *Child Devel.,* 1931, **2**, 96-101.
40. GUERNSEY, M. Eine genetische Studie über Nachahmung. *Zeit. f. Psychol.,* 1928, **107**.
41. HETZER, H., & RIPIN, R. Frühestes Lernen des Säuglings in der Ernährungssituation. *Zeit. f. Psychol.,* 1930, **118**, 82-127.
42. HETZER, & WOLF, K. Baby tests. *Zeit. f. Psychol.,* 1929, **107**.
43. JENSEN, K. Differential reactions to taste and temperature stimuli in new-born infants. *Genet. Psychol. Monog.,* 1932, **12**, 361-479.
44. JONES, M. C. The development of behavior patterns in young children. *Ped. Sem.,* 1926, **33**, 537-585.
45. ———. Emotional development. In *A Handbook of Child Psychology.* Worcester, Mass.: Clark Univ. Press, 1933. (Pp. 271-303.)
46. KAILA, E. Die Reaktionen des Säuglings auf das menschliche Gesicht. *Ann. Universitatis Aboensis,* 1932, **17**, 1-114.
47. KESTENBAUM, A. Zur Entwicklung der Augenbewegungen und des optokinetischen Nystagmus. *Arch. f. Ophthalmol.,* 1930, **124**, 115.
48. MAJOR, D. R. First Steps in Mental Growth: A Series of Studies in the Psychology of Infancy. New York: Macmillan, 1906.
49. MCGRAW, M. Growth. New York and London: Appleton, 1935.
50. MOORE, K. C. The mental development of a child. *Psychol. Rev. Monog.,* 1896, No. 3.
51. MORO, E. Das erste Trimenon. *Münch. Med. Woch.,* 1918, **65**, 1147-1150.
52. MURCHISON, C. A Handbook of Child Psychology. Worcester: Clark Univ. Press, 1933.
53. MURPHY, G., & MURPHY, L. B. Experimental Social Psychology. New York: Harper, 1931.
54. PIAGET, J. La Naissance de l'Intelligence chez l'Enfant. Neuchâtel and Paris: Delachaux & Niestlé, 1936.
55. PICHON, E. Le Développement psychique de l'Enfant et de l'Adolescent. Paris: Masson, 1936.
56. SEARL, M. N. The psychology of screaming. *Int. J. Psychoanal.,* 1933, **14**, 193-205.
57. SHERMAN, N., & SHERMAN, I. C. The Process of Human Behavior. New York: Norton, 1929.
58. SHINN, M. W. The Biography of a Baby. Boston: Houghton Mifflin, 1900.

59. SIGISMUND, B. Kind und Welt: I. Die fünf ersten Perioden des Kindesalters. Braunschweig: Vieweg, 1856.

60. SPITZ, R. A. Diacritic and coenesthetic organizations. *Psychoanal. Rev.*, 1945, 146-162.

61. ———. Hospitalism, an inquiry into the genesis of psychiatric conditions in early childhood. In *The Psychoanalytic Study of the Child: A Yearbook.* New York: International Univ. Press, 1945, 53-75.

62. STRACHEY, A. A New German-English Psychoanalytical Vocabulary. Baltimore: Williams & Wilkins, 1943.

63. TIEDEMANN, D. Beobachtungen über die Entwicklung der Seelenfähigkeiten bei Kindern. (Published in 1787, Translation by C. Murchison and S. Langer.) *Ped. Sem.*, 1927, **34**, 205-230.

64. WASHBURN, R. W. A study of the smiling and laughing of infants in the first year of life. *Genet. Psychol. Monog.*, 1929, **6**, 399-537.

65. WATSON, J. B. Behaviorism. New York: Norton, 1930.

9

Reprinted from pp. 16–23 of *Maternal Care and Mental Health,* J. Bowlby, World Health Organization, 1951 179 pps.

EVIDENCE ON EFFECTS OF DEPRIVATION. I

John Bowlby

Consultant in Mental Health, World Health Organization Director, Child Guidance Department, Tavistock Clinic, London

Direct Studies

Direct observations of the ill-effects on young children of complete deprivation of maternal care have been made by a large number of paediatricians, psychologists, and child psychiatrists and have shown that the child's development may be affected physically, intellectually, emotionally, and socially. All children under about seven years of age seem to be vulnerable and some of the effects are clearly discernible within the first few weeks of life.

Bakwin [7, 8] and Ribble [120] have each given detailed accounts of the adverse effects on physical health. Bakwin,[8] who gives a valuable survey of the paediatric literature on the subject which goes back at least to 1909, summarizes his own observations thus :

> " Infants under 6 months of age who have been in an institution for some time present a well-defined picture. The outstanding features are listlessness, emaciation and pallor, relative immobility, quietness, unresponsiveness to stimuli like a smile or a coo, indifferent appetite, failure to gain weight properly despite the ingestion of diets which, in the home, are entirely adequate, frequent stools, poor sleep, an appearance of unhappiness, proneness to febrile episodes, absence of sucking habits. "

These changes, he remarks, are not observable in the first 2-4 weeks of life, but can be seen any time thereafter, sometimes within a few days of the baby's separation from his mother. The failure of such babies to smile at the sight of a human face has been confirmed experimentally by Spitz & Wolf [135] while Gesell & Amatruda [57] have noted a diminished interest and reactivity to be characteristic as early as 8-12 weeks. A very careful study of the infant's babbling and crying by Brodbeck & Irwin [30] showed that babies from birth to six months in an orphanage were consistently less vocal than those in families, the difference being clearly discernible before two months of age. As will be seen, this backwardness in ' talking ' is especially characteristic of the institution child of all ages.

This diverse evidence from reputable workers leaves no room for dioubt that the development of the institution infant deviates from the norm at a very early age. If the regime is continued, the deviations become more pronounced. Gesell & Amatruda have listed their appearance (see table I).

These findings, while giving more detail, confirm in principle those of such early workers in the field as Ripin,[123] Vance, Prall, Simpson

TABLE I. ORDER OF APPEARANCE OF ADVERSE REACTIONS IN INSTITUTION INFANTS (GESELL & AMATRUDA)

Adverse reactions	Time of appearance
Diminished interest and reactivity	8 — 12 weeks
Reduced integration of total behaviour	8 — 12 weeks
Beginning of retardation evidenced by disparity between exploitation in supine and in sitting positions	12 — 16 weeks
Excessive preoccupation with strange persons	12 — 16 weeks
General retardation (prone behaviour relatively unaffected)	24 — 28 weeks
Blandness of facial expression	24 — 28 weeks
Impoverished initiative	24 — 28 weeks
Channelization and stereotypies of sensori-motor behaviour	24 — 28 weeks
Ineptness in new social situations	44 — 48 weeks
Exaggerated resistance to new situations	48 — 52 weeks
Relative retardation in language behaviour	12 — 15 months

& McLaughlin (reported by Jones & Burks[85]), and Durfee & Wolf.[50] Using the Hetzer-Wolf baby tests, the latter compared the developmental quotients (DQ)[b] of 118 infants in various institutions and correlated their findings with the amount of maternal care which the infants received. Although they discerned no differences before the age of three months, differences steadily increased so that the children who had been institutionalized for more than eight months during the first year showed such severe psychiatric disturbances that they could not be tested.

Spitz,[133] with Wolf, using the same tests, has more recently made a systematic study of the adverse effects which occur during the first year if the child is kept throughout in an institutional environment. They studied altogether four groups of children, in three of which the babies were with their mothers and one where they were not. Though the absolute levels of development, not unexpectedly, differed according to the social group the babies came from, there was no change of quotient during the year in the case of the babies, 103 in all, who lived with their mothers. The group of 61 brought up in an hygienic institution, on the other hand, showed a catastrophic drop of developmental quotient between the ages of 4 and 12 months. This is shown in table II.

At the earlier age the average DQ was 124 and second in magnitude of the four groups. By 12 months it had sunk to 72 and was by far the lowest. By the end of the second year it had sunk to 45. The last two figures indicate grave retardation.

In confirmation of earlier work, Spitz & Wolf's results show that most of the drop in DQ had taken place during the first six months of life.

---

[b] The developmental quotient, although calculated in a way similar to the intelligence quotient (IQ), is concerned with general physical and mental development, of which intelligence is only a part. A DQ of 90-110 represents average development.

2

TABLE II. MEAN DEVELOPMENTAL QUOTIENT OF INFANTS AT BEGINNING AND END OF FIRST YEAR WITH REGARD TO SOCIAL CLASS AND TO EXPERIENCE (SPITZ)

Social class	Presence or absence of mother	Number of cases	Developmental quotient	
			Average of 1st to 4th months	Average of 9th to 12th months
Unselected urban	absent	61	124	72
Professional . . .	present	23	133	131
Peasant	present	11	107	108
Delinquent unmarried mothers . .	present	69	101.5	105

It is true that these infants were living in conditions especially bad from the psychological point of view, as not only was there but one nurse to some seven children, but, for reasons of hygiene, the children were kept restricted to cots and cubicles in what amounted to solitary confinement. However, studies such as those of Rheingold [119] and Levy [92] make it plain that retardation may occur in conditions which are far from being as adverse as these. Rheingold studied 29 children aged from 6 months to 2½ years (mostly between 9 and 15 months) all of whom were awaiting adoption. All had been cared for by foster-mothers ; 15 with no other young children, the remainder with up to three others in the same foster-home. Those receiving all the foster-mother's attention were on the average accelerated in development while those who had to share it with other babies were retarded to a statistically significant degree. Levy also studied infants awaiting adoption. Her main sample was composed of 122 babies, 83 cared for in an institution and 39 in foster-homes, all of whom had come into the agency's care within their first two months of life, and had been tested around six months of age. Those in the institution were in one large nursery, which had accommodation for 17 babies and was staffed by a total of 10 practical nurses, there never being fewer than two in attendance during the day. The DQs on Gesell tests are shown to be slightly above average for the foster-home children and slightly below for the institutionalized, a difference which is statistically significant. Unfortunately, neither Rheingold nor Levy give their results in a form comparable to those of Spitz & Wolf, but it is clear that the drop in DQ in Levy's institutional group is far less than that of the group studied by Spitz & Wolf, a result which no doubt reflects the better psychological conditions in which they lived.

There are several studies showing similar retardation in *the second and later years*. One of the earliest was that of Gindl et al. [58] who, working in prewar Vienna, showed a difference of 10 points in mean DQ between a group of 20 children aged from 15 to 23 months who had spent six months or more in an institution and a similar group brought up in the poorest of homes. Confirmation comes from Denmark, France, and the USA.

Goldfarb,[66] in a very thorough study of 30 children aged 34-35 months, half of whom had lived in an institution and the other half in foster-homes from four months of age, found a difference of 28 points of IQ on the Stanford-Binet test between the two groups. The IQs of the foster-home group averaged 96, which is average, those of the institution children 68, which is seriously retarded and borders on mentally defective. The difference on the Merrill-Palmer test was less dramatic but none the less serious, figures being 91 and 79 respectively.

Simonsen,[130] using the Hetzer-Bühler tests, compared a group of 113 children, aged between one and four years, almost all of whom had spent their whole lives in one of some 12 different institutions, with a comparable group who lived at home and attended day nurseries. The mothers of these children were working and the homes often very unsatisfactory. Even so, the average DQ of the family children was normal—102—while that of the institution children retarded—93. This difference is found consistently at each of three age-levels, namely, children in the second, third, and fourth years of life.

TABLE III. COMPARATIVE DQs AND IQs OF INSTITUTION AND FAMILY CHILDREN AGED FROM ONE TO FOUR YEARS

Investigators	Tests	Time spent in institution	DQs/IQs	
			institution group	family group
Gindl et al.	Hetzer-Bühler	at least 6 months	90	100
Goldfarb	Stanford-Binet Merrill-Palmer	from about 4 months	68 79	96 91
Simonsen	Hetzer-Bühler	from birth	93	102
Roudinesco & Appell	Gesell	at least 2 months	59	95

Finally, Roudinesco & Appell [126] are at present making a similar study in Paris, taking as their sample children, also aged from one to four years, who have spent two months or more in an institution. This group numbers 40. The control group of 104 children of similar age and social class is drawn from nursery schools situated in poor districts. Using the Gesell tests, they found that the average DQ of the children living with their families was 95, that of the institution children as low as 59. As in Simonsen's study, the adverse effects seem to obtain throughout the age-range, though their numbers are still rather small for firm conclusions to be drawn. An important finding confirming the work of Durfee & Wolf and of Spitz & Wolf, though in this case it refers to an older age-group, is that the longer the child is in the institution, the lower becomes the DQ. Although numbers in each subgroup are small, totalling between 12 and 30, the consistency of the finding in each of the subtests suggests its reliability. The overall DQ drops from about 65 for those who have been in for between two and six months to about 50 for those in for more than a year.

These four studies from four different countries using as criteria four different tests are remarkably consistent. In each case the quotient of the control group averages about 100 while that of the institution group is retarded, very seriously so in the cases of Goldfarb and of Roudinesco & Appell. The results are conveniently tabulated in table III.

Although the results of tests of statistical significance are given only by Goldfarb, the internal consistency of the results of both Simonsen and of Roudinesco & Appell make it clear that in neither case can the results be due merely to chance.

So far only the overall scores on tests of development (Hetzer-Bühler and Gesell) and of intelligence (Standford-Binet and Merrill-Palmer) have been used as criteria. Studies, however, show that not all aspects of development are equally affected. The least affected is neuromuscular development, including walking, other locomotor activities, and manual dexterity. The most affected is speech, the ability to express being more retarded than the ability to understand. (Speech retardation is sometimes made good remarkably quickly, Burlingham & Freud [39] reporting that " when children are home on visits . . . they sometimes gain in speech in one or two weeks what they would have taken three months to gain in the nursery "). Midway in retardation between motor development and speech come social responses and what Gesell calls ' adaptivity '. Here again there is remarkable agreement between a number of different workers, among whom may be mentioned Gindl et al., Goldfarb (who gave special attention to speech), Burlingham & Freud, Simonsen, and Roudinesco & Appell.

Though there can be no mistaking the consistency of these findings, their import is frequently questioned on the grounds that many children in institutions are born of parents of poor stock, physically and mentally, and that heredity alone might well account for all the differences. Those who advance this objection do not seem to be aware that in the majority of the studies quoted care has been taken by the investigators to ensure that the control groups, brought up either in their own homes or in foster-homes, are of a similar social class and, as nearly as possible, spring from similar stock. Explicit data on this point are given by Brodbeck & Irwin,[30] Levy,[92] Spitz,[133] and Goldfarb,[66] while in the cases of Gindl et al.,[58] Rheingold,[119] Simonsen,[130] and Roudinesco & Appell,[126] sufficient care has been taken on the point to make it most improbable that heredity accounts for all the variation. Even so the only certain method of controlling heredity is by the use of a sample of identical twins. Though there are no human twin studies of the problem, Liddell (personal communication) is doing experimental work on twin goat kids, one of whom is separated from its mother for a brief spell each day and the other not. Except for the daily experimental period of 40 minutes, both kids live with and feed from their mother. During the experimental period the lights are periodically extinguished, a stimulus known to create anxiety in goats, and this produces very different behaviour in the twins. The one which is with its mother is at ease and moves around freely ; the isolated one is " psychologically frozen " (Liddell's words) and remains cowed in a corner. In one of the first experiments the isolated kid discontinued suckling from its mother and, the experimenters being unaware of this and so unable to help, died of dehydration after a few days. This is ample demonstration of the adverse effects of maternal deprivation on the mammalian young, and disposes finally of the argument that all the observed effects are due to heredity.

Moreover, positive evidence that the causative factor is maternal deprivation comes from innumerable sources. First, there are the very clear findings of Durfee & Wolf, of Spitz & Wolf, and of Roudinesco & Appell that the longer the deprivation, the lower falls the DQ. Secondly, there is experimental evidence that even if the child remains in the same institution, extra mothering from a substitute will diminish the ill-effects. Nearly twenty years ago Daniels studied two groups of two-year olds living in the same institution. " One group was given very little tenderness although adequately cared for in every other respect ", while in the other " a nurse was assigned to each child and there was no lack of tenderness and affection. At the end of half a year the first group was mentally and physically retarded, in comparison with the second." [c]

A comparable experiment has been done by Roudinesco & Appell [126] who arranged that each of 11 children, of ages ranging from 19 months to 3 years and 8 months, should have special attention comprising four sessions a week of three-quarters of an hour each with a special member of staff (in 10 cases the psychologist, in 1 case a nurse). Though in some cases therapeutic work was attempted, for most the session consisted of giving the child a chance of regular contact, away from the others, with a sympathetic adult. In several cases the results were very satisfactory. For instance, one child, whose DQ had fallen to 37 and had later (aged 18 months) become untestable, improved to 70 after three months of this treatment, and another of 2½ years, whose DQ had also fallen very low and had become untestable, improved to 100 (average) after a year's work.

[c] Reported by Bühler.[84] It is not clear whether in the second group each child had a separate nurse, which the text implies, or whether each child was assigned to a nurse, which seems more likely.

Finally, there is the evidence of spectacular changes in the child's condition following restoration to his mother. Bakwin,[7] after recording the views of the older generation of paediatricians, himself remarks :

"The rapidity with which the symptoms of hospitalism begin to disappear when an afflicted baby is placed in a good home is amazing. It is convincing evidence of the etiologic relation of the emotionally arid atmosphere of the hospital to the symptoms. The baby promptly becomes more animated and responsive ; fever, if present in the hospital, disappears in twenty-four to seventy-two hours ; there is a gain in weight and an improvement in the color."

He cites as an example a boy who at four months of age, the latter two in hospital, weighed less than at birth and whose condition was critical.

"His appearance was that of a pale, wrinkled old man. His breathing was so weak and superficial that it seemed as though he might stop breathing at any moment. When seen twenty-four hours after he had been at home he was cooing and smiling. Though no change had been made in his diet he started to gain promptly and by the end of the first year his weight was well within the normal range. He appeared to be in every way a normal child."

The dramatic and tragic changes in behaviour and feeling which follow separation of the young child from his mother and the beneficent results of restoring him to her are in fact available for all to see and it is astonishing that so little attention has been given to them hitherto. So painful, indeed, are the agonies which these children suffer on separation that it may well be that those who have their care shut their eyes in self-protection. Yet of their existence there can be no doubt, as distressingly similar pictures are given by numerous different investigators.

Bakwin's description of the typical separated infant—listless, quiet, unhappy, and unresponsive to a smile or a coo—has already been quoted. This clinical picture, in the age-range of 6 to 12 months, has been the subject of systematic study by Spitz & Wolf,[134] who named it 'anaclitic depression'. And depression it undoubtedly is, having many of the hallmarks of the typical adult depressive patient of the mental hospital. The emotional tone is one of apprehension and sadness, there is a withdrawal from the environment amounting to rejection of it, there is no attempt to contact a stranger and no brightening if this stranger contacts him. Activities are retarded and the child often sits or lies inert in a dazed stupor. Insomnia is common and lack of appetite universal. Weight is lost and the child becomes prone to intercurrent infections. The drop in DQ is precipitous.

In what conditions, it may be asked, does this syndrome develop ? In general, it is characteristic of infants who have had a happy relationship with their mothers up till six or nine months and are then suddenly separated from them without an adequate substitute being provided. Of 95 children studied by Spitz & Wolf and on whom a diagnosis was made, 20 % reacted to separation by severe depression and another 27 % by mild depression making nearly 50 % in all.[d] Almost all those with a close and loving relation

[d] In the original paper another 28 children are shown as "undiagnosed". Subsequent study, it is understood, showed a large number of these cases to fall in the category of "severe depression" so that the figures quoted here are under-estimates.

to their mothers suffered, which means that the depressive response to separation is a normal one at this age. The fact that a majority of those with unhappy relationships escaped indicates that their psychic development is already damaged and their later capacity for love likely to be impaired. The illness respected neither sex nor race—boys and girls, white and coloured, all being affected. Although recovery is rapid if the child is restored to his mother, the possibility of psychic scars which may later be reactivated cannot be disregarded, while, if the condition is permitted to continue, recovery is greatly impeded. Spitz & Wolf believe that there is a qualitative change after three months of deprivation, after which recovery is rarely, if ever, complete.

Spitz & Wolf report (verbal communication) that disturbances of development may also follow separation at an even earlier age. These disturbances are much less dramatic than in older babies and were at first described as ' mild depressions ', but further observation made this term seem wholly inappropriate since it became evident that the condition was neither mild nor, in the view of Spitz & Wolf, could it properly be classified as depression. These disturbances, to which infants of the age-group three to six months are prone, are insidious in development and much less easily reversed by restoration to the mother. The DQ falls slowly but steadily (not precipitously as in the older babies), and recovery is only partial—perhaps 25%-30% of the drop—instead of almost complete.

These very adverse results, it must be emphasized, can be partially avoided during the first year of life by the children being mothered by a substitute. Hitherto many have thought that substitute care could be completely successful during most of this year. Ribble [120] has expressed doubts, however, and Spitz & Wolf (verbal communication) are now definitely of the opinion that damage is frequently done by changes even as early as three months. Nevertheless, all are agreed that substitute care, even if not wholly adequate, is indispensable and should on no account be withheld. In the second and third years of life, the emotional response to separation is not only just as severe but substitute mothers are often rejected out of hand, the child becoming acutely and inconsolably distressed for a period of days, a week, or even more, without a break. During much of this time he is in a state of agitated despair and either screaming or moaning. Food and comfort are alike refused. Only exhaustion brings sleep. After some days he becomes quieter and may relapse into apathy, from which he slowly emerges to make a more positive response to his strange environment. For some weeks or even months, however, he may show a serious regression to infantile modes of behaviour. He wets his bed, masturbates, gives up talking, and insists on being carried, so that the less experienced nurse may suppose him to be defective.[e]

[e] Description based on unpublished observations of Robertson of the Tavistock Clinic, London.

[*Editor's Note:* In the original, material follows this excerpt.]

Editor's Comments on Papers 10 Through 13

CRITICAL PERIODS FOR SOCIAL ATTACHMENT IN SHEEP AND GOATS

Social Attachment and Primary Socialization in Mammals

As with birds, mammalian development has evolved in two directions, one toward precocity, in which the young are born in a highly advanced state, and the other toward neonatal prematurity, in which the young are born almost helpless except for their ability to nurse. The precocious mammals usually bear a single mature infant, in contrast to the multiple births that are typical with immature young. Like the birds, mammals show a process of social attachment in early development but, unlike them, many species of mammals lead semisolitary lives and among these the phenomenon of attachment is far from obvious. For example, a hand-reared wild Norway rat is obviously tame and easy to handle, but is it really attached to the handler? Rats do not normally follow each other and show obvious signs of separation distress, with the result that if the rat is attached, it is difficult to prove it.

In other species such as sheep and dogs, the attachment process is readily apparent. I have called it *primary socialization* in order to emphasize the point that the essential function of the process is the establishment of the young animal's first social relationship. These, in turn, lead to its becoming integrated into a social group, with all that this implies.

Attachment in Sheep

My own first introduction to the phenomenon of critical periods in primary socialization came as a result of pilot experiments with handreared bottle lambs that my wife and I raised as part of a general observational study of social organization in sheep (Scott, 1945). The results of the first experiment were striking. We took a newborn female from its mother and raised it on a bottle apart from other sheep, for the first ten days of life. Even though it was placed in the same field with the other sheep, it never became integrated with the flock and was still moving about independently three years later. Flocking is such a major part of sheep behavior that it seemed obvious that we were dealing with a major critical period. The lamb, of course, followed human beings and was obviously attached to them. A second experiment with a male lamb did not give such striking results. We were unable to obtain it until it was three days old and after it had some contacts with other sheep. Perhaps because of this, and perhaps because of sexual attraction, the male eventually became more integrated with the flock than had the female. However, his behavior and that of the flock showed that the critical period for attachment was regulated by the behavior of the females, who butted this strange lamb any time he tried to approach.

There are two kinds of critical period phenomena with respect to social attachment in sheep. While practical stock breeders had long known the difficulty of getting a mother sheep to nurse a strange lamb, the paper by Collias (Paper 10) was the first experimental demonstration of a critical period of approximately two hours after parturition during which a female would accept a strange lamb. Hersher et al. (Paper 11) did several experiments attempting to modify the critical period by restraining the mother and discovered that she would eventually accept such a lamb, but much more slowly. As far as I know, the physiological basis of this critical period has not been analyzed, but presumably it is based on hormonal changes.

A second kind of critical period is that of the attachment of the young lamb for its mother or for its foster mother. Following birth, this attachment can take place with dramatic speed, but the paper by Cairns (Paper 12) shows that young lambs can form attachments to other species at much later dates. In normal flock living, this would probably result in attachment to other flock members rather than to the mother. Whether or not these attachments are as strong and permanent as the primary ones is yet to be discovered, but the fact that they could be extinguished indicates that they are relatively weak.

Thus there are two critical periods for social attachment in these species: one for the mother, which is short and precisely defined, and the other for the infant, which is more extensive and probably involves attachment to other flock members, especially to young born in the same year. Observational evidence indicates that similar phenomena occur in other ungulates, but there is little information available concerning maternal attachment in other groups of mammals.

This research on sheep and goats suggested that there might be a similar but less restrictive critical period for the attachment of human mothers to their newborns. Klaus and his coworkers (Paper 13) explored this possibility by modifying the usual hospital technique of removing the baby immediately after birth, and reported that keeping the baby with the mother produced long-lasting effects on her responsiveness to it. Since then, they (Klaus and Kennell, 1976) have published a book detailing their recommendations for the management of mother-infant contacts.

10

Reprinted from *Ecology* **37**:228–239 (1956)

THE ANALYSIS OF SOCIALIZATION IN SHEEP AND GOATS

NICHOLAS E. COLLIAS

Cornell University, Ithaca, New York[1]

In recent years, the ecological significance of social behavior in animals has attracted increasing attention. In turn, social behavior has received more analytical investigation. A number of authors have observed that the establishment of normal social relations for the species often seems to depend on normal parent-young interactions at and shortly after birth or hatching (cf. review by Scott, 1956). This process of socialization is frequently difficult to analyze experimentally in sufficient detail and replication in wild animals, partly because they are wild, and studies on related domestic forms will help guide investigations on wild animals.

The purpose of this article is to describe and analyze mother-young interactions in sheep and goats with special reference to the process of socialization. The animals studied, with the exception of some initial observations on parturition in sheep at the University of Wisconsin, belonged to the Cornell Behavior Farm of Cornell University, where the author was a guest during 1952-53 as a research fellow of the National Institute of Mental Health, United States Public Health Service. I am indebted to those in charge of the University of Wisconsin Experimental Sheep Barn and to the staff of the Cornell Behavior Farm for their kind assistance in various ways.

The pattern of mother-young interactions will be illustrated by one example each for a domestic sheep and a domestic goat, for the first few hours after birth, followed by an interpretation of this behavior, with special reference to the establishment of the maternal-filial bond. Finally, some aspects of later social development will be summarized.

EXAMPLES OF MOTHER-YOUNG INTERACTION

The object of describing specific examples of mother-young interaction during and after the birth is to attempt to convey an objective and realistic conception of the complexity of the events that are involved.

[1] Present address: Illinois College, Jacksonville, Illinois.

Mother-Young Interactions in Sheep

This parturition was observed at the University of Wisconsin Experimental Sheep Barns, May 8, 1952. Because of limitations of space only the more significant portions of my notes are given in detail. Observations were continued for four hours. This ewe had had lambs for at least three previous years.

6:55 P.M. A translucent, yellow-brown water bag, about four inches in diameter, is protruding from the vaginal opening.

7:00. There is a gush of water from the vagina. The ewe is restless, blows through nostrils, and seems to nibble at ground. Keeps calling *ma-a-a-a-a.* Chews cud a little, and licks her lips.

7:05. Very restless. Once gets on knees and spreads hind legs a little, but rises at once. Water bag now hangs down a little farther.

7:07. Sniffs or blows through nostrils at ground and paws straw with one forefoot. Drops to knees momentarily. Rises, and one minute later lies down and gasps continually, with nose raised. In labor, *i.e.* belly contracts front to back, and ewe makes straining sounds as well as giving loud sniffs or sudden forcing of air out through nostrils.

7:14. Takes first rest. Soon resumes straining.

7:16. Rises to feet—water bag is broken and sticks to udder at lower end. Ewe puts nose to straw. Resumes labor while standing, and then rests.

7:18. Lies down and resumes labor.

7:20. Rests. Breathing rapidly.

7:22. Ewe rises and turns to face observer. Drops nose to straw, then lifts head, licks lips, lies down and resumes fast breathing with intermittent straining.

7:24. Rises again and noses restlessly about, turning in one spot.

7:25. Lies down and breathes heavily, intermittently contracting abdomen front to back—sometimes having a strong spell of contractions and lifting head, nose up.

7:27. Rises and mouths at straw, turns about 360°, lies down, and strains again for a while; then breathes heavily with mouth closed. Rests, then resumes straining.

7:29. Rises, picks up straw or hay in mouth and eats. Again eats hay or straw which disappears down its mouth once again. Circles and lies down and resumes straining. Chews cud a few times and breathes heavily—again strains. Each time it strains the first visible signs of the lamb to be born soon, appear as a slight protrusion from the opening of the vagina, being withdrawn when the ewe rests.

7:32. Rises, gives weak "maaa," turns and lies down again, and again labors. (Note that ewe largely stopped vocalizing since active labor began.)

7:35-8:15. Labor continues in the same restless fashion described above.

8:15. Lamb is born head first and feet down doubled beneath it while ewe is lying down. It starts to wriggle as soon as clear of mother. Ewe calls "maaa," rises, turns and at once eats and licks amniotic membranes off lamb, going over its whole body, and at times calling "maaaa" in a very low and rather gurgling voice. Lamb soon raises head, and also licks its lips, and in wobbly uncertain movements brings its head in contact with mother's head.

8:27. Ewe stops licking lamb for first time, and goes into labor again. Returns to lamb in a minute, licks it, again labors, stops labor and again goes to lamb.

8:30 First sound by lamb, a very weak "aaaaa." Soon repeated, as mother licks it.

8:31. Lamb starts to rise, and falls, again rises on hind legs and front knees, front legs apparently too weak to support it. Voice becomes stronger and mother answers.

8:35. Lamb works way to mother on front knees and on hind feet, nudges her abdomen, and suckles her abdomen and hind leg, coming close to teat, but missing it. Ewe continues to lick lamb, keeps circling it, but does not tread on it. Birth membranes protrude from her vaginal opening and hang to the ground.

8:41. Lamb wags its tail a little as it nudges breast of mother between her legs. Lamb keeps turning toward ewe and as she licks it, the lamb also makes licking movements with mouth.

8:42. Lamb wags tail vigorously as it nudges mother's breast.

8:43. Lamb stands up on all four feet for first time. Ewe keeps circling and so works lamb in and out of right position to nurse. Lamb continues to stand and wags tail sometimes, as ewe licks it, even when not trying to suckle.

8:47. Lamb for first time *walks* on all four feet—wobbly.

8:50. Note that ewe licked lamb almost continuously first 15 minutes with very few breaks, licked lamb most of second 15, and then licked lamb only about half the time during last five minutes. Ewe goes into labor again, picks up and eats a mouthful of straw briefly. Turns back to lamb and licks it.

8:57. Ewe lies down and labors.

8:58. Lamb shakes self for first time, while nudging neck of ewe. Note that ewe has answered every bleat of lamb with her "maaaa."

9:01. Ewe eats mouthful of hay. Lamb comes, puts its head along side of hers and takes hay into mouth, mouths but doesn't actually eat the hay.

9:04. Lamb lies down and rests. Ewe paws hay next to it with opposite forefoot, and then licks lamb again. Lamb raises head and licks lips. Thus far lamb has sucked at breast, leg, abdomen and udder, but hasn't hit teat yet.

9:05. Ewe lies down next to lamb and resumes labor. Lamb bleats and she doesn't answer for a moment, but eats mouthful of hay. Lamb bleats and she at once answers. After a few mouthfuls ewe labors again for about 20 seconds and then rises. Lamb continues to rest, and she goes and licks it.

9:10. Ewe lies down to labor, partly on lamb, and I frighten her off. She lies down on other side of pen and labors again, pants and rests.

9:12. Another lamb is starting to show at birth opening.

9:13. First lamb has been resting since 9:04. It bleats and ewe rises and licks it. She soon lies down and labors again, also calls occasionally.

9:15. Ewe rises, breathes heavily and rests, turns and lies down.

9:17. Second lamb is born—ewe stops and rests when lamb is more than half out. The lamb starts to move—ewe rises, and lamb falls out rest of way. She at once turns, licks and eats the membranes which cover the lamb.

9:20. The second lamb bleats when less than three minutes old (first lamb was calling).

9:23. First lamb finds teat and sucks teat for first time at 1 hour and 8 minutes after birth.

9:25. First lamb sucks briefly at membranes hanging from vagina of mother, and then it briefly licks the other lamb.

9:27. Ewe finished eating membranes off of second lamb.

9:30. Ewe stops licking the second lamb for first time, and looks around to see first lamb who has been sucking on a teat for over one minute.

8:31-10:00. First lamb (male) sucks two more times. Second lamb (female) stands at 9:49, and after pushing against neck and front part of abdomen of ewe many times, manages to find teat and sucks for first time at 10.01. Wagged its tail and ewe smells it under tail for first time. Loses teat after about 15 seconds.

10:04. Second lamb lies down to rest. Ewe has just about stopped licking it.

10:05. After-birth starts coming out.

10:07. Ewe starts eating afterbirth. Soon stops and apparently eats hay instead.

10:12-10:19. Ewe finishes eating the afterbirth. The two lambs are lying down together.

10:24. Second lamb apparently finds teat again and sucks; found teat when ewe stepped forward and turned slightly toward lamb which was nudging her in the fore part of abdomen. It soon loses teat. First lamb continues to lie down and rests, apparently asleep (immobile) for the first time.

Mother-Young Interactions in Goat

This parturition was observed at the Cornell University Behavior Farm, November 22, 1952. Female 7-49. Has had young before. For two days, Female 7-49 has stayed in barn, and has not gone out with the herd.

11:40 A.M. For one hour 7-49 has been lying down in hay in depression she made, and does not rise when I touch her. Does not chew her cud. Now starts rising restlessly at occasional intervals, turning about and at once lying down again. Also starts to strain with head and neck tensed and extended, chin almost in line with throat, ears laid stiffly back and mouth closed. Coincidentally there are movements of lower abdomen forcing backward, and tail is partly raised. Apparently female is in early labor. While standing she hunches her back up (vaguely suggestive of post-copulatory position).

11:45. She gives typical call of mother to kid, *i.e.* short, light, low-pitched series of notes with 3 to 5 notes in a group, and she looked back while calling. These vocalizations were uttered long before kid was born. She then lies down.

11:50. Female 7-49 starts to grunt occasionally, and a string of mucoid substance begins to protrude from the vaginal opening. The area beneath her tail trembles. Tail rises slowly above the horizontal, as she chews hay briefly from hay crib under her nose. Again tail rises slowly above the horizontal and region about birth opening trembles. Then she lies down again, and starts giving low, short bleats in series, with each series timed to her labor; this coincidence is repeated several times. The movements of labor begin with a straining grunt or groan given with the head forward. The female gets on her knees with tail raised high—then lies down again.

11:55. Mucoid substance from birth opening now extends downward to distance of about a foot. The goat rises, eats hay briefly, and again lies down. She starts to breathe rapidly with mouth closed. Actually eats hay, and later chews cud very briefly.

12:20 P.M. The external margins of the vagina gape whenever the female strains, and this straining is now commonly accompanied by low bleating. At same time the whole surrounding area of bare pink skin bulges outward as if kid is near mouth of birth canal.

12:32. Amniotic sac bulges out and breaks, and part of the kid protrudes outward. Female looks back, chin raised, and bleats repeatedly—then she yawns widely.

12:34. The kid is forced out at 12:34. The birth is apparently painful and the mother screams loudly several times, starting forward as the kid is born. The female then licks her own external genitalia, meanwhile bleating repeatedly in low, short notes. In the meantime, the kid snorts lightly, struggles to a sitting position, and then starts bleating in a very weak voice, like a tiny trumpet. Soon the kid begins to call more loudly, and the mother turns to it, touches it gently with her nose, yawns, and as the kid continues to bleat more loudly, she again touches it with her nose, and again yawns.

12:42. The mother then starts licking the kid, and the kid bleats less often and more lightly. The mother apparently eats the amniotic membranes as she licks them off the kid. She stops to yawn. The kid starts to struggle up on its hind legs, but soon slumps down again.

12:44. The mother stops licking kid to yawn again, and then lies down. A second kid is now born, coming out head first with front and rear legs extended and twitching. The mother apparently strained only once for this second birth. The kid immediately after birth starts snorting or sniffing, shakes its head from the damp membranes that cover and cling to it, and then lifts its head and rights itself within 20 seconds of birth. The mother at once starts to lick and eat the birth membranes commencing from the thigh region of the kid and proceeding forward. The second kid does not bleat immediately after its birth, unlike the first kid.

12:45. The first (older) kid stands up on all four feet for the first time; it is very wobbly and after about 10 seconds flops down again. It continually utters light and relatively low, single bleats, while the mother licks off the second (younger) kid.

12:49. The first kid walks for the first time, taking a few steps forward. It remains on all four feet for some time, although wobbling.

12:50. The mother bleats or grunts (low, short notes) for the first time since the birth of the first kid, and she leaves off licking the second kid to sniff at the rear end of the first kid. She then shakes herself for the first time since observations began this morning, and resumes her licking of the second kid. The first kid starts bleating again, and the mother licks at its rear end.

12:52. The mother yawns.

12:54. The second kid begins to suck hair on mother's leg, and it bleats briefly for the first time as it moves back toward teat. Meanwhile the first kid has wandered off some six feet and keeps on uttering a series of low bleats.

12:57. The second kid seizes and then loses the tip of a teat, but keeps trying and soon regains it. Its head wobbles so that it again loses the teat. Meanwhile the first kid starts sucking and pushing with its muzzle at the wooden wall of the barn, and wags its tail meanwhile. The second kid has just worked its way past the rear end of the mother.

1:00. The mother leaves the second kid to go and lick the first kid which was five feet away from her, and then the second kid starts to bleat. The first kid also bleats as she licks it. It has been on all four feet all this time. The first kid moves between the mother's front legs and stops bleating, and sucks at hair on her hind legs and abdomen, between the teats, at the udder and at the sides of teats which it nudges for the first time. It soon gets the tip of the swollen teat in its mouth and at once loses it.

1:05. The second kid is still bleating, while the first kid is silent with the mother still licking it.

1:07. The first kid grabs and holds a teat for the first time, wagging its tail while mother licks its rump. The mother occasionally grunts or utters low bleats consisting of one to three notes, especially when the second kid bleats after struggling to get close to her again, coming from a distance of five feet. The second kid starts sucking at hair on rear of udder, at hair on mother's legs, and then at side of teat; it also nudges her udder from the rear.

1:12. The first kid manages to seize a teat again, and then loses it, and sucks hair on the breast of the second kid. The second kid drops to its knees and sucks at the region of the udder of the first kid. The first kid moves off and sucks hair of mother between front legs. Note that both kids tend to work beneath the mother, who keeps on licking the first kid.

1:15. The kids keep trying repeatedly and persistently to suck, and often they seem to keep working toward udder. The first kid wags tail slightly when mother licks it, even when not trying to suck. Note that mother pays no attention to remnants of amniotic membranes that have slipped off kids to floor of barn, but only eats those remnants still on kids.

1:16. The first kid again gets a teat, and loses it in about 10 seconds. The mother started licking the second kid again, and it soon starts sucking at hair on her abdomen. It works its way back to region of udder, nudges the udder, and gets teat but the teat slips repeatedly out of its mouth.

1:20. The second kid manages to hold teat for about 5 seconds. The mother licks it on rear, and it keeps wagging its tail all the while.

1:22. The second kid gets and holds teat 7 seconds before losing it, then manages to hold it again for 7 seconds, and at 1:25 for about 15 seconds, and again at 1:27 for about 15 seconds, before losing it. Soon it is back on the teat again.

1:25. Mother yawns, and again at 1:28. Note that this female has done relatively little turning and shifting, and the kids seem to find the teats largely by their own efforts.

1:30. The first kid seizes a teat and sucks.

1:32. I lift up the first kid (still very damp), and move it about 8 feet from mother, and for the first time it gives loud, high, long (2 seconds) piercing screams of distress. I put it down, and the female goes part way to it and it goes rest of way to her and is nursed. She gave low grunts (in series of 1 to 4 grunts each) in response to its bleating (*eh-eh-eh-etc.*) as it moved toward her. The second kid also went to her right after she grunted ("bleated").

1:35. The mother again yawns. A bag of fluid, some 4 inches long, still dangles from her vagina as for some time now, and the afterbirth has not yet been passed. She has been licking the kids off and on ever since they were born, and they have been trying to suck ever since they could stand. Both of the kids have been on their feet most of the time since first they stood, walking about and under the mother in a rather wobbly way.

1:45. Observer leaves.

Establishment of the Bond between Mother and Young

In general, the pattern of behavior at parturition appeared to be basically similar in sheep and goats, although minor differences existed. A total of four cases including the instant of birth were observed in sheep and eleven in goats, while 7 additional cases in sheep and 19 in goats were observed within an estimated hour or less (often much less) after the birth had occurred. The observations on sheep agree with Scott's (1945) more general description of the development of behavior in sheep.

Most of these births were watched from a distance of a few feet, and with few exceptions the animals, most of which were very tame, seemed undisturbed by the presence of a human observer. Behavior of the mother and young in the hours subsequent to the birth was often watched through one-way glass in a laboratory room in which mother and young were placed.

In the 41 cases of mother-young interaction that were observed immediately or shortly after birth, individual variations in behavior of both mother and young were often observed. Repeated observation frequently combined with experiment helped to bring out the significant elements and to clarify the interpretation of mother-young interactions.

Some of the more significant phenomena determining the manner in which the social bond is established between mother and infant are suggested in the following sections, which deal in a step-wise fashion with the establishment of the bond between mother and young, starting from the instant of birth.

1. *Initial Responses at Birth*

In both sheep and goats parturition might take place with the mother lying down, or standing. In the case of only one female goat (described above) was the birth apparently very painful and accompanied by a loud scream of distress. As a rule the first response of the mother ewe or goat following the birth was to turn at once and begin licking the membranes from the newborn; occasionally the mother might lick her own external genitalia briefly before tending to her young one. Frequently, the mother would give a low-pitched, relatively short bleat (goat) or gurgle (sheep), which is the typical parturient voice, as she turned to face her newborn, but occasionally she might not begin this call for one-half hour or more. Sometimes a pregnant animal would give this call shortly before parturition.

A kid when born as a rule came out smoothly and head first; in one case (one of triplets) a kid was seen to come out feet first. Quite often the kid showed no movement until it was completely out of the birth canal and on the floor or ground. But one kid lifted and shook its head when partly out, another gasped as soon as its head was clear of the vagina, and in a third case, the kid's head was out for 10 to 20 seconds before the body was born and the kid bleated at this stage of the procedure. A kid or lamb on being born might bleat at once as might be expected since it is wet and roughly enters a colder environment than the one it has just left. But some kids or lambs did not call for some time after their birth.

In one case the head of a kid came out while the mother goat was lying down; she then arose, withdrew the head of the kid back into her body, turned and licked at the gelatinous fluid that had spilled out from beneath the kid, and all the while she continued bleating. The kid was born shortly afterwards.

It may be seen that the initial events at birth are quite variable in different cases. The most consistent and perhaps most significant event would appear to be the turning of the mother to face the newborn, associated with the fresh birth odor.

2. *Licking and Eating of the Birth Membranes*

What are the stimuli that cause the mother to lick and eat the birth membranes and fluid from the newborn? It is probable that some specific odor is one important stimulus. A ewe and a goat were seen to turn and lick a puddle of gelatinous fluid that had emanated from the vagina shortly before parturition started. A ewe was easily led from the pasture into the laboratory by holding a few inches from her nose her newborn lamb, which was not vocalizing nor moving very often, and with which the mother had not yet been permitted any contact. It was possible to attract this ewe for short distances by a rag rubbed in the fresh birth membranes, but not with a rag soaked in water.

The thirst of the mother may be a minor factor facilitating licking of the birth membranes. Ewes, particularly, are likely to drink much water during the first few hours after parturition. Once the kid or lamb is dry the mother licks it very little. One kid shortly after it had dried off, was made thoroughly wet again with water, but was not licked again by its mother, except for a few desultory licks normal for its age.

Specific hunger perhaps is a factor in licking and eating of the birth membranes, and might perhaps increase the sensitivity to special odors. Pregnancy involves considerable drain on the energy resources of the mother, and eating of the fetal membranes and placenta may help restore some essential nutrients to the mother. Usually the amniotic membranes were eaten, while the placenta often was not eaten. The degree of licking of the fetal membranes varies greatly in different females. One mother goat scarcely licked her two kids at all, but nevertheless accepted them.

3. *Vocalizations*

The young are stimulated to bleat on hearing the mother call, or on seeing her moving at a little distance away. The mother as a rule promptly replies to the bleating of her young with a characteristic series of low-pitched and short bleats in the goat, or with a low-pitched gurgling call in the ewe, and the mother at the same time goes to the young one. After it has been licked for a while by the mother, the young one is more likely to bleat whenever the mother for any reason leaves it to go more than a few feet away. Similarly, the mother which has had a chance to become conditioned to her young, is more likely to bleat or give distress calls when the young are taken from her. The distress call in both adult and young of sheep and goats is a relatively prolonged, loud and high-pitched scream or moan, and is given, for example, under stress of human handling as well as under a number of other conditions apparently indicative of distress (pain, hunger, etc.).

A lamb or kid isolated immediately at birth is likely to vocalize but little. One such lamb became attached to the human observer, would reply to his crude imitation of the maternal voice, and would also bleat promptly when he reappeared after a brief period of absence, even in the absence of vocal stimulation.

The initial importance of vocalizations in bringing mother and young together is correlated with a low threshold of maternal responsiveness to bleating of the young when compared with other aspects of maternal behavior. Thus, a mother sheep or goat often replies vocally to the bleating of any young one of its species, but she may then rebuff the approach of the young one by butting it away. A goat mother may even bleat in response to the distress cries of a lamb, or a ewe to those of a kid, but neither mother on smelling the young one of the other species will have anything further to do with it. One signal stimulating and permitting the kid or lamb to nurse is the abrupt cessation of movement by the mother who then stands still while the young one sucks. This maternal response has a definitely higher threshold of stimulation than does the maternal response to vocalizations of the young. Often a mother goat or sheep may answer and call her young one to her, but then withdraw from its attempts to suck.

4. *Maternal Defense of the Young*

Most of the observations on maternal defense were of goats. The mother goat defends her newborn against the approach of other goats, regardless of sex or age. This defense serves to prevent disturbance of the normal interaction between a mother and her newborn kid which is necessary for the establishment of a firm bond between the mother and kid. Older kids not infrequently try to suck mothers not their own, and if permitted this would often prevent smaller and weaker kids from being nursed by their proper mothers. A mother of low dominance may be driven from the vicinity of her kid by larger, stronger goats, as was seen in several cases. The newborn kid may then soon become lost in a crowd of goats, and being very indiscriminating in its attempts to suck, tries to suck strange females, males and older kids of either sex, alike. It is promptly butted away in most instances, receiving particularly bad treatment from the older male kids. This adverse treatment very probably serves to condition the kid against older goats, making difficult subsequently the establishment of a normal bond to its own mother.

An experienced mother with newborn kids generally defends them effectively, and may even attempt to drive from the vicinity of the kids, males much larger and stronger than herself. The normal adult males treat this aggression tolerantly and soon move off, but castrate males may react intolerantly by fighting and may even drive the mother temporarily from her young ones.

5. *The Young Stand Up*

Before the young one ever attempts to suck it usually struggles to its feet and stands up. The kid or lamb first succeeds in standing anywhere from 10 minutes to one-half hour or more after birth. Licking by the parent may stimulate its efforts to rise, but is not essential, since lambs or kids isolated at birth manage to stand and walk. Usually the lamb or kid sprawls flat shortly after first rising to its feet, but soon persists in struggling up again, and maintains balance longer with every effort. It is not long before it can easily stand for many minutes instead of seconds.

6. *Initial Sucking Attempts by the Young*

Its tendency to go toward a large moving object helps bring the young one in contact with the mother. Kids or lambs that had recently stood up for the first time and have not yet been nursed could often be induced to move directly away from the mother and to follow after a human observer who merely placed himself near the young one and then walked slowly away from it.

The inexperienced lamb or kid will first attempt to suck whatever object, animate or inanimate, or whatever part of the body of the mother, with which it happens to come in contact at the approximate level of its own height. It will particularly suck on protuberances, normally first at the hair on the mother's body. The tendency of the kid or lamb to work between the legs and beneath the body of the mother, combined with its persistence, eventually brings it near the udder and teats. Once having seized and held a teat the young one shows a greatly increased tendency to return directly to the teat on losing it, and soon succeeds in sucking regularly and effectively on the teat.

The mother ewe or goat sometimes appears to assist the attempts of her young to be nursed, by moving her hind quarters into position, and sometimes even lifting one hind leg on the same side as the young one. As an opposite tendency she frequently breaks off the nursing in order to lick the young one from some new position.

7. *Interactions during Nursing*

As soon as the young one is nursed it frequently but not always wags its tail, and the mother as a rule promptly smells beneath its tail. One's impression is that this is a relatively stable position. Presumably the wagging of the tail helps waft any scent that may be present. Tail wagging by the lamb or kid may be stimulated not only by sucking, but also by contact of the mother's nose with the region at the base of the tail, and at times tail wagging is associated with bleating, independently of contact or of sucking.

It seems not unlikely that one reason that a goat has a beard is to facilitate the reciprocal contact stimulation involved when a mother brings her nose near the rump and tail of her kid.

8. *Hiding of the Young after Initial Nursings*

After the newborn lamb or kid has been nursed more or less to satiation, it shows reduced responsiveness to the mother, lies down and sleeps. The mother may then leave it to go off and graze in the general vicinity, sometimes joining the herd when the latter happens to be nearby. Unlike goats, mother sheep rarely stray very far from the lambs, nor do lambs exhibit the marked immobility often displayed by very young kids on approach of a person (J. P. Scott, personal communication).

An example will be given. A kid born out in the pasture was led when dry by its mother into the nearby sheep shed, where she left it for almost four hours, and where it remained during her absence, lying down in exactly the same spot and in much the same position with head and throat flat on the straw. When the head was lifted and then released by the human observer it was allowed to flop down again, and when the head of the kid was placed to one side it was retained in this new position. The kid made no effort to rise and run away.

For two and one-half days this kid kept the same hiding place, being left alone by the mother for three hours on the morning of the second day. During the forenoon of the third day she came and led it away on the first long excursion of its life. She approached its hiding place in a very alert way—stopping every 20 or 30 feet to sniff the breeze, neck erect and ears pricked forward. I had to hide myself before she would come in to her kid. When she got within 30 feet of the shed she began to bleat, but her kid did not answer until she was visible to it through the entrance to the shed. It then bleated, rose, went to her, stretched its legs and shook itself. As soon as the mother saw her kid she changed the quality of her bleating to a lower, less "worried" pitch, went to it, smelled it, led it outdoors and nursed it. She then led it away, bleating when it fell behind, stopping briefly to permit it to catch up and sometimes to nurse, and soon she had the kid moving steadily behind her in the direction of the herd.

The Problem of Maternal Rejection

If a young lamb or kid be removed from the mother at or very shortly after its birth, and is kept away from her for two hours or more, she is likely to reject it on return to her. This rejection is evidenced by persistent withdrawal from the nursing attempts of the lamb or or kid and by the mother's actively butting it away when it comes near her. Maternal rejection under these conditions demonstrates that the first few hours after parturition are critical to the development of the social bond between mother and young in sheep and goats. The supporting data for this conclusion are presented in Table I. An abstract of these results has been published previously (Collias 1953). J. P. Scott recently informed me that sheep owners often have trouble with maternal rejection of the lamb, particularly where the lambs are taken away and warmed after they are born.

TABLE I. Maternal acceptance or rejection of young removed from the mother at birth, for various periods of separation from her.

	Length of separation	Number of young tested		Twin controls	
		Accepted	Rejected	Accepted	Rejected
Goats:	15 minutes	4	0	4	0
	2 hours	1	1	1	0
	3-3½ hours	0	2	..	..
Sheep:	40-45 minutes	2	0	2	0
	4½ hours	0	2	1	0

To summarize my experimental results: In 5 of 6 cases where the newborn was separated from the mother for 2 to 4½ hours before being returned to her, the young one was rejected, at least during the first hour after it was restored to the mother. In two of these cases, one of a goat and one of a sheep, the young one eventually died as a result of maternal rejection. The one exception was a kid that had been separated from an experienced mother goat for only 2 hours. It had been removed at the instant of birth without permitting the mother to lick or touch it in any way. It had no twin. It was accepted at once on return to the mother.

In all six cases where the newborn was separated from the mother for only 15 to 45 minutes, it was accepted at once on return to the mother.

There were 8 twins left with their mothers as controls for the separated twin. All the controls were at once accepted and were never butted by the mother.

There were also three cases, not included in Table I, of young not removed from the mother until one to two hours after birth. One of these, a kid, was restored to its mother after 2 hours of separation and was at once accepted. The other two cases were of lambs, one of which was returned to the mother after 3½ hours' separation and was at once accepted. The other lamb, separated for 1½ hours, was rejected for the first half hour and thereafter was accepted by its mother.

Although there are only five cases presented here of experimental maternal rejection of young temporarily removed at birth, these data are strengthened by the fact that only in these 5 instances out of 41 kids or lambs that were observed within one hour after birth was the young one ever seen to be butted by its own mother on the day of birth.

In these experiments, with one exception, it was always the young one and not the mother which was removed in separations. During the period of separation the young one was generally kept alone in a laboratory room. All of the mothers referred to in Table I had previously experienced parturition.[2]

A specific example of these separation experiments leading to maternal rejection will be cited. On April 8, 1953, a ewe (Female 23) had twin lambs, male and female, and the latter was removed at the instant of birth. Four and one-half hours later this female lamb, which in the interim had been kept alone in a laboratory room, was returned to the mother. At once the mother advanced gurgling, smelled and licked the female lamb and permitted it to make nursing attempts at various places on her body. The lamb persisted vigorously in these attempts and occasionally got the teat but soon lost it each time. Forty minutes later the mother as if becoming irritated at the unusually persistent attempts of the female lamb to suck, butted it from its feet as it came near her head. She then licked it and again butted it as it kept moving toward her, then butted it 15 more times, licking it a little and gurgling occasionally between butts. Every time it rose to its feet she butted it down flat. Her butts became harder and harder, slamming the female lamb off its feet to the floor. Occasionally she still licked this lamb, although she butted it 17 more times as it persisted in trying to nurse. She now withdrew promptly whenever the female lamb got anywhere near her teat or touched her udder, and kicked one hind leg up at these attempts, especially when made from the rear. After 14 minutes of this aggressiveness toward her female twin, the mother lay down, but when the female lamb came near her, she pushed it violently away with her snout 5 times, hissing or blowing each time that she did so.

Meanwhile, the male twin, who had been lying down rose to his feet, and shortly after the mother also got to her feet and butted away the female twin, and then permitted the male lamb to nurse for about 20 seconds, smelling and tolerating him. Then he lost the teat, and the female lamb seized and held a teat for 5 to 10 seconds; the mother smelled under the tail of this female lamb, and at once moved off. Again, the female twin tried to nurse and the mother withdrew so sharply that this lamb was caught by the movements of the ewe's legs and thrown head over heels. The female lamb persisted in its attempts to nurse, and the mother again commenced to butt it away.

Next day, the mother was locked in a stanchion to enable her female twin to get something to eat, and in subsequent days she gradually accepted and nursed it.

It remains to discuss the possible mechanisms in the maternal rejection of a lamb or kid which has been separated from its mother during the critical first few hours after its birth.

It was considered that partial drying of the fetal membranes and decline of the fresh birth odor might be important in causing the rejection. Gibson (1951) observed that a one-day old kid when rubbed with the afterbirth of a female not its mother, was immediately accepted by this female, which had previously rejected it. Mrs. Gibson also found that a newborn kid when cleaned and washed off with a strong detergent was nevertheless accepted by its mother. I confirmed this latter observation on a kid, and got similar results with a newborn lamb. Although it is possible that traces of the birth odor persisted in spite of the thorough washing, the fact remains that a mother may accept her young one after all visible traces of the fetal membranes have been artificially removed. Furthermore, I have successfully transferred a kid, 40 to 50 minutes old, from its mother to another (primiparous) mother, whose own kid was removed promptly at the instant of birth and at once exchanged for that of the older and experienced mother. Both adoptions were permanent in this cross-transfer, although the older kid had been completely licked off by its own mother before the transfer.

In another case a 2 day old kid was rubbed with the placenta of another mother whose own kids had been born about one hour before. She licked, tolerated and nursed the strange kid, but by the following morning was found to have rejected it, *i.e.* she then withdrew repeatedly from its attempts to nurse and often butted it away.

[2] Recently, Blauvelt has reported some experiments suggesting that maternal rejection may be more readily induced in primiparous mother goats (Cf. Josiah Macy, Jr. Foundation, Trans. 1st Confer. Group Processes, 1955).

It was concluded that the birth membranes facilitate but are not essential to the formation of the maternal-filial bond.

The physiological state of the mother at parturition is important to acceptance of the newborn. She is prepared to respond appropriately to the young even before they are born, and may lick puddles of birth fluid emitted shortly before parturition. A female goat, about one-half hour before her kids were born, responded to the distress cries of two strange kids with the typical call of the parturient female, and moved toward them. This call in both sheep and goats is relatively low-pitched, segmented and repetitive. Within a few hours after parturition it is given much less frequently, and gradually becomes higher in pitch. This change in voice of the mother suggests that her physiological state at parturition may be optimal for acceptance of the newborn.

This responsiveness apparently soon declines as suggested in Table I. Additional support for this conclusion is derived from 2 mother goats, who only 2 and 3 hours after themselves giving birth, would not lick nor stay with other kids presented to them (untouched by human hands in one case) immediately after birth of the kids.

The mother is less likely to terminate nursing on the first day than is a newborn lamb or kid, but after a week or two, it is generally the mother who terminates the nursing.

However, since mother goats or sheep may be experimentally induced to reject one but not the other young one in a pair of twins (Table I), it is evident that deficiency in maternal drive cannot have been the basic cause of maternal rejection in most of the cases here described. The mother, as it were, becomes fixated on one twin in the absence of the other.

From this it follows that a very rapid learning process is involved in the establishment of the social bond between a mother and her young. In one instance, three different female goats happened to have their kids within one to two hours of each other. During this period it was found possible to cross-transfer kids from one to another of these mothers and to have them tolerated and nursed, particularly if the kids from different mothers were of the same color. But when retested after several days these same kids were rejected by the same foster mothers, that previously had accepted them. In the interim these mothers and their kids had all been kept together in the same barn, as usual.

Odor and sound as well as color cues are probably used by females in learning their individual young. The frequency with which a mother goat smells a strange young one and the length of time engaged in smelling it are greatly increased when the strange kid closely resembles her own kid in size, color and general appearance.

Vocal cues to individual recognition were not thoroughly investigated. Often mothers and their kids or lambs were seen to reply to each other's bleating from behind partitions or walls as if able to recognize each other's voice. But when a kid, one or two days old, was held behind a partition separating it from its own and another mother, the distress screams of the kid were often answered by both mothers, neither of which could see the kid.

In the first few hours immediately following parturition it seems evident upon close observation that mother and young are becoming conditioned to one another during this very active period. Frequently the kid or lamb manages to seize the teat, and frequently it soon loses the teat because the mother moves in order to lick the young one from some new vantage point, or because of the wobbling, uncertain control that the young one has over its own movements at this stage. This make and break of sucking contacts would seem almost inevitably to lead to a rapid strengthening and specification of the developing bond between the mother and young. In effect the young one is subjected to a rapidly repeated series of learning trials serving to condition it to all sorts of significant and satisfying stimuli—tactile, olfactory, auditory, visual—that rain upon it during one of the most highly sensitive periods of its life. The same conclusion would seem to hold in almost every detail with respect to the reciprocal conditioning of the mother ewe or goat to her young.

Later Social Development

Independent feeding activity of the lamb or kid is associated with increasing indifference of the mother to her young as they grow older. Frequently lambs mouthed hay on the day of birth, but apparently did not chew or swallow it. As the lamb or kid learned to graze it was likely to forage farther and farther from the mother. However, in the event of some disturbance, the young one ran back to its mother.

The frequency of nursing decreases as lambs and kids get older, although a kid or lamb may be nursed occasionally for several months. During the weaning period lambs or kids could sometimes be seen to try and block the mother as she walked along by repeatedly crossing in front of her. If she stopped they would at once try to nurse. The greatest age at which a lamb was seen to be nursed was 4½ months. It is rare to see a kid nursed when more than six months old. However, one kid was nursed at 187 days of age, and right afterwards its mother went to another kid to which she had given birth 3½ days before and she nursed this kid for about two minutes. In only this one case was a mother goat ever seen to nurse her young from two different pregnancies, on the same day. As a rule the mother goats and sheep apparently discontinued nursing older young well before giving birth again.

Aggressive behavior in its early stages developed as play-fighting in which butting the heads together was generally brief, relatively, harmless and did not lead to any definite decision on dominance relations. "King of the hill" was a common game among kids. Kids under daily observation were first seen to butt other kids on the ninth day after birth. The young goats gradually developed consistent dominance relations with each other and with the rest of the herd. This dominance order, when finally established, was definite and very consistent with regard to any given pair of individuals. Within each sex, goats with horns regularly dominated goats without horns, so that the presence or absence of horns helped determine the place assumed by a young goat in the dominance order. All the kids were born without horns except as nubbins, and when present the horns begin to grow almost at once, although slowly.

The dominance order in adult ewes is much more indefinite and more of a give and take nature than in female goats, although placing ewes under stress of hunger and competition for a localized and restricted food supply often brought out consistent, unilateral dominance relations between certain individuals.

The development of sexual behavior was studied mainly among goats. The development of male behavior will be discussed first. Mounting of other kids, male or female, was first seen on the ninth day after birth. This was followed and accompanied by the appearance of pelvic thrusts (12th day) and erections (3 months). Kicking of one leg stiffly forward was first noted on the 12th day. The male call of sexual excitement, a segmented, rolling, low-pitched call, was one of the last elements to appear in male sex behavior. Normal adult males are more discriminating in their sexual behavior than are male kids, and unlike the latter, do not ordinarily mount other males, or mount from the front or side as the male kids sometimes do.

Infantile modes of response persisted for some time after male sex behavior had developed to the point where erection was possible. For example, a 3-month-old male kid followed and mounted an estrous female, but the instant she stopped moving —a signal to the adult male to mount, but to a kid to nurse—this kid dropped down and began to nurse the female. Possibly some frustration was involved in this switch of behavior response. Estrous female goats generally avoid the sex advances of the male kids, may butt them away, or go directly to an adult, full-grown male, who invariably chases the sexually active male kids away from the female. The earliest age of a male goat seen to copulate successfully with an estrous female was from 5 to 6 months.

The sexual behavior of the adult male seems to develop partly from a common basis with certain elements of maternal behavior. His call of sexual excitement is much like the attraction call of the parturient female to her newborn. The smelling and licking of the external genitalia of the female resemble the smelling and licking under the tail of a young kid by its mother. The moving contact of the mouth, nose and beard of the male over the posterior portions of the body of the estrous female also bears some similarity to maternal behavior.

Sexual behavior in male goats is also closely related to aggressive behavior, and the two types of behavior develop coincidently. Male kids, five to six months old, sometimes develop penile erections during prolonged fights with one another.

The sexual behavior of female goats in its development seems to make some use of pre-existing infantile responses, and indeed most kids become mothers long before they have attained their full body growth; they may have a small kid of their own by the approximate age of 11 months. Like a kid when its mother smells under its tail, the estrous female wags her tail whenever the male touches her external genitalia or runs his chin and beard along the side of the rump and flank of the female. Presumably the wagging of the tail serves to waft some special odor about.

The earliest age of a female goat seen to copulate was 5 to 6 months. The copulation was not forced, and this particular female, although not yet half-grown, appeared to be in estrus as judged by the pink and swollen external genitalia, by the persistent interest of the males, and by the way in which the female would stand when mounted instead of moving away. Less than 5 minutes after copulating with an adult male who was at least several times her size, this female kid went to her mother and was nursed. Less than five minutes after being nursed, she copulated with another adult male.

The masculine sex behavior pattern develops in females to some extent, but is seen rather uncommonly and under special circumstances. A female goat, victor in a fight, may pursue the losing female, give a male-like sex call (which in such a female sounds almost exactly like the parturition call), dart the tongue in and out, swing one leg stiffly forward while running the chin along side of the other female and may even mount. Such behavior is not peculiar to adult females, but develops early. A young female kid, coming into her first estrus at 5 to 6 months of age, was seen to show all of these elements of the masculine sex behavior pattern towards another estrous female kid of approximately the same age as herself.

The association between a mother goat and her female kids often persists long after the kids have become sexually mature adults and mothers. In the case of domestic sheep, Scott (1945) has observed that leadership of the flock may trace to the continued association of related ewes in overlapping generations.

Comparisons between Species

The number of similarities in the social behavior of sheep and goats is striking and is evident on almost every page of this report. The species differences in mother-young interactions are largely quantitative, and would require large series of data to bring out adequately. Species differences in behavior between adult goats and adult sheep are more pronounced. There is much less aggressive behavior within a flock of ewes than between female goats, correlated with somewhat closer flocking of the sheep. The manner of fighting differs in the two species; goats often rear up on their hind legs and then drop down smashing their horns together, while domestic sheep back up and then charge forward, butting their heads together. This difference in mode of fighting is paralleled by a related difference in manner of feeding. Both species graze, but in addition goats often rear up to browse, placing the forefeet against the trunk of a tree.

Detailed comparisons of sheep and goats with wild species of ungulates would necessitate another report (Scott 1945). The possible survival value of normal maternal-filial relations is suggested by the observation made in a winter concentration of white-tailed deer, that fawns (of the preceding year) without mothers were much less wary than fawns with mothers (Kabat, Collias and Guettinger 1953).

Summary

1. Examples are described of mother-young interaction at birth and during the first few hours after parturition in sheep and goats. The reciprocal and regulatory nature of this interaction as a basis for the establishment of the social bond between mother and young is developed.

2. If a lamb or kid is removed from the mother at or very shortly after its birth, and is kept away from her for a few hours, she is likely to reject it when it is returned to her. This rejection is evidenced by persistent withdrawal from the nursing attempts of the lamb or kid, and by actively butting it away when it approaches her.

3. Experimental evidence is presented that the probable reasons for the critical importance of the first few hours post-partum in the establishment of the social bond between mother and young in sheep and goats are: (1) facilitation by attraction of the mother to the fetal membranes and birth fluids as well as to the young one itself, (2) maternal drive is apparently highest at or near the time of parturition, and (3) a very rapid learning process results in early fixation of the female on her particular young.

4. Some aspects of later social development are described: (1) As a lamb or kid learns to graze it is likely to forage farther and farther from the mother, and the frequency of nursing decreases. (2) Aggressive behavior, starting as play-fighting among kids and lambs, develops into a consistent dominance order among the goats, while dominance relations are more of a give and take nature among adult ewes, although placing ewes on short rations often brings out consistent, unilateral dominance relations between certain individuals. (3) The development of sexual behavior was studied mainly in goats. Both male and female goats show the complete pattern of sexual behavior long before they have attained their full body growth. Male kids may mount from the front or side, and often mount other males as well as females, unlike adult males. The sexual behavior of male goats seems to develop partly from a common basis with certain elements of maternal behavior, and is also closely related to aggressive behavior. The sexual behavior of female goats in its development seems to make some use of preexisting infantile responses. The masculine sex behavior pattern also develops in female goats to some extent. (4) The companionship between a mother goat and her female kids often persists long after the kids have become sexually mature adults and mothers.

References

Collias, Nicholas E. 1953. Some factors in maternal rejection by sheep and goats. Bull. Ecological Society of America, **34**: 78.

Gibson, E. J. 1951. Maternal behavior in the domestic goat. Anatomical Record, **111**: 67.

Kabat, Cyril, Nicholas E. Collias, and Ralph C. Guettinger. 1953. Some winter habits of White-tailed

Deer and the development of census methods in the Flag Yard of northern Wisconsin. Wis. Conservation Dept., Tech. Wildlife Bulletin 7: 1-32

Scott, J. P. 1945. Social behavior, organization and leadership in a small flock of domestic sheep. Compar. Psychol. Monog., **18**(96): 1-29.

———. 1956. The analysis of social organization in animals. Ecology, **37**:

11

Reprinted from *Behaviour* **20**:311–319 (1963)

MODIFIABILITY OF THE CRITICAL PERIOD FOR THE DEVELOPMENT OF MATERNAL BEHAVIOR IN SHEEP AND GOATS [1])

by

LEONARD HERSHER, JULIUS B. RICHMOND, and A. ULRIC MOORE

(College of Medicine, State University of New York; Behavior Farm Laboratory, Cornell University.)

(Rec. 12-XII-1961)

INTRODUCTION

It has been demonstrated that in the development of many behavioral responses there exist certain critical stages in ontogeny during which particular environmental conditions may influence specific types of behavior for long periods of time and even for life, whereas exposure to those same environmental conditions at other stages has little or no effect.

Critical periods probably vary in duration for different kinds of behavior and for different types of organisms, from the entire juvenile or adult stage to very brief but crucial periods of time. Recently there has been considerable interest in these critical periods. Most investigations in this area have been conducted under the label of *imprinting*.

Several authors (HESS, 1959a; HINDE, 1955) have suggested that the length of the critical period for imprinting is determined by the time of onset of a response incompatible with the imprinted behavior, rather than by an innate "timetable" of development. In the *following behavior* of precocial birds, for example, it has been hypothesized that the critical period ends with the onset of flight response to novel stimuli. These flight responses are assumed to be incompatible with following behavior. HINDE (1955) has shown that the longer after hatching that flight behavior is delayed, the longer is the critical period for following behavior. Experimentally, HESS (1959a, 1959b) prolonged the critical period of following behavior by drug administration and by social facilitation, and JAYNES (1957) lengthened it by permitting his animals longer practice sessions with the imprinting object.

1) This study was carried out at the Behavior Farm Laboratory of Cornell University, directed by HOWARD S. LIDDELL, and was supported in part by grants from the Josiah Macy Jr. Foundation and the Ford Foundation. Thanks are due to FRANCES MOORE for many useful suggestions and assistance, and to Dr GRANT NEWTON for his careful criticism of the manuscript. Dr ROLF ZÜRBRUGG and Professor O. KOEHLER generously provided the German summary.

Although most studies of critical periods have focused upon the effects of early experience (BEACH & JAYNES, 1954; THORPE, 1956), there is evidence that brief critical periods later in life may be significant in the development of parental responses of fish (NOBLE & CURTIS, 1939), birds (TINBERGEN, 1936), and goats and sheep (COLLIAS, 1956; HERSHER, MOORE & RICHMOND, 1958).

The critical period for the development of individual-specific maternal behavior in goats and sheep is comparable in brevity to the critical period for following behavior in birds. Goats and sheep establish the identity of their own young immediately after birth, and thereafter vigorously repell any alien young that approach them (COLLIAS, 1956). However, goat dams separated from their young for 1 hour immediately after parturition fail to show normal, individual-specific maternal care (HERSHER, MOORE & RICHMOND, 1958).

This study is an attempt to prolong the critical period for the development of individual-specific maternal behavior in sheep and goats by preventing the occurrence of butting-isolation behavior. Further, the study is an investigation of the influence of species-dissimilarity between dam and young on maternal and filial behavior.

METHOD

The experiment was designed to prevent the mother's rejection of a young animal other than her own offspring after her initial contact with her own kid or lamb, and thus to provide an opportunity for the development of a social bond with an alien young.

All adoption attempts were begun within 12 hours after the mother had delivered a kid or lamb, although no mother was separated from her newborn during the first 2 hours after birth. The foster young varied in age from a few hours to several days. All young were chosen for the adoption attempts according to the order of their birth, and therefore selected randomly with respect to other variables. Mothers that delivered twins (9 dams) received one foster kid or lamb and kept one of their own.

Mothers and alien young were placed in small areas enclosed by low walls within a larger room, apart from the rest of the flock but within sight and hearing of the two or three other adopting mothers in the same room. Each mother was harnessed to a stanchion bolted to the wall so that the young could live in close proximity with her without being driven away.

Once each day the mother was removed from the stanchion and permitted free interaction with her young. Not until the mother fully accepted the alien kid or lamb by not butting it away and by permitting it to nurse, was the mother removed permanently from the stanchion. On the basis of these criteria, about 10 days was the average time for an adoption to occur, with a range from immediate adoption to over one month. Eventually, all adoptions attempted were completed.

Thus four adoptive groups were formed, two between different species and two within the same species: goats adopting lambs (5), sheep adopting kids (3), sheep adopting lambs (4) and goats adopting kids (4). Thus the total number of adoptions was 16. After they were removed from their stalls, all the members of each group were housed together, but the groups were kept separate from each other and from the rest of the flock where kids and lambs lived in normal relation to their mothers. When the young were two months of age, each kid or lamb was separated from its foster mother for an observation period of several hours. The experimenter took the adopted offspring from the mother in her full view and put the lamb or kid on the other side of a screen door which permitted the mother and young to see and to hear each other, but which prevented actual contact between them. The behavior of the mother in response to the separation was rated on three 4 point scales, from 0, no response, to 3, extreme response:

Scale 1) Alerting behavior was defined as any response in which the mother stopped her behavior in process and looked in the direction of the separated kid or lamb.

Scale 2) Pacing was defined as agitated walking near the door.

Scale 3) Bleating was rated in terms of frequency.

The ratings were made by two independent observers and had a reliability of .88. Any behavior for which the two ratings differed was assigned the mean rating of the two on the four point scale. This experimental procedure was repeated after a month and ratings were averaged for the two observation periods.

Mothers and young were thus separated for several hours, with only a screen door between them. Each mother individually was then led into the room containing her adopted kid and the other kids in her adoptive group. The experimenter made observations from behind a one-way vision glass and used electric counters and clocks activated by toggle switches to record the following behaviors for a 10 minute observational period:

1. Number of attempts to nurse the mother made by foster young and by all other young.
2. Time in seconds that the mother nursed her foster young.
3. Number of times the mother butted her foster young and all other young.

RESULTS

There was no relationship among the three aspects of maternal care studied: reaction to separation from the young, amount of nursing, and mother-young isolation behavior. Correlations among these variables did not differ significantly from zero.

Reaction to Separation.

The three measures of reaction to separation — alerting, pacing and bleating — varied positively with each other. Dams who showed some degree of response on one measure generally also showed it on at least one other measure, and usually to a similar degree. Occasionally a dam reacted on only one measure, but in each of these instances the reaction was mild alerting, a response which commonly occurs among sheep and goats after changes in the environment. Reaction to separation varied from active pacing before and butting against the door separating the mother from her young, along with continuous bleating, to no overt reaction of any kind.

TABLE I

Mean scores of maternal behavior

Dam-young combinations	Reaction to separation				Nursing time in seconds	Number of butts of alien young
	Alerts	Paces	Bleats	Total		
Ewe-kid	2.9	2.5	2.9	8.3	12.6	6.0
Ewe-lamb	0.6	0.3	0.4	1.3	17.3	1.4
Doe-kid	0.2	0.0	0.2	0.4	22.6	4.9
Doe-lamb	1.2	0.4	1.4	3.0	6.3	6.0
Days in stanchion						
>10	1.8	1.0	1.8	4.6	11.3	5.1
<10	0.8	0.4	0.6	1.8	16.6	4.2

The longer it took for maternal acceptance of the young to develop, the more reaction was observed during the separation test (Chi square $= 5.83$, $P < .02$) (Table I). Cross-species foster mothers reacted more vigorously than did dams who adopted a young animal of the same species (Chi square $= 4.06$, $P < .05$), the most extreme reactions occurring among ewes that adopted kids.

Among those dams that reared both a kid of their own and a foster kid, there was no difference in reaction score when they were separated from their own young compared to their reaction when separated from their foster young. Nor was there a difference in reaction to foster-young separation between those dams that reared both their own and a foster young and those that reared only a foster young.

Considering all mothers in the study population, mean degree of reaction to separation was no different whether the animal separated was the dam's own or her foster young. Sheep reacted more than goats when separated from foster young, but this difference merely approached statistical significance ($P = .10$).

Ratings also were made of the reaction shown by the separated young. All kids and all but two lambs showed an extreme reaction, but degree of reaction shown by the young was unrelated to reaction of the dam, even though mother and young could both see and hear each other. The lack of positive correlation between the two measures of reaction, however, may be a function of the restricted range of activity among the young.

Nursing.

Mean nursing time during the observation period was 13.6 seconds for foster kids, 19.0 seconds for natural kids. The small numerical difference was not statistically significant, although both means were highly different from the mean of 67 seconds found in a normal, non-experimental flock (HERSHER, MOORE & RICHMOND, 1958).

Foster mothers in the cross-species group nursed the foster young less than mothers in the within-species group ($t = 2.96$, $P < .02$), a finding in contrast to the data on reaction to separation (Table I). Dams rearing young of their own as well as foster young nursed no longer than dams rearing foster young only, the data again failing to demonstrate a social-facilitation effect. Evidence for the discrimination of the mother by the foster young is found in the data on the number of nursing attempts made by the young. Alien young seldom attempted to nurse, compared to foster young ($t = 4.40$, $P < .001$), but foster and natural young attempted to nurse with approximately equal frequency. Kids and lambs did not differ on this measure, nor did cross-species foster young compared to within-species foster young.

Maternal Isolation.

In a normal flock of sheep or goats alien young are butted or pushed away from the mother if they attempt to suck her. This butting behavior is similar to what has been described as "territoriality" among other animals, although in maternal butting among goats there is no fixed geographic boundary to protect. COLLIAS (1956) refers to this behavior as "maternal defense of the young", although it seems more likely to be protection of the mother, since she will butt alien kids who approach her even when she is separated from her own young. Maternal butting is referred to in this paper as maternal isolation. Alien young were butted approximately as often as observed in a normal flock exposed to a similar observation test. Only occasionally were the dams' own or foster young butted, and these instances seemed to occur only when the young were unusually aggressive in their attempts to nurse, and presumably before the dam could discriminate them as her own.

A dam that was vigorous in her attempts to maintain isolation needed little stimulation to butt alien young confined with her and her own young, such a mother frequently butting severely any alien young in the same room even though it made no attempt to suckle or even to approach her. The correlation between number of times a dam butted alien young and number of times those young attempted to nurse was not different from zero (Chi square = .006, $P > .90$).

The mean amount of butting among three of the experimental groups was approximately the same, only ewes rearing foster lambs butting alien young somewhat less than the mean for all groups. There was no difference in degree of maternal isolation between sheep and goats, or between cross- and within-species adoptions.

DISCUSSION

The Critical Period.

Though the appropriate stimulating conditions for the development of individual-specific maternal behavior in goats and sheep normally may be effective only during a brief time span shortly after parturition, results of this study suggest that the effective period may be considerably prolonged by enforced contact between dam and young after this post-partum period. Mother-young contact thus is a variable that affects maternal care, the duration of contact necessary for the development of maternal behavior being much longer after the post-partum period than during the period immediately following birth.

This enforced contact is made possible only by preventing the behavioral response (butting) the dam normally exercises to avoid contact with alien young. In sheep and goats, therefore, the development of individual-specific maternal care depends upon at least two distinct but inter-dependent interactive processes — contact and maternal isolation.

In the normal mother-young relationship contact and butting-avoidance appear soon after parturition, establishing within a few hours after birth the identity of the dam and her young for the entire nursing period and perhaps for life (SCOTT, 1958). However, if avoidance of alien young is prevented and contact between alien young and dam is forced, the dam develops a relationship with the alien young similar to the relationship she develops with her own. In the natural development of the individual-specific mother — young relationship, therefore, the onset of maternal isolation behavior probably marks the end of the critical period. Isolation behavior limits contact between young and adult to family members, an important process in these highly social kids and lambs who often attempt to nurse any mother in the flock.

Preventing butting-avoidance behavior toward one animal does not result in generalized inhibition of the response, since the foster mothers continue to avoid young other than their own or foster young even after avoidance behavior directed toward the foster young is completely extinguished. None of the foster mothers in this study was "indiscriminate", (HERSHER, MOORE & RICHMOND, 1958) *i.e.*, none accepted and nursed non-adopted alien young.

Animal species like rats (BEACH & JAYNES, 1956; MEYER & MEYER, 1944) and other small mammals (KAHMANN & v FRISCH, 1952), which do not show the vigorous maternal isolation behavior observed in sheep and goats, adopt alien young readily and, therefore, develop less discriminating mother-young relationships than the family-specific relationships characteristic of sheep and goats, pinnipeds (HAMILTON, 1934; PREBLE, 1923) and other animals. Maternal isolation behavior is a response incompatible with the development of this type of stimulus (young animal) generalization.

Whether the development of a maternal relationship after the 2-4 hour post-partum period takes place through essentially the same process as the development of maternal care during the post-partum period is a questionable point. In reference to the behavior designated as i m p r i n t i n g [several investigators (HERSHER, RICHMOND & MOORE, 1957; SCOTT, 1958) have suggested that maternal care in goats is a type of impinting], HESS (1959a) distinguishes between filial following originating before the onset of flight responses, and "learned" affiliation which may develop later. HESS argues that only following behavior that originates before the onset of flight responses may properly be labeled a consequence of the process of i m p r i n t i n g. Although in this study dams that developed a maternal relationship within the post-partum period nursed their young during the experimental test slightly (but not significantly) longer than dams that later adopted young, more definitive experiments are needed to determine whether the development of maternal care at these two different times is a function of two qualitatively dissimilar processes.

Species Similarity.

The factor of species similarity between dam and young clearly has an effect upon maternal behavior. In this investigation species differences resulted in more pronounced maternal behavior in the separation test, but in less maternal behavior in the nursing test, whereas isolation behavior did not distinguish the inter- and intra-species relationships. Little work has been done on this problem, although at least one other investigator has found more pronounced maternal behavior in cross-species adoptions than in same-species adoptions (RAMSAY, 1953).

These results may be related to the additional finding of this study that the longer the dam resisted accepting the foster young, the greater was her reaction later when separated, since there was a tendency for the cross-species adoptions to require a longer time to become established. One might expect somewhat more agitation in the separation test in dams that had experienced the greater degree of agitation during the early period when contact with the foster young was forced upon them, on the assumption that the agitation response became conditioned to a contact-separation stimulus. A difference, of course, lies in the fact that in the earlier condition the dam attempted separation from the young whereas is the separation test the young were separated from the dam. It should be noted, in reference to this problem, that the number of days required for an adoption to become established was not related to the amount of nursing, but was rather specific to separation reaction.

Whether the effect of species-similarity in the maternal behavior of goats and sheep is related to HESS' (1959b) finding that preference for an imprinting object is a positive function of the difference in form of that object from the natural object (the mother bird form), is an intriguing problem. HESS (1959b) also found in the chick very different color preferences for pecking than for following. Similarly, for maternal responses in sheep and goats, different threshold levels seem to exist for different form characteristics of the stimulus depending upon the specific maternal behavior observed.

SUMMARY

Sixteen sheep and goat dams were placed in a restraining harness between 2 and 12 hours after parturition, and were forced to remain continuously in close proximity to an alien young animal. Five of 9 goats were placed with lambs and 3 of 7 sheep with kids. All dams remained in restraint until, when released from the harness, they permitted the alien young to nurse and refrained from butting them.

Two and 3 months later the 2 inter-species and 2 intra-species adoptive groups were tested for maternal and filial behavior, with the following results:

1. All adoptions were established, with an average of 10 days required for maternal acceptance of the young.

2. There were no significant differences between natural young- and foster young-mother pairs in the dams' reaction to separation and in nursing time.

3. Cross-species foster mothers reacted more vigorously to separation and nursed less than same-species foster mothers.

4. There was a positive correlation between the length of time necessary for an adoption to be established and maternal reaction to separation, but no relationship between adoption time and amount of nursing.

The results are interpreted as evidence (a) that enforced contact between dam and young after the 2-4 hour post-partum period may considerably prolong the critical period for the development of individual-specific maternal care in sheep and goats and (b) that species-difference between dam and young differentially affects thresholds for different maternal behaviors.

REFERENCES

BEACH, F. A. & JAYNES, J. (1954). Effects of early experience upon the behavior of animals. — Psychol. Bull. 51, p. 239-263.

—— —— (1956). Studies of maternal retrieving in rats III: Sensory cues involved in the lactating female's response to her young. — Behaviour 10, p. 104-125.

COLLIAS, N. E. (1956). The analysis of socialization in sheep and goats. — Ecology 37, p. 228-239.

HAMILTON, J. E. (1934). The southern sea lion (*Otharia byronia* DeBlainsville). — Discovery Reports 8, p. 268-318.

HERSHER, L., J. B. RICHMOND, & A. U. MOORE (1957). Critical periods in the development of maternal care patterns in the domestic goat. — Paper read at Annual Convention of the Amer. Psychol. Ass'n., Chicago.

——, A. U. MOORE & J. B. RICHMOND (1958). Effect of postpartum separation of mother and kid on maternal care in the domestic goat. — Science 128, p. 1342-1343.

HESS, E. H. (1959a). Imprinting. — Science 130, p. 133-141.

—— (1959b). The relationship between imprinting and motivation. — Nebraska Symposium on Motivation VII, p. 44-83.

HINDE, R. A. (1955). The modifiability of instinctive behaviour. — Advanc. Sci., Lond. 12, p. 19-24.

JAYNES, J. (1957). Imprinting: the interaction of learned and innate behavior: II The critical period. — J. comp. physiol. Psychol. 50, p. 6-10.

KAHMANN, H. & O. v. FRISCH (1952). Relations between female and nestlings among small mammals. — Experientia 8, p. 221-223.

MEYER, B. J. & R. K. MEYER (1944). Growth and reproduction of the cotton rat, *Sigmodon hispidus hispidus,* under laboratory conditions. — J. Mammal. 25, p. 107-129.

NOBLE, G. K. & B. CURTIS (1939). The social behavior of the jewel fish, *Hemichromis bimaculatus,* Gill. — Amer. Mus. Nat. Hist. Bull. 76, p. 1-46.

PREBLE, E. A. (1923). Mammals of the Pribilof Islands. — N. Amer. Fauna 46, p. 102-120.

RAMSAY, A. O. (1953). Variations in the development of broodiness in fowl. — Behaviour 5, p. 51-57.

SCOTT, J. P. (1958). Animal Behavior. — Chicago, The Univ. of Chicago Press.

THORPE, W. H. (1956). Learning and Instinct in Animals. — London, Methuen & Co., Ltd.

TINBERGEN, N. (1936). Zur Soziologie der Silbermöve *L. a. argentatus* Pontopp. — Beitr. Fortpflanzungsbiol. Vögel, 12, p. 89-96.

12

Reprinted, by permission, from *J. Comp. Physiol. Psychol.* 62:298–306 (1966)

DEVELOPMENT, MAINTENANCE, AND EXTINCTION OF SOCIAL ATTACHMENT BEHAVIOR IN SHEEP[1]

ROBERT B. CAIRNS

Indiana University

Social attachment behavior of 20 purebred lambs was studied over a 6-mo. period. In the first of 3 experiments, the reinforcing properties of strong attachments formed by young lambs to the perceptually prominent objects, animate or inanimate, with which they had been continuously confined were demonstrated in a series of maze tests. The remaining 2 experiments dealt with the processes involved in the extinction of previously acquired social attachments by (a) analyzing some of the effects of short-term social and biological deprivation, and (b) examining the conditions under which the attachments might be reversed.

The experiments reported here had as their purpose the study of the mechanisms that control social attachment behavior in young sheep, a species for which gregarious behavior is presumed to be prepotent (Miller, 1951; Scott, 1945).

Experiment 1

On the basis of assumptions discussed elsewhere (Cairns, 1966), it was expected that lambs would form an attachment with respect to any salient object with which they had been continuously confined. While tactile stimlation might facilitate attachment formation, such stimulation was not seen as essential to the process. Nor was it required that the object be alive and capable of developing patterns of dyadic interaction. The rearing conditions of the present study permitted a preliminary evaluation of these expectations.

This experiment was also concerned with the quantification of the reinforcement properties of the experimentally produced attachments. Previous work has shown that the ongoing behavior of lambs is usually disrupted when the cohabitant is removed from the confinement compartment (Cairns & Johnson, 1965; Hersher, Richmond, & Moore, 1963). It was expected, again on the basis of the association hypothesis (Cairns, 1966), that measures of the extent of the disruption would provide reliable indices of attachment strength. This proposition implied that the greater the amount of disturbance observed upon cohabitant separation, the greater the effectiveness of the cohabitant as a "social" reinforcement event.

Method

Subjects. From birth until the beginning of the experiment, when they were 4–8 wk. old, 20 purebred lambs (Hampshire Down) lived with the maternal ewes and other lambs in a small flock. One lamb died after 7 wk. in the control condition and was replaced with an *S* of the same age and sex.[2] In addition, 5 Rambouillet ewes and 10 mongrel dogs were used as cohabitants.

Apparatus. A **U** maze of plywood and wire construction was used for the assessment of social preferences. The 30-in.-wide runways were enclosed by 48-in. plywood walls and covered by translucent netting material. In length, the runway segments were: stem (start compartment to choice point) 12 ft.; arm (choice point to 90° turn) 6 ft.; entry (turn to goal area) 4 ft. The 8 × 8 ft. goal areas were enclosed by 48-in. plywood walls. Guillotine doors were located at the start compartment and at either side of the choice point. Five television sets, of various makes and external dimensions, provided the remaining items of equipment. All sets operated continuously, presenting both auditory and visual patterns.

[1] The author expresses his thanks to D. L. Johnson and R. Webb for their help in the completion of these studies. This research was supported, in part, by grants from the Indiana University Foundation and the National Institute of Mental Health (07144-02 and 08757-01).

[2] The relevant statistical analyses were performed with and without the inclusion of the substitute control *S*. The results of the two sets of analyses were strictly comparable. Unless otherwise noted, the product-moment correlations reported in Experiment 1 were based upon 20 *Ss*. The corresponding two-tailed significance levels ($df = 18$) are: $r \geq .45$, $p < .05$; $r \geq .57$, $p < .01$; $r \geq .68$, $p < .001$.

Confinement compartments. Each of the 20 compartments was approximately 8 × 10 ft. in floor area, enclosed on all sides. Thus *S*s were permitted no visual contact with animals other than the cohabitant. Ten of the compartments were partitioned into two equal parts by a wire fence, 5 ft. high, which extended the length of the midline of the compartment. The fence interstices were 1⅞ × 3⅞ in.

Procedure. Five lambs were assigned at random to one of four confinement conditions. (*a*) Dog interaction: the lamb-dog pairs were housed in five different compartments. If the dog chewed, mauled, or otherwise abused the lamb, it was restricted by a neck harness to approximately one-half the compartment. It was necessary to so restrict two of the five dogs. All lambs were permitted free movement. (*b*) Dog separation: the two animals in each pair were housed together as above, except that the lamb was placed on one side of the wire partition, and the dog on the other. The interstices of the fence were small enough virtually to debar the animals from physical contact. (*c*) Inanimate: lambs were isolated from other animals, but were housed with a continuously operating television set. The sets emitted organized, but varied, patterns of visual and auditory stimulation. (*d*) Control: lambs were paired individually with nonmaternal Rambouillet ewes under conditions of restricted interaction, i.e., as in condition *b*. Once the experimental confinement had begun, the two animals were kept together 24 hr. per day, and separated only when required by the test sessions.

Two types of maze series were conducted: noncontrast, where the cohabitant was placed in one goal area, and the second goal compartment was empty; contrast, where a ewe was tethered in one goal area, and a dog was tethered or a television set was placed in the opposite compartment. One of the test objects was the lamb's cohabitant. The contrast stimulus for *S*s in the three experimental groups was a ewe; the contrast stimulus for the control group was a dog.

Sets of 10 noncontrast trials were completed after 7, 14, 21, 28, and 63 days of confinement. The position of the cohabitant was alternated in each set of trials for each *S*: e.g., left, for Trials 1–10; right, Trials 11–20, etc. Prior to the first test trial in every set, *S* was forced twice to either goal area in an ABBA or BAAB sequence by closing off one arm of the U. During all trials the noncorrection method was followed: i.e., a guillotine door was closed immediately after *S* passed the choice point. The *S* remained in the goal area for 60 sec. and then was returned for the next test trial. On a given trial, *S* was permitted 5 min. to traverse the stem distance and enter either arm.

On Days 70–71, two blocks of 10 contrast trials were completed for each *S*. The placement of the cohabitant was the same on both test days. On Day 70, *S*s were given four forced runs, two to either side, prior to the first test trial. On Day 71, prior to the beginning of the test series, *S*s were given an additional forced run to either side. In other respects the procedure was the same as that followed in the noncontrast series.

To obtain an assessment of behavioral disruption contingent upon cohabitant removal, sets of short-term separation tests were conducted after Weeks 1, 2, 3, and 9 of confinement. In each series, *S* was observed for six successive 60-sec. periods. During half of these observations (Minutes 1, 3, 5) the cohabitant was present; during the remainder (Minutes 2, 4, 6) the cohabitant was removed.

Response measures. The behavior observed during the cohabitant removal tests was the amount of vocalization, i.e., bleating, which occurred during cohabitant separation relative to nonseparation. The confinement vocalization index, VI_c, was a difference score based upon the effects of cohabitant removal as observed in the confinement compartment: mean bleats per minute emitted during cohabitant absence minus mean bleats per minute emitted during cohabitant presence. A parallel measure, the maze vocalization index, VI_m, was the vocalization that occurred during two 60-sec. periods of confinement in the U-maze goal compartments with and without the cohabitant during the 4 preliminary trials of each noncontrast series.

The maze trials yielded two measures: (*a*) proportion of trials within each block of 10 trials that *S*s selected the cohabitant; (*b*) running time, i.e., the time elapsed between the opening of the start compartment and *S*'s passing the choice point into one of the two arms. The time scores, recorded to the nearest .1 sec., were transformed to common logarithms for analysis.

Results

Behavioral disruption. Vocalization was almost perfectly controlled by the experimental operations of cohabitant removal and replacement. Summing over observations and conditions, the difference in mean bleats per minute during cohabitant presence (.50) and cohabitant absence (8.05) was significant ($t = 5.72$, $df = 19$, $p < .001$). With the exception of 2 *S*s assigned to the inanimate condition, every *S* tested demonstrated the essential disruption-quiescence pattern. As noted elsewhere (Cairns & Johnson, 1965; Hersher et al., 1963), recurrent bleating in this context was usually accompanied by agitated pacing, rapid breathing, and leaping against the walls of the enclosure.

To determine whether the magnitude of the disruption varied as a function of treatment conditions, a repeated-measures analysis of variance (4 × 4) was performed on the VI_c scores summarized in Table 1. The

TABLE 1

MEAN CONFINEMENT VOCALIZATION INDEX OF THE FOUR TREATMENT GROUPS FOR COHABITANT-REMOVAL TESTS CONDUCTED AFTER 1, 2, 3, and 9 WK. OF CONFINEMENT (EXPERIMENT 1)

Condition	Weeks				Total
	1	2	3	9	
Dog interaction	12.2	11.4	13.0	12.4	12.3
Dog separated	4.6	6.6	7.0	11.0	7.3
Inanimate	1.6	2.0	2.8	2.6	2.3
Control	11.0	11.4	11.8	15.0	12.3

main treatment effect was statistically significant ($F = 4.27$, $df = 3/16$, $p < .05$). All between-group differences between the three experimental groups (interaction, separation, inanimate) surpassed the critical values of the Newman-Keuls procedure (Winer, 1962) at $p < .05$. Neither the repeated Tests effect nor the Test × Treatment interaction was significant.

An independent assessment of separation vocalization was obtained in the preliminary trials of each noncontrast **U**-maze series. During the initial weeks of testing, the correlations between the two independently derived vocalization indices, VI_c and VI_m, were of moderate magnitude (r = .48, .46, and .36 for Weeks 1, 2, and 3, respectively). By Week 9 of confinement,

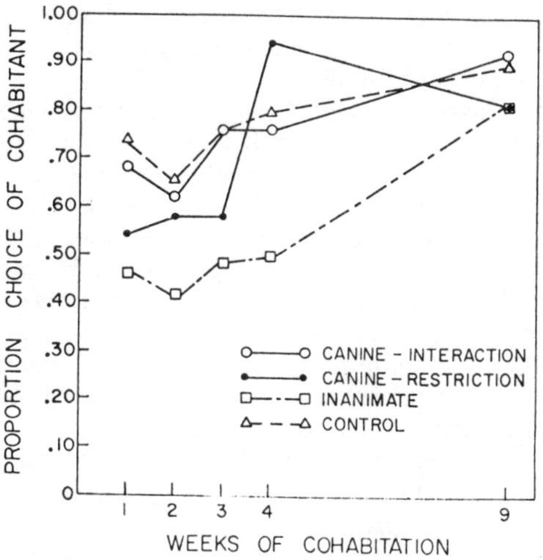

FIG. 1. Choice behavior of lambs in noncontrast maze series, with 10 trials at each test week (Experiment 1).

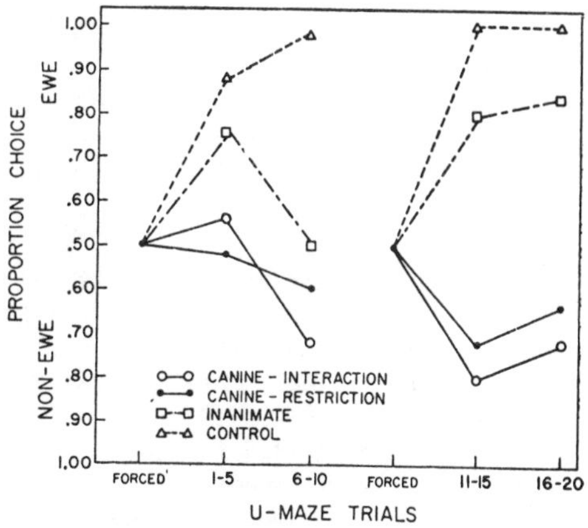

FIG. 2. Choice behavior of lambs in contrast maze series over 4 blocks of 5 trials (Experiment 1).

however, the vocalization scores obtained in the **U** maze were highly correlated with those obtained in the compartment cohabitant removal tests ($r = .90$). Both vocalization indices showed the expected differences in intensity of behavioral disruption as a function of treatment conditions.

Choice data. An analysis of variance of the noncontrast **U**-maze series data (Figure 1) indicated that the groups improved in performance over the successive five blocks of test trials ($F = 2.74$, $df = 4/64$, $p < .05$). In the final series (Week 9), *S*s' preference for the cohabitant was clearly above the chance level ($F = 14.49$, $df = 1/19$, $p < .005$). A comparison of the "correct" responses produced by the four groups indicated that the experimental conditions did not have a significant differential effect on *S*s' choice behavior in the noncontrast series. Neither the Treatment effect nor the Treatment × Trials interaction was statistically significant.

The contrast series permitted an assessment of the relative strength of the experimentally produced attachments. As shown in Figure 2, the experimental treatment effect was reliable ($F = 7.96$, $df = 3/16$, $p < .01$). Analysis by the Newman-Keuls procedure indicated that, with the exception of the two dog-paired groups, all group comparisons yielded significant differences: *Ss* in these two experimental conditions selected the ewe test object on fewer occasions than control *Ss* ($p < .001$) or *Ss* in the inanimate condition ($p < .01$) and the difference between the inanimate condition and the control condition was reliable ($p < .05$).

Running times. Over the five blocks of noncontrast trials, the lambs showed a systematic increase in the amount of time in mean log seconds (mls) that they remained in the stem of the maze prior to making a choice ($F = 8.65$, $df = 4/64$, $p < .01$). In all conditions, *Ss* tended to run faster in the first test series (Week 1 mls = .94) than they did in the final test series (Week 9 mls = 1.40). Unlike the choice scores, the running time index differentiated between the four treatment groups in the noncontrast series. The between-group effect was statistically significant, however, only in the final block of trials ($F = 4.20$, $df = 3/16$, $p < .05$). A Newman-Keuls analysis of these data indicated that control *Ss* required significantly less time (mls = .88) than *Ss* assigned to the inanimate condition (mls = 1.88). The remaining between-group differences were nonsignificant.

The contrast series running times failed to yield significant differences between the various treatment groups. It is of some interest to note, however, that the lambs ran reliably faster in the contrast (mls = 1.10) series than in the final noncontrast (mls = 1.40) series ($F = 12.24$, $df = 1/16$, $p < .01$). Analysis of the significant Test Type × Treatment interaction indicated that the main effect was due to the change in performance of one group: the inanimate condition. This group was the only one for which the contrast vs. final noncontrast latency difference was reliable ($t = 3.98$, $df = 4$, $p < .02$).

Predictors of maze performance. A principal aim of the experiment was to determine whether attachment strength could be reliably quantified. Specifically, it was expected that the vocalization indices of behavioral disturbance, VI_c and VI_m, would be significantly related to the lamb's choice of its cohabitant.

The results indicated that neither vocalization index was significantly related to the choice performance of *Ss* in the noncontrast trial blocks. However, both indices were highly correlated with *Ss*' performance in the contrast series. For the final VI_c, the product-moment correlation was .81; for the final VI_m, the correlation was .75. If *S* showed considerable disruption during cohabitant separation, it would likely move in the direction of its cohabitant during the contrast trials. The within-group correlations were, with the exception of the control group, of the same order as those based upon the entire sample. The product-moment correlations between VI_m and choice of cohabitant in the contrast series within the various groups were: dog-paired conditions, $r = .75$ ($df = 8$, $p < .05$); inanimate condition, $r = .88$ ($df = 3$, $p < .05$); control, $r = -.06$ ($df = 3$, $p > .10$).

Similar correlational analyses were performed for the vocalization indices and running times. The data show that all of the correlations were in the expected direction: the greater the disturbance of *S* upon being separated from its cohabitant, the shorter its response latencies. But the relationships were reliable only for *Ss*' performance in the noncontrast series. For VI_c, the correlations between weekly vocalization scores and running times for Weeks 1, 2, 3, and 9 were −.23, −.41, −.27, and −.50. The corresponding correlations for VI_m and running times were −.11, −.65, −.59, and −.56.

Observations of following behavior. One of the more striking behavior patterns to emerge as a consequence of these experimental manipulations was the development of a strong following response: the lamb remained close to its dog cohabitant even when both animals were placed in an open field outside the maintenance compartment. If the cohabitant walked, the lamb would walk; if the cohabitant ran, the lamb would run; if the cohabitant jumped over a fence, the lamb would try to follow by going over, or through, the barrier.[3] This behavior,

[3] A short research film of these behaviors, shown at the 1964 American Psychological Association convention, is available from the Film Library, Audio-Visual Center, Indiana University (16 mm., silent, 10 min.).

noted in earlier work (Cairns & Johnson, 1965), was specific to the cohabitant, and was obtained in all but two of the lambs assigned to the dog-paired conditions. Of the two *S*s that did not follow their cohabitants, one was in the dog-interaction condition, and the other was in the dog-separation condition.

Discussion

Familiar objects, animate or inanimate, can assume highly effective control over the behavior of young sheep. The attribution of reinforcement properties to a particular class of "social" objects, i.e., same-species animals, however, appears to be neither an inevitable nor an irreversible phenomenon. For lambs, at least, both the direction and the strength of social attachments are susceptible to experimental manipulation.

It should be noted that the experimentally produced attachments were often preceded by, or concurrent with, a same-species attachment. All *S*s in the present experiment had 4–8 wk. of constant exposure to various representatives of their own species prior to the experimental confinement. This experience presumably was sufficient for the lambs to develop a strong attachment response with respect to the same-species objects. Substantial evidence was later obtained (Experiment 3) which suggests that a same-species attachment not only had been established, but that it had not been entirely extinguished by the experimental procedures. This assumption —that the ewes possessed positive incentive properties for all lambs—was also consistent with the results of the choice and the time data of the present study. Indeed, the apparent conflicts between these two indices of incentive magnitude are resolved by this assumption.

Consider first the choice data. When obtained in single reward (noncontrast) series, the choice measure did not clearly differentiate between lambs that were strongly attached and those that were minimally attached to the cohabitant. All *S*s learned to approach the "correct" goal area. But when a second reward event was introduced to the testing context—permitting *S*s to select between the cohabitant and a presumably positive alternative—only the experimental *S*s that were strongly attached to their cohabitant persisted in a cohabitant-appropriate turning response. With the resultant increase in range of choice scores in the contrast series, the choice vs. vocalization correlation was enhanced.

The running time results also suggest that there was a residual, or rapidly learned, same-species attachment. Even though all lambs tended to move toward the location of the cohabitant in the noncontrast series, there were significant (and predictable) individual differences in how fast they got there. The most strongly attached animals, in terms of the VI measures, had shorter response latencies than *S*s that were least strongly attached to their cohabitants. But those experimental *S*s that had not formed strong alien-species social bonds, when tested in the contrast series, tended (*a*) to select the ewe test object instead of the cohabitant, and (*b*) to run faster to the ewe than they had to the cohabitant in the noncontrast trials. Under the particular conditions of this experiment, then, the time-dependent (latency) and time-independent (choice) measures of incentive magnitude yielded parallel and complementary results. In the light of the generally low or nonsignificant relationships that have been reported between incentive strength and discrimination learning (Pubols, 1960), the degree of the correlations obtained here between vocalization and maze performance was of particular interest.

Finally, preliminary support can be claimed for the hypothesized relationship between stimulus salience and attachment strength. As the cohabitant-removal tests demonstrated, the most salient objects in the lamb's compartment became the focus of an attachment response. Equally available, but less prominent, objects in the confinement context did not acquire effective control over the lamb's behavior. And the strongest attachments were formed within the conditions where the cohabitants were presumably most salient. Further evaluation of this hypothesis might include (*a*) the quantitative control of objective stimulus characteristics, such as intensity or mobility, and (*b*) assessments of the orienting behavior of the dependent animals.

Experiment 2

The principal aim of Experiment 2 was to determine the effects of various periods of short-term cohabitant separation on two indices of behavioral disruption (i.e., vocalization and gross movement). The study was also designed to yield information about the effects of water deprivation on these indices, and to permit thereby a direct comparison of the two different types of "deprivation."

Method

Subjects. Fourteen Hampshire lambs, all of which had participated as *Ss* in Experiment 1, were 17–21 wk. old at the time of the first deprivation series, and had been confined under conditions of experimental cohabitation for approximately 13 wk. (±1 wk.).

Water deprivation. Ten *Ss* were deprived of water for a 72-hr. period. The lamb's drinking dish was removed at 7:30 A.M. (±1 hr.) on the first day of deprivation. Immediately following water removal, and at the end of 1, 2, 4, 8, 24, 48, and 72 hr., *Ss* were observed for two consecutive 15-min. periods. After the first 15-min. observation, *Ss* were given access to 200 cc of water in a nippled bottle for a 60-sec. period. At the end of the 60-sec. interval, the water was removed and a second 15-min. observation was conducted.

The *Ss* were maintained with their respective cohabitants under the conditions of confinement described in Experiment 1. The cohabitants were permitted to drink ad lib for brief periods approximately three times daily outside the confinement compartment. Dry food (grain, alfalfa, "Master Mix" dog pellets manufactured by McMillen Feed) was continuously available for both animals.

Social deprivation. Exactly parallel operations were followed with 10 lambs in assessing the effects of short-term social deprivation. Instead of water removal, the cohabitant (dog for 5 *Ss* and ewe for 5 *Ss*) was removed at 7:30 A.M. (±1 hr.). The same observation schedule was followed. During the interval between each of the 15-min. observations, the cohabitant was reintroduced to the compartment for 60 sec., then removed. The *Ss* had ample food and water available at all times.

Six *Ss* were exposed to both types of deprivation separated by 1 wk., and the order of presentation counterbalanced (i.e., half of the group was exposed to the water deprivation treatment first, and the remainder to the social deprivation treatment first).

Measures. During the observation periods, two measures of behavioral disruption were recorded: (*a*) vocalization, and (*b*) gross movement. For each 15-min. period of continuous observation, the rate of vocalization was determined in mean bleats per minute. In addition to the vocalization measure, an index of general movement or locomotion, in mean number of occasions per minute that *S* entered a different quadrant of the compartment for each 15-min. observation period, was obtained.

Since each *S* was observed over 16 different 15-min. blocks in each deprivation series, it was possible to determine, for every *S*, the relationship between vocalization and movement. Ten independent correlations were computed from the social deprivation data and 10 from the water deprivation data. The median product-moment correlation between these two measures in the social deprivation series was $r = .89$ ($p < .001$), and in the water deprivation series, $r = .76$ ($p < .001$).

Results

The effects of water and social deprivation upon the vocalization and gross movement measures are shown in Figure 3. Both measures showed the expected in-

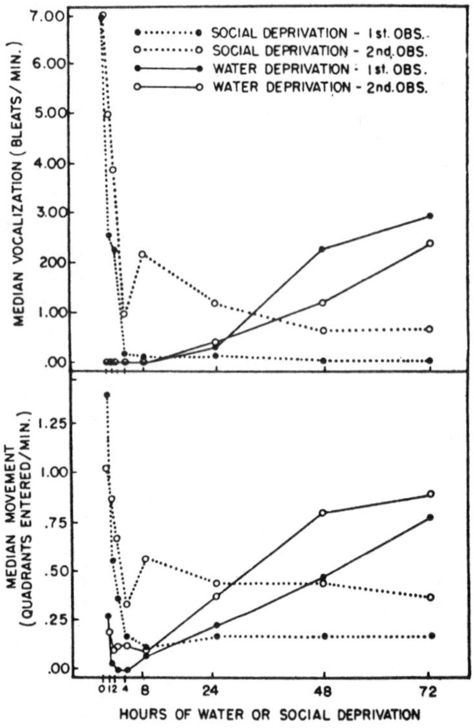

FIG. 3. Lamb vocalization and movement as a function of hours since separation from cohabitant or water removal (Experiment 2).

TABLE 2

DISTRIBUTION-FREE TREND TESTS (L) SHOWING EFFECTS OF WATER AND COHABITANT REMOVAL (EXPERIMENT 2)

Index	Water removal		Cohabitant removal	
	1st Obs.	2nd Obs.	1st Obs.	2nd Obs.
Vocalization	1879**	1924**	1900**	1909**
Movement	1817**	1865**	1788**	1765*

* $p < .01$.
** $p < .001$.

crease with number of hours of water deprivation. Increments in rate of bleating and movement directly paralleled increments in rate of water consumption. The L test (Page, 1963) indicated that, in every instance, the trends were significant (Table 2).

Rather than showing that behavioral disturbance increased with hours of social deprivation, the data indicated exactly the opposite trend. The greatest disturbance was observed immediately upon removal of the cohabitant, followed by a sharp decrement in both indices in the early postseparation observations. This effect was observed regardless of the species of the cohabitant. Note should be made that, except for the initial observation (i.e., 0 hr.), the amount of disruption occurring during the second set of observations (Minutes 16–30) was consistently greater than that observed in the first set (Minutes 1–15).

The Ls computed for the social deprivation curves surpassed the critical values for significance (Table 2).

Discussion

It appears that prolonged cohabitant separation provided the occasion for the initiation of an attachment-extinction process. It has been sometimes assumed that learned appetitive drives function in a fashion that is directly analogous to primary drives. In an extension of this model to social behavior, Gewirtz and Baer (1958) deduced that the longer the separation (presumably over a short-term period) from social objects, the higher the social drive level and the greater the reinforcement effectiveness of social events. Not only were the expectations of the primary drive analogue model not confirmed, but significant trends in the opposite direction were obtained. It must be noted, however, that concomitant changes in reinforcement effectiveness as a function of length of separation were not studied directly in this experiment.

EXPERIMENT 3

The final study in this series dealt with the reversal of a previously established social attachment.

Method

Subjects. Ten lambs from Experiment 1 were 23–25 wk. old at the beginning of the experimental procedures of this study.

Procedure. The original experimental conditions were reversed for *Ss*, i.e., 5 dog-paired lambs were reassigned to ewe cohabitants, and 5 control (ewe-paired) lambs were reassigned to the dog-paired conditions. The interaction-separation variable was ignored in the reassignment of all of the dog-paired *Ss*. The interchanges occurred after the lambs had been with the original cohabitant for 15–19 wk., excluding a 72-hr. period of social deprivation during Confinement Weeks 12–14.

Under the same procedure followed in the original contrast series, U-maze trials were conducted after 7, 21–22, 35–36, and 49–50 days in the interchanged conditions. The original cohabitant was placed in one goal area, the contemporaneous cohabitant in the other goal area. Ten trials were involved in the first series, after Day 7 of confinement, and 20 trials in each of the succeeding series.

Results and Discussion

Performance in the final 10 trials of the original contrast series (Days 70–71 of Experiment 1) was taken as the prereversal index of social preference. These results, and those for tests following the interchange manipulation, are shown in Figure 4. The consequences of the interchange were seen after the first week in the new setting. An almost complete reversal of preference occurred in the case of the lambs moved from dog cohabitation to ewe cohabitation; a minimal effect was observed in the opposite condition. By Day 50 of confinement, however, a significant reversal of preference was obtained in the latter group. Although the study was discontinued at this point, the trend in preferences seemed clear. Statistical analysis indicated that the Treatment × Time interaction was reliable ($F = 19.62$, $df = 4/32$, $p < .001$). Both experimental groups demonstrated a significant change in preference with respect to the dog cohabitants.

It has been suggested elsewhere (Cairns, 1966) that extended separation from an "attached" object would be associated with a progressive extinction of that relationship, coupled with the simultaneous development of an attachment to currently available stimuli. Certain factors might accelerate the relearning process: e.g., placement of the animal into an entirely unfamiliar setting, minimal or no contact with previously conditioned stimuli, or constant exposure to a highly salient stimulus in the "new" context. The very rapid reversal of attachments obtained in the dog to ewe interchanges may have been due to still another factor: the reestablishment of a previously acquired attachment response. It will be recalled that all lambs had been reared with sheep prior to the original (Experiment 1) confinement. The interchange manipulation was, for the animals assigned to the dog-paired condition in the original study, a reinstitution of the preexperimental context. For lambs assigned to the original control group, however, the reversal condition provided their first exposure to an alien animal in a nontest situation.

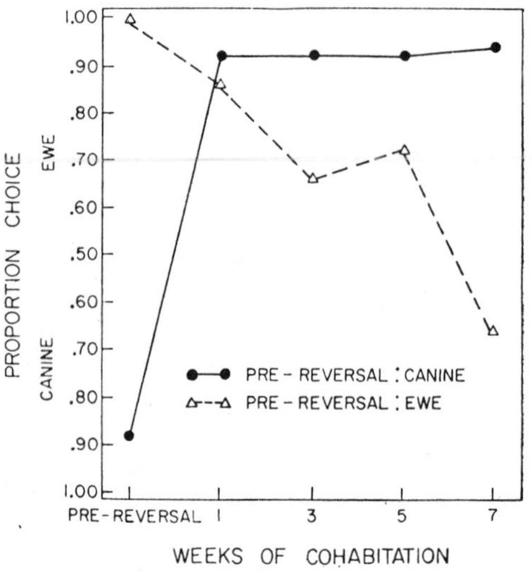

FIG. 4. Choice behavior of lambs in final 10 trials of the prereversal and postreversal contrast series (Experiment 3).

GENERAL DISCUSSION

Nonbiologic and derivative reinforcement events have been assigned a role of nuclear import in theories of personality and social behavior. It has been generally assumed that the reinforcement properties of such events will, under certain conditions, rival or exceed those which have been demonstrated for events more directly relevant to physiological need states. Only limited experimental evidence, however, can be cited in support of this proposition. Conditioned reinforcement events have rarely been shown to approach the stability or the intensity of primary reinforcers (Kelleher & Gollub, 1962; Myers, 1958). The present results provide a striking exception. Once acquired, the lamb's attachment to its cohabitant was strong and pervasive; its consequences were generalized across response systems and situations.

One of the more interesting findings of the present work was that the strength of the attachment response, and its corresponding reinforcement properties, could be experimentally manipulated. But the operation traditionally followed to enhance the effectiveness of primary reinforcement events diminished the effectiveness of social reinforcers. Though these deprivation effects appear to be contradictory, further analysis of the cue properties of drive stimuli involved suggest that the two functions represent one and the same process (Baumeister, Hawkins, & Cromwell, 1964; Cairns, 1966; Estes, 1958).

Finally, the limitations of the present studies due to species and organismic sample restrictions should be noted. The animals studied, young sheep, were ones in which gregarious behavior was readily elicited. Whether comparable effects might be obtained with older animals, or members of other species, requires further study. The results of other investigators indicate that the essential attachment-acquisition phenomena can be replicated, but at a diminished intensity, with a different species (Denenberg, Hudgens, & Zarrow, 1964), and with mature members of the same species (Hersher et al., 1963).

REFERENCES

BAUMEISTER, A., HAWKINS, W. F., & CROMWELL, R. L. Need states and activity level. *Psychol. Bull.*, 1964, **61**, 438–453.

CAIRNS, R. B. Attachment behavior of mammals. *Psychol. Rev.*, 1966, **73**, 409–426.

CAIRNS, R. B., & JOHNSON, D. L. The development of interspecies social attachments. *Psychon. Sci.*, 1965, **2**, 337–338.

DENENBERG, V. H., HUDGENS, G. A., & ZARROW, M. X. Mice reared with rats: Modification of behavior by early experience with another species. *Science*, 1964, **143**, 380–381.

ESTES, W. K. Stimulus-response theory of drive. In M. R. Jones (Ed.), *Nebraska symposium on motivation: 1958*. Lincoln: University of Nebraska Press, 1958. Pp. 35–69.

GEWIRTZ, J. L., & BAER, D. M. Deprivation and satiation of social reinforcers as drive conditions. *J. abnorm. soc. Psychol.*, 1958, **57**, 165–172.

HERSHER, L., RICHMOND, J. B., & MOORE, A. U. Modifiability of the critical period for the development of maternal behavior in sheep and goats. *Behaviour*, 1963, **20**, 311–320.

KELLEHER, R. T., & GOLLUB, L. R. A review of positive conditioned reinforcement. *J. exp. Anal. Behav.*, 1962, **5**, 543–597.

MILLER, N. E. Learnable drives and rewards. In S. S. Stevens (Ed.), *Handbook of experimental psychology*. New York: Wiley, 1951. Pp. 435–472.

MYERS, J. L. Secondary reinforcement: A review of recent experimentation. *Psychol. Bull.*, 1958, **55**, 284–301.

PAGE, E. B. Ordered hypotheses for multiple treatments: A significance test for linear ranks. *J. Amer. Statist. Assn.*, 1963, **58**, 216–230.

PUBOLS, B. H., JR. Incentive magnitude, learning, and performance in animals. *Psychol. Bull.*, 1960, **57**, 89–115.

SCOTT, J. P. Social behavior, organization and leadership in a small flock of domestic sheep. *Comp. Psychol. Monogr.*, 1945, **18**(4, Whole No. 96).

WINER, B. J. *Statistical principles in experimental design*. New York: McGraw-Hill, 1962.

13

Reprinted, by permission, from *New England J. Med.* **286**:460–463 (1972)

MATERNAL ATTACHMENT

Importance of the First Post-Partum Days

MARSHALL H. KLAUS, M.D., RICHARD JERAULD, B.S., NANCY C. KREGER, B.S., WILLIE MCALPINE, B.S., MEREDITH STEFFA, B.S., AND JOHN H. KENNELL, M.D.

Abstract To determine whether present hospital practices may affect later maternal behavior, we placed 28 primiparous women in two study groups shortly after delivery of normal full-term infants. Fourteen mothers (control group) had the usual physical contact with their infants, and 14 mothers (extended contact) had 16 hours of additional contact. Mothers' backgrounds and infants' characteristics were similar in both groups. Maternal behavior was measured 28 to 32 days later during a standardized interview, an examination of the baby and a filmed bottle feeding. Extended-contact mothers were more reluctant to leave their infants with someone else, usually stood and watched during the examination, showed greater soothing behavior, and engaged in significantly more eye-to-eye contact and fondling. These studies suggest that simple modification of care shortly after delivery may alter subsequent maternal behavior.

IN certain animals such as the goat, cow and sheep, separation of the mother and infant immediately after birth for a period as short as one to four hours often results in distinctly aberrant mothering behavior, such as failure of the mother to care for the young, butting her own offspring away and feeding her own and other infants indiscriminately.[1,2] In contrast, if they are together for the first four days and are then separated on the fifth day for an equal period, the mother resumes the protective and mothering behavior characteristic for her species when the pair is reunited. Thus, there is a special period immediately after delivery in the adult animal. If the animal mother is separated from her young during this period, deviant behavior may result. An early short period of separation does not produce as severe a distortion of mothering behavior in all species.[3]

In recent years several investigators have studied whether a similar phenomenon occurs in mothers of premature infants.[4,5] Does the prolonged separation experienced by the mother of a premature infant affect the formation of her affectional bonds and change her mothering behavior months and years after the delivery? Early results from these studies suggest that the long period of physical separation common in most nurseries may adversely affect maternal performance of some women.

Studies of human mothers of premature infants necessarily differ in design from the classic studies of separation in the animal mother. The gestation of the mothers is severely shortened, the infant is small and appears fragile, the period of separation after birth is greatly extended, and it has not been possible to provide close physical contact immediately after birth similar to the natural human and animal situation.

In most nurseries in the United States, however, even full-term mothers are separated from their infants for a short, but possibly important time. Thus, it seemed essential to determine whether present hospital practices for the mother of a full-term infant influence later maternal behavior. This report tests the hypothesis that there is a period shortly after birth that is uniquely important for mother-to-infant attachment in the human being.

MATERIAL AND METHODS

We placed each of 28 primiparous mothers of normal full-term infants in one of two study groups, depending on the day of delivery. Neither group knew of this study in advance or to our knowledge was aware of the arrangements made for the other. (The mothers, however, were not questioned on this subject.) The 14 mothers in the control group had

From the Department of Pediatrics, School of Medicine, Case Western Reserve University, Cleveland (address reprint requests to Dr. Klaus at the Department of Pediatrics, School of Medicine, Case Western Reserve University, 2103 Adelbert Rd., Cleveland, O. 44106).

Presented in part at the plenary session of the American Pediatric Society, Atlantic City, N.J., April 29, 1971.

Supported in part by the Grant Foundation and the Educational Foundation of America.

the traditional contact with their infants: a glimpse of the baby shortly after birth, brief contact and identification at six to 12 hours, and then visits for 20 to 30 minutes every four hours for bottle feedings. In addition to this routine contact, the 14 mothers in the extended-contact group were given their nude babies, with a heat panel overhead, for one hour within the first three hours after birth, and also five extra hours of contact each afternoon of the three days after delivery. (A heat panel was also placed over the control mothers' beds for one hour during the first three hours.)

To eliminate any influence from the enthusiasm or interest of the nurse that might obscure the results, the special nurses who cared for the mothers during the extended-contact period (five hours per day) spent an equal amount of time with the control mothers. After an initial standardized introductory statement they only answered questions, did not instruct any of the women in caretaking unless this was requested, and most of the time were available just outside the room.

The mean age, socioeconomic and marital status, color, premedication, sex of the infant and days hospitalized in both groups were nearly identical (Table 1). Only mothers who intended to keep their infants and to bottle-feed them were admitted to the study. The mean birth weights of the two groups of infants differed by 110 g.

Second question: "Have you been out since the baby was born, and who sat?" A score of 0 was given for "yes," and if the mother felt good and did not think about her infant while she was out. A score of 3 was given if she did not go out or leave the baby with anyone, or if she did go out but thought constantly about the baby.

The third question related to spoiling and could not be scored.

A second measure of maternal behavior was the observation of the mother during a standardized examination of her infant. A score of 3 was allotted if, during the examination of the infant, she was standing by the pediatrician and watching continuously; a score of 0 was given if she remained seated and looked elsewhere. We also noted whether or not the mother attempted to soothe the baby when it cried. If she did not interact with the baby, she was given a score of 0; if she was consistently soothing, she was given a score of 3. The scoring of the interview and observation of maternal performance was then determined by independent raters who did not know to which group the mothers belonged.

To study maternal behavior in another situation, we made time-lapse films of the mothers feeding their infants. They all knew they were being photographed and were told to spend as much time as they wished. Filming was done through a one-way mirror for 15 minutes at a speed of 60 frames per minute. Mothers' and babies' reactions could then be analyzed in detail at one-second intervals. Each frame of the first 600 was scored by analyzers who did not know which group the mothers were in. We analyzed each frame for 25 specific activities, ranging from caretaking skills (such as the position of the bottle) to measurements of maternal interest and affection such as "en face" (defined as when the mother aligned her face in the same vertical plane of rotation as the infant's[6]), whether the mother's body was touching the infant's trunk, and whether she fondled the infant. (We defined fondling as any active spontaneous interaction initiated by the mother not associated with feeding, such as stroking, kissing, bouncing or cuddling.) Inter-observer reliability coefficients were calculated for the individual behaviors. The average of the reliability coefficients was 0.83 for "en face" and 0.99 for fondling.

Table 1. Clinical Data for 14 Mothers in the Extended-Contact and 14 in the Control Group.

Group	Maternal Characteristics				Mean Score*			Nurses' Time	Hospital Stay	Mean Birth Weight	No. of Infants	
	age	married	N†	W‡	A	B	C				M§	F¶
	yr	*no. of mothers*						*min/day*	*days*	*g*		
Extended contact	18.2	4	13	1	6.7	6.7	4.9	13	3.8	3184	6	8
Control	18.6	5	13	1	6.5	6.9	4.9	14	3.7	3074	8	6

*In this (Hollingshead) scoring system, on a scale of 1 to 7, residence (A) of 7.0 = poorest housing, occupation (B) of 7.0 = unskilled workers, & education (C) of 5.0 = reaching 10th to 11th grade in high school.
†Negro. ‡White. §Male. ¶Female.

To determine if this short additional time with the infant early in life altered later behavior, we asked the mothers to return to the hospital a month after delivery for three separate observations. These observations were made between the 28th and 32d post-partum days and consisted of a standardized interview, an observation of maternal performance during a physical examination of the infant and a filmed study of the mother feeding her infant.

The first seven questions on the interview concerned the general health of the infant, such as the number of stools and the amount of milk taken. Three separate questions were related to caretaking and were scored 0, 1, 2, 3.

First: "When the baby cries and has been fed, and the diapers are dry, what do you do?" A score of 0 was given for letting the baby cry it out, and 3 for picking up the baby every time. An intermediate score was given for gradations of behavior.

Results

Analysis of the interview data is shown in Figure 1. The extended-contact group (the solid black bars) had scores of 2 and greater, whereas the control mothers (cross-hatched bars) were at the lower end of the scale. The chance of this occurrence is less than 0.05, with the use of the Mann–Whitney U-test.[7]

The two groups scored differently on the results of the observations during the physical examination (Fig. 2). The extended-contact group did not score below 3, whereas the scores of the control mothers were distributed from 1 to 6 (p less than 0.02).

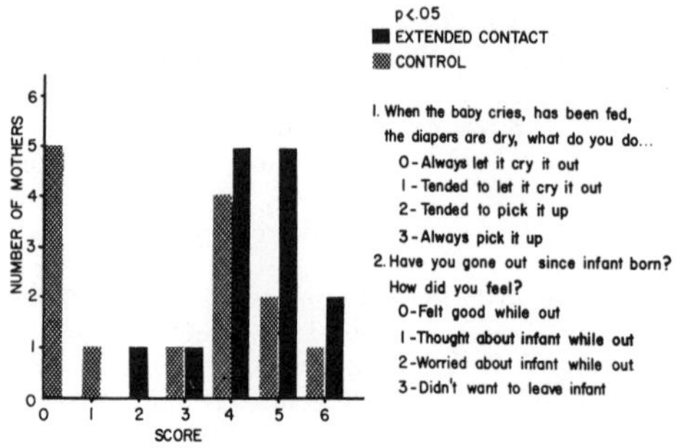

Figure 1. Maternal Scores from a Standardized Interview at One Month.

When the scores on the interview questions and the observations made during the examination are combined (Fig. 3), there is a separation of the scores of the two groups of mothers. The controls have scores of 2 to 10 spread out over the entire range, whereas mothers in the extended-contact group have scores ranging from 7 to 12 (p less than 0.002).

Figure 4 indicates the fondling and "en face" scores for both groups of mothers. Although the

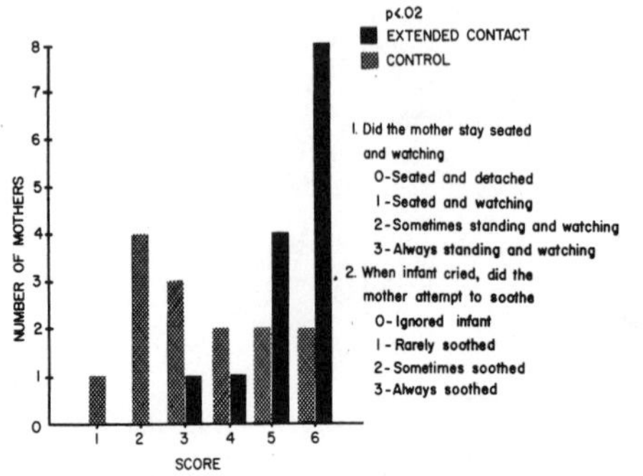

Figure 2. Scored Observations of the Mother Made during a Physical Examination of Her Infant at One Month.

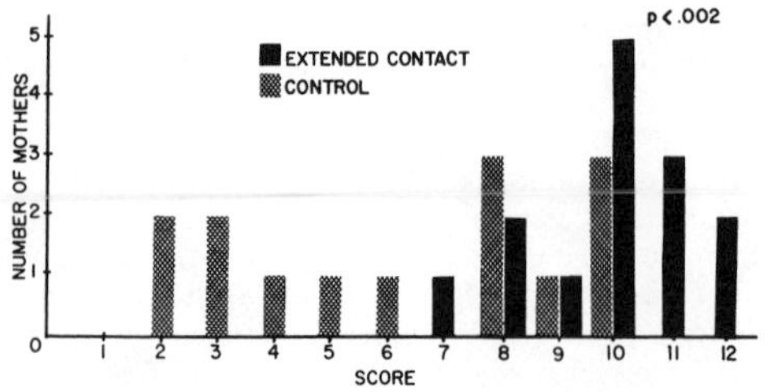

Figure 3. Summation of Scores of Performance from Both the Interview and the Observation of the Mother during an Office Visit at One Month Post Partum.

amount of time the mothers were looking at their babies was not significantly different in the two groups, the extended-contact mothers had significantly greater "en face" and fondling (11.6 per cent and 6.1 per cent of the total scored time, as compared to 3.5 per cent and 1.6 per cent in the control group). There were no significant differences in measures of caretaking, although the bottle was held away from the perpendicular more often in the control group. By all three measurements studied, differences between the two groups of mothers are apparent.

Discussion

It is surprising with the multitude of factors that influence maternal behavior[8] (such as the mother's genetic and cultural background, her relations with

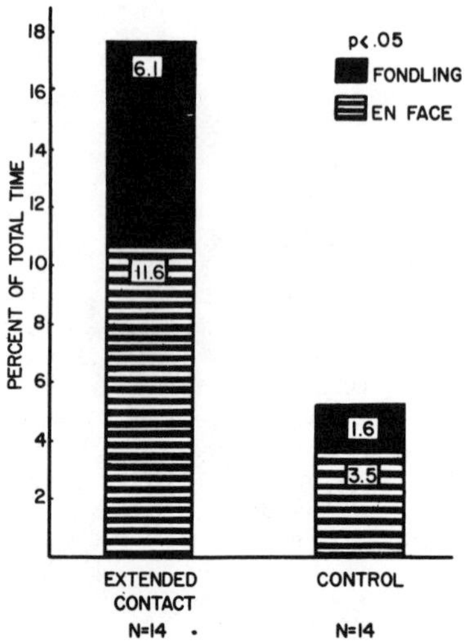

Figure 4. Filmed Feeding Analysis at One Month, Showing Percentage of "en Face" and Fondling Times in Mothers Given Extended Contact with Their Infants and in the Control Group.

her husband and family, the planning and course of her pregnancy, her own mothering as an infant, and her experiences in her family) that just 16 extra hours in the first three days had an effect that persisted for 30 days. From our study we are unable to determine if the initial hour, the five hours of additional contact per day or a combination produced the differences. The previously observed intensive interest of mothers[6,9] in their infants' eyes matched with the unusual ability of the newborn infant to attend and follow, especially in the first hour of life, suggest that the period immediately after birth may be uniquely important.

Though these findings suggest a special attachment period in the human mother somewhat similar to that described in animals, it is possible that the early presentation of a baby shortly after birth is taken by a mother as a special privilege or recognition that in itself may have altered her behavior. In either case, it does affect behavior.

Extensive studies have focused on the process by which the infant becomes attached to his mother. Our observations help in describing the process in the opposite direction — the attachment behavior of the mother. It is tempting to consider this a form of imprinting or a critical period for an adult human. However, this process does not fit the precise definition for either imprinting or a critical period.[10] Both processes are defined in terms of the infant animal and refer to events that occur only once in the life of an individual. Our data suggest that this may be a special attachment period for an adult woman — special in the sense that what happens during this time may alter the later behavior of the adult toward a young infant for at least as long as one month after delivery. It would be useful to have a special term for this period, such as "maternal sensitive period."

An understanding of this intricate process may be vital during planning for the mother of the full-term infant as well as for the mother of the high-risk infant, the premature infant and even the adopting mother. Should the adopting mother receive her baby immediately after delivery to optimize maternal attachment? If there is a "sensitive period," this question and many others require study.

The differences between the two groups in eye-to-eye contact and in tactile stimulation that have probably occurred in the first month in over 200 feedings, and in countless other encounters between mother and infant, may have definite effects on the infant. If these differences in attentiveness and in responsiveness to the babies' cries that we observed are to continue, they could assume additional consequence when taken in the light of the observations of Rubenstein,[11] Bell[12] and others, who have shown that increased maternal attentiveness facilitates exploratory behavior and the early development of cognitive behavior in infants. Early and extended contact for the human mother may have a powerful effect on her interaction with her infant and consequently its later development.

We do not know whether these differences in maternal behavior will disappear after two or three months, will be present in other social and economic groups, or will affect the later development of the two groups of infants. Thus, it is premature to make any recommendations regarding which caretaking regimen is preferable. Caution is recommended before any drastic changes are made in hospital policies as a result of this report, particularly in facilities for mother and infant care, where changes have been made in the past without study of the long-term effects on the mother and infant. It has been the custom of health professionals to make major changes affecting behavior and environment to promote what appeared to be a beneficial innovation without a careful study of the side effects.

We are indebted to Harriet Wolfe, Robin White, Susan Davis and the nursing staff for their helpful ideas and criticism.

REFERENCES

1. Collias NE: The analysis of socialization in sheep and goats. Ecology 37:228-239, 1956
2. Hersher L, Moore AU, Richmond JB: Effect of post partum separation of mother and kid on maternal care in the domestic goat. Science 128:1342-1343, 1958
3. Rheingold H: Maternal Behavior in Mammals. New York, John Wiley and Sons, 1963
4. Barnett CR, Leiderman PH, Grobstein R, et al: Neonatal separation: the maternal side of interactional deprivation. Pediatrics 45: 197-205, 1970
5. Klaus MH, Kennell JH: Mothers separated from their newborn infants. Pediatr Clin North Am 17:1015-1037, 1970
6. Robson K: The role of eye-to-eye contact in maternal-infant attachment. J Child Psychol Psychiatry 8:13-25, 1967
7. Siegel S: Non-parametric Statistics for the Behavioral Sciences. New York, McGraw-Hill Book Company, 1956
8. Bowlby J: Attachment and Loss. Vol I. New York, Basic Books Inc, 1969
9. Klaus M, Kennell JH, Plumb N, et al: Human maternal behavior at the first contact with her young. Pediatrics 46:187-192, 1970
10. Caldwell B: The usefulness of the critical period hypothesis in the study of filiative behavior. Merrill-Palmer Q 8:229-242, 1962
11. Rubenstein J: Maternal attentiveness and subsequent exploratory behavior in the infant. Child Dev 38:1089-1100, 1967
12. Bell S: The development of the concept of object as related to infant-mother attachment. Child Dev 41:291, 1970

Editor's Comments on Papers 14 Through 17

CRITICAL PERIOD FOR PRIMARY SOCIALIZATION IN DOGS

Dogs are the prototype of a highly social species whose young are born in an immature state. Unlike sheep, which can be induced to form attachments to humans only by isolation from their parent species, dogs normally form social attachments to both dogs and people. When we first began our experiments on genetics and the social behavior of dogs in 1946 (Scott and Fuller, 1965), only a few scattered studies of behavioral development in this species had been made. We therefore began systematic daily observations on the behavior of large numbers of puppies as they developed under standard conditions of rearing. These descriptive data clearly indicated a critical period for primary socialization beginning at about three weeks of age (Scott and Marston, Paper 14). Eight years later, we had studied many more puppies and were able to present some statistically accurate landmarks in puppy behavior (Scott, 1958). Changes in behavior were associated with changes in physiology and development of sense organs and we felt that we had, in part, established the physiological basis of the critical period.

It remained to make an experimental test of the reality of the critical period. The paper by Freedman et al. (Paper 15) summarizes the results of the most elaborate and definitive experiment of that sort. On this basis, we concluded that the end of the critical period for primary socialization occurred at approximately twelve weeks, with an optimum period between six and eight weeks.

Paper 16 by Cairns and Werboff showed that young puppies in the critical period could form social attachments to rabbits as well as to dogs and people. Provided the puppies could interact directly with rabbits, they began to show distress vocalization upon separation as soon as two hours after the initial contact, demonstrating how rapidly the attachment process takes place. Some attachment took place when the puppies could only see the rabbit. More recent studies (Pettijohn et al., 1977) with alleviation of separation distress show that the most effective alleviating agent is active, playful interaction with the puppy, which also seems to be the technique that produces the most rapid attachment.

The period is a critical one in more ways than one. It not only determines which animals shall be the close social relatives of the puppies, but also determines whether or not the puppies will enjoy good mental health. Melzack, Thompson, Hebb, and their colleagues (Melzack and Thompson, 1956) had reared young Scottish terrier puppies in isolation for long periods and reported gross disturbances of behavior. But the period of treatment was so long that it gave no information regarding critical periods. Fuller and Clark (1966a, 1966b) then did a series of studies that were more analytical in nature and whose results are summarized by Fuller (1967). Essentially, these studies showed that puppies could be reared in isolation during the early part of the critical period up to about seven weeks and still recover completely. They also showed that outside contacts of as little as two twenty-minute periods per week during the critical period could insure normal development. This demonstrates the ease with which dramatic effects on behavior can be achieved during critical periods.

Paper 17 summarizes abnormal behavior in dogs in relation to the critical period of primary socialization. These facts provide a formula for a developmental history (programming a life history) that will insure normal development in the dog with very little effort. In contrast, once maladaptive behavior has appeared as a result of other developmental experiences, it becomes extraordinarily persistent.

14

Reprinted from *J. Genet. Psychol.* 77:25, 32–42, 45–47, 57–60 (1950)

CRITICAL PERIODS AFFECTING THE DEVELOPMENT OF NORMAL AND MAL-ADJUSTIVE SOCIAL BEHAVIOR OF PUPPIES*

Division of Behavior Studies, Roscoe B. Jackson Memorial Laboratory

J. P. SCOTT AND MARY-'VESTA MARSTON[1]

A. INTRODUCTION

In 1945 the Roscoe B. Jackson Memorial Laboratory began an extensive program of research designed to test the relationship between heredity and social behavior, particularly in dogs. One of the important aspects of this work was the opportunity to study the interaction of environmental and hereditary factors in producing so-called "abnormal" behavior.

As necessary groundwork to the total program two things were done: (*a*) A descriptive and experimental study of the development of behavior was made under standard and as nearly optimal conditions as possible, out of which has come the conclusion that there are certain natural periods in development during which the puppy is unusually susceptible to environmental influences. It is with this study that the present paper is concerned. (*b*) Dogs have been studied under more or less free and natural conditions (30), from which it was possible to conclude that the behavior patterns exhibited by dogs toward human beings are essentially the same as those exhibited toward dogs, and that one sort of social relationship which can be set up between men and dogs is essentially similar to the parent-offspring relationship in either species.

[*Editor's Note:* Material has been omitted at this point.]

*Received in the Editorial Office on July 26, 1949.

[1]In the course of this extended piece of research the authors have received help from many sources and wish to specially thank the following persons: Miss Eleanor Mallay Smith for making the first preliminary study of behavior development and working out the technique of observation; Dr. C. C. Little and Miss Edna DuBuis for advice and help in setting up optimal conditions of rearing; Dr. John L. Fuller for help and advice in testing puppies; Miss Margaret Charles for help in collecting the data; Mr. Frank Clark and Mr. Gordon Gilbert for careful and conscientious care of the animals.

C. Development of Social Behavior in Puppies: Description by Periods

1. *Period I, Neonatal: From Birth Until Eyes Open*

a. Sense organs. The newborn puppies predominantly employ the thermal and tactile senses, reacting principally to cold and touch. Smell and taste are probably also present, since most puppies will taste fish if offered to them and react negatively to strong smelling substances such as oil of anise.

However, these senses are little used because the puppy takes in no food except milk and has little use for smelling objects. Puppies placed a few inches away from their mothers apparently did not detect her presence by smell, showing no unusual actions or orientation. Since the eyes are closed, sight, of course, is not used. The external auditory meatus is closed, and we have no evidence that hearing is present. Puppies do not react in any way to loud sounds or to high pitched sounds produced by the Galton whistle. The startle reaction is therefore missing, as is any fear response to falling (i.e., when lowered suddenly). On the other hand, they will extend the forelegs and sometimes whine when slipping off the edge of the scales.

b. Psychological abilities. We have no direct evidence in favor of conditioning, but judging from puppies that have been raised on the bottle, animals of this age gain facility in nursing or become used to rejecting the bottle. Animals which are well fed act quite differently from those not receiving an adequate milk supply, but this does not imply learning. There is no evidence regarding their ability to solve problems, but because of their limited motor and sensory abilities it would be very difficult to ascertain whether or not this ability was present.

c. Motor abilities. The puppies are able to crawl forward and to right themselves if turned upside down. They can lift their heads and move them unsteadily. The wink reflex in response to touch is present in some animals even though the eyes are closed. While sleeping the puppies show typical twitching reactions of the limbs. Periods of activity while eating are interspersed with long periods of quiet in which the animals may be presumed to be asleep.

d. Social behavior.

(1). *Ingestive behavior.* The newborn puppies in contact with the mother's breast suck at various points until they reach a nipple. As soon as feeding begins they push against the breast with the head, alternately push with the fore paws and hold themselves against it by pushing with the hind legs. The tail is held down and slightly out from the perineal region. This tail posture is typical also of adult dogs while feeding.

(2). *Eliminative behavior.* While feeding the puppies, the mother noses and licks the under side of the puppies, removing feces and urine. This apparently sets off appropriate reflexes in the young puppies. These same reflexes may occasionally be called forth by the handling of an experimenter.

(3). *Investigative behavior.* When cold or hungry the puppies typically crawl forward swinging the head from one side to another and stopping when the head touches some warm smooth surface such as provided by the mother or other puppies. Another investigative pattern which appears very early is that of sniffing.

(4). *Et-epimeletic behavior.* This has been previously defined as calling or signalling for care or attention (28). In connection with investigation, which is usually stimulated by discomfort of some kind, the puppies frequently whine, a reaction which often has the effect of attracting the attention of the mother. Increasing amounts of discomfort may cause these whines to increase in loudness to yelps. There is very seldom any other type of vocalization in puppies during the neonatal period.

(5). *Contactual behavior.* When the pupies are cold or wet they tend to crowd close to the mother or to pile themselves closely together if she is absent.

(6). *Agonistic or conflict behavior.* This is limited to escape behavior and yelping in reaction to pain. There is no allelomimetic behavior except that several puppies may react to the same stimulus at the same time, as when the mother offers to nurse. There is no recognizable sexual behavior, aggressive fighting, or epimeletic behavior.

In general, the stimuli responded to appear to be cold and pain externally and hunger internally. Behavior of the "emotional" sort is largely confined to the whining or et-epimeletic behavior described above. Neonatal puppies show signs of discomfort and satiation, but nothing that could be called fear.

All evidence seems to indicate that there is little development during this period except in growth and strength and that all of the above patterns of behavior are present both at birth and at the end of the period. Smith (32) found that there is a much higher correlation between genetically different litters of puppies during this period than in later periods.

Just as thermal and tactile reactions dominate in the sensory field, it may be said that et-epimeletic behavior is predominate in the social field, exclusive of ingestive and eliminative behavior which are essential to life. All types of social behavior present at this time will be profoundly modified later.

2. *Period II, Transition: From the Opening of the Eyes Until Leaving the Nest*

This is a fairly short period in which rapid changes take place in sensory and motor capacities. The period generally lasts from 10 days to two weeks, usually ending while the animal is between three and four weeks of age.

a. Sense organs. The time of the opening of the eyes is quite variable and has been recorded as occurring as early as 11 days and as late as 19. Since the gestation period is variable this probably reflects the fact that puppies may be born more or less immaturely, as well as exhibiting genetic differences in rates of development. The eyes are apparently used at once, as the puppies tend to crawl backwards as soon as they are open. However, it is probable that the puppies have to learn to use their eyes as has been reported in chimpanzees (25), since the wink reflex can be elicited by touch and not by moving objects and apparently has to be conditioned.

The pupillary reflex is present as soon as the eyes are open, as is nystagmus, although some individuals show at first simple rolling motion instead of quick jerks.

The first definite auditory reaction, the startle reflex to loud noises, has never been observed earlier than three weeks of age. This reaction usually consists of withdrawal and flattening of the body, although some animals merely erect the ears.

By the end of the period all sense organs are obviously functional, and tactile and thermal reactions are no longer dominant, their place being taken by responses given to visual, auditory, and olfactory stimuli.

b. Psychological abilities. There is no further evidence regarding conditioning. The same applies to the puppy's ability to solve problems, and until the end of this period the puppy is incapable of doing enough things so that satisfactory tests of this sort can be applied.

c. Motor abilities. Most puppies begin to walk in an unsteady fashion at about 18 days of age, although some have been recorded as early as 12 days. Along with this, the animal stands erect and crawling disappears. The puppies are more active and spend less time sleeping. They also begin to chew on each other, an action which seems to be correlated with the eruption of the teeth, beginning with canines and incisors.

d. Social Behavior.

(1). *Ingestive behavior.* Nursing is continued, but toward the end of this period the mother may nurse the puppies in a sitting position instead of lying down, and the periods of nursing appear to be shorter. Solid food is first taken at about three weeks of age, at approximately the same time as the teeth erupt. However, the teeth still cannot be used for masticating the food.

(2). *Eliminative behavior.* During this period the puppies begin to eliminate independently of the mother's actions, leaving the sleeping corner to do so, and at the end of the period regularly eliminate outside of the nest.

(3). *Investigative behavior.* The neonatal pattern of swinging the head from side to side disappears and investigation is apparently accomplished with eyes, nose, and ears. No definite adult patterns of investigation have appeared as yet. Movements are definitely oriented toward distant objects.

(4). *Et-epimeletic behavior.* The early pattern of whining is continued but is much less frequent. The tail wagging pattern of behavior does not appear yet.

(5). *Contactual behavior.* The puppies continue to crowd together when sleeping but apparently are much less sensitive to cold than in the early period.

(6). *Agonistic behavior.* Fighting play (the first aggressive form of conflict behavior) first appears near the end of this period and includes clumsy pawing and biting of the litter mates or portions of the mother's body. Growling is occasionally present but not barking. As noted above, the startle reaction is given to loud noises such as the growling of the mother, but not earlier than about three weeks.

There is still no allelomimetic, sexual, or epimeletic behavior present, and most of the neonatal patterns of behavior are still present, although in a weaker form. The period is primarily one of change in physiological capacities, both sensory and motor, which are reflected in changes in social behavior during the next period. At the end of this period, the puppy gives its first reactions which indicate a differentiation of social environment; e.g., it first pays attention to an observer. It also gives the first behavior and attitudes which indicate timidity or fear responses. The end of the period is also the time when the puppy begins to frequently leave the comparatively sheltered and uniform environment of the nest.

3. *Period III, Socialization/or Social Adjustment, Leaving Nest Until weaning (The Period May Also be Said to Begin When the Puppies First Notice the Observer)*

During this period the puppies first come into extensive contact with people and animals other than the mother and litter mates, and they explore the immediate environment of the nest. Under the conditions of rearing, this means that they come into contact with feeders and experimenters, and explore the entire nursery room. By the end of the period they have developed, at least in playful form, all of the main types of social behavior but epimeletic. The puppies make considerable progress in physical development, but even at the end of the period are still comparatively slow, helpless, and dependent compared to adults.

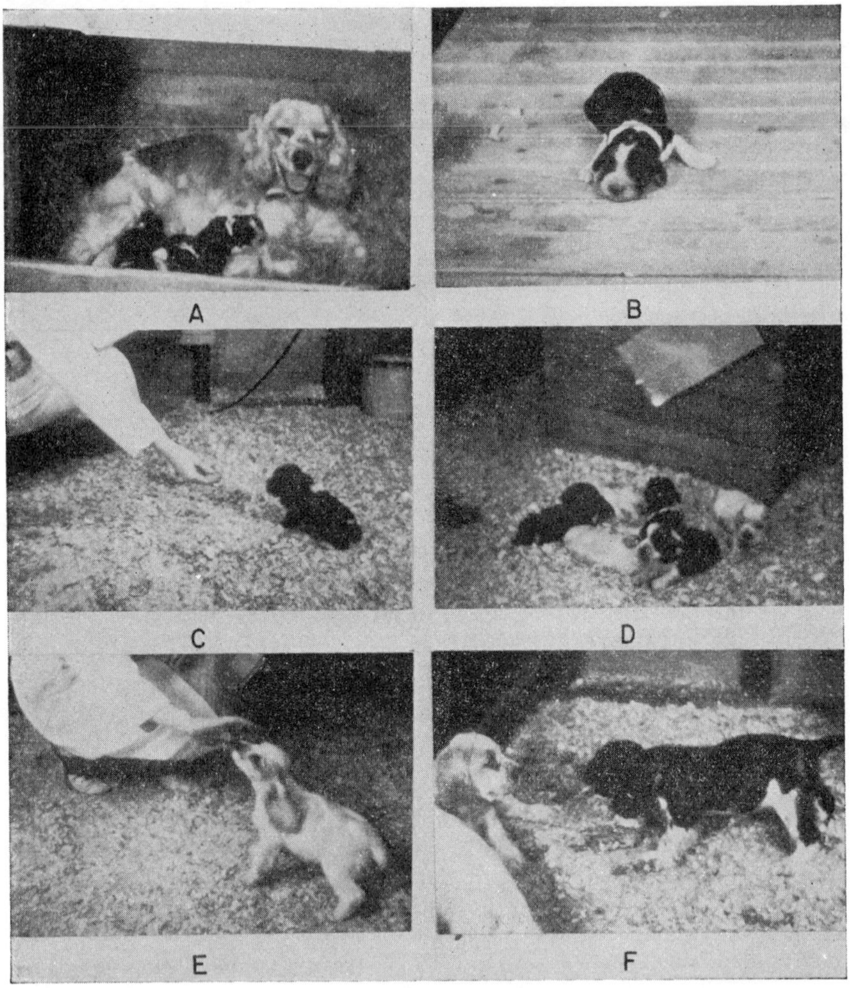

FIGURE 2

COCKER SPANIEL PUPPIES IN THREE STAGES OF DEVELOPMENT (PHOTOGRAPHS ENLARGED FROM 16 MM. MOTION PICTURE FRAMES)

A. Neonatal stage, nursing. *B*. Neonatal Stage, investigative behavior. The puppy crawls, swinging the head from side to side. *C*. Early Socialization Stage (27 days), reaction to handling. Note posture of withdrawal, and compare with *E* below. *D*. Same stage, startle reaction to sound of metal sheet struck against box. *E*. Early Juvenile stage, reaction to handling. The puppy approaches with wagging tail and attempts to lick the hand. *F*. Same stage, conflict behavior in presence of a bone. The puppy on the right succeeded in dominating the others in the litter, and barks at the more subordinate animal on the left.

a. Sense organs. All the sense organs appear to be functional, and the puppies apparently learn to recognize and differentiate objects. At first the puppies are very sensitive to sudden movements or loud noises, crouching down in reaction to them. By six weeks of age they apparently try to follow scent trails, and new objects are investigated with nose, eyes, and mouth.

b. Psychological abilities. Puppies can solve simple problems, such as the way around barriers, as early as six weeks. The stages usually include investigation, failure followed by random movements and whining, further investigation and solution. There is some evidence that puppies are able to generalize from one situation to another, and definite evidence of conditioning. By nine weeks puppies remember a feeding place after one trial.

c. Motor abilities. Puppies learn to run, although in a relatively awkward fashion, and the amount of chewing gradually increases so that coarser food can be utilized.

d. Social behavior.

(1). *Ingestive behavior.* Nursing is continued but it is less frequent and takes a shorter time. The mother often stands while allowing the pups to nurse. At the end of the period this pattern is, of course, discontinued. Throughout this period the pups drink water and milk, take solid food, and chew it more extensively.[3]

(2). *Eliminative behavior.* In this period (at 8½ weeks, according to Ross (26)), the puppies begin to defecate in a definite place, usually at a distance from both the sleeping place and the food. This habit is common to both dogs and wolves. Along with this behavior the pups show interest in feces.

(3). *Investigative behavior.* By six weeks of age the puppies make definite attempts at trailing, and the general adult patterns of investigation are established, although not necessarily in the adult form typical of the breed.

(4). *Et-epimeletic behavior.* The puppies are still dependent and whine and yelp if frustrated in any way, whether by barriers, lack of food, etc. Added to the vocalization, a new pattern of behavior appears under this category. The pup approaches another dog or a human being with wagging tail and will lick the face and gently paw the other animal. This reaction occurs more often if the pup is hungry or if the other animal has recently

[3]According to Martins (16), three mothers fed at a distance from the pups began disgorging behavior at the beginning of Period III (22-24 days), the pups feeding from the vomited material. This reaction occurs regularly in wolves (35). However, under our conditions of feeding disgorging behavior occurred regularly in only one female, a basenji.

been eating, and is probably primitively a food begging reaction. This pattern appears early in the period and increases as the period goes on.

(5). *Contactual behavior.* Under the nursery conditions the puppies are often seen sleeping apart, although they may crowd together if the temperature happens to fall.

(6). *Agonistic behavior.* There is a gradually increasing amount of playful fighting. The puppies throw themselves on each other, pawing, growling and chewing each other's ears. A puppy which is underneath may roll over on its back and extend the paws (pattern of extreme subordination in playful form). Dominance in fighting gradually develops but no marked dominance postures are present until the end of the period. The puppies begin to bark early in the period and this becomes gradually more frequent. In the latter half of the period it is frequent for two or three puppies to surround and playfully attack one individual.. This pattern is usually evoked by a scuffle between a pair of animals. One of them runs away and the rest follow and attack. Toward the end of the period a playful fight may occasionally become more serious, marked by louder growling and harder biting. This usually ends quickly, with the losing pup assuming a subordinate attitude.

(7). *Allelomimetic behavior.* The first evidences of coördinated group activity are seen in the group attacks referred to above (first observed about 6½ weeks) and in the tendency of puppies to rush together to the door of the pen when it is entered.

(8). *Sexual behavior.* No complete sexual behavior is present but puppies may show the "playful" attitude characteristic of courtship, and mount and clasp each other during their play. This behavior may be seen rather early in the period and becomes gradually more common, apparently as the testes descend in the male. This behavior is always interrupted if an observer is noticed, in contrast to adult sexual behavior.

By the end of this period the neonatal patterns of behavior have almost disappeared and all the main adult types of behavior are present, at least in playful form. From now on development is largely a matter of growth and learning of skills with but few sudden changes in behavior. By the end of this period most basic social relationships have been established.

4. *Period IV, Juvenile: Weaning Until Sexual Maturity (Studied in Detail to 16 Weeks)*

The time at which the puppies are shifted outside the nursery environment was arbitrarily chosen as one at which the puppies could take care of them-

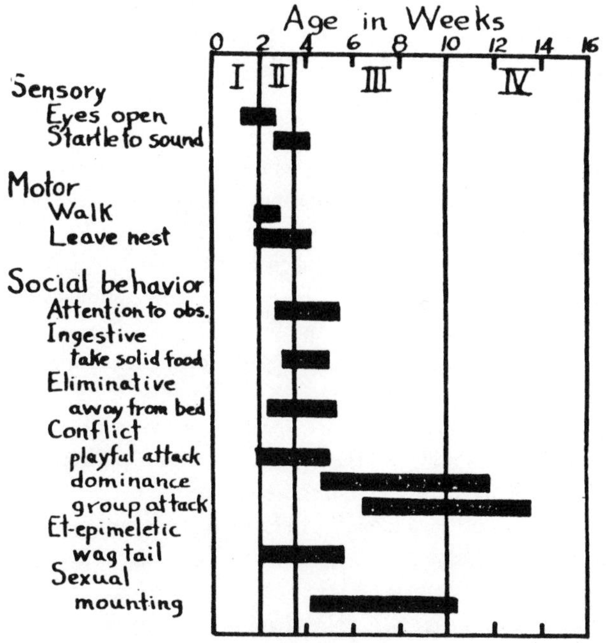

FIGURE 3

RANGE OF VARIABILITY OF TIME AT WHICH CERTAIN SIGNIFICANT DEVELOPMENTAL EVENTS WERE FIRST OBSERVED IN A LITTER. NOTE RELATIONSHIP TO THE STAGES OF DEVELOPMENT.

selves in the more rigorous outdoor environment. However, this choice had a slight natural basis, as four months is approximately the time that the second set of teeth appear. Thus there is some justification for making a minor division of the period. The length of this period varies considerably. The earliest date of fertile sexual behavior observed at this laboratory has been six months (both male and female), but many animals do not mature until well over a year.

a. Sense organs. No change.

b. Psychological abilities. In problem solving it appears that the puppies are still handicapped by inability to inhibit themselves and give a long attention span, but it is apparent that this ability develops gradually throughout the whole period. Puppies tested on a maze with a pattern consisting of one right, two left, and three right turns have so far never shown perfect scores after 10 trials at 13 weeks.

c. Motor abilities. At the beginning of the period the puppies are comparatively slow and awkward but by the time of sexual maturity are almost as capable as adults. Dogs are usually considered to reach maximum physical development at about two years of age.

d. Social behavior.

(1). *Ingestive.* The adult pattern of eating and drinking is present during all this period. There is no opportunity for adult dogs to feed the juvenile animals, although this might take place under other conditions.

(2). *Eliminative behavior.* According to Martins (15), the adult pattern of leg lifting in the males is developed at 5-8 months. Likewise, scratching after defecation appears during this period. The tendency to urinate at "scent posts" appears along with this pattern.

However, under our conditions these patterns are rarely seen unless strange animals are admitted to the pens.

(3). *Investigative behavior.* By the beginning of this period the puppies are alert to noises outside their own room and differentiate between stimuli having some significance and those which do not.

(4). *Et-epimeletic behavior.* The food begging reaction described above is still very prominent during this period and probably increases at least up to 16 weeks.

(5). *Contactual behavior.* No change.

(6). *Agonistic behavior.* By 15 weeks of age the playful fighting has been pretty well organized into a dominance system and there is, therefore, less actual bodily contact. By the end of Period IV the definite bodily postures of dominance (tail erect, growling, and placing fore feet on the other animal), and subordination (crouching with tail between legs or rolling on back with paws outstretched) have been developed. Severe fighting in which the animals actually hurt each other has been observed in only 2 out of 17 litters (both Foxterriers).

(7). *Allelomimetic behavior.* The litter tends to react more and more as a unit to any stimulation. If one animal is attracted by a noise or a movement and runs to investigate, the rest usually follow.

(8). *Sexual behavior.* The playful patterns described under the preceding period are continued but are not frequently seen unless the pups are unaware of the observer. Marking the end of the period, of course, are the first estrus periods of the females and the appearance of adult sexual patterns in both sexes.

In summary, this period is primarily one of growth and the development of skill in motor patterns already present in other periods. In free living animals this is the period which would be spent in learning to hunt and become self supporting.

Other periods, with which this paper is not concerned, are the adult reproductive period and the period of old age.

[*Editor's Note:* Material has been omitted at this point.]

E. Discussion and Conclusions: The Hypothesis of Critical Periods

In this paper the viewpoint has been presented that the development of puppies falls into several natural periods, which were first obtained by descriptions of social behavior and then confirmed by objective ratings of behavior traits, as well as by certain physiological and physical measurements. In reviewing these data, it would appear that there are distinct dividing lines between all of the periods except between the neonatal and transition periods. The opening of the eyes is a dramatic event but it does not as dramatically change the behavior of the puppies, and in some way it might be better to think of Period II, the transition period, as being the end of the neonatal period or at least very closely allied to it.

If this is done, it will be seen that all of the remaining periods are set off by changes in social relationships which naturally occur in the normal development of the puppy. This, together with certain observational data, leads to the idea that there are critical periods in development which correspond to the times when new social relations appear.

For example, a puppy at the beginning of the period of socialization is obviously extremely fearful, shrinking away from loud sounds and sudden movements of any kind. In one litter the mother became ill at this time and soon died. The puppies were much upset and became unusually attached to the human handlers. On the other hand, there is almost no evidence of disturbance in litters where the mothers are removed at the usual weaning time of 10 weeks.

In several litters of puppies, the tails have been removed during the neonatal period, as is usually done for certain breeds of dogs. There has so far been no evidence of gross differences in behavior between these animals and their litter mates. In short, where environmental disturbances have occurred, the evidence does not support the commonly held view that these should be more effective in the earlier stages of development, but rather leads to the hypothesis that disturbances are most important and effective when they occur at periods when new social relationships are being developed. In addition, the newborn animal is far from being sensitive. He appears to be emotionally undeveloped, and from a sensory point of view, protected from the environment, since he can neither see nor hear.

Thus there appear to be two major factors which determine which periods of life will be critical in the development of social behavior. One of these is the time at which any new social adjustment is made, which is almost inevitably important because of the well-known influence of primacy and successful adjustment on learning.

The other is the factor of maturation of the nervous system. In the dog, the greatest changes of this sort appear to coincide with the beginning of social adjustments outside the nest, which makes the period of socialization (III) a doubly critical one. At this time the puppy first shows something like complete emotional capacities, and simultaneously first becomes aware of potentially dangerous or helpful features of the environment. From the standpoint of learning, the puppy should have no standards of comparison as to what constitutes, for example, a dangerous experience, and no control of emotional reactions should have been built up through conditioning in non-dangerous situations. The puppy therefore over-reacts, giving all indications of extreme fear to loud but harmless noises and sudden but innocuous movements.

Applying these hypotheses, it may be stated that the critical periods of development in the early life of a puppy should be: (*a*) birth, at which the adjustment to nursing is a matter of life or death but not of psychological trauma; (*b*) the early part of Period III when the puppies develop social relationships with dogs outside the litter or with people, and establish new relationships within the litter, and during which the factor of maturation of the nervous system exerts its greatest effect. A third critical period, of course, should be that of sexual maturity, when new relationships with the opposite sex should be established.

These hypotheses have important implications for the study of abnormal behavior and for mental hygiene because from them it may be concluded that so-called "traumatic experiences" should be most effective during certain critical periods, particularly in Period III. This statement, of course, needs repeated experimental verification, some of which is being undertaken in this laboratory at the present time. It also implies that those hypotheses may be widely extended, and this possibility may be briefly examined in the light of available comparative evidence.

[*Editor's Note:* Material has been omitted at this point.]

G. Summary

1. Theoretical considerations lead to the hypothesis that in the development of any mammal (and perhaps any higher animal) the same experiences should lead to different behavioral results at different periods. This hypothesis may be labelled that of "critical periods."

2. One factor which is involved in this hypothesis is the nature of learning of the conditioning type, which indicates that first experiences in any situation are more important than later ones. A *CR* may be extinguished, but will show spontaneous recovery after rest. Primacy has also been shown to be important in human verbal memory. Applying this to social situations, it may be concluded that the times at which new social relationships are developed should be critical periods.

3. A second factor involved in the hypothesis is that of maturation of the nervous system. The time immediately following the development of the capacity for conditioning or memory should also be a critical one.

4. Seventeen litters of puppies belonging to seven different dog breeds and comprising 73 individuals have been studied under standard and as nearly optimum conditions as possible, emphasizing the development of patterns of social behavior and the sensory and motor factors which affect them. The conditions of rearing are described in detail.

5. The development of social behavior in the dog falls into four natural periods up to the time of sexual maturity:

a. Neonatal Period, approximately 0 to two weeks, from birth until opening of eyes. Locomotor and ingestive patterns of behavior adapted to infantile life only.

b. Transition Period, approximately from 2 to 3½ weeks, until the time the puppy leaves the nest and first notices observers. Unskilled adult patterns of locomotion and ingestion are developed in addition to the infantile ones.

c. Period of socialization, approximately from 3½ to 8-10 weeks, ending with weaning. First extensive social contacts with other individuals than parents, ending with cessation of infantile patterns of behavior.

d. Juvenile Period, approximately from 8-10 weeks to 7-14 months, from weaning till sexual maturity. Adult patterns fully developed except those involved in sex and reproduction.

6. The patterns of behavior characteristic of each period are described in detail up to the age of 16 weeks.

7. Average results of behavior tests which were regularly repeated show changes at about the times dividing these periods and confirm their reality.

8. It is concluded that for the puppy the most important critical period is the early part of the period of socialization, maturation of sensory, motor, and memory capacities apparently coinciding with the first development of outside social relationships.

9. Comparison with development in wolves shows close similarities except for earlier sexual development in the dog. The different periods of development are closely related to the natural social organization of the wild species.

10. Comparison with the mouse, sheep, and howling monkey shows wide differences in the relative length and importance of the various periods. Consideration of this fact may resolve certain apparently contradictory experimental results.

11. On the basis of information available, it is difficult to define the periods of development in human beings as accurately as those in animals because of cultural modification of behavior patterns. However, it would appear that human development, like that of the howling monkey, is distinguished by a relatively long transition period.

12. It is suggested that the hypothesis of critical periods may be fruitfully applied to human studies. On the basis of available data it would appear that the factor of maturation of the nervous system does not coincide as closely with the beginning of the period of socialization as it does in the dog, but probably acts at sometime during the transition period.

References

1. Baege, B. Zur Entwickling der Verhaltensweisen junger Hunde in den ersten drei Lebensmonaten. *Z. Hundeforschung,* 1933, **3**, 3-64.
2. Bahrs, A. M. Notes on the reflexes of puppies in the first six weeks after birth. *Amer. J. Physiol.,* 1927, **82**, 51-55.
3. Berg, I. A. Development of behavior: the micturition pattern in the dog. *J. Exper. Psychol.,* 1944, **34**, 343-368.
4. Carpenter, C. R. A field study of the behavior and social relations of howling monkeys (*Alouatta palliata*). *Comp. Psychol. Monog.,* 1934, **10**, 168 pp.
5. Dennis, W. Infant reaction to restraint: An evaluation of Watson's theory. *Trans. New York Acad. Sci.,* 1940, **2**, 202-218.
6. Freud, S. An Outline of Psychoanalysis. (Trans. by J. Strachey.) New York: Norton, 1949.
7. Fuller, J. L. Situational Analysis; a classification of organism-field reactions. *Psychol. Rev.,* 1950, **57**, 3-18.

8. GESELL, A., *et al.* The First Five Years of Life. New York: Harper, 1940.

9. ———. The ontogenesis of infant behavior. (Ch. 6 in *Manual of Child Psychology,* L. Carmichael, *ed.*) London: Wiley, 1946.

10. GESELL, A., & ILG, F. L. Infant and Child in the Culture of Today. New York, Harper, 1943.

11. ———. The Child from Five to Ten. New York: Harper, 1946.

12. LEVY, D. M. Experiments on the sucking reflex and social behavior in dogs. *Amer. J. Orthopsychiat.,* 1934, **4**, 203-224.

13. ———. Psychic trauma of operations in children. *Amer. J. Dis. Child,* 1945, **69**, 7-25.

14. LINDZEY, G. Experiments on the deprivation of sucking in beagle puppies from 11 to 16 days of age, 1947. (Unpublished.)

15. MARTINS, T. A atitude do cão na micção e os hormônios sexuais. *Memórias do Instituto Oswaldo Cruz,* 1946, **44**, 343-361.

16. ———. Disgorging of food to the puppies by the lactating dog. *Phys. Zoöl.,* 1949, **22**, 169-178.

17. MENZEL, R., & MENZEL, R. Welpe und Umwelt. *Kleintier und Pelztier,* 1937, **13**, 1-65.

18. MILLS, W. The Nature and Development of Animal Intelligence. London: Unwin, 1898.

19. MUNN, N. L. Learning in children. (Ch. 8, in *Manual of Child Psychology,* L. Carmichael, *ed.*) New York: Wiley, 1946.

20. MURIE, A. The wolves of Mount McKinley. U.S.D.I. Fauna Series No. 5. U. S. Govt. Printing Office, Washington, 1944.

21. ORLANSKY, H. Infant care and personality. *Psychol. Bull.,* 1949, **46**, 1-48.

22. PAVLOV, I. P. Conditioned Reflexes: An investigation of the physiological activity of the cerebral cortex. (G. V. Anrep. ed. and trans.) Oxford: Oxford U. Press, 1927.

23. PRATT, K. C. The neonate. (Ch. 4 in *Manual of Child Psychology,* L. Carmichael, *ed.*) New York: Wiley, 1946.

24. RIBBLE, M. A. The rights of infants. New York: Columbia U. Press, 1943.

25. RIESEN, A. H. The development of visual perception in man and chimpanzee. *Science,* 1947, **106**, 107-108.

26. ROSS, S. Some observations on the lair dwelling behavior of dogs. *Behaviour,* 1950, **2**, 144-162.

27. SCOTT, J. P. The embryology of the guinea pig: III. The development of the polydactylous monster. A case of growth accelerated at a particular period by a semi-dominant lethal gene. *J. Exper. Zoöl.,* 1937, **77**, 123-157.

28. ———. Social behavior, organization, and leadership in a small flock of domestic sheep. *Comp. Psychol. Monog.,* 1945, **18**, 1-29.

29. SCOTT, J. P. Studies on the early development of social behavior in puppies (abstract). *Amer. Psychol.,* 1948, **3**, 239-40.

30. ———. The social behavior of dogs and wolves; an illustration of sociobiological systematics. *Annals New York Acad. Sci.,* 1950, **51**, 1009-1021.

31. SCOTT, J. P., & MARSTON, M. V. The development of dominance in litters of puppies (abstract). *Anat. Rec.,* 1948, **101**, 696.

32. SMITH, E. M. A study of the development of social behavior in pups. (Jackson Laboratory Summer Student's Report, 1946. Unpublished.)

33. SNELL, G. D. Reproduction, Chapter II in the *Biology of the Laboratory Mouse.* Philadelphia: Blakiston, 1941.

34. WOODWORTH, R. S. Experimental Psychology. New York: Holt, 1938.
35. YOUNG, S. P., & GOLDMAN, E. A. The Wolves of North America. Washington. Amer. Wild Life Institute, 1944.

15

Reprinted from *Science* **133**:1016–1017 (1961)

CRITICAL PERIOD IN THE SOCIAL DEVELOPMENT OF DOGS

Daniel G. Freedman, John A. King, and Orville Elliot
Roscoe B. Jackson Memorial Laboratory, Bar Harbor, Maine

Abstract. Litters of puppies were isolated, with the bitch, in fenced acre fields from 2 to 14 weeks of age. They were removed indoors at different ages, played with for a week, and returned to the field. The pups manifested an increasing tendency to withdraw from human beings after 5 weeks of age and unless socialization occurred before 14 weeks of age, withdrawal reactions from humans became so intense that normal relationships could not thereafter be established.

The term *imprinting* is generally defined as a capacity of some species of birds to develop a permanent attachment to any species, including man, made available to it during a critical period in its early development. This period of primary socialization usually ends with a mounting tendency to flee from strange species (*1*). The present experiment demonstrates a similar phenomenon in a mammalian species.

This study derived from the observation that purebred cocker spaniels exhibited intense flight responses to humans after they had been raised in an acre field with a minimum of human contact prior to 14 weeks of age. Our unsuccessful attempts to tame or socialize them led us to examine the age when human contact would most effectively reduce the withdrawal response at 14 weeks of age.

Five litters of cocker spaniels ($N = 18$) and three litters of beagles ($N = 16$) were raised in acre fields bounded by an 8-foot high wooden fence. The mother and her litter were raised alone in the pen and received food and water through drops in the fence. Pups from each litter were taken from the field for a week of socialization at 2 weeks of age ($N = 6$), 3 weeks, of age ($N = 6$), 5 weeks of age ($N = 7$), 7 weeks of age ($N = 7$), and 9 weeks of age ($N = 3$), and then returned to the field. During this week indoors, pups were played with, tested, and cared for throughout three daily half-hour periods (*2*). Controls remained in the field ($N = 5$) until the entire litter was taken indoors for final testing at 14 weeks of age.

At the start of the week of socialization pups removed from the field at 5 weeks of age scored significantly higher on a test of attraction to a handler [Handling Test (*3*)] than those removed at 2, 3, or 9 weeks of age ($p = 0.01$ to 0.05; t, tests). The low scores of 2- and 3-week-olds were due simply to their physical and motor immaturity, while 9-week-olds exhibited low scores because they had a marked tendency to avoid the handler. By the end of the week of socialization, however, all save the still immature 2-week-olds were equally attracted to the handler.

The progressive development of avoidance responses was evident in daily, 10-minute tests of the amount of time a puppy spent in physical contact with a passive, reclining human. Two-week-olds, again, were too immature to do much but sleep, eat, or crawl about randomly; 3-week-olds were immediately attracted to the experimenter and spent most of the 10-minute period pawing, mouthing, and biting him and his garments; 5-week-olds exhibited wariness at first, but they became comparable to 3-week-olds before the end of the first play period; 7-week-old pups, however, were frightened and wary of contacting the experimenter over the first *two* days of socialization, while 9-week-old pups exhibited these reactions over the first three days. No *p* values are given since this test was administered only to the last three litters; however, notes taken on all animals reveal no exceptions to this pattern of progressive avoidance, and it was persistently observed in the other situations of the socialization period.

After removal from the field at 14 weeks of age a series of tests was administered over a 2-week period. The handling test was administered to all pups at the start and at the end of this period of testing, a period involving daily contact with humans. At 14 weeks the pups socialized in their second week, and the controls scored significantly lower in "attraction to the handler" than did the fifth, seventh, and ninth week groups ($p \lesseqgtr 0.05$, *t* tests). By the 16th week, however, only the control group remained significantly low, and it scored lower than all other groups ($p \lesseqgtr 0.02$, *t* tests). These results are illustrated in Fig. 1.

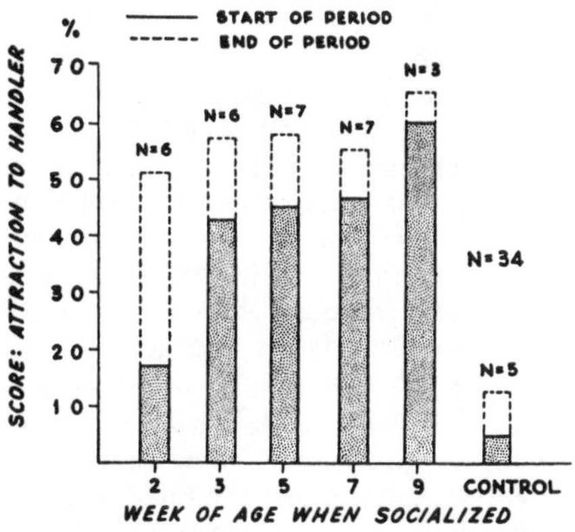

Fig. 1. Performance in the handling test. A measure of attraction to the handler, comparing performance at the start and at the end of the final period of testing (14 and 16 weeks of age).

Since the control animals appeared as timid on the final day of testing as on the first, one control animal, selected at random, was petted and fondled each day for a period of 3 months. The handling test was readministered at that time, and the animal showed only a slight positive change in score. It is our impression that any of the control pups would have been similarly resistant to socialization.

The leash-control test (*3*), devised to test an animal's resistance to training to a leash, was administered over a period of 10 days. There was significantly greater ease in the training of animals socialized at 5, 7, and 9 weeks of age than with the two younger groups and the controls ($p \lesseqgtr 0.01$, Wilcoxen rank test, and see Table 1). It appears that while socialization experiences during the second and third weeks of age were effective, as judged by the handling test, the stress conditions of leash training favored the scores of animals socialized during the fifth, seventh, or ninth week of age.

Table 1. Rank order for tests administered after 14 weeks of age. (The higher numbers rank low.)

Test	Rank at age socialized					Controls
	2 wk	3 wk	5 wk	7 wk	9 wk	
			Handling			
Initial attraction to handler	5	4*	3*	2*	1*	6
			Leash control			
Eating in strange situation	4	3	1.5*	1.5*	5	6
Fewer balks	4	5	3*	1*	2*	6
			Reactivity test			
Total activity	2	4	3	1	6	5
Heart rate	6	3	4	1	2	5
Vocal, panting, and tail wagging	2	3	4	1	5	6

*Distinctly superior rank

The final test was the reactivity test (*3*). Each pup was placed in a physiological harness and subjected to various stimuli such as cajoling and threat from a human, acoustic-startle, and electric shock. Heart rate, depth of respiration, and muscle tension were concurrently recorded in an electrocardiographic apparatus, while an observer made note of other aspects of the animal's reactions. This test appears to contrast ease of response (high score) with the tendency to "freeze" (low score). The controls were more inhibited than the seventh-week group on each of three subscores ($p = 0.05, 0.01, 0.01$, Mann-Whitney). In Table 1 we see that the seventh-week group ranked highest on all three subscores, indicating primacy in activity level, heart rate, vocal behavior, and tail wagging.

Although further work is necessary, the net results suggest that the seventh week of age was the period in which the pups were most receptive to socialization, and that 2½ to 9–13 weeks of age approximates a critical period for socialization to human beings. These figures are in accord with the findings of Pfaffenberger and Scott (*4*) and Scott and Marston (*5*). It is important to note that within this period motor and perceptual development reach maturity while, on the other hand, motivation to flee from strange species is not yet strong. We suspect that such a balance of factors is characteristic of a period that is critical for the formation of primary social relationships (*6*).

References and Notes

1. E. H. Hess, *Science* **130**, 133 (1959).
2. A detailed description of the socialization procedure may be obtained from us.
3. J. P. Scott and J. L. Fuller, *Manual of Dog Testing Techniques* (Jackson Memorial Laboratory, Bar Harbor, Maine, 1950).
4. C. J. Pfaffenberger and J. P. Scott, *J. Genet. Psychol.* **95**, 145 (1959).
5. J. P. Scott and M. V. Marston, *ibid.* **77**, 25 (1950).
6. The support of the Rockefeller Foundation and the Ford Foundation is gratefully acknowledged.
* Present address: Langley Porter Neuropsychiatric Institute, San Francisco, Calif.
† Present address: Department of Anthropology, Harvard University, Cambridge, Mass.

16

Reprinted from *Science* **158**:1070–1072 (1967)

BEHAVIORAL DEVELOPMENT IN THE DOG: AN INTERSPECIFIC ANALYSIS

Robert B. Cairns
Department of Pyschology, Indiana University, Bloomington

Jack Werboff
Hamilton Station, Bar Harbor, Maine

Abstract. *Young dogs were maintained in isolation from other dogs and under varying degrees of exposure to an alien species (mature rabbits). Parametric observations indicate that an interspecific social attachment develops during the initial hours of cohabitation. The later social interaction patterns of the dogs were influenced, but not irrevocably fixed, by the early cross-specific rearing experience.*

Immature animals that have been isolated from their own kind and reared with another species generally demonstrate a strong affinity for the "alien" animals (*1*). Despite the relevance of this curious phenomenon for the processes of species-identification and attachment behavior, it has been infrequently studied under laboratory conditions (*2*). Virtually no information is available with respect to the time-course of the process in mammals, or the extent to which the effects of early exposure to an alien species are enduring. To obtain parametric data on these issues, we reared young canines under various conditions of interaction with mature lagomorphs. We found that interspecific attachments develop with great rapidity in young dogs, an outcome which is in accord with the stimulus pattern theory of mammalian attachment behavior (*2*)

In our first experiment, 30 purebred dogs from the Jackson Laboratory were placed at 29 ± 2 days of age in individual compartments (1.2 by 0.8 by 1.2 m high) enclosed on four sides by opaque walls and open at the top. The rearing conditions permitted neither physical nor visual contact with other dogs. Ten animals were assigned to each of three conditions: (i) interaction, in which a dog was permitted continuous physical contact with a rabbit cohabitant; (ii) noninteraction, in which a dog and rabbit were separated by a double wire fence (2.5 by 5.1 cm interstices) down the midline of the compartment, which permitted visual and olfactory stimulation but no physical contact; and (iii) isolation, in which a dog was reared alone. The rearing conditions were comparable for all conditions save the varying degree of contact permitted with the alien cohabitant. Five pure breeds of dogs were used: basenjis ($N = 7$), beagles ($N = 4$), cocker spaniels ($N = 2$), Shetland sheepdogs ($N = 8$), and Telomians ($N = 9$). Within each sex-breed category, animals were assigned at random to the three experimental conditions. The cohabitants were mature rabbits obtained from the stocks of the Jackson Laboratory.

At the start of the experiment, the pups were placed alone in the compartment for 2 hours, after which the rabbit cohabitant was introduced. To investigate the development of attachment formation, a series of cohabitant removal-replacement tests was conducted. Each test ran for 18 minutes and involved six alternating periods in which the rabbit cohabitant was in the compartment for 3 minutes and then removed for 3 minutes. The indices of disturbance recorded were the number of vocalizations emitted by the young dog and the amount of locomotion shown by the dog in the cohabitant-absent periods relative to the cohabitant-present periods. For dogs reared alone in the isolation condition, these indices were recorded during the same time periods with no removal-replacement introduced. Removal-replacement tests were conducted with every animal after 0, 1, 2, 4, 8, 24, 48, 96, and 168 hours, and thereafter at weekly intervals.

The vocalization results over the first week of cohabitation are given in Fig. 1. By the end of the first day, animals in the interaction condition whined and yelped at high rates during those occasions when the rabbit was removed. Vocalization was accompanied frequently by the dogs' moving about the compartment and scratching at its walls. Similarly, a significant but less pronounced effect was observed after 1 week of experimental confinement for dogs in the noninteraction condition. Subsequent weekly tests indicated decreasing levels of vocal and motor disruption during the absence of the rabbit cohabitant, a finding which is consistent with the report of Elliot and Scott (*3*). However, the interaction group after 8 weeks of cohabitation continued to vocalize at a significantly elevated rate indicating a lack of habituation to this separation. Comparable results in terms of curve form and levels of statistical significance were obtained in the analysis of general activity (that is, locomotion). The results obtained in the noninteraction condition indicated that physical contact facilitates, but is not necessary for, the separation-disruption phenomena (*4*).

After 5 weeks of cohabitation, the dogs' "social" preferences were assessed in a series of learning trials in a Y maze with a noncorrective procedure. In this apparatus, the dogs could learn to choose either their rabbit cohabitant (or, in the case of dogs assigned to the isolation condition, a rabbit which had cohabited with another pup) or an empty goal area. Tests were conducted over a 5-day period, with two sets of three trials each day. For a given dog, the placement of his rabbit cohabitant was constant and he was required to learn a position response. If the dog did not enter one of the two goal areas within 6 minutes of the first day or within 3 minutes of succeeding days, he was placed in either the right or the left goal area. In all instances, the animals were permitted to remain in the goal area for 60 seconds prior to the beginning of the next trial. The index of preference obtained was the number of trials that the dog freely selected the rabbit minus the number of trials that he ran to the empty goal compartment.

No dog (0/10) in the interaction condition, 20 percent (2/10) in the noninteraction condition, and 60 percent (6/10) in the isolation condition selected the empty compartment more frequently than the compartment containing the rabbit. Furthermore, the amount of behavioral disruption (as assessed by amount of vocalization) observed among dogs in the interaction condition during the 5th-week removal-replacement test provided a remarkably reliable gauge of the pups' choice behavior. Thus the more disrupted the dog was by rabbit-cohabitant separation, the greater was the likelihood that he would approach the rabbit ($\rho = .81$, $P < .01$). A significant correlation was found only for the dogs in the interaction condition.

A final test series was conducted after 8 weeks of cohabitation. Over four test trials given daily, the dogs were permitted to approach a rabbit in a neutral 1.8 by 1.8m test chamber. On two trials, the test animal was the dog's cohabitant, or, in the case of isolated dogs, a rabbit that had cohabited with another pup. In the remaining trials, the test animal was a rabbit which had not been maintained in interspecific cohabitation. The latency recorded was the time elapsed from the dog's entry into the compartment to the point at which it made physical contact with the test animal. If the dog

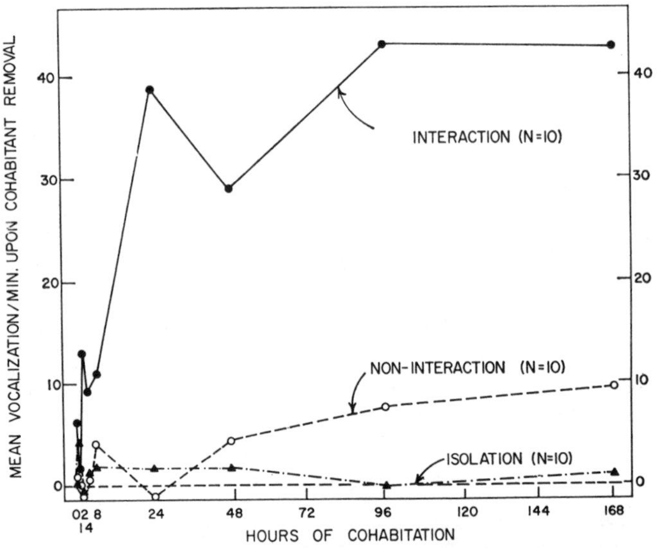

Fig. 1. Amount of vocalization, plotted as a function of number of hours of cohabitation for the three experimental conditions. These data represent the mean vocalization difference scores (vocalization when rabbit was removed minus vocalization when rabbit was present). Analysis by the *L* test (*13*) indicates that both the interaction ($P < .001$) and noninteraction ($P < .01$) conditions show increase in discriminative vocalization during the first week of cohabitation.

Table 1. Median latency (in seconds) for dogs to approach cohabitant and noncohabitant rabbits. Separate analyses of variance upon the scores obtained in a logarithmic transformation of the prime data indicate that the three groups of dogs differed in their latency in approaching both the familiar ($F = 6.61$, df $= 2/27$, $P < .01$) and unfamiliar ($F = 6.21$, df $= 2/27$, $P < .01$) test animals.

Condition	Test animal	
	Cohabitant	Noncohabitant
Interaction	4.0	9.0
Noninteraction	8.0	52.5
Isolation	128.0	193.0

did not approach the test animal within 5 minutes, the test was terminated. Again, the groups differed markedly in their approach behavior. Median latencies are presented in Table 1. Animals in the interaction condition had the shortest latencies, while animals in the isolation condition had the longest latencies, with the latter dogs frequently failing to contact the test rabbit in the entire 5-minute period (*5*). Apparently the essential phenomenon is trans-situational, and not restricted to a given test arrangement or limited to the particular rabbit with which the pup had cohabited.

These data are consistent in showing that interspecific rearing conditions have a pervasive influence on the young dog's response to another species to which it has been exposed. One of the more remarkable features of these results was the rapidity of formation of the interspecific attachment. Subsequent experiments confirmed that the phenomenon was not an artifact of the test procedures adopted nor of the response index employed. Independent removal-replacement results were obtained from a new group of 31 dogs maintained in an interaction condition similar to that of the first experiment, but tested only after 88 hours of cohabitation (*6*). These results, which were free of the influence of repeated testing, were not significantly different from those obtained after 96 hours of interaction-cohabitation in the first experiment. Nor were the effects restricted to the vocalization-disruption measure. After 4 days in the interaction condition, a significant shift was obtained in the preference of the experimental dogs for the rabbits. These data strongly suggest that significant changes in social preference occur over relatively short periods. A recently completed study by Fleener (*7*) indicates that human infants share this capacity for the rapid establishment of social preferences.

Observations of the animals in the first week of cohabitation yielded data which were consistent with the quantitative results. After an initial period of mutual avoidance, a considerable portion of the young dog's time was spent in grooming, lying upon, and gnawing at the extremities of his cohabitant. Such behavior continued throughout the duration of the experiment. As the dogs grew older and more capable of inflicting physical damage through grooming and "play" activities, the outcomes became increasingly more noxious to the rabbit cohabitant. By the 8th week of cohabitation, six of the ten rabbits in the interaction condition were severely injured and the pairings were discontinued. Contrary to the earlier reports of Kuo (*8*), continued cohabitation is not necessarily associated with the development and maintenance of peaceful relationships between species.

Preliminary information was obtained on the post-experimental sexual adaptation of dogs that had cohabitated with rabbits. A follow-up study of the subgroup of six female beagles used in the two experiments indicated that alien cohabitation does not necessarily inhibit the development of species-appropriate reproductive activities. Of the six animals observed in maturity, four were successfully mated and produced litters in their first heat. Parallel data on male dogs unfortunately were not obtained.

Our results clearly indicate that the young dog's experience prior to the 3rd week of life does not preclude the rapid establishment of a "new" social bond with respect to a member of another species. Moreover, early exposure to an animal of another species does not insure against the subsequent development of antagonistic patterns of interaction with that species.

The present findings thus are consistent with recent reports which emphasize the role of contemporary events, both endogenous and exogenous, in the control of the social behavior (*9*). Specifically, studies of the post-emergence behavior of dogs reared in complete isolation have demonstrated that the intensity of the treatment effects can be greatly modified by varying the conditions of emergence (*10*). Similarly, our previous work indicates that the primary effects of interspecific rearing in sheep can be reversed (*11*). While some long-term effects of early experience on social and sexual behavior patterns cannot be gainsaid (*12*), our data indicate that a critical examination of the conditions required for the persistence of such effects is in order.

References and Notes

1. V. H. Denenberg, G. A. Hudgens, M. X. Zarrow, *Science* **143**, 380 (1964); L. Hersher, J. B. Richmond, A. U. Moore, *Behaviour* **20**, 311 (1963); Z. Y. Kuo, *J. Comp. Physiol. Psychol.* **11**, 1 (1930); G. J. Romanes, *Nature* **12**, 553 (1875).
2. R. B. Cairns, *Psychol. Rev.* **73**, 409 (1966).
3. O. Elliot and J. P. Scott, *J. Genet. Psychol.* **99**, 3 (1961).
4. See also C. L. Pratt and G. P. Sackett, *Science* **155**, 1133 (1967); R. B. Cairns, *J. Comp. Physiol. Psychol.* **62**, 298 (1966).
5. It should also be noted that dogs maintained in isolation tended to approach rabbits which had previously cohabited with other dogs more rapidly than they approached rabbits that had not so cohabited (first and second columns, Table 1). This trend, of borderline significance ($.10 > P > .05$), suggests that the cohabitation experience modified the behavior of the rabbits as well as of the pups.
6. R. B. Cairns and J. Werboff, in preparation.
7. D. E. Fleener, thesis, Indiana University (1967).
8. Z. Y. Kuo, *J. Genet. Psychol.* **97**, 211 (1960). In this report Kuo indicated that attempts were made to inhibit fighting among dogs assigned to the experimental groups.
9. J. P. Scott, *Ann. Rev. Psychol.* **18**, 65 (1967).
10. J. L. Fuller and L. D. Clark, *J. Comp. Physiol. Psychol.* **61**, 251, 258 (1966).
11. R. B. Cairns, *ibid.* **62**, 298 (1966); R. B. Cairns and D. L. Johnson, *Psychon. Sci.* **2**, 337 (1965).
12. Including those effects related to the development of social preferences [see, for example, D. G. Freedman, J. A. King, O. Elliot, *Science* **133**, 1016 (1961)] and the sexual behaviors of dogs reared in isolation [see, for example, F. A. Beach in *Social Behavior and Organization among Vertebrates*, W. Etkin, Ed. (Univ. of Chicago Press, Chicago, 1964), p. 117].
13. E. B. Page, *J. Amer. Statist. Ass.* **58**, 216 (1963).

14. These experiments were conducted at the Jackson Laboratory while R.B.C. was on leave from Indiana University (PHS special fellowship 1-F3-NH-30, 205-10) and were supported in part by PHS research grants HD-01082 and GRS FR-05545-03-05 from NIH.

21 August 1967

17

Reprinted from pp. 21–31 of *The Postnatal Development of Phenotype*, S. Kazda and V. H. Denenberg, eds., Academia, 1970, 420 pp.

CRITICAL PERIODS FOR THE DEVELOPMENT OF SOCIAL BEHAVIOUR IN DOGS

J. P. SCOTT

Research Professor, Department of Psychology, Bowling Green State University, Ohio, United States of America

The general theory of critical periods states that organizational processes are most easily modified in the time when they are taking place most rapidly. The period at which this occurs therefore constitutes a critical or sensitive period in development (Scott, 1962). The organizational process with which this paper is chiefly concerned is that of primary socialization, defined as the formation of the young animal's first social relationships, principally including the formation of emotional attachments, but also the formation of certain kinds of mutual behavioural adjustments.

Timing of the Critical Period in the Dog

Unlike the situation with imprinting in precocious birds, the critical period in the dog does not occur immediately after birth. Its limits can be set on the basis of available evidence as approximately from the age of 3 to 12 weeks with a peak between 6 and 8 weeks.

One of the difficulties of studying this process in the dog is the ease and rapidity with which it occurs. As Fuller (1961) has shown with his isolation experiments, it requires only two 20-minute periods per week of social contact for a puppy to establish reasonably normal social relationships. Therefore, in order to experimentally establish the major effects of this process, complete visual and tactile isolation from the objects of socialization is necessary. This technique involves three environmental variables: (1) the presence or absence of dogs; (2) the presence or absence of people; and (3) the extension or restriction of the physical environment. Of the eight possible combinations of these factors, only two have been employed extensively (Table).

In one major experiment (Freedman, King and Elliot, 1961), people were absent, dogs present and the physical environment extended. Puppies were reared in a 1-acre field surrounded by a 7 ft high board fence and fed through a hole in the fence so that they never saw human beings. However, they were not restricted in other ways, having plentiful contact with other dogs and a large and varied physical environment. The results were dramatic. Puppies left in this situation until the age

TABLE

Major Experimental Variables Affecting the Process of Primary Socialization

People	*Dogs*	*Physical environment*	*Result*
Present	Present	Extended	Normal
Present	Present	Restricted	Kennel dog syndrome (Pfaffenberger and Scott, 1959)
Present	Absent	Extended	Confident in strange situations (Scott and Fuller, 1965)
Present	Absent	Restricted	Socially unresponsive to dogs (Fox and Stelzner, 1967)
Absent	Present	Extended	'Wild dog' (Freedman, King and Elliot, 1961)
Absent	Present	Restricted	Isolation syndrome (Fuller and Clark, 1966a; 1966b)
Absent	Absent	Extended	Unknown
Absent	Absent	Restricted	Isolation syndrome (Fuller and Clark, 1966a; 1966b; also, other authors)

of 14 weeks behaved like little wild animals; fearful, and attempting to bite when captured. They could be socialized only over a long period of time, using the same methods ordinarily used for training wild animals; that is, caging, enforced social contact and hand feeding.

Puppies reared in this field were taken from the litters one at a time into the laboratory and given extensive contacts with human beings for a week's time at ages covering the third, fourth, sixth, eighth and tenth weeks of life. These puppies were then returned to the field and kept with their litter mates until the age of 14 weeks, when all puppies were tested for the effects of previous socialization experience. Control puppies were removed only at 14 weeks. The smallest effects of the socialization experience were observed on the controls and those puppies taken during the third week, with the maximum effects at the sixth and eighth weeks and somewhat lessened effects during the tenth week. On the basis of this experiment by Freedman, King and Elliot (1961), we have concluded that the boundaries of the critical period can be set at the age of 3 and 12 weeks, with a peak effect coming between 6 and 8 weeks. This does not preclude the possibility that the process may continue at a low rate after 12 weeks and also that it may begin earlier than 3 weeks, again proceeding at a low rate.

The second method is to isolate each puppy individually in a small box. This is the most extreme kind of deprivation experiment, with both people and dogs absent and the physical environment restricted. The puppy's visual and tactile contact with the outside world is completely restricted, permitting no social contacts other than with the puppy himself, and no contact with physical objects except the limited and barren environment of the cage. Although the puppies grow normally and seem contented as long as they are in their cages, rearing them in such an environment from the age of 3 until 16 weeks produces striking deficits in social behaviour, both in response to human beings and to other dogs (Fuller and Clark, 1966 a; 1966 b). Fuller has found that puppies removed at any time up to the age of 7 weeks develop in a normal fashion, but that those remaining longer become increasingly disturbed in their behaviour when they are finally removed from the box. Thus, these experiments support the conclusion that the peak of the critical period is passed at the age of 7 weeks.

The maximum time during which puppies have been subjected to this treatment was approximately 6 months in the original isolation experiments done at McGill University (Clarke and colleagues, 1951). Such animals show somewhat greater disturbance and perhaps greater persistence of the effects, but it is clear that most of the effects have been produced before the age of 16 weeks.

Fox and Stelzner (1967) have used a less drastic form of isolation in which the puppies have contact with a human handler for about 6 minutes per day during routine feeding and cleaning. The total contact time is thus 42 minutes per week, approximately equal to the two 20-minute periods which Fuller found would permit normal development of isolated puppies and can be thus considered a minimal amount of contact necessary for socialization to human beings. In this technique, dogs are absent, people are present to a minimal degree, and the physical environment is restricted.

When all the puppies were tested at 12 weeks, the results indicated that puppies separated from the litter at 3½ weeks and given limited human socialization experience were much faster in their approach to a passive human handler than were puppies raised with the litter and not isolated in this fashion until the age of 8 weeks. Again, this experiment supports the conclusion that there is a lessened capacity for socialization beyond the age of 7 or 8 weeks, although the evidence is not conclusive in this case, as the 3½-week group had contact with people over approximately twice as long a period as did the 8-week group.

Experiments on the timing of the process of socialization have been done primarily with socialization to human beings, but the normal process of forming social attachments with other dogs appears to follow a similar course. In both Fisher's (1955) and Fuller and Clark's (1966 a; 1966 b) experiments with puppies completely isolated from the age of 3 until 16 weeks, there were severe disturbances of behaviour in response to other puppies as well as to human beings. These puppies tended to avoid contact with other puppies and play by themselves. In Fisher's experiment, wire-haired fox-terrier puppies showed a complete absence of fighting behaviour except when attacked by normal puppies. Beach (1965) found that male puppies reared in isolation during this period showed maladaptive sexual behaviour.

Fox and Stelzner (1967) reared beagle and mongrel puppies by hand until 3½ weeks and then in semi-isolation, as previously described, until 12 weeks. These puppies showed symptoms similar to those of Fisher's and Fuller's more completely isolated animals, being non-vocal, non-oral, non-aggressive, and passive when placed with more normal puppies. They rarely showed group play, even after considerable exposure to other animals, but eventually became aggressive, driving the other animals away.

A similar group of beagles and mongrels were raised with their mothers and litter mates until the age of 3½ weeks and then partially isolated as described. Some of these animals behaved normally when reintroduced to other puppies at 12 weeks, but others were similar to those which had been reared without any canine contact. The authors conclude that experience up to the age of 3½ weeks has a considerable effect on facilitating the development of normal canine social relationships. The puppies in this experiment should have had at least half a week and possibly as much as 1 week of contact with other puppies after they had entered the period of socialization, assuming that this period begins at the age of 3 weeks. Thus, we can conclude that the timing of the process of primary socialization to other canines is the same as that to human beings, and there is every reason to suppose that the same mechanisms are employed in both.

A final word should be said concerning the timing of developmental events. The times presented here are based on the averages of large groups of puppies, but even in early development there is considerable variation in the time of appearance of anatomical and behavioural characteristics, both between litters and between individuals within litters. This variation amounts to at least 3 or 4 days in either direction (Scott, 1958). Thus, if a large group of experimental puppies were given treatment beginning at the age of 3 weeks (the mean age for the inception of this period), we should expect that half of the animals would have entered the period of socialization and that the remaining half would enter it within the next 3 or 4 days. A group given treatment at 3½ weeks would, therefore, be expected to have 100 per cent of the animals in the socialization period. Fifty per cent of them would have at least half a week's experience in this period, while the other 50 per cent would have had none or lesser amounts of experience. Thus, some of the animals should be socialized and some not, as observed in Fox and Stelzner's (1967) results. This also emphasizes the technical point that it is highly desirable to measure individual development by behavioural indices as well as by arbitrary times since birth.

Limiting Processes of the Critical Period

The initial and terminal limits of the period appear to be principally the results of two subprocesses. One of these is the emotional response to the absence of familiar objects and individuals. Beginning at approximately 3 weeks of age a puppy that is temporarily isolated, either in its own pen or in a strange one, will begin to vocalize at a high rate and continue this over long periods. The rate is considerably higher in a strange pen and can be somewhat reduced by introducing a familiar, companion puppy (Scott and Bronson, 1964). The rate can also be reduced by permitting the puppy to become familiar with the strange situation. If a puppy is placed in a strange cage for 2 days in succession, the rate of vocalization is somewhat reduced. However, if a puppy is introduced for a 10-minute period no oftener than once a week, there is no effect of familiarization.

At ages much before 3 weeks a puppy will respond with distress vocalization to hunger, pain, cold and various other forms of discomfort, but as long as it is comfortable it adjusts very rapidly to any new situation and shows no distress vocalization. Therefore, the early limitation of the process of socialization is produced by the puppy's lack of sufficient sensory and learning capacities to distinguish between familiar and unfamiliar objects and individuals. While the eye is open at the age of 13 days in the average puppy, the retina does not develop into its adult form until approximately 28 days (Fox, 1963). A marked change in the rapidity with which conditioning is accomplished takes place at approximately 18–19 days (Fuller, Easler and Banks, 1950), and this point may be taken as the time when the puppy is sufficiently developed so that the process of primary socialization may proceed rapidly (Scott, 1967 a).

At the other end of the critical period, the limiting factor appears to be a rapidly developing fear response to strange individuals. Whereas the young puppy reacts primarily to the absence of the familiar and accepts strange individuals within a few minutes after a momentary startle response, at the age of 7 weeks it begins to show strong and prolonged fearful reactions to strange individuals that enter the environment (Freedman, King and Elliot, 1961). Under ordinary circumstances a puppy simply avoids contact with a strange individual and consequently, there is no opportunity for socialization to take place.

That socialization is possible if contact is enforced is shown by Woolpy and Ginsburg's (1967) experiment with wild-caught wolves. If such a wolf is isolated from other wolves and a human experimenter makes repeated close visual contact over a period of several weeks, the wolf will eventually become socialized to the experimenter and extend this to other human beings, although the relationship that has developed is quite different from that of a wolf cub socialized to people during the critical period. It is interesting that both this experiment and others with young puppies demonstrate that socialization takes place most effectively without any activity by the person concerned and with tactile contact made only by the animal. All that the person has to do is to be there, the socialization process taking place entirely within the puppy.

Mechanisms of Social Attachment

As already stated, beginning at approximately 3 weeks of age a puppy shows an almost instantaneous reaction of distress vocalization when isolated in a strange place. This is an almost reflex response which is activated by the ability of the puppy to become habituated or familiar with certain places and objects and to discriminate between those which have become familiar and those which are still unfamiliar. The reaction is adaptive in the sense that under natural conditions the vocalization would enable a care-taking animal to quickly locate a lost puppy.

In addition, this reaction could account for the development of emotional attachments in the following way. The puppy is distressed by the absence of familiar places and individuals, and he must very soon learn to associate the relief of this distress with the return of the familiar. He must also very quickly learn that he can avoid distress by staying in contact with familiar individuals and places. Indeed, we have observed that puppies reared in a large 1-acre field rarely wander more than 10 or 15 feet away from the familiar kennel area until they are approximately 12 weeks old. The emotional response itself is a strong one and its repetition should lead to a high degree of motivation for staying with the familiar. It is possible that there is also a positive emotion of pleasure arising from contact with the familiar, but the negative mechanism by itself is sufficient to account for emotional attachment.

I have also strongly stated the hypothesis that this response is the emotional and motivational basis for allelomimetic behaviour, the tendency for animals to move in groups and show other activities involving some degree of mutual imitation (Scott, 1967 b). If an animal is distressed by the absence of familiar individuals, he must soon learn that the way to avoid distress is to stay with the group, and the only way that he can stay with the group is to follow their movements. Thus, we are dealing with a response that has significance not only in early life, but also in later existence. Our evidence with older animals indicates that a mature dog isolated from familiar canine or human individuals becomes acutely distressed, but, rather than showing this entirely as a vocal response, he will also make violent attempts to escape and rejoin the group.

The Isolation Syndrome

This was first demonstrated by workers in Hebb's laboratory at McGill University (Clarke and colleagues, 1951). These workers were primarily interested in the effects of depriving young puppies of opportunities for perceptual experience and demonstrated not only that Scottish terriers raised in this fashion were severely handicapped in their learning capacities compared with normal dogs, but also, that they showed many abnormalities of social behaviour. The reality of these effects has been confirmed by Fisher (1955) and Fuller (1967), and the latter has done a brilliant series of analytic experiments which give us information as to how the effect is produced (Fuller and Clark, 1966 a; 1966 b). Puppies given some visual contact with the outside world through a window in the isolation cage are more normal than those raised with no visual contact, but puppies reared in pairs are no better off than those reared individually. Furthermore, rearing the puppy with playthings does little to alleviate the effect.

As observed in their isolation chambers, puppies appear to be normal in their behaviour and unusually calm, rarely giving any vocalization. Considered from the viewpoint of the mechanisms just suggested, a young puppy reared in this simple environment has no opportunity to experience emotional distress caused by the absence of the familiar and, consequently, no opportunity to become habituated to it or to learn how to alleviate it. In addition, a puppy should develop, from 7 weeks onwards, the capacity for an active fear response to the strange, reaching the adult level before the age of 16 weeks. As with the emotional response to the absence of the familiar, the isolated puppy should have no experience with this fear response, although fully capable of feeling it by the time he leaves the box. Consequently, the puppy first removed from the simple environment of the isolation box at the age of 16 weeks should experience, and for the first time, massive emotional responses of both kinds. These responses should be associated with the entire outside world and, like other fear responses, should be very persistent. Fuller (1967) concluded that the chief effects of the isolation experience, at least as exhibited by animals that are subjected to it no longer than to the age of 16 weeks, is primarily produced by emotional disturbance. It is not the conditions of early experience which produce disruption of behaviour, but the sudden and unexpected change in conditions. This is, then, a demonstration of a traumatic emotional experience induced by experimental means.

The Kennel-dog Syndrome

The foregoing results have great general theoretical interest, but, from a practical standpoint, the kennel-dog syndrome is perhaps a more important phenomenon. This syndrome is commonly encountered in pet animals which have been reared in kennels with minimal custodial care until the age of 4–6 months. Such animals are fearful and difficult to train and, while they can with careful handling be accustomed to their new environment, they become easily upset by any new circumstance. Similar effects are found in animals reared in laboratories. Krushinski (1962) found that a large number of dogs that had been reared in the Pavlovian laboratories of Russia could not be trained as war dogs. He also pointed out that breeds such as the German shepherd were more susceptible to this effect than were certain terrier breeds such as the Airedale.

In our experience at The Jackson Laboratory, we found that animals which had been well adjusted and trainable in our own laboratory became extremely fearful in new situations, even in other laboratories which were somewhat similar to our own. This behaviour persisted for years. Pfaffenberger and Scott (1959) found that guide dog puppies (chiefly German shepherds) that were left in the kennel beyond the age of 12 weeks before being sent to 4H homes (homes with rural families in which a child is taking part in a cooperative training programme) for normal family experience showed an increasing tendency to fail when trained as guide dogs at the age of 1 year.

There are three possible explanations of the maladaptive behaviour seen in the kennel-dog syndrome. One is that these animals have had an inadequate opportunity for human socialization and, hence, give a strong fear response to human beings which interferes with training. A second is that these animals are giving a fear response to strange physical environment, similar to that of puppies showing the isolation syndrome, but in a less severe form. This emotional response would also interfere with training. A third explanation is that, because of the lack of opportunity for learning in the simplified kennel environment, the puppies may develop negative learning sets; for example, a puppy might learn that anything outside his own pen had no significance for him.

We tried to test this last hypothesis by attempting to see if the puppy would develop a kennel dog syndrome in the absence of emotionally disturbing factors (Scott, Shepard and Werboff, 1967). We did this by giving two breeds of dogs a simple training task, in which they were taught to sit still on a square board placed in their home pens at three different ages, 4–6, 8–10 and 16–18 weeks. All puppies were given the same amount of handling and human contact so as to eliminate any fearful emotional responses to human contact, and all training was done in the home pen of the puppies so that they were not disturbed by strange physical surroundings. Results differed in the two breeds, perhaps because the task chosen was inhibitory in nature. In the African basenji, a breed resistant to inhibitory training, the results were poor at the age of 4–6 weeks and reached a plateau at the two later ages. In the Shetland sheep dog, a breed that readily receives inhibitory training, the results were relatively poor at 4–6 and 8–10 weeks, but became much better at 16–18 weeks.

When all puppies were retrained at 16–18 weeks, there was no significant effect of their age at previous training and amount of previous training, indicating that negative learning sets were not acquired either as a result of previous training or the lack of it. Thus, while there are large genetic differences in the capacity to accept this sort of training and in the age at which the capacity is developed, there is no indication that the ability to perform this task was decreased by simply living in kennel conditions. It must be concluded that the kennel-dog syndrome, like the isolation syndrome, is largely produced by emotional disturbances which result from a sudden change into an unfamiliar situation for which there has been no preparation in early life.

Genetic Differences in the Process of Primary Socialization

We have no evidence that there are any large breed differences in the overall timing of the period of socialization in dogs, although there are differences amounting to several days in certain developmental events, such as the opening of the eyes and ears (Scott and Fuller, 1965). The time of the appearance of these sensory capacities may conceivably modify the time of the onset of the process of socialization.

Krushinski (1962) and Fuller and Clark (1966 a; 1966 b) have found that terrier breeds are less susceptible to the kennel-dog and isolation syndromes. These breeds have been selected for their ability to be trained to attack both prey and other dogs. Other things being equal, they have less tendency to develop fearful behaviour and we can assume that they are, therefore, less likely to experience massive fear responses when introduced into a strange environment. It is probable, therefore, that the Scottish terriers used in the early McGill experiments (Clarke and colleagues, 1951) were less severely affected than another breed might have been.

As puppies, African basenjis show lower rates of distress vocalization in response to short periods of isolation than do Shetland sheep dogs (Scott, Deshaies and Morris, 1962). Their emotional reactions to temporary isolation are less persistent, and they form emotional attachments to people less readily when given minimal amounts of contact. Genetic differences in emotional responsiveness thus modify the general process of primary socialization.

Summary

(1) The general theory of critical periods states that organizational processes are most easily modified at the times when they are proceeding most rapidly. The time at which a developmental organizational process proceeds most rapidly is, therefore, a critical or sensitive period for that process.

(2) Experiments with the critical period of primary socialization in the dog involve three major variables: the presence or absence of people; the presence or absence of dogs; and the restriction or extension of the physical environment.

(3) Evidence from various experiments indicates that the process of primary socialization, whether directed toward people or other canines, proceeds most rapidly between the age of 3 and 12 weeks, with a peak between the age of 6 and 8 weeks.

(4) The initial and terminal limits of the critical period depend on two sub-processes. The first is the distress response to the absence of the familiar, whose appearance depends upon the sensory and learning capacities necessary to discriminate between familiar and unfamiliar individuals and objects. This response first appears at about the age of 3 weeks. The second process is the fear response to the strange, which remains at a low level until approximately 7 weeks of age,

rising thereafter until it reaches a point close to the adult capacity at approximately 12 weeks. A strong and persistent fear response effectively prevents even the minimal contact necessary for socialization.

(5) The principal mechanism of social attachment is the distress response to the absence of the familiar. This response acts as an internal reinforcing mechanism which punishes any behaviour that results in separation from familiar individuals and provides relief of distress on contact with familiar individuals. The same mechanism is probably the principal motivational basis of allelomimetic behaviour.

(6) The isolation syndrome consists of deficits in the ability to form adequate social relationships with either dogs or people, bizarre behaviour and deficits in learning capacities. According to the experiments of Fuller and Clark (1966 a; 1966 b), this syndrome results from a massive emotional disturbance following the introduction of an animal into an environment for which it has had no early preparation.

(7) The kennel-dog syndrome is a less drastic form of the isolation syndrome, consisting of persistent fearfulness and shyness and consequent deficits in trainability in animals removed from a kennel at a late age. Animals trained in the kennel environment show no such symptoms.

(8) All breeds of dogs appear to show the same general development and timing of the process of socialization. However, there are important breed differences in the times of developmental events that affect the onset of the process, and in the strength of emotional reactions involved in it.

References

Beach, F. A.: *Am. Zoologist* **5,** 687 (1965)

Clarke, R. S., Heron, W., Fetherstonehaugh, M. L., Forgyas, D. G. and Hebb, D. O.: *Can. J. Psychol.* **5,** 150 (1951)

Fisher, A. E.: *The Effects of Early Differential Treatment on the Social and Exploratory Behaviour of Puppies.* Pennsylvania State University. Ph. D. Thesis (1955)

Fox, M. W.: *J. Am. vet. med. Ass.* **143,** 968 (1963)

– and Stelzner, D.: *Anim. Behav.* **15,** 377 (1967)

Freedman, D. G., King, J. A. and Elliot, O.: *Science,* **133,** 1 016 (1961)

Fuller, J. L.: *Wld Conf. Psychiat., Montreal* **3,** 223 (1961)

–: *Science, N. Y* **158,** 1645 (1967)

– and Clark, L. D.: *J. comp. physiol. Psychol.* **161,** 251 (1966 a)

– –: *J. comp. physiol. Psychol.* **61,** 258 (1966b)

– Easler, C. and Banks, E.: *Am. J. Physiol.* **160,** 462 (1950)

Krushinski, L. V.: *Animal Behavior; Its Normal and Abnormal Development.* New York; Consultant's Bureau (1962)

Pfaffenberger, C. J. and Scott, J. P.: *J. genet. Psychol.* **95,** 145 (1959)
Scott, J. P.: *Psychosom. Med.* **20,** 42 (1958)
– : *Science, N. Y.* **138,** 949 (1962)
– : In *Early Experience.* Ed. by G. Newton and S. Levine. Springfield; Thomas (1967a)
– : In *Nebraska Symposium on Motivation.* Ed. by D. Levine. Lincoln, Nebraska, University of Nebraska Press (1967 b)
– and Bronson, F. H.: *In: Psychobiological Approaches to Behavior.* Ed. by P. H. Leiderman and D. Shapiro. Stanford; Stanford University Press (1964)
– and Fuller, J. L.: *Genetics and the Social Behavior of the Dog.* Chicago; University of Chicago Press (1965)
– Deshaies, D. and Morris, D. D.: Unpublished study (1962)
– Shepard, J. H. and Werboff, J.: *J. Psychol.* **66,** 237 (1967)
Woolpy, J. H. and Ginsburg, B. E.: *Am. Zoologist* **7,** 357 (1967)

Part IV

CRITICAL PERIODS FOR LEARNING

Editor's Comments on Paper 18

18 MONEY, HAMPSON, and HAMPSON
Imprinting and the Establishment of Gender Role

Learning is itself a developmental organizational process that characteristically involves intermittent critical periods (Paper 38). Repetition of a learned association or task produces more and more stable organization which becomes increasingly difficult to modify. The initial phase of each new learning situation is therefore a critical one with respect to the ease with which reorganization and the consequent modification of behavior can take place. A striking human instance is the critical period for the establishment of gender roles.

Certain human babies are born with ambiguous external genitalia. Among them, it occasionally turns out that the child has been assigned to the sex role that is imcompatible with its biological sex. If its gender assignment is then reversed, which of course involves changing its name and clothing, and occasionally some surgical modifications, this can be done with ease under the age of 2 years and 3 months (Money et al., Paper 18). After this age, many children get into difficulties and make unsuccessful adjustments.

A successful sexual reversal depends on both the child and its family. The timing of changes in effects, however, suggest that this critical period is related to that of language development, which begins at about twenty-one months, and possibly with the development of a self-concept. The child may already have learned to consciously think of himself as herself, for example. Another organizing process that might be involved is that of identification with male or female members of the family. This, of course, could be independent of language.

The numbers quoted in Paper 18 are quite small. Later research on the subject is summarized in the book by Money and Ehrhardt (1972).

18

Reprinted from *Arch. Neurol. and Psychiatr.* 77:333–336 (1957)

Imprinting and the Establishment of Gender Role

JOHN MONEY, Ph.D.; JOAN G. HAMPSON, M.D., and JOHN L. HAMPSON, M.D., Baltimore

Introduction

Psychologic study of hermaphrodites sheds some interesting light on the venerable controversy of hereditary versus environmental determinants of sexuality in its psychologic sense.

Human hermaphrodites of whatever variety are persons born with some degree of sexual ambiguity, anatomically and physiologically. Since they are neither exclusively male nor exclusively female, hermaphrodites are likely to grow up with contradictions existing between the sex of assignment and rearing, on the one hand, and various physical sexual variables, singly or in combination, on the other. These physical sexual variables are five in number, namely, (1) chromosomal sex, (2) gonadal sex, (3) hormonal sex and pubertal feminization or virilization, (4) the internal accessory reproductive structures, and (5) external genital morphology.

In view of the various ambisexual contradictions that may be found in hermaphroditism, one may ask whether the gender role and orientation that a hermaphrodite establishes during the course of growing up is concordant with the sex of assignment and rearing, or whether it is predominantly concordant with one or another of the five physical sexual variables.

Received for publication Nov. 2, 1956.

Read at the VIII International Congress of Pediatrics, Copenhagen, July, 1956.

From the Department of Psychiatry, The Johns Hopkins University School of Medicine.

The research summarized in this paper is supported by a grant from the Josiah Macy, Jr. Foundation and is under the aegis of John C. Whitehorn, Professor of Psychiatry, The Johns Hopkins University, and of Lawson Wilkins, Associate Professor of Pediatrics, Acting Pediatrician-in-Chief, Director of Pediatric Endocrinology at The Johns Hopkins Hospital.

Psychologic Studies

During the past five years, we have investigated the sexual psychology of 105 hermaphroditic patients[1-5] of different diagnostic varieties and of all ages. The majority of them were, after their initial hospital appearance, followed from year to year. From observational notes, recorded interviews, and formal psychological tests, we obtained enough data from these patients to be able to appraise their gender role and orientation as masculine, as feminine, or as ambiguous. It was then possible to compare the gender role and orientation that each patient had established with the sex which had been assigned in infancy and in which the patient had subsequently been reared. It was also possible to compare the gender role and orientation with each of the five physical variables of sex, taken severally.

The resulting comparisons demonstrated that the sex of assignment and rearing is consistently and conspicuously a more reliable prognosticator of a hermaphrodite's gender role and orientation than is the chromosomal sex, the gonadal sex, the hormonal sex, the accessory internal reproductive morphology, or the ambiguous morphology of the external genitalia. There were only 5 among the 105 patients whose gender role and orientation was ambiguous and deviant from the sex of assignment and rearing. By contrast, for each of the five physical sexual variables, there were between 23 and 30 patients—not always the same persons*—whose sex of assignment and rearing was incongruous. In some patients this incongruity involved only one physical variable, but in most of the patients more than one physical variable was involved. Thus, some patients were predominantly female with respect to the

* The individual patients represented in each of the five tables, one for each physical variable of sex, were not identical, owing to the inconsistencies of physical contradictions in hermaphroditism; but some patients required entering in more than one table.

physical variables of sex but, having been reared as boys, had the sexual psychology of a boy, or man—and vice versa for patients reared as girls.

The clinching piece of evidence concerning the psychologic importance of the sex of assignment and rearing is provided when, among persons of identical physical diagnosis, some are reared as boys, some as girls. It is indeed startling to see, for example, two children with female hyperadrenocorticism in the company of one another in a hospital playroom, one of them entirely feminine in behavior and conduct, the other entirely masculine, each according to upbringing. As a social observer, one gets no suspicion that the two children are chromosomally and gonadally female, for psychologically they are entirely different.

Further supportive evidence concerning the importance, psychologically, of the sex of assignment and rearing is provided by cases of reassignment of sex by edict. Among our cases there were 14 patients who underwent a reassignment of sex after the early neonatal weeks. Of these 14, there were 9 below the age of 2 years 3 months at the time of the change; with 3 exceptions, they appeared subsequently to have negotiated the change without even mild signs of psychologic nonhealthiness. By contrast, only one of the five children older than 2 years 3 months at the time of reassignment of sex could possibly be rated as psychologically healthy. One infers that once a person's gender role begins to get well established, an attempt at its reversal is an extreme psychologic hazard. Psychologic nonhealthiness was markedly less common in patients without a history of sex reassignment than in those with one.†

Practical Applications

The practical and clinical applications of our studies and findings have been spelled out in detail in two papers already published.[6,7] In briefest summary, our findings point to the extreme desirability of deciding, with as little diagnostic delay as possible, on the sex of assignment and rearing when a hermaphroditic baby is born. Thereafter, uncompromising adherence to the decision is desirable. The chromosomal sex should not be the ultimate criterion, nor should the gonadal sex. By contrast, a great deal of emphasis should be placed on the morphology of the external genitals and the ease with which these organs can be surgically reconstructed to be consistent with the assigned sex. In cases of female hyperadrenocorticism, good surgical feminization is possible almost without exception, and these patients can, of course, also be hormonally regulated as females when treated with cortisone. Other surgical considerations being equal, the earlier surgical reconstruction of the genitals is done, the better. When operations must necessarily be delayed until later childhood or adolescence, it is sound psychologic medicine to take children into one's confidence and explain the whys and wherefores of what is planned on their behalf. Clitoral amputation in patients living as girls does not, so far as our evidence goes, destroy erotic sensitivity and responsiveness, provided the vagina is well developed. If clitoridectomy is performed in early infancy, the chances of undesirable psychologic sequelae are negligible.

Theoretical Considerations

Theoretically, our findings indicate that neither a purely hereditary nor a purely environmental doctrine of the origins of gender role and orientation—of psychologic sex—is adequate. On the one hand, it is evident that gender role and orientation is not determined in some automatic, innate, or instinctive fashion by physical, bodily agents, like chromosomes, gonadal structures, or hormones. On the other hand, it is also evident that the sex of assignment and rearing does not automatically and mechanistically determine the gender role and ori-

† In actual fact, the incidence of psychologic nonhealthiness among our 105 patients was surprisingly rare; frank psychosis was entirely absent, except for one instance of schizophrenia of long duration.

entation: The small group of five patients whose sexual outlook diverged somewhat from that of the sex to which they had been assigned prevents so simple-minded a view of environmental determinism. Rather, it appears that a person's gender role and orientation becomes established, beginning at a very early age, as that person becomes acquainted with and deciphers a continous multiplicity of signs that point in the direction of his being a boy, or her being a girl. These signs range all the way from nouns and pronouns differentiating gender to modes of behavior, hair cut, dress, and personal adornment that are differentiated according to sex. The most emphatic sign of all is, of course, the appearance of the genital organs. Presumably, it is the very ambiguity of the external genitals that makes hermaphrodites so adaptable to assignment in either sex, though it requires to be emphasized that the less ambiguous our patients could be made to appear as a result of well-timed plastic surgery and hormonal therapy, consistent with their rearing, the sturdier was their psychologic healthiness.

The salient variable in the establishment of a person's gender role and orientation is neither hereditary nor environmental, in any purist sense of those terms, but is his own decipherment and interpretation of a plurality of signs, some of which may be considered hereditary or constitutional, others environmental. His decipherment of social and environmental signs, whether under the impact of deliberate training and inculcation or through the more casual and haphazard lessons of experience, appears to be markedly more significant than has traditionally been allowed in medical and scientific theories.

Establishment of one's gender role and orientation appears to have much in common with est: blishment of one's native language. Bilingualism may be native. So also may a gender role and orientation be ambivalent. A native language eventually becomes ineradicable. So also does a gender role and orientation.

Ineradicability of psychologic functions established after birth is seldom given credence in most psychologic theory. There are many medical analogies, however. Bone development, for example, can be effectively influenced in rickets and cretinism only before maturity is reached. Thereafter, deformities of bone growth associated with these diseases become ineradicable.

There are some recent findings in animal psychology that give credence to the viewpoint that psychologic functions, such as gender role and orientation, may become so ineradicable as to appear innately instinctive. We refer to the investigations of Dr. Konrad Lorenz, in Austria, and with one of his examples we shall close.[8] Guided by his own exemplary reasoning, Lorenz experimented and discovered that wild mallard ducklings, immediately upon being hatched, could be induced to react to him as if he were their mother. In contrast with graylag goslings, which unquestioningly accept the first living thing they meet as mother, the mallard ducklings were panicky until they heard the quacking noise usually made by the mother mallard duck. Lorenz imitated the quacking of a mallard mother for half a day, almost continuously, waddling about in a squatting position, lest his height-width ratio produce a visual configuration that dispersed the ducklings in terror. After quacking and waddling with the newly hatched creatures for the first half-day of their lives, Lorenz became established for them as mother. The truly amazing sequel, however, is that the ducklings responded to Lorenz as if he were their mother from that day onward. They trailed behind him on his local excursions, and from the sky or the fields they came flying or running at the sound of the mallard notes he imitated.

Summary

Over a period of five years, we have made a comprehensive psychologic study of over 100 patients born with divers varieties of hermaphroditism. With rare exceptions, it was found that the sexual psychology of these patients—their gender role and orientation—was consistent with their sex of assignment and rearing, even when the latter contradicted chromosomal sex, gonadal sex, hormonal sex, the predominant internal accessory reproductive structures, and the external genital morphology. Though the sex of rearing could transcend external genital morphology in psychologic importance, absence or correction of ambiguous genital appearance was psychologically beneficial. Reassignment of the sex of rearing after the early months of life was, without doubt, psychologically injurious.

The Johns Hopkins Hospital.

REFERENCES

1. Money, J.: Hermaphroditism, Gender and Precocity in Hyperadrenocorticism: Psychologic Findings, Bull. Johns Hopkins Hosp. 96:253-264, 1955.

2. Hampson, J. G.: Hermaphroditic Genital Appearance, Rearing and Eroticism in Hyperadrenocorticism, Bull. Johns Hopkins Hosp. 96:265-273, 1955.

3. Hampson, J. L.; Hampson, J. G., and Money, J.: The Syndrome of Gonadal Agenesis (Ovarian Agenesis) and Male Chromosomal Pattern in Girls and Women: Psychologic Studies, Bull. Johns Hopkins Hosp. 97:207-226, 1955.

4. Money, J.; Hampson, J. G., and Hampson, J. L.: An Examination of Some Basic Sexual Concepts: The Evidence of Human Hermaphroditism, Bull. Johns Hopkins Hosp. 97:301-319, 1955.

5. Money, J.; Hampson, J. G., and Hampson, J. L.: Sexual Incongruities and Psychopathology: The Evidence of Human Hermaphroditism, Bull. Johns Hopkins Hosp. 98:43-57, 1956.

6. Money, J.; Hampson, J. G., and Hampson, J. L.: Hermaphroditism: Recommendations Concerning Assignment of Sex, Change of Sex and Psychologic Management, Bull. Johns Hopkins Hosp. 97:284-300, 1955.

7. Hampson, J. G.; Money, J., and Hampson, J. L.: Teaching Clinic: Hermaphrodism: Recommendations Concerning Case Management. J. Clin. Endocrinol. 16:547-556, 1956.

8. Lorenz, K. Z.: King Solomon's Ring; New Light on Animal Ways, New York, The Thomas Y. Crowell Company, 1952.

Editor's Comments on Papers 19 and 20

19 LENNEBERG
Further Comments on the "Critical Period" for Language Acquisition

20 EIMAS et al.
Speech Perception in Infants

One of the most important critical periods in human behavioral development is the period for the acquisition of language. It has long been recognized that young children learn new language material, whether that of their native culture or another, much more readily than adults. It is extremely difficult, if not impossible, for a person past the age of twelve or so to learn a new language without a foreign accent. The material by Lenneberg (Paper 19) summarizes neurological evidence for the length and importance of this critical period. Accidental brain lesions at any age may produce an aphasic condition in which the patient has difficulty in recalling words and other aspects of language. Up through the age of ten, recovery from these injuries is usually complete, but after that time the symptoms become irreversible, at least to some degree.

Therefore, there is a very long critical period from approximately twenty-one months to ten years based on the gradually increasing organization of the language functions of the brain. As this process goes on, the resulting system becomes more and more stable and resistant to change.

An interesting therapeutic technique has recently emerged from the fact that the lesions which produce aphasia usually occur on only one side of the brain. Opposite the language area, there is a corresponding region in the other half of the brain that is ordinarily used for music and which in most individuals is relatively unorganized. In severe cases of aphasia, language can be newly acquired by singing it and so organizing an uninjured portion of the brain. In this "Musical Intonation Therapy," the words are first sung, then the musical tone dropped out, and finally the rhythm, so that natural use of words is accomplished.

A sad commentary on this subject is the fact that educational systems in the United States make almost no use of this critical period. Foreign language learning is traditionally delayed until high school, after the end of the critical period. Obviously, foreign language learning should begin in the early grades, and no later than the age of eight.

This critical period has an even more important implication for basic education. Any material taught in the schools is intricately enmeshed with language learning. It follows that a child should be introduced, at least in a preliminary way, to all basic parts of his future intellectual life during this critical period, and that the way in which this experience is organized (which to a large extent depends on how it is taught) will have important effects on future capabilities and performance.

The fact that foreign accents are difficult or impossible to eliminate after the age of thirteen or fourteen raises the possibility that a similar freezing of motor organization may also take place. This hypothesis could be tested by measuring the effects of accidental lesions in motor areas of the brain at different ages.

In the dog, we have on the basis of empirical evidence postulated a similar critical period for early learning between the ages of eight to twelve weeks. Within this period, it is advisable to introduce the dog to his future life activities, but we have no neurological evidence to back this up.

Using language involves not only the ability to talk but also the auditory capacity to recognize and to discriminate between sounds produced by another person. The paper by Eimas et al. (Paper 20) indicates that these basic perceptual abilities develop at a very early age and are probably well developed by the time that a child begins to talk almost two years later.

19

Reprinted from pp. 175–187 of *The Biological Foundations of Language,* E. H. Lenneberg, John Wiley and Sons, Inc., 1967, 489 pp.

FURTHER COMMENTS ON THE "CRITICAL PERIOD" FOR LANGUAGE ACQUISITION

E. H. Lenneberg

FURTHER COMMENTS ON THE "CRITICAL PERIOD" FOR LANGUAGE ACQUISITION

At first sight it might be tempting to relate the age-limited potential for language acquisition to a variety of other types of emergence of animal behavior that depend upon stimulation during a short period of the animal's infancy. Most important in this connection is the phenomenon of *imprinting* (Gray, 1958), a highly specialized type of behavioral development investigated most closely in certain birds. It occurs during early infancy at a specific developmental stage, usually a few hours or days after hatching. The chick will follow that moving object to which it is exposed during the critical period, and it will continue to follow that object during most of its "childhood." The response is established very rapidly and indiscriminately to essentially anything that moves at a given speed and is within certain limitations of size. The response resists extinction to a high degree, but it is not completely irreversible. Eventually it will be overshadowed or displaced by other responses. Failure to develop imprinted responses during infancy may cause behavioral abnormalities in the adult, and such a bird's behavior cannot be normalized by later training, (Hinde, 1961; Hess, 1962).

Age-limited emergence of behavior has also been described in mammals (Thorpe, 1961). It is possible that many types of social organizations among animals are based on somewhat similar mechanisms, the most elementary of which is infant-mother relationship (Bowlby, 1953; Ahrens, 1954; Scott, 1963). The inference we may draw from this material is that many animal forms traverse periods of peculiar sensitivities, response-propensities, or learning potentials. Insofar as we have made such a claim for language acquisition, we have postulated nothing that would be extraordinary in the realm of animal behavior.

But at the same time we must sound a warning. Merely the fact that there are critical periods for the acquisition of certain types of behavior among a number of species *does not imply* any phylogenetic relationship between them. Age-linked emergence of behavior may be due to such a variety of factors that this phenomenon by itself is of limited heuristic value when it comes to tracing evolutionary origins of behavior. In the case of language, the limiting factors postulated are cerebral immaturity on the one end and termination of a state of organizational plasticity linked with lateralization of function at the other end of the critical period. We do not know whether these or similar factors are responsible for limitations of critical periods in the case of other animals.

Do the time limitations postulated for language acquisition function across the board for all types of human learning? Probably not: there are many skills and tasks that are much better learned during the late teens than in early childhood and a great deal of general learning has no age limitation whatever. Nevertheless, an accurate answer to the question is very difficult. For instance, our ability to learn foreign languages tends to confuse the picture. Most individuals of average intelligence are able to learn a second language after the beginning of their second decade, although the incidence of "language-learning-blocks" rapidly increases after puberty. Also automatic acquisition from mere exposure to a given language seems to disappear after this age, and foreign languages have to be taught and learned through a conscious and labored effort. Foreign accents cannot be overcome easily after puberty. However, a person *can* learn to communicate in a foreign language at the age of forty. This does not trouble our basic hypothesis on age limitations because we may assume that the cerebral organization for language learning as such has taken place during childhood, and since natural languages tend to resemble one another in many fundamental aspects (see Appendix A), the matrix for language skills is present.

Would cerebral lateralization of function develop in the absence of language acquisition? If we were dealing with a laboratory animal, we could perform a number of decisive experiments to answer this important question. As it is, we must be satisfied with inconclusive but suggestive evidence. A total absence of language development is nowadays seen only in the worst cases of feeblemindedness and chronic childhood psychosis. Hand preference is poorly developed in the amented, probably a reflection of their extremely retarded state of development. Reliable surveys of hand preference in psychotic children are not available, but it is my impression that right-handedness may be observed in all of those psychotic children whose motor milestones are attained at normal age. In this population, however, we can never be certain about the degree of covert language acquisition. As mentioned earlier, unwillingness to communicate is not necessarily a sign of absence of language.

Congenitally deaf but otherwise healthy children whose language acquisition is delayed to their first years in school, say age seven, have a normal incidence of right-handedness which seems to emerge at the usual time and which is firmly established between four and five years. However, the diagrams of Fig. 4.16 show that hand preference is not an unfailing guide to knowledge about cerebral dominance. There is a

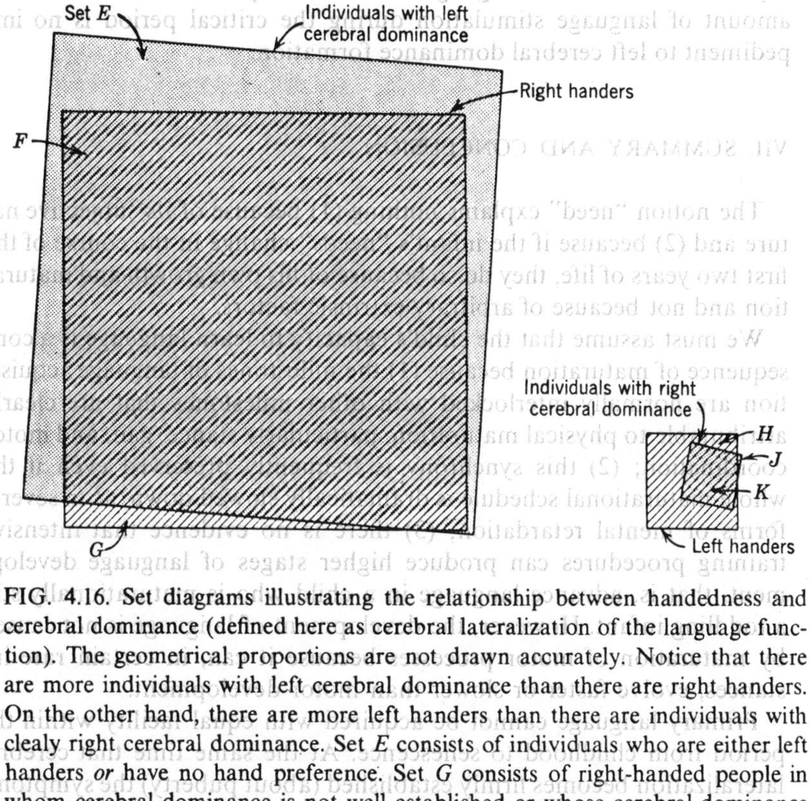

FIG. 4.16. Set diagrams illustrating the relationship between handedness and cerebral dominance (defined here as cerebral lateralization of the language function). The geometrical proportions are not drawn accurately. Notice that there are more individuals with left cerebral dominance than there are right handers. On the other hand, there are more left handers than there are individuals with clealy right cerebral dominance. Set *E* consists of individuals who are either left handers *or* have no hand preference. Set *G* consists of right-handed people in whom cerebral dominance is not well-established or whose cerebral dominance is predominantly in the right hemisphere (rare). Most individuals belong to Set *F*: right handed with left cerebral dominance. Half of the individuals in the set of left handers have right cerebral dominance (Set *K*) and half have either left dominance or bilateral cerebral representation (Set *H*). Set *J* consists of the very rare individuals who are not clearly left handers but who have definite right cerebral dominance.

small percentage of right-handers who have been found to have poorly established cerebral lateralization. Perhaps a relatively large percentage of the congenitally deaf falls into this category. Militating against this possibility is the fact that aphasia with right-sided paralysis has been reported in congenitally deaf persons, (Critchley, 1938; Douglas and Richardson, 1959; Grasset, 1896; Tureen et al., 1951). None of these four patients had had oral speech before their stroke; all four used sign language and finger spelling, and in all of them, manual language communication was disordered by left-hemisphere lesions. From these cases and the deaf population as a whole we may conclude that even delayed exposure of the child to language and a definitely unusual and decreased amount of language stimulation during the critical period is no impediment to left cerebral dominance formation.

VII. SUMMARY AND CONCLUSION

The notion "need" explains nothing (1) because of its subjective nature and (2) because if the infant's "needs" change in the course of the first two years of life, they do so because of his own growth and maturation and not because of arbitrary extrinsic factors.

We must assume that the child's capacity to learn language is a consequence of maturation because (1) the milestones of language acquisition are normally interlocked with other milestones that are clearly attributable to physical maturation, particularly stance, gait, and motor coordination; (2) this synchrony is frequently preserved even if the whole maturational schedule is dramatically slowed down, as in several forms of mental retardation; (3) there is no evidence that intensive training procedures can produce higher stages of language development, that is, advance language in a child who is maturationally still a toddling infant. However, the development of language is not caused by maturation of motor processes because it can, in certain rare instances, evolve faster or slower than motor development.

Primary language cannot be acquired with equal facility within the period from childhood to senescence. At the same time that cerebral lateralization becomes firmly established (about puberty) the symptoms of acquired aphasia tend to become irreversible within about three to six months after their onset. Prognosis for complete recovery rapidly deteriorates with advancing age after the early teens. Limitation to the acquisition of primary language around puberty is further demonstrated by the mentally retarded who can frequently make slow and modest beginnings in the acquisition of language until their early teens, at which time their speech and language status becomes permanently consolidated. Furthermore, according to Fry, the profoundly deaf must receive sound training and prosthetic aid as close to age two as possible to develop good speech habits. The reverse is seen in acquired deafness where even short exposure to language before the onset of deafness improves prognosis for speech and language, with the outlook becoming better in proportion to the length of time the patient had been in command of verbal skills.

Thus we may speak of a critical period for language acquisition. At the beginning it is limited by lack of maturation. Its termination seems to be related to a loss of adaptability and inability for reorganization in the brain, particularly with respect to the topographical extent of neurophysiological processes. (Similar infantile plasticity with eventual irreversible topographical representation in the brain has been demonstrated for many higher mammals.) The limitations in man may well be connected with the peculiar phenomenon of cerebral lateralization of function, which only becomes irreversible after cerebral growth-phenomena have come to a conclusion.

The specific neurophysiological correlates of speech and language are completely unknown. Therefore, emergence of the capacity for language acquisition cannot be attributed directly to any one maturational process studied so far. But it is important to know what the physical states of the brain are before, during, and after the critical period for language acquisition. This is the prerequisite for the eventual discovery of more specific neural phenomena underlying language behavior. We find that in almost all aspects of cerebral growth investigated about 60% of the mature values are attained before the onset of speech (roughly at two years of age, when speech and language become rapidly perfected), whereas the critical period comes to a close at a time when 100% of the values are reached. This statement must not be mistaken for a demonstration of causal relationship between the variables involved. It merely suggests what structural and physiological substrates there might be that limit the capacity for cerebral organization and reorganization.

Species differ in their embryological and ontogenetic histories. Brain-maturation curves of *Homo sapiens* are different from those of other primates. Man's brain matures much slower, and there is evidence that the difference is not merely one of a stretched time-scale, but that there are intrinsic differences. Thus man is not born as a fetalized version of other primates; the developmental events in his natural history are *sui generis*. The hypothesis is advanced that the capacity for language acquisition is intimately related to man's peculiar maturational history

TABLE 4.8. *Summary Survey*

Age	Usual Language Development	Effects of Acquired, Lateralized Lesions	Physical Maturation of CNS	Lateralization of Function	Equipotentiality of Hemispheres	Explanation
Months 0–3	Emergence of cooing	No effect on onset of language in half of all cases; other half has delayed onset but normal development	About 60–70% of developmental course accomplished	None: symptoms and prognosis identical for either hemisphere	Perfect equipotentiality	Neuro-anatomical and physiological prerequisites become established
4–20	From babbling to words					
21–36	Acquisition of language	All language accomplishments disappear; language is reacquired with repetition of all stages	Rate of maturation slowed down	Hand preference emerges	Right hemisphere can easily adopt sole responsibility for language	Language appears to involve entire brain; little cortical specialization with regard to language though left hemisphere beginning to become dominant towards end of this period
Years 3–10	Some grammatical refinement; expansion of vocabulary	Emergence of aphasic symptoms; disorders tend to recover without residual language deficits (except in reading or writing). During recovery period, two processes active: diminishing	Very slow completion of maturational processes	Cerebral dominance established between 3–5 years but evidence that right hemisphere may often still be involved in speech and language	In cases where language is already predominantly localized in left hemisphere and aphasia ensues with left lesion, it is possible to re-	A process of physiological organization takes place in which functional lateralization of language to left is prominent. "Physiological redundancy" is gradually reduced and polarization of activities between right and left hemisphere is established. As long

		aphasic interference and further acquisition of language		functions. About 1/4 of early childhood aphasias due to right-hemisphere lesions	establish language presumably by reactivating language functions in right hemisphere	as maturational processes have not stopped, reorganization is still possible
11–14	Foreign accents emerge	Some aphasic symptoms become irreversible (particularly when acquired lesion was traumatic).	An asymptote is reached on almost all parameters. Exceptions are Myelinization and EEG spectrum	Apparently firmly established but definitive statistics not available	Marked signs of reduction in equipotentiality	Language markedly lateralized and internal organization established irreversibly for life. Language-free parts of brain cannot take over except where lateralization is incomplete or had been blocked by pathology during childhood
Mid-teens to Senium	Acquisition of second language becomes increasingly difficult	Symptoms present after 3–5 months postinsult are irreversible	None	In about 97% of the entire population language is definitely lateralized to the left	None for language	

and the unique degree of lateralization of function. Table 4.8 presents the argument in tabular form.

REFERENCES

Ahrens, R. (1954), Beiträge zur Entwicklung des Physiognomie- und Mimikerkennens, *Z. exp. Angew. Psychol.* **2**:412–454; 599–633.

Ajuriaguerra, J. de (1957), Langage et dominance cérébrale, *J. Français d'Oto-Rhino-Laryngol.* **6**:489–499.

Altman, P. L. and Dittmer, D. S. (eds.) (1962), *Growth Including Reproduction and Morphological Development,* Federation of American Societies for Experimental Biology, Washington, D.C.

André-Thomas, Sorrel, E. and Sorrel-Dejerine, Mme., Un cas d'aphasie motrice par traumatisme craniocerebral chez l'enfant. *Rev. Neurol.* **63**:893–896.

Austerlitz, R. (1956), Gilyak nursery words, *Word* **12**:260–279.

Basser, L. S. (1962), Hemiplegia of early onset and the faculty of speech with special reference to the effects of hemispherectomy, *Brain* **85**:427–460.

Bateman, F. (1890), *On Aphasia, or Loss of Speech, and the Localisation of the Faculty of Articulate Language.* (2nd ed.) Churchill, London.

Benjamin, R. M. and Thompson, R. F. (1959), Differential effects of cortical lesions in infant and adult cats on roughness discrimination, *Exp. Neurol.* **1**:305–321.

Bernhard, C. G. and Skoglund, C. R. (1939), On the alpha frequency of human brain potentials as function of age, *Skandinav. Arch. f. Physiol.* **82**:178–184.

Bok, S. T. (1959), *Histonomy of the Cerebral Cortex.* Elsevier, Amsterdam.

Bowlby, J. (1953), Critical phases in the development of social responses in man and other animals, in *Prospects in Psychiatric Research; the proceedings of the Oxford Conference of the Mental Health Fund.* J. M. Tanner (ed.), Blackwell, Oxford.

Branco-LeFèvre, A. F. (1950), Contribuição para o estudo da psicopatologia da afasia em criança, *Arq. Neuropsiquiat.* (São Paulo) **8**:345–393.

Brante, G. (1949), Studies on lipids in the nervous system; with special reference to quantitative chemical determination and topical distribution, *Acta Physiol. Scand.* 18 Suppl. 63.

Brodbeck, A. J. and Irwin, O. C. (1946), The speech behavior of infants without families, *Child Development* **17**:145–156.

Brooks, C. and Peck, M. E. (1940), Effect of various cortical lesions on development of placing and hopping reactions in rats, *J. Neurophysiol.* **3**:66–73.

Brown, R. W. (1957), *Words and Things.* Free Press, Glencoe, Illinois.

Brown, R. W. and Bellugi, U. (1964), Three processes in the child's acquisition of syntax, in *New Directions in the Study of Language,* E. H. Lenneberg (ed.), M.I.T. Press, Cambridge, Massachusetts.

Brunner, H. and Stengel, E. (1932), Zur Lehre von den Aphasien im Kindesalter, *Z. Neur. Psychiat.* **142**:430–450.

Bühler, C. (1931), *Kindheit und Jugend* (3rd ed.) Hirzel, Leipzig.

Carmichael, L. (1926), The development of behavior in vertebrates experimentally removed from the influence of external stimulation, *Psychol. Rev.* **33**:51–58.

Carmichael, L. (1927), A further study of the development of behavior in vertebrates experimentally removed from the influence of external stimulation, *Psychol. Rev.* **34**:34–47.

Carmichael, L. (ed.) (1954), *Manual of Child Psychology.* John Wiley and Sons, New York.

Conel, J. LeRoy (1939–1963), *The Postnatal Development of the Human Cerebral Cortex.* Volumes I through VI. Harvard Univ. Press, Cambridge, Mass.

Critchley, MacD. (1938), Aphasia in a partial deaf-mute, *Brain* **61**:163–168.

Davis, K. (1947), Final note on a case of extreme isolation, *Am. J. Sociol.* **52**:432–437.

De Crinis, M. (1934), *Aufbau und Abbau der Grosshirnleistungen und ihre anatomischen Gründe,* Karger, Berlin.

Dennis, W. and Dennis, M. G. (1951), Development under controlled environmental conditions, in *Readings in Child Psychology,* W. Dennis (ed.), Prentice-Hall, Englewood Cliffs, New Jersey.

Dennis, W. and Najarian, P. (1957), Infant development under environmental handicap, *Psychol. Monogr.* **71,** No. 7, Whole No. 436F.

Doty, R. W. (1953), Effects of ablation of visual cortex in neonatal and adult cats, *Abstracts Comm. XIX Int. Physiol. Congr.,* p. 316.

Douglas, E. and Richardson, J. C. (1959), Aphasia in a congenital deaf-mute, *Brain* **82**:68–80.

Dreyfus-Brisac, C. and Blanc, C. (1956), Electro-encéphalogramme et maturation cérébrale, *Encéphale* **45**:204–241.

Ervin, S. M. (1964), Imitation and structural change in children's language, in *New Directions in the Study of Language,* E. H. Lenneberg (ed.), M.I.T. Press, Cambridge, Mass.

Ervin, S. M. and Miller, W. R. (1963), Language development, *Child Psychology,* 62nd Yearbook, National Society for the Study of Education. Univ. of Chicago Press, Chicago, Ill.

Fisichelli, R. M. (1950), *A study of prelinguistic speech development of institutionalized infants.* Unpublished Ph.D. dissertation, Fordham University. Quoted by McCarthy, 1954.

Flechsig, P. (1927), *Meine myelogenetische Hirnlehre mit biographischer Einleitung.* Springer, Berlin.

Folch-Pi, J. (1952), Chemical constituents of brain during development and in maturity, in *The Biology of Mental Health and Disease, The 27th Annual Conference of the Milbank Memorial Fund,* Hoeber, New York.

Folch-Pi, J. (1955), Composition of the brain in relation to maturation, in *Biochemistry of the Developing Nervous System; Proceedings of the First International Neurochemical Symposium,* H. Waelsch (ed.), Academic Press, New York.

Fry, D. B. (1966), The development of the phonological system in the normal and deaf child, in *The Genesis of Language: a psycholinguistic approach*. F. Smith and G. A. Miller (eds.), M.I.T. Press, Cambridge, Mass.

Gesell, A. and Amatruda, C. S. (1947), *Developmental Diagnosis; normal and abnormal child development, clinical methods and pediatric applications* (2nd ed.), Hoeber, New York.

Gibbs, F. A. and Knott, J. R. (1949), Growth of the electrical activity of the cortex, *EEG & Clin. Neurophysiol.* **1**:223–229.

Goldfarb, W. (1943), The effects of early institutional care on adolescent personality, *J. Exp. Educ.* **12**:106–129.

Goldfarb, W. (1945), Effects of psychological deprivation in infancy and subsequent stimulation, *Am. J. Psychiat.* **102**:18–33.

Grasset, J. (1896), Aphasie de la main droite chez un sourd-muet, *Le Progrès Médical,* Series 3, Vol. 4, No. 44, p. 281.

Gray, P. H. (1958), Theory and evidence of imprinting in human infants. *J. Psychol.* **46**:155–166.

Grohmann, J. (1938), Modifikation oder Funktionsregung? ein Beitrag zur Klärung der wechselseitigen Beziehungen zwischen Instinkthandlung und Erfahrung, *Z. Tierpsychol.* **2**:132–144.

Gutmann, E. (1942), Aphasia in children, *Brain* **65**:205–219.

Harlow, H. F., Akert, K., and Schiltz, K. A. (1964), The effects of bilateral prefrontal lesions on learned behavior of neonatal, infant, and preadolescent monkeys, in *The Frontal Granular Cortex and Behavior.* J. M. Warren and K. Akert (eds.), McGraw-Hill, New York.

Hécaen, H. and Ajuriaguerra, J. de (1963), *Les Gauchers, Prévalence Manuelle et Dominance Cérébrale.* Presses Universitaires de France, Paris.

Henry, C. E. (1944), Electroencephalograms of normal children, *Monograph, Society for Research in Child Development,* **9**, No. 3.

Hess, E. H. (1962), Ethology: an approach toward the complete analysis of behavior, *New Directions in Psychology.* R. W. Brown, E. Galanter, E. H. Hess, and G. Mandler (eds.), Holt, Rinehart and Winston, New York.

Hillier, W. F., Jr. (1954), Total left cerebral hemispherectomy for malignant glioma, *Neurology* **4**:718–721.

Hinde, R. A. (1961), The establishment of the parent-offspring relation in birds, with some mammalian analogies, in *Current Problems in Animal Behavior,* W. H. Thorpe and O. L. Zangwill, Cambridge University Press, Cambridge, England.

Irwin, O. C. (1948), Infant speech, *J. Speech and Hearing Disorders* **13**:224–225, 320–326.

Kaes, T. (1907), *Die Grosshirnrinde des Menschen in ihren Massen und in ihrem Fasergehalt,* Gustav Fischer, Jena.

Kety, S. S. (1955), Changes in cerebral circulation and oxygen consumption which accompany maturation and aging, in *Biochemistry of the Developing Nervous System; Proceedings of the First International Neurochemical Symposium,* H. Waelsch (ed.), Academic Press, New York.

Koehler, O. (1952), "Wolfskinder," Affen im Haus und Vergleichende Verhaltensforschung, *Folia Phoniatrica* **4**:29–53.

Kroeber, A. L. (1916), The speech of a Zuni child, *Am. Anthrop.* **18**:529–534.

Kummer, B. (1953), Untersuchungen über die Entwicklung der Schädelform des Menschen und einiger Anthropoiden, *Abhandlungen zur exakten Biologie,* fasc 3, L. v. Bertalanffy (ed.), Borntraeger, Berlin.

Laine, E. and Gros, C. (1956), *L'Hémispherectomie,* Masson, Paris.

Landau, W. M., Goldstein, R., and Kleffner, F. R. (1960), Congenital aphasia; a clinicopathologic study, *Neurology* **10**:915–921.

Lehrman, D. S. (1958*a*), Induction of broodiness by participation in courtship and nest-building in the Ring Dove *(Streptopelia risoria), J. comp. physiol. Psychol.* **51**:32–36.

Lehrman, D. S. (1958*b*), Effect of female sex hormones on incubation behavior in the Ring Dove *(Streptopelia risoria), J. comp. physiol. Psychol.* **51**:142–145.

Lenneberg, E. H.,(1962), Understanding language without ability to speak: a case report, *J. abnorm. soc. Psychol.* **65**:419–425.

Lenneberg, E. H. (1964), Speech as a motor skill with special reference to nonaphasic disorders, in *The Acquisition of Language,* Monograph of the Society for Research in Child Development. U. Bellugi and R. Brown (eds.), Serial No. 92, Vol. 29, No. 1.

Lenneberg, E. H., Nichols, I. A., and Rosenberger, E. F. (1964), Primitive stages of language development in mongolism, in *Disorders of Communication Vol. XLII: Research Publications,* A.R.N.M.D. Williams and Wilkins, Baltimore, Maryland.

Lenneberg, E. H., Rebelsky, F. G., and Nichols, I. A. (1965), The vocalization of infants born to deaf and to hearing parents, *Vita Humana* (Human Development) **8**:23–37.

Lindsley, D. B. (1936), Brain potentials in children and adults, *Science* **84**:354.

Lorenz, K. Z. (1958), The evolution of behavior, *Scientific American* **119,** No. 6, December, 67–78.

Luchsinger, R. and Arnold, G. E. (1959), *Lehrbuch der Stimm- und Sprachheilkunde* (2nd ed.), Springer, Wien.

Marks, M., Taylor M., and Rusk, H. A. (1957), Rehabilitation of the aphasic patient, *Neurology* **7**:837–843.

McCarthy, D. (1954), Language development in children, in *Manual of Child Psychology.* L. Carmichael (ed.), pp. 492–630.

McGraw, M. B. (1963), *The Neuromuscular Maturation of the Human Infant.* Hafner, New York.

Morley, M. (1957), *The Development and Disorders of Speech in Childhood.* Livingstone, London.

Peiper, A. (1961), *Die Eigenart der Kindlichen Hirntätigkeit* (3rd ed.), G. Thieme, Leipzig.

Poetzl, O. (1926), Ueber sensorische Aphasie im Kindesalter, *Z. Hals- N.-Ohrenhlk.* **14**:190–216.

Russell, W. R. and Espir, M. L. E. (1961), *Traumatic Aphasia,* Oxford University Press, Oxford, England.

Schadé, J. P. and Groenigen, W. B. van (1961), Structural organization of the human cerebral cortex; maturation of the middle frontal gyrus, *Acta anat.* **47**:74–111.

Scharlock, D. P., Tucker, T. J., and Strominger, N. L. (1963), Auditory discrimination by the cat after neonatal ablation of temporal cortex, *Science* **141** (Sept. 20):1197–1198.

Schultz, A. H. (1956), Postembryonic age changes, in *Primatologia: Handbook of Primatology,* Vol. I. H. Hofer, A. H. Schultz, and D. Starck (eds.), pp. 887–964. Karger, Basel.

Scott, J. P. (1963), The process of primary socialization in canine and human infants, *Monograph of the Society for Research in Child Development,* Serial No. 85, Vol. 28, No. 1.

Sholl, D. A. (1956), *The Organization of the Cerebral Cortex.* Methuen, London.

Singh, J. A. L., and Zingg, R. M. (1942), *Wolf Children and Feral Man.* Harper, New York.

Slobin, D. I. (1966), The acquisition of Russian as a native language, in *The Genesis of Language: a psycholinguistic approach.* F. Smith and G. A. Miller (eds.), M.I.T. Press, Cambridge, Mass.

Smith, J. R. (1941), The frequency growth of the human alpha rhythms during normal infancy and childhood, *J. Psychol.* **11**:177–198.

Smith, M. E. (1926), An investigation of the development of the sentence and the extent of vocabulary in young children, *Univ. Iowa Stud. Child Welfare,* Vol. 3, No. 5.

Sperry, R. W. (1961), Cerebral organization and behavior, *Science* **133**:1749–1757.

Sperry, W. M. (1962), The biochemical maturation of the brain, in *Mental Retardation,* L. C. Kolb, R. L. Masland, and R. E. Cooke (eds.), A.R.N.M.D., Vol. 39, Williams and Wilkins, Baltimore.

Teuber, H.-L. (1950), Neuropsychology, in *Recent Advances in Diagnostic Psychological Testing: a critical summary,* Chapter 3, pp. 30–52, C Thomas, Springfield, Illinois.

Teuber, H.-L. (1960), Perception, in *Handbook of Physiology, Section 1: Neurophysiology,* Vol. 3, Chapter 65, pp. 1595–1668, American Physiological Society, Washington, D.C.

Teuber, H.-L. (1962), Effects of brain wounds implicating right or left hemisphere in man: hemisphere differences and hemisphere interaction in vision, audition, and somesthesis, in *Interhemispheric Relations and Cerebral Dominance,* pp. 131–157. V. B. Mountcastle (ed.), Johns Hopkins Press, Baltimore.

Thomas, E. and Schaller, F. (1954), Das Spiel der optisch isolierten, jungen Kaspar-Hauser-Katze, *Naturwiss* **41**:557–558.

Thorpe, W. H. (1961), Sensitive periods in the learning of animals and men: a study of imprinting with special reference to the induction of cyclic behavior, in *Current Problems in Animal Behavior,* W. H. Thorpe and O. L. Zangwill (eds.), Cambridge University Press, Cambridge, England.

Tureen, L. L., Smolik, E. A., and Tritt, J. H. (1951), Aphasia in a deaf mute, *Neurology* **1**:237–244.

Vogt, O. (1911), Die Myeloarchitektonik des Isocortex parietalis, *J. Psychol. Neurol.* **18:** (Suppl. No. 2) 379–390.

Woodward, F. R. (1945), Recovery from aphasia; report of two cases, *Bull. Los Angeles Neurol. Soc.* **10:**73–75.

Yakovlev, P. I. (1962), Morphological criteria of growth and maturation of the nervous system in man, in *Mental Retardation,* A.R.N.M.D., Vol. 39, pp. 3–46, Williams and Wilkins, Baltimore, Maryland.

Zangwill, O. L. (1960), *Cerebral Dominance and its Relation to Psychological Function.* Oliver and Boyd, Edinburgh.

Note: Since the time of my original research for this chapter two recent articles have come to my attention that are relevant to the neurological material covered here. They are Alajouanine, T. and Lhermitte, F., Acquired aphasia in childhood. *Brain* (1965) **88:**653-662; and Penfield, W., Conditioning the uncommitted cortex for language learning, *Brain* (1965) **88:**787–798. Although there are some discrepancies both in facts and in interpretation between these articles and the material presented here, there appears to be perfect agreement on the basic issue, namely that the prognosis for acquired aphasia in childhood is definitely better than for similar pathology in the adult.

20

Reprinted from *Science* **171**:303–306 (1971)

SPEECH PERCEPTION IN INFANTS

Peter D. Eimas, Einar R. Siqueland, Peter Jusczyk and James Vigorito
Department of Psychology, Brown University

Abstract. *Discrimination of synthetic speech sounds was studied in 1- and 4-month-old infants. The speech sounds varied along an acoustic dimension previously shown to cue phonemic distinctions among the voiced and voiceless stop consonants in adults. Discriminability was measured by an increase in conditioned response rate to a second speech sound after habituation to the first speech sound. Recovery from habituation was greater for a given acoustic difference when the two stimuli were from different adult phonemic categories than when they were from the same category. The discontinuity in discrimination at the region of the adult phonemic boundary was taken as evidence for categorical perception.*

In this study of speech perception, it was found that 1- and 4-month-old infants were able to discriminate the acoustic cue underlying the adult phonemic distinction between the voi ed and voiceless stop consonants /b/ and /p/. Moreover, and more important, there was a tendency in these subjects toward categorical perception: discrimination of the same physical difference was reliably better across the adult phonemic boundary than within the adult phonemic category.

Earlier research using synthetic speech sounds with adult subjects uncovered a sufficient cue for the perceived distinction in English between the voiced and voiceless forms of the stop consonants, /b-p/, /d-t/, and /g-k/, occurring in absolute initial position (*1*). The cue, which is illustrated in the spectrograms displayed in Fig. 1, is the onset of the first formant relative to the second and third formants. It is possible to construct a series of stimuli that vary continuously in the relative onset time of the first formant, and to investigate listeners' ability to identify and discriminate these sound patterns. An investigation of this nature (*2*) revealed that the perception of this cue was very nearly categorical in the sense that listeners could discriminate continuous variations in the relative onset of the first formant very little better than they could identify the sound patterns absolutely. That is, listeners could readily discriminate between the voiced and voiceless stop consonants, just as they would differentially label them, but they were virtually unable to hear intraphonemic differences, despite the fact that the acoustic variation was the same in both conditions. The most measurable indication of this categorical perception was the occurrence of a high peak of discriminability at the boundary between the voiced and voiceless stops, and a nearly chance level of discriminability among stimuli that represented acoustic variations of the same phoneme. Such categorical perception is not found with nonspeech sounds that vary continuously along physical continua such as frequency or intensity. Typically, listeners are able to discriminate many more stimuli than they are able to identify absolutely, and the dis-

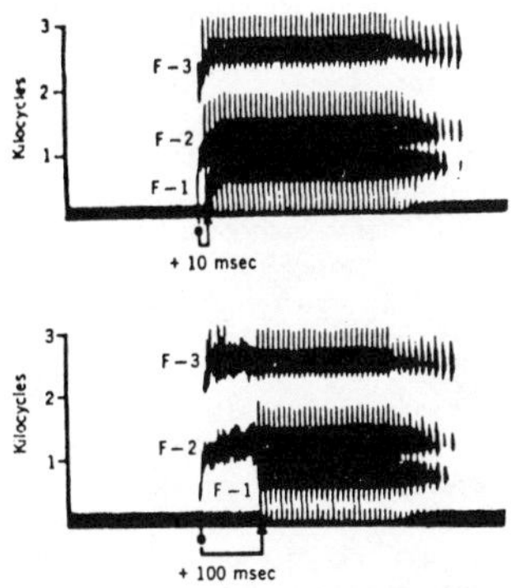

Fig. 1. Spectrograms of synthetic speech showing two conditions of voice onset time (VOT): slight voicing lag in the upper figure and long voicing lag in the lower figure. The symbols *F-1*, *F-2*, and *F-3* represent the first three formants, that is, the relatively intense bands of energy in the speech spectrum. [Courtesy of L. Lisker and A. S. Abramson]

criminability functions do not normally show the same high peaks and low troughs found in the case of the voicing distinction (*3*). The strong and unusual tendency for the stop consonants to be perceived in a categorical manner has been assumed to be the result of the special processing to which sounds of speech are subjected and thus to be characteristic of perception in the speech or linguistic mode (*4*).

Because the voicing dimension in the stop consonants is universal, or very nearly so, it may be thought to be reasonably close to the biological basis of speech and hence of special interest to students of language development. Though the distinctions made along the voicing dimension are not phonetically the same in all languages, it has been found in the cross-language research of Lisker and Abramson (*5*) that the usages are not arbitrary, but rather very much constrained. In studies of the production of the voicing distinction in 11 diverse languages, these investigators found that, with only minor exceptions, the various tokens fell at three values along a single continuum. The continuum, called voice onset time (VOT), is defined as the time between the release burst and the onset of laryngeal pulsing or voicing. Had the location of the phonetic distinctions been arbitrary, then different languages might well have divided the VOT continuum in many different ways, constrained only by the necessity to space the different modal values of VOT sufficiently far apart as to avoid confusion.

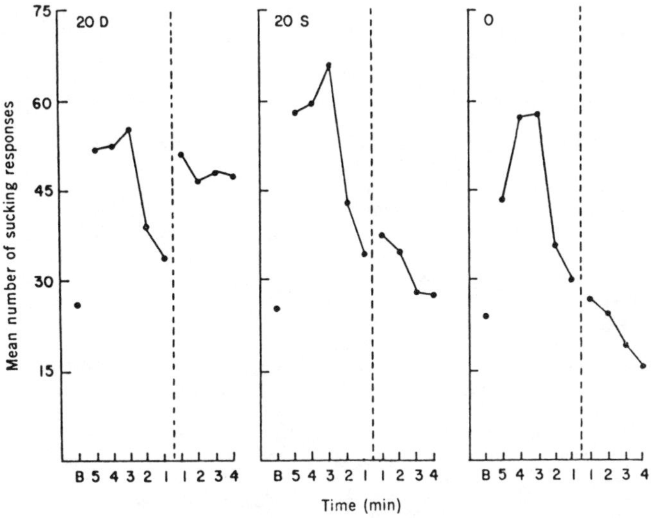

Fig. 2. Mean number of sucking responses for the 4-month-old infants, as a function of time and experimental condition. The dashed line indicates the occurrence of the stimulus shift, or in the case of the control group the time at which the shift would have occurred. The letter *B* stands for the baseline rate. Time is measured with reference to the moment of stimulus shift and indicates the 5 minutes prior to and the 4 minutes after shift.

Not all languages studied make use of the three modal positions. English, for example, uses only two locations, a short lag in voicing and a relatively long lag in voicing. Prevoicing or long voicing lead, found in Thai, for example, is omitted. Of interest, however, is the fact that all languages use the middle location, short voicing lag, which, given certain other necessary articulatory events, corresponds to the English voiced stop /b/, and one or both of the remaining modal values. The acoustic consequences for two modes of production are shown in Fig. 1; these correspond to short and long voicing lags, /b/ and /p/, respectively.

Given the strong evidence for universal—and presumably biologically determined—modes of production for the voicing distinction, we should suppose that there might exist complementary processes of perception (*6*). Hence, if we are to find evidence marking the beginnings of speech perception in a linguistic mode, it would appear reasonable to initiate our search with investigations of speech sounds differing along the voicing continuum. What was done experimentally, in essence, was to compare the discriminability of two synthetic speech sounds separated by a fixed difference in VOT under two conditions: in the first condition the two stimuli to be discriminated lay on opposite sides of the adult phonemic boundary, whereas in the second condition the two stimuli were from the same phonemic category.

The experimental methodology was a modification of the reinforcement procedure developed by Siqueland (*7*). After obtaining a baseline rate of high-amplitude, nonnutritive sucking for each infant, the presentation and intensity of an auditory stimulus was made contingent upon the infant's rate of high-amplitude sucking. The nipple on which the child sucked was connected to a positive pressure transducer that provided polygraphic recordings of all responses and a digital record of criterional high-amplitude sucking responses. Criterional responses activated a power supply that increased the intensity of the auditory feedback. A sucking rate of two responses per second maintained the stimulus at maximum intensity, about 75 db (13 db over the background intensity of 62 db).

The presentation of an auditory stimulus in this manner typically results in an increase in the rate of sucking compared with the baseline rate. With continued presentation of the initial stimulus, a decrement in the response rate occurs, presumably as a consequence of the lessening of the reinforcing properties of the initial stimulus. When it was apparent that attenuation of the reinforcing properties of the initial stimulus had occurred, as indicated by a decrement in the conditioned sucking rate of at least 20 percent for two consecutive minutes compared with the immediately preceding minute, a second auditory stimulus was presented without interruption and again contingent upon sucking. The second stimulus was maintained for 4 minutes after which the experiment was terminated. Control subjects were treated in a similar manner, except that after the initial decrease in response rate, that is, after habituation, no change was made in the auditory stimulus. Either an increase in response rate associated with a change in stimulation or a decrease of smaller magnitude than that shown by the control subjects is taken as inferential evidence that the infants perceived the two stimuli as different.

The stimuli were synthetic speech sounds prepared by means of a parallel resonance synthesizer at the Haskins Laboratories by Lisker and Abramson. There were three variations of the bilabial voiced stop /b/ and three variations of its voiceless counterpart /p/. The variations between all stimuli were in VOT, which for the English stops /b/ and /p/ can be realized acoustically by varying the onset of the first formant relative to the second and third formants and by having the second and third formants excited by a noise source during the interval when the first formant is not present. Identification functions from adult listeners (*8*) have indicated that when the onset of the first formant leads or follows the onset of the second and third formants by less than 25 msec perception is almost invariably /b/. When voicing follows the release burst by more than 25 msec the perception is /p/. Actually the sounds are perceived as /ba/ or /pa/, since the patterns contain three steady-state formants appropriate for a vowel of the type /a/. The six stimuli had VOT values of −20, 0, +20, +40, +60, and +80 msec. The negative sign indicates that voicing occurs before the release burst. The subjects were 1- and 4-month-old infants, and within each age level half of the subjects were males and half were females.

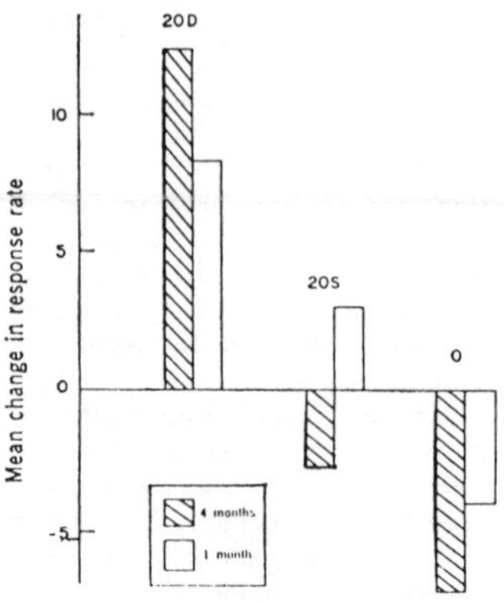

Fig. 3. The mean change in response rate as a function of experimental treatments, shown separately for the 1- and 4-month-old infants. (See text for details.)

The main experiment was begun after several preliminary studies established that both age groups were responsive to synthetic speech sounds as measured by a reliable increase in the rate of sucking with the response-contingent presentation of the first stimulus ($P < .01$). Furthermore, these studies showed that stimuli separated by differences in VOT of 100, 60, and 20 msec were discriminable when the stimuli were from different adult phonemic categories; that is, there was reliable recovery of the rate of sucking with a change in stimulation after habituation ($P < .05$). The finding that a VOT difference of 20 msec was discriminable permitted within-phonemic-category discriminations of VOT with relatively realistic variations of both phonemes.

In the main experiment, there were three variations in VOT differences at each of two age levels. In the first condition, 20D, the difference in VOT between the two stimuli to be discriminated was 20 msec and the two stimuli were from different adult phonemic categories. The two stimuli used in condition 20D had VOT values of +20 and +40 msec. In the second condition, 20S, the VOT difference was again 20 msec, but now the two stimuli were from the same phonemic category. In this condition the stimuli had VOT values of −20 and 0 msec or +60 and +80 msec. The third condition, 0, was a control condition in which each subject was randomly assigned one of the six stimuli and treated in the same manner as the experimental subjects, except that after habituation no change in stimulation was made. The control group served to counter any argument that the increment in response rate associated with a change in stimulation was artifactual in that the infants tended to respond in a cyclical manner. Eight infants from each age level were randomly assigned to conditions 20D and 20S, and ten infants from each age level were assigned to the control condition.

Figure 2 shows the minute-by-minute response rates for the 4-month-old subjects for each of the training conditions separately. The results for the younger infants show very nearly the identical overall pattern of results seen with the older infants. In all conditions at both age levels, there were reliable conditioning effects: the response rate in the third minute prior to shift was significantly greater than the baseline rate of responding ($P < .01$). As was expected from the nature of the procedure, there were also reliable habituation effects for all subjects. The mean response rate for the final 2 minutes prior to shift was significantly lower than the response rate for the third minute before shift ($P < .01$). As is apparent from inspection of Fig. 1, the recovery data for the 4-month-old infants were differentiated by the nature of the shift. When the mean response rate during the 2 minutes after shift was compared with the response rate for the 2 minutes prior to shift, condition 20D showed a significant increment ($P < .05$), whereas condition 20S showed a nonsignificant decrement in responding ($P > .05$). In the control condition, there was a fairly substantial decrement in responding during the first 2 minutes of what corresponded to the shift period in the experimental conditions. However, the effect failed to reach the .05 level of significance, but there was a reliable decrement when the mean response rate for the entire 4 minutes after shift was compared with the initial 2 minutes of habituation ($P < .02$). The shift data for the younger infants were quite similar. The only appreciable difference was that in condition 20S there was a nonsignificant increment in the response rate during the first 2 minutes of shift.

In Fig. 3 the recovery data are summarized for both age groups. The mean change in response rate (that is, the mean response rate for the initial 2 minutes of shift minus the mean response rate during the final 2 minutes before shift) is displayed as a function of experimental treatments and age. Analyses of these data revealed that the magnitude of recovery for the 20D condition was reliably greater than that for the 20S condition ($P < .01$). In addition, the 20D condition showed a greater rate of responding than did the control condition ($P < .01$), while the difference between the 20S and control conditions failed to attain the .05 level of significance.

In summary, the results strongly indicate that infants as young as 1 month of age are not only responsive to speech sounds and able to make fine discriminations but are also perceiving speech sounds along the voicing continuum in a manner approximating categorical perception, the manner in which adults perceive these same sounds. Another way of stating this effect is that infants are able to sort acoustic variations of adult phonemes into categories with relatively limited exposure to speech, as well as with virtually no experience in producing these same sounds and certainly with little, if any, differential reinforcement for this form of behavior. The implication of these findings is that the means by which the categorical perception of speech, that is, perception in a linguistic mode, is accomplished may well be part of the biological makeup of the organism and, moreover, that these means must be operative at an unexpectedly early age.

References and Notes

1. A. M. Liberman, P. C. Delattre, F. S. Cooper, *Language and Speech* **1**, 153 (1958); A. M. Liberman, F. Ingemann, L. Lisker, P. C. Delattre, F. S. Cooper, *J. Acoust. Soc. Amer.* **31**, 1490 (1959). It should be emphasized that the cues underlying the voicing distinction as discussed in the present report apply only to sound segments in absolute initial position.
2. A. M. Liberman, K. S. Harris, H. S. Hoffman, H. Lane, *J. Exp. Psychol.* **61**, 370 (1961).
3. P. D. Eimas, *Language and Speech* **6**, 206 (1963); G. A. Miller, *Psychol. Rev.* **63**, 81 (1956); R. S. Woodworth and H. Schlosberg, *Experimental Psychology* (Holt, New York, 1954).
4. A. M. Liberman, F. S. Cooper, D. P. Shankweiler, M. Studdert-Kennedy, *Psychol. Rev.* **74**, 431 (1967); M. Studdert-Kennedy, A. M. Liberman, K. S. Harris, F. S. Cooper, *ibid.* **77**, 234 (1970); M. Studdert-Kennedy and D. Shankweiler, *J. Acoust. Soc. Amer.*, in press.
5. L. Lisker and A. S. Abramson, *Word* **20**, 384 (1964).
6. P. Lieberman, *Linguistic Inquiry* **1**, 307 (1970).
7. E. R. Siqueland, address presented before the 29th International Congress of Psychology, London, England (August 1969); ——— and C. A. DeLucia, *Science* **165**, 1144 (1969).
8. L. Lisker and A. S. Abramson, *Proc. Int. Congr. Phonet. Sci. 6th* (1970), p. 563.

9. Supported by grants HD 03386 and HD 04146 from the National Institute of Child Health and Human Development. P.J. and J.V. were supported by the NSF Undergraduate Participation Program (GY 5872). We thank Dr. F. S. Cooper for generously making available the facilities of the Haskins Laboratories. We also thank Drs. A. M. Liberman, I. G. Mattingly, A. S. Abramson, and L. Lisker for their critical comments. Portions of this study were presented before the Eastern Psychological Association, Atlantic City (April 1970).

14 September 1970

Editor's Comments on Papers 21 Through 24

CRITICAL PERIODS IN THE ACQUISITION OF BIRD SONGS

Vocal communication in birds has some of the characteristics of human language. Certain young birds, such as crows, parrots, and mynah birds, can be easily taught to mimic human speech. In normal bird development, there are critical periods during which greater or lesser degrees of modification of the characteristic cries of a species can take place. Birds, however, lack the ability to organize vocalizations in different combinations and so convey varieties of meaning in the way that humans use language.

Many perching birds have easily recognizable songs that are characteristric of their own particular species. If one has a good ear, one can recognize a difference between birds coming from different geographical regions; the birds themselves can recognize small individual differences in their neighbors. Since the males do not sing until they are adults and approximately one year of age, one might advance the hypothesis that the characteristic song of the species, the regional dialects, and the individual variations all might be produced by genetic factors. However, the singing of many birds is modified by captivity, and research in recent years has established the fact that the nature of the song is determined during a critical period.

Long before modern methods of recording and analyzing sounds were invented, W. E. D. Scott (Paper 21) raised a pair of orioles by hand and observed that they developed a song which was unrecognizable as belonging to that particular species. He then went on to handrear other orioles in their company and found that they developed the same peculiar song. His paper is historically interesting because of its informal and discursive style and its wealth of detail, luxuries which modern scientific communication can no longer afford.

Many years later, Thorpe and Marler studied the acquisition of song in an English bird, the chaffinch. Paper 22 by Thorpe summarizes the early work in which they found that birds reared apart from others, as with the orioles, developed unusual songs. Modification of the song could only take place during the first ten months of life, after which the song was fixed and could never be modified again.

Marler and his students have gone on to demonstrate similar effects in many other species of birds (Marler and Mundinger, 1971). The paper by Marler and Tamura (Paper 23) describes the condition in the white-crowned sparrow. Young male birds, under natural conditions, hear adults singing during the first 100 days or so after fledging. They have the opportunity to learn the local dialect only during that period. Handreared birds cannot learn songs after 100 days. Thus, the critical period is even shorter in this species.

Paper 24 by Nottebohm develops a theoretical explanation of the critical period phenomenon. He concludes that there are actually two critical periods, involving respectively perceptual and motor learning. The ends of these critical periods are produced, not by age per se, but by a process he calls crystallization. In terms of systems theory, this would be equivalent to stable organization. Nottebohm suggests some alternate possibilities with respect to physiological organization that could produce this result.

21

Reprinted from *Science* **14**:522–526 (1901)

DATA ON SONG IN BIRDS. OBSERVATIONS ON THE SONG OF BALTIMORE ORIOLES IN CAPTIVITY

William E. D. Scott
Curator of Ornithology, Princeton University

MUCH has been written in regard to the songs of birds, and no small part of the literature of the subject has dealt with the problem of the way in which many kinds of birds have acquired the distinctive song that characterizes each different species.

In the eastern United States many of us recognize, without seeing, the singer, on hearing the song of one of our commoner native birds. We say, 'A robin is singing,' 'Listen to the bobolink,' 'That is a song sparrow.'

Some who pay close and particular attention realize that individuals of a given kind have sometimes slight, though marked, variations in the method of song that distinguish them from the mass of their kind and characterize them as individuals which are readily known by their *peculiar personal song*. So we say, 'This robin is a good singer,' 'The note of that thrush is particularly pleasing,' 'That oriole has some harsh notes.' Such comments are indicative of the taste or appreciation of the listener and are only introduced here to emphasize two facts. First, that the song of all the individuals of a given kind of bird, as the robins, is so characteristic that we call it the robin's song, readily recognize it, and know that, in the main, all the robins of a given region have a common song, so much alike that we do not individualize the singer. Second, that now and again individual birds of a given kind, robins again for example, are readily distinguishable as individuals by some turn or phrasing of the notes that gives to the individual singer an identity as a particular robin, with an individual song, different, to a greater or less degree, from the mass of robins in the same region.

The question at once suggests itself: How is this characteristic song acquired?

Is it a matter of inheritance? Or does each robin learn to sing? Is it inherent in the species or is this song of the robin a matter of education?

A. R. Wallace and Lloyd Morgan especially have advanced hypotheses to account for the matter of call notes and song, and Mr. Morgan's work is based on many careful experiments that are set forth in his book, 'Habit and Instinct.' But, so far, I am not aware of any prolonged or detailed account of the study of this factor, as it develops with, and extends through, the life of a given individual, nor has a second generation been carefully watched.

The following experiment, though imperfect and by no means as exhaustive as could be desired, seems, however, worthy of record, as from it certain conclusions may be drawn. The notes accumulated extend over a period of nearly five years and are briefly as follows:

On July 7, 1895, I took from a maple tree at Annisquam, Massachusetts, a nest of the Baltimore oriole (*Icterus galbula*), which contained three very young birds. They were quite naked and showed no signs of wing or tail feathers. They appeared to be about five days old. As a record to refer to, one was killed and preserved in alcohol. The other two were carefully reared by hand and throve well.

So far as I know, they did not hear, after coming into my possession, any birds sing, nor did any person whistle or sing to them.

At the age of between three and four weeks they were able to feed and care for themselves. They began then to fly from place to place about the room, and it became necessary to confine them in a cage. However, they were allowed the larger liberty of the sitting room for a portion of each day and were very tame and familiar, for a long period calling for food in the characteristic oriole way and begging with drooping fluttering wings of any one who came into the room.

By August 1 they were fully fledged and the downy first plumage of the head and body began to be replaced by the compact and finished plumage of the first autumn. The wing and tail feathers were, however, not moulted at this time.

During the first week in October, the birds were taken by me to Boston. Here I lived in rooms on the upper floor of a four-story house where there were no other birds in confinement, so that no song of any kind was heard by the birds while at this place.

Now I began to appreciate that both were female birds and also noted great temperamental differences in the two. One was timid, and the other taking advantage of this characteristic, scolded and chased the timid bird both in the cage and when at large in the room. So by name I began to distinguish them as Driver and Timid, which last soon became Timmy, a name always associated in my mind with Baltimore orioles.

At this time they had a single call note very like that of wild birds, but with a slightly different quality difficult to define, more abrupt, musical and much louder. They also had the peculiar rattling chatter associated with orioles. These were all their notes and were uttered rarely, the infant appeal so prevalent during the first four weeks of their lives having disappeared with their babyhood.

During the next few months their lives had no marked events. Each day they spent much time out of the cage at large in the room. Threads interested them, and hours were spent by the two birds in sewing, for I can use no other word, threads and strings into the wire bars of the cage they lived in. Without any semblance of weaving a nest or attempting to shape one, the birds simply tied and wove the threads into the wire until there were no loose ends. Ultimately thick bunches of thread and string on the bars characterized the cage.

I have told all this detail, really foreign to my thesis, because it seems important to record an inheritance so marked. The birds never learned to do more with threads than is here described, though they were ultimately allowed a room to live in with branches of trees to alight on, etc., and at least one of them laid eggs in an artificial nest.

On February 16, 1896, I took the birds by train from Boston to New York, where they spent the succeeding months until May 6 in a room in a large hotel. I wish to emphasize again two facts: both birds were females though I was not absolutely sure of it at this period, and, so far as I am aware, they heard no birds sing after I took them from their parents when about five days old, until after I took them to the country again on May 6, as will presently be related.

After reaching New York it was found expedient to keep them in separate cages when confined, though they were daily allowed much liberty at large in the room. During the last of February a partial moult occurred in both birds. This was chiefly the feathers of the head, throat and back. The wing and tail feathers were not shed.

Till now the two birds had looked so much alike, that in order to readily distinguish them I had early in October clipped the tips of the secondary feathers in one of Timmy's wings. This was a distinct mark even with the wings closed. But with the moult I am about to discuss, the birds ceased to be alike in appearance and were readily recognized.

Timmy in this moult acquired a distinct black throat patch, some black arrow-shaped marks in the feathers of the top of the head and decidedly dusky patches about the region of the ears. The throat patch extended over the throat proper. The entire period taken in completing this moult was about three weeks.

The other bird, Driver, did not acquire any decided black marking about the head, throat or ears, and only showed a few scattered tiny black feathers.

Before this moult was quite completed, during the latter part of February, the birds began to sing. The interval between the singing was sometimes several days, and only a very few minutes in each day were devoted to song. This song was very low and soft, and more or less broken, reminding one of the song of the white-throated sparrow (*Z. albicollis*) as it is heard during the fall and in the early spring migrations.

Timmy was the first to sing in this way, and the period of song when noticed was brief, not lasting more than about one minute. The song was not heard again for several days. Then it became of daily occurrence, and was gradually more prolonged and better sustained. About five days after Timmy began to sing, Driver sang also. Driver soon became the chief singer, so that Timmy's weaker song was not so noticeable. But both increased in volume, and frequency all through the month of March, and during April and the first half of May while daylight lasted, the song was incessant in both birds. It was now a loud clear series of notes of great brilliancy, and poured forth in such rapid succession as to be like that of the house wren (*T. aëdon*) in the intervals, and lasting about as long as the warble of that bird. Except for the 'rattle' which was now and then a part of the repertoire, this song had nothing in it that reminded one of the song of the Baltimore oriole as heard in New York, Massachusetts or at any point where the birds occur. Through the second week in May, the song of both birds gradually diminished.

I could generally, during the height of the song season, start the birds to sing by going to their cages, speaking to them and whistling a few notes. Here it seems essential to emphasize the fact that I in no way trained them to sing and made no effort to start them in song till long after their method of singing was established. In fact, the quality and phrasing of their singing was of such a character that none save an expert whistler could reproduce it.

Early in May of 1896 I took the birds to the country near New York, where we remained until July 20, 1897, a period of some fourteen months; then I moved to Princeton, New Jersey, where the remainder of their lives was passed. Both birds died during the winter of 1899–1900, apparently of old age.

To go back to the time of departure from New York in the spring of 1896. As has been stated, the birds' song became less frequent by the first week in May, and by the twentieth of that month they had ceased to sing. On June 6 I noticed the first signs of the summer moult and in a very few days it was in full progress.

It may be well to indicate some of the details of the change, though this is a divergence from the chief subject. Also, it should be borne in mind that native birds kept in confinement are generally about a month earlier in moulting and also in the song season, than are the representatives of the same species at liberty out of doors. This applies to all the species I have kept in confinement and when the birds are perfectly normal and healthy—so sound in health as to *breed in captivity*, which seems a good criterion. As examples, I may mention the bluebird (*S. sialis*), robin (*M. migratoria*), wood thrush (*H. mustelina*), catbird (*G. carolinensis*), brown thrasher (*H. rufus*), and the orchard oriole (*I. spurius*), all of which I have had live and breed and go through the song and moult seasons year after year in captivity.

The moulting period of the two orioles occupied a month, and early in July both were in most exquisite fall plumage. The deeper orange and rusty tint that is so characteristic of the species, and the suffusion of the black areas on the throat, were as marked and fine in detail as in wild birds. At this moult for the first time the larger wing and all the tail feathers were shed and replaced. The two birds were marvels of beauty at all times, but just after the full summer moult they filled those who saw them with admiration and wonder. After the moult there was a secondary song season of short duration. The song was of the same character, but not so prolonged or elaborate.

So I have endeavored to give an idea of a year, or rather more, of these birds' lives, and the succeeding years to the end were but repetitions with but slight variation.

Each year the wearing of the tips of the feathers was apparent in January, and a partial moult such as I have described took place late in that month or in February. Then began again the peculiar low soft song at infrequent intervals, presently becoming noticeable in volume and occurrence, till the song wave reached its height and died away. Each early June found the birds putting on an entirely new garment of feathers.

I have spoken before in this paper of the observations of a second generation. I find that this perhaps conveys a wrong impression. Let me say at once that the second generation consisted of a brood of young orioles in no way related to Timmy or Driver. However, for the purpose of my subject, really these were a second generation, of birds of a given kind, subject to the influence of older birds of their own species.

On June 15, 1897, when Timmy and

Driver had passed through the song seasons and had a well-established song formula of their own, I obtained a brood of Baltimore orioles which I believed to be about six days old. The birds were secured at South Orange, N. J., a point several hundreds of miles from the birthplace of my original birds, Timmy and Driver. I shall distinguish these birds, when speaking of them, as the brood of 1897. They were reared in the same way that the other orioles had been, except that they had the *society of, and were closely associated during their early lives with*, the two older orioles.

The moults occurred at the same intervals that I have indicated, and by the winter of 1897–1898 I was able to distinguish the sexes of my four new birds by the characteristics that correlate with sex. Three were males and assumed full nuptial plumage by a partial moult in late January and part of February. The fourth bird was a female.

On my coming to live in Princeton when these 1897 orioles were about seven weeks old, they, as well as Timmy and Driver, had an especial room given over to their use, and from that time on the birds knew little or nothing of cage life.

After the spring or, rather, late winter moult of 1898, Timmy and Driver began to sing as they had done in the two previous years. At this time friends, good field ornithologists, familiar with the conventional song of the Baltimore oriole, heard them both sing, and not having up to that time seen the birds, were at a loss to identify the song as being like anything they had ever heard.

Soon after Timmy and Driver began to sing, the 1897 birds one by one joined, and in a month all were singing a song not to be distinguished from that of the two older birds. They outlived Timmy and Driver a year or more and always sang as I believe they had been taught by older birds of their own kind. In short, only six orioles have ever sung this song, for I pursued the experiment no farther, other matters interfering.

My conclusion is that two birds, *isolated from their own kind and from all birds*, but with a strong inherited tendency to sing, originated a novel method of song, and that four birds, *isolated from wild representatives of their own kind, and associated with these two who had invented the new song*, learned it from them and never sang in any other way.

22

Reprinted by permission of Doubleday and Company, Inc., from pp. 501–507 of *Ideas in Modern Biology*, J. A. Moore, ed., Natural History Press, 1965.

SENSITIVE PERIODS AND IMPRINTING

W. H. Thorpe, SC.D., F. R. S.

Sub-Department of Animal Behavior, Madingley, Cambridge

I would like to start this section by referring to some experiments of my own on the song-learning of the chaffinch (*Fringilla coelebs*).

The first reference to a talking parrot antedates Aristotle by about a century; and it is obvious that as soon as man started to keep as pets birds such as parrots and starlings, he would have discovered that such species can imitate, with extraordinary accuracy, the sounds produced by beings very different from themselves. It was not, however, till the late seventeenth or early eighteenth century that naturalists seem to have realized that local song dialects can be developed in the wild as a result of song birds learning at least some details of their songs from their parents or neighbors, and so perpetuating a vocal tradition. But even this discovery led to no scientific development until the coming of high-fidelity recording and the electronic analysis of sound patterns at last made possible the scientific study of the subject. Since it is clear that in many, perhaps most, species of song birds the song is a reliable specific recognition mark, it follows that many bird songs must be an elaborate integration of inborn and learned components, the former constituting the basis for the latter. Such is the situation in the chaffinch (*Fringilla coelebs*).

A good example of a normal song of *Fringilla coelebs gengleri* is shown in Figure 17–1. The inborn component of the chaffinch song can be revealed by hand-rearing the young birds from early nestling life, either in acoustic isolation or at least out of contact with all chaffinch song. In the course of six experiments of this type, all the birds individually isolated produced songs of an extremely simple type (Figures 17–2 and 17–3) consisting of a song burst of approximately the correct length and made up of about the right number of notes. The fundamental frequency of these notes was somewhat lower than normal, and the songs produced by these isolates lacked the division into the three phrases so characteristic of the normal chaffinch song. Moreover, the final flourish and all the other fine details by which the chaffinch song is normally recognized were also absent. Of all the hundreds of wild and aviary-kept birds that have passed through our hands during the course of these experiments, none has produced songs of such extreme simplicity as these isolate birds, although such undeveloped songs are known to occur in the wild at times.

In contrast to the simple restricted song produced by the isolate birds, we find that if, after babyhood, two or more such birds are put together in a room, but still without the opportunity of hearing experienced chaffinches, they will develop more complex songs. It seems that the attempt to sing in company produces mutual stimulation that encourages the development of complexity. The members of each group of hand-reared birds thus kept together will, by mutual stimulation, build up a distinctive community pattern. What we have thus done is to make small communities of hand-reared birds, consisting of perhaps two, three, four, or five birds per group, the individuals of which can hear each other but are, as a group, still totally isolated from all experience of normal chaffinch song. In experiments of this kind the birds conform so closely to the chosen community pattern that it is sometimes barely possible to distinguish the song of one from another, even by electronic analysis. Figures 17–4, 17–5 and 17–6 show examples of song patterns for which this applied. It sometimes happens that, as Figure 17–6 shows, the song pattern produced by such birds is quite as complex as that of a normal wild chaffinch; but its complexity tends to be of a different kind, and the song thus produced may bear little resemblance to the characteristic utterance of the species.

If now, instead of taking young chaffinches from the nest, we catch them in the autumn of their first year so that, as juveniles, they will already have heard some song in the wild; and if we keep these birds singly and again isolated so that they cannot hear any other chaffinches, we find that they produce songs that are very much nearer normality than the birds treated in the experiments I have previously described. It is clear from the study of such songs that the birds have, during the autumn, learned that the

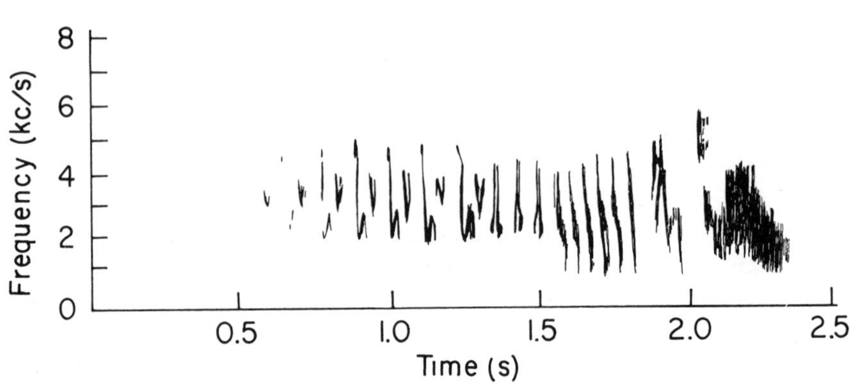

Figure 17–1. Chaffinch, *Fringilla coelebs gengleri*. Sound spectrogram of typical full song. (Madingley, Cambridge.)
Vertical scale: Frequency in kilocycles/second. Horizontal scale: time in seconds.

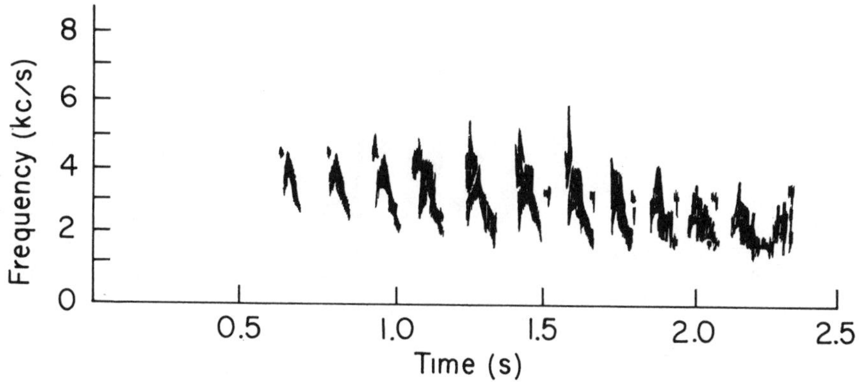

Figure 17–2. Song of chaffinch. Hand-reared in auditory isolation. Scales as in Figure 17–1.

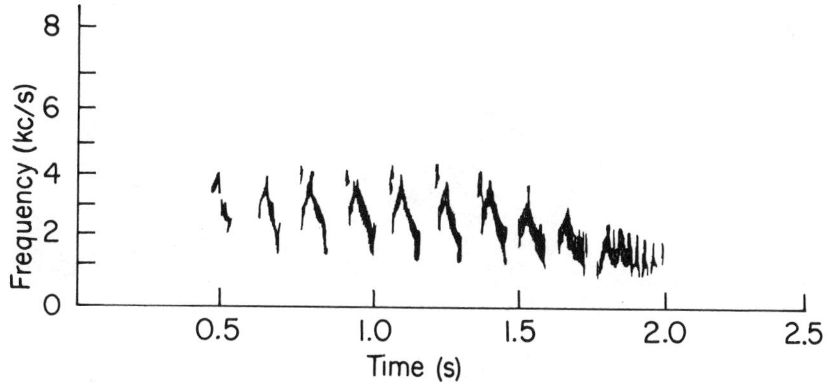

Figure 17–3. Song of hand-reared isolate, 24 June 1954. Scales as in Figure 17–1.

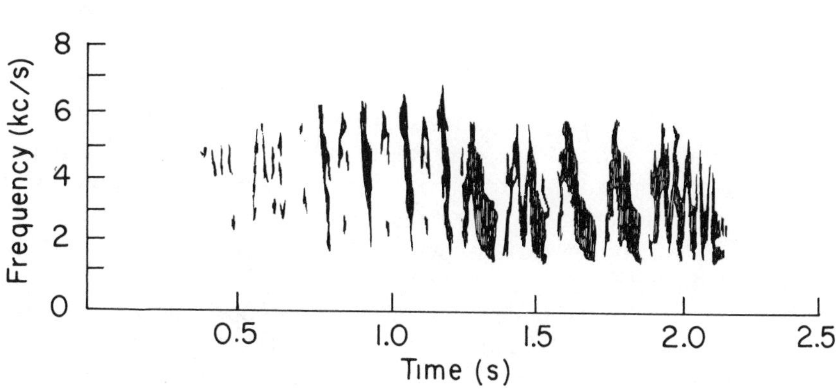

Figure 17–4. Song produced by one member of isolate group of two unrelated birds. Scale as in Figure 17–1.

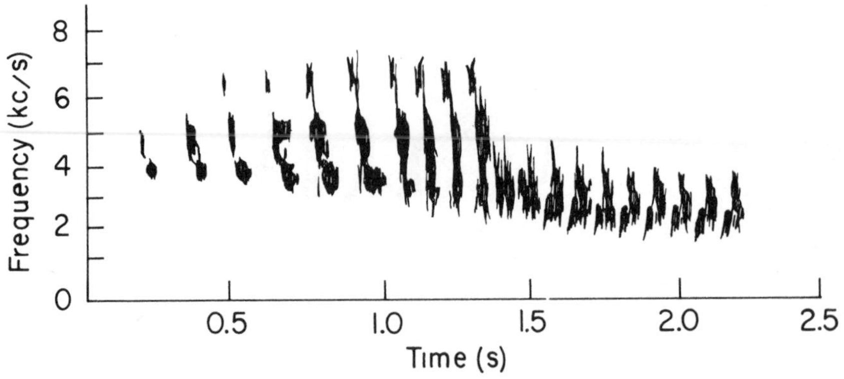

Figure 17–5. Full song of a member of an isolate group of five. Scales as in Figure 17–1.

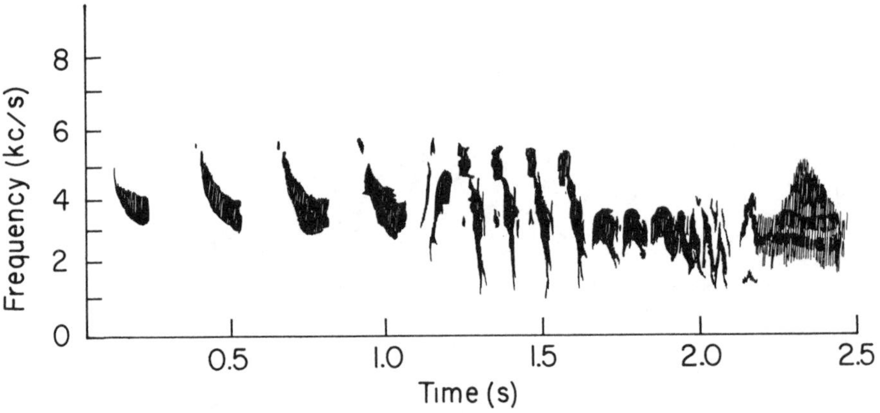

Figure 17–6. Full song of a bird from an isolate group of two. Scales as in Figure 17–1.

song "should be" divided into three sections and that a terminal flourish is an appropriate ending. The next step is to repeat this experiment but to keep the autumn-caught birds together in small isolated communities so that again a member of any one community will hear nothing but the songs of its community mates—that is, so that they can now, so to speak, pool the experience of their first few weeks of life.

Thus we now give the birds opportunity to develop in the spring songs constructed from (1) the inborn component, (2) material heard the previous autumn, and (3) material as elaborated by their cage mates of similar experience. Figure 17–7 shows what an autumn-caught first-year bird was able to produce by itself, and Figure 17–8 shows what such a

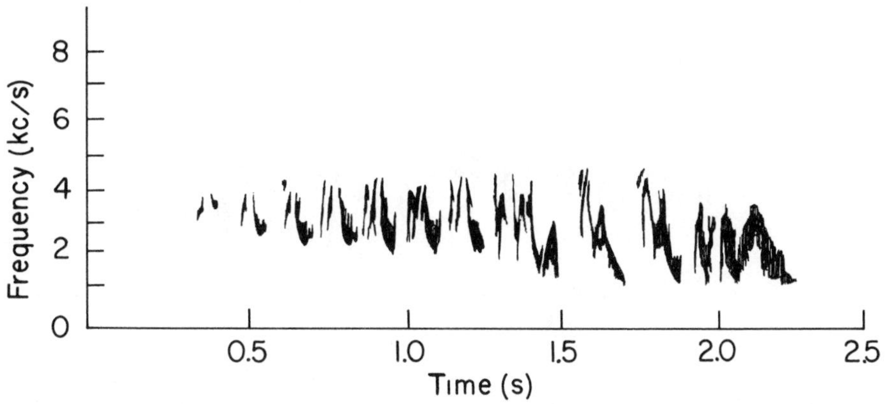

Figure 17–7. Song produced by a bird caught in the autumn of its first year and prevented from hearing full song of other chaffinches. The song is thus constructed out of the inborn component plus material heard in the previous autumn. Scales as in Figure 17–1.

bird was able to produce after it had had the experience of singing together with another bird of similarly restricted opportunities for a matter of about two weeks. Similarly, Figure 17–9 shows what a particular bird was able to produce from its previous song as a result of singing in company with one other bird of similar experience for a longer period. Thus these birds, by practicing together with other birds (Figure 17–10), were able to use the combination of their inborn blueprint and their previous autumn's experience to better advantage—that is, they were able to achieve a more normal song by means of group practice. Under these conditions it is found that there is a special tendency for the birds of the same group to match their song endings. There is little doubt that this is the way local song dialects are built up and perpetuated.

The important point to emphasize, as a result of this, is that in social animals the presence of social stimulation, even though it is apparently of a very inferior inexperienced kind, may be very important. In addition, it looks as though there are certain aspects of the song pattern that are so well coded, genetically, that the chaffinch can produce them without any help at all from any other individual.

There are other details of pattern that the mere singing in competition with other inexperienced individuals tends, so to speak, to realize—to bring to the surface. And, of course, there are yet other quite fine details of song pattern that are learned later and only from experienced individuals, and which can thus form the basis of local traditions in song. And so I think the one point coming from these studies that I wish particularly to emphasize, is *the importance, in animals that have any socialization at all, of the stimulus provided from siblings or other animals of the same age*. You see the same sort of thing in the "following" response of young

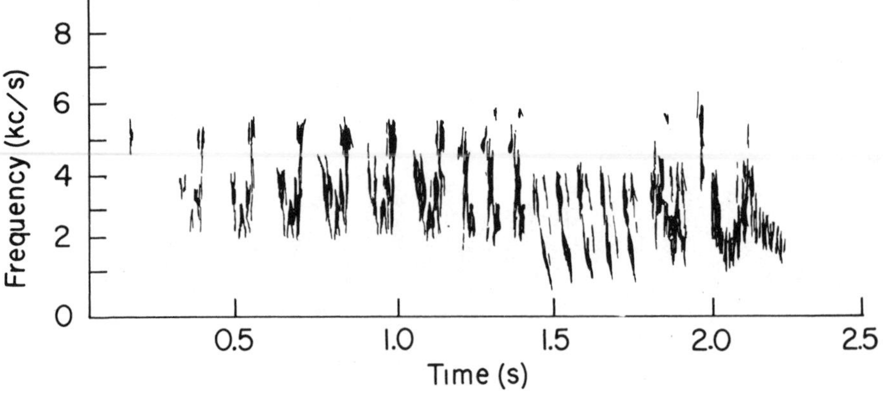

Figure 17–8. Song of autumn-caught chaffinch given opportunity the following spring to construct songs from (1) inborn component, (2) material heard the first autumn, (3) material as elaborated by cage mates of similar experience. Scales as in Figure 17–1.

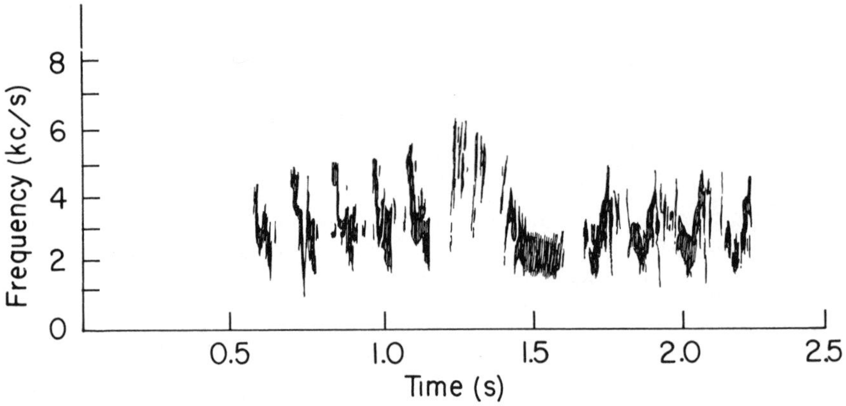

Figure 17–9. Re-articulated song produced for tutoring. End transferred to middle. Scales as in Figure 17–1.

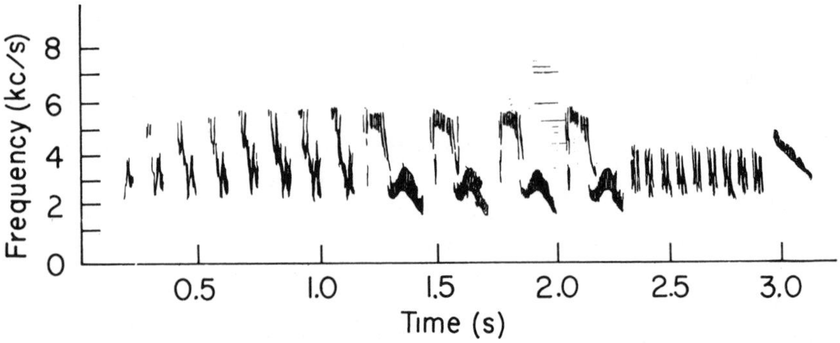

Figure 17–10. Continental tree pipit, *Anthus t. trivialis,* used as a model on song tutor. Scales as in Figure 17–1.

goslings—the following is greatly aided in the presence of siblings; they do much better than if they are kept alone.

From the experiments I have described, it appears that the difference between the hand-reared birds and those that had a normal fledgling and early juvenile life, but which were isolated from September onward, is explicable only on the assumption that some peculiarities of the normal song have been learned (or differentiated) in the earliest youth before the bird itself is able to produce any kind of full song. These peculiarities include, *first*, the tendency to produce a three-phrase song. In fact this must be due in part to latent components of the innate blueprint that are incapable of finding their expression in action without some help from associates. We know this from the fact that even the songs of isolated birds often show a slight trend in this direction of the production of three phrases—just enough to be indicative of an inborn tendency. *Second*, the birds that have had normal fledgling and early juvenile life appear to have learned that the terminal phrase should contain a more or less elaborate flourish—a performance the true isolates seem quite unable to emulate. Here again we have some evidence that there is an inherent tendency to pay attention to a flourish and that as soon as a flourish is heard under any circumstance, there is also a tendency to imitate it and tack it onto the end of the song. The details of this terminal phrase, with its flourish, are apparently not learned in September but are worked out by members of the group in competitive singing the following spring.

It seems therefore that, in the wild, young chaffinches must learn some details of song from their parents or from other adults in the first few weeks of life. At this stage the young bird appears to absorb the general pattern of division of the song into two or three phrases, with a flourish at the end; but not until the critical period during the following spring does the bird develop the finer details. This period is of course the time when the young wild chaffinch first sings in a territory in competition with neighboring birds of the same species, and there is good evidence that it learns the details of song from these neighbors. It may in fact learn two or three different songs, sometimes even more, from neighbors on different sides of its territory.

Thus we see that the full chaffinch song is an integration of an inborn (or self-differentiating) and of a learned (or socially-differentiated) song pattern; the former constitutes the basis for the latter. Although isolated chaffinches can work out for themselves very strange songs, those in the wild are presumably circumscribed by the general pattern of the chaffinch song characteristic of the locality, though of course they too may develop individual variations in the details.

23

Reprinted from *Science* **146**:1483–1486 (1964)

CULTURALLY TRANSMITTED PATTERNS OF VOCAL BEHAVIOR IN SPARROWS

Peter Marler and Miwako Tamura
Department of Zoology, University of California, Berkeley

Abstract. *Male white-crowned sparrows have song "dialects," acquired in about the first 100 days of life by learning from older males. In the laboratory an alien white-crowned sparrow dialect can be taught. Once the song is established further acoustical experience does not change the pattern. White-crowned sparrows do not copy recorded songs of other sparrow species presented under similar conditions.*

The white-crowned sparrow, *Zonotrichia leucophrys*, is a small song bird with an extensive breeding distribution in all but the southern and eastern parts of North America (*1*). Ornithologists have long remarked upon the geographical variability of its song. Physical analysis of field recordings of the several vocalizations of the Pacific Coast subspecies *Z. l. nuttalli* reveals that while most of the seven or so sounds which make up the adult repertoire vary little from one population to another, the song patterns of the male show striking variation (see *2*).

Each adult male has a single basic song pattern which, with minor variations of omission or repetition, is repeated throughout the season. Within a population small differences separate the songs of individual males but they all share certain salient characteristics of the song. In each discrete population there is one predominant pattern which differs in certain consistent respects from the patterns found in neighboring populations (Fig. 1). The term "dialect" seems appropriate for the properties of the song patterns that characterize each separate population of breeding birds. The detailed structure of syllables in the second part of the song is the most reliable indicator. Such dialects are known in other song birds (*3*).

The white-crowned sparrow is remarkable for the homogeneity of song patterns in one area. As a result the differences in song patterns between populations are ideal subjects for study of the developmental basis of behavior. If young male birds are taken from a given area, an accurate prediction can be made about several properties of the songs that would have developed if they had been left in their natural environment. Thus there is a firm frame of reference with which to compare vocal patterns developing under experimental conditions. Since 1959 we have raised some 88 white-crowned sparrows in various types of acoustical environments and observed the effects upon their vocal behavior. Here we report on the adult song patterns of 35 such experimental male birds. The several types of acoustical chamber in which they were raised will be described elsewhere.

In nature a young male white-crown hears abundant singing from its father and neighbors from 20 to about 100 days after fledging. Then the adults stop singing during the summer molt and during the fall. Singing is resumed again in late winter and early spring, when

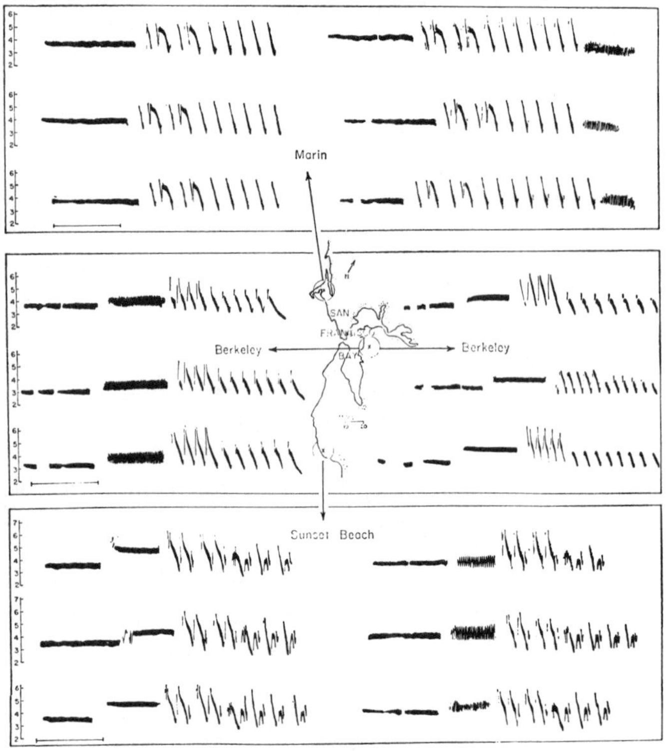

Fig. 1. Sound spectrograms of songs of 18 male white-crowned sparrows from three localities in the San Francisco Bay area. The detailed syllabic structure of the second part of the song varies little within an area but is consistently different between populations. The introductory or terminal whistles and vibrati show more individual variability. The time marker indicates 0.5 second and the vertical scale is marked in kilocycles per second.

the young males of the previous year begin to participate. Young males captured between the ages of 30 and 100 days, and raised in pairs in divided acoustical chambers, developed song patterns in the following spring which matched the dialect of their home area closely. If males were taken as nestlings or fledglings when 3 to 14 days of age and kept as a group in a large soundproof room, the process of song development was very different. Figure 2 shows sound spectrograms of the songs of nine males taken from three different areas and raised as a group. The patterns lack the characteristics of the home dialect. Moreover, some birds from different areas have strikingly similar patterns (*A3*, *B2*, and *C4* in Fig. 2).

Males taken at the same age and individually isolated also developed songs which lacked the dialect characteristics (Fig. 3). Although the dialect properties are absent in such birds isolated in groups or individually, the songs do have some of the species-specific characterisitcs. The sustained tone in the introduction is generally, though not always, followed by a repetitive series of shorter sounds, with or without a sustained tone at the end. An ornithologist would identify such songs as utterances of a *Zonotrichia* species.

Males of different ages were exposed to recorded sounds played into the acoustical chambers through loudspeakers. One male given an alien dialect (8 minutes of singing per day) from the 3rd to 8th day after hatching, and individually isolated, showed no effects of the training. Thus the early experience as a nestling probably has little specific effect. One of the group-raised isolates was removed at about 1 year of age and given 10 weeks of daily training with an alien dialect in an open cage in the laboratory. His song pattern was unaffected. In general, acoustical experience seems to have no effect on the song pattern after males reach adulthood. Birds taken as fledglings aged from 30 to 100 days were given an alien dialect for a 3-week period, some at about 100 days of age, some at 200, and some at 300 days of age. Only the training at the age of 100 days had a slight effect upon the adult song. The other groups developed accurate versions of the home dialect. Attention is thus focused on the effects of training between the ages of about 10 and 100 days. Two males were placed in individual isolation at 5 and 10 days of age, respectively, and were exposed alternately to the songs of a normal white-crowned sparrow and a bird of a different species. One male

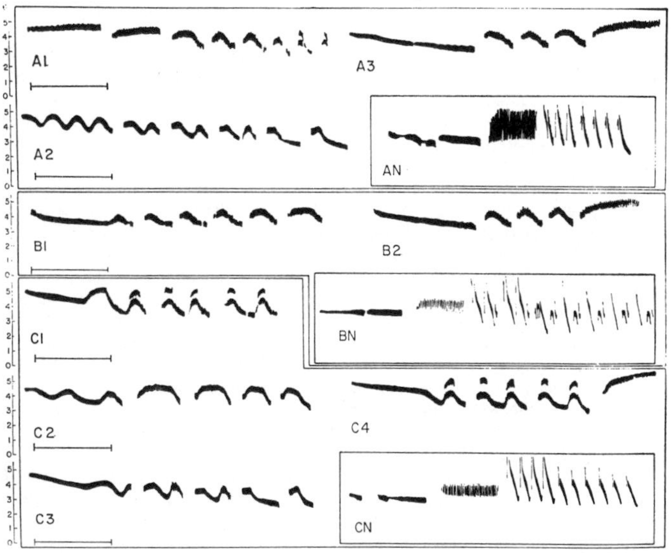

Fig. 2. Songs of nine males from three areas raised together in group isolation. *A1* to *A3*, Songs of individuals born at Inspiration Point, 3 km northeast of Berkeley. *B1* and *B2*, Songs of individuals born at Sunset Beach. *C1* to *C4*, Songs of individuals born in Berkeley. The inserts (*AN*, *BN*, and *CN*) show the home dialect of each group.

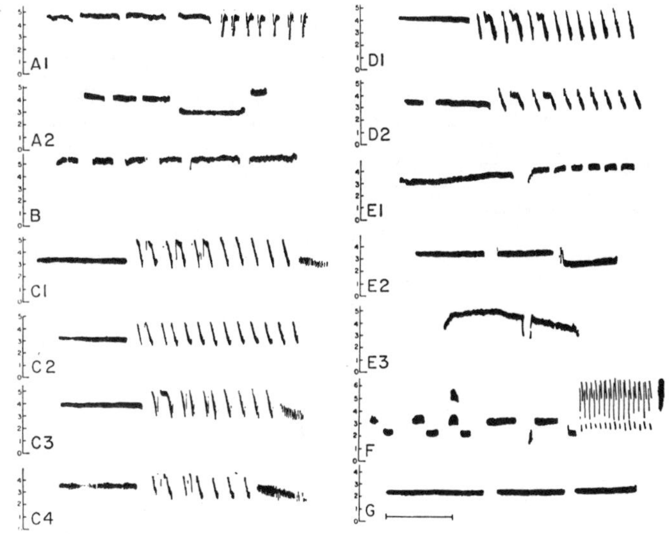

Fig. 3. Songs of 12 males raised under various experimental conditions. *A1* and *A2*, Birds raised in individual isolation. *B*, Male from Sunset Beach trained with Marin song (see Fig. 1) from the 3rd to the 8th day of age. *C1* to *C4*, Marin birds brought into the laboratory at the age of 30 to 100 days. *C1*, Untrained. *C2* to *C4*, Trained with Sunset Beach songs; *C2* at about 100 days of age, *C3* at 200 days, *C4* at 300 days. *D1*, Bird from Sunset Beach trained with Marin white-crowned sparrow song and a Harris's sparrow song (see *G*) from the age of 35 to 56 days. *D2*, Marin bird trained with Marin white-crowned sparrow song and a song-sparrow song (see *F*) from the age of 6 to 28 days. *E1* to *E3*, Two birds from Sunset Beach and one from Berkeley trained with song-sparrow song from the age of 7 to 28 days. *F*, A song-sparrow training song for *D2* and *E1* to *E3*. *G*, A Harris's sparrow training song for *D1*.

was exposed at 6 to 28 days, the other at 35 to 56 days. Both developed fair copies of the training song which was the home dialect for one and an alien dialect for the other. Although the rendering of the training song is not perfect, it establishes that the dialect patterns of the male song develop through learning from older birds in the first month or two of life. Experiments are in progress to determine whether longer training periods are necessary for perfect copying of the training pattern.

The training song of the white-crowned sparrow was alternated in one case with the song of a song sparrow, *Melospiza melodia*, a common bird in the areas where the white-crowns were taken, and in the other case with a song of a Harris's sparrow, *Zonotrichia querula*. Neither song seemed to have any effect on the adult patterns of the experimental birds. To pursue this issue further, three males were individually isolated at 5 days of age and trained with song-sparrow song alone from about the 9th to 30th days. The adult songs of these birds bore no resemblance to the training patterns and resembled those of naive birds (Fig. 3). There is thus a predisposition to learn white-crowned sparrow songs in preference to those of other species.

The songs of white-crowned sparrows raised in isolation have some normal characteristics. Recent work by Konishi (*4*) has shown that a young male must be able to hear his own voice if these properties are to appear. Deafening in youth by removal of the cochlea causes development of quite different songs, with a variable broken pattern and a sibilant tone, lacking the pure whistles of the intact, isolated birds. Furthermore, there is a resemblance between the songs of male white-crowned sparrows deafened in youth and those of another species, *Junco oreganus*, subjected to similar treatment. The songs of intact juncos and white-crowns are quite different. Konishi also finds that males which have been exposed to the dialect of their birthplace during the sensitive period need to hear themselves before the memory trace can be translated into motor activity. Males deafened after exposure to their home dialects during the sensitive period, but before they start to sing themselves, develop songs like those of a deafened naive bird. However, once the adult pattern of singing has become established then deafening has little or no effect upon it. Konishi infers that in the course of crystallization of the motor pattern some control mechanism other than auditory feedback takes over and becomes adequate to maintain its organization. There are thus several pathways impinging upon the development of song patterns in the white-crowned sparrow, including acoustical influences from the external environment, acoustical feedback from the bird's own vocalizations, and perhaps nonauditory feedback as well.

Cultural transmission is known to play a role in the development of several types of animal behavior (*5*). However, most examples consist of the reorientation through experience of motor patterns, the basic organization of which remains little changed. In the development of vocal behavior in the white-crowned sparrow and certain other species of song birds, we find a rare case of drastic reorganization of whole patterns of motor activity through cultural influence (*6*). The process of acquisition in the white-crowned sparrow is interesting in that, unlike that of some birds (*7*), it requires no social bond between the young bird and the emitter of the copied sound, such as is postulated as a prerequisite for speech learning in human children (*8*). The reinforcement process underlying the acquisition of sound patterns transmitted through a loudspeaker is obscure.

References and Notes

1. R. C. Banks, *Univ. Calif. Berkeley Publ. Zool.* **70**, 1 (1964).
2. P. Marler and M. Tamura, *Condor* **64**, 368 (1962).
3. E. A. Armstrong, *A Study of Bird Song* (Oxford Univ. Press, London, 1963).
4. M. Konishi, in preparation.
5. W. Etkin, *Social Behavior and Organization Among Vertebrates* (Univ. of Chicago Press, Chicago, 1964).
6. W. Lanyon, in *Animal Sounds and Communication, AIBS Publ. No. 7*, W. Lanyon and W. Tavolga, Eds. (American Institute of Biological Sciences, Washington, D.C., 1960), p. 321; W. H. Thorpe, *Bird Song. The Biology of Vocal Communication and Expression in Birds* (Cambridge Univ. Press, London, 1961); G. Thielcke, *J. Ornithol.* **102**, 285 (1961); P. Marler, in *Acoustic Behaviour of Animals*, R. G. Busnel, Ed. (Elsevier, Amsterdam, 1964), p. 228.
7. J. Nicolai, *Z. Tierpsychol.* **100**, 93 (1959).
8. O. H. Mowrer, *J. Speech Hearing Disorders* **23**, 143 (1958).

9. M. Konishi, M. Kreith, and J. Mulligan cooperated generously in locating and raising the birds and conducting the experiments. W. Fish and J. Hartshorne gave invaluable aid in design and construction of soundproof boxes. We thank Dr. M. Konishi and Dr. Alden H. Miller for reading and criticizing this manuscript. The work was supported by a grant from the National Science Foundation.

14 September 1964

24

Reprinted from *Ibis* **111**:386–387 (1969)

THE "CRITICAL PERIOD" FOR SONG LEARNING

Fernando Nottebohm

Rockefeller University and New York Zoological Society

The restriction of song learning to a certain period in the bird's life has already been described for several species. Some authors (Koehler 1951, 'J. Orn. Lpz'. 93 : 3–20; Poulsen 1954, 'Dansk orn. Foren. Tidsskr.' 48 : 32–37; Thorpe 1958, 'Ibis' 100 : 535–570) have likened the "critical period" for song learning to the processes occurring during imprinting: the song is learned during a sensitive period; after the end of this sensitive period further acoustic stimuli do not alter the bird's song repertoire.

It is not always clear, however, *what* kind of learning is restricted to the "critical period". In two cases, at least (Lanyon 1957, 'Publs Nuttall orn. Club' 1 : 1–67; Thorpe 1958, *loc cit.*), the evidence presented only refers to an end in the observed capacity to acquire new *motor* patterns of song. In two other cases (Marler & Tamura 1964, 'Science' 146: 1,483–1,486; Immelmann 1966, 'Verh. dt. zool. Ges.' 320–332) the "critical period" refers specifically to the bird's ability to acquire the *auditory* information after which it will shape its own song.

In the Chaffinch *Fringilla coelebs*, the critical period for song learning lasts during the first ten months of the bird's life (Thorpe 1958, *loc. cit.*). At the end of these ten months the bird establishes its song themes in their final stereotyped pattern, a process known as "crystallization" of song. Once this process comes to an end a Chaffinch will not alter its song themes nor add new ones. Its song repertoire remains virtually unchanged in future years.

What factors determine the onset and closure of the critical period for song learning? Is it a strictly age-dependent phenomenon occurring during a particular stage in the maturation of the nervous system, or does its incidence depend on more subtle hormonal and experiential factors? In the Chaffinch singing behaviour is under the control of rising testosterone levels (Collard & Grevendal 1946, 'Gerfaut' 2 : 89–107; Poulsen 1951, 'Behaviour' 3 : 216–228). Song makes its first appearance in early spring, when birds born the previous season are some nine months old.

The following experiment was undertaken. A young male Chaffinch was trapped near Cambridge, England, during December 1964. This bird was castrated on 7 January 1965, and placed in a room where it could hear other wild Chaffinches singing. With the onset of spring the beak of this bird did not turn blue, as is usually the case in males under the influence of rising testosterone levels (Collard & Grevendal 1946, *loc. cit.*). A year later, on 31 January 1966, this bird was placed in a sound-proof box under a schedule of 16 hours daylight and eight hours darkness. This procedure was continued until 1 March, without the bird ever being heard to produce song or subsong. During this time the beak did not turn blue, showing that there had been no significant regrowth of testicular tissue.

In the spring of 1966 this bird was two years old, and as yet had had no singing experience. On 1 March of that year it was subcutaneously implanted with a 10 mg testosterone propionate pellet (trade mark: Oreton, produced by the Schering Corporation, Bloomfield, New Jersey). On 6 March it was heard doing rather complex subsong. On 7 and 8 March it was recorded doing "plastic" full song (Plate 15)—i.e., the song themes were still being developed and had not crystallized. Sound-spectrographic analysis of the recording of 8 March showed the bird was developing normal song (Nottebohm 1967, 'Proc, XIV Int. orn. Congr.': 265–280; 1968, 'Ibis' 110: 549–568), and permitted a reasonable prediction of what the future full song of this bird would be like after it crystallized. Taking into account this prediction, a tutor tape was produced with two full-song themes (Plate 15) with a syllabic composition different from

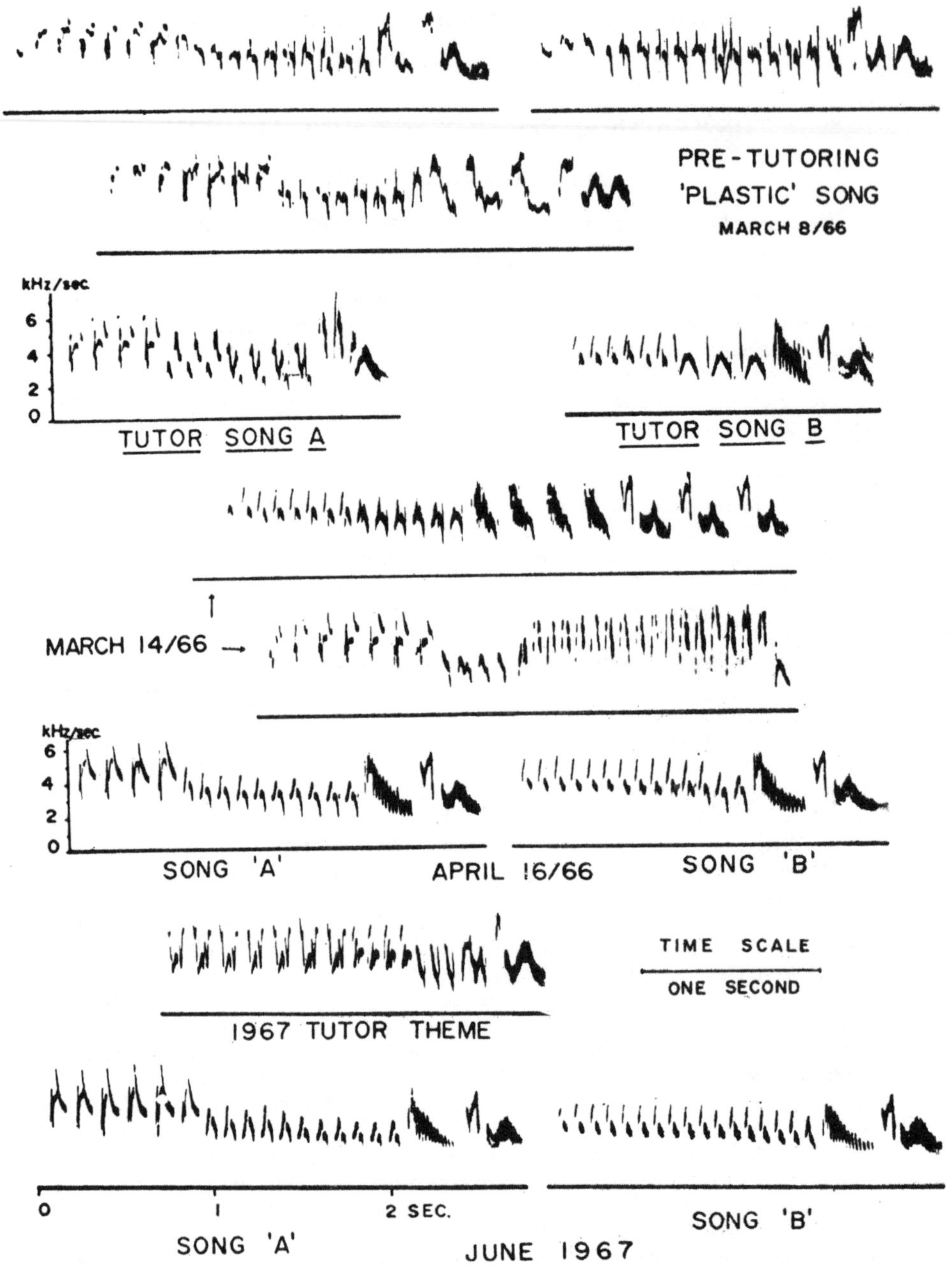

PLATE 15. Pre- and post-tutoring song of a castrate male Chaffinch. Elements from tutor songs A and B were imitated during "plastic" song (14 March 1966). Components of tutor song B were retained in the final version of songs 'A' and 'B' (16 April 1966). Their two songs were repeated with small changes in the following year (June 1967). The tutor theme used in 1967 had no effect on the song structure of the experimental bird.

the song of the experimental bird. These two full song themes were recorded from two wild-caught adult Chaffinches.

Tutoring with this tape, for two or three hours daily, started in the afternoon of 8 March and was continued until 20 March. On 14 March the experimental bird was recorded doing plastic song which included many imitated components from tutor themes A and B (Plate 15). On 16 April it was heard producing full song in a very stereotyped and repetitive fashion. On that day its two full song themes, ' A ' and ' B ', showed unmistakably the influence of tutor song B (Plate 15).

The 1966 tutoring experiment was repeated in the spring of 1967, under similar conditions, with the same bird and using a different wild-type tutor theme. Results were negative (Plate 15), the song repertoire of the previous year being retained with little change and without new additions.

These observations show that a Chaffinch can develop a normal *motor* pattern of song well after the usual " critical period " for song learning is over. Furthermore, at two years of age a Chaffinch that has not yet sung retains the ability to incorporate new auditory stimuli into its song. The end of the critical period for song learning is not an age-dependent phenomenon. Rather, it follows the crystallization of song, at whatever age this occurs. It is not possible at this time, however, to decide whether this termination results from the crystallization of song as a motor pattern, or whether it is determined by its accompanying high testosterone levels.

The observed loss of readiness to acquire new songs could be brought about by different mechanisms: (1) a loss of motor plasticity to develop new songs; (2) a loss of the ability to acquire new auditory song templates—i.e., auditory models with reference to which the bird might develop its own song (Konishi 1965, ' Z Tierpsychol.' 22 : 770–783). Either loss could be an absolute one and reflect physiological changes in the nervous tissue concerned, affecting the ability to acquire new sensory or motor information. Or the loss could be a motivational one, affecting the bird's predisposition to acquire new auditory templates and convert them into a motor pattern.

In species such as the White-crowned Sparrow *Zonotrichia leucophrys* (Marler & Tamura 1964, *loc. cit.*) and the Zebra Finch *Taenopygia guttata* (Immelmann 1965, ' Naturwiss.' 7 : 169–170; Immelmann 1966, *loc. cit.*), the end of the " critical learning period " occurs before the actual incidence of full song. Motor learning in this case cannot be invoked as the immediate cause for the observed end of the critical period. It is conceivable, however, that even in these species postponement of the motor learning of song would result in a " critical period " recurring in successive years, under normally recurring hormonal conditions.

It seems likely that the critical period for song learning in birds is not a unitary phenomenon, but rather results from the interaction of two critical periods: one for the learning of the auditory template, and one for motor learning. The two periods may overlap or not, and to varying extents in different species. In the Chaffinch the termination of both periods seems to occur simultaneously. In this case a temporally restricted motor learning may impose an end to the *manifestation* of further auditory learning. An independent manipulation of these two phenomena should throw considerable light on our understanding of the " critical period for song learning " and the physiological events underlying it.

The author is indebted to Professor W. H. Thorpe for space and facilities made available for him at Madingley, Cambridge University. Professor Peter Marler, Rockefeller University, read the manuscript and made helpful suggestions. The work reported here was supported by NSF GB 5274 to Professor Marler.

Editor's Comments on Papers 25 and 26

25 **HEBB**
Experiment: Infant Experience and Adult Problem-Solving

26 **FORGAYS and READ**
Crucial Periods for Free-Environmental Experience in the Rat

EFFECTS OF ENRICHING THE ENVIRONMENT

D. O. Hebb (Paper 25) was impressed by the barrenness of the environment in which most captive animals live and hypothesized that this very limited kind of experience would lower their ability to deal with problem-solving experiences in later life. He therefore took some rats home, let his children play with them as pets, and found them highly superior to the control rats that had been raised in the usual laboratory conditions. Later experimenters standardized the enriching experience by providing large cages filled with obstacles, playthings, and/or other rats. These rats also were superior to those raised in barren cages. Forgays and Read (Paper 26) found that the standard enriching experience was most effective if given from weaning up through ninety days of age, which is roughly the time of maturity in the rat. A slightly greater effect was noticed during the first three weeks after weaning. Similar experience at later ages gave much poorer results, indicating that the rat brain had become stably organized by this time.

These results are reminiscent of the prepubertal critical period for intellectual organization which we have hypothesized for humans. Actually, this line of research had a tremendous effect on the attempts to compensate for ghetto experience in school children and was largely responsible for such programs as Head Start, which aims at giving disadvantaged children a much wider sort of early experience. The first evaluation of the results of these programs was somewhat discouraging (Weikart and Lambie, 1970), but there are now indications of long-range benefits (White, 1977). In both rats and humans, the indicated critical period for these effects is long, extending from weaning to puberty. This being the case, the enrichment experience could profitably be extended in humans until at least ten years of age.

25

Reprinted from pp. 296–299 of *The Organization of Behavior,* Donald O. Hebb, John Wiley and Sons, Inc., 1949, 335 pp.

EXPERIMENT: INFANT EXPERIENCE AND ADULT PROBLEM-SOLVING

Donald O. Hebb

When we test human intelligence, we always assume that the subject has had a certain body of experience common to all "normal" children in the community, the experience whose *lack* may invalidate comparison of the innate potential of subjects from different communities. Apart entirely from controversy about the effect of special experiences on the IQ, we are all agreed, in this sense, on the effect of a certain kind of experience (which is not, however, well defined).

One purpose of the experimental work briefly described here was to find out more about how the ordinary experience of infancy affects mature behavior. It was not certain that such effects could be found in rat behavior, even if they exist for man;

but if one could find some trace of them in rat behavior their nature could be investigated much more easily in a species that reaches maturity in three months than in one that takes fifteen years. Also, the clinical evidence reviewed in this chapter has indicated that the effect of early experience is not found equally in all forms of behavior. Accordingly, these were exploratory experiments, with the main object of establishing the existence of some lasting effect of early experience on the later problem-solving of the rat. The first explorations gave wholly negative results, but they have the value of showing that some behavior is *not* affected by early experience; that is, they serve to delimit the effect.

In the first part of the study, one group of 7 animals were blinded in infancy, and a group of 7 littermates were blinded at maturity. Both groups were handled frequently, and were allowed daily to run outside their cages in a large space in which there were a number of objects. The question asked was this. Would the group with vision during growth learn something about finding their way around that they would retain after being blinded at maturity? Would this affect their behavior permanently, in other situations than those in which their visual experience occurred?

At the age of five months—two months after the second group were blinded—the rats were trained to find food in one of four containers in an open field. Two hundred trials were given, and the learning was not complete for most of the animals in this time—so this presumably is to be classed as rote learning rather than insightful. A second period of training in a similar task also appeared to give rote learning, and in neither could any significant difference be found between the two groups, early- and late-blinded.

At this point, however, a chance observation suggested the possibility that an "intelligence test" for the rat (Hebb and Williams, 1946) might reveal differences between the groups. Although the test had been meant for normal animals, it might work with the blind as well.

The test showed a clear difference between the groups. By this time the experiment was being done with only 3 late-blinded animals and 4 early-blinded, a small number for statistical significance. However, there was no overlap of scores in the two groups—all 3 late-blinded were better than all 4 early-blinded, which is certainly significant.*

Before repeating and confirming this result, it appeared profitable to explore further. The effect of vision during development, on the behavior of rats after being blinded at maturity, was great; would other variations of experience also have effects that could be detected by this—apparently sensitive—method of testing? The obvious experiment was to compare rats reared in ordinary small cages with others that had had the run of a wider environment. Two litters were taken home to be reared as pets,† a first group of 3 (after 1 mortality at home) and a second group of 4. They were out of their cages a good deal of the time and running about the house. While this was being done, 25 cage-reared rats from the same colony were tested.

When the pet group were tested, all 7 scored in the top third of the total distribution for cage-reared and pets. More important still, the pets improved their relative standing in the last 10 days of testing, following 10 days of preliminary training, and 11 days of testing (a total of 21 tests was used). One explanation of the better scores of the pets is just that they were tamer, more used to handling, and less disturbed by testing. But, if this were so, the longer the cage-reared animals were worked with the closer they would come to the pet group, as the cage-reared became tamer with prolonged handling. On the contrary, the pets improved more than the cage-reared. This means that *the richer experience of the pet group during development made*

* The experiments described in this section are now being repeated and carried further by B. Hymovitch and H. Lansdell, and will be reported in detail later. The method has been considerably improved since the first report of Hebb and Williams; it will be described in detail in a separate publication. The essential features of the method are: (1) 10 to 14 days' preliminary training gets the animal used to handling, to the test situation, and to daily changes in the route he must take to food, and teaches him where the food is to be found (its position is constant throughout); (2) the test itself is a series of 20 to 24 separate problems, each relatively easy for the seeing rat; he is given between 6 and 10 trials with each, and his score is the total number of entries into error zones (see figure 17, p. 137).

† Grateful acknowledgments are due to the Misses Jane and Ellen Hebb, ages seven and five, for their enthusiastic assistance in the investigation.

them better able to profit by new experiences at maturity—one of the characteristics of the "intelligent" human being. Furthermore, a measure of motivation and tameness in the cage-reared was available, and the correlation of this with the test score was negligible (0.13 ± 0.19).

These results show a permanent effect of early experience on problem-solving at maturity: "permanent," because, in the first experiment with early- and late-blinded, visual experience that ended at three months of age had marked effects at eight months of age (a long period in the life of a rat); and because, in the second experiment, the pet group improved its standing compared to the others as experience increased. Differences of early experience can produce differences in adult problem-solving that further experience does not erase.

These preliminary results are already being confirmed by more elaborate experiments now going on, and a principle is established that, first, is fully in accord with other evidence showing lasting and generalized effects of early experience (Chapter 6) and, secondly, clarifies the interpretation of existing data concerning human intelligence-test performance.

26

Reprinted from *J. Comp. Physiol. Psychol.* 55:816–818 (1962)

CRUCIAL PERIODS FOR FREE-ENVIRONMENTAL EXPERIENCE IN THE RAT[1]

DONALD G. FORGAYS AND JANET MICHELSON READ

Rutgers University

Psychologists have known for some time that the type of early experience provided an animal can influence his adult performance on a variety of tasks (Beach & Jaynes, 1954). Recently, researchers (Bingham & Griffiths, 1952; Forgays & Forgays, 1952; Forgus, 1954; and others) have demonstrated that rats reared in large complex environments are superior in problem-solving ability to rats reared under more restricted conditions. In addition, Hymovitch (1952) found evidence indicating that the enriched experience must occur before maturity if it is to lead to the reported effect. In a study using form discrimination as the response measure, Forgus (1954) reported that the enriched experience must occur extremely early in the life of the rat. In this latter study, testing of the two groups of animals constituting the design was accomplished well before full maturity of the rats so that in this sense, at least, the results cannot be compared directly with those of Hymovitch.

As yet there has not been reported a systematic investigation of several quite important aspects of the early-experience issue; namely, just how much experience is necessary in these complex environments to produce a superior adult animal, and when, specifically, during early life must this experience occur, assuming that it must take place before full maturity. A still more interesting matter is the interaction of these two dimensions, that is, the possibility that a greater amount of experience occurring during one developmental period produces the same results in the adult animal as a smaller quantity of such experience during another period. Moreover, it would be desirable in any such studies to examine the functioning of the adult animals on a variety of intellectual, emotionality, and other measures.

The present study is an attempt to investigate in part the second of the issues raised above; that is, When, specifically, during the relatively short maturation period of the rat, must a limited amount of exposure to a complex environment occur in order to effect superior problem-solving ability in the adult animal?

[1] This study was supported in part by a research grant from the Rutgers University Research Council.

METHOD

Apparatus

Exposure to the complex environment was provided by placing the animal *S*s for certain periods of time during early life in a large box 49 in. long, 28 in. wide, and 11 in. high. The box had wire-mesh sides and top; in it were placed several wooden and metal objects ("playthings") which have been described elsewhere (Forgays & Forgays, 1952). This setting is referred to below as Free Environment (FE).

Subjects

This study was run in a modified replication design in two phases. In the initial phase, data on Groups 3, 4, 5, and nine animals of Group 2 were collected (see Table 1 for group descriptions). In the second phase, run several months later, data on Groups 1 and 6 and the remaining eight animals of Group 2 were collected.

In the initial phase of this study, 36 male albino rats of the Rutgers University Psychology Laboratory strain were assigned at random to four groups of 9 animals each. These animals were all members of eight litters born within a few days of each other. For the second phase of the study, 24 rats of the same strain were assigned at random to three groups of 8 each. These animals were all members of five litters born within a few days of each other.

Procedure

In the initial phase of the study, when the animals averaged 21 days of age, the first group of nine animals was placed in the FE box; the other three groups were placed in small laboratory cages in the same general location of the laboratory as the FE box. Twenty-one days later, the second group of nine animals was placed in the FE box and the first group removed to the small cages. This procedure was repeated in subsequent 3-week periods for the remaining two groups. When the fourth group was taken out of the FE box, all of these animals averaged 111 days of age; all *S*s were then housed in small cages.

In the second phase of the study, the first group of eight animals was placed in the FE box within 20 hr. after birth and remained until 21 days of age. One of the mother animals, of the five available, was placed in the box with the pups to care for them during this period. When this first group averaged 21 days of age, it was removed and replaced with another group of eight animals which were 22 days of age upon entry to the FE box and 43 days old when they were removed

TABLE 1

MEAN ACTIVITY SCORES AND MEAN ERROR AND STANDARD DEVIATION SCORES OF THE SIX GROUPS OF *S*s ON THE HEBB-WILLIAMS TEST AND *t*'S OF THE VARIOUS MEAN COMPARISONS

Group	N	Time of Enriched Experience (Days of Age)	Mean Entries of Y Maze	Hebb-Williams Test		*t*				
				Mean Error Score	Standard Deviation	2	3	4	5	6
1	8	0–21	74.88	174.25	15.56	2.53*	1.30	1.08	0.21	2.15*
2	17	22–43	73.59	153.29	25.29		0.64	0.56	2.07*	3.70**
3	9	44–65	67.67	160.33	25.34			0.02	1.22	2.70*
4	9	66–87	63.67	160.56	31.94				1.07	2.37*
5	9	88–109	61.00	176.67	28.00					1.38
6	8	No enriched experience	69.52	195.75	25.41					

* $p < .05$.
** $p < .01$.

to the small laboratory cages from which they had come. This group is a replication of one of the groups of the earlier phase. A third group of eight animals (Control) received no experience in the FE box.

All animals were weaned at 21 days of age. During rearing, the FE box and small cages were cleaned once a week; care was taken at these times to handle all animals equally. Animals of all groups were confined in the small laboratory cages in groups of four or five rats.

When the animals were approximately 114 days old, each was placed for two 5-min. trials, one per day, on an elevated Y maze, the arms of which were 30 in. long and 6 in. wide. The total amount of activity (in terms of number of 10-in. sections entered), the number of urinations, and the number of boli excreted were recorded for each animal.

When the animals were about 123 days old, they began training on the Hebb-Williams maze (Rabinovitch & Rosvold, 1951). After training for 1 week, the rats were exposed to the 12 test problems at the rate of one per day. They were food-deprived for approximately 23 hr. prior to running each problem and were fed for an hour after each.

RESULTS

The results of the two phases of this study are presented and discussed together below. Data obtained from Group 2 animals, split over the two phases, were quite comparable over the two runnings for all measures and thus are combined.

Incidence of urination and defecation on the Y maze was negligible and is not reported here; there were no group differences on the basis of few such responses. Results of the activity measure averaged for the two trials are presented in Table 1. As seen there, the differences among the six groups of this study are slight, the animals having had the earliest FE exposure demonstrating a bit more activity than the other groups. None of these means is significantly different from any other.

The mean error scores of the six groups of animals on the 12 Hebb-Williams closed-field problems are given in Table 1. As seen there, Group 2 animals, which had the FE exposure from 22 to 43 days, made the fewest errors; Group 6 animals, which had no FE exposure, made the greatest number of errors; and the remaining four groups of animals made error scores at points between these extremes.

Statistical analysis of the significance of the differences between the various mean error scores was made by *t* test and the results are reported with appropriate probability statements in Table 1. As seen there, the animals which had no FE exposure (Group 6) made significantly more errors, at the .05 level of confidence or better, than all other groups of the study except the group of animals which had the FE exposure at a time when a rat could be considered a mature animal, between 88 and 109 days of age (Group 5).

As can also be seen in Table 1, Group 2, which received the FE exposure for 3 weeks immediately after weaning, made significantly fewer errors on the closed-field test than Group 1 (FE exposure during the first 3 weeks of life) and Group 5 (FE exposure at about the time of maturity), in addition to the Group 6 difference mentioned above.

DISCUSSION

While reference to Table 1 reveals reasonably large percentage differences among the activity scores of the various groups of animals tested, none of the 15 possible comparisons is significant, likely reflecting the considerable variability in the distributions of this measure. As indicated above, the incidence of urination and defecation by these animals was negligibly low; special care was taken to handle all animals equally and often in an attempt to dissipate emotionality differences among groups which may be the result of differential handling experiences. Activity, urination, and defecation measures have been used by others as indices of emotionality in the rat (Forgus, 1956; Hall, 1934). Whatever is being measured by such indices, it must be concluded that the six groups constituting the present design are equivalent on these bases.

It is difficult to compare the results of this study with those few other relevant studies available in the literature. However, the treatment accorded Group 5 in this study was quite similar to that of the group of animals in Hymovitch's study (1952) which received FE exposure at the end of the growth period; in his study this group was found to be no different in problem-solving ability from animals restricted to small cages throughout rearing (similar to Group 6 in the present study). The present results may be seen as substantiating those of Hymovitch on this specific point.

It is noteworthy that Group 1 animals were found to be adult problem-solvers superior to Group 6 animals. The eyes of the animals of Group 1 did not open until the middle of their FE exposure period, and they spent much of the total period nestled with the mother rat provided. The significant difference in mean error score found would suggest that a very brief exposure to the wider environment in early life can have rather lasting effects.

The results of this study may be viewed as generally confirming the finding of Hymovitch (1952) that FE experience, as described above, must occur before maturity if it is to result in adult rats of superior problem-solving ability, at least as measured by the Hebb-Williams test. In addition, the results are in essential agreement with the finding of Forgus (1954) that such experience must occur in early infancy. Our results show clearly that there is a "critical" period for such exposure. Within the limitations of this study, the period seems to occur long before maturity and soon after the eyes of the rat are first open. Much additional research is necessary, however, before we will have acceptably complete answers to questions concerning the interaction of time of FE exposure and amount of such experience.

Summary

This experiment studies in the rat the effect upon adult problem-solving ability of exposure to a complex environment at different periods during growth. It was found that animals having had no such exposure were significantly poorer adult problem-solvers than animals having had 3 weeks of such experience at several different times before 90 days or so of age. It was also found that animals exposed immediately after weaning at 21 days of age were significantly better adult problem-solvers than animals which had the experience either earlier or later. It was concluded that there is a critical period for such exposures but that considerable additional research is required before we will know exactly how much experience is necessary to produce such effects and the specific period when it must occur.

References

Beach, F. A., & Jaynes, J. Effects of early experience upon the behavior of animals. *Psychol. Bull.*, 1954, **51**, 239–262.

Bingham, W. E., & Griffiths, W. J., Jr. The effect of different environments during infancy on adult behavior in the rat. *J. comp. physiol. Psychol.*, 1952, **45**, 307–312.

Forgays, D. G., & Forgays, J. W. The nature of the effect of free-environmental experience in the rat. *J. comp. physiol. Psychol.*, 1952, **45**, 322–328.

Forgus, R. H. The effect of early perceptual learning on the behavioral organization of adult rats. *J. comp. physiol. Psychol.*, 1954, **47**, 331–336.

Forgus, R. H. Advantage of early over late perceptual experience in improving form discrimination. *Canad. J. Physiol.*, 1956, **10**, 147–155.

Hall, C. S. Emotional behavior in the rat: I. Defecation and urination as measures of individual differences in emotionality. *J. comp. Psychol.*, 1934, **18**, 385–403.

Hymovitch, B. The effects of experimental variations on problem solving in the rat. *J. comp. physiol. Psychol.*, 1952, **45**, 313–321.

Rabinovitch, M. S., & Rosvold, H. E. A closed-field intelligence test for rats. *Canad. J. Psychol.*, 1951, **5**, 122–128.

(Received September 6, 1961)

Part V

CRITICAL PERIODS IN PHYSIOLOGICAL ORGANIZATION

Editor's Comments on Paper 27

27 **RAKUSAN and POUPA**
Ecology and Critical Periods of the Developing Heart

In this section, I have included certain critical period phenomena which are primarily behavioral but whose physiological basis is relatively well known. In these cases, differential experience modifies an ongoing organizational process at the physiological level; this in turn has important consequences for future behavior. All organizational processes for individual behavior must have underlying physiological bases, but in many instances these are still unknown, and the phenomena have therefore been treated in other sections. I have omitted one of the oldest and best-known examples of physiological organization, the critical period for the modification of the secondary sex organs and the consequent modification of sexual behavior, as this is included in the Benchmark volume *Hormones and Sexual Behavior* (Carter, 1974).

Critical Period for Development of Heart Muscle Capillaries

Paper 27 presents an instance of behavioral modification of a physiological developmental process. Rakušan and Poupa demonstrated that exercise has a very different effect at different ages on the development of heart muscle in rats. In adults, the effect of heavy exercise is to increase the size of the muscle fibers without increasing the capillary circulation, with the result that blood flow to the heart is actually poorer than before. In young animals, the number of capillaries increases along with the size of the fibers, producing a much more efficient heart. The critical period for the best results of exercise ends at about fifty days of age, forty days before physiological maturity. These results have obvious human implications for the control of heart disease by proper exercise during critical periods of development.

27

Reprinted from pp. 364–368 of *The Postnatal Development of Phenotype,* S. Kazda and V. H. Denenberg, eds., Academia, 1970, 420 pp.

ECOLOGY AND CRITICAL PERIODS OF THE DEVELOPING HEART

K. Rakušan and O. Poupa

[*Editor's Note:* In the original, material precedes this excerpt.]

It was found that some of the parameters described in the previous chapter develop synchronously. Some of them are listed in *Figure 29.8*, together with the development of blood pressure and the development of growth activity of explanted heart tissue *in vitro* (Rakušan and colleagues, 1965). On the basis of these results it is possible to outline four characteristic periods during post-natal development of the heart (*Figure 29.7*).

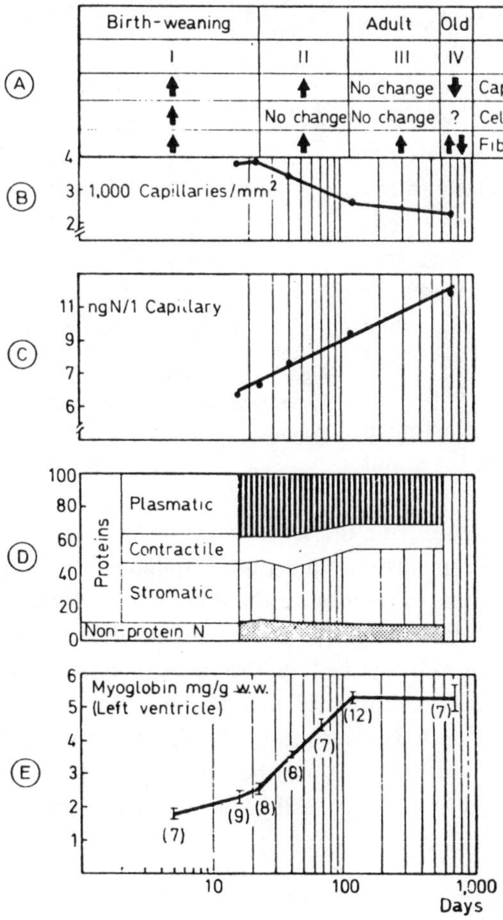

Figure 29.7 Summary of some data concerning the ontogeny of the rat heart

The first period is characterized by an increase in the number of muscle fibres and their diameters as well as in the number of capillaries. The increase in capillaries is more rapid than that in muscle fibres and hence the fibre/capillary ratio falls from 4 to 1·5. The heart grows at the same rate as the body. Therefore, the relative heart weight is unchanged. The growth activity of explanted heart tissue is considerable and the blood pressure is rapidly increased. This period commences with birth and terminates during the fourth post-natal week.

In the second period the heart grows more slowly and, hence, the relative heart weight decreases. The number of muscle fibres remains unchanged and only their diameter continues to grow larger. The number of capillaries increases more slowly, and the fibre/capillary ratio falls from 1·5–1 during the seventh week of life. The diffusion distance, which is the shortest at the start of this period, increases proportionally to the heart growth, and the growth activity of explanted heart tissue gradually disappears. On day 30, 49 per cent of fragments still grew, while none grew on day 40. The blood pressure still rises slightly. This transient period starts during the fourth post-natal week and lasts for about 3 weeks.

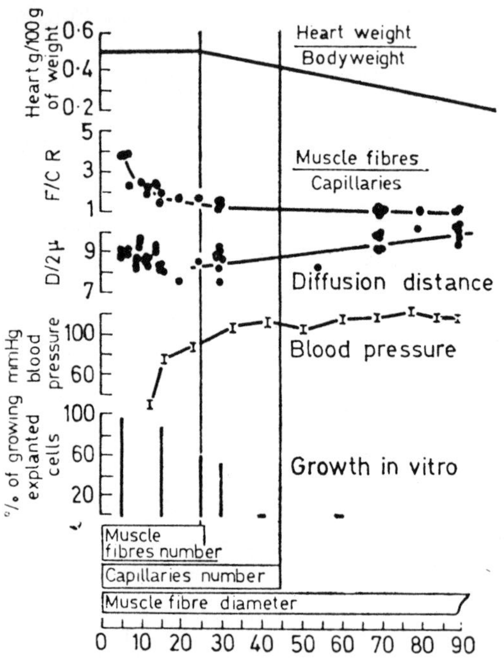

Figure 29.8 Post-natal development of the relative heart weight, the fibre/capillary ratio, the diffusion distance, blood pressure and growth of the explantates in vitro in the rat

The third period starts during the seventh week of life. The number of muscle fibres and capillaries now remains constant (fibre/capillary ratio = 1). The diffusion distance continues to increase in relation to the muscle fibre diameter growth. Tissue fragments do not grow and the blood pressure does not rise significantly.

The fourth period was described in the heart muscle of very old animals (over the age of 2 years). The number of muscle fibres/mm^2 is unchanged and the number of capillaries/mm^2 is lower, resulting in a significantly higher fibre/capillary ratio and a longer diffusion distance. It may be concluded that the disappearance of capillaries can be detected at this age. All these important developmental periods are summarized in *Figure 29.8*.

Critical Periods as a Determining Factor of the Structural Development of the Heart

From the data given here it may be assumed that the developmental stage determines when the heart can react to growth stimuli with hyperplasia and simultaneous growth of capillaries and when only with hypertrophy of contractile elements. To prove this hypothesis for abnormal heart growth also, the capillary blood supply in cardiomegalies produced by experimental aortic stenosis in rabbits of different ages was studied (Rakušan and colleagues, 1967). The capacity of the terminal vascular bed as an indicator of the capillary density was determined in these experiments by means of albumin ^{131}I in the rabbit myocardium.

Cardiomegaly was produced by experimental aortic stenosis in rabbits aged 3–14 weeks and in adult animals. The results are in *Figure 29.9*. An average increase of the left venricular weight was approximately the same in both groups. On the other hand, no changes were found in young animals in contrast to cardiomegaly in adults, where the vascular capacity was significantly lower. This finding supports the hypothesis of the importance of the critical period when the work load on the heart muscle is applied.

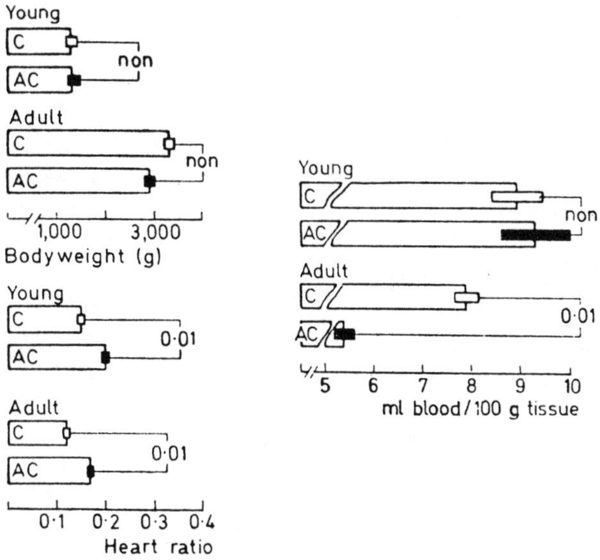

Figure 29.9 Heart of the rabbit with aortic constriction in different age. Capacity of the terminal vascular bed determined by albumin ^{131}*I expressed in ml blood/*100 g *of cardiac tissue.* C—*controls,* AC—*aortic constriction, experimentally produced in young and adult animals* (*Rakušan and colleagues 1967*)

For a detailed analysis of this phenomenon the development of the terminal vascular bed in the cardiac muscle of the rabbit during normal and pathological growth was studied. First, we examined the hypothesis that the capacity of the terminal vascular bed is constant. If this is true, the vascular capacity would decrease hyperbolically according to the heart weight in relation $y = k/x$, where x is the weight of the left ventricle and septum in mg and y is ml of blood/g of the left ventricle and septum and k is a constant calculated on the basis of numerical values in the group of normal adult rabbits.

In *Figure 29.10* such results are calculated on the basis of this equation in

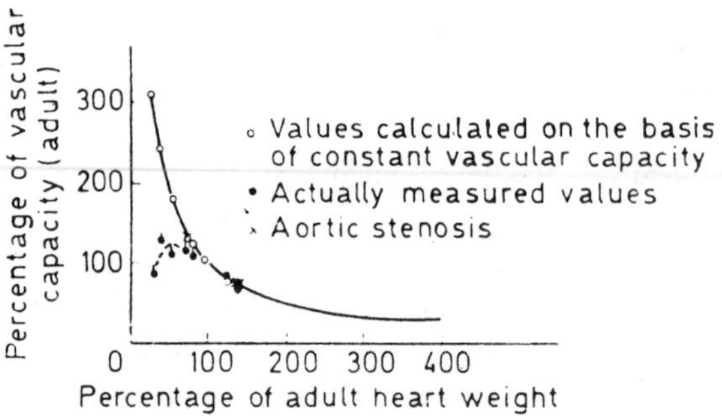

Figure 29.10 Relative changes of the vascular capacity in the heart muscle. Calculated (solid line) and measured (dashed line) values of the capacity of the terminal vascular bed during the post-natal development of the heart: 100 *per cent represents the capacity of terminal vascular bed in hearts of normal adult animals. Closed circles—actually measured values; open circles—values calculated on the assumption that the total vascular bed is constant during post-natal development of the heart;* X—*experimental aortic constriction (Rakušan and colleagues, 1967)*

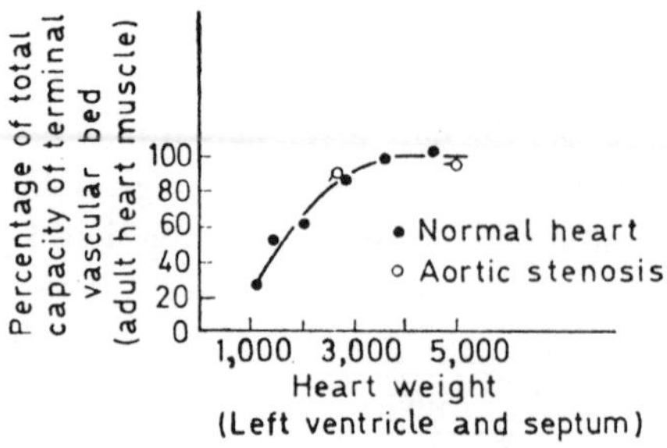

Figure 29.11 Growth of total capacity of termin al vascular bed of the heart muscle of a rabbit. Growth of the total capacity of the terminal vascular bed during post-natal development of a rabbit. 100 *per cent represents the total capacity of the terminal vascular bed in normal adult animals (Rakušan and colleagues, 1967)*

comparison to directly measured values. It may be seen that the vascular capacity cn the normal adult heart, and in cardiomegaly in adult animals as well as in the hearts of old animals follow this pattern, i. e. the capacity of the terminal vascular bed is constant and any further increase in the heart weight, results in a decrease of the vascular capacity per tissue unit. This is not true for younger animals.

The difference between the calculated and measured values makes it possible to calculate the percentage of the total capacity of the terminal vascular bed which was already formed. These values are given in *Figure 29.11*, which demonstrate the rate of growth of the terminal vascular bed in the heart muscle of the rabbit. This growth is very rapid in the first post-natal weeks. Later,

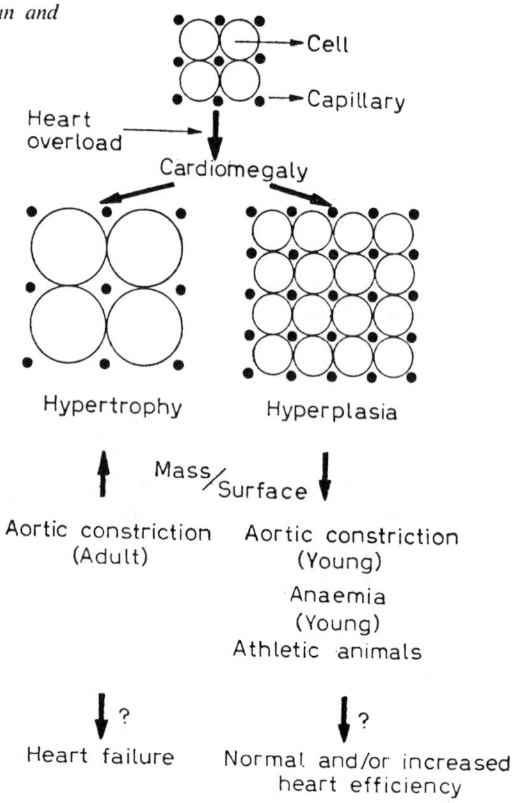

Figure 29.12 Summary of concluding remarks

it becomes slower and finally no growth of capillaries can be detected in adult and old animals. Curiously enough, this is valid not only for the normal heart development but also for the pathological growth of the heart.

CONCLUSIONS

On the basis of the detailed analysis of the development of the heart, four characteristic periods in post-natal ontogeny were described. The first period is characterized by a rapid growth of capillaries and muscle fibres. This period terminates at the time of weaning. During the next 3–4 weeks the growth of capillaries is less pronounced and starts to disappear while the total number of muscle fibres does not change. In adult animals the total number of capillaries as well as the number of muscle fibres is constant. In the heart muscle of very old animals (over the age of 2 years) a disappearance of capillaries can be detected.

The growth of the terminal vascular bed probably follows the same trend during the pathological increase in the heart weight irrespective of the type of cardiomegaly. In young animals, growth of the overloaded heart is accompanied by the growth of capillaries, while in adult animals the total number of capillaries is unchanged and the capillary density decreases proportionally to the heart growth. Similar changes probably occur in the number of muscle fibres, i.e. cardiomegaly in a young organism will be of the hyperplastic type while in adults it will be hypertrophic only, according to the critical period in which the stimulus was applied. Our concept is schematically drawn in *Figure 29.12*.

REFERENCES

Ošťádal, B., Wachtlová, M., Bílý, J., Rakušan, K. and Poupa, O.: *Physiologia bohemoslov.* **16,** 111 (1967)

Rakušan, K. and Poupa, O.: *Physiologia bohemoslov.* **12,** 220 (1963)

– –: *Gerontologia* **9,** 107 (1964)

– –: *Physiologia bohemoslov.* **14,** 320 (1965)

– –: *Physiologia bohemoslov.* **15,** 132 (1966)

– Korecký, B., Roth, Z. and Poupa, O.: *Physiologia bohemoslov.* **12,** 518 (1963)

– Jelínek, J., Korecký, B., Soukupová, M. and Poupa, O.: *Physiologia bohemoslov.* **14,** 32 (1965)

– du Mesnil de Rochemont, W., Braasch, W., Tschopp, H. and Bing, R. J.: *Circulation Res.* **21,** 163 (1967)

Editor's Comments on Papers 28 and 29

28 **BRONSON and DESJARDINS**
Aggression in Adult Mice: Modification by Neonatal Injections of Gonadal Hormones

29 **EDWARDS**
Mice: Fighting by Neonatally Androgenized Females

CRITICAL PERIOD FOR THE ORGANIZATION OF AGONISTIC BEHAVIOR IN MICE

In laboratory strains of house mice, females will ordinarily not fight, either as young animals or adults. Males, however, can be stimulated to fight at about the time of sexual maturation, when the male hormone first appears in quantity.

It has long been known that the gonadotropic hormones of a mammalian mother stimulate the gonads of her offspring to produce sex hormones before their birth and that the newborn animals continue to produce these for a few days following parturition.

Almost simultaneously, Bronson and Desjardins (Paper 28) and Edwards (Paper 29) independently tried the experiment of castrating newborn female mice and injecting them with male hormones. At the time of sexual maturity, if these animals are again injected with the male hormone, they will fight like males, whereas untreated controls will not. Whitsett et al. (1972) demonstrated that there is a quite short critical period for the effect of single injections. The effect is not an absolute one, however, since larger doses of hormones will produce similar effects at slightly later ages. The critical period is produced by the fact that the brains of newborn rats take up testosterone much more rapidly than they do at later ages. Neonatal testosterone thus appears to modify the organization of the neuroendocrine system, an effect which is similar to the mechanism explaining the result of neonatal stimulation which is described in the next section.

28

Reprinted from *Science* **161**:705–706 (1968)

AGGRESSION IN ADULT MICE: MODIFICATION BY NEONATAL INJECTIONS OF GONADAL HORMONES

F. H. Bronson and Claude Desjardins

Jackson Laboratory, Bar Harbor, Maine

Abstract. *Incidence of spontaneous aggression in adult male mice given a single injection of estradiol benzoate (0.4 milligram) when they were 3 days old was less than that of controls injected with oil. Aggressiveness was increased among adult females injected with either estradiol or testosterone propionate (1 milligram) at the same age. The increased aggressiveness noted among females given androgen was further documented during subsequent mating tests, when these females often attacked, wounded, and, in one case, killed naive males.*

The sexual differentiation of particular behavioral or neuroendocrine control systems may be influenced by the presence of gonadal hormones during infancy in rodents (*1*). For example, neonatal administration of androgens to females results in an acyclic, male-like secretion of gonadotropin during adulthood rather than in the cyclic pattern characteristic of normal adult females (*2*). Similarly, sexual behavior of female rats may be masculinized to a degree if they are given neonatal injections of androgen, or that of males may be feminized if they are castrated during infancy, provided that appropriate gonadal hormones are administered during adulthood (*1*, *3*). Estrogens, depending upon the time and dose of their injection, may mimic some of these effects of androgens (*4*). We hypothesized that aggressive behavior could also be modified following treatment with androgens or estrogens during infancy. Our results demonstrate that aggressiveness was increased in adult female mice if they were given either androgen or estrogen as neonates; aggressiveness in adult males was partially suppressed if they were injected with estrogen during infancy.

Complete litters of 3-day-old C57BL/6J mice of both sexes were injected subcutaneously with 0.05 ml of corn oil containing either 1 mg of testosterone propionate, 0.4 mg of estradiol benzoate, or nothing. Mice were weaned at 21 to 25 days of age and housed singly until tested for aggressiveness at 80 to 90 days of age. Spontaneous aggression (*5*) was measured in test chambers (12 by 12 by 6 inches) with removable partitions in the middle. Single mice of the same sex and treatment were placed on either side of the partition. It was removed 20 minutes later and the mice were observed until a fight was initiated, or for a maximum of 15 minutes (Table 1). The same pair of mice was tested once daily for three consecutive days, after which vaginal smears were obtained for five consecutive days from all females. All males and 12 females from each group were then autopsied to verify the expected effects of neonatal injections on reproductive tract morphology. Ovaries, uteri, and testes were weighed and examined histologically. Seminal vesicles were homogenized in water and analyzed for fructose (*6*).

The remaining females from each of

Table 1. Number of pairs (of same sex) in which fighting occurred at least once during three encounters and total number of fights occurring during all three encounters.

Neonatal treatment	Fighting at least once (No.)	Fights in three encounters (No.)
	Males	
Oil	23/24	51/72
Testosterone	18/19	46/57
Estradiol	10/20	20/60
	Females	
Oil	1/24	1/72
Testosterone	5/18	10/54
Estradiol	4/14	5/42

Table 2. Number of male-female pairs in which severe fighting occurred within the first hour after pairing and number in which wounding of one member occurred within 18 hours. Females had been previously tested in the primary experiment (Table 1), after which they were given progesterone daily for 8 days and then paired with naive males.

Neonatal treatment of females	Fighting (1st hour)	Wounding (18 hours)
Oil	0/20	0/20
Testosterone	12/23	5/23*
Estradiol	4/14	0/14

* One pair in which female was wounded, three pairs in which male was wounded, and one pair in which male was killed.

the three groups received subcutaneous injections of progesterone (0.3 mg per mouse per day) for 8 days to induce estrous cycles (*7*). On the afternoon of the 8th day, they were paired with naive males in the females' home cages. Our purpose in this secondary experiment was to verify the lack of mating in females treated neonatally with testosterone or estradiol and to follow a suggestion by Barraclough that changes in aggressiveness might be more obvious in such a situation (*8*). Incidence of fighting was recorded for the first hour after pairing, and all pairs were inspected for wounding and presence of vaginal plugs on the following three mornings. Males used in this experiment were about 100 days old, intact, and sexually and experimentally inexperienced; each male had been housed with four or five others since weaning.

The results of the primary experiment, in which mice were given the opportunity to fight only members of the same sex and treatment group, are presented in Table 1. Spontaneous fighting occurred at least once during three encounters in all but one pair of males in each of the two groups that received injections of either oil or testosterone during infancy. Neonatal injections of estradiol reduced the incidence of fighting in adult males to 50 percent ($P<.01$). Only 4 percent of the control females fought, whereas fighting among pairs that had received neonatal injections of either testosterone or estradiol increased to 28 and 29 percent, respectively ($P < .05$ in both cases).

The secondary experiment, in which females were injected with progesterone for 8 days and then paired with normal males, revealed marked aggressiveness on the part of females injected neonatally with testosterone (Table 2); fighting among such pairs was often vicious and usually initiated by the females. Females treated with estradiol also fought with males, but both the incidence and severity of fights were lower. No fighting was noted among pairs in which the female had been injected only with oil in infancy. No vaginal plugs were found in any females receiving steroid neonatally, but 55 percent of the females injected with oil had plugs during the 3 days after pairing.

The effects of neonatal injections of estradiol or testosterone on vaginal cycles and reproductive tracts were similar to previous findings (*2*, *4*) and will be reported here only to an extent necessary for correlation with the behavioral data. Neonatal injections of estradiol in males resulted in decreased body and reproductive organ weights and relative aspermia. Injections of testosterone in infancy also decreased weights of male organs but to a lesser extent than that caused by estradiol (Table 3). All vaginal smears obtained from all females injected neonatally with either steroid contained approximately 80 percent cornified cells and 20 percent leukocytes, and ovaries of such females were polyfollicular and devoid of corpora lutea. Body and uterine weights were increased among females injected neonatally with testosterone.

Androgen is a necessary prerequisite for attack behavior in inexperienced male mice (*9*), whereas estrogen administered during adulthood has no effect on aggressiveness of males (*10*). The reduction in spontaneous aggression shown by males injected with estrogen in our study was correlated with large changes in their reproductive tracts, and secretion of testicular androgen was probably considerably reduced. Weights of reproductive organs were also lower in males given neonatal injections of androgen, but they were as aggressive as control males. These facts suggest that those males injected with androgen neonatally probably had sufficient androgen in their circulation during adulthood to permit a high degree of aggressive behavior, whereas those that received estrogen did not. The amount of fructose in seminal vesicles, a good correlate of androgen titers (*6*), was reduced by 72 percent among males given estradiol in infancy compared to that in controls given oil (Table 3). The comparable figure for males receiving testosterone neonatally was only 21 percent and, hence, the postulate appears reasonably good on this basis.

The low incidence of spontaneous aggression found among control females agrees well with observations of other workers using mice (*11*). Androgen will not increase aggressiveness in either immature or mature gonadectomized females (*12*). However, neonatal injections of testosterone, and to a lesser extent estradiol, increase aggressiveness in females after maturity. These effects were significant in both experiments although more dramatic in the uncontrolled secondary experiment where some previously tested females were paired with naive males in the females' home cages after receiving progesterone to induce estrous cycles. Under such conditions mating did not occur, and the females usually attacked and sometimes wounded males. Wounding was sufficiently severe to cause death in one case. The reasons for the dramatic effects observed in this experiment are not readily obvious because of its uncontrolled nature and the data are presented only as an extreme example of a phenomenon observed in the primary experiment. Two investigators have reported that "masculine or aggressive responses" interfered with normal female sexual behavior when rats were treated with estrogen or testosterone in infancy (*13*) but not to the extent shown in the present study with mice.

A reasonable hypothesis to explain the increased aggressiveness of females treated neonatally with gonadal hormones is the alteration of a neural

able 3. Body weight, relative (paired) organ weights, and fructose concentrations in seminal vesicles of males treated neonatally with oil, stosterone, or estradiol; body and relative uterine weights of similarly treated females (mean ± standard error).

Neonatal treatment	Males					Females		
	No.	Body wt. (g)	Testes (mg/g body wt.)	Seminal vesicle (mg/g body wt.)	Seminal vesicle fructose (μg)	No.	Body wt. (g)	Uterus (mg/g body wt.)
il	48	27.8 ± 0.4	7.53 ± 0.52	2.42 ± 0.27	174.0 ± 6.3	12	22.6 ± 0.7	3.19 ± 0.31
estosterone	37	27.3 ± 0.5	5.93 ± 0.20*	1.98 ± 0.08*	137.0 ± 5.4*	12	28.2 ± 1.0*	5.23 ± 0.67*
stradiol	40	24.4 ± 0.4*	4.61 ± 0.41*	1.07 ± 0.15*	48.2 ± 4.7*	12	23.1 ± 0.8	2.37 ± 0.38

Significantly different from oil controls, as determined by analysis of variance, with a probability of at least $P < .05$.

mechanism whose sexual differentiation is normally regulated by androgen in infancy. Such a concept parallels the conclusions of many studies dealing with either sex behavior or the hypothalamic control of gonadotropin secretion, and some degree of experimental mimicking of androgen by estrogen is well documented in this respect. It does not seem reasonable at this time, however, to suspect the hypothalamus at the expense of other neural structures because the number of brain areas known to function in aggression is relatively large (*14*). Furthermore, as evidenced by changes in body weight in both sexes, the effects of early administration of steroids may be widespread.

References and Notes

1. S. Levine and R. F. Mullins, *Science* **152**, 1585 (1966).
2. C. A. Barraclough, *Endocrinology* **68**, 62 (1961); R. A. Gorski, *J. Reprod. Fertil. Suppl.* **1**, 67 (1966).
3. R. E. Whalen and D. A. Edwards, *Anat. Rec.* **157**, 173 (1967).
4. G. W. Harris and S. Levine, *J. Physiol. London* **181**, 379 (1965).
5. J. P. Scott, *Amer. Zool.* **6**, 683 (1966).
6. J. S. Davis and J. E. Gander, *Anal. Biochem.* **19**, 72 (1967).
7. C. A. Barraclough, *Fed. Proc.* **15**, 9 (1956).
8. ———, personal communication.
9. E. A. Beeman, *Physiol. Zool.* **20**, 373 (1947); E. B. Sigg, C. Day, C. Colombo, *Endocrinology* **78**, 679 (1966).
10. J. E. Gustafson and G. Winokur, *J. Neuropsychiat.* **1**, 182 (1960).
11. E. Fredericson, *J. Comp. Physiol. Psychol* **45**, 89 (1952).
12. J. V. Levy, *Proc. West Virginia Acad. Sci.* **26**, 14 (1954); J. Tollman and J A. King, *Brit. J. Anim. Behav.* **6**, 147 (1956).
13. H. H. Feder, *Anat. Rec.* **157**, 79 (1967); A. A. Gerall, *ibid.*, p. 97.
14. J. M. R. Delgado, *Amer. Zool.* **6**, 669 (1966).
15. This investigation was supported in part by PHS grants FR-05545-05 and HD-00767.

29

Reprinted from *Science* **161**:1027–1028 (1968)

MICE: FIGHTING BY NEONATALLY ANDROGENIZED FEMALES

David A. Edwards
Department of Psychobiology, University of California, Irvine

Abstract. *Administration of testosterone propionate to female mice on the day of birth resulted in increased fighting after administration of testosterone during adulthood. This fighting, comparable to fighting among normal male mice, suggests that early androgenic stimulation organizes neural structures mediating aggression in the mouse.*

When two male mice that have been socially isolated for some time are placed together, aggression is invariable. Relatively little is known about the development of the neuroendocrine determinants of this behavior. One report (*1*) indicates that, if the male mouse is castrated before puberty, fighting is rare. Treatment of the castrate with exogenous testosterone results in arousal of the propensity to fight. Unlike males, adult female mice do not fight when testosterone is administered (*2*). This difference in response by male and female mice to testosterone may reflect differences in the nature or sensitivity of brain systems underlying aggression. Much research on the neural mechanisms underlying sexual behavior (*3*) indicates that males do differ from females with respect to some brain characteristics, and that these differences result from differential androgenic stimulation during a limited critical period of development. I sought to determine whether or not differences between adult males and females in fighting also are determined by the presence or absence of early stimulation by androgens.

Some Swiss-Webster litters of mice were injected subcutaneously with 0.5 mg of testosterone propionate within 24 hours of birth. The result was genital virilization characterized by small vaginal opening and hypertrophied clitoris in all females. Control litters received injections of peanut oil within 24 hours of birth, without genital effect. The young mice were kept with the mother until 30 days of age, when all were weaned and gonadectomized; they remained in the litter of birth until 60 days of age, when the males that had received testosterone at birth were eliminated from the study, the remainder being individually caged.

The remainder constituted three groups: (i) males treated with oil at birth (OM), (ii) females treated with oil at birth (OF), and (iii) females treated with testosterone propionate at birth (TPF). During the 1st week of isolation all mice were injected subcutaneously daily with 0.05 ml of oil. On the 6th and 7th days of the 1st week, all mice were tested for fighting; none fought. Successively during each of the subsequent 5 weeks, all subjects received daily injections of 10, 20, 50, 100, and 500 μg of testosterone; on the 6th and 7th days of each week they were tested for fighting. Thus during successive weeks they were tested under progressively higher doses of testosterone.

For testing, two mice from the same group were paired in a neutral cage. If they fought within 10 minutes, the latency from the start of the test to the beginning of the fight was recorded to the nearest minute, and the test was terminated by restoration of each mouse to its home cage. A "fight" was scored if one mouse (or both) persistently attempted to bite the other. The same individuals were paired for each test.

More than 90 percent of the pairs of virilized females showed fighting during at least one test. One hundred percent of the pairs of males fought. Only one pair of group OF ever fought. Once fighting occurred, it persisted in most subsequent observations under conditions of increased dosage of testosterone.

For each pair in the OM and TPF groups, a mean latency to fighting was calculated for those tests on which fighting occurred. Analysis of variance of the data on latency (Table 1) failed to indicate any significant difference between males and virilized females.

When the dose of testosterone during adulthood was increased, the proportions of pairs of males and of virilized females showing fighting were increased (Fig. 1). The close correspondence of the curves for the OM and TPF groups indicates that these groups were little different in their response to testosterone; at no dose level was the difference in proportion of pairs fighting statistically significant. In constrast, females treated with only oil at birth failed to fight even when given large doses of exogenous testosterone in adulthood. Chi-square comparisons of group OF with group TPF are significant beyond the 0.05 level at all dose levels greater than 20 μg per day.

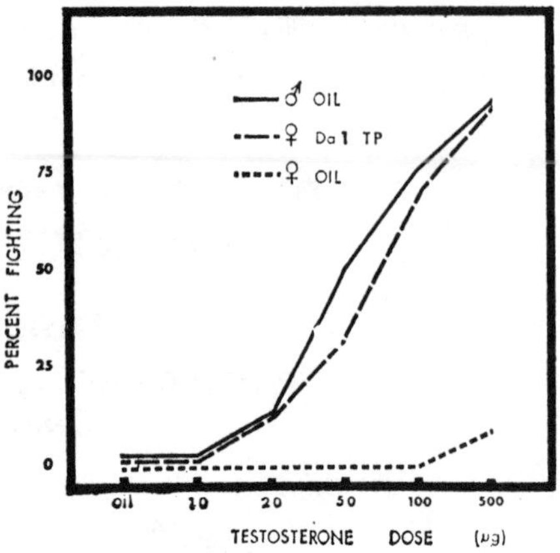

Fig. 1. Effects of neonatal stimulation by testosterone on adult fighting in mice. Represented are the percentages of pairs in each group fighting at various dosages of testosterone during adulthood.

Table 1. Percentages of pairs of mice fighting at least once, and mean latencies to fighting when fighting occurred.

Group	Pairs No.	Pairs Fighting (%)	Latency (min)
OM	16	100.0	5.1
TPF	16	93.8	5.0
OF	12	8.3	

These data clearly indicate that administration of testosterone to the neonatal female mouse facilitates the display of testosterone-aroused fighting in adulthood; they suggest that the usually observed difference between normal male and female mice, with respect to fighting, is due to the fact that males are stimulated by testicular androgens early in life. One may presume that the stimulation by endogenous testosterone in the male (and exogenous testosterone in the female) can "organize" or cause the differentiation of a neural substrate for fighting.

The ability of early androgenic stimulation to affect adult patterns of behavior has been clearly documented in several species for a variety of sexually dimorphic behaviors (*3*). In these instances, androgenic stimulation affected behavioral differentiation only when this stimulation occurred during a particular and limited period during maturation. It is not yet clear to what extent the "organizing" capacity of androgens with respect to adult fighting in mice is similarly time-limited. Data now being collected in our laboratory (*4*) suggest that the period, during which administration of testosterone promotes fighting in the female mouse, may extend well beyond the 10th day after birth.

References and Notes

1. E. A. Beeman, *Physiol. Zool.* **20**, 373 (1947).
2. D. A. Edwards, in preparation.
3. C. H. Phoenix, R. W. Goy, A. A. Gerall, W. C. Young, *Endocrinology* **65**, 365 (1959); R. W. Goy, *J. Anim. Sci.* **25**, 21 (1966); R. E. Whalen and D. A. Edwards, *Anat. Rec.* **157**, 173 (1967).
4. J. Tollman and J. A. King, *Brit. J. Anim. Behav.* **6**, 147 (1956).
5. Supported by PHS predoctoral fellowship 2F1-MH 30315-03. I thank R. E. Whalen for advice and encouragement. The hormones were supplied by P. Perlman, Schering Corp., Bloomfield, N.J.

Editor's Comments on Papers 30 Through 36

CRITICAL PERIOD FOR EARLY STIMULATION IN RATS AND HUMANS

Research in this area provides a fascinating story of the discovery of a critical period, a story whose pages unfolded one at a time with each adding a bit to the total picture of the phenomenon. The first paper in this area was that by Bernstein (Paper 30), who was interested in the effects on performance of the social relationship between an experimenter and the rats that he used in experimental work. Laboratory rats are traditionally weaned twenty-one days after birth, a time when the young can survive on their own but still have not been weaned from the breast by their mothers. Bernstein began gently handling and petting his rats at twenty-one days of age and continued it until sixty days, when the experiment was begun. As in now known, rats are not really physiologically mature until around ninety days. But Bernstein found that animals given extra gentling were superior in a discrimination task to those that had either been given minimal handling or none. The handled animals also gained more weight. (Incidentally, these experiments with gentling, which might be equivalent to studies with attachments in dogs and other mammals, have never been followed up.)

It then occurred to several investigators that it the ettects of handling were so pronounced in older animals, they might be even more striking in animals handled at earlier ages. Hunt and Otis (1963) had handled rats from seven through twenty-one days and found that their handled rats were superior on tests measuring emotionality. Schaefer (Paper 31), who was a graduate student at the University of Chicago with Hunt at this time, did his dissertation on a similar set of experiments but subdivided the preweaning handling experience into three periods of one week each. He found that the major effects occurred in animals handled during the first week of life. Later experimenters reduced this critical period to the first five days following birth, or possibly less.

A second problem was to analyze the nature of the handling experience, i.e., what the rat actually experienced, as opposed to what the experimenter read into it. To make a long story short, Levine and Lewis (Papers 32 and 33) found that any sort of stimulation would produce the same effect as handling, whether gentle or not. Schaefer found that cold stress—simply chilling the infant animals without tactile stimulation—would also produce the effect. They concluded that the essential phenomenon was physiological stress in the young rat pups, and Levine advanced the theory that physiological stress activated the endocrine system in such a way that it and the organization of the brain were permanently modified. He produced evidence that the animal really was stressed (Paper 34) and also demonstrated that stressful handling as late as fifty days of age had no effect (Levine, 1956). The complete details of this process were worked out in a long series of experiments reviewed in the paper by Denenberg and Zarrow (Paper 35).

All experimenters found that rats stimulated during the critical period became superior animals with respect to emotional stability, performance on various learning tasks, and also in their growth rates. The implication was that infant rats in the laboratory environment are disturbed so little that they do not achieve their complete physiological and behavioral potentials.

Landauer and Whiting (1964) wondered if similar effects might not take place in human infants. On the basis of a cross-cultural survey, they found that adults in those cultures in which young infants were subjected to some form of stress, such as cold baths, circumcision, etc., were superior in average height to adults in those societies in which babies were treated more gently. Paper 36, (Whiting, Landauer, and Jones, 1968) suggests that part of the increase in stature observed in modern Western cultures over the past two centuries may be related to the prevalence of innoculations against smallpox. Data collected from individuals whose medical histories were known support this hypothesis. Such results raise questions regarding the desirability of obstetrical practices that call for extremely gentle handling of newborn infants. If humans are like rats, infants who experience some stress are better able to cope with stress in later life.

30

Reprinted from *Psychol. Bull.* **49**:38–40 (1952)

A NOTE ON CHRISTIE'S: "EXPERIMENTAL NAÏVETE AND EXPERIENTIAL NAÏVETÉ"

LEWIS BERNSTEIN
Veterans Administration Hospital, Denver, Colorado

A recently completed investigation at the University of Colorado Laboratories, the first of a series suggested by Benjamin (1), relates directly to the provocative issues raised by Christie (2) concerning the pre-experimental experience of rats. Although the results of this study are not yet ready for publication, it is felt that some of our preliminary findings should be made known at this time.

Our study was a test of Benjamin's (1) relationship-reinforcement hypothesis. More specifically, an attempt was made to establish empirically that a relationship between the experimenter and experimental animals does affect the course of learning. Special emphasis was given to the effect of an interrupted relationship upon the course of retention during a period of experimental extinction. Relationship, for purposes of this investigation, was defined in terms of the amount of handling of the experimental animals.

Fifty albino rats were used in this study. Each litter was separated according to sex, and split into three groups at the time of weaning (21 days after birth).[1]

Group *EH* (extra handling) was handled and petted by the experimenter for ten minutes per day per animal, from weaning through completion of the experiment. This handling was in addition to the handling required for experimental procedures.

Group *IH* (intermediate handling) was not handled until the animals were 50 days of age, at which time they were tamed by handling, for a period of 10 days. Thereafter, they were handled only as required by experimental procedures. The purpose of this handling was to reduce situational anxiety. No attempt was made to establish a relationship with these animals.

Group *NH* (no handling) was not handled at all. Special procedures were devised for introducing these animals into and removing them from the experimental apparatus without handling.

The experiment began when all animals were 60 days old. They were trained to go to the lighted side of a T-shaped discrimination box in a corrective situation, under hunger-food tension. As each animal reached the criterion of learning, it was assigned to a new subgroup, and 40 extinction trials followed. For half the animals in Group *EH*, the daily extra handling was continued throughout the extinction trials; and for the other half, handling was interrupted. Similarly, half the animals in Group *NH* continued to be unhandled while the other half received handling for the first time. Group *IH* continued to be handled for experimental purposes throughout the extinction trials.

[1] The relevant pre-experimental variables suggested by Christie (2, p. 333) will be reported in a future publication.

Our data for the original learning show that in terms of (a) number of trials required to master the habit, and (b) number of errors, Group *EH* was significantly superior to Groups *IH* and *NH;* and Group *IH* was significantly superior to Group *NH.*

Our extinction data show that: (a) Animals who were handled throughout both parts of the experiment made significantly fewer errors than animals who were unhandled throughout the experiment, or who received intermediate handling throughout the experiment. (b) Unhandled animals who were handled for the first time during extinction trials made fewer errors than animals who continued to be unhandled. This difference, which was not statistically significant, can possibly be explained by the fact that the handling of these animals lasted for only four days. (c) Animals who were handled throughout both parts of the experiment made significantly fewer errors than animals who were handled for the first time during extinction trials. (d) Handled animals with whom the relationship was interrupted made significantly more errors than animals with whom the relationship was continued during extinction trials. In fact, the animals with whom the relationship had been interrupted made more errors than the unhandled animals. In other words, an interrupted relationship produced more errors than a minimal relationship.

It was noted throughout the experiment that the extra-handled animals were more active and lively than the unhandled animals. This was apparent not only in maze behavior, but also in home cage activity. In the maze, the handled animals vigorously explored the apparatus —testing the wire-mesh covers, learning to open sliding doors with paws and nose, and pushing the glass food-dish aside. In marked contrast, the unhandled animals ran directly to the goal-box, without any apparent exploratory behavior. After eating the goal-food, they entered directly into the delay-chamber to await the next trial, without any exploration of the goal-box. None of the unhandled animals learned to open the doors in the apparatus. It was also noted that the unhandled animals attempted to hoard food following their daily feeding periods, whereas there was no such attempt on the part of the handled animals. On this basis, a repetition of Hunt's (4) hoarding study, introducing the variable of relationship, is being planned.

These quantitative, as well as qualitative, findings are offered as further evidence for Christie's point of view in regard to pre-experimental experience. However, these same findings suggest an alternate interpretation to Christie's (2) and Hebb's (3) emphasis on the importance of early exploratory training. Possibly a second factor was operative in Hebb's study: the pet animals may have had the benefit of a relationship with the experimenter as well as a richer experience. Of the two possible variables operative, Hebb has chosen to use the one of broader experience as an explanatory concept. It is of some interest, therefore, to note that Shurrager (5), whose animals were treated in a fashion similar to Hebb's, emphasizes the relationship between the animals and the experimenter, rather than the concept of broader experience.

Being aware of these two variables, our animals were handled just outside their living cages in order to eliminate, as far as possible, the contamination of the relationship variable with that of broader experience. For this same reason, all animals were housed in the experimental room and none was taken outside the room. Furthermore, the position of the cages on the rack was systematically shifted twice each week, so that every cage twice occupied each position on the rack. To compensate for any additional experience which might have accrued to the handled animals by being handled outside their cages, the unhandled animals were required to run through a portable alleyway, placed between the home cages and the feeding cages, in order to obtain their daily ration. The handled animals were placed in the feeding cages by hand.

We do not mean to minimize the importance of Hebb's and Christie's emphasis on the value of early exploratory experience. We do wish to suggest, however, that in light of our findings, the following hypothesis might be tested: with breadth of early exploratory experience held constant, the group of animals with whom the experimenter establishes a relationship (through extra petting and handling) will show learning superior to that of the animals that have only broad early exploratory experience.

Finally, in connection with Christie's (2) suggestion of investigating genetic hypotheses, using animal subjects, our data show that the extra-handled and unhandled animals were equated for weight at weaning. By the age of 46 days, the mean weight gain of the extra-handled animals was significantly greater than that of the unhandled animals. Unfortunately, it cannot be stated at the present time whether this was due to better physiological use of the food consumed or to greater quantities of food consumed. We hope to resolve this question in future experiments by weighing the animals' food.

REFERENCES

1. Benjamin, J. D. Methodological considerations in the validation and elaboration of psychoanalytical personality theory. *Amer. J. Orthopsychiat.*, 1950, **20**, 139–156.
2. Christie, R. Experimental naïveté and experiential naïveté. *Psychol. Bull.*, 1951, **48**, 327–339.
3. Hebb, D. O. *Organization of behavior.* New York: Wiley, 1949.
4. Hunt, J. McV. The effects of infant feeding frustration upon adult hoarding. *J. abnorm. soc. Psychol.*, 1941, **36**, 338–360.
5. Shurrager, P. S. "Spinal" cats walk. *Sci. Amer.*, 1950, **183**, 20–22.

Received August 8, 1951.

31

Reprinted from *Trans. N. Y. Acad. Sci.* **25**:871–889 (1963)

EARLY "EXPERIENCE" AND ITS EFFECTS ON LATER BEHAVIORAL PROCESSES IN RATS: II. A CRITICAL FACTOR IN THE EARLY HANDLING PHENOMENON*

Theodore Schaefer, Jr.
Columbia University, New York, N.Y.

It was in 1956, in the context of the contradictory interpretations of the handling phenomenon discussed by Hunt, that I began the line of research described here. These experiments were aimed at determining which features of the handling procedure could be assigned primary responsibility for the effects obtained.

Experiment 1. The Critical Period†

The first experiment was designed to establish the age at which handling is most effective in reducing emotionality. If it can be shown that there is a particular time, a critical period in life, during which a given treatment has a maximal effect, several advantages ensue: First, one can compare the developmental stages when apparently similar treatments are reported to have similar effects in other species (e.g. tender loving care in human infants and gentling in young rats); second, one can begin to consider how the treatment produces its effect (through gentling or traumatizing, for example) by evaluating the organism's capacity for experiencing the treatment; third, one can gain insight into underlying mechanisms by considering what developmental changes are taking place in particular organs or processes during such a critical period (Scott *et al.*, 1951; King, 1958; Thompson and Schaefer, 1961; Scott, 1962).

With regard to establishing a critical period for handling in rats, Bernstein (1952) had reported that rats handled during early adulthood were inferior, on several tests, to animals handled immediately after weaning. Levine and Otis (1958) had found, early

* This paper was the second of three presented at a meeting of the Division on May 20, 1963.

† The first three experiments reported herein were done at the Institute for Psychosomatic and Psychiatric Research and Training at Michael Reese Hospital, Chicago, Illinois. These experiments were supported by Grant M-1057 of the National Institutes of Mental Health, under the general direction of Sheldon J. Korchin. This portion of the report is based on a dissertation submitted in partial fulfillment of requirements for the PhD at the University of Chicago under the sponsorship of Eckhard H. Hess.

Experiment IV, on temperature change, was done at the University of Chicago, under Grant MY-3651 from the National Institute of Mental Health. Experiment V was done at Columbia University with funds from Grant MH-07929-01, National Institute of Mental Health.

in 1956, that handling throughout the 21 days prior to weaning was more effective in reducing stress-reactivity than handling for 21 days immediately after weaning. Therefore, it was assumed in designing the following experiment that a critical period for the maximal effectiveness of handling might occur at some time during the 21 days of life prior to weaning.

Subjects. Ten litters containing 8 to 10 pups each were selected from the litters born to 25 multiparous Holtzman Sprague-Dawley albino mothers. Two litters were assigned randomly to each of five groups for different treatments during the 21 day nursing period: Group NH constituted the nonhandled controls, left undisturbed until weaning; pups in group H1 were handled daily on days one through seven; those in group H2 were handled daily on days 8 through 14; H3 on days 15 through 20; and group HΣ3 contained pups handled daily all three weeks. All litters were whelped and nursed in identical 9 by 9 by 12 inch metal cages, on wood shavings for nest material.

Procedure. For handling, the pups were removed from the mother's cage and placed on a tray of wood shavings. A single pup was grasped in each hand, held for a minute and a half, then placed in an adjoining tray of shavings. When all pups had been handled the litter was returned to its mother. Thus, in addition to handling, each pup was exposed for approximately ten minutes to the open, well-lighted room in the absence of its mother.

All pups were weaned on day 21 and placed in large cages, one litter per cage, on *ad libitum* food and water until observed for emotionality in a 3½ by 6½ foot, brightly lighted, open-field test at 52 to 59 days of age. The mean age of treatment groups at testing did not vary more than a few days.

As the animal was placed in the center of the field, a stop watch was activated and the experimenter stepped behind a one-way vision screen to record the time spent in the center before going to a wall, activity (number of grid lines crossed), and instances of defecation and urination. Crouching time was accumulated on another stop watch. At the end of two minutes the experimenter flicked a toggle switch to provide a sudden, rather loud click, after which crouching time, activity, and elimination were again recorded for a two-minute period. Then the rat was removed from the open-field, earmarked, and placed in a large cage with others of the same sex and early treatment to await later testing to be described in Experiment III.

Results

Quantitative behavioral differences between sexes necessitated separating the data for males and females to avoid misleading group differences due to the nonuniform sex ratios in the early treatment groups. Unless otherwise stated the Mann-Whitney *U* (Auble, 1953) was used to determine significance levels of differences between groups.

The amount of time spent crouching during the two minutes following presentation of the click provided the clearest, single measure of emotionality. Since the other measures gave congruent results, only the post-click crouching scores will be presented. FIGURE 1 illustrates the group differences in crouching behavior.

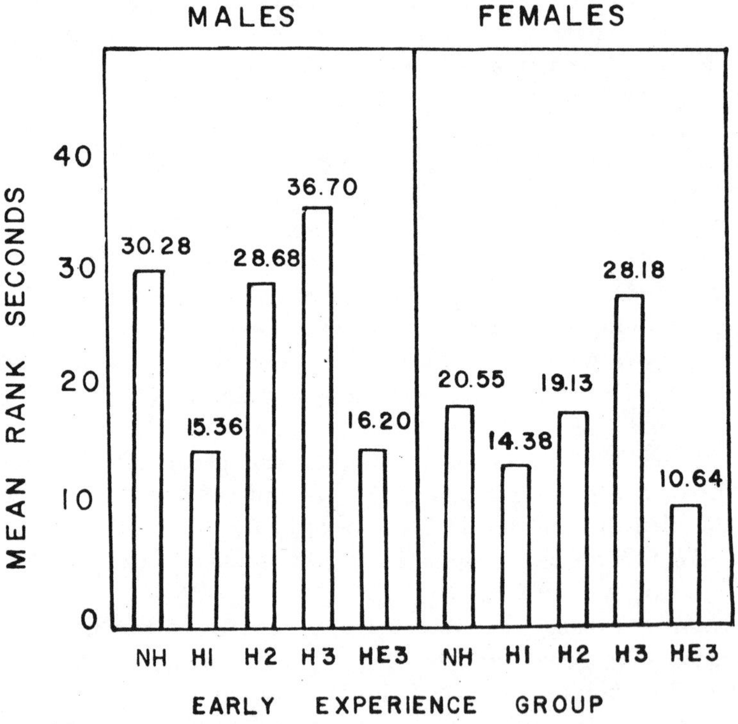

FIGURE 1. Amount of post-click crouching for each early experience group.

These differences were quite similar in both sexes. Analysis of variance between treatment groups for amount of crouching after the click, using the Kruskal-Wallis *H* statistic (1952), resulted in probabilities beyond the .05 level for females and the .001 level for males. For the males, animals handled only during the first week of life (Group H1) and those handled throughout the 21-day nursing period (HΣ3) crouched significantly less than the non-handled controls (NH), the second-week handled (H2) and third-week handled (H3) animals. Animals handled during the second week (H2) did not differ from the nonhandled controls, while those handled only during the third week of life (H3) crouched somewhat more than the controls. For the females, the only significant difference was that the HΣ3 animals crouched less than those in the NH and H3 groups. In general, the females crouched much less than the males (see TABLES 1 and 2) reducing the magnitude of differences between groups. In addition, it should be noted that there were only four females in group H1 which, like the H1 males, crouched less than the controls, but not significantly.

TABLE 1

MEAN NUMBER OF SECONDS SPENT CROUCHING AFTER THE CLICK, MEAN RANKS, AND LEVELS OF SIGNIFICANCE* OF DIFFERENCES BETWEEN GROUPS OF MALE RATS IN EXPERIMENT I.

Group	NH N=9	H1 N=11	H2 N=11	H3 N=7	HΣ3 N=10
Mean seconds crouching	45.2	2.2	28.9	48.9	13.8
Mean rank	30.3	15.4	28.7	36.7	16.2
Nonhandled	—	<.05	none	none	<.05
Handled first week only		—	<.[illegible]	<.002	none
Handled second week only			—	<.20	<.05
Handled third week only				—	<.01

* As determined by the Mann-Whitney *U* test.

Mean ranks are presented in FIGURE 1 because the Mann-Whitney is based on ranks, and mean ranks are more representative of group performance when, for example, one animal in a group crouches throughout the 120-second observation period and all

TABLE 2

MEAN NUMBER OF SECONDS SPENT CROUCHING AFTER THE CLICK, MEAN RANKS, AND LEVELS OF SIGNIFICANCE* OF DIFFERENCES BETWEEN GROUPS OF FEMALES IN EXPERIMENT I.

Group	NH N=9	H1 N=4	H2 N=8	H3 N=11	HΣ3 N=7
Mean seconds crouching	5.9	3.3	8.3	59.8	2.0
Mean rank	20.6	14.4	19.1	28.2	10.6
Nonhandled	—	none	none	<.10	<.05
Handled first week only		—	none	<.08	none
Handled second week only			—	<.08	<.20
Handled third week only				—	<.002

* As determined by the Mann-Whitney *U* test.

others crouch for only a few seconds. Mean ranks were determined by inter-ranking all same-sex animals across treatment groups, and dividing the sum of the ranks in each group by the number of rats in that group. TABLES 1 (males) and 2 (females) present for each treatment group, the number of animals, the mean number of seconds spent crouching, mean ranks, and significance levels of the differences between treatment groups.

According to these results, emotionality, as measured by the amount of crouching in an open-field, was significantly reduced in animals handled throughout the 21-day period constituting infancy, a finding which was consistent with previous reports (Weininger, 1953; Levine *et al.*, 1956; Levine & Otis, 1958) in which handling was administered throughout the nursing period. However, those animals handled only during the first week of life exhibited as marked a reduction in emotionality as the animals handled all three weeks. Animals handled exclusively during the second week did not differ from nonhandled control animals, while handling only during the third week was related to somewhat increased crouching. These results suggest that the reduction in emotionality produced by handling during infancy is related to a critical period in the first week of life. After this period, handling seems ineffective in reducing emotional behavior.

Experiment II. Separation of the Mother and Pups

The handling procedure described in the first experiment required separating pups from their mother for approximately ten minutes on each handling day. This separation of the mother and pups (a factor confounded in all handling studies at the time of this study) was selected for investigation for several reasons, including the following. Lidell (1954) found that electrophysiological indicants of emotionality were greater in baby goats subjected to electric shocks during their mother's absence than in kids similarly treated with the mother present. This can be interpreted to indicate that maternal absence is traumatic. Levine *et al.*, (1956), on the basis of their findings that animals shocked daily in infancy showed behavioral effects in adulthood similar to handled animals, interpreted the effects of handling in terms of an assumed traumatic aspect of the handling operation. It was hypothesized, therefore, that separation from the mother may thus be a crucial factor in handling, providing a traumatic experience similar to electric shock.

Method

Subjects. The parent stock for this experiment had been inbred from Sprague-Dawley animals for five years in Albert Tannenbaum's Cancer Research Laboratory, Michael Reese Hospital, Chicago, Illinois. Rats in this strain are a little smaller and less docile than the animals used in Experiment I. Fertility is somewhat reduced, as is viability of the young, compared with the Holtzman Sprague-Dawleys used in the first experiment. Litters used in this experiment were produced by brother-sister matings and each mother had reared one litter previously.

Procedure. Three nest cages were modified by attaching light, freely swinging, hanging doors in the openings where food hoppers had been mounted. These doors opened into galvanized metal covered runways (4 by 4 by 24 inches) which provided access to 8 by 8 by 10 inch wire mesh cages containing a food hopper and water bottle which were not available in the nest cages. The door and the rather high position of the opening prevented pups from entering the runways. Mercury switches attached to the swinging doors on two of these cages facilitated electrical recordings of the mothers' absences.

Three litters were assigned randomly to each of five groups for the following treatments throughout infancy:

Group NH..................Nonhandled controls
Group HΣ3..............Handled daily, all three weeks
Group R10................Mother removed, ten minutes per day
Group R6H..............Mother removed, six hours per day
Group RF..................Mother free to leave at will

Groups NH and HΣ3 were treated exactly like NH and HΣ3 in the first experiment. (It should be noted that this experiment was initiated before completion of the first experiment which indicated that treatment during the first week was sufficient to produce the effect.) Mothers in group R10 were removed from their nest cages for a ten-minute period each afternoon. This approximates the period of separation from the mother that handled animals undergo during each handling session. Pups in group R6H were subjected to a daily maternal absence of six hours. The mothers in groups R10 and R6H were removed with a gloved hand and placed, alone with food and water, in small wire mesh cages for the designated period of time.

Litters in group RF were whelped in the modified nest cages. Only one of the three litters survived the nursing period, and this litter numbered only three males and three females. It is unlikely that the mortality was related to the unusual nest cage arrangement: Two litters of stock Sprague-Dawley animals, reared in the special cages in a preliminary test of the feasibility of including group RF in this experiment, survived to maturity with no fatalities. Moreover, three out of the 12 litters of the inbred strain whelped in normal nest cages failed to survive, and several other inbred litters suffered one or more losses prior to weaning.

Group RF was included as a control for the experimenter's presence during removal and handling, as well as an attempt to simulate the natural environment of nonlaboratory rats. The frequency, duration, and periodicity of absences of two of the mothers were recorded automatically throughout the nursing period and for approximately four days before birth to permit a later comparison of absenteeism in this group with the enforced absences of the mothers in groups R10 and R6H. The absenteeism data (Schaefer, 1959) also provided information about a maternal behavior pattern in a situation similar to that in nature in which the mother must leave her pups to obtain food and water.

Procedures for weaning, maintenance, and testing were those described for Experiment I. The open-field test was administered at 43 to 53 days of age. Average age at testing did not vary between treatment groups by more than a few days.

Results

In general, the inbred animals used in this experiment exhibited more signs of emotionality than the stock Sprague-Dawley rats in Experiment I. Brief crouching during the first two minutes in the open-field, a relatively rare occurrence in the stock Sprague-Dawleys used in the first experiment, was exhibited by animals in each group except HΣ3. Defecation and urination were also more frequent than in the previous experiment, occurring in 66 per cent of the animals in the NH and the RF groups, 44 per cent of the R6 group, and 39 per cent and 38 per cent of the animals in the R10 and HΣ3 groups, respectively. This distribution yields a X^2 of 15.91 with three degrees of freedom, significant at the .01 confidence level, probably indicating that the nonhandled animals differed from the handled animals, the groups with the extreme scores. More specific statistical comparisons were not possible because of the small number of occurrences of defecation or urination in any one group.

The clearest measure of emotionality, as in the first experiment, was the amount of crouching after the click. Mean ranks and mean number of seconds spent crouching, along with N for each group, are presented in TABLE 3. The only significant difference was the lower amount of crouching by the males in group HΣ3 compared to group NH ($p < .01$). The extreme crouching score of the RF group is uninterpretable because of the low number of animals ($N = 3$ for both sexes). The behavior of noninbred Sprague-Dawley animals which had been reared in the RF cages in a preliminary trial of the cages did not differ from a simultaneously tested litter of nonhandled animals of the same age. These extra tests were conducted at the conclusion of Experiment II to resolve doubts about the high crouching scores of group RF.

TABLE 3

NUMBER OF ANIMALS, MEAN CROUCHING TIME, AND MEAN RANKS FOR EACH TREATMENT GROUP IN EXPERIMENT II

	Males			Females		
	N	Mean Crouching (Seconds)	Mean Rank	N	Mean Crouching (Seconds)	Mean Rank
Nonhandled	12	52.3	24.5	20	27.5	25.5
Handled all three weeks	11	16.1	11.9	4	16.8	22.9
Mother removed 10 min./day	7	45.4	21.1	11	28.4	21.0
Mother removed 6 hr./day	7	39.0	22.5	9	15.6	22.2
Mother free to leave	3	82.0	30.0	3	56.3	40.2

Summary. The reduced crouching and the lower frequency of defecation and urination of handled animals in this experiment substantiates the finding, in Experiment I, of reduced emotionality in $H\Sigma 3$ animals. Failure to obtain consistent differences between nonhandled controls and animals whose mothers had been absent for varying daily periods during infancy indicates, insofar as the open-field is an adequate test, that separation from the mother is not a crucial aspect of the handling situation. It will be seen later that the somewhat reduced scores of those groups whose mothers were removed may be interpretable in the light of subsequent experiments.

The records of maternal absences in group RF in which the mothers had to leave the nest cage to obtain food and water, or were free to leave when they wished, can be summarized briefly. This summary is based on two stock Sprague-Dawley mothers who had reared litters in the two cages arranged to record exits and entrances, as well as the two inbred mothers in group RF who reared their litters in these cages. In both strains the pattern of absences was the same.

Twenty-four hour, round-the-clock, kymographic records were obtained, starting approximately four days before birth of the pups and continuing until weaning. The results group themselves into three categories: (1) Prebirth behavior, based on records taken during the last week of gestation; (2) behavior of the mothers during the first three days following birth; and (3) behavior throughout the remainder of the nursing period. Before the pups were born the pregnant females spent 30 per cent to 40 per cent of each 24-hour period away from the nest cages. The average duration of absences was about 15 minutes, with a more or less daily, long period of two or three hours. This was certainly more than enough time for eating and drinking and, in fact, much of the time away from the nest cage was passed in the runway between the nest cage and the food cage. Most of the absenteeism before the birth of pups occurred during the early morning and early evening hours, a cyclic pattern which may have been structured by the daily lab routine where only the early morning and early evening, dinner, hours were free of disturbing human activity.

In marked contrast to this pre-birth pattern, the immediate post-birth behavior consisted of frequent short absences, usually less than a minute, rarely more than 15 minutes in duration. These brief absences were distributed more uniformly throughout the day. There were, typically, approximately 24 absences per day, approaching one each hour, although a tendency for longer absences in the early evening and early morning hours still persisted along with a corresponding tendency for longer gaps between absences to occur during the daylight hours. In all, the nursing mothers spent only one to twelve per cent of the first three days away from the litter, compared to the 30 per cent to 40 per cent absenteeism of the pregnant animals.

FIGURE 2 illustrates the contrast between the two behavior patterns. In this 24-hour excerpt from the actual record, the top line of dashes in both segments of the kymograph paper represents the absences of a pregnant female and the bottom line of dashes indicates the shorter absences of a nursing mother on the day after

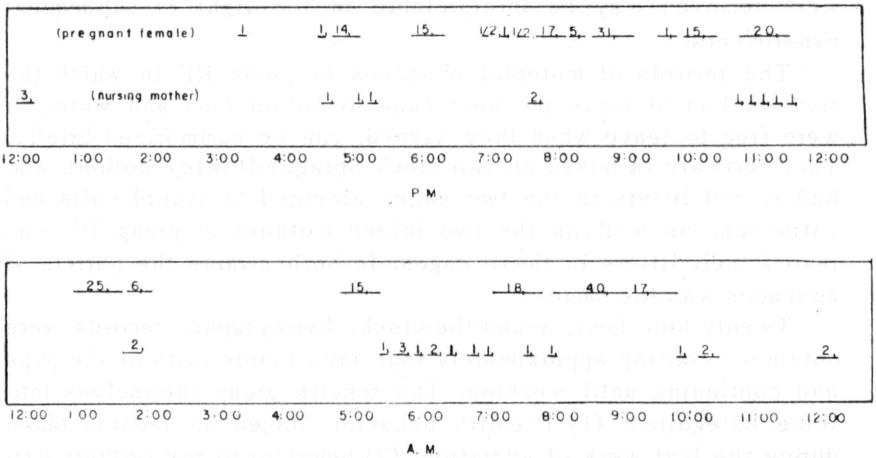

FIGURE 2. A 24-hour excerpt from the record of the absences of a pregnant female and the mother of two-day old pups. See text for explanation.

her litter was born. The length of each dash is roughly proportional to the length of absence, and the numbers above each dash indicate the duration in minutes. During this 24-hour period the pregnant animal was absent from her nest cage on 19 separate occasions, for an average of 12.8 minutes per absence and a total of 243 minutes or 17 per cent of the 24 hours. This percentage, and the average length of absence, are unusually low because the typical prolonged two- to three-hour absence did not occur.

During this same time-period the nursing mother was absent on 23 separate occasions for an average of 1.4 minutes per absence, a total of 33 minutes or 2 per cent of the time. The longest absence was three minutes and the distribution of absences was more regular.

Rather suddenly, by about the third or fourth day after the pups are born, the mothers' absences became longer, averaging between 7 and 12 minutes. In addition, a more or less daily absence of up to an hour begins to appear. After the fourth day, the chief differences between pre- and post-birth behavior are the smaller total amount of time away from the nest and the lack of two or three hour absences for the nursing mother. By weaning, at 21 days, pre- and post-birth absence patterns are virtually indistinguishable.

The very similar patterns of absenteeism in mothers of two different genetic strains, who also differed in age and pre-birth experience, suggests that this aspect of maternal behavior is a fundamental, species-specific behavior pattern. As such, it is probably related to the developmental pattern of the infant animals. The dramatic change in the mothers' behavior after the third or fourth day emphasizes the importance of this stage of development, suggesting that this period may encompass a critical period in development.

Experiment III. Perceptual Capacities or Emotionality

This experiment was based on Hebb's (1949) notion that early visual experience is a factor influencing the way in which an adult animal reacts to its environment. The experiment was designed to test the hypothesis that the lowered emotionality of handled animals is related to better visual ability. Added visual experience provided by handling might be sufficient to improve the visual capacities of handled animals, even though the added visual stimulation amounts to only 10 minutes per day (Hymovitch, 1952; Forgays & Forgays, 1952; Forgus, 1954). Reduced emotionality might result from a more adequate perception of the testing situation in animals which had been handled during early development. In previous handling studies most tests of emotionality or resistance to stress had involved more or less open, well-lighted situations like the open-field (Weininger, 1956), a transparent plastic double-grill box (Levine, *et al.*, 1956), open or elevated runways (Hunt & Otis, 1955), or fastening the animal supine upon a table top (Weininger, 1953). Thus, handling could affect emotionality indirectly through improving visual perception in certain test situations rather than directly, by modification of mechanisms underlying emotional behavior or emotionality, *per se*. Such a visual experience factor in handling would be implicated if it could be demonstrated that handled animals differ from nonhandled animals in visual capacities.

The Hebb-Williams maze (Hebb & Williams, 1946) was selected for comparing visual abilities of handled and nonhandled animals because, in addition to providing supplemental measures of emotionality in initial adaptation trials, it facilitates the separate analysis of emotionality and visual abilities by requiring pretraining until all signs of timidity and emotionality have disappeared. Only then is testing for visual capacities begun. Control of variations in emotionality between handled and nonhandled animals is essential to prevent emotional differences between the animals from affecting maze performance.

Method

The male subjects of Experiment I were used in this study. When they reached approximately 100 days of age, they were placed on a 22 hour food deprivation schedule and given daily training in the Hebb-Williams maze. This maze is a 36 by 36 inch enclosed surface with a start box diagonally across from a goal box where food is available. After the animal has learned to run directly, without hesitation, from start box to goal box, barriers of pine board painted black can be arranged in various patterns to form alleyways and detours to the goal box. Twelve such arrangements have been standardized as test items by Hebb and Williams. After 22 training trials without barriers, each animal was given three trials in quick succession on each item, one item per day. Surprisingly, perhaps, most animals ran most items perfectly on the second and third trials. On these trials any deviation from the shortest, most direct route through the barriers was scored an error.

Results

In terms of latency to leave the goal box, crouching, and defecating, the animals handled only during the first week of life, and those handled all three weeks, were less emotional during initial training trials on the Hebb-Williams maze than the nonhandled, second-week, or third-week handled animals. Thus, the open-field data of experiment 1 were nicely confirmed by these further measures of emotionality. But in terms of error scores on the test items, after all signs of emotionality had disappeared, there were no appreciable differences between any of the groups. This result has been confirmed, recently, by Denenberg & Morton (1962). Apparently, handled and nonhandled animals do not differ in visual abilities, the determining factor in performance on the test items in the Hebb-Williams maze.

Discussion

The indication in Experiment I that there is, during the first week of life, a critical period for handling has since been confirmed by several investigators. Karas (1957) reported a maximal effect on emotionality as measured by avoidance conditioning in animals handled during the first five days, compared with animals handled at other times during infancy. Levine and Lewis (1959) found that animals handled during the first week (days two through five) showed a significant depletion in adrenal ascorbic acid (AAA) in response to cold stress at the age of 12 days while nonhandled animals, and animals handled after the first five days, do not show a significant depletion until the 16th day of age (Levine, Alpert & Lewis, 1958). More recently, Bell, Reisner & Linn (1961) have reported another critical period study: Blood sugar level is significantly higher 24 hours after electro-convulsive shock in nonhandled animals and animals handled at times other than the first five days, than in animals handled during the critical period.

The results of Experiments II and III are also consistent with location of the critical period during the first 7 days. The fact that the eyes of rats are not open during this critical period precludes visual stimulation as a factor of importance in the handling procedure, and failure in Experiment III to find differences between groups in performance on Hebb-Williams test items could have been predicted. Consideration of the poorly developed sensory apparatus of week-old rats, which are eyeless, hairless, and apparently deaf (Small, 1899), also suggests that separation from the mother would not be an important aspect of the handling situation because the mother's absence could not be perceived, as such, by the infant rat. Negative results with respect to the effect of the mother's absence in Experiment II confirm this expectation.

Location of a critical period during the first week limits the range of hypotheses for explaining the handling phenomenon. Since the sensory capacities of one week-old rats are probably limited to gustatory, olfactory, temperature, tactual, and kinesthetic stimuli, the handling procedure must be considered in terms of its effectiveness in providing a change in one or more of these stimuli. Explanations of the handling phenomenon in terms of "relationship reinforcement" (Bernstein, 1952), "gentling" (Weininger, 1953; 1956), and "trauma" (Levine *et al.*, 1956) seem to assume complex perceptual and response processes that are beyond the sensory capacities of young rats. Progress in understanding the handling phenomenon would seem most probable through studies of the effects of varying the amount of stimulation in each of the available sensory modalities of the young rat.

Experiment IV. Temperature Change Without Handling

In an attempt to specify a feature of the handling procedure which could, conceivably, be effective during the first week of life, Levine and Lewis (1959) investigated the tactual stimulation which might be provided by handling. They administered tactual stimulation without actually handling by placing the entire cage containing the litter, but with the mother removed, on a laboratory shaker for three minutes of shaking. In addition to handled and nonhandled comparison groups, they included a shaker control group treated exactly like the shaker group, but with the shaker not operating. When they found, again using adrenal ascorbic acid depletion to cold stress as a measure of the stress resistance of early treatment groups, that the shaker control group showed as much effect as the shaker group, they concluded that the effects of handling are due to "any of several modes of extra-stimulation."

In considering what features of handling might possibly produce some effect on the infant rat during the first week of life, temperature change, a concomitant of the typical handling procedure, emerges as a prime candidate. Young mammals are generally unable to regulate body temperature nicely, and the young, hairless rat with a high surface-area to body-volume ratio can be expected to lose heat rapidly unless insulated by the mother, the nest, or the other pups. Before moving the nest cage, Levine and Lewis had removed the mother. In our laboratory this procedure scatters the pups, unless special care is taken. As Hutchings will show in the next paper, this scattering exposes the pups to cooler air outside the nest, resulting in a measureable drop in body temperature if the exposure is a few minutes in duration. Handling also exposes the pup to cooler air outside the nest, perhaps providing the extra stimulation suggested by Levine via temperature receptors in the skin. This exposure might also lower the body temperature sufficiently to alter ongoing enzymatic reactions involved in developmental processes, possibly producing permanent changes in physiological mechanisms underlying emotional- and stress-reactivity.

Direct measurements of skin and body temperature, and of neurologic, metabolic, or physiological changes would be needed to verify these speculations. Because of the technical difficulties of obtaining such data, and because it would still remain to be demonstrated that such temperature changes could produce the effects of handling, Frank Weingarten, a graduate student at the University of Chicago, and Jack C. Towne of the Veterans Administrative Research Hospital and Northwestern University Medical School, Chicago, Illinois, and I undertook the following experiment (Schaefer, *et al.*, 1962) as an initial test of the hypothesis that the effects of handling are due to lowered skin or body temperature.

Method

Subjects. Thirteen Holtzman Sprague-Dawley litters, totaling 118 pups, were assigned by litter to one of four treatment groups. The pups in group H (N=30) were handled daily for two minutes. Those in group NH (N=31) were not handled. Litters in group CE (N=31) were exposed daily to low temperature, and animals in group CC (N=26) were treated exactly like those in group CE, but were not exposed to cold.

Procedure. Pups in group CE were exposed to cold by placing the nest cage, containing mother and litter, in a refrigerator at 7° to 10° Celsius. Cages housing pups in group CC were placed in a nonfunctioning refrigerator maintained at room temperature (23° C). Groups CE and CC remained in their refrigerators for 12 minutes, the approximate time that group H litters were out of their cages during the handling procedure. Cages were transported gently to minimize disturbance and scattering. All treatments began on the day following birth and continued for six days, thus encompassing the first week, the critical period for handling.

Depletion of adrenal ascorbic acid in response to cold stress was selected to evaluate the effectiveness of treatments because it yields clear-cut differences between handled and nonhandled animals at an early age, and because it permitted us to replicate some of Levine's excellent work (previously cited). At 12 days, the earliest age for significant depletion by cold stress (Levine, *et al.*, 1958), half the pups in each litter were sacrificed and the adrenals were removed, weighed, and analysed for ascorbic acid content. The remaining pups were placed in small metal containers inside a refrigerator for a 90-minute cold stress at 5° C preceding removal of adrenals and assay. The assay method and data treatment were those described by Levine *et al.*, (1958).

Results

The results are graphed in FIGURE 3. Mean depletions of ascorbic acid, expressed in milligrams per hundred grams of tissue weight, were determined by subtracting the mean value of the stressed animals from that of the nonstressed animals within each treatment group. The Mann-Whitney *U* test of the differences between stressed and nonstressed animals within each group demonstrated significant reductions in AAA for the stressed animals in the handled and cold-exposed groups. There were no significant differences in ascorbic acid levels between stressed and nonstressed animals in the nonhandled or the cold-control groups. Kalberer (1961) has also reported that daily, brief exposure to a lowered ambient temperature (in a metal can) produces one of the effects of handling, increased weight gain.

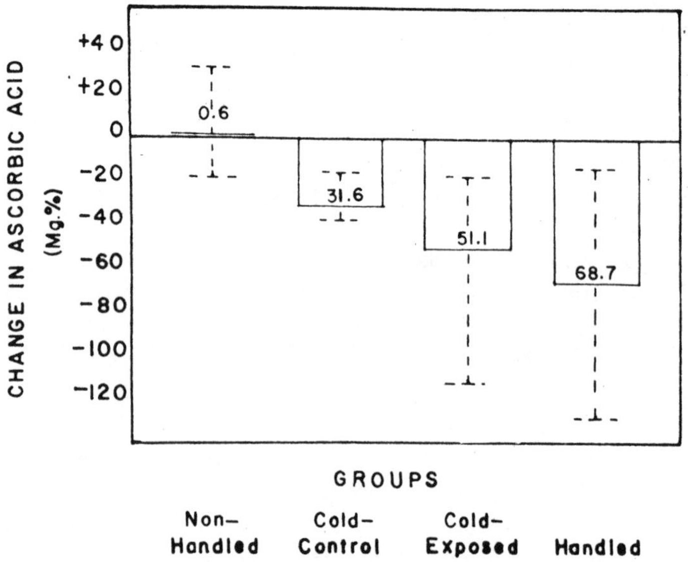

FIGURE 3. Comparison of adrenal ascorbic acid depletion in groups of 12-day-old rats which differed in early treatment during first week of life. Bars represent mean depletion, dashed lines indicate range among litters within each group. Mean values are lettered on the bars. Mg %, milligrams per 100 grams.

Discussion

These results indicated that an essential aspect of the handling procedure is a drop in environmental temperature accompanying removal from the nest. Subjecting the pups to low temperature without handling on days two through seven, although they were somewhat insulated in the nest by the mother, produced the same effect as handling (which exposed the pups to room temperature for the same amount of time). The small, but nonsignificant, depletion in adrenal ascorbic acid in the cold control group, we attributed to the mother's leaving the nest briefly when the cage was moved. When the mother leaves, the pups are dispersed and exposed to room temperature until they are returned to the nest by the mother after the cage is put down. It seems likely that AAA depletion in Levine's cage-moved, shaker-control group resulted not from merely moving the cage, but from exposing the scattered pups to room temperature for two minutes during the mother's absence. Hutchings will show that this exposure, longer than in our cold control group can produce a marked change in body temperature. On the other hand, Levine's animals were assayed at 14 days and are not entirely comparable with our cold-control animals assayed at 12 days since amount of depletion increases with age. It is also likely that a change in body temperature explains the slight effect obtained in the mother-removal groups in Experiment II, reported earlier. Although care was taken in that study not to scatter the nest when the mothers were removed, and Hutchings has shown that the body temperature of pups does not drop appreciably in the mother's absence if the nest is left intact, occasional scattering could have produced the slight reduction in emotionality in that experiment.

Experiment V. Handling Without Temperature Change

More recently, at Columbia, Donald Hutchings, Edward Atkins, Samira Hazen, and I have been engaged in a further study of the temperature factor in handling. In this study we are systematically varying the temperature to which pups are exposed while keeping the amount of handling constant.

Method

Subjects. To test the hypothesis that handling cannot produce the effect in the absence of a change in ambient temperature, 12 litters of Wistar Albino pups were assigned randomly at birth to three treatment groups.

Procedure. Group NH was a nonhandled control group; pups in group WH were removed from their nest on days 2, 3, 4, and 5 and placed for eight minutes on a cardboard surface in an incubator. The incubator was maintained at 34° to 36° Celsius, a temperature which, it was determined empirically, will maintain the pups' body temperature, measured rectally with a rapid-registering thermistor, at 36° to 37° Celsius, the normal temperature while in the nest. Pups in group CH were treated exactly like group WH, except that the incubator was maintained at room temperature, 22° Celsius. This treatment is very similar to that used in many handling studies in which the pup is merely picked up, put aside in some container for a few minutes and then returned to the mother. Hunt and Otis (1955) have shown that this type of handling is as effective as actually holding the pups in the hand.

At thirteen days of age each litter was sacrificed for AAA determination as in the previous study.

Results

FIGURE 4 shows the results: Only the pups exposed to room temperature showed appreciable depletion, significantly more, according to the Mann-Whitney *U* statistic, than that of the WH or the NH groups, which did not differ from each other.

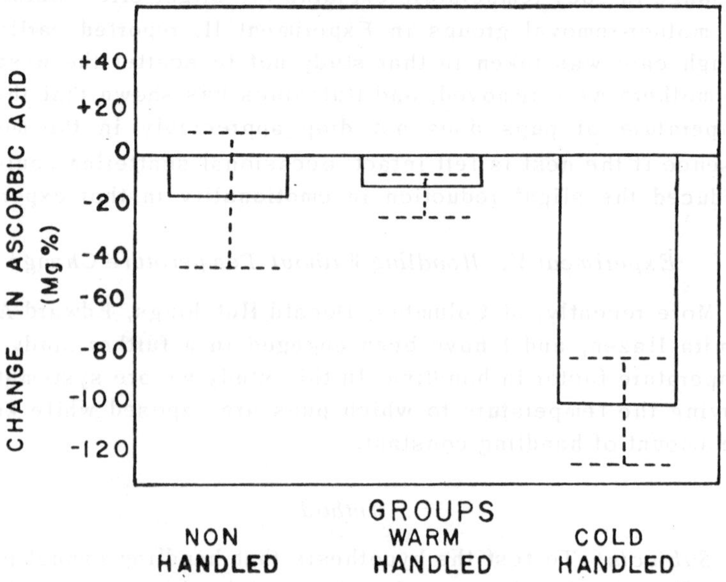

FIGURE 4. Comparison of adrenal ascorbic acid depletion in groups of 13-day-old rats which differed in early treatment during first five days of life. Bars represent mean depletion, dashed lines indicate range among litters within each group. Mg %, milligrams per 100 grams.

Discussion

This study demonstrates that handling is ineffective unless it is accompanied by a temperature change. The previous study showed that the effect of handling could be obtained without handling if the pups were merely exposed to a lower ambient temperature. Together, these two studies – suggested by the finding in the first experiment that handling is maximally effective at a time when rats are too poorly developed to be influenced by any but the most basic factors in the environment – provide strong evidence that temperature change is the basic variable in the early handling phenomenon. Hutchings, in the next paper, will present further research on the temperature factor in handling and discuss some of its implications.

References

AUBLE, D. 1953. Extended tables for the Mann-Whitney statistic. Bull Inst. Educ. Res. Indiana Univer. **1**: 2.

BELL, R. W., G. REISNER & T. LINN. 1961. Recovery from electroconvulsive shock as a function of infantile stimulation. Science. **133**: 1428.

BERNSTEIN, L. 1952. A note on Christie's "Experimental naivete and experiential naivete." Psychol. Bull. **49**: 38-40.

DENENBERG, V. H. & J. R. C. MORTON. 1962. Effects of preweaning and postweaning manipulation upon problem-solving behavior. J. Comp. Physiol. Psychol. **55**: 1096-1098.

FORGAYS, D. C. & J. W. FORGAYS. 1952. The nature of the effect of free environmental experience in the rat. J. Comp. Physiol. Psychol. **45**: 322-328.

FORGUS, R. H. 1954. The effect of early perceptual learning on the behavioral organization of adult rats. J. Comp. Physiol. Psychol. **47**: 331-336.

HEBB, D. O. 1949. The organization of behavior. Wiley, New York, N.Y.

HEBB, D. O. & K. WILLIAMS. 1946. A method of rating animal intelligence. J. Gen. Psychol. **34**: 59-65.

HUNT, H. F. & L. S. OTIS. 1955. Restricted experience and "timidity" in the rat. Am. Psychologist. **10**: 432. (Abstract).

HYMOVITCH, B. 1952. The effects of experimental variations on problem solving in the rat. J. Comp. Physiol. Psychol. **45**: 313-321.

KALBERER, W. D. 1961. Paper presented at Midwest Psychological Assoc. Meeting, Chicago, Illinois, 6 May 1961.

KARAS, G. C. 1957. The effect of the time and amount of infantile experience upon later avoidance learning. Unpublished master's thesis. Purdue Univer.

KING, J. A. 1958. Parameters relevant to determining the effect of early experience upon the adult behavior of animals. Psychol. Bull. **55**: 46-58.

KRUSKAL, W. H. & W. A. WALLIS. 1952. Use of ranks in one-criterion variance analysis. J. Am. Stat. Assoc. **47**: 583-621.

LEVINE, S., M. ALPERT & G. W. LEWIS. 1958. Differential maturation of an adrenal response to cold stress in rats manipulated in infancy. J. Comp. Physiol. Psychol. **51**: 774-777.

LEVINE, S., J. A. CHEVALIER & S. J. KORCHIN. 1956. The effects of shock and handling in infancy on later avoidance learning. J. Pers. **24**: 475-493.

LEVINE, S. & G. W. LEWIS. 1959. Critical period for the effects of infantile experience on maturation of stress response. Science. **129**: 42.

LEVINE, S. & G. W. LEWIS. 1959. The relative importance of experimenter contact in an effect produced by extra-stimulation in infancy. J. Comp. Physiol. Psychol. **52**: 368-369.

LEVINE, S. & L. S. OTIS. 1958. The effects of handling before and after weaning on the resistance of albino rats to later deprivation. Canad. J. Psychol. **12**: 103-108.

LIDELL, H. S. 1954. Conditioning and emotions. Sci. Amer. **190**: (1), 48-57.

SCHAEFER, T. 1959. Frequency, duration, and periodicity of voluntary absences of mother rats. Am. Psychologist. **14**: 334. (Abstract).

SCHAEFER, T., F. S. WEINGARTEN & J. C. TOWNE. 1962. Temperature Change: The basic variable in the early handling phenomenon? Science. **135**: 41-42.

SCOTT, J. P., E. FREDERICSON & J. L. FULLER. 1951. Experimental exploration of the critical period hypothesis. Personality. **1**: 162-183.

SCOTT, J. P. 1962. Critical periods in behavioral development. Science. **138**: 949-958.

SMALL, W. S. 1899. Notes on the psychic development of the young rat. Am. J. Psychol. **11**: 80-100.

THOMPSON, W. R. & T. SCHAEFER. 1961. Early environmental stimulation, in D. W. Fiske & S. R. Maddi. Functions of Varied Experience, Dorsey, Homewood, Ill.

WEININGER, O. 1953. Mortality of albino rats under stress as a function of early handling. Canad. J. Psychol. **7**: 111-114.

WEININGER, O. 1956. The effects of early experience on behavior and growth characteristics. J. Comp. Physiol. Psychol. **49**: 1-9.

32

Reprinted from *J. Comp. Physiol. Psychol.* **52**:368–369 (1959)

THE RELATIVE IMPORTANCE OF EXPERIMENTER CONTACT IN AN EFFECT PRODUCED BY EXTRA-STIMULATION IN INFANCY[1]

SEYMOUR LEVINE AND GEORGE W. LEWIS

Columbus Psychiatric Institute and Hospital, Ohio State University

In a recent study, Levine, Alpert, and Lewis (1958) reported that infant rats which had been manipulated (handled) once daily from birth responded to cold stress with a significant depletion of adrenal ascorbic acid (AAA) as early as 12 days of age, whereas nonmanipulated infant *S*s did not show significant AAA depletion until 16 days of age. These results were interpreted as indicating an acceleration of the physiological maturation of a response to stress as a function of the manipulation during infancy.

However, in the above study, and most of the studies reported dealing with the effects of prior experience on development and later behavior, procedures have been utilized which have involved handling the *S* to some degree. The degree of the handling has varied from a few minutes (Levine et al., 1958) to 10 min. (Weininger, 1956) per day.

The present experiment was designed to determine the effects of various types of extra-stimulation in infancy, in the absence of handling, on the development of the AAA depletion response to cold stress in the 14-day-old rat. The hypothesis under examination was that extra-stimulated infant *S*s, although not handled, would show a significant depletion of AAA following stress at 14 days of age.

METHOD

Subjects

One hundred and fifty-nine infant Sprague-Dawley-Holtzman albino rats were used as *S*s. The *S*s came from 17 females bred in this laboratory. The *S*s were assigned to one of five conditions as they were born. All *S*s were born and housed in cages measuring 9 in. by 15 in. by 9 in. In order to maintain a relatively constant home-cage environment, the cages were covered with a galvanized iron top so that all sides of the cage, with the exception of the front, were enclosed.

Procedure

The five conditions in this experiment were as follows:

Shaker ($N = 27$). Once daily, starting one day after birth, the whole cage was removed from the rack on which the cage was housed. The cage cover, water bottle, and mother were removed. The cage was then placed on an Eberbach Laboratory Shaker and shaken for 2 min. at 180 oscillations per minute. The cage cover, water bottle, and mother were then replaced and the cage returned to the rack. At no time until the test day were the *S*s handled.

Shaker Control ($N = 29$). This group received the same treatment as the Shaker group, but were placed on the shaker for 2 min. without shaking.

Shock ($N = 28$). These *S*s were removed from the nest, and each *S* was placed on a grid for a 2-min. period. The shock was turned as soon as the *S* was placed on the grid, kept on for the full 2 min., and turned off just before the *S* was removed. A shock of 0.1 ma. was delivered by a Grason Stadler Model E1064GS Shock Generator.

Manipulated ($N = 38$). The procedure for this group was identical to that previously described (Levine et al., 1958) and consisted of removing the pup from the nest, placing it in a 3-in. by 4-in. by 6-in. compartment for 3 min., and then returning it to the breeding cage.

The procedure for the groups which were stimulated was initiated on Day 1 and continued daily until the *S*s were 13 days of age.

Control ($N = 37$). The control or nonmanipulated *S*s remained in the breeding cages and received no treatment until the test day.

On Day 14, approximately half the pups within each litter were randomly assigned to the stress conditions. On the experimental day, the nonstressed *S*s were removed from their cages, killed by cervical spinal separation, and weighed. Their adrenals were removed immediately, weighed on a 25-mg. Roller-Smith balance, and prepared for AAA analysis.

The stressed *S*s were removed from their cages and were subjected to a cold stress of 5° C. for 90 min. They were then killed, and their adrenals removed, weighed, and prepared for assay. The analysis for AAA content and determination of depletion were made by the method previously described (Levine et al., 1958).

RESULTS AND DISCUSSION

The major findings are presented in Figure 1. The hypothesis that infant *S*s receiving stimulation in the *absence* of handling during infancy would show a significant depletion of AAA to cold stress at 14 days of age was clearly verified. All groups which received some form of extra-stimulation during infancy, with or without being handled, showed a significant depletion of AAA at 14 days, whereas the control (nonmanipulated) group failed to show significant depletion. Comparisons between the

[1] This investigation was supported by Research Grant PHS M-1630 from the National Institute of Mental Health of the National Institutes of Health, U. S. Public Health Service.

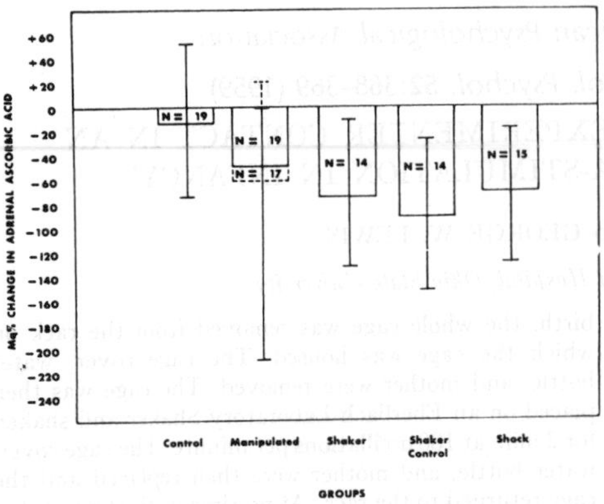

FIG. 1. Comparison of the various groups in AAA depletion to cold stress. The bars indicate the mean depletion, and the lines the range of depletion within each group.

groups (Mann Whitney *U* tests) revealed no significant differences in the amount of AAA depletion between the four experimental groups. All experimental groups did differ significantly from the control group. The differences were beyond the .01 level of probability when the control group was compared with Shock, Shaker, and Shaker Control *S*s. It should be noted that in Figure 1 the depletion for the manipulated *S*s is presented in two ways. When the total 19 stressed *S*s in the manipulated group are compared with the control *S*s, the difference closely approaches significance at the .05 level. A *U* of 132 is obtained, and a *U* of 130 is needed for significance at the .05 level. However, if the 2 *S*s (see Fig. 1) which showed a relative increase are not included, the difference between the manipulated and the control *S*s is significant beyond the .01 level.

The results of the present experiment indicate that the effects reported in the present study and the previous study related to AAA depletion in *S*s stimulated in infancy are not primarily due to contact with the *E*, but to any of several modes of extra-stimulation.

SUMMARY

In order to evaluate the importance of *E* contact in the effects of early experience on the development of adrenal ascorbic acid depletion to cold stress, the above study involved various forms of daily extra-stimulation during infancy. These modes of stimulation were manipulation and shock, which involved contacts with *E*, and shaking and moving about, which did not involve *E* contact.

At 14 days of age treated groups of *S*s were compared with *S*s which had received no extra-stimulation in infancy, in terms of adrenal ascorbic acid depletion to 90 min. of 5° C. cold. It was found that all treatment groups differed significantly from the control group and that there was no significant difference between experimental groups.

The obtained data indicate that experimenter contact is not a major variable in determining the effects of infantile extra-stimulation on the maturation of the adrenal ascorbic acid depletion response to stress.

REFERENCES

LEVINE, S., ALPERT, M., & LEWIS, G. W. Differential maturation of an adrenal response to cold stress in rats manipulated in infancy. *J. comp. physiol. Psychol.*, 1958, **51**, 774–777.

WEININGER, O. The effects of early experience on behavior and growth characteristics. *J. comp. physiol. Psychol.*, 1956, **49**, 1–9.

33

Reprinted from *Science* **129**:42–43 (1959)

CRITICAL PERIOD FOR EFFECTS OF INFANTILE EXPERIENCE ON MATURATION OF STRESS RESPONSE

Seymour Levine and George W. Lewis

Ohio State University Health Center

Abstract. Manipulated infant rats respond to cold with depletion of adrenal ascorbic acid (AAA) significantly earlier than nonmanipulated infants. The study discussed in this report examined the critical period for infantile manipulation on the depletion of AAA. It was found that infant rats manipulated immediately following birth exhibited significant AAA depletion, whereas infants manipulated later did not exhibit depletion.

Recently it has been reported (*1*) that infant rats which had been manipulated (handled) once daily fron birth responded to cold stress with a significant depletion of adrenal ascorbic acid as early as 12 days of age, whereas nonmanipulated infant rats did not show significant AAA depletion until 16 days of age. One question which arose from this study was whether the age at which the experimental treatment of manipulation was initiated is a significant factor in the accelerated maturation of the systems which result in AAA depletion with stress.

The experiment discussed in this report (*2*) was directed, therefore, toward answering the question of whether there exists a critical period in the development of the organism during which manipulation has its greatest effect on the AAA depletion response to stress. The existence of such a period seemed likely, since critical periods have been documented for many other aspects of development (*3*).

Seventy-six infant Sprague-Dawley albino rats were used as subjects. The subjects were assigned at birth to one of four groups. For the infants in group I ($N = 20$), the treatment was initiated on the second day following birth and continued through day 5. The treatment was started on day 6 and was continued through day 9 for group II infants (N = 20). The treatment for the group III subjects (N = 20) was given from day 10 through day 13. The last group, group IV, received the treatment from day 2 through day 13. The experimental treatment was identical to that previously described (*1*) and consisted of removing the pup from the nest, placing it in a 2.5- by 3.5- by 6-in. compartment for 3 minutes, and then returning it to the nest. This procedure was followed once daily during the period assigned to the subject. At 14 days of age, approximately half the pups within each group were randomly assigned to either the stress or control condition to test for AAA depletion with stress.

The stress conditions and method of analysis for AAA are fully described in previous reports (*1*) and, therefore, will be only briefly described here. The nonstressed subjects within each group were killed by cervical spinal separation and weighed. The adrenals were removed, weighed, and assayed for AAA by the modified method of Glick *et al.* The stressed infants were subjected to a cold stress of 5°C for 90 minutes before removal of the adrenals and determination of AAA.

The results of this experiment are shown in Fig. 1 and are expressed in terms of milligrams percent change in AAA level. Change in AAA level was determined by subtracting the AAA present in the stressed animals from the mean for the nonstressed subjects.

The data clearly indicate that the age during which the infant rat is manipu-

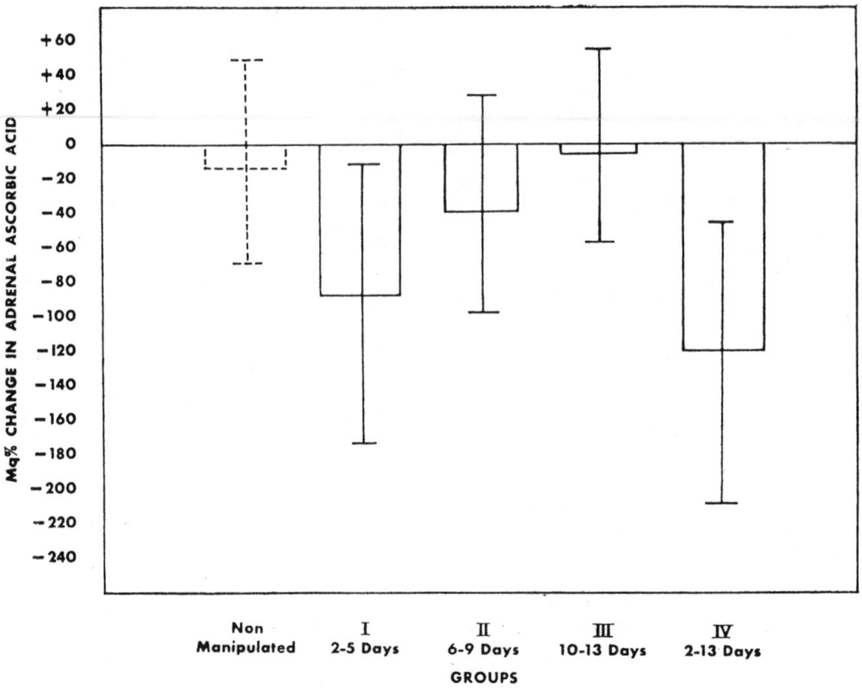

Fig. 1. Comparison of depletion in AAA in the various groups of infant albino rats of the study. The bar represents the mean depletion; the lines, the range. The dotted bar and dotted line represent untreated animals that had previously been tested.

lated is a major variable in the effect described in this report. Only the animals in groups I and IV showed significant AAA depletion. In terms of percentage, the group I subjects showed a 25-percent depletion and the group IV subjects showed a 32-percent depletion. The depletion in AAA in the group II and group III animals (9 percent and 0 percent, respectively) did not differ significantly from that in the respective controls. Thus, in the groups (I and IV) which had been manipulated during the period directly following birth, a significant depletion in AAA is evidenced in response to cold stress at 14 days of age, whereas the groups manipulated later in infancy do not show significant AAA depletion.

Recent evidence has indicated that the early postnatal period is also critical for behavioral changes during adulthood. Schaefer (*4*) found that handling during the first 7 days produced the greatest reduction in adult emotionality measured in terms of behavior in an open field situation. Denenberg (*5*) reports that handling during the first 10 days of life resulted in avoidance learning superior to that found when handling was initiated later. In both of these studies, the period during which the treatment was initiated includes the critical period found in the experiment discussed in this report. Whether behavioral difference can be detected in experiments with such restricted age groups as were tested in this experiment remains to be determined.

References and Notes

1. S. Levine, M. Alpert, G. W. Lewis, *J. Comp. Physiol. Psychol.*, in press.

2. This investigation was supported by research grant PHS M-1630 from the National Institute of Mental Health of the National Institutes of Health, U.S. Public Health Service.

3. J. P. Scott, *Psychosom. Med.* 20, 42 (1957).
4. T. Schaefer, Ph.D. dissertation, University of Chicago (1957).
5. V. Denenberg, paper presented at the 1958 meeting of the American Psychological Association.

31 July 1958

34

Reprinted from *J. Comp. Physiol. Psychol.* **51**:774–777 (1958)

DIFFERENTIAL MATURATION OF AN ADRENAL RESPONSE TO COLD STRESS IN RATS MANIPULATED IN INFANCY[1]

SEYMOUR LEVINE, MORTON ALPERT,[2] AND GEORGE W. LEWIS

Columbus Psychiatric Institute and Hospital, Ohio State University

During the past several years there has been a marked resurgence of experimentation related to the effects of prior experience on adult behavior. Investigators have reported differences in adulthood in learning (1, 6, 10), emotionality (4, 6, 7, 16), and physiological resistance to stress (8, 16) as a function of experience during the preweaning and immediately postweaning periods. Although there have been numerous experiments concerning the effects of infantile (preweaning) and early (postweaning) experience on adult behavior, there has been little work concerning the effects of infantile experience on the physiological development of the infant organism.

A review of the experiments concerning infantile experience and subsequent behavior indicates that one of the major differences between *S*s manipulated in infancy and nonmanipulated *S*s is observed in the relative differences in emotionality of these *S*s. Characteristically, rats that are left in the breeding cage and not manipulated in any manner prior to weaning show more responses associated with emotionality (defecation, freezing) in adulthood than *S*s that were either shocked or picked up and placed in a small compartment once daily during the first 21 days of life. Since emotional responses are usually made to stressful situations in adulthood, the present study was designed to investigate the maturation of the physiological response of adrenal ascorbic-acid depletion to stress in infant *S*s as related to prior manipulation.

Jailer (5) reported that infant rats subjected to cold stress failed to show adrenal ascorbic-acid depletion prior to 16 days of age, when a 19% depletion was found. Infant animals as young as 4 to 8 days do show ascorbic-acid depletion to injection of ACTH and large doses of epinephrine, and to the surgical trauma of laparotomy (5, 12). One hypothesis offered to account for these results is the lack of development of the hypothalamo-hypophysial system, which appears to be essential in the reaction to certain types of stress (5). Since it has been previously suggested that infantile manipulation modifies later reactivity of the central nervous system under conditions of stress (8), it was hypothesized that manipulation in infancy would affect the rate of development and the intensity of the stress response in the infant organism.

METHOD

Subjects

Two hundred and seventy-eight infant Sprague-Dawley Holtzman albino rats were used as *S*s. The *S*s came from 31 females bred in this laboratory. The experimental treatments of manipulation and nonmanipulation were assigned alternately to litters as they were born.

Procedure

The *S*s were run at 10, 12, 14, and 16 days of age. Half the litters within each age group were manipulated prior to the experimental day. The manipulation procedure was identical to that previously described as handling (6) and consisted of removing the pup from the nest, placing it in a 2½ by 3½ by 6-in. cardboard compartment for 3 min. and then returning it to the breeding cage. This procedure was followed once daily from Day 1 through the day prior to the experimental day for each of the age groups.

At 10, 12, 14, and 16 days approximately half the pups within each litter were randomly assigned to the stress condition. There were thus four groups at each age point: (*a*) manipulated, nonstressed; (*b*) manipulated, stressed; (*c*) nonmanipulated, nonstressed; and (*d*) nonmanipulated, stressed. The total *N* for each condition is presented in Table 1.

On the experimental day the nonstressed animals were removed from their cages, killed by cervical spinal separation, and weighed. Their adrenals were removed immediately, weighed on a 25-mg. Roller-Smith balance, and analyzed for ascorbic-acid content. The stressed animals were removed from their cages, placed in small individual stainless-steel compartments, and subjected to a cold stress of 5° C. for 90 min. They were

[1] This investigation was supported by Research Grant PHS M-1630 from the National Institute of Mental Health of the National Institutes of Health, U. S. Public Health Service. The authors are indebted to Benjamin Pasamanick, Director of Research, for his assistance throughout this investigation.

[2] Department of Anatomy, Ohio State University.

TABLE 1
Summary Table of t Tests

Group	Condition	N	Depletion (mg. %)	S	t	p
16-Day manipulated	Stressed	15	110.1	13.0	8.47	<.005
	Nonstressed	15				
16-Day non-manipulated	Stressed	18	68.8	9.1	7.56	<.005
	Nonstressed	17				
14-Day manipulated	Stressed	20	49.7	21.3	2.15	<.025
	Nonstressed	18				
14-Day non-manipulated	Stressed	19	16.2	13.1	1.24	>.20
	Nonstressed	18				
12-Day manipulated	Stressed	19	47.4	20.0	2.37	<.025
	Nonstressed	20				
12-Day non-manipulated	Stressed	19	+4.1	18.3	0.22	>.80
	Nonstressed	17				
10-Day manipulated	Stressed	16	+7.1	15.0	0.47	>.60
	Nonstressed	16				
10-Day non-manipulated	Stressed	15	2.7	14.2	0.19	>.80
	Nonstressed	16				

then killed, and their adrenals were removed, weighed, and assayed.

Adrenal ascorbic acid was assayed by a modification of a micro technique (3). After weighing, the adrenals were placed in a 15-ml. ground-glass stoppered centrifuge tube and thoroughly ground in 2 ml. of 0.5% oxalic acid. Five milliliters of n-amyl alcohol was added to the tube followed by 3 ml. of a 4-mg.% aqueous solution of sodium 2,6-dichlorophenol indophenol dye. The tubes were then thoroughly shaken and centrifuged. The colored alcohol layer was then removed and its optical density determined on the Beckman D U spectrophotometer at a wave length of 546 mμ. The obtained optical density was then converted to micrograms of ascorbic acid by reading it on a standard curve obtained with known quantities of ascorbic acid. The obtained value was expressed as milligrams of ascorbic acid per 100 gm. of adrenal weight, or mg.%. The amount of depletion of ascorbic acid was determined by subtracting the adrenal ascorbic acid present in the stressed *S*s from the mean of the nonstressed *S*s.

RESULTS

The major findings are presented in Figure 1.

The animals manipulated during infancy evidenced a physiological response to cold stress earlier, and consistently to a greater extent than did the nonmanipulated animals. The manipulated animals first showed a significant depletion in adrenal ascorbic acid at 12 days of age, whereas the nonmanipulated animals failed to show significant depletion until 16 days of age. At 10 days, neither group showed significant depletion. At 12 days of age, the nonmanipulated *S*s showed no depletion, whereas the manipulated *S*s showed a depletion of 47 mg.%. At 14 days, the nonmanipulated animals evidenced a depletion of 16 mg.% (not significantly different from zero), while the manipulated animals showed 50 mg.% depletion. Sixteen-day-old nonmanipulated *S*s had an average depletion of 69 mg.%, whereas the manipulated *S*s had a depletion of 110 mg.%, a level which is not normally observed until adulthood (Fig. 1). Table 1 consists of a summary of t tests between experimental and control groups at the various age points.

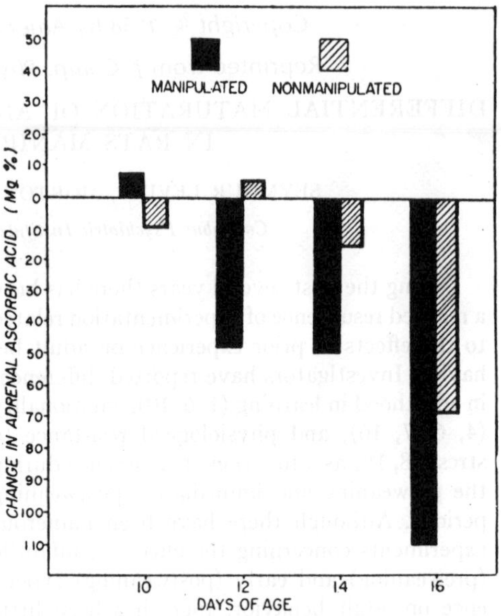

FIG. 1. Adrenal ascorbic-acid depletion in manipulated and nonmanipulated infant rats.

DISCUSSION

The results of this experiment clearly indicate that manipulated infant rats exhibit a physiological response to stress at an earlier age than do nonmanipulated infants. It should be further noted that at 16 days, when both groups exhibit significant depletion, the manipulated *S*s show significantly greater depletion (9) than the nonmanipulated *S*s. The 16-day nonmanipulated *S*s showed 20% depletion, corresponding to the 19% depletion obtained by Jailer for this age group, whereas the manipulated group had a depletion of 30%. The 30% depletion exhibited by the manipulated animals closely resembles the adult response to cold stress, which has been reported to be between 30 and 60% depletion. It appears that manipulation during infancy results in accelerated maturation in the systems involved in response to cold stress, as evaluated by ascorbic-acid depletion.

It has been suggested that there exists a dual mechanism which is responsible for activation of the pituitary-adrenal system under stress. One of these mechanisms involves blood concentration of ACTH and adrenal-cortical hormones and is considered as a self-regulating hormonal system (13). The other involves the response of the central and autonomic nervous systems. For certain types of stress, such as histamine and epinephrine injection, and laparatomy, there is evidence (2, 11) that the self-regulatory hormonal system can operate in the absence of an intact hypothalamo-hypophysial system. However, neurotropic stress such as restraint, intense sound, and cold apparently do not occur unless the hypothalamo-hypophysial system is functioning. It would appear, therefore, that one of the effects of manipulation in infancy is accelerated maturation of the systems involved in the response to neurotropic stress. Since the exact mechanisms involved in the response under investigation are not known, it is difficult to implicate the exact site of action. Furthermore, this study investigated only one response mechanism, and it is possible that many other developmental processes are affected by the manipulation procedures employed, including that of the central nervous system. In general, the results of the study demonstrate an interaction between experience and maturation. The extent of this interaction remains to be determined.

There are two additional points which warrant consideration. First, it should be noted that throughout this paper the term "manipulation" has been used to describe a procedure which has previously been called "handling." Since handling has been used (1, 14, 16) to describe a procedure which involves fondling, stroking, and gentling, it is necessary to distinguish between the handling procedure which involves gentling and the handling procedure which consists merely of transporting the *S* from one place to another. It is apparent that these different procedures differ markedly in the manner in which the *S* is manipulated, and there is no reason to assume at this time that the effects produced by these different procedures are the same. It is possible that subsequent research will show that the critical aspects of these procedures which result in the changes observed in adulthood and infancy might be the same, but for the present it is important, in order to avoid confusion and erroneous comparisons, to make a clear distinction between what is involved in so-called handling or gentling and what is done in what we are now calling manipulation.

Second, there has been a noticeable tendency among many investigators in this area to use the terms "early" and "infantile" experience interchangeably (14, 16). In the majority of studies in which infantile and early experience are considered as one and the same thing, the experimental treatment is not initiated until the *S* is weaned, approximately 21 days of age. Unlike the extremely dependent and undeveloped infant, 21-day-old rats are fully able to maintain themselves under normal laboratory conditions and are far advanced physiologically. In view of the evidence concerning critical periods in development (15), it is erroneous to assume that experimental treatments initiated during the preweaning period give rise to the same effects produced by experimental treatments given during the postweaning period. It is critical, therefore, that in the future a clear distinction be made between preweaning (infantile), postweaning (early), and other prior experiences.

SUMMARY

The present study was performed to investigate the effects of infantile manipulation upon the development of a stress response to cold as measured by adrenal ascorbic-acid depletion.

Groups of manipulated and nonmanipulated infant rats were run at 10, 12, 14, and 16 days of age. Approximately half the animals were stressed by placing them in a small compartment at a temperature of 5°C. for 90 min. The remaining nonstressed *S*s were killed and their adrenals immediately assayed to determine initial adrenal ascorbic-acid levels. The adrenal ascorbic-acid content of the stressed *S*s was then assayed and depletion determined.

The manipulated *S*s showed significant depletion at 12, 14, and 16 days of age, whereas the nonmanipulated rats failed to show significant depletion until 16 days, a finding in line with that previously reported. In addition, at 16 days, the manipulated *S*s evidenced a depletion of 110 mg. % which approximates the level normally seen in adult rats to the same stress, whereas the nonmanipulated *S*s showed a depletion of 68 mg. %, a level approximating that previously reported for the 16- to 25-day-old rat.

The implication of the results was discussed in terms of the effects of infantile experience on the maturation of the organism, and the possibility of a permanent alteration in stress-response reactivity was presented. In addition, the need for clarification of the term "handling" and the clear differentiation of infantile from early experience was emphasized.

REFERENCES

1. Bernstein, L. The effects of variations in handling upon learning and retention. *J. comp. physiol. Psychol.*, 1957, **50**, 162–167.
2. Fortier, C. Dual control of adrenocorticotrophin release. *Endocrinology*, 1951, **49**, 782.
3. Glick, D., Alpert, M., & Stecklein, H. C. Studies in histochemistry: XXVII. The determination of L-ascorbic acid, and dehydro-L-ascorbic acid plus diketo-L-gulonic acid in microgram quantities of tissue. *J. histochem. cytochem.*, 1953, **1**, 326–335.
4. Hunt, H. F., & Otis, L. S. Restricted experience and "timidity" in the rat. *Amer. Psychologist*, 1955, **10**, 432. (Abstract)
5. Jailer, J. W. The maturation of the pituitary-adrenal axis in the new-born rat. *Endocrinology*, 1950, **46**, 420–425.
6. Levine, S. A further study of infantile handling and adult avoidance learning. *J. Pers.*, 1956, **25**, 70–80.
7. Levine, S. Infantile experience and consummatory behavior in adulthood. *J. comp. physiol. Psychol.*, 1957, **50**, 609–612.
8. Levine, S. Infantile experience and resistance to physiological stress. *Science*, 1957, **126**, 405.
9. Levine, S., Alpert, M., & Lewis, G. W. Infantile experience and maturation of the pituitary-adrenal axis. *Science*, 1957, **126**, 1347.
10. Levine, S., Chevalier, J. A., & Korchin, S. J. The effects of shock and handling in infancy on later avoidance learning. *J. Pers.*, 1956, **24**, 475–493.
11. Long, C. N. H. The role of epinephrine in the secretion of the adrenal cortex. In *Ciba colloquia on endocrinology*, Vol. IV. Boston: Little, Brown, 1952. P. 139.
12. Rinfret, A. P., & Hane, S. Depletion of adrenal ascorbic acid following stress in the infant rat. *Endocrinology*, 1955, **56**, 341–344.
13. Sayers, G. The adrenal cortex and homeostasis. *Physiol. Rev.*, 1950, **30**, 241–320.
14. Scott, J. H. Some effects at maturity of gentling, ignoring, or shocking rats during infancy. *J. abnorm. soc. Psychol.*, 1955, **51**, 412–414.
15. Scott, J. P., & Marston, M. V. Critical periods affecting the development of normal and maladjustive social behavior of puppies. *J. genet. Psychol.*, 1950, **77**, 25–60.
16. Weininger, O. The effects of early experience on behavior and growth characteristics. *J. comp. physiol. Psychol.*, 1956, **49**, 1–9.

Received December 9, 1957.

35

Reprinted from pp. 40, 49–57, 62–64 of *Early Childhood: The Development of Self-Regulatory Mechanisms,* D. W. Walcher and D. L. Peters, eds. Academic Press, 1971, 249 pp.

EFFECTS OF HANDLING IN INFANCY UPON ADULT BEHAVIOR AND ANDRENOCORTICAL ACTIVITY: SUGGESTIONS FOR A NEUROENDOCRINE MECHANISM

Victor H. Denenberg and M. X. Zarrow
University of Connecticut

EFFECTS OF HANDLING IN INFANCY UPON LATER BEHAVIOR

When one looks back on the brief history of experimental research on early experiences, one finds that the first sets of studies were done using a postweaning animal in which the "richness" of the animal's environment was manipulated to see how this affected later perceptual and problem-solving behavior. This work was stimulated by Hebb's exciting book, *The Organization of Behavior,* published in 1949. It was not until several years later that experimenters turned to the newborn, or infant, animal for experimental investigations.

The first report concerning the effects of handling infant animals was probably the brief abstract by Hunt and Otis (1955) of a paper which they presented at the annual meeting of the American Psychological Association. Unfortunately, these researchers waited until 1963 before they published a formal report of their research (Hunt & Otis, 1963). The first full-fledged experimental research report on the effects of handling was a paper by Levine, Chevalier, and Korchin in 1956. In that study the authors were primarily interested in the effects of shock upon the infant animal's later ability to learn an avoidance response. However, being good experimenters, they were aware that their shocked group also had the experience of being removed from their home cages, being placed into a strange apparatus, etc., in addition to receiving the electric shock. Thus, they included a second experimental group which was manipulated in the same manner as their shocked group except that shock was omitted. This "handled" group was found to be as effective at avoidance learning as the animals in the shocked group, and both groups were better than a nondisturbed control.

In his next study, therefore, Levine (1956) omitted the shocked group and studied the effects of handling as an experimental variable. He had one group which was handled for the first 20 days of life, and a second experimental group which was handled at 50-70 days of age. The control group, of course, was not disturbed between birth and weaning, nor after weaning until avoidance testing began at 71 days. Levine found that the animals handled in infancy were significantly better in avoidance learning than the late-handled group or the control group, while the latter two groups did not differ from each other.

This experiment, in conjunction with the prior one by Levine *et al.* and the brief abstract by Hunt and Otis, established that handling, a seemingly mild form of stimulation in infancy, would have long-lasting effects upon the rat. In addition Levine's (1956) study also showed that handling in later life did not have the same consequences as handling in infancy.

[*Editor's Note:* Material has been omitted at this point.]

STUDIES INVOLVING CORTICOSTERONE AS PART OF THE MECHANISM OF INFANTILE STIMULATION

One of the very important principles coming out of the work on neonatal sex hormones is that hormones either prenatally or in early infancy can act upon and modify brain organization. Though this has just been established for the sex hormones, it seems reasonable to conclude that other hormones may also have this function. When one now looks at the data on infantile stimulation and compares them with the neonatal sex hormone data, certain interesting parallels are seen. First of all, the effects of infantile stimulation are limited to the period of infancy, and the sex hormones also have their impact during very early infancy. [Remember that Levine (1956) showed that handling between 50-70 days of age had no effect upon behavior as compared to handling between 1-20 days of age.] Also, most of the effects of handling during the first 20 days of life can be obtained by handling animals for the first 5 days (see the two 5-day groups in Figure 3 and compare them with the 20-day group). Second, handling has long-term essentially permanent effects on the behavior of an animal, and the same is true with the neonatal sex hormones. (This statement does not imply that it is impossible to reverse these effects. It merely states that given a constant set of conditions under which animals are maintained, one is able to demonstrate these effects throughout the lifetime of the animal.) Finally, corticosterone is a steroid and, as such, belongs to the same class of hormones as testosterone, estrogen, and progesterone.

Because of these various considerations, we adopted the working hypothesis that stimulation in infancy brought about the release of corticosterone into the bloodstream, and that the corticosterone went to the brain, presumably to the hypothalamus, where it acted to modify brain organization, thus resulting in an animal which was less emotionally reactive. We set out to test this hypothesis in a series of experiments which we will now briefly describe.

If our hypothesis is true, the first thing which must be established is that corticosterone can be found in the blood of a neonatal animal. Interestingly enough this had not been demonstrated previously and, indeed, there was some evidence that corticosterone was not present. We will get to that in a moment.

In considering how to attack this problem we decided that the safest thing to do was to use very powerful stressors to try to elicit the corticosterone response. Therefore we selected electric shock and heat. We used 0.8 mA of shock delivered to the young animal on a brass grid floor. For heat stress the animals were suspended in a nylon mesh basket in a thermal-regulated chamber maintained at 63°C. The animals were exposed to these stressors for 3 minutes. They were then removed, placed in a can containing shavings for an additional 15 minutes, after which they were decapitated, and both plasma and adrenal corticosterone were determined. Since we had no knowledge as to the age at which the animals would be sensitive to these stressors, if at all, we decided to do a developmental study. Different groups of animals were stressed and assayed at 1, 2, 3, 4, 5, 7, 9, 11, and 21 days of age (Haltmeyer, Denenberg, Thatcher, & Zarrow, 1966). Figure 4 shows the data for the amount of corticosterone in the plasma, while Figure 5 presents the findings for the amount of corticosterone obtained in the adrenal cortex itself.

The plasma corticosterone data in Figure 4 clearly demonstrate that the newborn rat is capable of secreting significant amounts of corticosterone into its bloodstream as a function of exposure to electric shock and heat stress, with heat having a greater effect than shock during the first 5 days of life. Another interesting thing to note about the curves in Figure 4 is that there is a considerable amount of corticosterone present at birth, that the levels drop to a minimum at approximately 7 days of age, and then rise again at 21 days for the experimental animals to values approximating those of the normal adult. This is an important point to which we will return later in the paper. Figure 5, which shows the amount of corticosterone which can be measured in the adrenal gland, presents a slightly different picture. Heat has a measurable effect starting with the first day of life, but electric shock had no significant effect upon increasing corticosterone output until the animals were 7 days old.

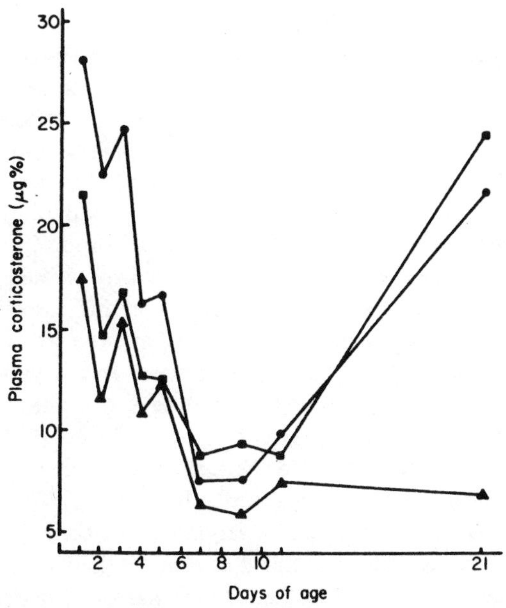

Fig. 4. Plasma corticosterone concentrations in the immature rat following exposure to heat stress, electric shock, or no stimulation. ■, Shock; ●, heat; ▲, control. From Haltmeyer *et al.* (1966).

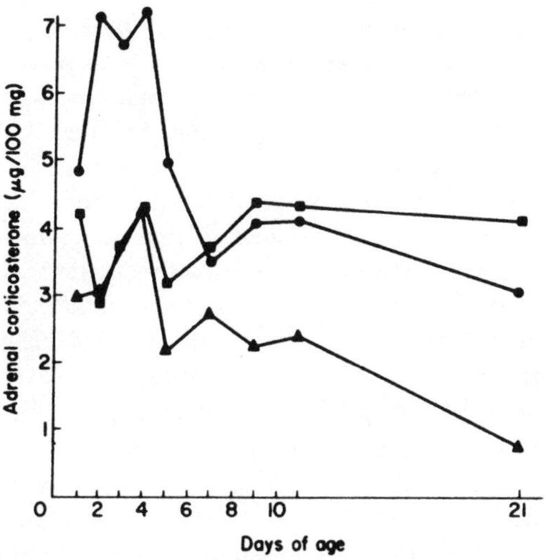

Fig. 5. Adrenal corticosterone concentrations in the immature rat following exposure to heat stress, electric shock, or no stimulation. ■, Shock; ●, heat; ▲, control. From Haltmeyer *et al.* (1966).

These results were consistent with our working hypothesis, which gratified us. However, the results were contradictory to other findings in the literature, and this perplexed us. Several researchers had reported over the years that the neonatal rat did not respond to stressors with any evidence of an adrenal reaction. In fact, Schapiro and his associates (Schapiro, 1962; Schapiro, Geller, & Eiduson, 1962) had formalized this observation by coining a term for it. They stated that the rat had a "stress-nonresponsive period" during the first 6 to 8 days of life during which time stressors would not produce any adrenal activity.

We were now faced with the question as to why we had found evidence of significant adrenal activity while Schapiro and his associates had not. To investigate this discrepancy in findings we carried out a second experiment using rats which received heat or electric shock stress at 2 days when, according to Schapiro, they are nonresponsive and at 9 days when they are known to be responsive (Zarrow, Haltmeyer, Denenberg, & Thatcher, 1966). At both 2 and 9 days the animals were subjected to the same electric shock or heat stress for a period of 3 minutes as had been described previously. They were then placed into shaving cans and were killed at varying times thereafter. In order to get resting levels, some animals were killed as soon as they were removed from the home cage. Figures 6 and 7 show the data for plasma corticosterone and adrenal corticosterone, respectively, in this experiment.

As compared to resting level values (designated by the letters RL in Figures 6 and 7) the plasma corticosterone response of those animals which received either heat or electric shock stimulation at 2 and 9 days of age was significantly increased, which is consistent with our prior findings. Also in Figure 6, it will be noted that there is a greater response at 2 days of age than at 9 days of age, again consistent with our previous study. The discrepancy between our results and those of Schapiro and his associates was explained by the adrenal corticosterone data. In the left-hand panel of Figure 7 we see that electric shock stimulation has no measurable effect upon the amount of corticosterone found in the adrenal gland. Thus both we and Schapiro failed to find any evidence of an adrenal response when 2-day old rats were stressed with electric shock, killed an hour afterwards, and assayed for adrenal corticosterone. If the first or third of these parameters is changed, significant effects are obtained. Thus, the stress-nonresponsive hypothesis was based upon an artifact generated by selecting an unfortunate combination of parameters to investigate this phenomenon. In Figure 7 we again found evidence confirming our previous study that heat has a very marked effect both at 2 days and 9 days of age, and that electric shock also has a significant effect at 9 days.

Our first two experiments have established that the newborn rat could respond to stressors such as heat and shock with a significant rise in adrenal corticosterone. Our next concern was whether other forms of stressing agents could also elicit a significant increase in adrenal activity in the 2-day old rat

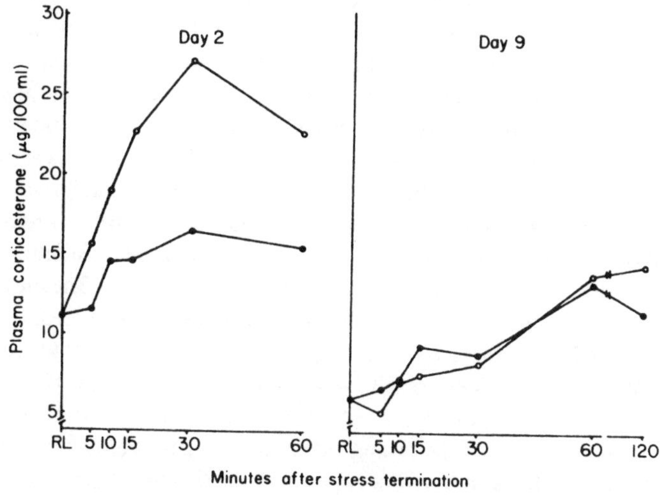

Fig. 6. Time course of plasma corticosterone following exposure to heat (○–○) and electric shock (●–●) in the 2-day and 9-day old rat. From Zarrow *et al.* (1966).

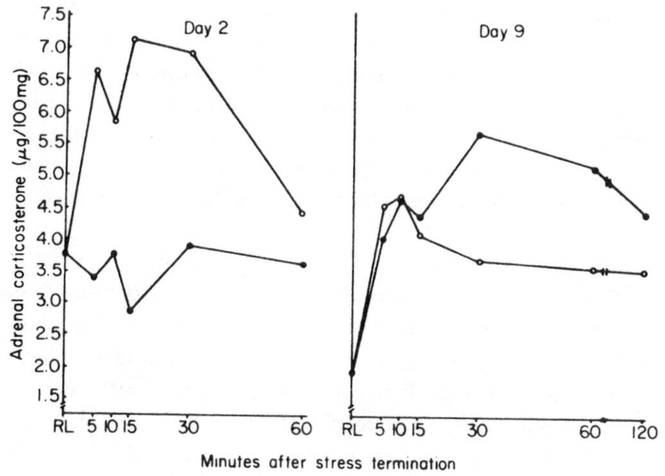

Fig. 7. Time course of adrenal corticosterone following exposure to heat (○–○) and electric shock (●–●) in the 2-day and 9-day old rat. From Zarrow *et al.* (1966).

(Zarrow, Denenberg, Haltmeyer, & Brumaghim, 1967). When ACTH and histamine were used as stressors, significant rises in corticosterone were obtained. When the animals were exposed to cold stress by being placed on crushed ice, only a marginal effect was obtained.

There was one stressor in this experiment which did not have any measurable effect, namely ligation: surgical silk was tied tightly just above the knee of the right hind leg and the ligature was tight enough to cause the animals to squeal. Yet in spite of this squealing, which we take to be evidence of a painful stimulus, we found no evidence of an increase in either plasma or adrenal corticosterone as compared to controls. We consider this finding of the ligature experiment to have rather broad implications. Fortier (1951, 1966) has suggested two classes of stressors, one "neural" and the other "systemic" according to whether they activate ACTH release solely by the mediation of the nervous system or whether they act on the pituitary through the systemic circulation. The outstanding feature of the stimulus involved in the ligature experiment appears to be its neural nature (the ligature was not tied tightly enough to cut off blood circulation in the limb). These results would tend to indicate that the pituitary–adrenal axis is operative in the 2-day old rat but that the neural component in the system is not active as yet. This finding would also suggest why we found a lesser effect with electric shock in our first experiment of this series (see Figures 4 and 5) than with heat since electric shock has a large neural component involved while heat would have its effects mediated primarily through systemic activity.

These findings had started us off on the right track by showing that it was possible to get the adrenal gland to release corticosterone into the blood stream when strong stressing agents such as heat, shock, histamine, or ACTH were used. But the technique we had used to stimulate infant rats in our early experience work was the handling procedure which certainly appears to be much more innocuous than the various stressors enumerated above. The experimental question to which we next addressed ourselves was whether the standard handling procedure was a sufficient stimulus to elicit a measurable corticosterone response in the neonate (Denenberg, Brumaghim, Haltmeyer, & Zarrow, 1967).

On the first day of life litters were cut back to eight animals, but they were not handled at this age because we wanted to keep this experiment comparable to our previous studies. On Day 2 the pups were removed from their maternity cage, two were killed immediately from each litter to obtain resting levels, and the other six were placed into handling cans where they were left for 3 minutes. At the end of the 3 minutes they were placed back with their mother in the maternity cage. This procedure, it will be noted, is identical to our standard handling techniques except that six rather than eight animals were returned to the mother. Thirty minutes after being returned, two pups were removed from the litter and were killed. We found that those pups which had received handling had a significantly greater amount of plasma corticosterone than their resting level littermate controls.

We also found two other techniques which would elicit a significant adrenocortical response. The first was to leave the pups along in handling cans for 33 minutes, and the second was to place the pups into an empty maternity cage for a half hour after the usual 3 minutes in handling cans. These two procedures demonstrated that it was not necessary to return the young to the mother in order to obtain a significant response. The importance of this was in eliminating the mother as necessarily a causal variable. The mother, upon the return of the pups, will pick the young up, run around with them, prepare a new nest for them, and engage in much "handling" activity with them. Thus, it is possible that it is the mother's behavior toward the pups after they are returned to the nest box which is the major stimulus that affects the pups' subsequent behavior. (We are in agreement that the mother's behavior toward the pups does have a significant effect, but it is also important to understand clearly that the handling procedure, independent of the mother's behavior, can also elicit a significant corticosterone response.)

Another part of this study investigated the question as to whether the temperature loss brought about as a function of being removed from the warm nest and being placed into a handling can alone was a significant factor in eliciting the corticosterone response. If temperature loss was the critical variable, then the corticosterone response should be prevented if rats were placed into handling cans maintained at a temperature equivalent to that present when the rats were packed together in the maternity cage. The average temperature in a packed nest was 35.5°C. When 2-day old pups were placed into handling cans maintained at this temperature, their corticosterone levels did not differ from that of resting level controls, while other experimental animals placed in handling cans at ambient temperature did show the usual significant rise in plasma corticosterone.

But one should not suppose from this that the change in temperature is the only variable affecting the corticosterone response. In Figure 3 there was one group of animals which had been handled for 5 days in infancy at body temperature, and this group also had a significantly lesser corticosterone response to the novel stimulus of an open field than did nonhandled controls. Thus one is able to handle animals without reducing their body temperature and can still obtain significant effects. We suggest that these significant effects may be mediated through the mother's behavior toward the pups after they are returned to the nest box.

Let's pause for a moment and recall our working hypothesis which set us off on this series of studies. It was that stimulation in infancy would bring about a release of corticosterone from the adrenal cortex into the blood stream and that this hormone would act upon the central nervous system, presumably the hypothalamus, in order to change the neural organization of the brain. We have gotten corticosterone into the blood stream by our handling procedure as well as by other more severe stressing agents. The next question was: where does the corticosterone go from there? To answer that question we took radioactive-labeled corticosterone and injected it into 2-day old rats. Different groups were killed 10, 30, 60, or 120 minutes after the injection, and we removed muscle tissue, and liver, the hypothalamus, and the rest of the brain, and we counted the amount of corticosterone present using a liquid scintillation system. The radioactive corticosterone was taken up in significant amounts both by the hypothalamus and by the rest of the brain throughout the 2-hour interval of the study. More important, however, was that the hypothalamus showed a greater uptake of radioactivity than the rest of the brain both at 10 minutes and 30 minutes after injection (Zarrow, Philpott, Denenberg, & O'Connor, 1968). At the same time McEwen, Weiss, and Schwartz (1968) showed a selective retention of corticosterone by the hippocampus and septum.

Now let us change focus for a moment. The technique of using radioactive-labeled corticosterone had been useful in demonstrating that this hormone is taken up by the brain, with a greater amount in the hypothalamus. Recall that in all the experiments described above our various manipulations had been mediated by the experimenter. However, in nature no experimenter is present, and so if we believe that corticosterone is having an effect upon the newborn animal in its natural setting and if we believe that handling has some counterpart in a biological context, we have to find some natural biological mediator for these events. It seems reasonable to assume that the mother would be the mediator during both the prenatal stage and the postnatal stage of development.

Consider, first, prenatal development. A number of studies have demonstrated that a pregnant rat which is emotionally upset will have offspring which are also emotionally upset (Ader and Belfer, 1962; Thompson, 1957). On the other hand, Ader and Conklin (1963) demonstrated that when pregnant rats are handled during their gestation, the offspring are less emotional. If corticosterone from the pregnant mother is able to pass the placental barrier, it is possible that this hormone might act upon the central nervous system of the developing fetus to affect its neural organization and, thus, its emotional behavior. To test this hypothesis, we injected radioactive corticosterone into pregnant rats the day before they were due to deliver their young (Zarrow, Philpott, & Denenberg, 1970a). Thirty minutes later the mothers were decapitated, the fetuses were removed, and tissues from muscle, liver, hypothalamus, and the rest of the brain were evaluated to determine that amount of radioactivity present in the fetuses. We found that the hypothalamus and the rest of the brain had taken up a significant amount of radioactive corticosterone and again, as in our prior experiment, the hypothalamus had a significantly greater uptake than did the rest of the brain. Thus maternal corticosterone is able to cross the placental barrier and can localize in the brain of the fetus, thereby indicating that this is a possible mechanism for the effects of prenatal stimulation.

The next question we asked was whether corticosterone could get through the mammary glands of the mother while the young were nursing (Zarrow, Philpott, & Denenberg, 1970a). On the second day after birth the mothers were separated from their pups for 4 hours and were then injected with radioactive corticosterone. The pups were then returned and allowed to nurse for 55 minutes. We were able to find evidence of a measurable amount of radioactive corticosterone in the blood of the neonatal animals and in their stomach contents, but in no other tissues. Furthermore, only a very small percentage of the injected hormone was found in the offspring, which agrees with findings of others that labeled steroids are transferred through the milk in only extremely small amounts. Thus, it seems unlikely that corticosterone in the mother's milk has much effect upon the infant animal's behavior. It is much more likely that the mother affects her offspring by means of her behavioral interactions with them rather than through her milk supply. Evidence supporting this position has been recently reviewed by Denenberg (1970) with respect to the effects of maternal factors upon the aggressive behavior, open-field activity, and adrenocorticosterone response of mice.

This brings us up to date with respect to our research on the hypothesis that corticosterone is involved in mediating the effects of infantile stimulation. So far each experiment that we have done has been completely consistent with our hypothesis, though we recognize that this does not establish its validity. To summarize briefly, we have shown that corticosterone is released in the neonatal rat as a function of intense stressors such as shock, heat, histamine, and ACTH. We have also shown that our standard handling procedure will bring about a significant release of corticosterone in the 2-day old animal. We have been able to obtain a corticosterone response in the newborn animal without returning it to its mother, thereby demonstrating that we can get an effect mediated entirely by the experimenter. This does not mean that the mother has no effect. Instead, it suggests that our handling procedure may do some of the same things that the mother does toward her young between birth and weaning, as if we are, in a sense, simulating certain characteristics of the mother's behavior. McEwen *et al.* (1968) have shown a retention of corticosterone by the hippocampus and septum, and we have been able to demonstrate that the corticosterone, after it gets into the blood stream, goes to the brain and more of it is taken up in the hypothalamus than in the rest of the brain. Our results indicate that this is true for the newborn animal and is also true for the fetus, thus suggesting a mechanism whereby emotional upset on the part of the mother during pregnancy may have an effect upon her unborn offspring's subsequent emotional behavior. When we look at the nursing female, we find evidence that only a very small amount of corticosterone in the milk supply has any major effect upon the animal's behavior. Instead, we think it more reasonable that the mother's behavior toward her young results in stimulation that brings about a release of endogeneous corticosterone.

[*Editor's Note:* Material has been omitted at this point.]

SUMMARY

This paper starts with a review of the data on the effects of handling as a technique for introducing stimulation in infancy. One of the major consequences of handling rats in early life is to bring about a reduction in emotional reactivity as measured by a variety of behavioral tests. We then discuss the effects of handling in infancy upon the corticosterone response of the adrenal cortex, and demonstrate an experimental relationship between behavioral measures of emotionality and the amount of corticosterone found in the adult animal.

Next, we briefly discuss some of the research involving neonatal sex hormones to develop the principle that the function of these hormones in very early life is to organize the brain with respect to maleness or femaleness while the function of the hormones in adulthood is to activate an already organized brain. Using this as a model we propose that stimulation in infancy acts to release corticosterone from the adrenal cortex, that this hormone acts upon the brain, presumably the hypothalamus, to modify neural organization and to make an animal less emotional. We then present our experimental data based on this hypothesis. To date all experiments we have carried out have been consistent with the hypothesis, but as yet the data are still not adequate to draw any firm conclusions concerning the validity of the hypothesis. Finally, we briefly discuss some of our research investigating the physiological characteristics of the adrenal cortex of the newborn animal and its relation to the pituitary gland.

REFERENCES

Ader, R., & Belfer, M. S. Prenatal maternal anxiety and offspring emotionality in the rat. *Psychological Reports,* 1962, vol. 10, 711-718.

Ader, R., & Conklin, P. M. Handling of pregnant rats: Effects on emotionality of their offspring. *Science,* 1963, vol. 142, 411-412.

Campbell, H. J. The development of the primary portal plexus in the median eminance of the rabbit. *Journal of Anatomy,* 1966, vol. 100, 381-387.

Denenberg, V. H. Critical periods, stimulus input, and emotional reactivity: A theory of infantile stimulation. *Psychological Review,* 1964, vol. 71, 335-351.

Denenberg, V. H. Stimulation in infancy, emotional reactivity, and exploratory behavior. In D. C. Glass (Ed.), *Neurophysiology and emotion.* New York: Rockefeller University Press and Russell Sage Foundation, 1967.

Denenberg, V. H. The effects of early experience. In E. S. E. Hafez (Ed.), *The behaviour of domestic animals.* London: Bailliere, Tindall and Cassell, 1969. (a).

Denenberg, V. H. Open-field behavior in the rat: What does it mean? *Annals of the New York Academy of Science, 1969,* vol. 159, 852-859. (b).

Denenberg, V. H. The mother as a motivator. In W. J. Arnold (Ed.), *Nebraska symposium on motivation.* Lincoln, Neb.: University of Nebraska Press, 1970, in press.

Denenberg, V. H., Brumaghim, J. T., Haltmeyer, G. C., & Zarrow, M. X. Increased adreno-cortical activity in the neonatal rat following handling. *Endocrinology,* 1967, vol. 81, 1047-1052.

Denenberg, V. H., & Haltmeyer, G. C. Test of the monotonicity hypothesis concerning infantile stimulation and emotional reactivity. *Journal of Comparative and Physiological Psychology,* 1967, vol. 63, 394-396.

Fortier, C. Dual control of adrenocorticotropin release. *Endocrinology,* 1951, vol. 49, 782-788.

Fortier, C. Nervous control of ACTH secretion. In G. W. Harris and B. T. Donovan (Eds.), *The pituitary gland,* Vol. 2. Berkeley: University of California Press, 1966.

Glydon, R. St. J. The development of the blood supply of the pituitary in the albino rat, with special reference to the portal vessels, *Journal of Anatomy,* 1957, vol. 91, 237-244.

Haltmeyer, G. C., Denenberg, V. H., Thatcher, J., & Zarrow, M. X. Response of the adrenal cortex of the neonatal rat after subjection to stress. *Nature (London),* 1966, vol. 212, 1371-1373.

Haltmeyer, G. C., Denenberg, V. H., & Zarrow, M. X. Modification of the plasma cortico-sterone response as a function of infantile stimulation and electric shock parameters. *Physiology and Behavior,* 1967, vol. 2, 61-63.

Hebb, D. O. *The organization of behavior.* New York, New York: Wiley, 1949.

Hess, J. L., Denenberg, V. H., Zarrow, M. X., & Pfeifer, W. D. Modification of the corticosterone response curve as a function of handling in infancy. *Physiology and Behavior,* 1969, vol. 4, 109-111.

Hunt, H. F., & Otis, L. S. Restricted experience and "timidity" in the rat. *American Psychologist,* 1955, vol. 10, 432. (Abstract)

Hunt, H. F., & Otis, L. S. Early "experience" and its effects on later behavioral process in rats: I. Initial experiments. *Transactions of the New York Academy of Science,* 1963, vol. 25, 858-870.

Levine, S. A further study of infantile handling and adult avoidance learning. *Journal of Personality,* 1956, vol. 25, 70-80.

Levine, S. Plasma-free corticosteroid response to electric shock in rats stimulated in infancy. *Science,* 1962, vol. 135, 795-796. (a).

Levine, S. The psychophysiological effects of infantile stimulation. In E. L. Bliss (Ed.), *Roots of behavior.* New York: Harper, 1962. (b).

Levine, S. Sex differences in the brain. *Scientific American,* 1966, vol. 214, 84-90.

Levine, S., & Mullins, R. F., Jr. Hormonal influence on brain organization in infant rats. *Science,* 1966, vol. 152, 1585-1592.

Levine, S., Chevalier, J. A., & Korchin, S. J. The effects of early shock and handling on later avoidance learning. *Journal of Personality,* 1956, vol. 24, 475-493.

Levine, S., Haltmeyer, G. C., Karas, G. G., & Denenberg, V. H. Physiological and behavioral effects of infantile stimulation. *Physiology and Behavior,* 1967, vol. 2, 55-59.

McEwen, B. S., Weiss, J. M., & Schwartz, L. S. Selective retention of corticosterone by limbic structures in rat brain. *Nature (London),* 1968, vol. 220, 911-912.

Newton, G., & Levine, S. (Eds.) *Early experience and behavior.* Springfield, Ill.: Charles C. Thomas, 1968.

Philpott, J. E., Zarrow, M. X., & Denenberg, V. H. Prevention of drop in adrenocortical activity in the 7-day-old rat by pretreatment with ACTH. *Proceedings of the Society for Experimental Biology and Medicine,* 1969, vol. 131, 26-29.

Schapiro, S. Pituitary ACTH and compensatory adrenal hypertrophy in stress-nonresponsive infant rats. *Endocrinology,* 1962, vol. 71, 986-989.

Schapiro, S., Geller, E., & Eiduson, S. Neonatal adrenal cortical response to stress and vasopressin. *Proceedings of the Society for Experimental Biology and Medicine,* 1962, vol. 109, 937-941.

Thompson, W. R. Influence of prenatal maternal anxiety on emotionality in young rats. *Science,* 1957, vol. 125, 698-699.

Whimbey, A. E., & Denenberg, V. H. Experimental programming of life histories: the factor structure underlying experimentally created individual differences. *Behaviour,* 1967, vol. 29, 296-314. (a).

Whimbey, A. E., & Denenberg, V. H. Two independent behavioral dimensions in open-field performance, *Journal of Comparative and Physiological Psychology,* 1967, vol. 63, 500-504. (b).

Young, W. C., Goy, R. W., & Phoenix, C. H. Hormones and sexual behavior. *Science,* 1964, vol. 143, 212-218.

Zarrow, M. X., Denenberg, V. H., Haltmeyer, G. C., & Brumaghim, J. T. Plasma and adrenal corticosterone levels following exposure of the two-day-old rat to various stressors. *Proceedings of the Society for Experimental Biology and Medicine,* 1967, vol. 125, 113-116.

Zarrow, M. X., Haltmeyer, G. C., Denenberg, V. H., & Thatcher, J. Response of the infantile rat to stress. *Endocrinology,* 1966, vol. 79, 631-634.

Zarrow, M. X., Philpott, J. E., & Denenberg, V. H. Postnatal changes in the pituitary-adrenal axis of the rat. *Proceedings of the Society for Experimental Biology and Medicine,* 1968, vol. 128, 269-272.

Zarrow, M. X., Philpott, J. E., & Denenberg, V. H. Passage of ^{14}C-4-corticosterone from the rat mother to the fetus and neonate. *Nature (London),* 1970, vol. 226, 1058-1059. (a).

Zarrow, M. X., Philpott, J. E., & Denenberg, V. H. Responsiveness of the adrenal gland of the neonatal rat. In S. Kazda and V. H. Denenberg (Eds.), *The Postnatal Development of Phenotype.* Prague: Academia, 1970. (b).

Zarrow, M. X., Philpott, J. E., Denenberg, V. H., & O'Connor, W. B. Localization of ^{14}C-4-corticosterone in the 2-day old rat and a consideration of the mechanism involved in early handling. *Nature (London),* 1968, vol. 218, 1264-1265.

36

Reprinted from *Child Dev.* **39**(1):59–67 (1968)

INFANTILE IMMUNIZATION AND ADULT STATURE

JOHN W. M. WHITING

Harvard University

THOMAS K. LANDAUER and THOMAS M. JONES

Stanford University

In a previous study, which used a cross-cultural method, apparently stressful infant-care practices, including immunological inoculations, were found to be associated with greater adult stature. In the present study, data from 2 longitudinal-growth studies were analyzed. With parental stature held constant statistically, the adult stature of individuals inoculated before 2 years of age was significantly greater than that of individuals not so inoculated. This and a variety of other sources of evidence bearing on the possible growth-accelerating influence of early physiological stress were compared and the present status of the question evaluated.

There is substantial evidence that unusually stimulating events during early infancy can cause acceleration of growth in rats (see Landauer & Whiting, 1964; Levine, 1960, for reviews of this evidence). It has been postulated (Levine, 1960) that the acceleration of growth results from an alteration in endocrine balance which is brought about by the occurrence of a physiological stress reaction at an early, perhaps critical, period. Whether or not this is the proper explanation of the phenomenon, it is nevertheless empirically clear that apparently stressful experiences in early life lead to increased size at maturity in rats.

In looking for a parallel effect in humans, Landauer and Whiting

---

We are very grateful to Lester Sontag, director of the Fels Research Institute, and to Stanley Garn as member of the staff responsible for the materials on physical growth; to Millah Ayoub for overseeing the abstracting of materials from the Fels Institute files; to Jean Macfarlane and Marjorie Honzik of the Berkeley Guidance Study for providing us with the opportunity to use their excellent data as the basis of the study reported here; to Lincoln Moses and R. S. Srivastava for help in the statistical analyses; and to Henry Harpending who served as research assistant. J. W. M. Whiting's address: William James Hall, Harvard University, Cambridge, Massachusetts 01541,

(1964) studied the relation between apparently stressful infant-care practices and the adult stature of males in two independent cross-cultural samples. They found that adult males in societies in which scarification, circumcision, inoculation, or repeated molding and shaping of the limbs or cranium was practiced before the age of 2 years were a statistically significant 2½ inches taller, on the average, than adult males in societies without such practices. The relation between infant experience and adult stature was independent of cross-cultural measures of diet, race, and several geographical factors.

There are other data which may also be interpreted as suggesting an effect of stimulation on growth in humans parallel to that observed in lower animals. Gunders (1961), in a cross-cultural study, investigated the effect on growth of separation of an infant from its mother in the first days of life, which she interprets as a stressor. She found such separation to be significantly associated with greater stature in adults. Gunders and Whiting (1964) studied the relation between hospital birth and growth. Their assumption was that hospital deliveries ordinarily involve many of the same features as do the mother-separation practices of Gunders' cross-cultural study; notably, the child is removed from the warm bed of his mother and may not be fed for 24 hours or so. They studied children born in a relocation camp in Israel in which the distribution of which individuals were born in the hospital and which at home seemed to be primarily determined by how far the family's assigned tent was from the camp hospital at the time of birth. Those children born in the hospital were found to be significantly heavier at ages 3 and 4 than those born at home.

Graham et al. (Graham, 1966; Graham, Ernhart, Thurston, & Craft, 1962) found that infants who suffered anoxia at birth showed a significant faster rate of growth than a normal control group. Many of the same children were studied again at age 7. Those who had suffered perinatal anoxia were significantly ($p < .01$) taller and heavier than normals (Corah, Anthony, Painter, Stern, & Thurston, 1965). Again, it is possible to interpret anoxia at birth as a stressful stimulus which might lead to the same changes which underlie the growth-accelerating effects of early stress in animals.

While none of these data can be taken as clear evidence of a causal relation between early stress and increased growth in humans, they may all be so interpreted; and the considerable variation among them, with the exception of the commonality of their probable stressfulness to the infant, suggests that the stress-growth hypothesis is worthy of further study. In an effort in this direction, we have reanalyzed data from two longitudinal-growth studies carried out in the United States: the Fels Study (Garn, 1962; Kagan, 1964), and the Berkeley Guidance Study (Macfarlane, 1938). We have searched the medical records of the cases from these studies for the occurrence of stressful events during early life. As suggested by the results of the earlier cross-cultural work, the age of 2 years was taken as an empirical cutoff point between early and later childhood. This cutoff is used as a matter of convenience only, based on our previous results, but with the possibility held open that examination of new data will lead to its modification.

Of the various infant-care practices which were associated with increased adult stature in the cross-cultural study, in the longitudinal study samples only inoculation was found in the necessary intermediate frequency which would allow a comparison of those who had been exposed to it with those who had not been so exposed. Inoculation may be presumed to be stressful on several counts. First of all it involves a pain at the time of occurrence, but this is probably the least significant of its stressful effects. An infant who has been inoculated for smallpox ordinarily shows symptoms of distress up to 2 or 3 weeks thereafter (Spock, 1957). In addition, recent evidence (Marshall, 1966) indicates that smallpox and other inoculations are associated with the formation of bone lines, which have often been thought to be associated with stress (Tanner, 1962, p. 130).

It is important to enter a caveat to our argument at this point. It is obvious that early inoculations in the U. S. population may be associated with many other things. Those parents who have their children inoculated early almost certainly differ in many ways from those who do not. For example there may be an association between this medical procedure and other forms of medical care. We by no means reject the possibility that the association with growth which we have observed and will report below is due to these other factors rather than to stress per se. However, we feel it is important, as a first step, to see whether inoculation, which was associated with increased stature in a cross-cultural sample of primitive societies, is similarly associated with increased stature among members of our own society. Once this empirical question has been answered, a discussion of its interpretation will become more fruitful.

While we did not present cross-cultural data separately for inoculation as compared to other forms of stress in the original report (Landauer & Whiting, 1964), a significant relation between inoculation and stature existed in those data, as indicated by the following reanalysis. There were 5 societies in the sample of 65 that were reported to systematically inoculate children before the age of 2 years. The mean stature of the adult males in these five societies was 66.8 inches as compared to 64.2 inches for the remainder of the sample, and 63.0 for those societies in which no stress before the age of 2 was reported. Each case is a society in which at least 25 individuals were measured and their heights recorded in ethnographic literature and for which detailed data on child rearing were available. The ratings on the child-care practice and stature were done by independent (blind) raters. The differences are statistically significant (for inoculated vs. not inoculated $t = 2.61$, $df = 63$, $p < .02$ two-tailed; for inoculated vs. not stressed in any way $t = 4.46$, $df = 32$, $p < .001$ two-tailed).

METHOD

Materials

From the Fels study we obtained inoculation and vaccination histories, and stature measurements made at age 18 for 77 boys and 69 girls born between 1928 and 1944 in or near Yellow Springs, Ohio. From the Berkeley Guidance Study we obtained inoculation, vaccination, and summary medical histories as well as yearly stature measurements up to maturity, from 80 boys and 90 girls, all born in 1928–29 in Berkeley, California. The two samples are roughly comparable with respect to socioeconomic and racial factors. However, the Fels sample contains a much larger number of children from poor and rural backgrounds, while the Berkeley sample is almost entirely urban. We also obtained adult height data, most from actual measurements, some from report, for the mothers and fathers of all children in both samples.

In an attempt to control for parental stature, and factors which might operate through association with parental stature, a statistical correction for height of mother and father was used. For these data, it was found that the sum of mother's and father's height gave the most efficient prediction of the child's terminal stature, and this sum was used as the covariate control variable in all the comparisons to be reported below. A covariance technique was used in which the height of individuals was adjusted with respect to the best fit within-group linear regression of children's stature (separately for boys and girls and for the two samples) on sum of parental heights.

For each individual in both samples, the age at which the first immunological vaccination or inoculation of any kind occurred was determined. For over half of the cases, this procedure consisted of smallpox vaccination. Following the results of the cross-cultural study, we divided the samples into those individuals who did or did not receive one or more such treatments before the age of 2 years. The number of cases was too small to make the analysis of finer age ranges possible.

RESULTS

Table 1 gives the mean 18-year statures for boys and girls in the two samples separated according to whether or not they received an immunological vaccination or inoculation before the age of 2 years. The means presented have been adjusted for heights of mothers and fathers. Separate analyses of covariance were performed for each of the four groups. The associated F ratios are given in Table 1. Only the difference for males in the Fels sample is significant by itself ($p < .04$), but the difference between the two treatment groups is in the same direction in all four groups, and the lack of significance is probably due to the rather small numbers in each. Combining the significance values for the four groups by a z transformation yields a probability of less than .02 for the full set of data. It thus appears reasonably clear that, on the average, the treated children exceeded the stature predicted from that of their parents to a greater extent than did those not treated.

TABLE 1

MEAN 18-YEAR STATURE ADJUSTED FOR PARENTAL STATURE OF CHILDREN WITH AND WITHOUT EARLY IMMUNIZATION

Sample and Sex	Immunization Treatment before 24 Months	*N*	Adjusted (and Raw) Mean 18-Year Stature (Cm.)	*F*
Berkeley Guidance Study:				
Male	1 or more	38	180.31 (180.66)	1.073
	None	42	179.05 (178.74)	
Female	1 or more	48	166.61 (167.00)	2.116
	None	42	164.97 (164.52)	
Fels Growth Study:				
Male	1 or more	52	178.51 (178.73)	6.161
	None	25	175.99 (175.53)	
Female	1 or more	45	165.45 (166.35)	1.107
	None	25	164.08 (162.46)	

Interpretation

It remains to determine what interpretation may most reasonably be put on the finding that early immunization is associated with greater adult stature. One interpretation is that the relation is another instance of the growth-accelerating effect of early stress. But there are obviously other possibilities. One is that early immunization, through the protection afforded and/or through correlation with other forms of medical care, may result in less illness during the growth period and that a lack of illness contributes to adult stature. We were able to investigate the notion that illness during the growing period might be related to adult stature with the data from the Berkeley Guidance Study. Medical histories for each child were examined, abstracted, and rated by a person who did not have access to stature data for the same cases. The ratings were made in terms of the estimated number of days during which the individual had either an elevated temperature or elevated steroid hormone levels. Estimates of elevated temperature were made either from direct information given in the medical histories or from the usual course of a recorded illness, as described by standard pediatric texts. Estimates of elevated steroid levels had to be based on educated guesses, as direct evidence as to their usual course in common diseases and injuries is lacking.

Both illnesses and injuries were rated; such disparate items as severe allergic reactions, accidental ingestion of poison, rickets, infected ears, and mumps were all considered. The raters relied most heavily upon such signs as level and duration of fever, number of days of bed rest, descriptions of disability, and number of days of absence from school. When such information was only partially available, the raters relied on medical texts to determine the average course of a disease in order to make a rating. In general each illness or accident was given a rating in terms of presumed days of significantly heightened steroid levels. Each illness was given a duration rating and a severity rating. The severity ratings (1, 2, or 3) were generally "1." Ratings of "2" or "3" were reserved for definite indications of elevated steroid levels such as high fever. The total rating for each illness or accident was the product of the duration rating and the severity rating. Totals were tabulated for the years 0–2 and 2–18. A reliability coefficient of .88 was obtained between ratings on 36 separate 1-year records. While these ratings are obviously crude, they are probably sufficient for present purposes. There was an immense range—from 31 to 195 for summary ratings for 0–18 years among children in the sample—and it is thus quite clear that large differences in the amount of illness were being reflected. Certainly if gross amount of illness has an important influence on overall growth, children with such wide differences in rated illness histories should provide some evidence thereof.

To test the relation between illness and stature, we divided the groups at the median illness rating into those with much illness in their histories and those with little illness. The mean 18-year statures, adjusted for parental height, for those with much or little illness from birth to 2 years and from 2 to 18 years are given in Tables 2 and 3. It is clear that illness, as rated, bears no appreciable relation to stature. The *F* ratios obtained from analyses of covariance for these data are all insignificant. Moreover, the average illness ratings for those with and without early immunization also do not

TABLE 2

ADJUSTED MEAN 18-YEAR STATURE OF BERKELEY GUIDANCE STUDY SUBJECTS IN RELATION TO ILLNESS HISTORY DURING FIRST TWO YEARS

Sex and Amount of Illness	*N*	Adjusted Mean (and Raw) 18-Year Stature (Cm.)	*F*
Male:			
High	31	180.68 (179.48)	< 1
Low	33	179.32 (180.45)	
Female:			
High	33	166.03 (165.77)	< 1
Low	37	166.78 (167.02)	

TABLE 3

ADJUSTED MEAN 18-YEAR STATURE OF BERKELEY GUIDANCE STUDY SUBJECTS IN RELATION TO ILLNESS HISTORY BETWEEN THE AGES OF 2 AND 18

Sex and Amount Illness	N	Adjusted Mean (and Raw) 18-Year Stature (Cm.)	F
Male:			
High............	30	179.58 (179.22)	< 1
Low.............	34	180.33 (180.65)	
Female:			
High............	33	167.21 (167.10)	1.328
Low.............	37	165.73 (165.83)	

differ appreciably (mean illness ratings were 77.4 and 78.8 for those with and without early immunization, respectively: $F < 1.$). Thus, as far as we could determine, early immunization was not associated with less illness during the growing period, and differences in illness were not associated with 18-year stature. Thus it is implausible that the observed correlation between early immunization and adult stature could have been mediated by either direct or indirect association of early immunization with decreased morbidity.

This is not to say, of course, that better medical or other care may not still be the mediator of the immunization-growth relation observed here. It is possible that early immunization is correlated, in these samples, with more frequent correction of serious malnutrition, with supplementary vitamin therapy, with better diets, or with any one or more of a large number of potential growth-accelerating factors. The present data, unfortunately, provide no information on such matters. The present data cannot, therefore, be used to reject these many plausible alternatives. Other evidence is needed.

DISCUSSION

This seems an appropriate place to summarize the case to date concerning the hypothesis that infantile stress leads to increased growth in humans. No single definitive test of this hypothesis has been made, nor is one likely to appear in the future, because the experimental study of the effect of early stress is not possible with human subjects as it has been with laboratory animals. To explore the hypothesis with humans it is necessary to rely on correlational data with all its well-known pitfalls. Nonetheless, confidence in the likelihood of a particular interpretation may be gradually increased by the addition of new sources of confirmatory evidence in which various alternative interpretations are successively controlled. In the original cross-cultural study, it was possible to show that the association between early stress and adult stature was independent of race, geography, and diet. It was not possible to show that the causal relation might not be in the opposite direction, that is, that tall people stressed infants, with these data, however, since parental stature could not be controlled. Nor was it possible to assess the contribution of illness during growth since such information could not be obtained. In addition, these data left open the possibility of the effect being due to other cultural variables correlated with stressful infant-care practices. Perhaps most important, the cross-cultural evidence left open the possibility of selective differential mortality resulting from early stress.

In the present study, (a) culture was held relatively constant; (b) it was possible to control for parental stature by statistical means, making the directionality of the effect, from treatment to stature rather than vice versa, more plausible; (c) the possible contribution of decreased illness could be explored; and (d) there was essentially no mortality in the sample. But it was not possible, with the present data, to control for a variety of possible third-factor effects such as diet, which *were* controlled in the cross-cultural study.

In the same way, the assignment of treatment to individuals was probably anything but random in the present study. But in the Gunders study of hospital births (Gunders & Whiting, 1964), the initial treatment at least approached random assignment, the proximity of parents to the camp hospital being, apparently, the chief determinant of whether infants were born in the hospital or at home. Thus, self-selection of early stress by parents who might have other features contributory to growth, such as wealth and status, were controlled in Gunders' study, but in none of the others' to date, while in her study many of the other possibilities were not controlled.

Finally, in both the Gunders hospitalization study and the present investigation of immunization, the treatment was one generally thought to be benign, and thus some question of whether its stressful aspects were the crucial ones is raised. On the other hand, this is not true of many of the treatments considered in the cross-cultural studies, nor of the birth-anoxia effect reported by Corah et al. (1965), and by Graham (1966) and Graham et al. (1962).

In summary, there now exist a number of reports of enhanced growth associated with treatment in early infancy which have been interpreted as potential stressors. While no one of the studies controls for all possible artifacts, the following possible extraneous sources of the correlation have been at least partially controlled in at least one study: diet; race; geography, including sunlight and rain; parental stature; illness and selective mortality; self-selection of treatment by parents; and direct benign effects of the treatment.

What links all of these studies and leads to comparison of their results in the first place, of course, is the interpretation that they are all instances of infantile stimulation or stress. This assumption is for the most part made on insufficient evidence, and this is probably the weakest link in the case at present. What is needed is direct evidence of a common physiological effect of such growth-enhancing infant-care practices as mother separation, hospital birth, immunization, and birth anoxia, etc., and a real understanding of how such a physiological effect, if it exists, leads to acceleration of growth.

The lack of clear understanding of the mechanism, or of definitive evidence concerning the nature and site of action of infantile experiences on growth, should not, however, obscure the existence of a very real and important relationship. It is certain that there is an association between a variety of apparently stressful infant experiences and increased growth. Elucidation of the reason for this relation cannot help but shed significant light on the processes by which differences in growth rates are determined.

REFERENCES

Corah, N. L., Anthony, E. J., Painter, P., Stern, J. A., & Thurston, D. Effects of perinatal anoxia after seven years. *Psychological Monographs,* 1965, **79,** (Whole No. 596).

Garn, S. M. Genetics of normal human growth. In L. Gedda (Ed.), *De genetica medica.* Rome: Greyor Mendel, 1962.

Graham, F. Personal communication 1966.

Graham, F., Ernhart, C. B., Thurston, D. S., & Craft, M. Development three years after perinatal anoxia and other potentially damaging newborn experiences. *Psychological Monographs,* 1962, **76** (Whole No. 522).

Gunders, S. M. The effects of periodic separation from the mother during infancy upon growth and development. Unpublished doctoral dissertation, Harvard University, 1961.

Gunders, S. M., & Whiting, J. W. M. The effects of periodic separation from the mother during infancy upon growth and development. Paper presented at International Congress of Anthropological and Ethnological Science, Moscow, August, 1964.

Kagan, J. American longitudinal research on psychological development. *Child Development,* 1964, **35,** 1–32.

Landauer, T. K., & Whiting, J. W. M. Infantile stimulation and adult stature of human males. *American Anthropologist,* 1964, **66,** 1007–1028.

Levine, S. J. Stimulation in infancy. *Scientific American,* 1960, **202,** 80–86.

Macfarlane, J. Studies in child guidance. I. Methodology of data collection and organization. *Monographs of the Society for Research in Child Development,* 1938, **3,** No. 6 (Whole No. 19).

Marshall, W. Personal communication. 1966.

Spock, B. *Baby and child care.* New York: Pocket Books, Inc., 1957.

Tanner, J. N. *Growth at adolescence.* (2d ed.) Oxford: Blackwell Scientific, 1962.

[*Child Development,* 1968, **39,** 59–67. © 1968 by the Society for Research in Child Development, Inc.]

Part VI

THE THEORY OF CRITICAL PERIODS

Editor's Comments on Papers 37, 38, and 39

37 DENENBERG
Critical Periods, Stimulus Input, and Emotional Reactivity: A Theory of Infantile Stimulation

38 SCOTT, STEWART, and DE GHETT
Critical Periods in the Organization of Systems

39 SCOTT
Critical Periods in Organizational Processes

Most of the early historical work on critical periods was not highly theoretical but consisted largely of detailed descriptions of various phenomena that seemed to involve such periods. This was followed by experimental studies designed to test the reality of critical period responses to environmental changes and to define the boundaries of such responses. Denenberg (1968) outlined the necessary experimental designs.

In some cases, such as that of infantile stimulation, experimental work preceded description. Ideally, descriptive work should come first. If the approximate boundaries of a critical period are known through description; the experiential variables can be applied systematically before the critical period, during its maximum phase, and after it. If, on the other hand, experiental factors are applied at random times, they may give inconclusive results. Even though the rise and decline of an organizational process may be quite rapid in a given individual, a population tested at corresponding times should show approximately half the animals in the critical period and half outside it. Such data would give misleading impressions of gradualness of organizational change and the extent of individual unresponsiveness.

Denenberg was one of the first authors to develop theoretical formulations concerning critical periods based on the work by himself and his colleagues on early stimulation in rats. He concluded (1962) that the strength of stimulation affected the results, which could be expressed in a U-shaped curve whose center was an optimal level of stimulation. He also stated that there may be more than one critical period: ". . . there may be as many critical periods as there are combinations of independent variable parameters and dependent variable measures."

These formulations have certain limitations. The conclusions only apply to the phenomena associated with early stimulation in rats. The theoretical approach is a mechanistic one, i.e., the assumption that there is a one-to-one relationship between a causal and dependent factor. Applied to the early stimulation phenomenon, the simplest explanatory theory of this sort is that of multiple effects of a single stimulus. Further, Denenberg at that time did not attempt to relate the changes in physiological organization to behavior. Rather, he considered the physiological changes as dependent variables and only later identified changes in the neuroendocrine systsem as basic. Considering the latter as an intermediate organizational process, one can hypothesize that this single process is affected by many sorts of stimuli and that its reorganization leads to many different effects. As pointed out in an earlier section, there is good evidence that this physiological change can be produced by a variety of stimuli. The questions of how it in turn affects such diverse phenomena as body weight, avoidance scores, and emotionality have never been answered.

Denenberg's thinking foreshadows but does not specifically state the possibility that multiple organizing processes with different or overlapping critical periods could exist. It is distinctly possible that electric shock, one of the experiential variables used by Denenberg, may affect processes other than the endocrine stress response, especially if it is continued into later periods of development, when it should affect the process of learning, if nothing else. Some of Denenberg's results, particularly those shown in Figure 5 (Paper 37) resemble the theoretical result of two organizational processes with different critical periods. Furthermore, Denenberg correctly placed emphasis on the detailed analysis of the nature of critical periods. It is especially important to discover the nature of the organizational process or processes that may be involved.

In response to stimulation by Denenberg and others, I began to develop a general theory of critical periods based on the organization of systems. This was briefly stated (Scott, 1970) in the preface to the Liblice Symposium held in 1967 and was developed further in my presidential address to the International Society for Developmental Psychobiology (Paper 38). In the present book, I have combined the theoretical portion of this paper with that of a later and more general paper (Paper 39).

One major outcome of these theoretical considerations is that the theory of critical periods should apply to systems on any level of organization including the social. While this conclusion is sufficient for most practical applications (e.g., it is quite easy to bring about new forms of organization in a new and developing university but almost impossible to do so in an old one except by adding new sections to the university), this book contains no data of this sort. Empirical studies on critical periods in the organization of nonhuman social groups are few and far between, although Stewart's (1974) work with the modification of agonistic behavior and resulting dominance organization of groups of dogs provides some stimulating suggestions. Studies on critical periods in the organization of human groups, whether they involve the dyadic social relationship of a marriage or the organization of an entire culture, are still to be done.

37

Reprinted from *Psychol. Rev.* **71**:335–351 (1964)

CRITICAL PERIODS, STIMULUS INPUT, AND EMOTIONAL REACTIVITY:

A THEORY OF INFANTILE STIMULATION [1]

VICTOR H. DENENBERG [2]

Purdue University

Experiments, using rats and mice, do not support the critical period hypothesis that there are certain limited time periods in infancy during which a particular class of stimuli will have profound effects upon subsequent behavior. Where findings are consistent with the hypothesis, further research has shown that the "critical period" is a complex function of amount of infantile stimulation. The central hypothesis of this paper is that amount of stimulus input in infancy acts to reduce emotional reactivity in a monotonic fashion. From this it follows that an inverted U function should be obtained between amount of infantile stimulation and adult performance for tasks involving some form of noxious element and which are of "moderate" difficulty. For tasks which are "easy" or "difficult," the relationships between performance in adulthood and infantile stimulation should be monotonic, though opposite in slope. Data supporting this theory are discussed.

This paper has two purposes. The first is to question certain aspects of the critical period hypothesis (Scott, 1958, 1962). The second, and more important, purpose is to develop a somewhat different hypothesis: that stimulation in infancy reduces the organism's emotional reactivity; this reduction is a monotonic function of amount of stimulus input. In turn, this hypothesized change in emotional reactivity offers a useful mechanism by which one can explain a number of disparate and seemingly unrelated changes in adult performance.

The data to be considered, and the generalizations therefrom, come specifically from research with rats and mice which have received various forms of stimulation between birth and weaning. For more general reviews of early experience research and the critical period hypothesis see Denenberg (1962b) and Scott (1962).

Critical Periods

Recently Scott (1962) has suggested that there are three major kinds of critical period phenomena: one for the formation of basic social relationships,

[1] Much of the research described in this paper was supported, in part, by Grant M-1753 from the National Institute of Mental Health, National Institutes of Health, United States Public Health Service, and by several grants from the Purdue Research Foundation.

[2] It is a pleasure to acknowledge the contributions of Mark W. Stephens, whose incisive comments, both conceptual and editorial, have significantly improved this paper.

a second concerned with optimal periods for learning, and a third involving infantile stimulation. This discussion is concerned only with the last of these.

There are at least two different ways in which the critical period hypothesis has been interpreted. One is that the same physical stimulation at different ages has different effects upon *S*; this says, simply, that *S*'s age is an important parameter and can scarcely be questioned. The second interpretation is that there are certain *limited* time periods in development during which a particular class of stimuli will have particularly profound effects and that the same stimulation before or after this interval will have little, if any, effect upon the developing organism. This approach stems directly from the embryological meaning of critical periods, and it is in this context that Scott (1958, 1962; Scott & Marston, 1950; Williams & Scott, 1953) has developed and described the critical period hypothesis. The term, critical periods, when used in this paper, will refer to this second interpretation.

Operationally, a test of the critical period hypothesis requires several experimental groups which receive the same stimulation at different ages and a control group which does not receive the stimulation at all. If some of the experimental groups do not differ from the control while others do, this may be construed as evidence supporting the critical period hypothesis. (On the other hand, any significant differences among the experimental groups are support for the first meaning of the hypothesis.)

Although it is obvious that the age at which *S* is stimulated is an important parameter, when one carefully examines experiments investigating critical periods in infancy in rats and mice, there is little evidence supporting the hypothesis that stimulation must occur only during certain delimited time intervals to affect the organism's subsequent behavior. Interestingly, the only unequivocal demonstrations of critical periods are to be found in papers which used physiological, rather than behavioral, endpoints (Bell, Reisner, & Linn, 1961; Levine & Lewis, 1959a).

The general conclusion noted above might not be apparent from a casual inspection of the literature. There are several studies which, if taken in isolation, appear to support the hypothesis. For example, two early experiments on critical periods (Denenberg, 1958, 1960) seemed to support the concept. In the first study mice initially conditioned between 20 and 40 days of age had essentially the same reconditioning scores at 50 days, and all these scores were significantly higher than either a 50-day control group or a group which was initially conditioned at 16 days. These data suggested a critical period around 20 days of age such that conditioning experience prior to that date did not affect subsequent reconditioning performance; experience after that date appeared to have the same effect upon reconditioning, regardless of the original age of conditioning or the actual amount of conditioning. A subsequent study with older *S*s (Denenberg, 1960) established that it was indeed the age of the animals rather than the time interval between conditioning and reconditioning which mediated the effects.[3]

[3] A number of investigators have also shown, with the rat, that stimulation in infancy has different consequences as compared to equivalent stimulation in adulthood. (These include handling in infancy and early adulthood, Levine, 1956; raising rats in groups of 6 or 12 during infancy or adulthood, Seitz, 1954; subjecting rats to handling and auditory stimulation in infancy and

However, another study with the mouse, though not directly comparable to the two above, disclosed some complexities concerning critical period phenomena which cast doubt on the degree of generality of the hypothesis. Denenberg and Bell (1960) studied avoidance learning in adulthood as a joint function of age of infantile stimulation (i.e., critical periods), intensity of stimulation in infancy, and intensity of electric shock during adult performance. These latter two parameters had been held constant in prior research. Analyses of the learning data revealed that critical periods were not significant as a main effect; but the Periods × Adult Shock and the Periods × Adult Shock × Infantile Stimulation interactions were significant. The disturbing thing was that the age variable (i.e., critical periods) was dependent upon the particular level of stimulation used in the adult learning task. By the selection of certain combinations of infantile stimulation levels and adult shock levels one could "prove" that stimulation during certain "critical periods" could facilitate, have no effect, or interfere with avoidance learning in adulthood. The phenomena, then, appear to be far more complex than previously recognized in the generalizations afforded by the critical period hypothesis.

These data suggest that any single "critical period" is, at least in part, dependent upon the parameter of stimulus intensity. Thus, Denenberg's prior studies (1958, 1960) should be looked upon with caution since different shock levels may have yielded very different findings.

Critical period research with the rat has generally used the procedure called *handling* rather than shock. This consists of removing the pups from the home cage, and placing the young into containers (e.g., cans containing wood shavings, small wooden compartments, grid-floored boxes). The pups are left there for a short duration (generally 2 to 3 minutes though some *E*s have used intervals of 8 minutes or longer) and are then returned to the home cage. This is generally done once a day for different prescribed periods.

In a series of experiments Denenberg and Karas (1960, 1961) found that rats handled for the first 10 days of life were superior with respect to body weight, avoidance learning, and survival capability to ones handled during the second 10 days. In general, both 10-day groups were superior to *S*s which had been handled for 20 days in infancy.

These data suggested that it might be possible to handle *S*s for fewer than 10 days and possibly isolate specific critical periods related to different dependent variables. Therefore Denenberg (1962a) handled different groups of rats for 3- or 5-day intervals at different ages during the first 10 days of life. Measures of body weight, avoidance learning behavior, and survival time, with one exception, did *not* support the critical period hypothesis. The exception was that *S*s handled for the first 5 days of life were not significantly better than controls in avoidance learning while *S*s handled on Days 6–10 were superior to controls and equal to *S*s handled on Days 1–10.

Though the avoidance learning findings are compatible with the critical period hypothesis, another possibility, based upon the Denenberg and Bell mouse study, is that the failure to modify avoidance learning by handling during the first 5 days was because the stimulation induced by handling was

adulthood, Spence & Maher, 1962a; and temporarily blinding or deafening rats in infancy or later life, Wolf, 1943.)

not sufficiently intense to affect *S*. Denenberg and Kline (1964) tested this hypothesis by giving different groups of rats electric shock (0.2 milliampere) on Days 1–5, 1–3, 3–5, 2, or 4. The shocked groups (with the exception of the group shocked only on Day 2) were significantly better in avoidance learning than a nondisturbed control group.

In conclusion, experimental research with the mouse and rat investigating stimulation between birth and weaning has established that the critical period hypothesis is not sufficient to account for the findings. In instances where the data are consistent with the hypothesis further study has found that the "critical period" is a complex function of the parameter of stimulus intensity. Research to date indicates that, for the rat and mouse at least, there may be as many "critical periods" as there are combinations of independent variable parameters and dependent variable measures (Denenberg, 1962a). Meyers (1962) and Lindholm (1962) have recently arrived at a similar conclusion.

Then should the term "critical periods" be abandoned when discussing the effects of infantile stimulation? Not at the present time, certainly. The concept has had, and will continue to have, great heuristic value. However, conclusions concerning critical periods must be limited to the particular experimental operations involved until enough empirical evidence has been obtained to indicate the limits of generalization. In terms of current research strategy it appears more reasonable to study the functional relationships among various classes of independent and dependent variables between birth and weaning than to design experiments which try to isolate critical periods during this crucial stage of development.

THEORY OF INFANTILE STIMULATION AND ADULT PERFORMANCE

One approach to the problem of understanding the effects of stimulation in infancy is by means of the critical period hypothesis. A different approach is to examine the diverse research findings to see if any common factor can be discerned. Such an examination of the literature leads to the conclusion that stimulation administered between birth and weaning brings about a reduction in "emotional reactivity." Furthermore, the greater the stimulation in infancy, the less emotional *S* will be in adulthood. The central hypothesis of this paper is that *emotional reactivity is reduced as a monotonic function of amount of stimulus input in infancy.*

Before discussing this hypothesis in detail, and showing some of its consequences, it is first necessary to define "emotional reactivity" and show that this intervening variable is modified by stimulation in infancy. This will be done by showing, on the stimulus side, that different methods of stimulating *S* in infancy have similar consequences in adulthood; and, on the response side, by showing that different operational measures of emotional reactivity yield internally consistent results (Miller, 1959). The two most common methods of stimulating *S*s in infancy have been handling and shocking. Emotional reactivity has been measured by procedures as divergent as open-field testing, consummatory behavior, behavior in a learning situation, and behavior when given an opportunity to emerge from the home cage.

Handling and Emotional Reactivity

Open-field Behavior. In two experiments Denenberg and Morton (1962a) found that rats handled daily between birth and weaning were significantly more active and had a significantly smaller defecation rate than nonhandled controls. Similar findings were obtained by Denenberg and Whimbey (1963). Rats handled for the first 10 or 20 days of life were found to be significantly more active and to defecate significantly less than nonhandled controls (Denenberg, Morton, Kline, & Grota, 1962). In a study relating infantile stimulation to age of testing Denenberg and Smith (1963) handled or shocked rats during the second 10 days of life and tested independent groups at 50, 100, 150, or 200 days of age. Both groups which received stimulation in infancy were significantly more active than the controls and had a significantly lower defecation percentage. The open-field test was also used by Schaefer (1963), but his index of emotionality was the amount of time spent crouching during the 2 minutes after presentation of a sharp click. Handled *S*s crouched significantly less than nonhandled controls.

Consummatory Behavior. Levine (1957, 1958) handled, shocked, or did not disturb rats between birth and weaning. When adult, the *S*s were deprived of water for 18 hours and then given the opportunity to drink. Levine (1957),

> hypothesized that since deprivation constitutes a novel internal stimulus complex for nonhandled *S*s, the novelty should result in greater emotional disturbance and produce reduced water consumption following a period of deprivation [p. 609].

In both experiments handled and shocked *S*s consumed significantly more water than nondisturbed controls. In a similar type of experiment Spence and Maher (1962a) also found that handled *S*s consumed significantly more water than controls.

Emergence-from-Cage Behavior. Hunt and Otis (1963) exposed their experimental rats to a variety of stimulus conditions in infancy, including handling. In their first two experiments their measure of emotionality was a "timidity" test. The home cage of an *S* which had been deprived of food and water for 22 hours was placed on an open alley upon which were placed pellets of food. Handled *S*s were found to emerge significantly further into the runway than nondisturbed controls. In their third experiment they recorded *S*'s behavior when *E* opened the cage door to attach a plastic milk cup to it, scoring *S* with respect to the degree of "boldness" manifested. Subjects not disturbed in infancy were found to be significantly more timid than those receiving stimulation in infancy.

Behavior in a Learning Situation. Several indexes of emotional behavior were recorded by Levine (1956) while testing handled and nonhandled *S*s for avoidance learning. These were defecation and activity during habituation trials, percentage of *S*s freezing after the first shock trial, and the number of trials on which *S*s showed freezing behavior. On all four measures nonhandled controls were found to be significantly more emotional than *S*s handled in infancy.

Electric Shock and Emotional Reactivity

Open-field Behavior. Subjects receiving 0.25 milliampere of current for 3 minutes daily on Days 11–20 were significantly more active and defecated significantly less than nondisturbed controls when tested at 50, 100, 150, or 200 days of age (Denenberg & Smith, 1963). Rats given 3 minutes of either 0.5 milliampere or 0.8 milliampere shock on Day 4 of life were significantly more active than *S*s receiving the same stimulation on Day 2; the latter group did not differ from nondisturbed controls (Kline & Denenberg, unpublished). The effect of electric shock is measurable at weaning as well. Rats given 30 seconds of 0.2 milliampere current on Days 1 and 2 of life were significantly less emotional than nondisturbed controls at the time of weaning as measured by time to emerge into the open field and activity in the field (Denenberg, Carlson, & Stephens, 1962).

Consummatory Behavior. Rat pups were given 3 minutes of electrical stimulation (variable current from 0.10 milliampere to 0.37 milliampere, disregarding *S*'s resistance) from Day 1 through Day 20. These *S*s consumed significantly more water in adulthood than nondisturbed controls; the findings were replicated in a second experiment (Levine, 1957, 1958). A similar finding was obtained by Lindholm (1962) who shocked rats for the first 10 days, the second 10 days, the first 20 days of life, and did not disturb a control group. No specified shock level was used; instead, the shock was set high enough to make the *S*s move and squeal in the apparatus. The intensity of the shock was increased as *S* matured. When adult, the *S*s were deprived of water for 24 hours and then given an opportunity to drink. The *S*s shocked in infancy took significantly less time to initiate drinking and consumed significantly more water than the nondisturbed group. A subsequent analysis determined that the differences in consummatory behavior could all be attributed to the latency to approach the water tubes.

Stimulus Input and Emotional Reactivity: The Monotonicity Hypothesis

The data summarized above are sufficient to justify the conclusion that stimulation in infancy will result in a reduction in emotional reactivity in adulthood. It remains to be demonstrated that a monotonic relationship obtains between amount of stimulus input in infancy and emotional reactivity. Two experiments have explicitly tested this hypothesis (Denenberg, Carlson, & Stephens, 1962; Denenberg & Smith, 1963). In addition, there are three other experiments in the literature which offer support for the hypothesis (Levine, 1957, 1958; Lindholm, 1962).

Amount of stimulus input was varied by Denenberg and his co-workers by handling rats for 0 (control), 10, or 20 days in infancy. In adult open-field testing the controls had the highest defecation rate while the group handled for 20 days had the lowest rate; all differences were significant. In the second study (Denenberg & Smith, 1963) one group of rats received 3 minutes of shock daily from Day 11 through Day 20, a second group was placed on the unelectrified grid (handled group), and a third group was not disturbed. Figure 1 shows the percentage of *S*s in each group defecating before and after adult avoidance learning training. The greater the stimulus input in infancy, the smaller (significantly) was the percentage of defecators in adulthood. Furthermore, the shocked *S*s were the only

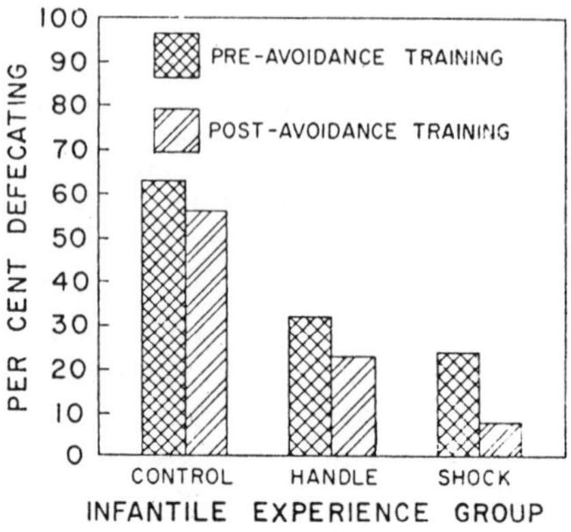

FIG. 1. Percentage of rats defecating before and after avoidance learning as a function of infantile stimulation (from Denenberg & Smith, 1963).

ones whose defecation percentage was significantly reduced following avoidance learning training.

Levine (1957, 1958) compared water consumption following 18 hours of thirst for *S*s which had been shocked, handled, or not disturbed in infancy. In both experiments the shocked *S*s consumed the most water, followed by the handled group, with the controls consuming the least. The difference between shocked and handled *S*s approached significance in the first study ($p < .10$) and was significant in the second study; nonhandled controls consumed significantly less than either experimental group in both studies.

In the Lindholm (1962) experiment rats were shocked for the first 10 days of life, the second 10 days, or the first 20 days, while a control group was not disturbed (his postweaning experimental group is not pertinent to this discussion). Consummatory behavior following 24 hours of thirst found that the controls had the greatest latency and consumed the least amount of water, followed by the two 10-day groups, with the 20-day group having the shortest latency and ingesting the greatest amount of water.

To summarize: Stimulus input in infancy has been varied by number of days of handling (0, 10, 20) (Denenberg et al., 1962), number of days of shock (0, 10, 20) (Lindholm, 1962), and form of stimulation (nondisturbed controls, handled, shocked) (Denenberg & Smith, 1963; Levine, 1957, 1958). Emotional reactivity has been measured by open-field behavior and consummatory behavior. In each instance the greater the amount of stimulus input in infancy the less was the level of *S*'s emotional reactivity in adulthood. Figure 2 presents an idealized curve showing this theoretical relationship. The negatively accelerated form of the curve is suggested by

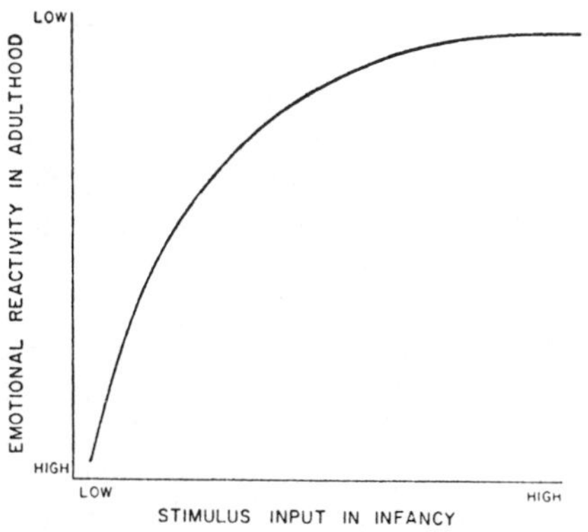

FIG. 2. Theoretical curve relating stimulus input in infancy to emotionality in adulthood.

the findings of the five experiments cited above. In each instance the greatest change in behavior occurred between the control group and the group receiving the intermediate amount of stimulation.

Relationship between Emotional Reactivity and Adult Performance

When one examines the dependent variables used in studies of infantile stimulation, it is apparent that many of them contain some form of noxious element (avoidance learning, underwater swimming, thirst, starvation). Obviously, then, *S*'s emotionality or level of arousal will have a significant effect upon his performance in such tasks. It is reasonable to expect that there will be an optimal level of emotionality for efficient performance. As one moves away from this optimal level, performance should drop off, thus resulting in an inverted U function (cf. Hebb, 1955).

However, another parameter is needed. The Yerkes-Dodson Law (Broadhurst, 1957) posits that the optimal level of motivation for a task decreases as task difficulty increases. Assuming that the more emotional *S* is more motivated, it follows that highly emotional *S*s should have the best performance when the level of task difficulty is quite low while the least emotional *S*s should be the best performers when the task is very difficult (Broadhurst, 1957; Karas & Denenberg, 1961). In both of these instances the relationship between performance and emotionality should be monotonic, through opposite in slope. It is only when a task is of "moderate" difficulty that one should expect to obtain the nonmonotonic inverted U function. Figure 3 presents the theoretical relationship between adult performance and *S*'s emotionality for tasks of different levels of difficulty.[4]

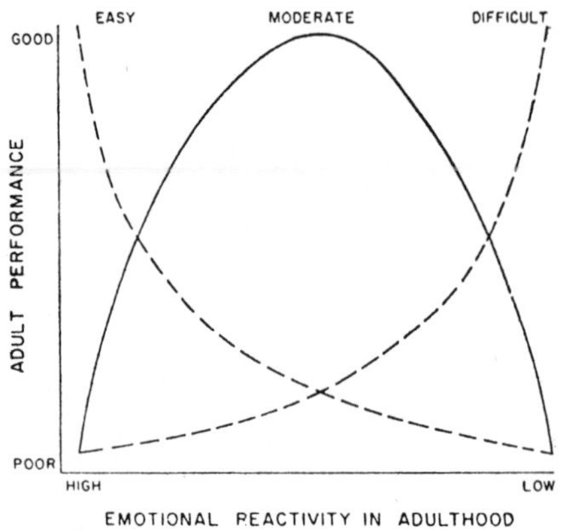

FIG. 3. Theoretical relationship between performance in adulthood and emotionality level for tasks of varying degrees of difficulty.

Some Relationships between Stimulus Input in Infancy and Adult Performance

A number of experiments have been carried out, the results of which are consistent with the predictions made by the theory depicted in Figures 2 and 3. For example, Karas and Denenberg (1961) explicitly tested the theory by assuming that the greater the number of days of handling in infancy, the greater the reduction in emotional reactivity in adulthood. In addition, they assumed that "spaced" handling would result in greater emotional reduction than "massed" handling. Experimental rats were space or mass handled for 10 or 20 days while controls were not disturbed. The criterion task was an underwater discrimination Y maze similar to the one used by Broadhurst (1957) who had shown that maze performance was related to *S*'s level of emotionality. The discrimination task was an "easy" one (86.6% correct choices, highly comparable to Broadhurst's value of 86.4% errorless trials on his "easy" task), thus leading to the deduction that the most emotional *S*s should exhibit the best performance with a monotonic decline in performance as emotional reactivity decreased (see Figure 3). Analysis of the swimming time scores found that the rank order of the five groups was as predicted, thus confirming the hypotheses.

Several studies have found an inverted U relationship between amount of stimulation in infancy and later performance. In the experiments by Denenberg (1962a) and Denenberg and Karas (1960, 1961) rat pups were handled for 0 (controls), 3, 5, 10, or 20 days in infancy. One can average the data for the 3-day, 5-day, and 10-day groups (irrespective of age of stimulation), add in the findings of the control and 20-day groups, and plot the functional relationship between number of days of handling in infancy and later performance. The averaging procedure acts to partially balance out

[4] Still another parameter which may be relevant is rate of development. Denenberg and Karas (1959), in comparing the effects of handling upon the rat and mouse, point out that the mouse is a more rapidly developing organism and they suggest the hypothesis that the more rapid an organism's development, the greater the effect of infantile experience.

the age of stimulation. One can, in other words, disregard "critical periods" between birth and weaning and examine amount of stimulation within that period. Such an analysis is shown in Figure 4 for 21- and 69-day body weight, avoidance learning, and survival time (Denenberg, 1962a). The general function of these data may be described by an inverted U curve.

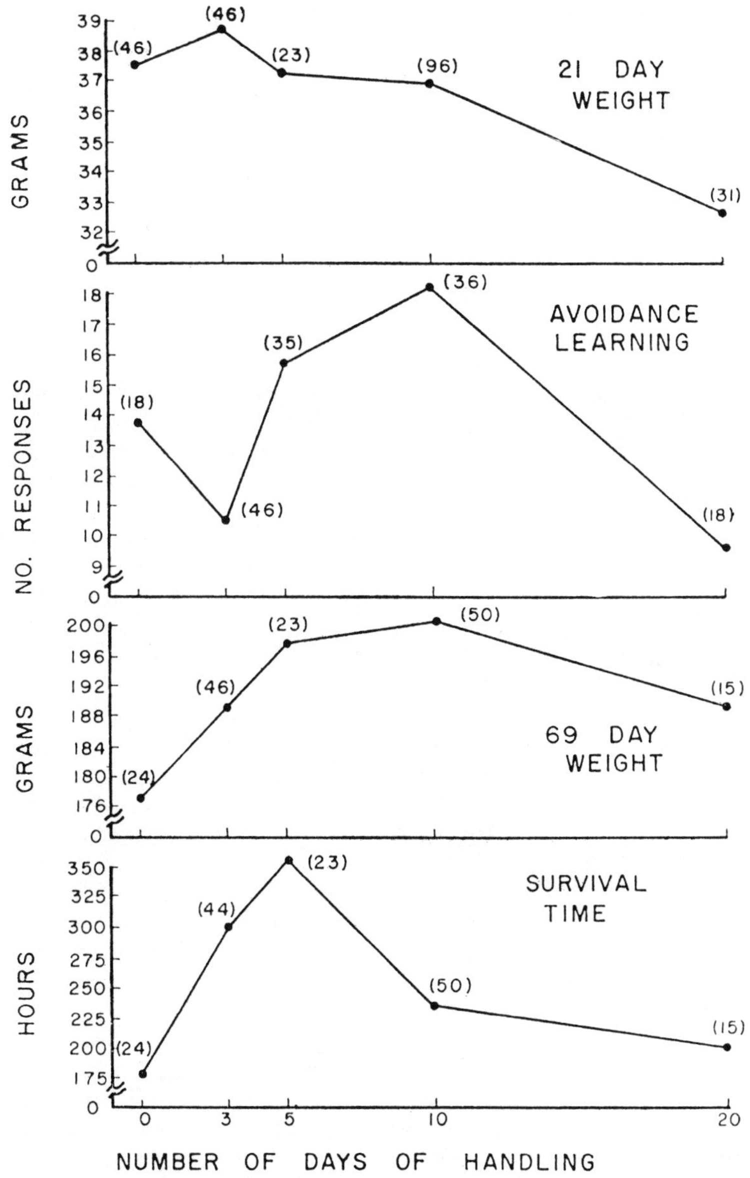

FIG. 4. 21-day body weight, avoidance learning, 69-day body weight, and survival time in rats as a function of number of days of handling in infancy. (Numbers in parentheses indicate the *N* per point, from Denenberg, 1962a.)

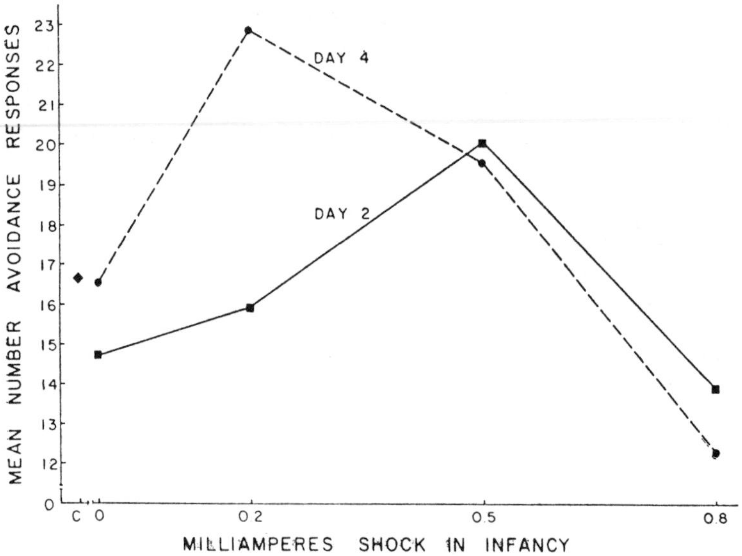

FIG. 5. Number of avoidance learning responses in rats as a function of infantile shock intensity on Day 2 or Day 4 (from Kline & Denenberg, 1964).

Both too much and too little handling led to less than optimal performance. The optimal amount of handling varied with different dependent variables.

This same general function was obtained when electric shock was used to stimulate *S*s in infancy. Rats were shocked on the second or fourth day of life using 0.2 milliampere, 0.5 milliampere, or 0.8 milliampere electricity; one group of controls was handled, another not disturbed (Denenberg & Kline, 1964; Kline & Denenberg, 1964). The *S*s were given avoidance learning training between 60 and 69 days of age. Figure 5 presents the relationship between intensity of stimulation in infancy and adult learning. The inverted U function is clearly present.

Evidence that this inverted U function has some degree of interspecies generality is seen in Figures 6 and 7, which show the performance of mice. Figure 6 summarizes an experiment by Denenberg (1959) in which *S*s were given classical buzzer-shock conditioning at 25 days under 0.2 milliampere, 0.5 milliampere, or 0.8 milliampere shock. At 50 days they were taken to an extinction criterion, split into thirds, and reconditioned under 0.2, 0.5, or 0.8 milliampere shock. The adult reconditioning data are plotted as a function of shock level at 25 days. The inverted U function adequately describes all three curves.

Bell and Denenberg (1963) gave mice 0.1 milliampere, 0.3 milliampere, or 0.5 milliampere shock in infancy, handled other groups (0.0 milliampere) and did not disturb still others. Adult avoidance learning performance, plotted in Figure 7, again reveals the inverted U function.

The relationship between stimulus input in infancy and adult performance aids in interpreting other data. For example, Levine, Chevalier, and Korchin (1956) found that rats handled for the first 20 days of life performed best in an adult avoidance learning task, followed by *S*s which had been

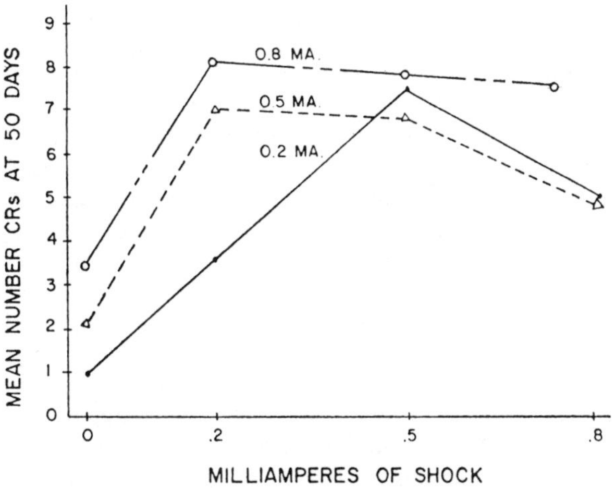

FIG. 6. 50-day conditioning scores in mice for three shock levels as a function of infantile shock intensity (from Denenberg, 1959).

handled and shocked, with nonhandled controls the poorest learners. These data exhibit a rough inverted U function with the group receiving the intermediate amount of stimulation exhibiting the best performance.

The theory depicted in Figures 2 and 3 leads to the prediction that *S*s with the greatest amount of stimulus input in infancy should have the best performance when the task is quite difficult. There are, as yet, no data relevant to this prediction.

It should be possible to generalize the parameter of "task difficulty" beyond the usual learning context. For example, the inverted U curves for body weight and survival time in Figure 4 were obtained after *S*s had undergone avoidance learning training. For *S*s which did *not* receive avoidance training, the controls lived longest, followed by *S*s handled for 10 days, with the 20-day group dying earliest. In other words, those data parallel the "easy" curve in Figure 3 while the results of the groups which had avoidance training follow along the

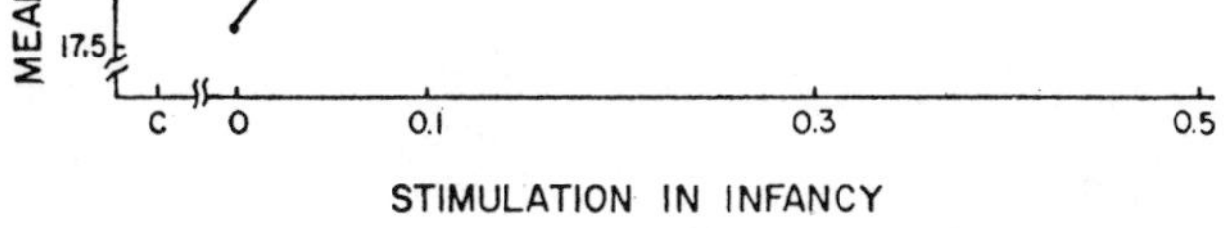

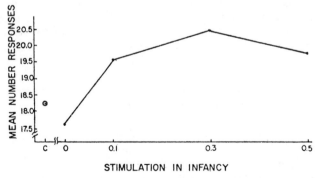

FIG. 7. Number of avoidance responses in mice as a function of stimulation in infancy. (C: nonstimulated controls; O: handled, nonshocked; 0.1, 0.3, 0.5: milliamperes of shock, from Bell & Denenberg, 1963.)

curve of the "moderate" group. Since avoidance learning has been shown to be a stressor (Brady, Porter, Conrad, & Mason, 1958; Denenberg & Karas, 1961), this suggests the hypothesis that stress experience, prior to a terminal stress, may act in a manner similar to the task difficulty parameter. This leads to the interesting prediction that *S*s subjected to a severe, but nonlethal stress, would be best able to survive a subsequent lethal stress, if they had received a considerable amount of stimulation in infancy.

It is pertinent to ask here about the relationship between stimulation in infancy and performance on a task which minimizes the emotional component. One would expect little or no relationship between infantile stimulation and later behavior. This is exactly what Denenberg and Morton (1962b) found in a series of three experiments. Handling in infancy did not have any effect upon problem-solving behavior as measured by the Hebb-Williams maze test. The authors concluded that,

> These findings suggest that preweaning stimulation such as shock and handling affects emotional processes but does not have any direct effect upon perceptual or problem-solving behavior [p. 1098].

Schaefer (1963) has obtained similar results.

Similarly, Spence and Maher (1962b) suggested that the obtained differences in learning performance between *S*s stimulated in infancy and controls may be a function of emotional rather than learning factors. Their experiment on this point, while equivocal, does offer some support for this position.

Comparisons with Bovard's Theory

Though Bovard's (1958) theory is concerned with the effects of handling upon viability, there are certain points of agreement and disagreement to be noted between his position and the one presented here. The major point of disagreement is that Bovard combines the results of preweaning and postweaning handling (the term "gentling" has been commonly used to describe the procedure of manually manipulating rodents postweaning), while this theory has been limited to preweaning stimulation. There are logical and empirical reasons for making such a distinction. The postweaning rat is a very different organism, behaviorally and biologically, from the preweaning animal, and it is not logical to assume that stimulation administered to the immature, recently born rat has the same consequences as the same stimulation administered to a weanling. The experiments cited in Footnote 3 offer general support for this conclusion. Clear evidence that handling and electric shock after weaning do not affect rats in the same manner as handling and shock before weaning can be found in the monograph by Brookshire, Littman, and Stewart (1961).

A paper directly relevant to this issue is the one by Levine and Otis (1958). They either handled or gentled rats before or after weaning; a control group was not disturbed. Preweaning handling or gentling had the same effect of significantly increasing body weight and survival rate while postweaning handling or gentling had no significant effect, compared to the control group. In addition to showing that preweaning stimulation has different consequences from postweaning stimulation, the Levine and Otis (1958) paper failed to substantiate Weininger's (1953, 1956) results which Bovard used as part of the empirical base for his theory. Ader (1959) and J. H. Scott (1955) have also failed to replicate Weininger's findings. Even the Hammett (1922) reference cited by Bovard is not supportive of his position, since the experimental data reported in that paper was not concerned with the effects of gentling rats. Hammett does refer back to his 1921 paper, and it is that portion of Hammett's paper which Bovard refers to in his reference to Hammett. Several other researchers have also cited the Hammett (1921) paper when discussing the positive effects of postweaning gentling. This is most interesting, since Hammett presents absolutely no data supporting such a conclusion. Hammett (1921) carried out five experiments concerning the effects of parathyroidectomy or thyroidectomy upon survival. The first three studies do not permit a valid evaluation of the effects of gentling because of lack of appropriate controls (though the experiments were valid for Hammett's purposes). The fourth and fifth experiments (see Hammett, 1921, p. 201) can be used to evaluate the effects of gentling since Hammett shifted the rats at weaning from one colony room to the other, thus balancing environmental conditions for the two different stocks of animals. The only significant effect in the fourth experiment was that the two colony stocks differed in genetic make-up; gentling failed to have any effect. And the fifth experiment contradicts this: all rats, regardless of genetic stock or whether or not they were gentled, survived the parathyroidectomy operation. One can only conclude that those who have cited Hammett's work as proof that gentling enhances survival ability have allowed their fertile imagination to inhibit their reading comprehension. All these experiments suggest that the postweaning handling (or gentling) phenomenon is rather tenuous with respect to modification of the rat's physiology.

There is some degree of agreement between Bovard's theory and the present one concerning preweaning stimulation. In so far as behavioral indices of emotional reactivity correlate with what Bovard (1958) calls stress, then the two theories are in agreement that "early [preweaning] handling raises the threshold for response to stress [p. 259]." Bovard, however, does not believe that handling is stressful while Levine (1956) and Denenberg (1959) have taken the opposite position. Bovard believes that "early stress lowers resistance to later stress [p. 260]." Since electric shock—a stimulus typically considered to be stressful—and handling have similar functional properties *vis à vis* emotional reactivity, the Levine and Denenberg position appears to be on firmer ground. Further evidence that stressful stimulation in infancy can have beneficial results, rather than the deleterious results predicted by Bovard, is discussed in the next section.

DISCUSSION

The hypothesis that emotionality decreases as a monotonic function of stimulus input may not appear reasonable at first glance because of our knowledge of conditioned fears, traumatic experiences in childhood, etc. It must be emphasized that this hypothesis is based upon, and is restricted to, data obtained on rodents which have been stimulated prior to weaning. Weaning has been used as a criterion point, not because of any clinical implications concerning mother-young separation, but because all of *S*'s senses are functioning by this time and because it is only after weaning that there is any evidence of long-term retention of a learned fear response (Campbell & Campbell, 1962; Denenberg, 1958, 1959; Lindholm, 1962). Furthermore, the consequences of handling or electric shock after weaning have been shown to be very different from their effects prior to weaning (Brookshire, Littman, & Stewart, 1961).

Scott (1962) has made a similar suggestion and has indicated that the transition point may occur at about 16 days of age, when the eyes open. Up to that age the critical factor mediating infantile stimulation is hypothesized by Scott to be the adrenal cortical stress mechanism while the psychological process of reduction of fear through familiarity is presumed to predominate between 17 days when the eyes open and 30 days.

The traditional assumption that traumatic experiences in infancy must inevitably have deleterious effects in later life is clearly not consonant with many of the studies cited above. Several other experiments, in fact, may also be noted which contradict this classical assumption. Baron, Brookshire, and Littman (1957) found that rats given 1.25 milliamperes of electric current continuously for 3 minutes on Days 20 and 21 were better escape and avoidance learners in adulthood than controls. Infant rats either placed on a laboratory shaker which oscillated 180 times per minute or shocked with 0.1 milliampere electricity were found to exhibit earlier maturation of the adrenal ascorbic acid depletion response to stress (Levine & Lewis, 1959b). Using the same dependent variable Schaefer, Weingarten, and Towne (1962) showed that placing rat pups into a refrigerator at 7° to 10° Centigrade also resulted in earlier maturation of the adrenal responses. Finally, Werboff and Havlena (1963) induced febrile convulsions in 3-day old rats by means of microwave diathermy. The *S*s so treated weighed significantly more at weaning and were significantly more resistant to audiogenic seizures.

Certain parallels may be noted between this theory and the arousal or activation theories of Hebb (1955), Duffy (1957), and Malmo (1959). All the theories are concerned with the intensity dimension of stimulation or arousal, and the inverted U function relating the intensity dimension to performance is common to all. The theory proposed here contributes to general arousal theory in two ways. First, intensity of infantile stimulation is specifically implicated as a major parameter affecting later differences in "chronic" or general level of arousal. Brookshire et al. (1961) have isolated what may be a similar phenomenon with the postweaning rat. They suggest that their "pure shock" residual factor of shock trauma may act to modify *S*'s arousal level. The second contribution is a methodological one: the techniques used in infantile stimulation are also procedures for experimentally generating individual differences in chronic arousal level. This opens up a new avenue of attack for those interested in individual differences in arousal level.

Though the proposed theory does account for a considerable number of experimental findings, contrary data are to be noted. For example, Spence and Maher (1962a) subjected rats to intense auditory stimulation between birth and weaning, handling a second group but did not give them auditory stimulation, moved the cages of a third group, and did not disturb a fourth group. Using water consumption as their index of emotionality no differences were found among the experimental groups though the stimulated *S*s consumed significantly more water than the undisturbed controls. No reason can be suggested to account for the failure to find a monotonic relationship between stimulus intensity in infancy and consummatory behavior.

Finally, this theory is not meant to be a substitute for the critical period hypothesis. In fact, the functional relationships are most clearly seen when *S*s are stimulated at different ages (but for the same number of days) and the date averaged so that age of stimulation is equated. Ultimately, any general theory of infantile stimulation will have to account for both age of stimulation and stimulus input and will have to relate these to the psychology and biochemistry of ontogeny (Levine, 1962).

REFERENCES

ADER, R. The effects of early experience on subsequent emotionality and resistance to stress. *Psychol. Monogr.*, 1959, **73**(2, Whole No. 472).

BARON, A., BROOKSHIRE, K. H., & LITTMAN, R. A. Effects of infantile and adult shock-trauma upon learning in the adult white rat. *J. comp. physiol. Psychol.*, 1957, **50**, 530–534.

BELL, R. W., & DENENBERG, V. H. The interrelationships of shock and critical periods in infancy as they affect adult learning and activity. *Anim. Behav.*, 1963, **11**, 21–27.

BELL, R. W., REISNER, G., & LINN, T. Recovery from electroconvulsive shock as a function of infantile stimulation. *Science*, 1961, **133**, 1428.

BOVARD, E. W. The effects of early handling on viability of the albino rat. *Psychol. Rev.*, 1958, **65**, 257–271.

BRADY, J. V., PORTER, R. W., CONRAD, D. G., & MASON, J. W. Avoidance behavior and the development of gastroduodenal ulcers. *J. exp. Anal. Behav.*, 1958, **1**, 69–73.

BROADHURST, P. L. Emotionality and the Yerkes-Dodson law. *J. exp. Psychol.*, 1957, **54**, 345–352.

BROOKSHIRE, K. H., LITTMAN, R. A., & STEWART, C. N. Residue of shock-trauma in the white rat: A three-factor theory. *Psychol. Monogr.*, 1961, **75**(10, Whole No. 514).

CAMPBELL, B. A., & CAMPBELL, E. H. Retention and extinction of learned fear in infant and adult rats. *J. comp. physiol. Psychol.*, 1962, **55**, 1–8.

DENENBERG, V. H. Effects of age and early experience upon conditioning in the C57BL/10 mouse. *J. Psychol.*, 1958, **46**, 211–226.

DENENBERG, V. H. The interactive effects of infantile and adult shock levels upon learning. *Psychol. Rep.*, 1959, **5**, 357–364.

DENENBERG, V. H. A test of the critical period hypothesis and a further study of the relationship between age and conditioning in the C57BL/10 mouse. *J. genet. Psychol.*, 1960, **97**, 379–384.

DENENBERG, V. H. An attempt to isolate critical periods of development in the rat. *J. comp. physiol. Psychol.*, 1962, **55**, 813–815. (a)

DENENBERG, V. H. The effects of early experience. In E. S. E. Hafez (Ed.), *The behaviour of domestic animals.* London: Bailliere, Tindall, & Cox, 1962. Pp. 109–138. (b)

DENENBERG, V. H., & BELL, R. W. Critical periods for the effects of infantile experience on adult learning. *Science*, 1960, **131**, 227–228.

DENENBERG, V. H., CARLSON, P. V., & STEPHENS, M. W. Effects of infantile shock upon emotionality at weaning. *J. comp. physiol. Psychol.*, 1962, **55**, 819–820.

DENENBERG, V. H., & KARAS, G. G. Effects of differential handling upon weight gain and mortality in the rat and mouse. *Science*, 1959, **130**, 629–630.

DENENBERG, V. H., & KARAS, G. G. Interactive effects of age and duration of infantile experience on adult learning. *Psychol. Rep.*, 1960, **7**, 313–322.

DENENBERG, V. H., & KARAS, G. G. Interactive effects of infantile and adult experiences upon weight gain and mortality in the rat. *J. comp. physiol. Psychol.*, 1961, **54**, 685–689.

DENENBERG, V. H., & KLINE, N. J. Stimulus intensity *vs.* critical periods: A test of two hypotheses concerning infantile stimulation. *Canad. J. Psychol.*, 1964, **18**, 1–5.

DENENBERG, V. H., & MORTON, J. R. C. Effects of environmental complexity and social groupings upon modification of emotional behavior. *J. comp. physiol. Psychol.*, 1962, **55**, 242–246. (a)

DENENBERG, V. H., & MORTON, J. R. C. Effects of preweaning and postweaning manipulations upon problem-solving behavior. *J. comp. physiol. Psychol.*, 1962, **55**, 1096–1098. (b)

DENENBERG, V. H., MORTON, J. R. C., KLINE, N. J., & GROTA, L. J. Effects of duration of infantile stimulation upon emotionality. *Canad. J. Psychol.*, 1962, **16**, 72–76.

DENENBERG, V. H., & SMITH, S. A. Effects of infantile stimulation and age upon behavior. *J. comp. physiol. Psychol.*, 1963, **56**, 307–312.

DENENBERG, V. H., & WHIMBEY, A. E. Infantile stimulation and animal husbandry: A methodological study. *J. comp. physiol. Psychol.*, 1963, **56**, 877–878.

DUFFY, E. The psychological significance of the concept of "arousal" or "activation." *Psychol. Bull.*, 1957, **64**, 265–275.

HAMMETT, F. S. Studies of the thyroid apparatus. I. The stability of the nervous system as a factor in the resistance of the albino rat to the loss of the parathyroid secretion. *Amer. J. Physiol.*, 1921, **56**, 196–204.

HAMMETT, F. S. Studies of the thyroid apparatus. V. The significance of the comparative mortality rates of parathyroidectomized wild Norway rats and excitable and non-excitable albino rats. *Endocrinology*, 1922, **6**, 221–229.

HEBB, D. C. Drives and the C.N.S. (conceptual nervous system). *Psychol. Rev.*, 1955, **62**, 243–254.

HUNT, H. F., & OTIS, L. S. Early "experience" and its effects on later behavioral processes in rats: I. Initial experiments. *Trans. N. Y. Acad. Sci.*, 1963, **25**, 858–870.

KARAS, G. G., & DENENBERG, V. H. The effects of duration and distribution of infantile experience on adult learning. *J. comp. physiol. Psychol.*, 1961, **54**, 170–174.

KLINE, N. J., & DENENBERG, V. H. Qualitative and quantitative dimensions of infantile stimulation. Unpublished manuscript, Purdue University, Department of Psychology, 1964. (Ditto)

LEVINE, S. A further study of infantile handling and adult avoidance learning. *J. Pers.*, 1956, **25**, 70–80.

LEVINE, S. Infantile experience and consummatory behavior in adulthood. *J. comp. physiol. Psychol.*, 1957, **50**, 609–612.

LEVINE, S. Noxious stimulation in infant and adult rats and consummatory behavior. *J. comp. physiol. Psychol.*, 1958, **51**, 230–233.

LEVINE, S. The psychophysiological effects of early stimulation. In E. Bliss (Ed.), *Roots of behavior.* New York: Hoeber, 1962.

LEVINE, S., CHEVALIER, J. A., & KORCHIN, S. J. The effects of early shock and handling on later avoidance learning. *J. Pers.*, 1956, **24**, 475–493.

LEVINE, S., & LEWIS, G. W. Critical periods and the effects of infantile experience on maturation of stress response. *Science*, 1959, **129**, 42–43. (a)

LEVINE, S., & LEWIS, G. W. The relative importance of experimenter contact in an effect produced by extra-stimulation in infancy. *J. comp. physiol. Psychol.*, 1959, **52**, 368–369. (b)

LEVINE, S., & OTIS, L. S. The effects of handling before and after weaning on the resistance of albino rats to later deprivation. *Canad. J. Psychol.*, 1958, **12**, 103–108.

LINDHOLM, B. W. Critical periods and the effects of early shock on later emotional behavior in the white rat. *J. comp. physiol. Psychol.*, 1962, **55**, 597–599.

MALMO, R. B. Activation: A neuropsychological dimension. *Psychol. Rev.*, 1959, **66**, 367–386.

MEYERS, W. J. Critical period for the facilitation of exploratory behavior by infantile experience. *J. comp. physiol. Psychol.*, 1962, **55**, 1099–1101.

MILLER, N. E. Liberalization of basic S-R concepts: Extensions to conflict behavior, motivation and social learning. In S. Koch (Ed.), *Psychology, a study of a science.* Vol. 2. New York: McGraw-Hill, 1959. Pp. 196–292.

SCHAEFER, T., JR. Early "experience" and its effects on later behavioral processes in rats: II. A critical factor in the early handling phenomenon. *Trans. N. Y. Acad. Sci.*, 1963, **25**, 871–889.

SCHAEFER, T., WEINGARTEN, F. S., & TOWNE, J. C. Temperature change: The basic variable in the early handling phenomenon? *Science*, 1962, **135**, 41–42.

SCOTT, J. H. Some effects at maturity of gentling, ignoring, or shocking rats during infancy. *J. abnorm. soc. Psychol.*, 1955, **51**, 412–414.

SCOTT, J. P. Critical periods in the development of social behavior in puppies. *Psychosom. Med.*, 1958, **20**, 42–54.

SCOTT, J. P. Critical periods in behavioral development. *Science*, 1962, **138**, 949–958.

SCOTT, J. P., & MARSTON, M. V. Critical periods affecting the development of normal and maladjustive social behavior in puppies. *J. genet. Psychol.*, 1950, **77**, 25–60.

SEITZ, P. F. D. The effects of infantile experiences upon adult behavior in animal subjects: I. Effects of litter size during infancy upon adult behavior in the rat. *Amer. J. Psychiat.*, 1954, **110**, 916–927.

SPENCE, J. T., & MAHER, B. A. Handling and noxious stimulation of the albino rat: I. Effects on subsequent emotionality. *J. comp. physiol. Psychol.*, 1962, **55**, 247–251. (a)

SPENCE, J. T., & MAHER, B. A. Handling and noxious stimulation of the albino rat: II. Effects on subsequent performance in a learning situation. *J. comp. physiol. Psychol.*, 1962, **55**, 252–255. (b)

WEININGER, O. Mortality of albino rats under stress as a function of early handling. *Canad. J. Psychol.*, 1953, **7**, 111–114.

WEININGER, O. The effects of early experience on behavior and growth characteristics. *J. comp. physiol. Psychol.*, 1956, **49**, 1–9.

WERBOFF, J., & HAVLENA, J. Febrile convulsions in infant rats, and later behavior. *Science*, 1963, **142**, 684–685.

WILLIAMS, E., & SCOTT, J. P. The development of social behavior patterns in the mouse, in relation to natural periods. *Behaviour*, Leiden, 1953, **6**, 35–64.

WOLF, A. The dynamics of the selective inhibition of specific functions in neurosis: A preliminary report. *Psychosom. Med.*, 1943, **5**, 27–38.

38

Reprinted, with permission, from *Dev. Psychobiol.* 7:489–503 (1974)

Critical Periods in the Organization of Systems

J. P. SCOTT
JOHN M. STEWART
VICTOR J. DE GHETT
Bowling Green State University
Bowling Green, Ohio

The general theory of critical periods applies to organizational processes involved in the development of any living system on any level of organization and states that the time during which an organizational process is proceeding most rapidly is the time when the process may most easily be altered or modified. Complex organizational processes involving 2 or more interdependent subprocesses may show 1 to several critical periods, depending on the time relationships of the subprocesses. The nature of the relationships between interdependent processes operating on different levels is again dependent on time and is a more meaningful formulation than that of the old "innate-acquired" dichotomy. These theoretical considerations lead to the conclusion that understanding a critical-period phenomenon rests on analyzing the nature of the organizational process or processes involved. An example is given in a review of research on the critical period for primary socialization (social attachment) in the dog. Evidence that attachment has taken place consists of discriminative behavior in relation to familiar and unfamiliar objects and rests on a minimum of 3 processes: 1) organization of the separation distress response; 2) visual and auditory sensory capacities; and 3) long-term associative memory capacities. Once these capacities are developed, the overall attachment process proceeds very rapidly (the critical period for such attachment). Thus the critical periods for the organizational subprocesses precede or slightly overlap that for the overall process. Deeper analyses of these processes must rest on neurophysiological research. The theory of critical periods is a general one that should apply to any developmental organizational process which proceeds at grossly different rates at different times.

General Theory of Critical Periods

As presently understood, the theory of critical periods is a general theory of organization. Therefore, it is applicable to a wide variety of organizational phenomena, ranging from embryonic development to the formation of organizations between nations. The only exceptions are those based on the nature of specific organizational processes—those that are continuous and proceed at uniform rates—rather than on the entities which are being organized. Such exceptions are relatively rare and, therefore, one may safely assume that any new or unknown organizational process has a high probability of showing a critical period. The theory of critical periods is thus related to and should be compatible with other theories of organization.

Concept of Systems

The theory of organization largely depends on the concept of systems, which is an old idea in biology, and one so familiar and pervasive that most biologists rarely stop to think about it in the abstract but simply employ the concept in most of their work and ideas.

In its simplest definition, a system is a group of interacting entities. These entities may be anything from planets to people, but they must interact in the true sense: the activities of each affect those of the others. They do not interact in the sense of independent action on a common object, nor in the statistical sense of 1 entity affecting the activity of another but not being affected in return.

A group of entities might act on each other without being organized. An example would be a group of gas molecules striking each other within a chamber. The degree to which a group is organized can be measured by the probability that a given activity on the part of 1 entity in the system will be followed by a given response by other entities. Thus systems can range between being organized to a very low degree, with predictability approaching zero, to systems which are highly organized, with predictability approaching one.

A system is different from a mechanism in that while the action of a mechanism may be highly predictable, its definition does not require that the entity that is affected will in turn have an effect on the machine, or upon the entity which set the mechanism in motion. A mechanism may, however, be part of a system. Thus a mechanistic concept of behavior produces quite different results from a systemic one, but the 2 concepts are not incompatible.

Furthermore, the conventional concept of causality becomes difficult to apply to systems as wholes, in that the usual experimental models assume only that A affects B, and not that B will affect A in turn. The latter phenomenon has led to the concept of equilibrium, which has been applied in many different sorts of systems, including nonliving chemical reactions in which reactions are assumed to go in both directions, and on a grander scale in the ideas of homeostasis in individual living systems and the balance of nature with respect to ecosystems.

We, however, are interested primarily in living systems and in the phenomenon of development, which may be defined as a change in the degree of organization of a system. When we relate such organizational change to a time scale, we enter the particular aspect of the organization of systems to which the concept of critical periods applies.

Theory of Critical Periods

In its simplest and most general form, the theory of critical periods states that the organization of a system is most easily modified during the time in development when organization is proceeding most rapidly. This is essentially a descriptive statement of a phenomenon that has been empirically established in relation to a wide variety of organizational processes. Whether or not a critical period exists depends upon the nature of the organizational process. If an organizational process proceeds at a uniform rate during the life or existence of the system involved no critical period exists, as the process can be modified as easily at one time as another (Fig. 1A). At the opposite extreme, an

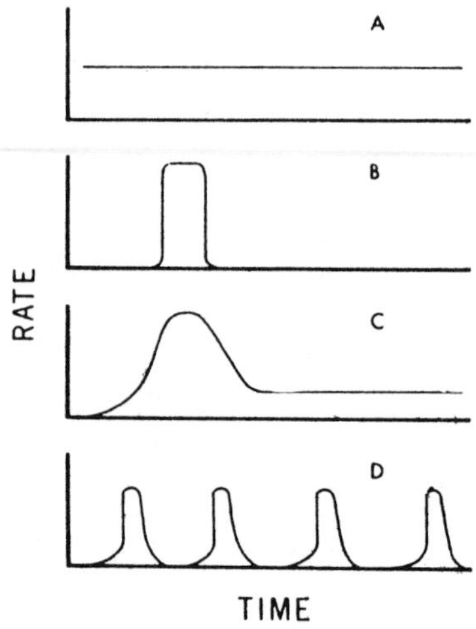

Fig. 1. Organizing processes and critical periods. A: Uniform rate of organization; no critical period. B: High rate of organization during limited time period; precisely defined critical period. C: Process operates at a high rate at one period; at a much reduced level later. D: Intermittent operation of process; repeated critical periods.

organizational process may proceed rapidly at only 1 limited period and is completely halted either before or afterwards (Fig. 1B). This is, of course, the most extreme example of a critical period, i.e., only 1 limited period during which organization may be modified. In between these 2 extremes is what is probably a more common condition, one in which a process proceeds slowly at first, then more rapidly for a time, and then slows down again but never returns to zero (Fig. 1C). An example is the process of social attachment. Still another possibility is that an organizational process may proceed intermittently, with periods of rapid organization, separated by periods in which little or no organization takes place (Fig. 1D). Such a process has many critical periods, and a good example is the process of learning.

Critical Periods in Complex Processes

Because many organizational processes are complex, we need to consider the theoretical implications of combining 2 or more simple processes. The least-complicated model is that of 2 interdependent processes, each having a single critical period. Figure 2 shows how these may be related with respect to time. The assumption is that both component processes are necessary to the completion of the total process.

In Figure 2A, processes P_1 and P_2 have critical periods occurring at the same time. Modification of either process during the critical period produces modification of the total process, and the critical period for the total process will of course be identical with that of both subprocesses. Depending on their natures, each subprocess might be affected by different factors. In such a case, a combination of these factors acting at the same time

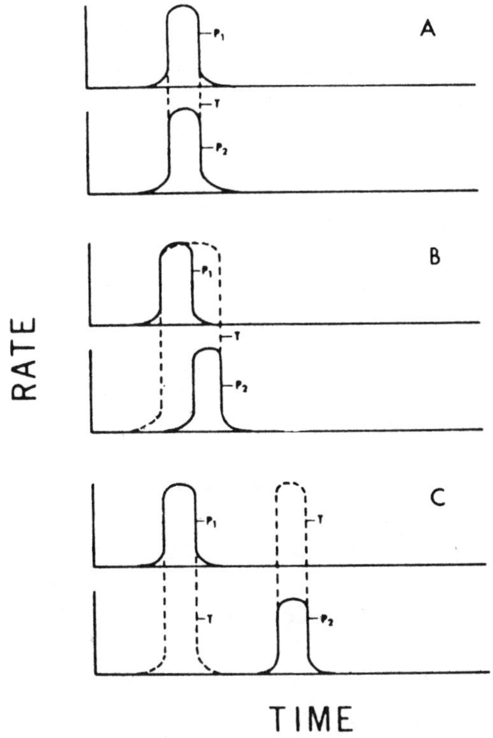

Fig. 2. Critical periods in relation to complex organizing processes. A: Processes P_1 and P_2 coincide in time. T, the critical period for combined processes, coincides with both. B: Processes P_1 and P_2 are immediately consecutive, extending T. C: Processes P_1 and P_2 operate at 2 different times producing 2 critical periods for combined process T.

will produce more severe effects. In general, when critical periods coincide, to demonstrate experimentally that 2 subprocesses do, indeed, exist is difficult, as any result could be explained equally well as an additive effect of 2 factors on a single process. The demonstration of 2 processes therefore depends on some form of independent evidence, such as that provided by genetic variation in 1 process but not the other.

Figure 2B represents the case of interdependent processes whose critical periods immediately succeed each other in time. Such is the case where the completion of 1 process is necessary before the 2nd can begin. The critical period for the entire complex process therefore includes both the critical periods of the component processes. If the 2 processes are affected by similar modifying factors, the main effect is to extend the critical period, and simple experimental techniques will not reveal the existence of the 2 processes. If, on the other hand, the 2 are affected by different factors, 2 critical periods will appear experimentally, 1 immediately succeeding the other.

Finally, in Figure 2C, if processes P_1 and P_2 are separated in time, the net effect is 2 separate critical periods. If the subprocesses are affected by different modifying factors, the situation is not changed. Of the 3 cases, this is obviously the one in which the presence of 2 subprocesses can be most easily demonstrated by the technique of experimental modification. Note, however, that Figure 2C superficially resembles Figure 1D, representing repeated critical periods in a single intermittent process.

We can extend the above reasoning to complex processes involving 3, 4, or more processes, anticipating nothing more than greater complexity of results. The larger the number of processes, the more likely the critical periods of each will overlap, and if a sufficient number of such processes exist, the probability is good that all periods in development will be critical for something. This essentially is the case if we consider the development of an organism as a single process, the view that Schneirla and Rosenblatt (1963) advanced in their critique of the theory of critical periods. It also approaches the situation depicted in Figure 1A, although it is unlikely that even the inclusive process of all development proceeds at a uniform rate. This is to say that the theory of critical periods is not inconsistent with the inclusive or holistic approach to development, but rather that each has its own validity. On a scale of complexity of organizational processes, the critical-period theory applies best to simple processes.

It is therefore apparent that the usefulness of the *theory* of critical periods (apart from the *phenomenon* of critical periods, which has enormous practical utility) depends on discovering the nature of organizational processes, particularly in the case of complex organizational phenomena which can only be understood in terms of their component parts. Hypotheses are the lifeblood of research, and we hope that the present theoretical formulation will inject new life into the field of early experience.

Destruction of Organization in Relation to Critical Periods

In most cases, the interest in critical periods is derived from the potential modification of organization. However, we may also be interested in the complete destruction of organization, if only to be able to explain the naturally occurring cases of this phenomenon. Figure 3 illustrates the effect of applying a strongly destructive factor at 3 points in time: before, during, and after a critical period. Supposing that this destructive factor affects only the particular organization studied, we predict that prior to the critical period, when the organization does not yet exist, there will be no effect; that during the critical period there will be a partial effect; and that at any time afterward there will be a complete effect. For the result of destruction, then, there is no critical period (unless one wishes to consider the entire life following the cessation of the organizational process as such), but rather a *critical point* (C) beyond which the effect is absolute.

This theoretical result is consistent with the empirical experimental results of destructive lesions of the nervous system. Done early enough in development, such lesions have little or no effect, somewhat later there may be partial recovery, and still later there may be no recovery.

A complicating factor in the above formulation is differential resistance to destructive agents. A general property of living systems is the tendency to maintain organization under a great variety of potentially disrupting conditions, with the result that they are most susceptible to destructive agents during the process of organization. A mildly destructive agent therefore demonstrates the critical-period phenomenon in a way no different from that of modifying factors.

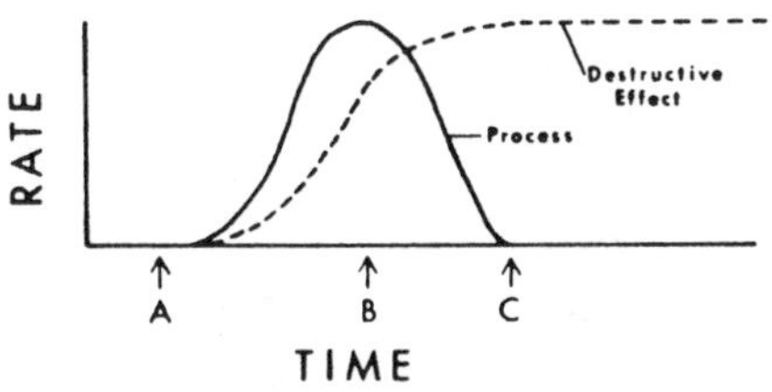

Fig. 3. Destructive effect in relation to timing of an organizational process. The same destructive agent is ineffective at time "A," partially effective at "B," and completely effective at "C."

From a general viewpoint, the young developing organism should therefore be more or less resilient with respect to traumatic injury, depending on the timing of the organizing process or processes involved. Contrary to some of the early theories as to the effects of early experience, one would anticipate that in certain respects an infantile organism is less susceptible to traumatic injury than an adult organism because organizing processes are not yet completed. In particular cases, this depends on the nature of the organizational process involved and whether or not it has gone to completion and so was in fact destroyed. These considerations bring up the further point that any modifying factor (as opposed to a destructive one) should be more effective if applied throughout the entire organizational process (critical period), rather than at only 1 point during the period.

Relationship Between Higher and Lower Levels of Organizational Processes

Until now we have considered only those complex processes which operate on the same level, but any complete consideration of such processes must consider the possible interrelationships between processes operating on different levels of organization. Table 1 is a simplified representation of the principal organizational processes that take place at different levels, and lists processes acting, respectively, on the intraorganismal level, the organismal one, and on the social level. Each level is in part determined by that below it, but not completely so.

Of particular interest is the relationship between intraorganismal factors that are ordinarily classed as physiological with those above it, since any aspect of behavior must have a physiological basis. Such physiological processes fall into at least 3 classes: (a) those which maintain organization but are not themselves organizational, as for example metabolism, nutrition, and blood circulation; (b) those which form the physiological bases for

TABLE 1. Relationships Between Organizational Processes On Different Levels.

Level of Organization	Organizational Process
Social	Formation of Social Relationships (including Attachment Process)
Organismal	Learning
Intraorganismal	Growth and Differentiation

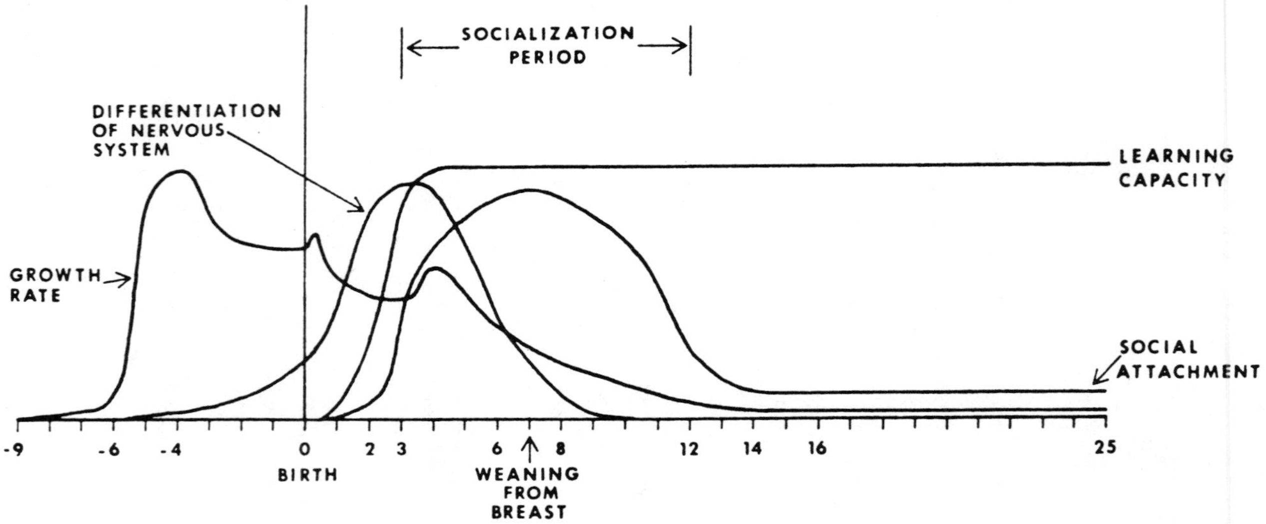

Fig. 4. Time relationships of certain developmental organizational processes in the dog. Processes are indicated semidiagrammatically in terms of weeks prior to and after birth.

organizational processes on higher levels, e.g., the physiological basis of learning; and, (c) those which are themselves organizational, such as growth and differentiation. Considered from the viewpoint of development of an organism, organizational physiological processes (c) precede maintenance processes (a), which in turn precede physiological processes basic to higher organizational processes (b). However, there may be considerable overlap in time in all 3 of these processes. Just how extensive this overlap may be is illustrated in Figure 4, which strikingly illustrates the artificiality of dichotomizing development into "innate" and "acquired" organizational processes on the basis of a single event of birth or hatching, and suggests that this old problem should be abandoned in favor of a more meaningful approach.

Because organizational processes on different levels obviously proceed simultaneously (Fig. 4), a fascinating and fundamental problem arises: what are the relationships between organizing processes at different levels? To begin with, it is well known that organizational processes on a higher level may influence physiological maintenance processes on a lower level, an example being the influence of learning on the process of salivation, as was originally shown by Pavlov. The extent to which higher level processes can influence physiological organizational processes is an open one, but it is at least possible for learning to influence growth through the organization of feeding behavior. Conversely, it is obvious that the outcome of lower level processes can influence the operation of upper level processes, if in no other way than by affecting the capacity to exercise higher level processes.

The effect of a lower level process on an upper one is related to time. If there is an overlap in time, both lower and upper level processes modifying the lower level may have more effect at an early stage than at a time close to the final stage of organization. Once a lower level process has achieved its final stage of stable organization, the effect is to limit processes on the higher level. We may therefore conclude that the relationship between lower and higher level processes depends on the stability of organization achieved in the lower level. If it is unstable, it will produce corresponding instability in the higher processes. If higher processes can influence the lower ones, they could theoretically produce instability in them, thus leading to a circular situation in which organization never proceeded to a final stage of stability.

Further, if a lower level process is unstable, this creates the possibility that it may be in the process of being organized by a higher level process. If this in turn proceeded to completion, the lower level organizational process might thus achieve stability in a different fashion.

It follows also that higher level processes can affect organization at lower levels only if these organizational processes overlap in time. There is now abundant evidence that this actually does occur in the development of learning processes in the higher organisms, i.e., the capacity for learning appears well before final physiological organization of the nervous system takes place, and long before physiological growth and maturation are completed (see Fig. 4). Further, if a lower level process does not run to completion, a higher level process may impose a continuous effect on organizing processes at lower levels.

In attempting to summarize these relationships, we can say that in general there is a hierarchical relationship between higher and lower level processes, in the sense that higher level processes can impose organization on the lower ones but the latter can only influence higher level organization by providing basic capacities, but not by controlling the organization itself.

Incidentally, one of the consequences of these theoretical findings is that they bring about a reconsideration of the process of adaptation. Organizing processes tend to proceed in the direction of stability, but effective adaptation to a changing environment demands flexibility. We would therefore expect that processes might be evolved that would tend to inhibit the completion of organization to a final steady state. For example, in the process of learning there is a tendency to organize behavior in fixed and stereotyped habit patterns. At the same, time, there appears to be in higher organisms a counterprocess which leads to variation in behavior, and in any particular case the end result is a balance between these processes. Fixed and completely stable organization of behavior is adaptive only in cases where the environment is completely stable.

Analysis of the Critical Period for Primary Socialization in the Dog: an Example

From our theoretical introduction it follows that a basic empirical problem in the analysis of any critical-period phenomenon is determining the nature of the organizational process or processes involved. As a general strategy, a 1st approach is to try to discover the process or processes that appear at the beginning and disappear at the end of the period. In order to do this, the boundaries of the period need to be determined as precisely as possible by experimentally varying a factor which is known to modify the organization of behavior during the critical period. Once the relevenat processes are determined, they can be experimentally analyzed on an individual basis.

Discovery of the Critical Period for Primary Socialization in the Dog

Ordinarily, the discovery of such a period can take place in 2 ways: either by detailed observation of behavioral development or by accidental or deliberate administration of an experimental factor that modifies organization. An example of the latter sort of technique was the discovery of the critical period for early stimulation in rats, which came about as the result of systematic study of the effects of handling on later behavior (Denenberg & Zarrow, 1971; Levine & Lewis, 1959; Schaefer, 1968).

In the case of the dogs, both methods contributed to the discovery. Originally, we did a detailed observational study of behavioral development involving some 500 puppies from 5 pure breeds and hybrids between 2 of them (Scott & Fuller, 1965; Scott & Marston, 1950). As a result of classifying this material, we concluded that the early development of the puppy naturally fell into 3 periods marked by different organizational processes. The *neonatal* period, extending from birth until the opening of the eyes at approximately 2 weeks of age, is chiefly marked by the establishment of the process of neonatal nutrition. All behavior at this time is adaptive to an existence in which the mother takes complete care of the pups. The 2nd or *transition* period, extending from approximately 2-3 weeks (more precisely, from 13 to 19 days on the average), extends from the opening of the eyes to the appearance of the startle response to sound. This period is marked by several transition processes: that from neonatal to adult forms of locomotion (crawling to walking and running), from neonatal nutrition to the adult form (nursing to eating of solid food), from relatively slow-learning capacities to the rapid capacities of adults, the acquisition of adult sensory capacities of sight and vision, and finally the acquisition of the capacity to rapidly form attachments to strange individuals, whether they be dogs, people, or other living animals. We later realized that the puppies also develop a capacity to become attached to particular places, paralleling that of attachment to living things.

The 3rd period, known as the period of *primary socialization*, is characterized by the process of forming attachments to conspecifics, other animals including humans, and to particular places. On the basis of observation, we set the end of this period at the time of final weaning from the breast, which takes place on the average at 7-10 weeks, on the logical grounds that weaning marked a strong change in social relationships.

Separation experiments provided a method of modifying the normal processes of social attachment and site attachment. Results from these tended to verify conclusions from observational studies. For example, in 1 early experiment (Scott, Fuller, & Fredericson, 1951) a puppy taken from the mother at 2 weeks (1 week prior to the beginning of the socialization period) readily adjusted to human care, but 1 taken at 4 weeks showed violent emotional reactions upon separation. On the basis of this and other preliminary experiments, a more extensive experiment was designed.

Experiments Determining the End of the Critical Period

Carrying out this design, Freedman, King, and Elliot (1961) performed the most elegant and extensive experimental test of the critical-period hypothesis that has so far been carried out. They placed pregnant mothers in 1-acre fields with high board fences and allowed them to give birth to their pups and rear them without any direct human contact, except when the experimenters entered briefly to remove 1 of the pups. In a given litter 1 pup would be taken out when 2 weeks old and given opportunity for socialization with human beings during the following week. Subsequent puppies were removed at 3, 5, 7, and 9 weeks and given similar treatment. Finally, the whole litter was brought in and tested for individual responses to human beings at 14 weeks of age.

The results were unequivocal (Fig. 5). Puppies taken at 2 and 3 weeks were relatively unresponsive to human contacts and performed little better than untreated controls at 14 weeks. Those taken at 5 and 7 weeks were highly responsive and also showed maximum levels of performance at 14 weeks. Those taken at 9 weeks were intermediate in both respects. Puppies that were not brought in until 14 weeks showed severe and permanent deficits in their behavior, being extremely fearful in initial contacts, never forming close attachments to human beings, and always showing preferences for dogs. The results with the 9-week-old puppies were unexpected in that they adjusted to human contact effectively but more slowly than younger ones.

It was obvious that the end of the critical period could not be set at 8 weeks, and that it should be placed somewhere between 9 and 14 weeks. Had we anticipated this result we could have tested additional groups of puppies at later ages. As it was, other experiments gave us additional clues as to the duration of the critical period. In an entirely different sort of experiment, Fuller (1967) raised puppies in complete isolation from 3 weeks on, i.e., from the onset of the critical period. Puppies left in isolation until 16 weeks showed drastic disturbances of behavior on being removed, again of such severity that recovery was never complete. Puppies removed as late as 7 weeks, however, appeared to be completely normal in their later behavior. Those taken out at later ages

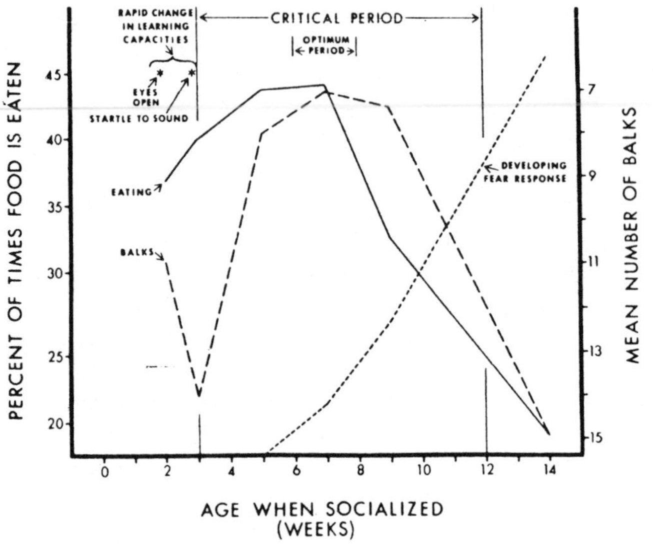

Fig. 5. Nature of the critical period for primary socialization (primary attachment) in the dog. Scores for eating and balks are inversely related, as indicated by the reversed scale on the right.

showed increasing distortions of behavior. Scott and Fuller (1965) concluded that the peak of the socialization process occurred at approximately 7 weeks, and that its end should be placed considerably later.

Stanley (1965) did a somewhat similar experiment, except that he raised puppies apart from human beings in small rooms. Before 9 weeks, such puppies immediately approached human experimenters without hesitation. At 9 weeks they showed obvious fearful reactions when exposed to people for the 1st time. Data on guide dogs retained in kennels until 12 weeks or longer before being placed in homes indicated that the probability of failure in later training increased after 12 weeks (Pfaffenberger & Scott, 1959). Somewhat arbitrarily, then, Scott (1970) placed the end of the critical period at approximately 12 weeks and concluded that a major limiting factor was the development of a fear response to the strange, which would have the effect of limiting any contacts with new individuals to very brief periods and thus interfere with the process of attachment.

Waller and Fuller (1961) did the only experiment in which the fear response was manipulated. They kept puppies in isolation from 3 weeks onward under constant treatment with chlorpromazine, which has the effect of decreasing anxiety in human beings and therefore might be presumed to control fear responses. The assumption was that this would prevent the development of fear responses. However, such puppies, when taken off drugs and removed from isolation at 16 weeks, were no different from controls, leading to the conclusion that the capacities for the fear response develop even when it is not evoked. Fuller (1967) later found that if he gave puppies chlorpromazine at the time of emergence it did have some beneficial effect, although it did not produce completely normal puppies. Thus the developing fear response is 1 factor that brings about the end of the critical period, but not the only one.

Subsequent observations on puppies that had undergone isolation showed that they could, given sufficient time, develop attachments at later periods. Woolpy and Ginsburg's

(1967) experiments on socializing wild-caught adult wolves lead to a similar conclusion. If daily contact with a human experimenter is enforced on such a wolf over a period of several weeks, its initial reaction is one of extreme fear, persisting for many contacts. Eventually, the wolf will overcome this, make positive contacts, and form an attachment, albeit not one of the same kind that is formed by a young wolf cub during the critical period. The speed of attachment is much slower, covering a period of weeks rather than hours.

We now believe that the canine attachment process which is, of course, a process of organizing a social relationship, can take place at any time in life subsequent to 3 weeks, provided there is not too much interference. There are at least 4 interfering factors. The 1st of these is the developing capacity for fear responses to the strange, which becomes increasingly important after 7 weeks and reaches a maximum by 14 weeks. A 2nd factor is the separation reaction itself. An animal that has already developed a strong attachment to other individuals or places will show an acute and long-lasting emotional distress reaction when separated from them. Under these conditions formation of new attachments is impossible, unless this separation reaction can be relieved in some way. A 3rd factor is interference from previously formed attachments. If an animal is attached to particular individuals or places he tends to stay with these, and thus not to have extensive contacts with new individuals and places unless forcibly kept under such conditions. A 4th factor is the development at sexual maturity of territorial defense reactions, including a tendency to attack strange individuals. This, of course, inhibits both the process of attachment between adult dogs and that between adult dogs and strange people. The first 3 of these interfering or limiting factors become increasingly strong after 7 weeks and have parallel effects that may in combination strongly limit the process of social attachment after 12 weeks.

Optimum Period for Transfer of Relationships

One of the outcomes of this research is that we have been able to define with considerable exactitude the critical period of primary socialization as extending from 3 until 12 weeks of age, and to recommend to prospective dog owners that the optimum period for achieving attachment of a puppy to a human master is somewhere between 6 and 8 weeks of age. A puppy will still do reasonably well up until 12 weeks, but as it grows older it becomes increasingly difficult to control and train, as well as not becoming attached as rapidly.

An interesting additional bit of evidence is the discovery by Theberge and Pimlott (1969) that wolves normally move their litters from the den to another location at about 2 months of age, the same age that we have defined as being an optimal period for making the change from dog to human society. This new area, called a rendezvous site, is usually near a small lake. Here, the litter is left to explore the environment and rest while the pack goes off to hunt.

Also, Woolpy and Ginsberg (1967) have found that wolf cubs that socialized during the critical period and later returned to a zoo pack acted like wild animals as adults. This suggests that there may be a 2nd critical period when the attachment becomes "nailed down," so to speak. This possibility should also be explored in dogs, but does not invalidate the existence of an early critical period when attachment is easy to initiate.

With respect to the original problem of determining the nature of the organizing processes in social attachment, these experiments were somewhat disappointing. Rather than finding a process that ceased with the end of the critical period, we found only a set of interfering factors that limited it. We therefore concluded that more definite clues might be found near the beginning of the critical period.

Experimental Evidence Regarding the Onset of the Critical Period

We may now consider the organizational processes accompanying the onset of the critical period. First, there is the organization of the separation distress response. Fredericson [see Scott et al. (1951)] first studied the phenomenon and discovered that a puppy 2 weeks of age made a rapid adjustment to being removed from a litter and reared in a home; a similar puppy, taken at 4 weeks of age, vocalized for 24 hr without stopping, showing that strong attachments had already been formed. Later, Elliot and Scott (1961) showed that puppies separated from their familiar social companions and placed alone either in the home room or in a strange room otherwise identical with their own would vocalize at high rates as early as 3 weeks of age.

Second, there are gross changes in learning capacity. In studying the development of learning, Fuller, Easler, and Banks (1950) found that pronounced qualitative changes in the ability to respond to classical conditioning techniques took place around 18-19 days of age. After this age, a pupply could form associations as rapidly as an adult. Scott and Marston (1950) then hypothesized that this change in learning capacities accounted for the onset of the process of attachment, i.e., that the younger pupply simply could not remember that he had seen or had contact with a particular individual before. Scott and Marston also stated, on the bases of Fuller's experiment and certain observational data, that puppies appeared to learn little or nothing before this point in development, and hypothesized that the capacities for simple associative learning developed suddenly at this point. Fuller and Christake (1959) challenged this statement and showed that pupples could form associations prior to this age, albeit at a slower rate. Stanley (1970) also challenged the hypothesis of nonlearning in the neonatal puppy and, in a brilliant and careful series of experiments, was able to show that the puppies could be conditioned even very early in the neonatal period. Stanley further showed that the model of operant conditioning was more appropriate than classical techniques in studying sucking, which is 1 of the few kinds of behavior that the neonatal puppy emits, and hence that can be modified by operant learning.

However, it is still true that gross quantitative changes in the capacity for learning do take place during the transition period. Russian experimenters (Klyavina, Kobakova, Stelmakh, & Troshikhin, 1958) have shown that the kind of behavior involved determines the rate at which classical conditioning takes place. The number of pairings to criterion is much lower with respect to feeding behavior than escape behavior. In addition, there are certain qualitative changes which take place. Bacon (1971) has shown that although neonatal puppies can learn to make discriminations, their behavior lacks 1 of the elements of such behavior in adults. The puppies form positive associations in respect to discriminated stimuli, but not negative ones. Finally, 1 result obtained by Fuller and Christake (1959) has never been followed up. They hypothesized that conditioned responses formed through the autonomic system might develop earlier than those developed through voluntary responses (a reasonable assumption based on the commonly held belief that learned emotional responses are important in early development), but obtained quite the opposite results, being unable to condition heart rates until 5 weeks or so, long after good conditioned responses in overt behavior can be obtained.

None of these experiments cover 1 of the most basic factual issues in this field. We still do not have good studies of developmental change in various learning capacities from birth to 3 weeks of age. These results, however, raise some very interesting questions with respect to the effects of experience on infantile animals. The data indicate that young puppies are protected against the consequences of traumatic experiences in early life, and that they do not have the ability to develop inhibitions as the result of such experiences. Furthermore, it has not been established how long memories acquired in the neonatal period last, and whether the information so stored can be retrieved at later ages. This is an extremely interesting theoretical and practical problem now being studied by Misanin, Nagy, Keiser, and Bowen (1971), who have found in another species (rats) that the memory capacity for retaining associations more than 1 hr does not develop until several days after birth. What the situation is in the dog is now being tested by Z. M. Nagy (unpublished data).

Nature of the Organizational Process

The organizational changes that take place in the nervous system as an animal becomes attached to another individual or place are, of course, physiological in nature. At the present time nothing is known directly about such a process or processes, and they must be inferred from behavioral evidence. As indicated above, 2 organizational processes may be inferred to accompany the onset of social attachment: organization of the separation response and that of learning. An obvious hypothesis is therefore that social attachment is the outcome of a process of learning, and various theories have been proposed in the past to account for it on this basis. We can now cite the following evidence concerning the relationship between the attachment and learning processes.

As to the nature of social attachment itself, we can conclude that all that is necessary for the process to take place is some form of perceptual contact. Early experiments by Brodbeck (1954) and W. C. Stanley (private communication) showed that feeding was unnecessary, as attachment would take place even if puppies were fed mechanically, provided they had contact with human beings. Cairns and Werboff (1967) showed that during the early part of the critical period, puppies would begin to show separation distress after 1-2 hr of contact with new animals and that direct interaction with physical contact produced a more rapid effect than mere visual contact. Stanley and Elliot (1962) showed that puppies would learn to run and show improvement in performance when the goal was a completely passive individual. We can conclude that although the attachment process may be slightly modified by external circumstances, it must be primarily an internal one. Even when puppies are punished for making contact with human experimenters, they still become attached (Fisher, 1955). Thus we have a learning process that is not dependent upon either positive or negative external reinforcement. What is it?

To set up the simplest possible hypothesis that will account for the results, the animal must have developed 2 capacities. One is the ability to discriminate between familiar and unfamiliar objects, which in turn depends on the development of adequate sensory capacities. The 2nd is the capacity for memory, i.e., perceiving that an object is familiar would depend on memory of the fact that it had been previously seen or sensed in some other way. Following this reasoning, we conclude that associative learning is an essential part of the attachment process. Repeated exposure to an object renders the association stronger, in accordance with the laws of learning.

It is also possible that the perception of a familiar object evokes a pleasurable emotion that might have a reinforcing function, but this has not been established. What is definite is that separation from a familiar individual or place will evoke distress. From the viewpoint of reinforcement, such distressing experiences should result in the puppy being internally punished for separation and rewarded for reunion. Repeated separations, then, should result in a strengthening of attachment. At the same time, repeated exposures to the familiar object, even when no separation is involved, should result in increasingly strong associations and memories of the familiar object. Thus learning processes should strengthen attachment in 2 ways, but do not themselves comprise the whole process.

Returning to the theoretical problem of the relationships between interdependent organizing processes, we see that the recognizable processes involved include development of: (1) distress vocalization (present at birth but not yet organized with respect to separation); (2) sensory capacities (tactile and olfactory capacities present at birth, visual capacities increasingly organized from 13 to 28 days after birth, and auditory capacities appearing at approximately 19 days); and (3) learning capacities (associative processes becoming increasingly organized from approximately Day 6 to Day 21).

There is obviously a great deal of overlap in the time of rapid organization of sensory and learning capacities, and their critical periods sould consequently overlap during the transition period. However, until both kinds of capacities become well organized, the overall process of social attachment cannot proceed rapidly. We therefore predict that social attachment takes place slowly prior to 3 weeks, but at a gradually rising rate. Thus the critical periods for the component processes take place immediately prior to that of the overall process. This is similar to the situation in Figure 2B, except that in this case the organization of component processes can be altered by quite different modifying factors from that of the overall attachment process, and hence be separately recognizable.

39

Reprinted from *Human Growth: A Comprehensive Treatise,* Vol. III, F. Falkner and J. M. Tanner, eds., Plenum Press, in press.

CRITICAL PERIODS IN ORGANIZATIONAL PROCESSES

John Paul Scott

Center for Research on Social Behavior, Bowling Green State University, Bowling Green, Ohio

OPTIMAL PERIODS AND CRITICAL PERIODS

The time of most rapid organization in a particular process is not only a critical period for decisions but is also an optimal period for producing desirable (or at least desired) changes in organization. Change cannot be produced before the organizational process begins nor after it has ceased.

The Optimal Period for Adoption in Dogs

When adopting a dog the usual desired effect is for it to be a well-adjusted member of both canine and human societies. If a puppy is removed from its canine companions before the critical period begins and no later than 4 weeks from birth and is given no further contact with other dogs, it will form all of its social relationships with humans but none with other dogs and consequently be maladjusted in its relationships with canines. A male pupply adopted at four weeks into a human family may as an adult be antagonistic toward all dogs, even females in estrus. On the other hand, if a puppy is kept with other dogs and has no contact with humans, it develops strong relationships with other dogs but never develops them with people. If such a puppy is given no human contact for fourteen weeks after birth, it becomes acutely maladjusted in human relations although it can be laboriously tamed like a wild animal. The situation is somewhat modified when there is minimal contact with humans, such as dogs would receive in an ordinary kennel. The dogs will show signs of social attachment to humans during the critical period even if they are only able to see them from a distance (Scott and Fuller, 1965). On the basis of these empirical facts, we have placed the optimal time for adoption at six to eight weeks of age, with a week or two leeway thereafter. The best results are obtained if the puppy is adopted at approximately eight weeks. As it happens in wolf packs, the age of approximately two months is also the time when the adults will move a litter from the den and relocate it at a somewhat distant spot known as a rendezvous site (Theberge and Pimlott, 1969). This optimal period is, therefore, associated with a change in site attachment that has obvious practical implications in a hunting animal. If wolf puppies were kept permanently in a den and became attached only to that locality, they would have difficulty in making the kind of adjustments that are necessary for a wide ranging hunting animal.

Adoption in Humans

With human adoption the desired result is to have a child that is well adjusted and strongly attached to its close social relatives. Attachment to the personnel of an orphanage or to the natural parents is, in this case, undesirable. Since the period of most rapid social attachment in human beings occurs from approximately five to six weeks to six to seven months of age, the optimal period for adoption should be as early as possible within this period and preferably soon after birth when no complications could occur. The longer the adoption procedure is put off beyond six months, the more difficulties could develop. Since such adoptions are often necessary, however, it is possible to minimize difficulties through an understanding of the attachment process itself. There are two things that interfere with new attachments after the critical period. The first is the development of fear responses toward strangers. Every precaution should be taken to not frighten such a child. Also, young infants in an orphanage could be brought into frequent contact with strangers so that being adopted by a stranger would not be as frightening.

Second, and even more important, is the emotional disturbance resulting from breaking previous social and site attachments. The old method of adoption was to remove the infant immediately and completely from all early contact, automatically insuring maximum emotional disturbance. A better way is to proceed more gradually in order to reduce emotional disturbance. In the beginning, the adoptive parent should visit the infant several times in its own familiar setting and attempt to establish pleasant relations by active social interaction. Later the infant could be taken away to visit the new home for several short periods of a few hours before finally moving there permanently. It would be well to visit the old environment occasionally so the infant could maintain some continuity between its earlier and later environments (Scott, 1971).

Xenophobia, the fear of strangers, is one of the major obstacles to human understanding and world peace. It would be desirable if young infants became attached not only to their own social relatives but to the entire human race. It is not possible for a young infant to have contact with large and widespread samples of human populations, but it should be helpful to expose the young infant to as many kinds of people as possible during early infancy and childhood. The racial integration of the public schools is a desirable step in this direction, but the age of six may already be beyond the optimal period. Empirical studies could be made of the behavior of children who are being brought up in restricted or isolated conditions in order to determine the reality of these effects.

Optimal Periods for Site Change

In the dog the optimal period for site change coincides with the optimal period for adoption. The period is also one in which young puppies are reasonably mature in their motor capacities and are beginning to move out and investigate new parts of the adjacent environment. Human infants, on the other hand, are not capable of leaving their parents for even short distances until long after the period of socialization. Infants begin to walk on the average at about fourteen months and do not become really active until somewhat later. Rheingold and Eckerman (1973) have studied this phenomenon of the child leaving its mother. On the basis of their work and some observations of the ages at which young children get lost by straying too far from their parents, I would estimate that the optimal time for changing a child's environment is around two years of age. This change could, of course, be either in the form of a vacation trip or a permanent move. Since moving is such a common practice in our society, it would be desirable to get some empirical data on the effects of moving at differeng ages. It may turn out that there are other optimal periods as well.

Optimal Period for Motor Learning

In spite of its obvious practical implications, very few studies on the optimal period for motor learning have been done. McGraw's (1935) early study on identical twins that were given differential training was marred by the fact that her twins later turned out not to be identical. The study, nevertheless, produced certain interesting suggestions. One twin could be taught to do such things as swimming and roller-skating at an astonishingly early age, before it had even learned to walk well, but showed no benefit over the other twin when retaught at a later age. In fact, if anything, roller-skating was more difficult because it had been learned at an age when the proportions of leg length and body length were not fully developed, and that skill therefore had to be relearned. One would predict that motor learning involving whole body coordination could be acquired most rapidly at the time when the nervous system, sensory capacities, and motor organs were close to the adult form. Judging from the development of the EEG, brain development is not complete until seven or eight years of age although there is a great deal of individual variation. It is around this time that most children first begin to be physically well-coordinated. In the absence of better information, we could predict that six or seven would be a good age in which to initiate the development of physical skills.

McGraw herself stated that there was a different optimal time for learning each kind of coordinated physical activity. These learning processes are complicated by many different factors that might determine that specific ages are good for specific skills. For example, learning to ride a tricycle at any early age should not interfere with learning to ride a bicycle later since the two skills are quite different and learning the first might contribute to later confidence. Motivation is another complicating factor in any learning process and it may be a major factor in determining an optimal period. The child must have at least some interest in learning, and his motivation will be strengthened or diminished by his success or failure. Therefore, it is important not to try to attempt learning any activity before the age when success is possible.

Optimal Periods for Intellectual Learning

Many of the same considerations apply to the learning of intellectual skills as apply to motor skills. Of these, motivation is perhaps the most important. In the dog, young puppies achieve a mature EEG at about eight weeks. For the next four weeks or so, puppies are interested in almost any new activity and are quite easy to teach, provided one does not require skilled motor performance or long continued persistence. The usual rule is to achieve one or perhaps two successes and then quit for the day.

Similarly, in human children there are ages in which there is active intellectual curiousity but poor staying power. This is particularly noticeable in children around the age of eight and during the next few years prior to puberty, but it may also exist much earlier with respect to certain activities. In humans the basic intellectual skill is language. One of the things that children begin to learn and actively try to learn at a very early age is language itself.

Indeed the acquisition and organization of language forms an almost classical case of a critical period (Lenneberg, 1967). The period is a long one extending between the ages of approximately two and twelve years. During the early part of this period, the organization of language may be easily modified in almost any direction, i.e., any language may become the native language of an individual who is adopted from one culture into another at an early age. Toward the end of the period, it becomes more and more difficult (though not impossible) to learn a second language. By the age of thirteen or so, it can only be learned with a foreign accent. It appears, then, that the optimal time for learning a second language is during the time the child is learning a primary one. However, it has never been satisfactorily demonstrated exactly when during the learning of the primary language the learning of the second should take place because a second language may interfere with mastery of the first.

Should one try to enlarge a child's vocabulary when he or she is just beginning to learn words? The answer is possibly that undue emphasis on individual words may interfere with sentence learning and the acquiring of skills in rapid, uninterrupted speech. Emphasis might better be placed on learning organized language rather than its isolated parts.

Similarly, the optimal period for acquiring secondary language skills such as reading and writing has never been determined. The obvious guideline would be the time at which the child can do these things easily and is also well motivated to do them. One would expect that reading would come before writing and, in fact, when writing skills are first acquired at an early age, they tend to persist in an immature and somewhat unskilled fashion because of the early formation of habits. There is also a tendency to try to teach skills at the same age in all children, in spite of obvious differences in developmental rates. The age of six may be too early for one child to learn to read and later than the optimal period for another.

The critical period for language acquisition can be more precisely defined by the evidence from children who have suffered brain lesions from various accidents. Before twenty months of age, language development may be delayed in some cases, but otherwise there is no deficit. This is prior to the age when language appears, and obviously the organization process has not yet begun. From twenty-one to thirty-six months, a lesion has the effect of destroying all language abilities, which then reappear as they did in the beginning. From three to ten years, lesions may produce aphasia; but eventually there is complete recovery except for some effects on reading and writing. At the same time, the child will continue to acquire new language skills in addition to the old. By eleven to fourteen years, some changes produced by lesions are irreversible; and after age fourteen, the symptoms that remain five months after the injury tend to be irreversible.

The evidence concerning the organization of language acquisition is similar in form to that of socialization, namely, that there is an early period of very rapid organization which then falls off to a lower rate but never goes down to zero. These facts concerning language organization then bring up the problem of the relationship between the optimal periods and periods that are vulnerable to injury.

VULNERABLE AND SENSITIVE PERIODS

In contrast to the concept of optimal periods, which implies the modification of organization in a favorable direction either by speeding it up or modifying it, the concept of vulnerability implies that the organizing process is unfavorably affected either by slowing it down or by distorting it. The concept of sensitivity similarly implies damage to an organizing process although of a less serious degree. For example, a bird becoming attached to a human being instead of to its own species has obviously been damaged but not to the extent that its existence is threatened. The period in which such events occur easily is called a sensitive period by some authors (Hinde, 1970; Hess, 1973).

If an injurious agent or event is applied to an organizational process and affects only that process, it should act as follows (Scott et al., 1974). Prior to the critical period, defined as the time during which the organizational process is taking place, the agent should produce no effect. During the critical period, it should produce effects proportional to the speed of organization and inversely proportional to time. That is, if the agent is applied early in the period when organization is still proceeding slowly, it should produce relatively little effect and, because reorganization is possible, there should be almost complete recovery. Later, the effect should be more serious because the process is proceeding more rapidly and also because there is less time for reorganization and recovery. Finally, once the organizational process is complete, the agent should produce no effect.

On the other hand, if the injurious agent affects not the organizing process but the organized system itself, the results should be minimal early in the critical period when reorganization is still possible, and increase as the organization becomes stable and fixed. Once the organizational process ceases, the system can be destroyed and never recover. Such effects as these can be observed with lesions of the nervous system.

The general theory of critical periods states that an organizational process is most easily modified when it is proceeding most rapidly. Such modifications can produce either favorable or unfavorable effects. Thus, vulnerable periods and optimal periods should be essentially the same with respect to the time periods involved, the distinction between these concepts being the nature of their effects on organization.

With respect to critical periods, a further distinction can be made on the basis of basic and developmental research. The concept of critical periods is concerned with basic research in the description and identification of organizational processes. The concepts of optimality and vulnerability, on the other hand, lead to applied and developmental research and practical uses of this information.

CONCLUSION

As presented in this paper, the theory of critical periods is a general one applying to developmental change in the organization of any living system. It applies equally well to growth processes, to behavioral development, and even to organizational change in social systems. The application of the critical period concept to both embryology and behavioral development is no mere analogy but is based on the fundamental nature of all living systems.

At the same time, organizational processes differ at different levels of system organization. The critical nature of any given decision made during organizational change depends on three variable factors: 1) its importance for survival or adaptive value, 2) the degree of irreversibility; i.e., the degree of system stability, and 3) the ease with which the organizational processes can be modified.

Comparing growth processes with those of behavorial development, it can be generally stated that the decisions made in behavioral development are somewhat less important for survival, are somewhat more reversible, and are considerably easier to modify in optimal directions. These generalities may not hold true in every pair of processes that may be compared, as certain behavioral systems may achieve extraordinary stability while certain physiological systems are relatively labile.

A major new theoretical contribution of this paper is the distinction made between maintenance processes, which organize external materials to be included in a living system, and developmental processes, which produce organizational change of the system itself. Being more or less continuous, maintenance processes should not show critical periods, whereas the developmental processes must exhibit critical periods as they produce stable systems or subsystems. Further, the critical nature of a given developmental decision is variable, depending on the degree of stability of organization of the resulting system. Finally, the concepts of optimality, vulnerability, and sensitivity are related to that of critical periods.

The usefulness of a theory depends on its ability to provide a causal explanation of a given set of facts and one that will give predictable results when controlling factors or processes are manipulated. The theory of critical periods meets this test. In addition, a theory is scientifically valuable if it leads to further research. As presented here, the theory of critical periods demands in each particular case the identification of organizing processes and the measurement of time relationships between them.

REFERENCES

Beadle, G. W., and E. L. Tatum, 1941. Genetic Control of Biochemical Reactions in Neurospora, *Proc. Nat. Acad. Sci.* **27**:499.

Bowlby, J., 1951. *Maternal Care and Mental Health.* Geneva: World Health Organization Monograph.

Bronson, F. H., and C. Desjardins, 1968. Aggression in Adult Mice: Modification by Neonatal Injections of Gonadal Hormones, *Science* **161**:705.

Cairns, R. B., 1972. Attachment and Dependency: a Psychol-Biological and Social Learning Synthesis, in *Attachment and Dependency.* J. L. Gerwirtz, ed., New York: V. H. Winston. pp. 29–80.

Cairns, R. B., and J. A. Werboff, 1967. Behavior Development in the Dog: an Interspecific Analysis, *Science* **158**:1070.

Child, C. M., 1921. The Origin and Development of the Nervous System. Chicago: University of Chicago Press.

Collias, N. E., 1956. The Analysis of Socialization in Sheep and Goats, *Ecology* 37:228.

Denenberg, V. H., and M. X. Zarrow, 1971. Effects of Handling in Infancy upon Adult Behavior and Adrenal Activity: Suggestions for a Neuroendocrine Mechanism, in *Early Childhood: The Development of Self-regulatory Mechanisms.* D. N. Walcher and D. L. Peters, eds., New York: Academic Press, pp. 39–71.

Fleener, D. E., 1967. Attachment Formation in Human Infants. Doctoral dissertation, Indiana University. Ann Arbor, Michigan: University Microfilms, No. 6872-12.

Gurski, J. C., K. L. Davis, and J. P. Scott, 1974. Onset of Separation Distress in the Dog: The Delaying Effect of Comfortable Stimuli. Paper presented at the International Society for Developmental Psychobiology, St. Louis.

Harlow, H. F., and M. K. Harlow. 1965. The Affectional Systems, in *Behavior of Nonhuman Primates.* A. M. Schrier, H. F. Harlow, and S. F. Stollnitz, eds., New York: Academic Press, pp. 287–334.

Heinroth, O., 1910. Beitrage zur Biologie, namentlich Ethologie und Psychologie der Anatiden, *Verh. des V. Internationalen Ornithologen-Kongresses* **5**:589.

Hess, E. H., 1973. *Imprinting,* New York: D. Van Nostrand.

Hinde, R. A., 2nd ed. 1970. *Animal Behavior: A Synthesis of Ethology and Comparative Psychology.* New York: McGraw-Hill.

Kaufman, I. C., and L. A. Rosenblum, 1969. Effects of Separation from Mother on the Emotional Behavior of Infant Monkeys, *Ann. N. Y. Acad. Sci.* **159**:681.

Klinghammer, E., 1967. Factors Influencing Choice of Mate in Altricial Birds, in *Early Behavior.* H. W. Stevenson, E. H. Hess, and H. L. Rheingold, eds., New York: Wiley, pp. 5–42.

Lenneberg, E. H., 1967. *The Biological Foundations of Language.* New York: Wiley.

Lorenz, K., 1935. Der Kumpan in der Umwelt des Vogels, *Jour. f. Ornithologie* **83**:137.

Marler, P., and P. Mundinger, 1971. Vocal learning in birds, in *Ontogeny of Vertebrate Behavior.* H. Moltz, ed., New York: Academic Press, pp. 389–450.

Mason, W. A., 1963. The Effects of Environmental Restriction on the Social Development of Rhesus Monkeys, in *Primate Social Behavior.* C. H. Southwick, ed., New York: Van Nostrand. pp. 161–173.

Mason, W. A., and M. D. Kenney, 1974. Redirection of Filial Attachments in Rhesus Monkeys: Dogs as Mother Surrogates, *Science* **183**:1209.

McGraw, M. B., 1935. *Growth: A Study of Johnny and Jimmy.* New York: Appleton-Century.

Money, J., and A. A. Ehrhardt, 1972. *Man and Woman, Boy and Girl.* Baltimore: Johns Hopkins Press.

Moore, A. U., 1960. Studies on the Formation of the Mother neonate Bond in Sheep and Goats, *Amer. Psychologist* **15**:413.

Moore, K. L., 1974. *The Developing Human: Clinically Oriented Embryology.* Philadelphia: Saunders.

Rakusan, K., and O. Poupa, 1970. Ecology and Critical Periods of the Developing Heart, in *The Post Natal Development of Phenotype.* S. Kazda, and V. H. Denenberg, eds., Prague: Academia, pp. 359–368.

Reinisch, J. M., 1974. Fetal Hormones, the Brain, and Human Sex Differences: A Heuristic, Integrative Review of the Recent Literature, *Arch. Sex. Behavior* **3**:51.

Rheingold, H. L., and C. O. Eckerman, 2nd ed. 1973. The Infant Separates Himself from his Mother, in *Child Development and Behavior.* F. Rebelsky, and L. Dormon, eds., New York: Alfred A. Knopf.

Schein, M. W., 1963. On the Irreversibility of Imprinting, *Zeits. f. Tierpsychol.* **20**:462.

Scott, J. P., 1937. The Embryology of the Guinea Pig. III. Development of the Polydactylous Monster. A Case of Growth Accelerated at a Particular Period by a Semidominant Lethal Gene, *J. Exp. Zool.* **77**:123.

Scott, J. P., 1945. Social Behavior, Organization and Leadership in a Small Flock of Domestic Sheep, *Comp. Psych. Monog.* No. 96, **18**(4):1.

Scott, J. P., 1962. Critical periods in Behavioral Development, *Science* **138**:949.

Scott, J. P., 1963. The Process of Primary Socialization in Canine and Human Infants, *Monographs Soc. Res. Child Devel.* **28**(1):1.

Scott, J. P., 1971. Attachment and Separation in Early Development, in *The Origins of Human Social Relations.* H. R. Schaffer, ed., London: Academic Press. pp. 227–243.

Scott, J. P.., and J. L. Fuller, 1965. *Genetics and the Social Behavior of the Dog.* Chicago: University of Chicago Press.

Scott, J. P., and M. V. Marston, 1950. Critical Periods Affecting Normal and Maladjustive Behavior in Puppies, *J. Genet. Psychol.* **77**:25.

Scott, J. P., J. M. Stewart, and V. J. DeGhett, 1974. Critical Periods in the Organization of Systems, *Devel. Psychobiol.* **7**:489.
Spalding, D. A., 1873. Instinct, with Original Observations on Young Animals, *McMillan's Magazine* **27**:282.
Stockard, C. R., 1907. The Artificial Production of a Single Median Cyclopian Eye in the Fish Embryo by Means of Sea Water Solutions of Magnesium Chloride, *Arch. f. Entwicklungsmech.* **23**:249.
Stockard, C. R., 1921. Developmental Rate and Structural Expression, *Am. J. Anat.* **28**:115.
Theberge, J. B., and D. H. Pimlott, 1969. Observations of Wolves at a Rendezvous Site in Algonquin Park, *Canadian Field Naturalist* **83**:122.
Thorpe, W. H., 1965. The Ontogeny of Behavior, in *Ideas in Modern Biology.* J. A. Moore, ed., Garden City, New York: Natural History Press, pp. 483–518.
Young, C., W. Goy, and H. Phoenix, 1964. Hormones and Sexual Behavior, *Science* **143**:212.
Waddington, C. H., 1962. *New Patterns in Genetics and Development.* New York: Columbia University Press.

EDITOR'S REFERENCES

(This is by no means an exhaustive list of the literature on the subject of critical periods. Additional references can be found in the reprinted articles.)

Ainsworth, M. D. S. 1973. The Development of Infant-Mother Attachment, in *Review of Child Development Research, Vol. 3,* B. M. Caldwell and H. N. Ricciuti, eds., Chicago: University of Chicago Press, pp. 1–94.

Bowlby, J. 1969. *Attachment and Loss. I. Attachment.* New York: Basic Books.

Carter, C. S., ed., 1974. *Hormones and Sexual Behavior.* Stroudsburg, Pa.: Dowden, Hutchinson & Ross, Inc.

Dareste, C. 1891. *Recherches sur la Production Artificielle des Monstruosites, ou Essais de Teratogenie Experimentale.* Paris: C. Reinwald Cie, p. 587.

Denenberg, V. H. 1962. An Attempt to Isolate Critical Periods of Development in the Rat, *J. Comp. Physiol. Psychol.* **55**:813–815.

Denenberg, V. H. 1968. A Consideration of the Usefulness of the Critical Period Hypothesis as Applied to the Stimulation of Rodents in Infancy, in *Early Experience and Behavior: The Psychobiology of Development.* G. Newton and S. Levine, eds., Springfield, Illinois: Charles C. Thomas.

Denenberg, V. H., ed. 1970. *Education of the Infant and the Young Child.* New York: Academic Press.

Fleener, D. E. 1967. *Attachment Formation in Human Infants.* Ph.D. dissertation, Indiana University. Ann Arbor, Michigan: University Microfilms No. 6872–12.

Fuller, J. L. 1967. Experiential Deprivation and Later Behavior, *Science* **158**:1645–1652.

Fuller, J. L., and L. D. Clark. 1966a. Genetic and Treatment Factors Modifying the Post-isolation Syndrome in Dogs, *J. Comp. Physiol. Psychol.* **61**:251–257.

Fuller, J. L., and L. D. Clark. 1966b. Effects of Rearing with Specific Stimuli upon Post-isolation Behavior in Dogs, *J. Comp. Physiol. Psychol.* **61**: 258–263.

Gray, P. H. 1963. The Descriptive Study of Imprinting in Birds from 1873 to 1953, *J. Gen. Psychol.* **68**:333–346.

Hess, E. H. 1973. *Imprinting.* New York: D. Van Nostrand.

Hunt, H. F., and L. S. Otis. 1963. Early "Experience" and its Effects on Later Behavioral Processes in Rats: I. Initial Experiments, *Trans. N. Y. Acad. Sci.* **25**:858–870.

Klaus, M. H., and J. H . Kennell. 1976. *Maternal-Infant Bonding.* St. Louis: C. V. Mosby.

Landauer, T. K., and J. W. M. Whiting. 1964. Infantile Stimulation and Adult Stature of Human Males, *Am. Anthropol.* **66**:1007–1028.

Levine, S. 1956. A Further Study of Infantile Handling and Avoidance Learning, *J. Pers.* **25**:70–80.

Marler, P., and P. Mundinger. 1971. Vocal Learning in Birds, in *Ontogeny of Vertebrate Behavior.* New York: Academic Press, pp. 389–450.

Melzack, R., and W. R. Thompson. 1956. Effects of Early Experience on Social Behaviour, *Canad. J. Psychol.* **10**:82–90.

Money, J., and A. A. Ehrhardt. 1972. *Man and Woman, Boy and Girl.* Baltimore: Johns Hopkins University Press.

Money, J., J. G. Hampson, and J. L. Hampson. 1957. Imprinting and the Establishment of the Gender Role, *Arch. Neurol. and Psychiatry* **77**: 333–336.

Pettijohn, T. F., T. W. Wong, P. D. Ebert, and J. P. Scott. 1977. Alleviation of Separation Distress in Three Breeds of Young Dogs, *Devel. Psychobiol.* **10**:373–381.

Schaffer, H. R. 1958. Objective Observations of Personality Development in Early Infancy, *Brit. J. Med. Psychol.* **31**:174–183.

Schaffer, H. R., and P. E. Emerson. 1964. The Development of Social Attachments in Infancy, *Monogr. Soc. Res. Child Dev.* **29**:1–77.

Scott, J. P. 1945. Social Behavior, Organization, and Leadership in a Small Flock of Domestic Sheep, *Comp. Psychol. Monogr.* **18**:1–29.

Scott, J. P. 1958. Critical Periods in the Development of Social Behavior in Puppies. *Psychosom. Med.* **20**:42–54.

Scott, J. P. 1963. The Process of Primary Socialization in Canine and Human Infants, *Monogr. Soc. Res. Child Dev.* **28**(1):1–47.

Scott, J. P. 1970. Foreword, in *The Postnatal Development of Phenotype.* S. Kazda and V. H. Denenberg, eds., Prague: Academia.

Scott, J. P., and J. L. Fuller. 1965. *Genetics and the Social Behavior of the Dog.* Chicago: University of Chicago Press.

Stewart, J. M. 1974. *Social Disorganization and the Control of Fighting in Dogs.* Ph.D. dissertation. Bowling Green, Ohio: Bowling Green State University.

Weikart, D. P., and D. Z. Lambie. 1970. Early Enrichment in Infants, in *Education of the Infant and Young Child,* V. H. Denenberg, ed., New York: Academic Press.

White, S. H. 1977. The Nature and Meaning of Sleeper Effects, in *AAAS Symposium: Found: Long Term Gains from Early Intervention.* AAAS 143rd Annual Meeting, Denver, Colorado, February 23, 1977, p. 70.

Whitsett, J. M., F. H. Bronson, P. J. Peters, and T. H. Hamilton. 1972. Neonatal Organization of Aggression in Mice: Correlation of Critical Period with Uptake of Hormone, *Horm. and Behav.* **3**:11–21.

AUTHOR CITATION INDEX

SUBJECT INDEX

About the Editor

JOHN PAUL SCOTT is Regents' Professor of Psychology and director of the Center for the Study of Social Behavior at Bowling Green State University. He first became interested in critical periods while studying embryology as an undergraduate at the Marine Biological Laboratory at Woods Hole, Massachusetts. After taking a degree in zoology at Oxford as a Rhodes Scholar, he did research in developmental genetics at the University of Chicago under Professor Sewall Wright and discovered a critical period for gene action in the guinea pig.

His later research centered around the interaction of genetic and experiential factors affecting the development of social behavior in mammals, and he described a critical period for social attachment in the lamb. Later, he and his colleagues at the Jackson Laboratory described and analyzed a similar period in the dog. In recent years, he has developed a general organizational theory of critical periods which is described in this book.

Among other honors, he has been president of the International Society for Developmental Psychobiology, the International Society for Research on Aggression, and the Behavior Genetics Society.